2022 release

# Adobe® Photoshop®
## The Professional Portfolio

**AGAINST THE CLOCK**

mastering graphic technology

Managing Editor: Ellenn Behoriam
Cover & Interior Design: Erika Kendra

The fonts utilized in these training materials are the property of Against The Clock, Inc. and are supplied to the legitimate buyers of the Against The Clock training materials solely for use with the exercises and projects provided in the body of the materials. They may not be used for any other purpose, and under no circumstances may they be transferred to another individual, nor copied or distributed by any means whatsoever.

Against The Clock and the Against The Clock logo are trademarks of Against The Clock, Inc., registered in the United States and elsewhere. References to and instructional materials provided for any particular application program, operating system, hardware platform, or other commercially available product or products do not represent an endorsement of such product or products by Against The Clock, Inc.

Photoshop, Acrobat, Illustrator, InDesign, Flash, Dreamweaver, and PostScript are trademarks of Adobe Systems Incorporated. Macintosh is a trademark of Apple Computer, Inc. Word, Excel, Office, Microsoft, and Windows are either registered trademarks or trademarks of Microsoft Corporation.

Other product and company names mentioned herein may be the trademarks of their respective owners.

Cover image by Image by  Isabel Iniesta/Pixabay.com.

10   9   8   7   6   5   4   3   2   1

Print ISBN: 978-1-946396-71-6
Ebook ISBN: 978-1-946396-72-3

4710 28th Street North, Saint Petersburg, FL 33714
800-256-4ATC • www.againsttheclock.com

## About Against The Clock

Against The Clock, long recognized as one of the nation's leaders in courseware development, has been publishing high-quality educational materials for the graphic and computer arts industries since 1990. The company has developed a solid and widely respected approach to teaching people how to effectively use graphics applications, while maintaining a disciplined approach to real-world problems.

Having developed the Against The Clock and the Essentials for Design series with Prentice Hall/Pearson Education, ATC drew from years of professional experience and instructor feedback to develop The Professional Portfolio Series, focusing on the Adobe Creative Suite. These books feature step-by-step explanations, detailed foundational information, and advice and tips from professionals that offer practical solutions to technical issues.

## About the Author

Erika Kendra holds a BA in History and a BA in English Literature from the University of Pittsburgh. She began her career in the graphic communications industry as an editor at Graphic Arts Technical Foundation, and has been a full-time professional graphic designer since 1999.

Erika is the author or co-author of more than forty books about Adobe graphic design software. She has also written several books about graphic design concepts such as color reproduction and preflighting, and dozens of articles for industry online and print journals. Working with Against The Clock for almost twenty years, Erika was a key partner in developing The Professional Portfolio Series of software training books.

## Contributing Editors and Artists

A big thank you to the people whose comments and expertise contributed to the success of these books:

- **Roger Morrissey,** technical editor
- **Gary Poyssick,** technical editor
- **Rob McAllister,** copy editor

Images used in the projects throughout this book are in the public domain unless otherwise noted. Individual artists' credit follow:

**Interface Project:**
glass.jpg photo by Free-Photos on Pixabay.com
potter.jpg by Marcel Kessler on Pixabay.com
weaver.jpg by Wei Zhu on Pixabay.com
welder.jpg by Janno Nivergall on Pixabay.com

**Project 1:**
Sunrise.jpg photo by Stefan Kunze on Unsplash.com.
Lightning.jpg photo by David Mourn on Unsplash.com
Tornado.jpg photo by Jean Beaufort on Publicdomainpictures.net

**Project 2:**
amg.jpg photo by Mike on Pexels.com
inset1.jpg photo by Kyle Murfin on Unsplash.com
inset2.jpg photo by Jake Weirick on Pexels.com
inset3.jpg photo by Sergiusz Rydosz on Publicdomainpictures.net
tires.jpg photo by Imthaz Ahamed on Pexels.com

**Project 3:**
Museum images in this project are courtesy of the Metropolitan Museum of Art's Open Access Program, which makes images of artworks it believes to be in the public domain widely and freely available for unrestricted use. www.metmuseum.org/about-the-met/policies-and-documents/image-resources

**Project 4:**
Images used in this project are copyright Against The Clock, Inc. Roshambo.jpg photo by Charlie Essers.

**Project 5:**
Photos used in this composition are by skeeze on Pixabay.com

**Project 6:**
Images used in this project are copyright Against The Clock, Inc. Images in the supplied banner ad are photos by Jesse Darland and Dark Rider on Unsplash.com

**Project 8:**
culture1.jpg by Pixabay.com
culture2.jpg by Liam Penjur on Pexels.com
culture3.jpg by skeeze on Pixabay.com
culture4.jpg by Miguel Bruna on Unsplash.com
fantasy1.jpg by Anthony Tran on Unsplash.com
fantasy2.jpg by Ambar Simpang on Unsplash.com
fantasy3.jpg by Darcy Delia on Pexels.com
fantasy4.jpg by Couleur on Pixabay.com
feature1.jpg by Joy Anne Pura on Pexels.com
feature2.jpg by Vinicius Vilela on Pexels.com
feature3.jpg by Kathleen Sullivan on Pexels.com
theater1.jpg by Sasint on Pixabay.com
theater2.jpg by Cesira Alvarado on Unsplash.com
theater3.jpg by A. Zuhri on Unsplash.com

## Project Goals

Each project begins with a clear description of the overall concepts that are covered. These goals closely match the different "stages" of the project workflow.

## Project Meeting

Each project begins with the client's comments about the job, and the project Art Director provides fundamental advice and production requirements.

The Project Meeting also includes a summary of the specific skills required to complete the project.

## Real-World Workflow

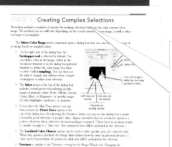

Projects are broken into logical lessons or "stages" of the workflow. Brief introductions at the beginning of each stage provide vital foundational material for completing the task.

## Step-by-Step Exercises

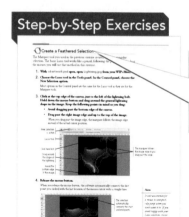

Every stage of the workflow is broken into multiple hands-on, step-by-step exercises.

## Resource Files

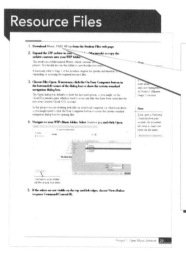

All images and fonts required to complete the step-by-step projects are included in the online student resources, which you can access using the individual code on the inside back cover of this book.

## Visual Explanations

Concepts and processes throughout the book are extensively illustrated. Wherever relevant, screen captures are annotated to help you quickly identify important information.

## Supplementary Videos

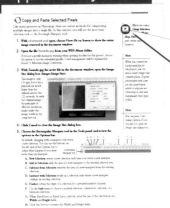

Wherever you see the "Play" icon, log on to your student resources page to view a video tutorial about the current topic.

## Project Review

Test your understanding of the concepts in the project and practice for the online quiz by answering the fill-in-the-blank and short-answer questions at the end of each project.

## Photoshop Foundations

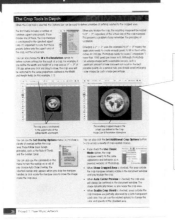

Underlying design concepts, additional functionality, and related tools are presented in Foundations discussions throughout the book.

## Portfolio Builder Projects

Each step-by-step project is accompanied by a freeform project assignment in which you practice skills and exercise creativity, resulting in an extensive and diverse portfolio of finished work.

## Advice and Warnings

Throughout the book, sidebars provide shortcuts, warnings, or useful tips about the topic at hand.

## Visual Summary

Using an annotated version of the finished project, the Visual Summary quickly identifies the skills used to complete different aspects of the job.

## Prerequisites

To use *The Professional Portfolio Series,* you should have a basic understanding of foundational computer skills, including:

- How to use your mouse to point and click.

- How to drag items around the screen.

- How to resize and arrange windows on your desktop to maximize your available space.

- How to use drop-down menus, checkboxes, and radio buttons.

- How your operating system organizes files and folders, and how to navigate your way around them.

## Software Versions

This book was written and tested using the original release of Adobe Photoshop 2022 (version 23.0) from October 2021.

You can find the specific version number in the Splash Screen that appears while your application is launching, or by choosing About Photoshop in the Photoshop/ Help menu.

Because Adobe releases periodic upgrades throughout the year, some features and functionality might have changed since publication.

Please check the Errata section of the Against The Clock website for any significant issues that might have arisen from these periodic upgrades.

## System Requirements

*The Professional Portfolio Series* was designed to work on Macintosh or Windows computers; where differences exist from one platform to another, we include specific instructions relative to each platform.

One issue that remains different from Macintosh to Windows is the use of different modifier keys (Command/ Control, Option/Alt, etc.) to accomplish the same task. When we present key commands, we always follow the same Macintosh/Windows format — Macintosh keys are listed first, then a slash, followed by the Windows key commands.

## Account and Book Registration

To access the online resources that accompany this book, you must create an account at www.againsttheclock.com:

### If you purchased an ebook:

You already have an account, and the book you purchased is already registered to the email address that you used when you purchased the ebook.

### If you purchased a print book:

You must create a free account at againsttheclock.com. Click the Sign In button in the top-right corner, then choose Create an Account from the drop-down menu. Fill in the required information, and be sure to include:

- The version of the software you are using.

- Whether you are a student or an instructor.

- The school you attend (enter "Self Learner" if you do not attend a specific school).

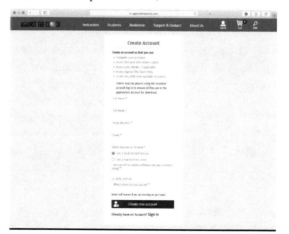

After you have created your account, you can sign in to register your book, as well as to access required fonts, project resource files, video tutorials and online quizzes:

- Click the Sign In button in the top-right corner of the page, then choose Sign In from the drop-down menu.

- Enter your email and password in the appropriate fields, then click Log In.

- Click the My Account button in the top-right corner, then choose My Account and Files from the drop-down menu.

- In the Get My Student Resource Files block, register your print book using the unique code printed on the inside back cover.

## Project Resource Files

All of the files you need to complete the projects in this book — except, of course, the Adobe software — are on your My Account and Files page at againsttheclock.com.

The primary archive for the book contains of all the Resource File (RF) and Portfolio Builder (PB) zip archives for every project in this book.

At the beginning of each project, we tell you which specific archive you need to access required project assets (e.g., **Music_PS22_RF.zip**).

If a Portfolio Builder project requires using "client-supplied" content, we also tell you which archive you need to access those files (e.g., **Eury_PS22_PB.zip**).

## Against The Clock Fonts

You must also download and install the ATC fonts from the My Account page to ensure that your exercises and projects will work as described in the book.

## Supporting Videos

Registering your book gives you access to a library of online tutorial videos that support or extend the concepts you are learning. Throughout this book, videos to watch are identified by the icon shown to the right. Videos play directly in the browser window without the need for external plug-ins or video players.

## Online Tests

As you work through the projects in this book, you can complete online fill-in, multiple-choice, and short-answer quizzes to check for understanding. See your results immediately, including correct answers to questions you missed. If you entered your school name when you created your account, quiz results may be automatically sent to your instructor.

Before downloading your ebooks, download the required ebook reader for your operating system here.

If you need to register a book, do so in this block.

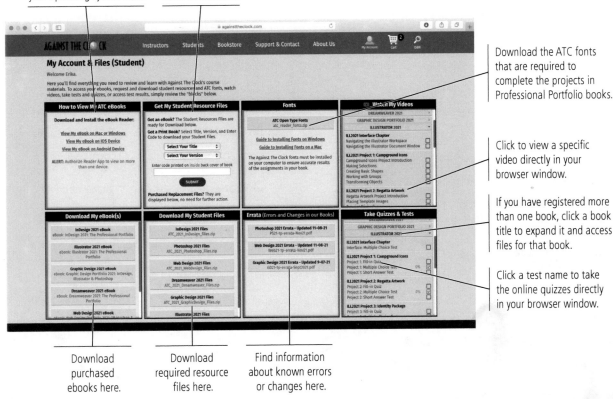

Download the ATC fonts that are required to complete the projects in Professional Portfolio books.

Click to view a specific video directly in your browser window.

If you have registered more than one book, click a book title to expand it and access files for that book.

Click a test name to take the online quizzes directly in your browser window.

Download purchased ebooks here.

Download required resource files here.

Find information about known errors or changes here.

Against The Clock's *The Professional Portfolio Series* teaches graphic design software tools and techniques entirely within the framework of real-world projects; we introduce and explain skills where they would naturally fall into a real project workflow.

The project-based approach in *The Professional Portfolio Series* allows you to get in-depth with the software beginning in Project 1 — you don't have to read several chapters of introductory material before you can start creating finished artwork.

Our approach also prevents "topic tedium" — in other words, we don't require you to read pages and pages of information about text (for example); instead, we explain text tools and options as part of a larger project (in this case, as part of a postcard series).

Clear, easy-to-read, step-by-step instructions walk you through every phase of each job, from creating a new file to saving the finished piece. Wherever logical, we also offer practical advice and tips about underlying concepts and graphic design practices that will benefit students as they enter the job market.

The projects in this book reflect a range of different types of Photoshop jobs, from creating a magazine ad, to correcting menu images or building a web page. When you finish the eight projects in this book (and the accompanying Portfolio Builder exercises), you will have a substantial body of work that should impress any potential employer.

The eight Photoshop projects are described briefly here; more detail is provided in the full table of contents (beginning on Page x).

## project 1

## New Music Artwork

- ❏ Compositing Images and Artwork
- ❏ Managing Layers
- ❏ Creating Complex Selections
- ❏ Saving Files for Multiple Media

## project 2

## Car Magazine Cover

- ❏ Enlarging Source Files
- ❏ Working with Vector Tools
- ❏ Applying Styles and Filters

## project 3

## Museum Image Correction

- ❏ Retouching Damaged Images
- ❏ Correcting Lighting Problems
- ❏ Correcting Color Problems
- ❏ Preparing Images for Print
- ❏ Working with HDR Images

Our goal in this book is to familiarize you with the majority of the Photoshop tool set, so you can be more productive and more marketable in your career as a graphic designer.

It is important to keep in mind that Photoshop is an extremely versatile and powerful application. The sheer volume of available tools, panels, and features can seem intimidating when you first look at the software interface. Most of these tools, however, are fairly simple to use with a bit of background information and a little practice.

Wherever necessary, we explain the underlying concepts and terms that are required for understanding the software. We're confident that these projects provide the practice you need to be able to create sophisticated artwork by the end of the very first project.

## Project 7
## House Painting — 365

## Project 8
## Web Page Design — 425

Adobe Photoshop is the industry-standard application for working with pixels — both manipulating existing ones and creating new ones. Photo retouching, artistic painting, image compositing, and color correction are only a few of the types of work you can create with Photoshop. Our goal in this book is to teach you how to use the available tools to succeed with different types of jobs you might encounter in your professional career.

The simple exercises in this introduction are designed to let you explore the Photoshop user interface. Whether you are new to the application or upgrading from a previous version, we highly recommend following these steps to click around and become familiar with the basic workspace.

## Explore the Photoshop Interface

The first time you launch Photoshop, you will see the default user interface (UI) settings as defined by Adobe. When you relaunch after you or another user has quit, the workspace defaults to the last-used settings — including open panels and the position of those panels on your screen. We designed the following exercises so you can explore different ways of controlling panels in the Photoshop user interface.

1. **Create a new empty folder named WIP (Work in Progress) on any writable disk (where you plan to save your work).**

2. **Download the Resource File archive for this book from the My Account and Files page at againsttheclock.com**

   This folder contains all the Resource File (RF) and Portfolio Builder (PB) archives for every project in this book.

3. **Locate the downloaded file (from Step 2) on your local drive and open the PS22 RF Files folder in the downloaded files.**

4. **Macintosh users: Place the InterfacePS_PS22_RF.zip archive in your WIP folder, then double-click the file icon to expand it.**

   **Windows users: Double-click the InterfacePS_PS22_RF.zip archive file to open it. Click the folder inside the archive and drag it into your primary WIP folder.**

   The resulting **InterfacePS** folder contains all the files you need to complete the exercises in this introduction.

*Note:*

*Although not intended as a layout-design application, many people create advertisements, book covers, and other projects entirely in Photoshop. We do not advocate doing all or even most layout composite work in Photoshop, but because many people use the application to create these designs, we feel the projects in this book portray a realistic workflow.*

*Watch the video* ***Navigating the Photoshop Workspace*** *in your online student resources.*

**Macintosh:** Double-click the archive file icon to expand it.

**Windows:** Open the archive file, then drag the InterfacePS folder from the archive to your WIP folder.

5. **Macintosh users: While pressing Command-Option-Shift, launch Photoshop. Click Yes when asked if you want to delete Settings files.**

   **Windows users: Launch Photoshop, and then immediately press Control-Alt-Shift. Click Yes when asked if you want to delete the Settings files.**

6. **Macintosh users: Open the Window menu and make sure the Application Frame option is toggled on.**

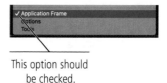

This option should be checked.

   Many commands in Photoshop are **toggles**, which means they are either on or off. When an option is already checked, that option is toggled on (visible or active). You can toggle an active option off by choosing the checked menu command, or toggle an inactive option on by choosing the unchecked menu command.

   On Windows, the Application Frame menu command is not available; you can't turn off the Application Frame on the Windows OS.

7. **In Photoshop, review the options in the Home screen.**

   The default user interface shows a stored "Home" workspace. No panels are visible in this workspace. Instead, you have buttons to create a new file or open an existing one; links to tutorial videos about new features; and one-click access to recently opened files (if any).

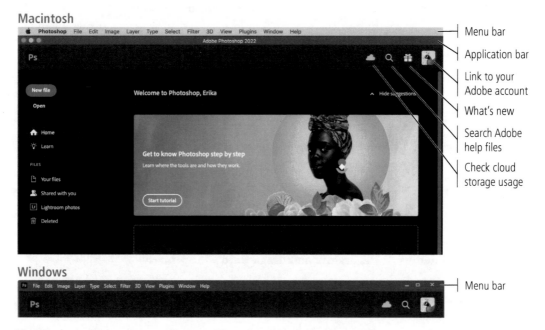

   The Home workspace appears whenever Photoshop is running, but no file is open. As soon as you open or create a file, the interface reverts to show the last-used workspace arrangement.

   The Macintosh and Windows workspaces are virtually identical, with a few primary exceptions:

   • On Macintosh, the Close, Minimize, and Restore buttons appear on the left side of the application bar, and the Menu bar is not part of the Application frame.

   • On Windows, the Close, Minimize, and Restore buttons appear at the right end of the Menu bar, which is part of the overall Application frame.

   • On Macintosh, the Apple menu provides access to system-specific commands. The Photoshop menu follows the Macintosh system-standard format for all applications; this menu controls basic application operations such as About, Hide, Preferences, and Quit.

## Understanding the Application Frame

On Windows, each running application is contained within its own frame; all elements of the application — including the Menu bar, panels, tools, and open documents — are contained within the Application frame.

Adobe also offers the Application frame to Macintosh users as an option for controlling the workspace. When the Application frame is active, the entire workspace exists in a self-contained area that can be moved around the screen. All elements of the workspace (excluding the Menu bar) move when you move the Application frame.

The Application frame is active by default, but you can toggle it off by choosing Window>Application Frame. If the menu option is checked, the Application frame is active; if the menu option is not checked, it is inactive. On Windows, the Application Frame menu command is not available. You can't turn off the Application Frame on the Windows OS.

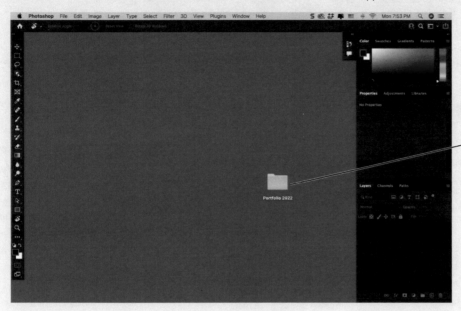

When the Application frame is not active, the desktop is visible behind the workspace elements.

8. **In Photoshop with no file open, click the Photoshop icon in the top-left corner of the Home screen.**

   Clicking this icon enters into the Photoshop workspace so you can access the various panels, even when no file is open.

Click this icon to enter the Photoshop workspace.

**Note:**

*When a file is open, you can always return to the Home workspace by clicking the Home icon in the left side of the Options bar.*

9. **Choose Window>Workspace>Essentials (Default).**

   The software includes a number of built-in saved workspaces, which provide one-click access to a defined group of panels, designed to meet common workflow needs.

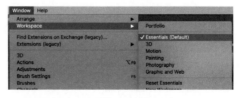

10. **Choose Window>Workspace>Reset Essentials.**

   This step might or might not do anything, depending on what was done in Photoshop before you started this project. If you changed anything, and then quit the application, those changes are remembered when Photoshop is relaunched. You are resetting the interface in this step so what you see matches our screen captures.

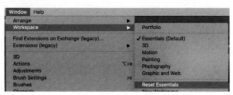

**11. Macintosh users: Choose Photoshop>Preferences>Interface.**
**Windows users: Choose Edit>Preferences>Interface.**

Remember that on Macintosh systems, the Preferences dialog box is accessed in the Photoshop menu. Windows users access the Preferences dialog box in the Edit menu.

Preferences customize the way many of the program's tools and options function. When you open the Preferences dialog box, the active pane is the one you choose in the Preferences submenu. Once open, however, you can access any of the categories by clicking a different option in the left pane. The right side of the dialog box displays options related to the active category.

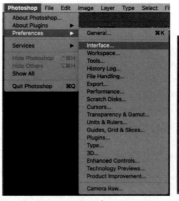

Macintosh                    Windows

In the User Interface preferences, you control the overall appearance of the workspace:

- **Color Theme.** You might have noticed the rather dark appearance of the interface background. Photoshop uses the medium-dark "theme" as the default.

- **Color and Border.** You can use the four options below Color Theme — Standard Screen Mode, Full Screen with Menus, Full Screen, and Artboards — to change the color of the area around an open file (sometimes called the pasteboard), as well as the border that appears around the canvas (the actual file area) for each screen mode. (The various screen modes are explained beginning on Page 23.)

- **UI Language.** If you have more than one localized version of the software, you can use this menu to change the language used throughout the interface.

- **UI Font Size.** You can use this option to increase the size of type that appears in Photoshop's user interface elements (panels, and so on).

- **Scale UI To Font.** If you check this option, all UI elements — tabs, tools, etc. — will be enlarged to match the font size if you choose a different UI Font Size than the default Small.

- **Show Channels in Color.** If this option is checked, individual color channels appear in shades of the representative color instead of the default grayscale. (Color channels are explained in Project 1: New Music Artwork.)

- **Show Menu Colors.** Some built-in workspaces include colored menu items. You can also edit application menus to define custom highlight colors to appear behind specific menu commands. When this option is checked, any defined colors appear behind the related items in the application menus. If you uncheck this option, all menu items appear in the application's default color theme, regardless of the defined color.

- **Dynamic Color Sliders.** If the Color panel appears in a mode that includes sliders for the various color components (CMYK, RGB, etc.), the sliders default to show the composite color that results from the values in all available sliders. If you uncheck this option, each slider shows only the color of that slider (for example, the cyan slider shows only a gradient of cyan.)

**12.** **In the Color Theme section, choose any option you prefer.**

We use the Light color theme option throughout this book because text in the interface elements is easier to read in printed screen captures.

Use these options to lighten or darken the user interface.

**13.** **Click OK to close the Preferences dialog box.**

**14.** **With Photoshop open, review the options in the user interface.**

The default Essentials workspace includes the Tools panel on the left side of the screen, the Options bar at the top of the screen, and a set of panels attached to the right side of the screen. The area where the panels are stored is called the **panel dock**.

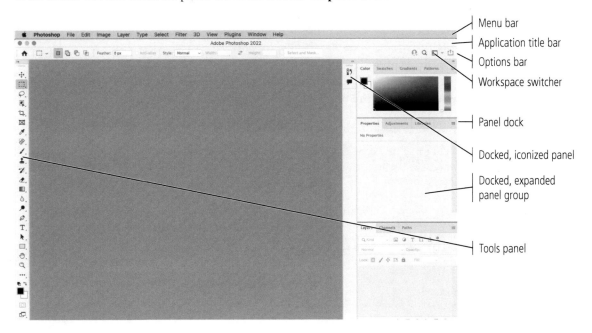

Menu bar

Application title bar

Options bar

Workspace switcher

Panel dock

Docked, iconized panel

Docked, expanded panel group

Tools panel

**15.** **Continue to the next exercise.**

# Explore the Arrangement of Photoshop Panels

As you gain familiarity with Photoshop, you will develop personal artistic and working styles. Adobe recognizes this wide range of needs and preferences among users. Photoshop includes a number of options for managing the numerous panels so you can customize the workspace to suit your specific needs.

We designed the following exercise so you can explore different ways of controlling Photoshop panels. The projects in this book instruct you to use certain tools and panels, but because workspace preferences are largely a matter of personal taste, where you place those elements within the interface is up to you.

1. **Make sure the Essentials workspace is visible in Photoshop.**

2. **Control/right-click the title bar above the right column of docked panels. Choose Auto-Collapse Iconic Panels in the contextual menu to toggle on that option.**

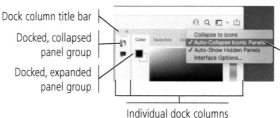

Dock column title bar

Docked, collapsed panel group

Docked, expanded panel group

Individual dock columns

This option should be checked (active) after you select it.

As we explained in the Getting Started section, when commands are different for the Macintosh and Windows operating systems, we include the different commands in the Macintosh/Windows format. In this case, Macintosh users who do not have right-click mouse capability can press the Control key and click to access the contextual menu. You do not have to press Control *and* right-click to access the menus.

Control/right-clicking a dock title bar opens the dock contextual menu, where you can change the default panel behavior. If you toggle on the Auto-Collapse Iconic Panels option — which is inactive by default — a panel collapses as soon as you click away from it. Auto-Collapse Iconic Panels is also available in the Workspace pane of the Preferences dialog box, which you can open directly from the dock contextual menu.

***Note:***

*If you're using a Macintosh and don't have a mouse with right-click capability, we highly recommend you purchase one.*

3. **In the left column of the panel dock, hover your mouse cursor over the top button until you see the name of the related panel ("History") in a tool tip.**

4. **Click the History button to expand that panel group.**

If you expand an iconized panel that shares a group with other panels, the entire group expands; the button you clicked is the active panel in the expanded group.

Tool tips identify collapsed panels when you hover your mouse cursor over the icon.

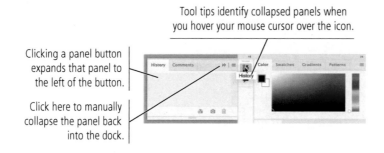

Clicking a panel button expands that panel to the left of the button.

Click here to manually collapse the panel back into the dock.

***Note:***

*Collapsed panels are referred to as **iconized** or **iconic**.*

**5.** **Click away from the expanded panel, anywhere in the workspace.**

Because the Auto-Collapse Iconic Panels option is toggled on (from Step 2), the History panel collapses as soon as you click away from the panel.

**6.** **Click the History panel button to re-expand the panel. Control/right-click the panel group drop zone (to the right of the two panel tabs) choose Close Tab Group from the contextual menu.**

The panel group's contextual menu is the only way to close a docked panel. You can also choose Close to close only the active panel.

Closing all panels in a column effectively removes that column from the dock.

The area behind a panel group's tabs is called the drop zone.

Control/right-click the drop zone to access that panel group's contextual menu.

**7.** **If any other panel remains in the left dock column, repeat the process from Step 6 to close it as well.**

**8.** **In the remaining dock column, Control/right-click the drop zone of the Properties/Adjustments/Libraries panel group and choose Close Tab Group from the contextual menu.**

When you close a docked group, other panel groups in the same column expand to fill the available space.

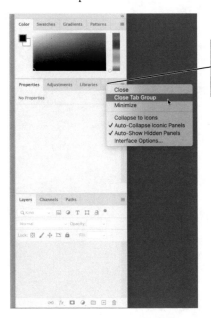

Control/right-click the panel group drop zone to access the contextual menu.

The remaining groups in the dock column expand to fill the available space.

9. **Click the Layers panel tab and drag left, away from the panel dock.**

A panel that is not docked is called a **floating panel**. You can iconize floating panels (or panel groups) by double-clicking the title bar of the floating panel group.

**Macintosh**          **Windows**

Click the panel tab and drag to move the panel.

When you release the mouse button, the panel floats over the workspace.

Floating panel Close button

10. **Click the Layers panel tab (in the floating panel group). Drag between the two existing docked panel groups until a blue line appears, then release the mouse button.**

To move a single panel to a new location, click the panel tab and drag. To move an entire panel group, click the panel group drop zone and drag. If you are moving panels to another position in the dock, the blue highlight indicates where the panel (or group) will be placed when you release the mouse button.

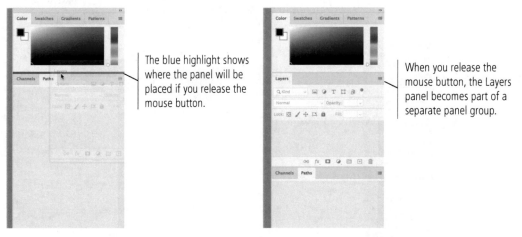

The blue highlight shows where the panel will be placed if you release the mouse button.

When you release the mouse button, the Layers panel becomes part of a separate panel group.

To add a panel to an existing group, drag the panel to the target group's drop zone. A blue highlight will surround the group where the moved panel will be added.

To create a new dock column, drag a panel or panel group until a pop-out "drawer" outlines the edge where the new column will be added.

11. **Control/right-click the drop zone behind the Colors/Swatches/Gradients/ Patterns panel group, and choose Minimize from the contextual menu.**

When a group is minimized, only the panel tabs are visible. Clicking a tab in a collapsed panel group expands that group and makes the selected panel active.

You can also double-click a panel tab to minimize the panel group.

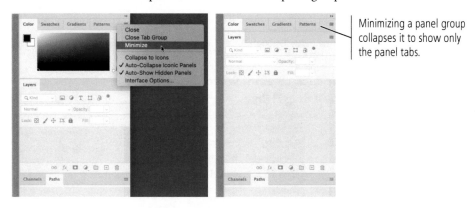

Minimizing a panel group collapses it to show only the panel tabs.

12. **Move the cursor over the line between the Layers and Channels/Paths panel groups. When the cursor becomes a double-headed arrow, click and drag up or down until the Layers panel occupies approximately half of the available dock column space.**

You can drag the bottom edge of a docked panel group to vertically expand or shrink it. Other panels in the same column expand or contract to fit the available space.

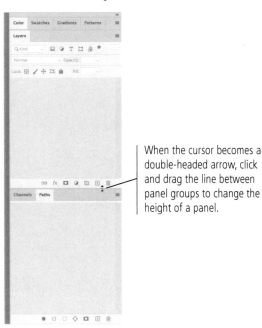

When the cursor becomes a double-headed arrow, click and drag the line between panel groups to change the height of a panel.

**13. Double-click the title bar above the column of docked panels to collapse those panels to icons.**

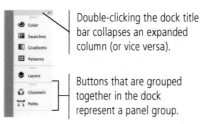

Double-clicking the dock title bar collapses an expanded column (or vice versa).

Buttons that are grouped together in the dock represent a panel group.

**14. Move the cursor over the left edge of the dock column. When the cursor becomes a double-headed arrow, click and drag right.**

If you only see the icons, you can also drag the dock edge to the left to reveal the panel names. This can be particularly useful until you are more familiar with the application and the icons used to symbolize the different panels.

Click here and drag right to hide the panel names.

*Note:*

*Dragging the left edge of a dock column changes the width of all panels in that dock column. This works for both iconized and expanded columns.*

**15. On the left side of the workspace, double-click the Tools panel title bar.**

The Tools panel can't be expanded, but it can be displayed as either one or two columns; double-clicking the Tools panel title bar toggles between the two modes.

The one- or two-column format is a purely personal choice. The one-column layout takes up less horizontal space on the screen, which can be useful if you have a small monitor. The two-column format fits in a smaller vertical space, which can be especially useful if you have a widescreen monitor.

The Tools panel can also be floated by clicking its title bar and dragging away from the edge of the screen. To re-dock the floating Tools panel, simply click the title bar and drag back to the left edge of the screen; when the blue line highlights the edge of the workspace, releasing the mouse button puts the Tools panel back into the dock.

Double-click the Tools panel title bar to toggle between the one- and two-column layouts.

*Note:*

*Throughout this book, our screen captures show the Tools panel in the one-column format. Feel free to work with the panel in two columns if you prefer.*

**16. Continue to the next exercise.**

## Customizing the Tools Panel

Near the bottom of the Tools panel, the Edit Toolbar button ⋯ provides access to a dialog box where you can customize the options that appear in the Tools panel. If you click and hold on this button, you can choose the Edit Toolbar option in the pop-up menu.

In the Customize Toolbar dialog box, you can select and move individual tools or entire groups of tools into the Extra Tools window. Any tools in that window are moved from their regular position in the default Tools panel to a single position, nested under the Edit Toolbar option.

You can toggle the buttons in the bottom-left corner of the dialog box to show or hide several options in the Tools panel. From left to right:

- Edit Toolbar
- Default Foreground and Background Colors
- Edit in Quick Mask Mode
- Change Screen Mode

If you choose to hide the Edit Toolbar option, any tools in the Extra Tools list are simply hidden; you will not be able to access them unless you customize the Tools panel again. (In this case, you can accomplish this task by choosing Edit>Toolbar.)

Clicking the Restore Defaults button in the Customize Toolbar dialog box resets all tools and options in the panel to their original default positions and visibility.

Click and drag tools from the Toolbar list to the Extra Tools list.

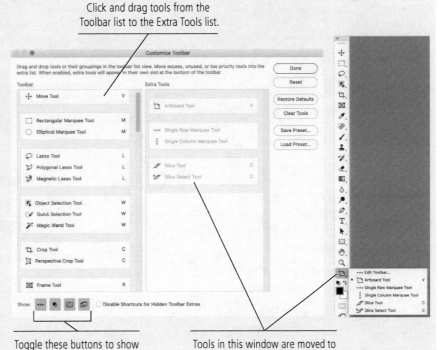

Toggle these buttons to show and hide extra options at the bottom of the Tools panel.

Tools in this window are moved to a single group at the bottom of the Tools panel, nested below the Edit Toolbar option.

# Accessing Photoshop Tools

In the Tools panel, tools with a small mark in the lower-right corner have **nested tools**.

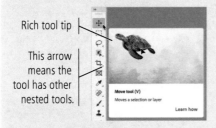

Rich tool tip

This arrow means the tool has other nested tools.

If you hover your mouse over a tool, a rich **tool tip** shows the name of the tool, keyboard shortcut (if any), a small animation related to that tool, and a link to video tutorials related to the specific tools.

You can disable overall tool tips or rich tool tips in the Tools pane of the Preferences dialog box. If you disable only rich tool tips, you would see only the tool name and keyboard shortcut when you hover over a tool.

You can access nested tools by clicking the primary tool and holding down the mouse button, or by Control/right-clicking the primary tool to open the menu of nested options.

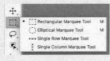

If a tool has a defined shortcut, pressing that key activates the associated tool. Most nested tools have the same shortcut as the default tool. By default, you have to press Shift plus the shortcut key to access the nested variations. You can change this behavior in the Tools pane of the Preferences dialog box by unchecking the Use Shift Key for Tool Switch option; when unchecked, you can simply press the shortcut key multiple times to cycle through variations.

Finally, if you press and hold a tool's keyboard shortcut, you can temporarily call that tool (called **spring-loaded keys**). After releasing the shortcut key, you return to the previous tool. For example, you might switch temporarily from the Brush to the Eraser tool while painting.

The following chart offers a quick reference of nested tools, as well as the shortcut for each (if any). Nested tools are shown indented.

- Move tool (V)
  - Artboard tool (V)
- Rectangular Marquee tool (M)
  - Elliptical Marquee tool (M)
  - Single Row Marquee tool
  - Single Column Marquee tool
- Lasso tool (L)
  - Polygonal Lasso tool (L)
  - Magnetic Lasso tool (L)
- Object Selection tool (W)
  - Quick Selection tool (W)
  - Magic Wand tool (W)
- Crop tool (C)
  - Perspective Crop tool (C)
  - Slice tool (C)
  - Slice Select tool (C)
- Frame tool (I)
- Eyedropper tool (I)
  - 3D Material Eyedropper tool (I)
  - Color Sampler tool (I)
  - Ruler tool (I)
  - Note tool (I)
  - Count tool (I)
- Spot Healing Brush tool (J)
  - Healing Brush tool (J)
  - Patch tool (J)
  - Content Aware Move tool (J)
  - Red Eye tool (J)
- Brush tool (B)
  - Pencil tool (B)
  - Color Replacement tool (B)
  - Mixer Brush tool (B)
- Clone Stamp tool (S)
  - Pattern Stamp tool (S)

- History Brush tool (Y)
  - Art History Brush tool (Y)
- Eraser tool (E)
  - Background Eraser tool (E)
  - Magic Eraser tool (E)
- Gradient tool (G)
  - Paint Bucket tool (G)
  - 3D Material Drop tool (G)
- Blur tool
  - Sharpen tool
  - Smudge tool
- Dodge tool (O)
  - Burn tool (O)
  - Sponge tool (O)
- Pen tool (P)
  - Freeform Pen tool (P)
  - Curvature Pen tool (P)
  - Add Anchor Point tool
  - Delete Anchor Point tool
  - Convert Point tool
- Horizontal Type tool (T)
  - Vertical Type tool (T)
  - Vertical Type Mask tool (T)
  - Horizontal Type Mask tool (T)
- Path Selection tool (A)
  - Direct Selection tool (A)
- Rectangle tool (U)
  - Ellipse tool (U)
  - Triangle tool (U)
  - Polygon tool (U)
  - Line tool (U)
  - Custom Shape tool (U)
- Hand tool (H)
  - Rotate View tool (R)
- Zoom tool (Z)

# Create a Saved Workspace

You have extensive control over the appearance of your Photoshop workspace. You can choose which panels are visible, where they appear, and even the size of individual panels or panel groups. Over time you will develop personal preferences — the Layers panel always appears at the top, for example — based on your work habits and project needs. Rather than re-establishing every workspace element each time you return to Photoshop, you can save your custom workspace settings so they can be recalled with a single click.

**Note:**

*Because workspace preferences are largely a matter of personal taste, the projects in this book instruct you regarding which panels to use, but not where to place those elements within the interface.*

1. **Choose Window>Workspace>New Workspace.**

   Saved workspaces can be accessed in the Window>Workspace submenu, as well as the Workspace switcher on the Options bar.

   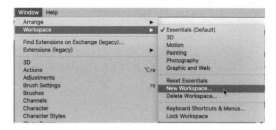

2. **In the New Workspace dialog box, type Portfolio and then click Save.**

   You didn't define custom keyboard shortcuts, menus, or toolbars, so those options are not relevant in this exercise.

**Note:**

*The Delete Workspace option opens a dialog box where you can choose a specific user-defined workspace to delete. You can't delete the default workspaces that come with the application.*

3. **Open the Window menu and choose Workspace>Essentials (Default).**

   Calling a saved workspace restores the last-used state of the workspace. You made a number of changes since calling the Essentials workspace at the beginning of the previous exercise, so calling it now restores the last state of that workspace. In essence, nothing changes from the saved Portfolio workspace.

   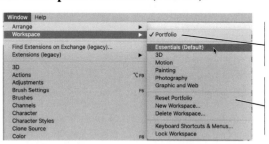

   Custom workspaces appear at the top of the list.

   Options in this submenu are also available in the Workspace switcher.

   Access saved workspaces in the Workspace Switcher.

4. **Open the Workspace switcher and choose Reset Essentials (or choose Window>Workspace>Reset Essentials).**

Remember, saved workspaces remember the last-used state. Calling a workspace again restores the panels exactly as they were the last time you used that workspace. For example, if you close a panel that is part of a saved workspace, the closed panel will not be reopened the next time you call the same workspace. To restore the saved state of the workspace — including opening closed panels or repositioning moved ones — you have to use the Reset option.

*Note:*

*If you change anything and quit the application, those changes are remembered, even when Photoshop is relaunched.*

5. **Using the Window>Workspace menu or the Workspace switcher, call the saved Portfolio workspace.**

6. **Continue to the next exercise.**

## Customizing Keyboard Shortcuts and Menus

People use Photoshop for many different reasons; some use only a limited set of tools to complete specific projects. Photoshop allows you to define the available menu options and the keyboard shortcuts that are associated with menu commands, panel menus, and tools.

At the bottom of the Edit menu, two options (Keyboard Shortcuts and Menus) open different tabs of the same dialog box. If you don't see the Keyboard Shortcuts or Menus options in the Edit menu, choose Show all Menu Items to reveal the hidden commands.

Once you have defined custom menus or shortcuts, you can save your choices as a set so you can access the same custom choices again without having to redo the work.

Click here to access existing saved sets.    Save the changes to the current set.    Save the changes as a new set.    Delete the selected set.

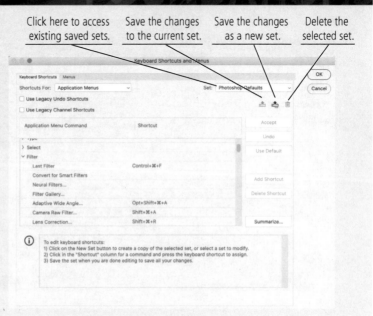

# Explore the Photoshop Document Views

There is much more to using Photoshop than arranging the workspace. What you do with those panels — and even which panels you need — depends on the type of work you are doing in a particular file. In this exercise, you open a Photoshop file and explore interface elements that will be important as you create digital artwork.

*Watch the video* ***Navigating the Photoshop Document Window*** *in your online student resources.*

1. **In Photoshop, choose File>Open.**

2. **If necessary, click the On Your Computer button in the bottom-left corner of the dialog box to show the system-standard navigation dialog box.**

Click here to access folders and files on your local drives.

**Note:**

*Press Command/ Control-O to access the Open dialog box.*

3. **Navigate to your WIP>InterfacePS folder and select glass.jpg in the list of available files. Press Shift, and then click welder.jpg.**

   The Open dialog box is a system-standard navigation dialog. This is one area of significant difference between Macintosh and Windows users.

   On both operating systems, this step selects all files, including those between the two you click. Pressing Shift allows you to select multiple consecutive files in the list. You can also press Command/Control and click to select multiple, non-consecutive files.

Macintosh                    Windows

### 4. Click Open.

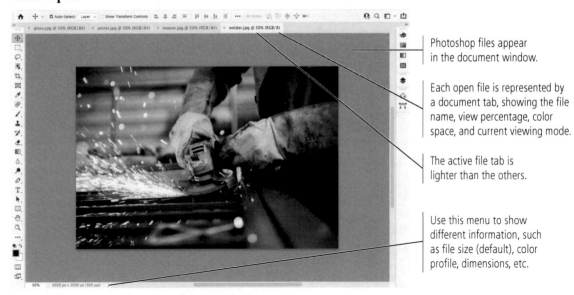

Photoshop files appear in the document window.

Each open file is represented by a document tab, showing the file name, view percentage, color space, and current viewing mode.

The active file tab is lighter than the others.

Use this menu to show different information, such as file size (default), color profile, dimensions, etc.

### 5. Click the glass.jpg tab to make that document active.

### 6. Highlight the current value in the View Percentage field (in the bottom-left corner of the document window). Type 80, then press Return/Enter.

Different people prefer larger or smaller view percentages, depending on a number of factors (eyesight, monitor size, and so on). As you complete the projects in this book, you will see our screen captures zoom in or out as necessary to show you the most relevant part of a particular file. Unless it is specifically required for the work being done, we do not tell you which view percentage to use for an exercise.

**Note:**

*Macintosh users: If you turn off the Application frame, opening multiple files creates a document window that has a separate title bar showing the name of the active file.*

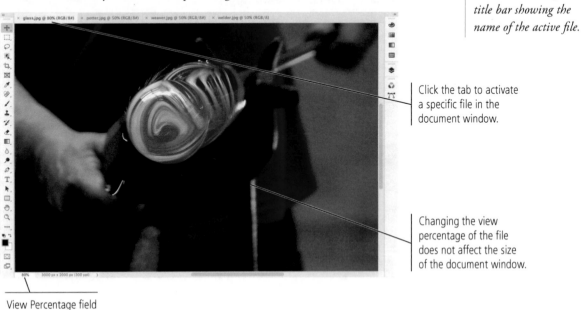

Click the tab to activate a specific file in the document window.

Changing the view percentage of the file does not affect the size of the document window.

View Percentage field

7. **Choose View>100%.**

These options affect the file's view percentage.

8. **Click the Hand tool (near the bottom of the Tools panel). Click in the document window, hold down the mouse button, and drag around.**

The Hand tool is a very easy and convenient option for changing the area of an image currently visible in the document window.

If the Scroll All Windows option is checked in the Options bar, dragging in one window affects the visible area of all open files.

Hand tool cursor

## 9. Click the Zoom tool in the Tools panel. Press Option/Alt, and then click anywhere in the document window.

Again: we list differing commands in the Macintosh/Windows format.
On Macintosh, you need to press the Option key; on Windows, press the Alt key.
We will not repeat this explanation every time different commands are required for the different operating systems.

Clicking with the Zoom tool enlarges the view percentage in specific, predefined percentage steps. Pressing Option/Alt while clicking with the Zoom tool reduces the view percentage in the reverse sequence of the same percentages.

If Scrubby Zoom is not active in the Options bar, clicking and dragging with the Zoom tool enlarges the selected area to fill the document window. If Scrubby Zoom is active, clicking and dragging dynamically enlarges (if you drag right) or reduces (if you drag left) the image in the document window.

You can zoom a document between approximately 0.098% and 3200%. We say approximately because the actual smallest size is dependent on the original image size. You can zoom out far enough to show the image as a single tiny square, regardless of the percentage of the image that represents.

When the Zoom tool is active, pressing Option/Alt changes the cursor to the Zoom Out icon.

## 10. In the Options bar, click the Fill Screen button.

The Options bar appears by default at the top of the workspace below the Menu bar. It is context sensitive, which means it provides different options depending on which tool is active. When the Zoom tool is active:

- If **Resize Windows to Fit** is checked, zooming in a floating window affects the size of the actual document window.

- If **Zoom All Windows** is checked, zooming in one window affects the view percentage of all open files.

- **Scrubby Zoom** enables dynamic image zooming depending on the direction in which you drag in the document window.

- The **100%** button changes the view percentage to 100%.

- The **Fit Screen** option changes the image view to the percentage necessary to show the entire image in the document window. This has the same effect as choosing Window>Fit on Screen.

- The **Fill Screen** button changes the image view to whatever percentage is necessary to fill the available space in the document window.

**Note:**

*You can toggle the Options bar on or off by choosing Window>Options.*

**Note:**

*If you check the Enable Narrow Options Bar option in the Workspace pane of the Preferences dialog box, many options in the Options bar will appear as small icons that you can click to toggle on and off. This saves horizontal space on narrow monitors.*

The Fit Screen command automatically calculates view percentage based on the size of the document window.

11. **In the Tools panel, choose the Rotate View tool (nested under the Hand tool). Click in the top half of the document window and drag right to turn the document clockwise.**

The Rotate View tool turns an image without permanently altering the orientation of the file; the actual image data remains unchanged. This tool allows you to more easily work on objects or elements that are not oriented horizontally (for example, working with text that appears on an angle in the final image).

In the Options bar, you can type a specific angle in the Rotation Angle field, or click the rotation proxy icon, to dynamically rotate the view. At any time, you can click the Reset View button to restore the original rotation (0°) of the image. If Rotate All Windows is checked, dragging in one window affects the view angle of all open files.

The red arrow of the compass indicates the image's original North.

Rotate View tool cursor

12. **In the Options bar, click the Reset View button.**

As we said, the Rotate View tool is **non-destructive** (i.e., it does not permanently affect the pixels in the image). You can easily use the tool's options to define a specific view angle or to restore an image to its original orientation.

Resetting the view restores the image's original orientation.

13. **Continue to the next exercise.**

Most Photoshop projects require some amount of zooming in and out to various view percentages, as well as navigating around the document within its window. As we show you how to complete different stages of the workflow, we usually won't tell you when to change your view percentage because that's largely a matter of personal preference. However, you should understand the different options for navigating around a Photoshop file so you can easily and efficiently get to what you want, when you want to get there.

### View Percentage Field

You can type a specific percentage in the View Percentage field in the bottom-left corner of the document window.

### View Menu

The View menu also provides options for changing the view percentage, including the associated keyboard shortcuts. The Zoom In and Zoom Out options step through the same predefined view percentages the Zoom tool uses.

| | |
|---|---|
| Zoom In | Command/Control-equals (=) |
| Zoom Out | Command/Control-minus (-) |
| Fit On Screen | Command/Control-0 (zero) |
| Actual Pixels (100%) | Command/Control-1 |

### Zoom Tool

You can click with the **Zoom tool** to increase the view percentage in specific, predefined intervals. Pressing Option/Alt with the Zoom tool allows you to zoom out in the same predefined percentages.

If Scrubby Zoom is active in the Options bar, you can click and drag left to reduce the view percentage, or drag right to increase the view percentage. (The Scrubby Zoom option does not follow predefined stepped percentages.) If Scrubby Zoom is not active, clicking and dragging with the Zoom tool enlarges the selected area to fill the document window.

### Hand Tool

At any view percentage, you can use the **Hand tool** to drag the file around in the document window. The Hand tool changes only what is visible in the window; it has no effect on the actual pixels in the image.

### Mouse Scroll Wheel

If your mouse has a scroll wheel, rolling the scroll wheel up or down moves the image up or down within the document window. If you press Command/Control and scroll the wheel, you can move the image right or left within the document window. You can also press Option/Alt and then scroll the wheel up to zoom in or down to zoom out.

In the General pane of the Preferences dialog box, the Zoom with Scroll Wheel option is unchecked by default. If you check this option, scrolling up or down with no modifier key zooms in or out and does not move the image within the document window.

### Navigator Panel

The **Navigator panel** is another method of adjusting how close your viewpoint is, and what part of the page you're currently viewing if zoomed in close enough that you're only seeing a portion of the image. The Navigator panel shows a thumbnail of the active file. A red rectangle represents exactly how much of the document shows in the document window.

Drag the red rectangle to change the visible portion of the file.

Use the slider and field at the bottom of the panel to change the view percentage.

Explore the Arrangement of Multiple Documents

You will often need to work with more than one Photoshop file at once. Photoshop incorporates a number of options for arranging multiple documents. We designed the following simple exercise so you can explore these options.

1. **With all four files from the WIP>InterfacePS folder open, click the weaver.jpg document tab to make that the active file.**

2. **Choose Window>Arrange>Float in Window.**

   You can also separate all open files by choosing Window>Arrange>Float All In Windows.

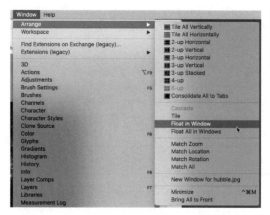

Floating a document separates the file into its own document window.

The title bar of the separate document window shows the same information that was in the document tab.

3. **Choose Window>Arrange>4-up.**

   The defined arrangements provide a number of options for tiling multiple open files within the available workspace. These arrangements manage all open files, including those in floating windows.

   The options' icons suggest the result of each command. The active file remains active; this is indicated by the brighter text in the active document's tab.

*Note:*

*All open files are listed at the bottom of the Window menu.*

glass.jpg
potter.jpg
✓ weaver.jpg
welder.jpg

*Note:*

*If more files are open than what a specific arrangement indicates, the extra files will be consolidated as tabs into the window with the active file.*

### 4. Choose Window>Arrange>Consolidate All to Tabs.

This command restores all documents — floating or not— into a single tabbed document window.

### 5. At the bottom of the Tools panel, click the Change Screen Mode button and hold down the mouse button.

Photoshop has three different **screen modes**, which change the way the document window displays on the screen. The default mode, which you saw when you opened these three files, is called Standard Screen mode.

*Note:*

*Press F to cycle through the different screen modes.*

### 6. Choose Full Screen Mode with Menu Bar from the Change Screen Mode menu.

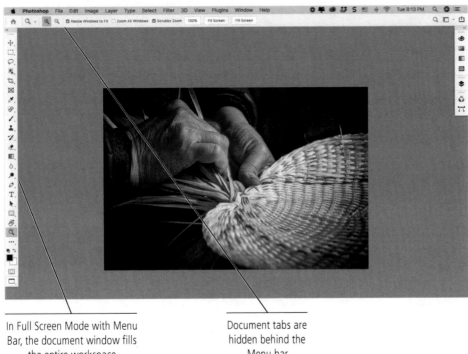

In Full Screen Mode with Menu Bar, the document window fills the entire workspace.

Document tabs are hidden behind the Menu bar.

7. **Click the Change Screen Mode button in the Tools panel and choose Full Screen Mode.**

In Full Screen Mode, the Menu bar, title bar, and all panels are hidden.

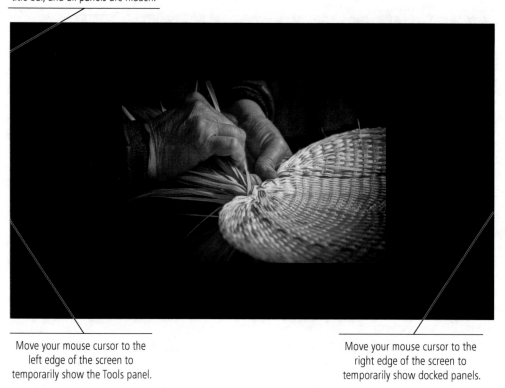

Move your mouse cursor to the left edge of the screen to temporarily show the Tools panel.

Move your mouse cursor to the right edge of the screen to temporarily show docked panels.

8. **Press the Escape key to return to Standard Screen mode.**

9. **Click the Close button on the weaver.jpg tab.**

10. **Macintosh: Click the Close button in the top-left corner of the Application frame.**

Closing the Macintosh Application frame closes all open files, but does *not* quit the application.

**Windows: Click the Close button on each document tab to close the files.**

Clicking the Close button on the Windows Menu bar closes all open files *and* quits the application. To close open files *without* quitting, you have to manually close each file.

Closing the Application frame closes all open files.

Macintosh

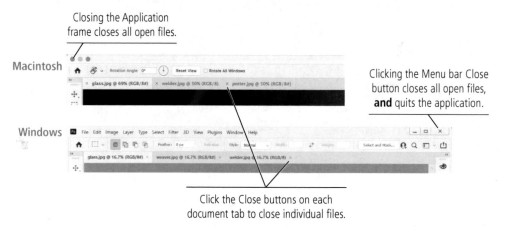

Clicking the Menu bar Close button closes all open files, **and** quits the application.

Windows

Click the Close buttons on each document tab to close individual files.

# 1

# New Music Artwork

You have been hired to create the artwork for a local band's new collection release. The final artwork will be used for an old-school vinyl album sleeve, in CD cases, on digital music libraries, and in advertisements in a variety of printed media (newspapers, magazines, and so on).

This project incorporates the following skills:

❑ Creating a composite ad from multiple supplied images

❑ Compositing multiple photographs, using various techniques to select the focal object in each image

❑ Incorporating graphics as rasterized layers and Smart Object layers

❑ Moving and transforming layer content in relation to the page and to each other

❑ Managing individual layout elements using layers and layer groups

❑ Saving versions of a file to meet different output requirements

## Videos to Watch

Access these helpful videos in your online student resources:

▶▶ New Music Art Project Introduction

▶▶ Understanding Resolution

▶▶ Cropping Images

▶▶ Using Selection Tools (Part 1)

▶▶ Using Selection Tools (Part 2)

client comments

Our new disc, Waiting For the Storm, kind of tells a story across the 11 tracks. The husband goes away on military service, the wife waits for him, he comes home but doesn't remember her, and she looks for answers to his amnesia.

Our band is a combination of rock, country, and alternative/punk. We want the artwork for the new collection to be dramatic, and reflect both our personalities, and the story we are telling.

We're actually releasing this first as a limited-edition album on vinyl. The sleeve for that version is 10″, square. We also need files for a standard-size printed CD insert, and for digital libraries like iTunes.

**Watch the video** New Music Art Project Introduction in your online student resources.

art director comments

The band loved the initial concept sketch I submitted last week, so we're ready to start building the files. In addition to the band's logo, I've gathered the photographs I want to use. I also already created a title treatment in Photoshop, so I'll send you that file as well.

The special edition LP will be 10″, square, but you need to incorporate a 1/8″ bleed allowance and a 1/4″ margin since the cover sleeve will be printed.

The 10″ file should be large enough for most print advertising applications, so we can just use the same file for those projects.

A standard CD insert is 4.75″, square. That version needs to incorporate 1/8″ bleeds as well, but it only needs 1/8″ safe margin according to our printer.

For digital media, use the current standards for iTunes music cover art. They require artwork to be at least 3000 × 3000 pixels, and delivered as high-quality JPEG or PNG files. That format should be sufficient for most other online catalogs.

project objectives

To complete this project, you will:

❏ Resize a raster image to change resolution

❏ Composite multiple images into a single background file

❏ Incorporate both raster and vector elements into the same design

❏ Transform and arrange individual layers to create a cohesive design

❏ Create layer groups to easily manage related layer content

❏ Use selection techniques to isolate images from their backgrounds

❏ Save different types of files for different ad requirements

# STAGE 1 / Compositing Images and Artwork

Technically speaking, **compositing** is the process of combining any two or more objects (images, text, illustrations, etc.) into an overall design. The ad you're building in this project requires compositing three digital photographs, as well as title treatment and logo files that were created in Adobe Illustrator by other designers. The various elements that make up the finished artwork are fairly representative of the type of work you can (and probably will) create in Photoshop.

## *Types of Images*

There are two primary types of digital artwork: vector graphics and raster images.

**Vector graphics** are composed of mathematical descriptions of a series of lines and shapes. Vector graphics are **resolution independent**; they can be freely enlarged or reduced, and they are automatically output at the resolution of the device being used to print them. The shapes that you create in Adobe InDesign, or in drawing applications, such as Adobe Illustrator, are vector graphics.

**Raster images**, such as photographs, are made up of a grid of independent pixels (rasters or bits) in rows and columns (called a **bitmap**). Raster files are **resolution dependent**; their resolution is fixed, and is determined when you scan, photograph, or otherwise create the file. You can typically reduce raster images, but you cannot significantly enlarge them without losing image quality.

**Line art** (also called a bitmap image) is actually a type of raster image, made up entirely of 100% solid areas. The pixels in a line-art image have only two options: they can be all black or all white. Examples of line art are UPC bar codes or pen-and-ink drawings.

## *Screen Ruling*

The file that you will be building in this project is intended to be printed, so you have to build the new file with the appropriate settings for commercial printing. When reproducing a photograph on a printing press, the image must be converted into a set of printable dots that fool the eye into believing it sees continuous tones. Prior to image-editing software, pictures that were being prepared for printing on a press were photographed through a screen to create a grid of **halftone dots** that simulate continuous tone, resulting is a **halftone image**. Light tones in a photograph are represented as small halftone dots; dark tones become large halftone dots.

The screens used to create the halftone images had a finite number of available dots in a horizontal or vertical inch. That number was the **screen ruling**, or **lines per inch (lpi)** of the halftone. A screen ruling of 133 lpi means that in a square inch; there are 133 × 133 (17,689) possible locations for a halftone dot. If the screen ruling is decreased, there are fewer total halftone dots, producing a grainier image. If the screen ruling is increased, there are more halftone dots, producing a clearer image.

**Line screen** is a finite number based on a combination of the intended output device and paper. You can't randomly select a line screen. Ask your printer what line screen will be used before you begin creating your images. If you can't find out ahead of time or if you're unsure, follow these general guidelines:

- Newspaper or newsprint: 85–100 lpi

- Magazine or general commercial printing: 133–150 lpi

- Premium-quality-paper jobs (such as art books or annual reports): 150–175 lpi; some specialty jobs might use 200 lpi or more

## Image Resolution

When an output device creates halftone dots, it calculates the average value of a group of pixels in the raster image and generates a spot of appropriate size. A raster image's resolution — measured in **pixels per inch (ppi)** — determines the quantity of pixel data the printer can read. Images need to have sufficient resolution so the output device can generate enough halftone dots to create the

appearance of continuous tone. In the images above, the same raster image is reproduced at 72 ppi (left) and 300 ppi (right). Notice the obvious degradation in quality in the 72-ppi version.

Ideally, the printer will have four pixels for each halftone dot created. In the image to the right, each white square represents a pixel. The highlighted area shows the pixel information used to generate a halftone dot. If an image only has 72 pixels per inch, the output device has to generate four halftone dots per pixel, resulting in poor printed quality.

The relationship between pixels and halftone dots defines the rule of resolution for raster-based images — the resolution of a raster image (ppi) should be two times the screen ruling (lpi) that will be used for printing.

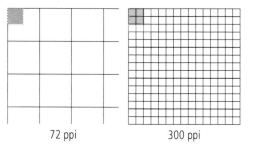

72 ppi                300 ppi

 Open and Resize an Image

Every raster image has a defined, specific resolution that is established when the image is created. If you scan an image to be 3″ high by 3″ wide at 150 ppi, that image has 450 pixels in each vertical column and 450 pixels in each horizontal row. Simply resizing the image stretches, or compresses, those pixels into a different physical space, but does not add or remove pixel information. If you resize the 3″ × 3″ image to 6″ × 6″ (200% of the original), the 450 pixels in each column or row are forced to extend across 6″ instead of 3″, causing a marked loss of quality.

The **effective resolution** of an image is the resolution calculated after any scaling is taken into account. This number is equally (perhaps more so) as important as the original image resolution. The effective resolution can be calculated with a fairly simple equation:

> Original resolution ÷ (% magnification ÷ 100) = Effective resolution

If a 300-ppi image is magnified 150%, the effective resolution is:

> 300 ppi ÷ 1.5 = 200 ppi

In other words, the more you enlarge a raster image, the lower its effective resolution becomes. In general, you can make an image 10% or 15% larger without significant adverse effects. The more you enlarge an image, however, the worse the results. Even Photoshop, which offers very sophisticated formulas (called "algorithms") for sizing images, cannot guarantee perfect results.

Effective resolution can be a very important consideration when working with client-supplied images, especially those that come from consumer-level digital cameras. Many of those devices capture images with a specific number of pixels rather than a number of pixels per inch (ppi). In this exercise, you will explore the effective resolution of an image to see if it can be used for a full-page printed magazine ad.

**Note:**

*For line art, the general rule is to scan the image at the same resolution as the output device. Many laser printers and digital presses image at 600–1200 dots per inch (dpi). Imagesetters used to make printing plates for a commercial press typically output at much higher resolution — possibly 2400 dpi or more.*

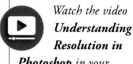 *Watch the video* ***Understanding Resolution in Photoshop*** *in your online student resources.*

1. **Expand the Music_PS22_RF.zip archive in your WIP folder (Macintosh) or copy the archive contents into your WIP folder (Windows).**

   This results in a folder named **Music**, which contains all of the files you need for this project. You should also use this folder to save the files you create in this project.

   If necessary, refer to Page 1 of the Interface chapter for specific information on expanding or accessing the required resource files.

2. **Choose File>Open. If necessary, click the On Your Computer button in the bottom-left corner of the dialog box to show the system-standard navigation dialog box.**

   The Open dialog box defaults to show the last-used option, so you might see the Cloud Documents pane, which is used to access any files that have been saved directly into your Creative Cloud (CC) account.

   In this project you are working with files on your local computer (or other local drive), so you might need to click the Your Computer button to access the system-standard navigation dialog box for opening files.

*Note:*

*We are intentionally overlooking issues of color space for the sake of this project. You will learn about color spaces and color management in Project 3: Museum Image Correction.*

3. **Navigate to your WIP>Music folder. Select Sunrise.jpg and click Open.**

*Note:*

*If you open a Photoshop Cloud file from your account, the document tab shows a cloud icon before the file name.*

Click here to access folders and files on your local drives.

4. **If the rulers are not visible on the top and left edges, choose View>Rulers (or press Command/Control-R).**

5. **Control/right-click the horizontal ruler and choose Inches as the default unit of measurement.**

As you can see in the rulers, this image has a very large physical size.

Use the contextual menu to make sure rulers are displayed in Inches.

*Note:*

*You can change the default unit of measurement in the Units & Rulers pane of the Preferences dialog box. Double-clicking either ruler opens the appropriate pane of the Preferences dialog box.*

6. **Choose Image>Image Size.**

The Image Size dialog box shows the number of pixels in the image, as well as the image dimensions and current resolution. You can change any value in this dialog box, but you should understand what those changes mean before you do so.

As you can see, this image is approximately 69″ wide and 46″ high, but it was captured at 72 pixels/inch. For most commercial printing, you need at least 300 ppi. You can use the principle of effective resolution to change the file to a high enough resolution for printing.

The actual number of pixels in the image is the most important information.

Use this widget to change the preview percentage.

Click and drag in the preview window to show a different area.

*Note:*

*Press Command-Option-I/Control-Alt-I to open the Image Size dialog box.*

7. **Check the Resample option at the bottom of the dialog box (if necessary).**

The options in this dialog box remember the last-used choices. The Resample option might already be checked in your dialog box.

**Resampling** means maintaining the existing resolution in the new image dimensions; in other words, you are either adding or deleting pixels to the existing image. When this option is turned on, you can change the dimensions of an image without affecting the resolution, or you can change the resolution of an image (useful for removing excess resolution or **downsampling**) without affecting the image size.

When the Resample option is checked, you can use the attached menu to tell Photoshop how to generate extra pixel data when increasing the image size, or which pixels to discard when reducing the image size. Each option also includes a parenthetical notation about when it is best used (enlargement, smooth gradients, etc.).

8. **Change the Resolution field to 300 pixels/inch.**

When you change resolution with resampling turned on, you do not change the file's physical size. To achieve 300-ppi resolution at the new size, Photoshop needs to add a huge number of pixels to the image. You can see at the top of the dialog box that this change would increase the number of pixels from 4943 × 3300 to 20596 × 13750.

You can also see that changing the resolution of an image without affecting its physical dimensions would have a significant impact on the file size. Changing the resolution to 300 ppi at the current size would increase the file size to over 810 megabytes.

When Resample is checked, changing the Resolution value adds or removes pixels.

Higher resolution means larger file sizes, which translates to longer processing time for printing, or longer download time over the Internet. When you scale an image to a smaller size, simply resizing can produce files with far greater effective resolution than you need. Resampling allows you to reduce physical size without increasing the resolution, resulting in a smaller file size.

The caveat is that once you delete pixels, they are gone. If you later try to re-enlarge the smaller image, you will not achieve the same quality as the original file before it was reduced. You should save reduced images as copies instead of overwriting the originals.

9. **Press Option/Alt and click the Reset button to restore the original image dimensions in the dialog box.**

In many Photoshop dialog boxes, pressing the Option/Alt key changes the Cancel button to Reset. You can click the Reset button to restore the original values that existed when you opened the dialog box.

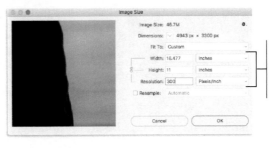

Pressing Option/Alt changes the Cancel button to Reset.

10. **Uncheck the Resample option at the bottom of the dialog box.**

11. **Change the Resolution field to 300 pixels/inch.**

Resizing *without* resampling basically means distributing the same number of pixels over a different amount of physical space. When you resize an image without resampling, you do not change the number of pixels in the image. In fact, those fields in the dialog box become simple text; the fields are unavailable and you cannot change the number of pixels in the image.

When the Resample option is unchecked, these three fields are all linked.

You can see how changing one of the linked fields (Resolution) directly affects the other linked fields (Width and Height). By resizing the image to be 300 ppi — enough for most commercial print quality — you now have an image that is approximately 16.5″ × 11″.

**12. Click OK to apply the change and return to the document window.**

The rulers change to reflect the new dimensions of the file.

Because you did not resample the image, the screen display does not change.

**13. Choose File>Save As.**

The File>Save command save changes to the active file in the current format and location.

The File>Save As command allows you to save a file with a different name, in a different format, and/or in a different location.

The File>Save a Copy command allows you to easily save a variation of a file in a different format — for example, a flat JPEG file from a layered native Photoshop file. This command offers a certain level of protection against accidentally overwriting a file when that is not your intent. When you use this command, the word "copy" is automatically added to the name of the new file you are saving (although you can delete that word if you choose).

**14. In the resulting dialog box, click the Save on Your Computer button.**

When you save a file in Photoshop, you now have a choice to save the file as a Photoshop Cloud document, or a regular Photoshop file on your desktop. If you choose the Save to Cloud Documents button, the file is saved in your Creative Cloud account with the special extension ".psdc".

**15. If necessary, navigate to your WIP>Music folder as the target location.**

**16. In the Save As/File Name field, change the word "Sunrise" to cd-artwork.**

Since this is a basic image file with only one layer (so far), most of the other options in the Save As dialog box are grayed out (not available).

**17. Choose Photoshop in the Format/Save As Type menu and then click Save.**

You can save a Photoshop file in a number of different formats, all of which have specific capabilities, limitations, and purposes.

While you are still working on a file, it's best to keep it as a native Photoshop (PSD) file. When you choose a different format, the correct extension is automatically added to the file name.

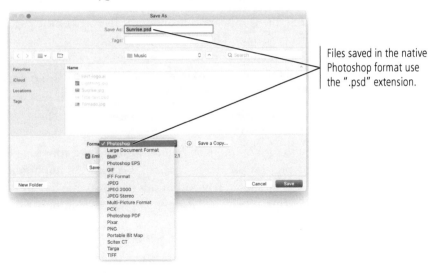

Files saved in the native Photoshop format use the ".psd" extension.

**18. Continue to the next exercise.**

---

## Understanding File Saving Preferences

You can control a number of options related to saving in the File Handling pane of the Preferences dialog box.

**Image Previews.** You can use this menu to always or never include image thumbnails in the saved file. If you choose Ask When Saving in this menu, the Save As dialog box includes an option to include the preview/thumbnail.

On Macintosh, you have an additional option to include a thumbnail in the saved file; if checked, the image thumbnail appears in dialog boxes instead of the Photoshop file icon. If you choose Ask When Saving in this preference menu, the Save As dialog box will include a Thumbnail checkbox in the lower half; you can then use that checkbox to include a thumbnail in individual files.

**File Extension.** File extensions are always added to saved files, even if you delete it from the Save As/File Name field. This preference menu has only two options: Use Upper Case and Use Lower Case.

**Save As to Original Folder.** When this option is checked, choosing File>Save As automatically defaults to the location where the original file is located.

**Save in Background.** The Save process occurs by default in the background; in other words, you can continue working even while a file is being saved. This can be a significant time saver because you don't have to sit and wait the several minutes it might take to save a very large file.

When a file is being saved in the background, the completed percentage appears in the document tab.

× aftermath.psd @ 16.7% (Layer 6, RGB/8) – Saving 25%

**Automatically Save Recovery Information Every...** When checked, this option means that your work is saved in a temporary file, every 10 minutes, by default. If something happens — such as a power outage — you will be able to restore your work back to the last auto-saved version. In other words, the most you will lose is 10 minutes of work!

**Enable legacy "Save As".** If you check this option, the Save As and Save a Copy dialog boxes revert to behavior from older versions of the software, including an "As a copy" checkbox option in either dialog box.

**Do not append "copy" to filename when saving a copy.** Choosing File>Save a Copy allows you to save a new copy of a file, and the word "copy" is added to the filename by default. If you check this preference, the word "copy" is not automatically added to the filename when you choose the Save a Copy command.

Crop the Canvas and Place Ruler Guides

Watch the video
*Cropping Images in Photoshop* in your online student resources.

The final step in preparing the workspace is defining the live area of the page. **Trim size** is the actual size of a page once it has been cut out of the press sheet. According to your client, the final required artwork has a trim size of 10″ × 10″.

Any elements that print right to the edge of a page (called **bleeding**) must actually extend beyond the defined trim size. The **bleed allowance** is the amount of extra space that should be included for these bleed objects. Most applications require at least a 1/8″ bleed allowance on any bleed edge.

Because of inherent variation in the mechanical printing and trimming processes, most printing projects also define a safe or **live area**. All important design elements — especially text — should stay within this live area. The live area for this project is 9.5″ × 9.5″ (leaving a 0.25″ safe margin on each edge of the artwork).

*Note:*

*You should familiarize yourself with the most common fraction-to-decimal equivalents:*

*1/8 = 0.125*

*1/4 = 0.25*

*3/8 = 0.375*

*1/2 = 0.5*

*5/8 = 0.625*

*3/4 = 0.75*

*7/8 = 0.875*

1. **With cd-artwork.psd open, choose the Crop tool in the Tools panel.**

   When you choose the Crop tool, a crop marquee appears around the edges of the image. The marquee has eight handles, which you can drag to change the size of the crop area.

Crop tool

Marquee handles allow you to resize the crop area before finalizing the crop.

2. **In the Options bar, make sure the Delete Cropped Pixels option is checked.**

   When this option is checked, areas outside the crop area are permanently removed from all layers in the file. If this option is not checked, cropped pixels remain in the file, but exist outside the edges of the canvas. The Background layer, if one exists, is converted to a regular layer (you'll learn more about Background layers later).

   This is an important distinction — by maintaining cropped pixels, you can later transform or reposition layers to reveal different parts of the layer within the newly cropped canvas size.

3. **Click the right-center handle of the crop marquee and drag left until the cursor feedback shows W: 10.250 in.**

When you drag certain elements in the document window, live cursor feedback (also called "heads-up display") shows information about the transformation. When dragging a side crop marquee handle, for example, the feedback shows the new width of the area.

You might need to zoom into at least 50% view percentage to achieve the exact dimensions needed for this project.

**Note:**

*You can rotate a crop marquee by placing the cursor slightly away from a corner handle.*

Use the cursor feedback to find the appropriate measurement.

Click and drag the marquee handle to resize the marquee area.

4. **Repeat Step 3 with the top-center handle until feedback shows the area of H: 10.250 in.**

**Note:**

*At the time of this writing, a bug in the software might cause rulers to temporarily disappear when you begin dragging a crop handle.*

**Note:**

*It might be helpful to toggle off the Snap feature (View>Snap), which causes certain file elements to act as magnets when you move a marquee or drag a selection.*

Remember, the defined trim size is 10″ × 10″ for this ad. Anything that runs to the page edge has to incorporate a 0.125″ bleed allowance, so the actual canvas size must be large enough to accommodate the bleed allowance on all edges:

[Width]    10″ + 0.125″ + 0.125″ = 10.25″

[Height]    10″ + 0.125″ + 0.125″ = 10.25″

**Note:**

*You can press the Escape key to cancel the crop marquee and return to the uncropped image.*

When the Crop tool is selected, the Options bar can be used to define a number of settings related to the cropped area.

The first menu includes a number of common aspect ratio presets. If you choose one of these, the crop marquee is constrained to the specified aspect ratio. It's important to note that these presets define only the aspect ratio of the crop, not the actual size.

You can also choose the **W x H x Resolution** option to define custom settings for the result of a crop. For example, if you define the width and height of a crop area as 9″ × 9″ at 300 ppi, when you click and drag to draw, the crop area will be restricted to the same proportions defined in the Width and Height fields (in this example, 1:1).

When you finalize the crop, the resulting image will be resized to 9″ × 9″, regardless of the actual size of the crop marquee. This presents a problem if you remember the principles of resolution.

Enlarging a 3″ × 3″ area (for example) to 9″ × 9″ means the application needs to create enough pixels to fill in the 6 extra inches. At 300 ppi, Photoshop needs to create ("interpolate") more than 1800 pixels per linear inch. Although Photoshop can enlarge images with reasonable success, such a significant amount of new data will not result in the best possible quality. As a general rule, you should avoid enlarging raster images by such a large percentage.

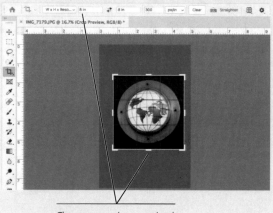

The crop area is constrained to the aspect ratio of the defined width and height.

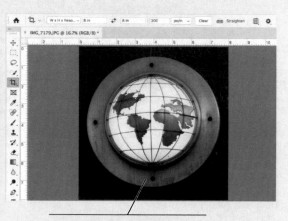

The resulting cropped image is the actual size defined in the Crop Image Size & Resolution dialog box.

You can use the **Set Overlay Options** menu (⊞) to show a variety of overlays within the crop area; these follow basic design principles, such as the Rule of Thirds and the Golden Spiral.

You can also use the commands in this menu to turn the overlay on or off. If you choose Auto Show Overlay, the selected overlay only appears when you drag the marquee handles or click inside the marquee area to move the image inside the crop area.

You can also click the **Set Additional Crop Options** button (✿) to access a variety of crop-related choices.

- If you check the **Use Classic Mode** option, the crop marquee reverts to the same appearance and behavior as in previous versions of Photoshop.

- When **Show Cropped Area** is checked, the area outside the crop marquee remains visible in the document window until you finalize the crop.

- When **Auto Center Preview** is checked, the crop area will always be centered in the document window. The image dynamically moves as you resize the crop area.

- When **Enable Crop Shield** is checked, areas outside the crop marquee are partially obscured by a semi-transparent solid color. You can use the related options to change the color and opacity of the shielded area.

When the Crop tool is selected, you can click the **Straighten** button in the Options bar, and then draw a line in the image to define what should be a straight line in the resulting image. The image behind the crop marquee rotates to show what will remain in the cropped canvas. The line you drew is adjusted to be perfectly horizontal or vertical.

Click the Straighten button, then draw a line representing what you want to be "straight" in the cropped image.

The image is rotated behind the crop marquee to be "straight" based on the line you drew.

You can draw a crop area larger than the existing canvas to effectively enlarge the canvas.

Using the default settings, new areas outside the original canvas size become transparent on regular layers, or filled with the background color on the locked Background layer.

If you check the **Content-Aware** option in the Options bar, Photoshop generates new pixels based on the existing image, filling the new pixels with content that better matches the previous image edges.

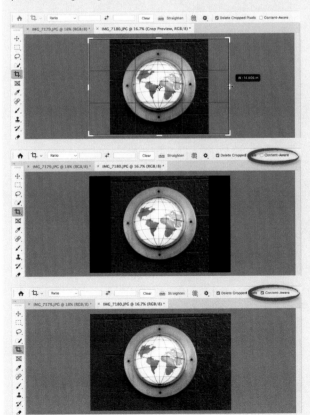

The **Perspective Crop tool** (nested under the Crop tool) can be used to draw a non-rectangular crop area. To define the area you want to keep, simply click to place the four corners of the area, then drag the corners in any direction as necessary. When you finalize the crop, the image inside the crop area is straightened to a front-on viewing angle. You should use this option with care, however, because it can badly distort an image.

In the following example, we used apparent lines in the photograph to draw the perspective crop marquee. After finalizing the crop, the building appears to be straight, rather than the original viewing angle at which it was photographed.

5. **Zoom out until you can see the entire canvas in the document window.**

6. **Click inside the crop area and drag to reposition the image so that the woman's silhouette is on the left side of the crop area (use the following image as a guide).**

When you change the marquee size, the area outside the marquee is "shielded" by a darkened overlay so you can get an idea of what will remain after you finalize the crop.

You can drag the image inside the crop area to change the portion that will remain in the cropped image. By default, the crop area remains in place; the image moves behind the crop area.

*Note:*

*You can also use the Arrow keys on your keyboard to "nudge" the image in a specific direction.*

*Note:*

*The X coordinate refers to an object's horizontal position and Y refers to the vertical position.*

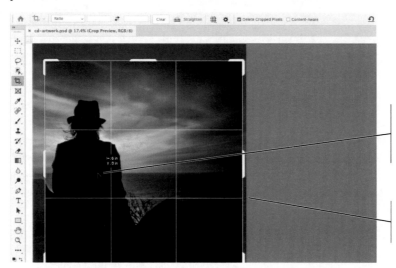

Click and drag inside the crop area to change the portion of the image inside the crop.

Areas outside the crop marquee are partially obscured.

7. **Press Return/Enter to finalize the crop.**

8. **Choose View>New Guide Layout.**

This dialog box makes it very easy to define a page grid using non-printing guides. The dialog box defaults to add 8 columns with a 20-pixel (0.067 in) gutter. In the document window, you can see the guides (blue lines) that will be created based on the active settings in the New Guide Layout dialog box.

9. **Uncheck the Columns option and check the Margin option. Change all four margin field values to 0.125.**

You can use the Margin fields to place guides at specific distances from each edge of the canvas. You don't need to type the unit of measurement because the default unit for this file is already inches. Photoshop automatically assumes the value you type is in the default unit of measurement.

10. **Click OK to return to the document and add the required trim guides.**

At this point you should have four guides – two vertical and two horizontal, each 1/8″ from the file edges. These mark the trim size of your final 10″ × 10″ file.

11. **Choose View>100%.**

It helps to zoom in to a higher view percentage if you want to precisely place guides. To complete the following steps accurately, we found it necessary to use at least 100% view.

12. **In the top-left corner of the document window, click the zero-point crosshairs and drag to the top-left intersection of the guides.**

You can reposition the zero point to the top-left corner of the bleed allowance by double-clicking the zero-point crosshairs.

Zero-point crosshairs

Drag to here to change the 0/0 point of the rulers.

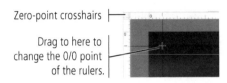

This new zero point will be the origin for measurments.

**13. Choose the Move tool, and then open the Info panel (Window>Info).**

As we explained in the Interface chapter, the panels you see depend on what was done the last time you (or someone else) used the Photoshop application. Because workspace arrangement is such a personal preference, we tell you what panels you need to use, but we don't tell you where to put them.

Remember, for this file, the live area should be a 0.25″ inset from the trim edge. In the next few steps you will add guides to identify that live area.

**14. Click the horizontal page ruler at the top of the page and drag down to create a guide positioned at the 1/4″ (0.25″) mark.**

If you watch the vertical ruler, you can see a marker indicating the position of the cursor. In addition to the live cursor feedback, the Info panel also shows the precise numeric position of the guide you are dragging.

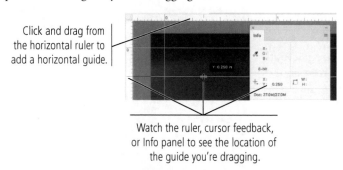
**15. Click the vertical ruler at the left and drag right to place a guide at the 0.25″ mark.**

Watch the marker on the horizontal ruler to judge the guide's position.

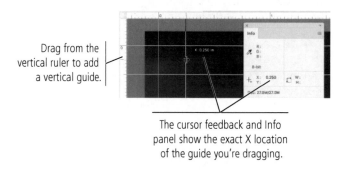

Drag from the vertical ruler to add a vertical guide.

The cursor feedback and Info panel show the exact X location of the guide you're dragging.

**16. Zoom out so you can see the entire canvas in the document window.**

**17. Choose View>New Guide. In the resulting dialog box, choose the Horizontal option, type 9.75 in the field, and click OK.**

This measurement results in the same 0.25″ margin that you created by manually dragging guides on the left and top edges of the canvas.

*New Guide dialog box:*
Orientation
○ Horizontal
○ Vertical
Position: 9.75 in
OK / Cancel

*Note:*

*Use the Move tool to reposition placed guides. Remove individual guides by dragging them back onto the ruler.*

*If you try to reposition a guide and can't, choose View>Lock Guides. If this option is checked, guides are locked; you can't move them until you toggle this option off.*

*Note:*

*Press Option/Alt and click a guide to change it from vertical to horizontal (or vice versa). The guide rotates around the point where you click, which can be useful if you need to find a corner based on the position of an existing guide.*

*Note:*

*You can press Command/Control-; to toggle the visibility of page guides.*

18. **Choose View>New Guide again. Choose the Vertical option and type 9.75 in the field. Click OK.**

Step 18

Step 19

19. **Double-click the zero-point crosshairs (where the two rulers meet in the top-left corner of the document window).**

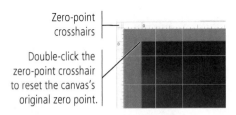

Zero-point crosshairs

Double-click the zero-point crosshair to reset the canvas's original zero point.

This resets the file's zero point to the original position (the top-left corner of the canvas).

20. **Click the View menu and make sure a check mark appears to the left of Lock Guides. If no check mark is there, choose Lock Guides to toggle on that option.**

After you carefully position specific guides, it's a good idea to lock them so you don't accidentally move or delete them later. If you need to move a guide at any point, simply choose View>Lock Guides to toggle off the option temporarily.

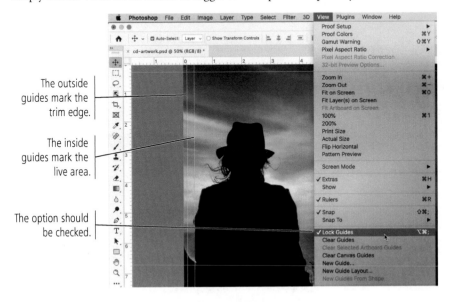

The outside guides mark the trim edge.

The inside guides mark the live area.

The option should be checked.

21. **Save the file and continue to the next exercise.**

Because you have already saved this working file with a new name, you can simply choose File>Save, or press Command/Control-S to save without opening a dialog box. If you want to change the file name, you can always choose File>Save As.

## Copy and Paste Selected Pixels

Like many processes in Photoshop, there are various methods for compositing multiple images into a single file. In this exercise, you will use the most basic selection tool — the Rectangle Marquee tool.

*Watch the videos **Using Selection Tool in Photoshop, Parts 1 and 2** in your online student resources.*

1. **With cd-artwork.psd open, choose View>Fit on Screen to show the entire image centered in the document window.**

2. **Open the file Tornado.jpg from your WIP>Music folder.**

   If you see a profile mismatch warning when opening the files for this project, choose the option to use the embedded profile. Color management will be explained in Project 3: Museum Image Correction.

3. **With Tornado.jpg the active file in the document window, open the Image Size dialog box (Image>Image Size).**

   This image is only 150 ppi, but it has a physical size much larger than the defined size for the CD artwork. As with the original image, the principle of effective resolution might make this image usable in the composite ad.

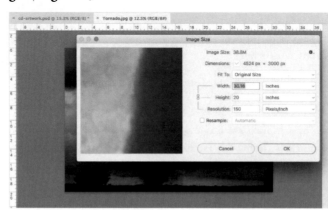

**Note:**

*When you created the background file for this project, you created a raster image that contains pixels. Digital photographs and scans are also pixel-based, which is why you use Photoshop to edit and manipulate those types of files.*

**Note:**

*You can press Command-Option-I/Control-Alt-I to open the Image Size dialog box.*

4. **Click Cancel to close the Image Size dialog box.**

5. **Choose the Rectangular Marquee tool in the Tools panel and review the options in the Options bar.**

   By default, dragging with a marquee tool creates a new selection. You can use the buttons on the left end of the Options bar to define what happens if you draw more than one marquee.

   Rectangular Marquee tool

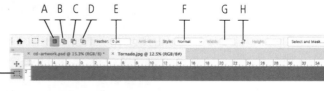

   A. **New Selection** creates a new selection each time you create a new marquee.

   B. **Add to Selection** adds the area of a new marquee to the existing selected area.

   C. **Subtract from Selection** removes the area of a new marquee from the existing selection.

   D. **Intersect with Selection** results in a selection only where a new marquee overlaps an existing selection.

   E. **Feather** softens the edges of a selection by a specified number of pixels.

   F. Use the **Style** menu to choose a normal selection, a fixed-ratio selection, or a fixed-size selection.

   G. When Fixed Ratio or Fixed Size is selected, enter the size of the selection in the **Width** and **Height** fields.

   H. Click this button to reverse the Width and Height fields.

6. **Choose the New Selection option in the Options bar. Click outside of the top-left corner, drag down past the bottom edge of the image, and drag right to create a selection area that is approximately 20.5″ wide.**

You can't select an area larger than the current canvas, so the top, left, and bottom edges of the selection snap to the canvas edges. The live cursor feedback, as well as the mark on the horizontal ruler, help to determine the selection area's width.

*Note:*

*Press Shift while dragging a new marquee to constrain the selection to a square (using the Rectangular Marquee tool) or circle (using the Elliptical Marquee tool).*

Selection marquee

Rectangular Marquee tool cursor

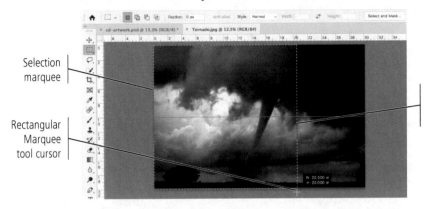

"Marching ants" identify the selected area.

7. **In the Options bar, choose the Subtract from Selection option.**

8. **Click outside the top-left corner of the image, and drag down and right to create a selection area that is wider than the original selection area and approximately 2″ high.**

*Note:*

*Command/Control-clicking a layer thumbnail results in a selection around the contents of that layer.*

Subtract from Selection is active.

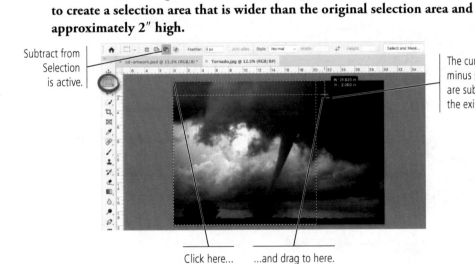

The cursor shows a minus sign because you are subtracting from the existing selection.

Click here...       ...and drag to here.

When you release the mouse button, the area you drew in this step is removed from the original selection area:

*Note:*

*When the New Selection option is active, you can move a selection marquee by clicking inside the selected area with the Marquee tool and dragging to the desired area of the image.*

*The live cursor feedback shows how far you have moved the area. The pink horizontal lines that appear as you drag are smart guides, which help you to reposition objects (including selection marquees) relative to other objects or to the canvas.*

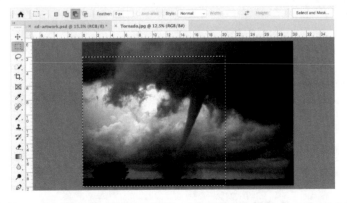

9. **Choose Edit>Copy.**

The standard Cut, Copy, and Paste options are available in Photoshop, just as they are in most applications. Whatever you have selected will be copied to the Clipboard, and whatever is in the Clipboard will be pasted.

10. **Click the Close button on the Tornado.jpg document tab to close that file.**

11. **With the cd-artwork.psd file active, choose Edit>Paste.**

The copied selection is pasted in the center of the document window. If you remember from the Image Size dialog box, the tornado image was approximately 30″ × 20″ at 150 ppi. Photoshop cannot maintain multiple resolutions in a single file. When you paste the copied content into the cd-artwork file, it adopts the resolution of the target file (in this case, 300 ppi). The concept of effective resolution transforms the selected area (20.5″ × 18″) of the tornado image to approximately 10.25″ × 9″ at 300 ppi.

12. **Open the Layers panel (Window>Layers).**

The original cd-artwork.psd file had only one layer — Background. When you copy or drag content from one file into another, it is automatically placed on a new layer with the default name "Layer *n*," where "n" is a sequential number.

The document tab shows the name of the active layer.

A new layer (Layer 1) is added to contain the contents that you pasted from the Tornado.jpg file.

The Background layer contains the original Sunrise.jpg file content.

13. **Choose File>Save, and then read the resulting message.**

Because this is the first time you have saved the file after adding new layers, you should see the Photoshop Format Options dialog box with the Maximize Compatibility check box already activated. It's a good idea to leave this check box selected so that your files will be compatible with other Adobe applications and other versions of Photoshop.

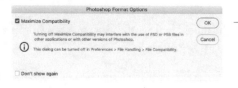

14. **Make sure the Maximize Compatibility check box is selected, click OK, and then continue to the next exercise.**

*Note:*

*If you want to move a marquee, make sure the Marquee tool is still selected. If the Move tool is active, clicking inside the marquee and dragging will actually move the contents within the selection area.*

*Note:*

*When creating a new selection with a marquee tool, pressing Option/Alt places the center of the selection marquee at the point where you click; when you drag out, the marquee is created around that point.*

*Note:*

*When the New Selection option is active, press Shift to add to the current selection or press Option/Alt to subtract from the current selection.*

*Note:*

*If you don't see this warning, check the File Handling pane of the Preferences dialog box. You can set the Maximize PSD and PSB File Compatibility menu to Always, Never, or Ask.*

Create a Feathered Selection

The Marquee tool you used in the previous exercise created a basic rectangular selection. The basic Lasso tool works like a pencil, following the path where you drag the mouse; you will use that method in this exercise.

1. **With cd-artwork.psd open, open Lightning.jpg from your WIP>Music folder.**

2. **Choose the Lasso tool in the Tools panel. In the Control panel, choose the New Selection option.**

   Most options in the Control panel are the same for the Lasso tool as they are for the Marquee tools.

3. **Click at the top edge of the canvas, just to the left of the lightning bolt. Hold down the mouse button and drag around the general lightning shape in the image. Keep the following points in mind as you drag:**

   - **Avoid dragging past the bottom edge of the canvas.**

   - **Drag past the right image edge and up to the top of the image.**

     When you drag past the image edge, the marquee follows the image edge instead of the actual cursor position.

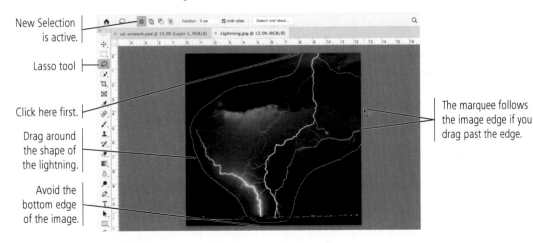

New Selection is active.

Lasso tool

Click here first.

Drag around the shape of the lightning.

Avoid the bottom edge of the image.

The marquee follows the image edge if you drag past the edge.

4. **Release the mouse button.**

   When you release the mouse button, the software automatically connects the first point you clicked with the last location of the mouse cursor with a straight line.

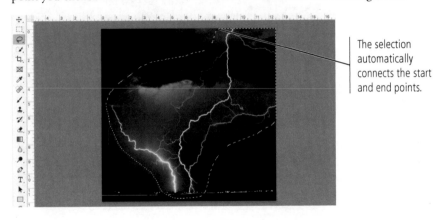

The selection automatically connects the start and end points.

*Note:*

*It isn't uncommon for a mouse to unexpectedly jump when you don't want it to. If you aren't happy with your Lasso selection, choose Select>Deselect, and then try again.*

5. **With the marching ants active, choose Select>Modify>Feather.**

Photoshop offers a number of options for modifying an existing selection marquee.

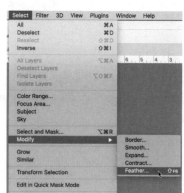

- **Select>Grow** expands the selection to include all adjacent pixels that fall within the tolerance defined for the Magic Wand tool.

- **Select>Similar** expands the selection to include all pixels throughout the image that fall within the tolerance range, even if they are not adjacent to the active selection.

- **Select>Transform Selection** shows bounding-box handles around the selection marquee, which you can use to transform the selection as you would transform layer content.

In the Select>Modify menu:

- **Border** creates a selection of a defined number of pixels around the edge of the active marquee.

- **Smooth** helps to clean up stray pixels at the edge of a selection. Within a defined radius from the selection edge, pixels with less than half of the surrounding pixels are excluded from the selection.

- **Expand** and **Contract** enlarge and shrink, respectively, a selection by a defined number of pixels.

- **Feather** creates a blended edge to the active selection area.

6. **In the resulting dialog box, type 100 in the Feather Radius field. Make sure Apply Effect at Canvas Bounds is not checked, then click OK.**

**Feathering** means to soften the edge of a selection so the image blends into the background instead of showing a sharp line around the edge. The Feather Radius defines the distance from solid to transparent.

If the Apply Effect... check box is active, the feathering will be applied at the top and right edges of the canvas, where you dragged past the image edge while making the selection. You want these edges to remain hard, so the option should remain unchecked.

7. **Click the Edit in Quick Mask button at the bottom of the Tools panel to toggle into Quick Mask mode.**

Marching ants do not show degrees of transparency. Quick Mask mode creates a temporary red overlay (called an Alpha channel) that shows the feathered selection. By default, the overlay is semi-transparent, which allows you to see the underlying image.

The semi-transparent overlay shows the smooth transition that was created by feathering the selection.

Edit in Quick Mask button

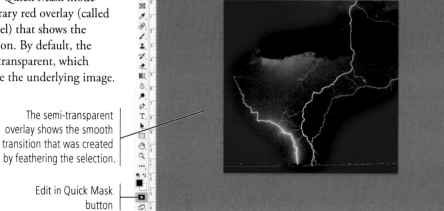

8. **Click the Edit in Standard Mode button at the bottom of the Tools panel to toggle off the Quick Mask.**

    When Quick Mask mode is active, the Edit in Quick Mask mode toggles to become the Edit in Standard Mode button.

9. **Choose Edit>Copy to copy the active selection.**

10. **Click the Close button on the Lightning.jpg document tab to close that file. Click Don't Save when asked.**

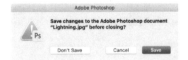

11. **With cd-artwork.psd active, choose Edit>Paste.**

    The feathered selection is pasted into the file as a new layer.

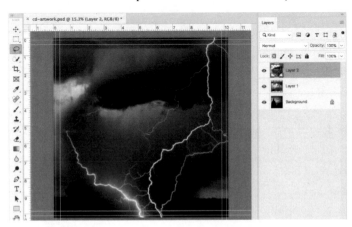

12. **Save the file, then continue to the next exercise.**

---

## Understanding the Lasso Tool Variations

The **Polygonal Lasso tool** creates selections with straight lines, anchoring a line each time you click. To close a selection area, click the first point in the selection.

Polygonal Lasso tool cursor

Click each spot to anchor the selection line.

The **Magnetic Lasso tool** snaps to high-contrast edges. You can use the Options bar to control the way Photoshop detects edges:

- **Width** is the distance from the edge the cursor can be and still detect edges; set this higher to move the cursor farther from edges.

- **Contrast** is how different the foreground can be from the background and still be detected; if there is a sharp distinction between the foreground and background, you can set this value higher.

- **Frequency** is the number of points that will be created to make the selection; setting this number higher creates finer selections, while setting it lower creates smoother edges.

Magnetic Lasso tool cursor

Drag near the edges of the object and the selection snaps to the edges.

Rasterize a Vector File

Logos and title treatments — such as the ones you will use in this project — are commonly created as vector graphics. Although Photoshop is typically a pixel-based application, you can also open and work with vector graphics created in illustration programs like Adobe Illustrator.

1. **With cd-artwork.psd open, choose File>Open. Select HHT-logo.ai (in your WIP>Music folder) and then click Open.**

   This is an Adobe Illustrator file of the band's logo. When you open a vector file (Illustrator, EPS, or PDF) in Photoshop, it is rasterized or converted to a raster graphic. The resulting Import PDF dialog box allows you to determine exactly how to rasterize the file. (Illustrator uses PDF as its underlying file structure.)

   The Crop To options determine the outside dimensions of the opened file. Depending on how the file was created, some of these values might be the same as others:

   - **Bounding Box** is the outermost edges of the artwork in the file.
   - **Media Box** is the size of the paper as defined in the file.
   - **Crop Box** is the size of the page/artboard, including printer's marks.
   - **Bleed Box** is the trim size, plus any defined bleed allowance.
   - **Trim Box** is the trim size as defined in the file.
   - **Art Box** is the area of the page as defined in the file.

   The Image Size fields default to the settings of the bounding box you select. You can change the size, resolution, color mode, and bit depth by entering new values. You can check the Constrain Proportions option to keep the height and width proportional to the original dimensions.

2. **Make sure Bounding Box is selected in the Crop To field, and the Resolution field is set to 300 pixels/inch.**

3. **Click OK.**

   The logo file opens in Photoshop. The checkered area behind the text indicates that the background is transparent. If you look at the Layers panel, you will see that Layer 1 isn't locked; because it's transparent, it is not considered a background layer.

**Note:**

*If you're opening a multi-page PDF or an Illustrator file with more than one artboard, the preview window on the left side of the dialog box shows thumbnails of each "page" in the file. You can click a specific thumbnail to select anything other than Page 1. Press Shift and click to select multiple consecutive pages, or press Command/Control and click to select multiple, nonconsecutive pages.*

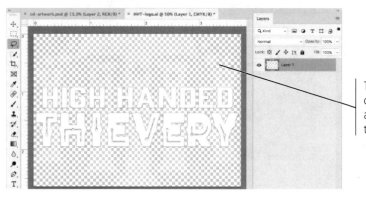

The gray-and-white checked pattern identifies areas of transparency in the layer content.

4.  **Open the Window>Arrange menu and choose 2-up Vertical to show both open files at one time.**

    As you saw in the Interface chapter, these options are useful for arranging and viewing multiple open files within your workspace.

5.  **Choose the Move tool in the Tools panel.**

6.  **Click in the HHT-logo.ai image window and drag into the cd-artwork.psd image window, then release the mouse button.**

    Basic compositing can be as simple as dragging a selection from one file to another. If no active selection appears in the source document, this action moves the entire active layer from the source document.

*Note:*

*On Windows, the cursor shows a plus sign to indicate that you are adding the image as a new layer in the document to which you dragged.*

Move tool

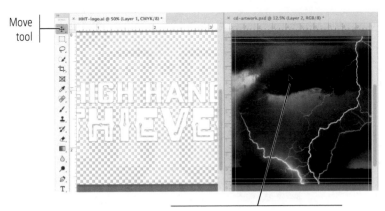

This cursor shows that you are dragging a layer. In this case, you're dragging it into another document window.

7.  **Click the Close button on the HHT-logo document tab to close that file. Click Don't Save when asked.**

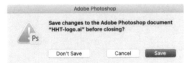

    After closing the logo file, the cd-artwork.psd document window expands to fill the available space.

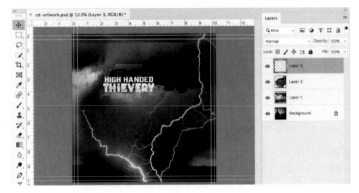

8.  **Save cd-artwork.psd and continue to the next exercise.**

Place Files as Smart Object Layers

As you have seen in the last few exercises, copying layer content from one file to another results in new regular layers for the pasted content. Photoshop also supports Smart Object layers, in which you place one file into another instead of pasting layer content. Smart Objects provide a number of advantages over regular layers, which you will explore later in this project. In this exercise, you will create a Smart Object layer for the remaining image element.

*Note:*

*Smart Objects enable tight integration between Photoshop and Illustrator. You can take advantage of the sophisticated vector-editing features in Adobe Illustrator, and then place those files into Photoshop without losing the ability to edit the vector information.*

1. **With cd-artwork.psd open, choose File>Place Embedded.**

   Two options in the File menu — Place Embedded and Place Linked — give you the option to embed the placed file data into the active file, or to place smart objects as links to the original placed file. (See Page 51 for more about placing linked files.)

2. **Choose the Title-text.psd file (in your WIP>Music folder) and click Place.**

   The placed file appears centered in the document window, with bounding-box handles and crossed diagonal lines. The placement isn't final until you press Return/Enter. You can press the Escape key to cancel the placement. If you check Skip Transform when Placing in the General pane of the Preferences dialog box, you will not see the diagonal lines and handles when you place a Smart Object layer.

   In the Options bar, you can see that the placed image has been scaled to approximately 70% to fit into the document where it is being placed.

The placed image is centered in the document window.

It has been scaled to fit into the active canvas.

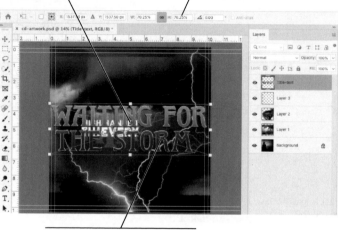

Crossed diagonal lines and bounding-box handles indicate that the placement is not yet final.

3. **Press Return/Enter to finalize the placement.**

   After you finalize the placement, the bounding-box handles and crossed diagonal lines disappear. In the Layers panel, the placed file has its own layer. This layer, however, is automatically named, based on the name of the placed file.

   The layer's thumbnail indicates that this layer is a **Smart Object**. Because you placed this file using the embedded option, it is not dynamically linked to the original file. Instead, Photoshop maintains the original file data within the Smart Object layer. The advantages of this technique will become clear in the next stage of this project.

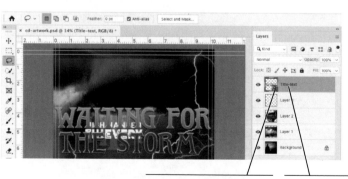

This icon identifies an embedded Smart Object layer.

The layer adopts the name of the placed file.

4. **Save the file and continue to the next stage of the project.**

## Working with Embedded and Linked Smart Objects

In this project you used the Place Embedded option to create a Smart Object layer containing the placed file data; the embedded file data became a part of the parent file.

If you double-click the thumbnail icon of an embedded Smart Object, the embedded file opens in an application that can edit the stored data — AI files open in Illustrator; PSD, TIFF, and JPEG files open in Photoshop.

When you first open a Smart Object file, the application provides advice for working with Smart Objects:

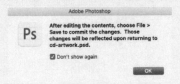

After you make necessary changes, you can save the file and close it, and then return to Photoshop (if necessary). Your changes in the Smart Object file will automatically reflect in the parent file where the Smart Object layer is placed.

**Important note:** Do not use the Save As option when editing Smart Object layers. The changes will not reflect in the parent file if you save changes with a different file name.

If you choose the Place Linked option in the File menu, the Smart Object layer stores a link to the original file data rather than embedding that data inside the parent file.

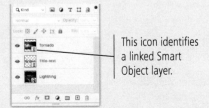

This icon identifies a linked Smart Object layer.

This provides an opportunity for maintaining consistency because you only need to change one instance of a file to reflect those changes anywhere the file is placed.

Say you place a logo created in Illustrator into a Photoshop file. The same logo is also placed as a link in an InDesign file. If you open the logo in Illustrator and change the main color (for example), when you save the changes in the original logo file, the new color automatically reflects in any file — whether InDesign or Photoshop — that is linked to the edited logo.

If you use the Place Embedded option in Photoshop, the Smart Object layer is not linked to the original, edited logo file; you would have to open the embedded Smart Object and make the same color change a second time.

Linked files also have potential disadvantages. As we mentioned previously, double-clicking a Smart Object layer thumbnail opens the linked or embedded file in an application that can edit the relevant data. If you are working with *linked* Smart Object layers, any changes you make affect the original file data. This means your changes appear not only in the parent Photoshop file where it is linked, but also in any other file that links to the same data.

For a file to output properly, linked Smart Object layers must be present and up to date at the time of output.

If the linked file has been modified while the parent file is open, the changes automatically reflect in the parent file when you return to that document. If the parent file is not open in Photoshop when the linked file is edited, you will see a Modified icon for the linked Smart Object layer.

If the linked file is deleted or moved to another location after it has been placed, the parent file will show a Missing icon for the linked Smart Object layer.

If a linked Smart Object has been moved while the parent file is not open, you will see a warning dialog box when you open the parent Photoshop file. You can use that dialog box to locate the missing link, or close it and use the options in the Layers panel to correct the problem.

Control/right-clicking a linked Smart Object layer name opens a contextual menu with options to update modified content and resolve broken links.

This icon identifies a linked, modified Smart Object layer.

This icon identifies a linked, missing Smart Object layer.

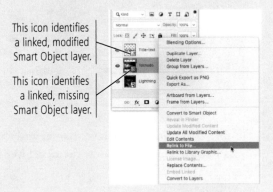

To avoid potential problems with missing linked files, you can use the File>Package command to create a job folder. The parent file is copied to a new folder, along with a Links subfolder containing any files placed as linked Smart Object layers.

# STAGE 2 / **Managing Layers**

Photoshop includes a number of options for managing layers: naming layers for easier recognition, creating layer groups so multiple layers can be manipulated at once, moving layers around on the canvas, transforming layers both destructively and non-destructively, controlling individual layer visibility, and arranging the top-to-bottom stacking order of layers to determine exactly what is visible. You will use all of these options in this stage of the project.

## Name Layers and Layer Groups

It's always a good idea to name your layers because it makes managing the file much easier — especially when you work with files that include dozens of layers. Even with only four unnamed layers in this file (counting the Background layer), it would be tedious to have to toggle each layer to find the one you want.

1. **With cd-artwork.psd open, review the Layers panel.**

2. **Option/Alt-click the eye icon for Layer 1 to hide all other layers.**

   Toggling layer visibility is an easy way to see only what you want to see at any given stage in a project.

   Clicking the Eye icon for a specific layer hides that layer. Clicking the empty space where the Eye icon should be shows the hidden layer. To show or hide a series of consecutive layers, click the visibility icon (or empty space) for the first layer you want to affect, hold down the mouse button, and drag down to the last layer you want to show or hide.

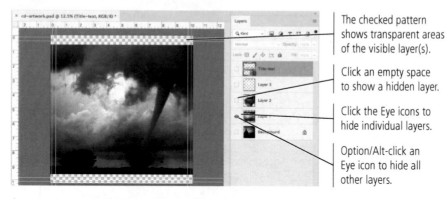

The checked pattern shows transparent areas of the visible layer(s).

Click an empty space to show a hidden layer.

Click the Eye icons to hide individual layers.

Option/Alt-click an Eye icon to hide all other layers.

3. **Double-click the Layer 1 layer name, and then type Tornado. Press Return/Enter to finalize the new layer name.**

   You can rename any layer by simply double-clicking the name and typing.

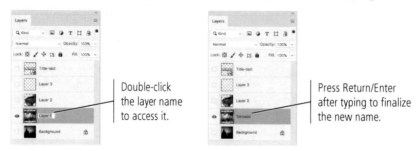

Double-click the layer name to access it.

Press Return/Enter after typing to finalize the new name.

4. **Click the Eye icon to hide the renamed Tornado layer, and then click the empty space to the left of Layer 2 to show only that layer.**

5. **Double-click the Layer 2 name, then type Lightning. Press Return/Enter to finalize the new layer name.**

6. **Repeat Steps 4–5 to rename Layer 3 as Logo.**

7. **Click the spaces on the left side of the Layers panel (where the Eye icons were) to show all hidden layers.**

8. **In the Layers panel, click the Title-text layer to select it.**

9. **Press Shift and click the Logo layer to select that layer as well.**

   Press Shift and click to select consecutive layers in the Layers panel. Press Command/Control and click to select nonconsecutive layers in the Layers panel.

10. **With the two layers selected, click the Create a New Group button at the bottom of the panel.**

    This button creates a group that automatically contains the selected layers. The new group is named "Group N" (where N is simply a sequential number). Of course, you can rename a layer group just as you can rename a layer. You can also choose New Group from Layers in the panel Options menu.

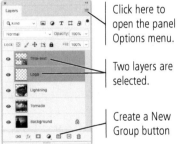

Click here to open the panel Options menu.

Two layers are selected.

Create a New Group button

The new group automatically contains the selected layers.

To create a new empty layer group, make sure nothing is selected in the Layers panel before clicking the Create a New Group button. Alternatively, choose New Group in the panel Options menu; this results in an empty layer group even if layers are selected.

11. **Double-click the Group 1 name in the Layers panel to highlight it, then type Logotypes. Press Return/Enter to finalize the new layer group name.**

    As with any other layer, you should name groups based on what they contain so you can easily identify them later.

*Note:*

*Deselect all layers by clicking in the empty area at the bottom of the Layers panel.*

*Note:*

*You can create up to ten levels of nested layer groups (groups inside of other groups).*

**12.** Click the arrow to the left of the Logotypes group name to expand the layer group.

You have to expand the layer group to be able to access and edit individual layers in the group. If you select the entire layer group, you can move all layers within the group at the same time. Layers in the group maintain their position relative to one another.

**13.** Save the file and continue to the next exercise.

*Note:*

*You can click the Eye icon for a layer folder to hide the entire layer group (and all layers inside the folder).*

##  Move and Transform a Smart Object Layer

Photoshop makes scaling, rotating, and other transformations fairly easy to implement, but it is important to realize the potential impact of your transformations.

**1.** With **cd-artwork.psd** open, click the **Title-text** layer (in the Logotypes folder) in the Layers panel to select only that layer.

**2.** Choose the Move tool in the Tools panel.

As the name suggests, the Move tool is used to move a selection around on the canvas. You can select a specific area, and then click and drag to move only the selection on the active layer. If there is no active selection area, you can click and drag to move the contents of the entire active layer.

**3.** In the Options bar, make sure the Auto-Select option is not checked.

When Auto-Select is checked, you can click in the image window and drag to move the contents of the layer containing the pixels where you click; you do not need to first select the layer in the Layers panel before moving the layer content. This is very useful in some cases, but not so much in others — for example, when the contents of multiple layers are stacked on top of each other (as is the case with your file as it exists now).

**4.** Click in the image window and drag until the Title-text layer content snaps to the top and left live-area guides.

If you toggled off the Snap feature when you used the Crop tool, you should turn it back on now by choosing View>Snap.

Uncheck this option.

Select the layer you want to move, then click and drag in the document window to move the layer content.

# Understanding Smart Guides

As you dragged the layer in the previous exercise, you might have noticed a series of pink lines appearing in different locations. These lines are a function of Smart Guides, which make it easier to align layer content to other layers or the overall canvas.

Smart Guides are active by default, but you can toggle them on and off in the View>Show submenu.

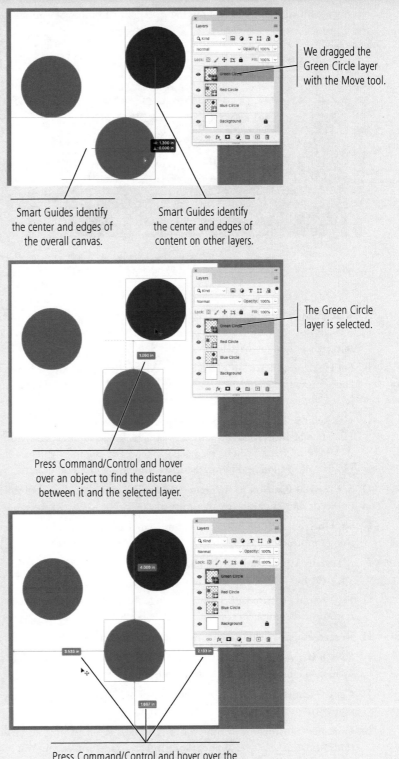

We dragged the Green Circle layer with the Move tool.

Smart Guides identify the center and edges of the overall canvas.

Smart Guides identify the center and edges of content on other layers.

The Green Circle layer is selected.

Press Command/Control and hover over an object to find the distance between it and the selected layer.

Press Command/Control and hover over the canvas to find the distance between the selected layer content and the canvas edges.

5. **With the Title-text layer still active, choose Edit>Free Transform.**

When you use the transform options, bounding-box handles surround the selection in the document window. The Options bar gives you a number of options for controlling the transformations numerically:

Bounding box handles
surround the content that
is being transformed.

**A Reference Point Location.** This point determines the point around which transformations are made. It always defaults to the center point. To choose a different reference point, you have to check the related box.

**B Set Horizontal Position of Reference Point.** This is the X position of the reference point for the content being transformed. If the center reference point is selected, for example, this is the X position of the center point of the active content.

**C Use Relative Positioning for Reference Point.** If this option is active, the Set Horizontal Position and Set Vertical Position fields default to 0; changing these values moves the reference point by the value you type. For example, typing "–25" in the Set Horizontal Position field moves the active content 25 pixels to the left.

**D Set Vertical Position of Reference Point.** This is the Y position of the reference point for the content being transformed.

**E Set Horizontal Scale.** Use this field to change the horizontal scale percentage of the transformed content.

**F Maintain Aspect Ratio.** When active, the horizontal scale and vertical scale fields are locked to have the same value.

**G Set Vertical Scale.** Use this field to change the vertical scale percentage of the transformed content.

**H Rotate.** Use this field to rotate the transformed content by a specific angle.

**I Switch Between Free Transform and Warp Modes.** If available, click this button to apply a built-in warp to the active selection.

**J Cancel Transform.** Click this button (or press the Esc key) to exit Free Transform mode without applying any transformation.

**K Commit Transform.** Click this button (or press Return/Enter) to finalize the transformation that you applied while in Free Transform mode. You can also simply click away from the area in the bounding box to finalize the transformation.

6. **In the Options bar, make sure the Maintain Aspect Ratio option is active.**

7. **Click the bottom-right bounding-box handle, and then drag up and left until the title treatment fits inside the live area guides on both sides of the canvas.**

The selection (in this case, the entire Title-text layer) dynamically changes as you scale the layer.

Because the Maintain Aspect Ratio option is active, Photoshop automatically constrains the selection's height-to-width proportions. (When Maintain Aspect Ratio is active, you can press Shift while you drag a handle to transform the selection nonproportionally.)

When you release the mouse button, the handles remain in place until you finalize ("commit") the transformation.

This button appears darker when the option is active.

Manual transformations in the document window reflect in the Options bar fields.

Click and drag a handle to scale the content proportionally.

8. **Press Return/Enter to finalize the transformation.**

After finalizing the transformation, the bounding-box handles disappear.

9. **With the Title-text layer still active, press Command/Control-T to enter Free Transform mode again and look at the Options bar.**

Because the Title-text layer is a Smart Object layer, the W and H fields still show the scaling percentage based on the original.

It is not uncommon for a placed image to have slightly different height and width percentages when it is placed. The change will be slight, but it's a good idea to check this issue so that you maintain the integrity of the placed artwork.

10. **In the Options bar, change the W field to 65%.**

Click to activate this option.

The W and H percentages are now the same value.

You can type in Options bar fields to apply specific numeric transformations.

When the Maintain Aspect Ratio option is active, the X and Y percentage fields are forced to the same values; changing the W value also changes the value in the H field.

11. **Click the Commit Transform button on the Options bar (or press Return/Enter) to finalize the transformation.**

If you press Return/Enter, you have to press it twice to finalize the transformation. The first time you press it, you apply the change to the active field; the second time, you finalize the transformation and exit Free Transform mode.

12. **Save the file and continue to the next exercise.**

## Move and Transform Regular Layers

Smart Object layers enable non-destructive transformations, which means those transformations can be changed or undone without affecting the quality of the layer content. Transforming a regular layer, on the other hand, is destructive and permanent.

1. **With cd-artwork.psd open, hide all but the Tornado layer. Click the Tornado layer in the Layers panel to select it.**

2. **Using the Move tool, drag the layer content up so there is no transparent area at the top of the canvas.**

3. **Choose Edit>Transform>Flip Horizontal.**

   The Transform submenu commands affect only the selected layer.

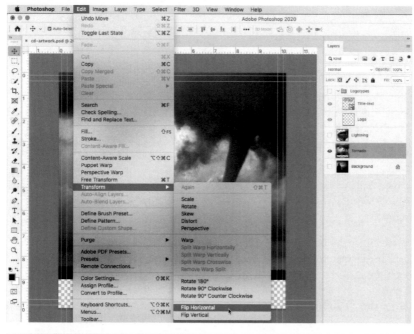

*Note:*

*When the Move tool is active, you can move the selected object or layer 1 pixel by pressing the Arrow keys. Pressing Shift with any of the Arrow keys moves the selected object/layer by 10 pixels.*

*Note:*

*You can also use the Edit>Transform submenu to apply specific transformations to a layer or selection.*

4. **Show and select the Lightning layer, then press Command/Control-T to enter Free Transform mode.**

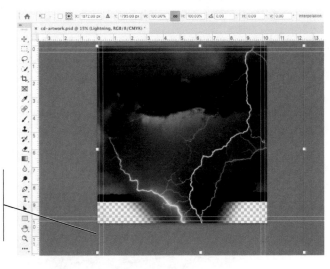

Some handles might not be visible within the boundaries of the document window. If necessary, zoom out so you can see all eight handles of the layer content.

5. **Click inside the bounding-box area and drag until the layer content snaps to the top and right canvas edges.**

The edge of the bounding box shows that some parts of the layer do not fit within the current file dimensions.

6. **On the left side of the Options bar, check the box for the Reference Point option and then choose the top-right reference point.**

The reference point, which defaults to the center point, is the point around which numeric transformations are made. To choose a different reference point, you must first activate the check box in the Option bar, and then choose the desired point in the 9-square proxy.

Activate the Reference Point option...

then choose a reference point.

7. **Place the cursor over the W field label to access the scrubby slider for that field.**

When you see the scrubby slider cursor, you can drag right to increase or drag left to decrease the value in the related field.

Place the cursor over a field label to access the "scrubby slider" for that field.

8. **Click and drag left until the W field shows approximately 75%.**

Because you selected the top-right reference point, the top-right corner of the layer remains in place when you scale the selection. The bottom-left corner moves based on the scaling you define.

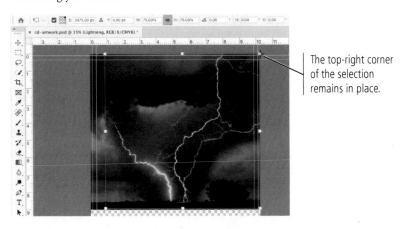

The top-right corner of the selection remains in place.

9. **Press Return/Enter to finalize the transformation.**

10. **With the Lightning layer still active, press Command/Control-T to re-enter Free Transform mode.**

Once you commit the transformation on a regular layer, the transformation is final. Looking at the Options bar now, you can see that it shows the layer at 100%, instead of the 75% from Step 8.

If you transform a Smart Object layer, the scale percentage is maintained even after you finalize the change, unlike scaling a regular layer, where the layer recalibrates so the new size is considered 100% once you finalize the scaling.

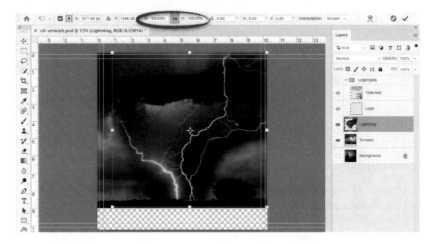

11. **Press Esc to exit Free Transform mode without changing anything.**

12. **Save the file and continue to the next exercise.**

##  Transform the Background Layer

Your file currently has a number of layers, most of which were created by pasting or placing external files into the original file. Because every photograph and scan (and some images that you create from scratch in Photoshop) begins with a default locked Background layer, it is important to understand the special characteristics of that layer:

- You can't apply layer transformations, styles, or masks to the Background layer.

- You can't move the contents of the Background layer around in the document.

- If you delete pixels from the Background layer, you must determine the color that will be used in place of the deleted pixels.

- The Background layer cannot include transparent pixels, which are necessary for underlying layers to be visible.

- The Background layer is always the bottom layer in the stacking order. You can't add or move layers lower than the Background layer.

In the final composite file for this project, you need to flip the woman's silhouette from left to right, and remove the sunset from the image background. For either of these options to work properly, you need to convert the default Background layer to a regular layer.

**Note:**

*If you crop an image that includes a Background layer, the Background layer is automatically converted to a regular layer if the Delete Cropped Pixels option is not checked.*

1. **With cd-artwork.psd open, show only the Background layer.**

2. **Click the Background layer to select it and then choose Edit>Transform.**

   The Transform submenu commands are not available for the locked Background layer.

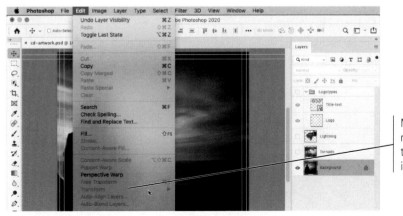

Many commands are not available because the Background layer is locked.

3. **With the Background layer still selected, choose Image>Image Rotation> Flip Canvas Horizontal.**

   To affect the locked background layer, you have to flip the actual canvas.

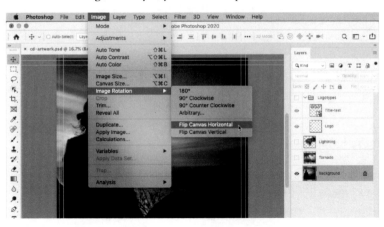

*Note:*

*Although the Background layer exists by default in many files, it is not a required component.*

4. **Show the Logotypes layer group.**

   Because you flipped the canvas, the Title-text and Logo layers are also flipped left-to-right. Rotating or flipping the entire canvas affects all layers in the file; this is obviously not what you want to do.

Because you flipped the canvas, the logos are now backward.

Showing the layer group shows all layers in that group.

5. **Choose Edit>Undo Layer Visibility.**

   The Undo command affects the last action you performed. The actual Undo menu command changes to reflect the action that will be undone.

6. **Choose Edit>Undo Flip Canvas Horizontal.**

   Photoshop supports multiple Undo commands. You can use the Undo command to step back through multiple actions.

**Note:**

*You can press Command/Control-Shift-Z to redo the last undone action.*

7. **In the Layers panel, click the Lock icon on the Background layer.**

   Clicking the Lock icon unlocks the layer and immediately converts the previous Background layer to a regular layer named "Layer 0."

   Click the lock icon to unlock the Background layer.

   The layer is automatically converted to a regular layer named Layer 0.

8. **Double-click the Layer 0 layer name to highlight it, then type Sunrise to rename the layer. Press Return/Enter to finalize the new layer name.**

9. **With the Sunrise layer selected, choose Edit>Transform>Flip Horizontal.**

   Because the layer is no longer locked, you can now access and apply the transform commands that affect only the selected layer.

10. **Show the Logotypes layer group again.**

    Because you flipped only the selected layer, the Title-text and Logo layers are not flipped; they appear in the correct position and orientation.

11. **Choose the Logo layer in the Layers panel.**

12. **Using the Move tool, move the Logo layer content until it snaps to the bottom and right live area guides.**

13. **Save the file and continue to the next stage of the project.**

# Navigating the Photoshop File History

In addition to using the Undo command to step back through each previous action, you can use the History panel (Window>History) to navigate back to earlier stages.

Every action you take is recorded as a state in the History panel. You can click any state to return to that particular point in the document progression. You can also delete specific states or create a new document from a particular state using the buttons at the bottom of the panel.

Snapshot thumbnails

Individual history states

Source for the History Brush

Create new document from current state

Create new snapshot

Delete current state

By default, the History panel stores the last 50 states; older states are automatically deleted. You can change that setting in the Performance pane of the Preferences dialog box. Keep in mind, however, that storing a larger number of states will increase the memory that is required to work with a specific file.

Keep the following in mind when using the History panel:

- The default snapshot is the image state when it was first opened.

- The oldest state is at the top of the list. The most recent state appears at the bottom.

- You can save any particular state as a snapshot to prevent it from being deleted when that state is no longer within the number of states that can be stored.

- The history is only stored while the file is open. When you close a file, the history and snapshots are not saved.

- When you select a specific state, the states below it are dimmed so you can see which changes will be discarded if you go back to a particular history state.

- Selecting a state and then changing the image eliminates all states that come after it.

- Deleting a state deletes that state and those after it. If you choose Allow Non-Linear History in the History Options dialog box (accessed in the History panel Options menu), deleting a state deletes only that state.

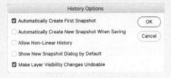

If you need to keep a record of a file's history even after you close the file, you can activate the History Log option in the History Log pane of the Preferences dialog box. When this option is checked, you can save the history log as metadata, in a text file, or both. You can also determine the level of detail that will be recorded in the history log.

- Sessions Only records each time you launch or quit, and each time you open and close individual files.

- Concise adds the text that appears in the History panel to the Sessions information.

- Detailed gives you a complete history of all changes made to files.

# STAGE 3 / **Creating Complex Selections**

Photoshop includes a number of options for making selections based on the color content of an image. The method you use will vary depending on the actual content of your image, as well as what you hope to accomplish.

The **Select>Color Range** menu command opens a dialog box that you can use to select areas of an image based on sampled colors.

- On the right side of the dialog box, the **Eyedropper tool** is selected by default. You can click a color in the image, either in the document window or in the dialog box preview window, to define the color range you want to select (called **sampling**). You can then use the Add to Sample and Subtract from Sample eyedroppers to refine your selection.

Eyedropper tool

Add to Sample

Subtract from Sample

Click in the image to define the color range you want to select.

Light areas are selected.

Dark areas are not selected.

Gray areas are partially selected.

- The **Select** menu at the top of the dialog box includes several presets for isolating specific ranges of primary colors (Reds, Yellows, Greens, Cyans, Blues, or Magentas), or specific ranges of color (highlights, midtones, or shadows).

- If you select the Skin Tones preset, you can then activate the **Detect Faces** option at the top of the dialog box. By adjusting the Fuzziness slider, you can use this dialog box to make reasonably good selections of people's skin. (Again, remember that no automatic option is a perfect substitute when subjective decision-making is required. Other tones in an image might be similar enough to a "skin tone" that unwanted areas will be included in the selection.)

- The **Localized Color Clusters** option can be used to select specific areas of a selected color. When this option is checked, the Range slider defines how far away (in physical distance) a color can be located from the point you click and still be included in the selection.

- **Fuzziness** is similar to the Tolerance setting for the Magic Wand tool. Changing the Fuzziness value expands (higher numbers) or contracts (lower numbers) the selection. Be careful, though, as higher fuzziness values can eliminate fine lines and detail.

- The Selection Preview menu determines how the selection appears in the document window:
  - **None** shows the normal image in the document window.
  - **Grayscale** shows the entire image in shades of gray. Selected areas are solid white and unselected areas are solid black.
  - **Black Matte** shows unselected areas in solid black. Selected areas appear in color.
  - **White Matte** shows unselected areas in solid white. Selected areas appear in color.
  - **Quick Mask** adds a partially transparent overlay to unselected areas.

- You can check the **Invert** box to return a selection that is the opposite of the color range you select. This is useful if you want to isolate (select) the background instead of the actual areas you selected in the dialog box.

The **Object Selection tool** allows Photoshop to make a selection based on what it determines to be the "object" of the photo. This tool does a remarkably good job creating an initial selection, which you can then modify and fine-tune to create the exact selection you need.

If the Object Finder checkbox is active in the Options bar, moving the tool cursor over an area of the image reveals a blue overlay that identifies the "object" that would be selected by clicking.

When the Object Selection tool is active, you have a number of choices in the Options menu:

Object Selection tool cursor

- By default, the Object Finder automatically refreshes as you work. If this option is turned off in the Set Additional Options menu, you can click the **Refresh Object Finder** ( ↻ ) to manually refresh the object finder.

- Clicking the **Show All Objects** ( ▣ ) button reveals all "objects" that the software identifies on the active layer.

- You can click the **Set Additional Options** ( ✿ ) button to turn off automatic refresh, change the color of the object overlay, and determine when the overlay is visible (automatically, always, or never).

- If you turn off the Object Select checkbox, you can draw a specific selection area to define the area you want the software to evaluate. In the **Mode menu**, choose a Rectangle or Lasso in the Options bar Mode menu to determine what type of selection you want to draw.

- Finally, you can check or uncheck the **Hard Edge** option to determine whether the resulting selection will have a hard or soft (feathered) edge.

> **Note:**
>
> *When any of the Selection tools are active, you can click the **Select Subject** button in the Options bar to cause Photoshop to analyze the entire layer instead of only a specific, selected area.*

The **Quick Selection tool**, nested under the Object Selection tool, essentially allows you to "paint" a selection. As you drag, the selection expands and automatically finds edges in the image.

- In the Options bar, you choose to create a new selection, add to, or subtract from the current selection.

- Open the Brush Options to change the brush size, so that your selection includes a smaller or wider range of color.

- **Auto-Enhance** allows the software to refine the edges of the selection based on internal algorithms. (Although many "auto" features in the software are very useful starting points, never rely entirely on this type of automatic result.)

The **Magic Wand tool**, also nested under the Object Selection tool, is an easy way to select large areas of solid color.

- The first options in the Options bar are the same as those for the Marquee tools (New, Add To, Subtract From, and Intersect).

- **Tolerance** is the degree of variation between the color you click and the colors Photoshop will select. Higher tolerance values select a larger range based on the color you click.

- The **Anti-alias** check box allows edges to blend more smoothly into the background, preventing a jagged appearance. Anti-aliasing is the process of blending shades of pixels to create the illusion of sharp lines.

- When **Contiguous** is selected, the tool only selects adjacent areas of the color; unchecking this option allows you to select all pixels within the tolerance, even if some are noncontiguous.

- By default, selections relate to the active layer only. You can check **Sample All Layers** to make a selection of all layers in the file.

Create and Refine a Color-Based Selection

Many images have both hard and soft edges, and/or very fine detail that needs to be isolated from its background (think of a model's blowing hair overlapping the title on the cover of a magazine). In this exercise, you are going to use two techniques to isolate the woman's silhouette and the ground on which she is sitting in the Sunrise image layer.

1. **With cd-artwork.psd open, hide all but the Sunrise layer. Click the Sunrise layer to make it active.**

2. **Choose View>Show>Guides.**

    Now that the file elements are in place, you can turn off the guides so that they do not distract from the work you will do in the rest of this project.

    You can also press Command/Control-; to toggle the visibility of guides.

3. **Choose the Quick Selection tool in the Tools panel.**

4. **In the Options bar, make sure the Sample All Layers option is not checked.**

    You only want to select an area based on the Sunrise layer content, so you do not want to make a selection based on the content of other layers in the file.

5. **Click near the bottom-left corner of the image, then drag right and up into the person's head.**

    The resulting selection marquee shows that the software does a good job of isolating the obvious foreground elements of the image (the ground and the person's silhouette). If you look closely, however, areas of fine detail — the person's hair and the grass in front of the water — are not included. You will need to use a different method to refine the selection edge and add the areas of detail.

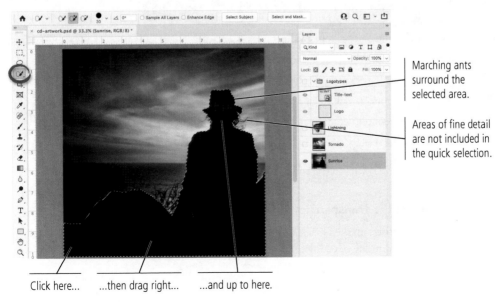

Marching ants surround the selected area.

Areas of fine detail are not included in the quick selection.

Click here...      ...then drag right...      ...and up to here.

## 6. Click the Select and Mask button in the Options bar.

The Select and Mask workspace is a specialized workspace that contains only the tools you need to refine a complex selection.

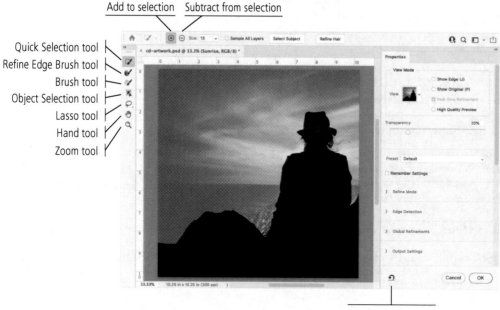

Add to selection
Subtract from selection

Quick Selection tool
Refine Edge Brush tool
Brush tool
Object Selection tool
Lasso tool
Hand tool
Zoom tool

Reset the Workspace

## 7. In the Properties panel, open the View menu and make sure Onion Skin is selected.

The different types of preview change the way your image appears while you refine the edges within the workspace.

- **Onion Skin**, the default, shows unselected (masked) areas as semi-transparent, based on the value in the Transparency slider. You can make the masked areas more or less transparent by increasing or decreasing (respectively) the Transparency value.
- **Marching Ants** shows the basic standard selection.
- **Overlay** shows the unselected areas with a Quick Mask overlay.
- **On Black** shows the selection in color against a black background.
- **On White** shows the selection in color against a white background.
- **Black & White** shows the selected area in white and the unselected area in black.
- **On Layers** shows only the selected area. Unselected areas are hidden so that underlying layers are visible in masked areas in the preview.

## 8. In the Properties panel, set the Transparency slider to 50%.

Using the 50% transparency setting, masked pixels are partially visible, so that you can see the areas you want to add to the selection.

9. **Expand the Refine Mode options and click the Object Aware mode button. Read the resulting warning and then click OK.**

   The default **Color Aware** mode performs well when isolating objects from high-contrast backgrounds, or with backgrounds that do not include much detail.

   If you expand the Refine Mode options in the Properties panel, you can activate the **Object Refine** mode, which creates better results when fine details exist in front of a more detailed background.

Click these arrows to expand each category of properties.

Click the Object Aware button.

10. **Zoom into the woman's head in the image, then choose the Refine Edge Brush tool.**

    This tool has edge detection capabilities, which means you can simply "paint" over areas to identify edges of very small areas of detail.

*Note:*

*You can use the Zoom and Hand tools, as well as their associated short-cuts, to change the image preview in the Select and Mask workspace.*

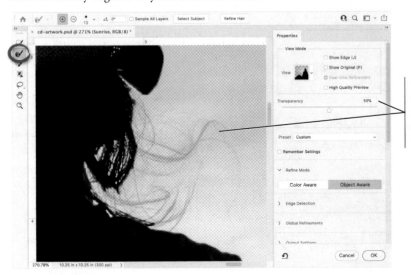

Changing the onion skin transparency changes the view of unselected areas of the image layer.

11. **Click and drag over the wispy areas of the woman's hair.**

    You might not see much of a difference as you drag, but when you release the mouse button, you should see some of the thin details appear solid (selected) instead of transparent (not selected).

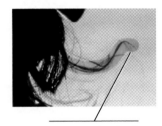

Paint over the detail areas that are currently unselected.

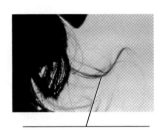

Details appear solid (selected) after you paint over them and release the mouse button.

**12. Continue to drag over the details on both sides of the woman's head until you are satisfied with the results.**

You don't need to be precise when you drag over the details, although dragging approximately over the details generally does produce better results.

Original Selection

Refined Selection

**13. Using the Refine Edge Brush tool, paint over the grass (near the woman's arm) to add those fine details to the selection.**

It might be helpful in this area to reduce the onion skin transparency, so that you can better see the details in this portion of the image.

Original Selection

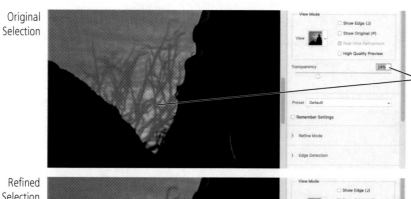

Reducing the transparency allows you to better see the unselected details.

Refined Selection

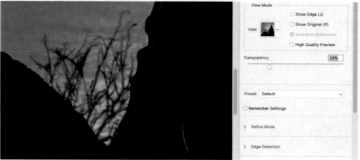

**Note:**

*When the Select and Mask workspace is active, the Refine Hair button in the Options bar does an excellent job of identifying and refining obvious hair in an image. It would not, however, select the grasses in this image, so you should still know how to use the various tools and settings individually.*

14. **If necessary, expand the Edge Detection and Global Refinements sections of the Properties panel, then review those options.**

- **Radius** is the number of pixels around the edge that are affected. Higher radius values result in softer edges and lower values result in sharper edges.

- **Smart Radius** automatically adjusts the radius for hard and soft edges found in the border region. You should turn off this option if your selection area has all hard edges or all soft edges.

- **Smooth** reduces the number of points that make up your selection and, as the name suggests, makes a smoother edge. You can set smoothness from 0 (very detailed selection) to 100 (very smooth selection).

- **Feather** softens the selection edge, resulting in a transition that does not have a hard edge (in other words, blends into the background). You can feather the selection up to 250 pixels.

- **Contrast** is the degree of variation allowed in the selection edge. Higher Contrast values (up to 100%) mean sharper selection edges.

- **Shift Edge** shrinks or grows the selection edge by the defined percentage (from −100% to 100%).

- **Invert** reverses the mask; selected areas become unselected and vice versa.

15. **Experiment with the adjustments until you're satisfied with the selection edge.**

We increased the Smooth value to 10 to reduce jagged effects at the selection edge.

16. **Expand the Output Settings in the Properties panel and choose the Layer Mask option in the Output To menu.**

The Output options can be used to create a new layer or file (with or without a mask) from the selection. (You might need to scroll in the panel to find the Output menu, or you can collapse the Edge Detection and Global Refinements sections.)

The **Decontaminate Colors** can be checked to remove a certain percentage of color from the edge of a selection.

17. **Click OK to accept your refined selection. Choose View>Fit on Screen to show the entire image.**

When you pasted the feathered selection from the original Lightning.jpg file, you pasted only the pixels inside the selection area; unselected pixels from the original image are not a part of the composite file.

The resulting layer mask hides areas that were not selected.

Rather than actually excluding or deleting pixels, a **layer mask** hides unwanted pixels. The mask you just created is a raster-based pixel mask. Unselected (masked) areas are hidden but not deleted, so you can later edit the mask to change the visible part of the image. This is a non-destructive way to hide certain elements of a layer without permanently deleting pixels. You can edit or disable the layer mask at any time.

> **Note:**
>
> *A layer mask is basically an Alpha channel that is connected to a specific layer.*

18. **Control/right-click the mask thumbnail and choose Disable Layer Mask from the contextual menu.**

When you disable the mask, the background pixels are again visible. This is one advantage of using masks — masked pixels are not removed, they are simply hidden.

Control/right-click the thumbnail to open the mask's contextual menu.

When the mask is disabled, masked pixels are visible.

A red X indicates that the mask is disabled.

19. **Control/right-click the mask thumbnail and choose Apply Layer Mask from the contextual menu.**

This option applies the mask to the attached layer, permanently removing the masked pixels from the layer.

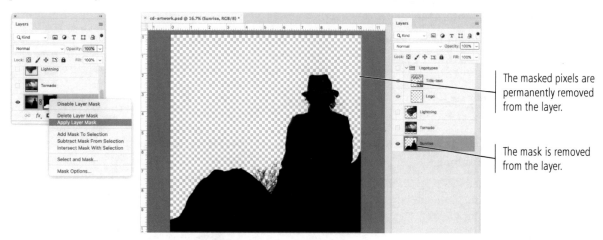

The masked pixels are permanently removed from the layer.

The mask is removed from the layer.

20. **Choose Edit>Undo Apply Layer Mask to restore the layer mask.**

As you saw in the previous step, applying a mask permanently removes the masked pixels. This essentially defeats the purpose of a mask, so you are restoring it in this step.

# Automatically Selecting and Replacing the Sky

If you choose Select>Sky, Photoshop automatically analyzes the image and creates a selection based on what it determines to be the sky. The function does a remarkable job, but does have some limitations. In the base image for this project, for example, it does not include the water area that you want to replace. We always encourage you to learn manual options for fine-tuning rather than relying only on automatic features.

Choosing Edit>Sky Replacement offers a dialog-box based option for changing the sky in an image, driven by the same process that creates the selection if you choose Select>Sky. You can open the Sky menu and choose any of the built-in alternatives, or click the New Sky button to add your own images into the dialog box.

Once you have selected a replacement sky, you can use the options in the dialog box to adjust how the sky is merged with the existing image:

While the dialog box's Move tool is active, you can click on the canvas and drag to reposition the replacement sky relative to the overall canvas.

You can also use the Sky Brush tool to extend or reduce the sky area.

In the lower section of the dialog box, you can adjust settings that affect the way the new sky image blends into the foreground of the base image:

Move tool

Sky Brush tool

Click to open the menu of available skies.

Click a specific sky thumbnail to apply it.

Create New Sky button

- Shift Edge expands or contracts the boundary between the image foreground and the sky.
- Fade Edge feathers the boundary between the foreground and the sky.
- Sky Adjustments:
  - Brightness adjusts the brightness of the replacement sky.
  - Temperature adjusts the color temperature of the replacement sky. (Higher-temperature lights, such as you might find in an office building, have a blue cast and are considered to be cooler. Lower-temperature lights have a yellow cast and are considered to be warmer.)
  - Scale adjusts the size of the replacement sky.
  - Flip reverses the replacement sky image horizontally.
- Foreground Adjustments:
  - Lighting Mode defines whether the lighting adjustment is applied using the Multiply or Screen blending mode.

- Lighting Adjustment controls the opacity of the lighting adjustment that is applied to the foreground image.
- Color Adjustment controls the opacity of color harmonizing that is applied to the foreground image.

In the Output menu, you determine how the new sky is applied. By default, the New Layers option results in a layer group with several component layers that make the replacement work.

If you choose Duplicate Layers, the result of the replacement is flattened into a single new layer; you can't access the individual component layers that created the replacement.

## Understanding Channels

You need a bit of background about channels to understand what's happening in the Quick Mask you will use in the next exercise. (You will use channels extensively in later projects.)

Every image has one channel for each component color. Each channel contains the information for the amount of that component color in any given pixel. An RGB image has three channels: Red, Green, and Blue (right top). A CMYK image has four channels: Cyan, Magenta, Yellow, and Black (right bottom).

In RGB images, the three additive primaries can have a value of 0 (none of that color) to 255 (full intensity of that color). Combining a value of 255 for each primary results in white. A value of 0 for each primary results in black.

In CMYK images, the three subtractive primaries plus black are combined in percentages from 0 (none of that color) to 100 (full intensity of that color) to create the range of printable colors. Channels in a CMYK image represent the printing plates or separations required to output the job.

### Understanding Alpha Channels

An Alpha channel is a special type of channel in which the value determines the degree of transparency of a pixel. In other words, a 50% value in the Alpha channel means that area of the image will be 50% transparent.

When working in Quick Mask mode, a temporary Quick Mask channel stores the degree of transparency based on the current selection. A semi-transparent red overlay shows areas being masked (i.e., the areas that are not included in the current selection).

Quick Masks are useful when you need to work with a temporary selection, or if you are still defining the exact selection area. As long as you stay in Quick Mask mode, the temporary Alpha channel remains in the Channels panel (listed as "Quick Mask"). If you return to Standard mode, the Quick Mask disappears from the window and the panel.

You can save a Quick Mask channel as a permanent Alpha channel by dragging the Quick Mask channel onto the New Channel button at the bottom of the panel. This adds a channel named "Quick Mask copy," which remains even if you exit Quick Mask mode. You can then double-click the Alpha channel name in the panel to rename it, as we did in the following image (naming the channel "Lion Head").

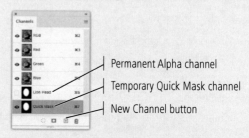

Permanent Alpha channel

Temporary Quick Mask channel

New Channel button

You can change the appearance of an Alpha channel mask by double-clicking a channel thumbnail in the Channels panel. In the top half of the resulting dialog box, you can change the overlay to show selected areas instead of the default masked areas.

Clicking the Color swatch opens a Color Picker, where you can change the color of the Quick Mask overlay. You can also use the Opacity field to change the transparency of the overlay (the default is 50%). Keep in mind that these settings only affect the appearance of the mask in Photoshop; the density of the selection is not affected by changing the overlay opacity.

21. **Control/right-click the mask thumbnail and choose Enable Layer Mask from the contextual menu.**

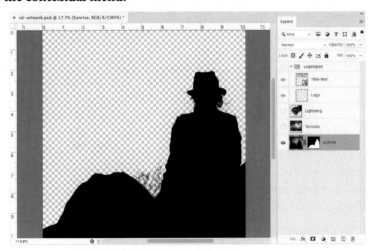

22. **Save the file and continue to the next exercise.**

 ## Edit Layer Mask Properties

The most important thing to understand in this series of exercises is that layer masks are non-destructive. You can change the mask to change the visible area of the layer, temporarily hide the mask to show the entire layer, or even delete the mask entirely if you decide you don't want or need it. You can also edit a number of mask properties to further refine the mask and its effect on the masked layer contents.

1. **With cd-artwork.psd open, open the Channels panel (Window>Channels).**

2. **In the Channels panel, click the empty space on the left side of the panel to make the Sunrise Mask channel visible.**

   Layer masks are not visible by default; you have to turn them on in the Channels panel to see them. Although you can edit a mask without seeing it, it is easier (at least when you're first learning) to be able to see what you're doing.

Making the mask channel visible allows you to see the red overlay in the image.

3. **Double-click the Sunrise Mask channel icon in the Channels panel.**

### 4. Change the Opacity field to 100%, then click OK.

Remember, this change only affects the transparency of the mask, not the degree of transparency applied to the layer. By setting the mask opacity to 100%, you will be better able to see the results of your choices in the following steps.

Anything solid red will be hidden and anything with no red will be visible; shades of red will be partially transparent.

### 5. If necessary, click the empty space on the left side of the Channels panel to make the Sunrise Mask channel visible.

There is a minor bug in the software that might cause the mask channel to be hidden when you change the mask opacity.

### 6. In the Layers panel, click the Sunrise layer mask thumbnail to select it.

These corner icons indicate that the base layer is selected.

Clicking the layer mask thumbnail selects the mask so you can edit it.

### 7. Open the Properties panel (Window>Properties).

Like the Options bar, the Properties panel is contextual. Different options are available in the panel depending on what is selected in the Layers panel. When a layer mask is selected, you can manipulate a variety of properties related to the selected mask.

The layer mask must be selected in the Layers panel.

The Properties panel can be used to edit the selected mask.

*Note:*

*The Select and Mask button opens the Select and Mask workspace. The Color Range button opens the [Select] Color Range dialog box.*

The Density slider changes the opacity of the overall mask. If you reduce the density to 80%, for example, underlying layers will be 20% visible through the mask. (Don't confuse this with the opacity of an alpha channel, which only affects the appearance of the mask onscreen.)

8. **In the Properties panel, change the Feather value to 25 px.**

   If you feather a selection and then make a layer mask from that selection, the feathering becomes a permanent part of the mask. The Properties panel allows you to adjust the feathering of a hard-edge mask, and then later change or even remove the feathering if necessary, without painting on the mask.

Use the Properties panel to feather the mask edge nondestructively.

9. **Change the Feather value to 1 px.**

   This small feathering value will help to remove (or at least minimize) any remaining background artifacts around the edges of your mask.

10. **Double-click the Sunrise Mask channel icon in the Channels panel.**

11. **Change the Opacity field back to 50%, then click OK.**

   Remember, the Layer Mask Display Options setting only affects the mask's visibility in the document window. This does *not* affect the degree to which the mask affects pixels on the masked layer.

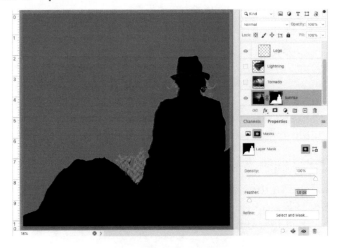

**12. If the mask channel remains visible, click the eye icon for the Sunrise Mask channel in the Channels panel to hide it.**

Even when the actual mask channel is not visible, the mask remains intact on the layer.

The mask remains intact and enabled, even though the mask channel is not visible.

**13. Save the file and continue to the next exercise.**

 **Arrange Layer Position and Stacking Order**

The ad is almost final, but a few pieces are still not quite in position. You already know you can use the Move tool to move the contents of a layer around on the canvas. You can also move a layer to any position in the **stacking order** (the top-to-bottom position of a layer) by simply dragging it to a new position in the Layers panel.

**1. With cd-artwork.psd open, make all layers visible.**

**2. Click the Sunrise layer in the Layers panel and drag up. When a heavy bar appears above the Lightning layer, release the mouse button.**

The line identifies where the layer will be positioned when you release the mouse button.

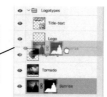

After you restack the layers, you might see that a small blank space appears in the bottom-left corner. (Yours might be slightly different, depending on how you painted the mask in the previous exercise.)

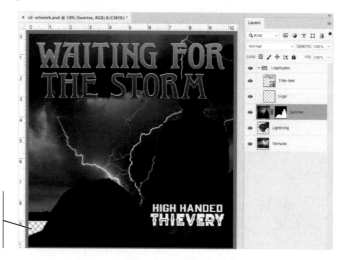

This transparent area needs to be filled for the overall composition to be complete.

*Note:*

*Be careful when dragging layers near a layer group. If the border appears around a layer group, releasing the mouse button would place the dragged layer inside of the group.*

*Note:*

*If your original selection does not result in the problem described in Step 2, skip to Step 7.*

*Note:*

*Press Command/Control-[ (left bracket) to move a layer down in the stacking order.*

*Press Command/Control-] (right bracket) to move a layer up in the stacking order.*

# Filtering Photoshop Layers

When you work with complex files, you might find yourself with dozens — or even hundreds — of layers. Descriptive names can help you navigate through the layers, but you still have to scroll through the panel to find what you need.

Layer filtering, available at the top of the Layers panel, allows you to narrow down the panel to only layers that meet certain criteria, making it much easier to locate a specific layer.

Use this menu to filter layers by a number of criteria.

Filter for:
Smart objects
Shape layers
Type layers
Adjustment layers
Pixel layers

When **Kind** is selected in the menu, you can use the associated buttons to show only certain types of layers (adjustment layers, smart objects, etc.).

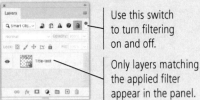

Use this switch to turn filtering on and off.

Only layers matching the applied filter appear in the panel.

When **Name** is selected, you can type in the attached field to find layers with names that include the text you enter in the field. The defined text string does not need to be at the beginning of the layer name. For example, typing "r" would return both Sunrise and Tornado layers in the file for this project.

When **Effect** is selected, you can use the secondary menu to find only layers with a specified effect (applied using the Layer>Layer Style submenu).

When **Attribute** is selected, you can choose from a number of layer attributes (visible, linked, clipped, masked, etc)..

When **Color** is selected, you can choose any of the built-in colors from the secondary menu. These colors, which appear around the layer's visibility icon, can be assigned to individual layers in each layer's contextual menu.

When **Mode** is selected, you can use the secondary menu to find only layers to which a certain blending mode has been assigned.

When **Smart Object** is selected, you can use the buttons at the top of the panel to find linked layers, layers with modified source data, layers with missing source data, or embedded layers. These buttons are nonexclusive, which means you can select more than one option at a time (for example, all layers with missing and modified source data).

The **Selected** option shows a subset of layers that exist in Isolation mode. To create a subset, select one or more layers in the Layers panel, and then choose Select>Isolate Layers. The Layers panel automatically shows a subset of only the selected layers, and Selected appears in the Filter By menu.

3.  In the Layers panel, select the Tornado layer as the active one.

4.  Press Command/Control-T to enter Free Transform mode.

5.  Drag the bottom-right corner handle of the layer down until any transparent area in the bottom-left corner is filled.

    Keep in mind that you are enlarging a raster-image layer, which can cause loss of detail. Because this is a very small increase, and because the layer is the background image behind several other elements, you can make this enlargement without ruining the integrity of the composition.

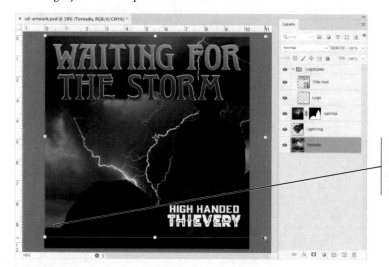

Drag the bottom-right handle to enlarge the active layer until this area is filled.

6.  Press Return/Enter to finalize the transformation.

7.  Select the Lightning layer in the Layers panel, then change the layer opacity to 35%.

    Layer opacity is the degree to which you can see underlying layers through the layer you are editing. Because you made the lightning only 35% opaque, the underlying tornado image is strongly visible through the lightning.

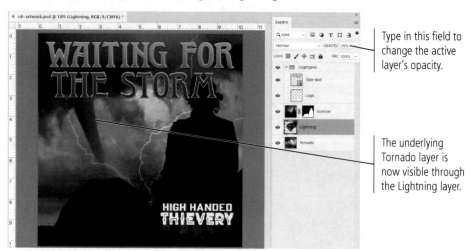

Type in this field to change the active layer's opacity.

The underlying Tornado layer is now visible through the Lightning layer.

8.  Save the file and then continue to the final stage of the project.

# STAGE 4 / Saving Files for Multiple Media

Many Photoshop projects require saving the completed file in more than one format. Many artists prefer to leave all files in the native PSD format, as there is then only one file to track. Others prefer to send only flattened TIFF files of their artwork because the individual elements can't be changed. Ultimately, the formats you use will depend on where and how the file is being placed.

Many Photoshop projects are pieces of a larger composition, and the overall project defines the format you need. The art you just created, for example, might be placed in magazine layouts, which will be built in a page-layout application such as Adobe InDesign. Although the current versions of industry-standard page-layout applications can support native layered PSD files, older versions can't import those native files. As the Photoshop artist, you have to save your work in a format that is compatible with the process being used by the magazine designer.

As you know, the artwork you created will be used in a variety of ways. You need to save three different versions of the artwork to meet those requirements.

Photoshop can save files in a number of common formats, including:

- **Photoshop**, with the extension PSD, is the native format.

- **JPEG** is a lossy compressed file format that does not support transparency.

- **Photoshop PDF** can contain all required font and image information in a single file, which can be compressed to reduce file size.

- **PNG** is a raster-based format that supports both continuous-tone color and transparency. It is more commonly used in digital publishing (specifically, web design), and does not support CMYK color, which is required for commercial printing.

- **TIFF** is a raster-based image format that supports layers, alpha channels, and file compression.

##  Save a Flattened TIFF File

The TIFF format is commonly used for print applications. Although the format can include layers, many designers prefer to send flattened files for output to avoid any potential problems that might be caused by older output devices, which is still an issue, as many service providers do not update very expensive output equipment until it becomes absolutely necessary.

In this exercise you will save the finished artwork as a flattened TIFF file that can be used for the album cover sleeve, as well as for most print advertising requirements.

1. **With cd-artwork.psd open, choose File>Save a Copy.**

   The CD artwork is complete in the native Photoshop file. In the next few exercises you are going to make changes that you don't want to become a permanent part of the file. Saving it now, if you haven't already, means the finished artwork file won't be compromised in the following exercises.

2. **Click the Save on Your Computer button if necessary.**

   From this point on throughout this book, you should assume you are saving the files to a local drive. We will not continue to repeat the instruction to click the Save on Your Computer button.

3. **If necessary, navigate to your WIP>Music folder as the target location.**

The Save a Copy dialog box defaults to the last-used location. If you continued the entire way through this project without stopping, you won't have to navigate.

4. **In the Save As/File Name field, change the word "copy" in the default file name to -album (including the space before the word "copy"). Leave the extension in the file name.**

5. **Click the Format/Save As Type menu and choose TIFF.**

6. **In the bottom half of the dialog box, uncheck the Layers option.**

Because this file contains layers, the Layers option was checked by default.

If your file contained alpha channels, annotations, or spot colors, those check boxes would also be available.

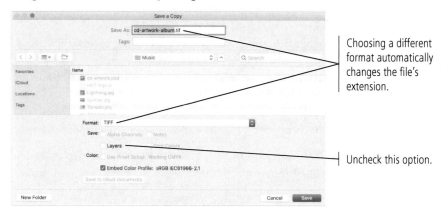

Choosing a different format automatically changes the file's extension.

Uncheck this option.

7. **Leave the remaining options at their default values and click Save.**

8. **In the resulting TIFF Options dialog box, make sure the None image compression option is selected.**

TIFF files can be compressed (made smaller) using three methods:

- **None** applies no compression to the file. This option is safe if file size is not an issue, but digital file transmission often requires files to be smaller than a full-page, multilayered Photoshop file.

- **LZW** (Lempel-Ziv-Welch) compression is **lossless**, which means all file data is maintained in the compressed file.

- **ZIP** compression is also lossless, but is not supported by all desktop-publishing software (especially older versions).

- **JPEG** is a **lossy** compression scheme, which means some data will be thrown away to reduce the file size. If you choose JPEG compression, the Quality options determine how much data can be discarded. Maximum quality means less data is thrown out and the file is larger; minimum quality discards more data and results in a smaller file size.

9. **Leave the Pixel Order radio button at the default value, and choose the Byte Order option for your operating system.**

    **Pixel Order** determines how channel data is encoded. The Interleaved (RGBRGB) option is the default. Per Channel (RRGGBB) is called "planar" order.

    **Byte Order** determines which platform can use the file on older versions of desktop publishing software. This option is largely obsolete because most modern software can now read either byte order.

    **Save Image Pyramid** creates a tiered file with multiple resolution versions; this isn't widely used or supported by other applications, so you can typically leave it unchecked.

    If your file contains transparency, the **Save Transparency** check box will be available. If you don't choose this option, transparent areas will be white in the saved file.

10. **In the Layer Compression area, make sure Discard Layers is selected.**

    These three options explain — right in the dialog box — what they do.

11. **Click OK to save the file, then continue to the next exercise.**

*Note:*

*Some experts argue that choosing the order for your system can improve print quality, especially on desktop output devices.*

 ## Reduce the Physical File Size

The CD insert artwork needs to be approximately half the size of the album artwork. Reducing the file's physical size is an easy process, although you need to check the positioning of various elements to make sure they meet the output requirements. In this exercise you will reduce the file's physical size, and then make necessary layer adjustments to meet the needs of the CD insert.

1. **With cd-artwork.psd open in Photoshop, choose Image>Image Size.**

2. **Make sure the Resample option is checked.**

    You are resizing this image, which means you are changing the physical dimensions (and the actual number of pixels in the file). If Resample was not checked, you would simply be redistributing the same number of pixels across a different physical space.

3. **With Inches selected in the Width and Height Units menus, type 5 in the Width field.**

    The CD insert is 4.75″ square, but it requires 1/8″ bleeds on all four sides:

    $$4.75'' + 0.125'' + 0.125'' = 5''$$

    Because the width and height are constrained by default, changing one value applies a proportional change to the other value.

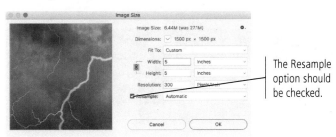

The Resample option should be checked.

4. **Click OK to change the file size.**

5. **Choose View>Show>Guides. Zoom in to the top-left corner and review the position of the guides.**

   Reducing the file size affects all elements of the file, including guides. As you can see, the position of the various guides is reduced by approximately half (for example, the bleed guides are near the 1/16″ mark instead of the 1/8″ mark).

   Guides are moved proportionally based on the reduced file size.

6. **Choose View>Clear Guides.**

   Rather than manually dragging each guide on the page, you are going to simply replace them with new ones. This command removes all existing guides from the canvas.

7. **Choose View>New Guide Layout.**

8. **With the Column option unchecked and the Margin option checked, set all Margin four fields to 0.125 in. Click OK to add the new guides.**

   This set of guides defines the trim size of the CD insert, marking a 1/8″ bleed allowance on all four edges of the file.

   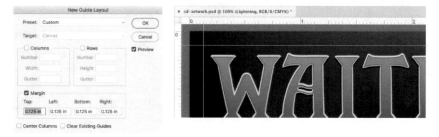

9. **Choose View>New Guide Layout again.**

10. **With the Margin option checked, change all four fields to 0.25 in. Click OK to add the new guides.**

   This second set of guides defines the live area, marking the required 1/8″ safe margin. Although they are 1/4″ from the canvas edge, they are 1/8″ from the trim guides.

11. **Zoom out so you can see the entire top of the artwork.**

12. **Choose the Move tool in the Tools panel. In the Options bar, make sure the Auto-Select option is checked and Layer is selected in the attached menu.**

    When active, clicking in the document window automatically selects the layer containing the layers where you click.

    Because Layer is selected in the menu, only the relevant layer will move, even if it is part of a layer group. If you want all layers in a group containing the selected layer to move, you can choose Group in the menu.

13. **Click any of the letters in the album title and drag until the layer snaps to the top and left margin guides.**

    Auto-Select    Layer is selected
    is active.      in the menu.

    Click any pixel in the title text and drag to move the layer.

14. **Press Command/Control-T to enter Free Transform mode. Click and drag the bottom-right bounding-box handle until the title fits inside the margin guides in the reduced file.**

    Drag the bottom-right handle to fit the title into the live area.

15. **Press Return/Enter to finalize the transformation.**

16. **With the Move tool still active, click any pixel in the logo and drag until it snaps to the bottom and right margin guides.**

    Because the Auto-Select option is active, you don't need to first select the target layer in the Layers panel to move the content.

    Click any pixel in the logo artwork and drag to move the layer content.

17. **Choose File>Save a Copy. Using the same method as in the previous exercise, save this file as a flat TIFF file named cd-artwork-insert.tif. Click OK to accept the default TIFF options.**

 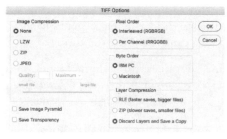

18. **With cd-artwork.psd still active, choose File>Revert.**

This command restores the file to the last-saved version. Because you saved the completed artwork at the beginning of this stage, the command restores the artwork to its original, 10.25" file size.

Because enlarging a raster image to such a degree (more than 200% to go from 5" to 10.25") would almost certainly cause image degradation, you are restoring the larger version instead of saving the smaller one.

19. **Continue to the next exercise.**

 ## Save a JPEG File for Digital Media

The final file required for this project is a 3000 × 3000 pixel, high-quality JPEG file.

1. **With cd-artwork.psd open and restored to its last-saved state, choose Image>Image Size.**

2. **Make sure the Resample option is checked, then choose Pixels in the Width menu.**

3. **Change the Width field to 3000.**

Again, you are defining the actual number of pixels to include in the file. If the resample was not checked, changing the width or height would only change the distribution of pixels instead of changing the actual number of pixels in the file.

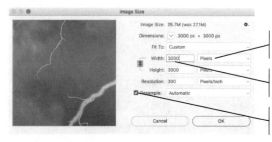

Choose Pixels in the Width menu.

Change the number of pixels in this field.

The Resample option should be checked.

4. **Click OK to finalize the new size.**

   This file is not being printed, so you don't need to worry about the bleed and margin areas. Because the size reduction is slight in this case, no further adjustment is required before saving the JPEG file for digital music libraries.

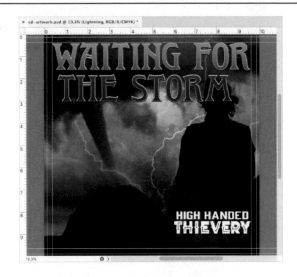

5. **Choose File>Save a Copy.**

6. **Choose JPEG in the Format/Save As Type menu, then change the file name to cd-artwork-digital.jpg.**

   The JPEG format does not support layers, alpha channels, or spot colors, so those options are unavailable in the bottom of the dialog box.

7. **Click Save.**

8. **In the resulting JPEG Options dialog box, choose High in the Image Options Quality menu.**

   This menu determines how much compression will be used in the resulting file:

   Type a quality level (1–12) in this field...

   ...or choose a quality level in this menu.

   - Higher values mean less compression, better quality, and larger file size.

   - Lower values mean more compression, lower quality, and smaller file size.

9. **Click OK to save the JPEG file.**

10. **Close the cd-artwork.psd file without saving.**

1. _____ is likely to cause degradation of a raster image when it's reproduced on a printing press.

2. A _____ is a linked file that you place into another Photoshop document.

3. The _____ is context sensitive, providing access to different functions depending on which tool is active.

4. The _____ is the final size of a printed page.

5. The _____ tool is used to draw irregular-shaped selection marquees.

6. The _____ tool is used to select areas of similar color by clicking and dragging in the image window.

7. The _____ tool can be used to drag layer contents to another position within the image, or into another open document.

8. When selecting color ranges, the _____ value determines how much of the current color range falls into the selection.

9. A _____ can be used to non-destructively hide certain areas of a layer.

10. _____ is a lossy compression method that is best used when large file size might be a problem.

1. Briefly describe the difference between raster images and vector graphics.

2. Briefly explain three methods for isolating an image from its background.

3. Briefly explain the concept of a layer mask.

Use what you have learned in this project to complete the following freeform exercise.
Carefully read the art director and client comments, then create your own design to meet the needs of the project.
Use the space below to sketch ideas. When finished, write a brief explanation of the reasoning behind your final design.

**art director comments**

Your client's friend liked your work on the new music artwork. She would like to hire you to create an early-release ad concept for a new movie that is expected to be a major release next year.

To complete this project, you should:

❏ Use the client-supplied title artwork, studio logos, and rating placeholder file in the **Eury_PS22_PB.zip** archive (in your student resources).

❏ Find or create appropriate background and foreground images to illustrate the movie theme (see the client's comments at right).

❏ Composite all the various elements into a single completed ad layout using the following specifications:

- Trim: 8.5″ wide × 11″ high
- Bleeds: 0.125″ all four sides
- Margins: 0.375″ all four sides

**client comments**

The movie is titled *His Eury*. It's a modern suspense/fantasy loosely based on the greek myth of Orpheus and Eurydice. Think medieval weapons and magic but set in a modern metropolitan setting.

Orlan's wife Eury is kidnapped, and he sets out to find and rescue her. Along the way, he discovers a hidden underworld — the Greek gods are real and living among us. Some are helpful and some are devious, while some are downright deadly.

We don't have any specific imagery in mind for the early promotional pieces, and we're still finalizing the cast so we can't use pictures of the cast yet. We did create a title treatment concept that plays on the similarity between Eury and the word "fury" (this is not a children's movie about teenage heros).

This movie is a joint venture between Sun and Tantamount Studios, so both logos need to be included in the artwork. It isn't rated yet, either, so please use the rating placeholder artwork for now.

**project justification**

Making selections is one of the most basic — and most important — skills that you will learn in Photoshop. Selections are so important that Photoshop dedicates an entire menu to the process.

As you created the music artwork in this project, you used a number of techniques that you will apply in many (if not all) projects you build in Photoshop. You learned a number of ways to make both simple and complex selections, and you will learn additional methods in later projects. You also learned how to work with multiple layers, which will be an important part of virtually every Photoshop project you create, both in this book and throughout your career.

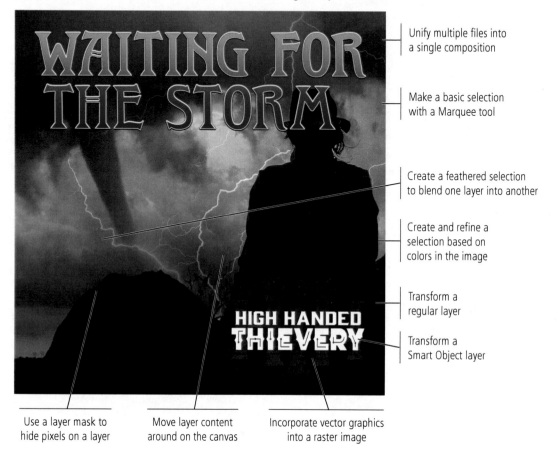

Unify multiple files into a single composition

Make a basic selection with a Marquee tool

Create a feathered selection to blend one layer into another

Create and refine a selection based on colors in the image

Transform a regular layer

Transform a Smart Object layer

Use a layer mask to hide pixels on a layer

Move layer content around on the canvas

Incorporate vector graphics into a raster image

# 2 Car Magazine Cover

Your client publishes a monthly magazine for car enthusiasts. Your agency has been hired to take over the magazine design and you have been tasked with designing the cover for the next issue.

This project incorporates the following skills:

❑ Resizing and resampling supplied images

❑ Creating complex vector paths and shape layers

❑ Compositing images as Smart Objects

❑ Applying non-destructive styles, effects, and filters

❑ Developing a custom artistic background

## Videos to Watch

Access these helpful videos in your online student resources:

▶ Car Magazine Cover Project Introduction

▶ Changing the Canvas Size

▶ Creating Vector Shapes

▶ Using the Pen Tool

**client comments**

Every month, the magazine cover includes one main featured car, and three smaller images related to other articles in the issue. In addition to those images and the magazine title, we also always include several text blurbs with teasers for secondary articles in the issue, and a QR code that links to the website.

We're looking for a new way to present these elements. Once we finalize a general layout, we'll use that layout going forward for every new issue.

The only thing we're fixed on is the trim size, which is 8″ × 10″, with a 1/8″ bleed allowance.

**Watch the video** Car Magazine Cover Project Introduction **in your online student resources.**

**art director comments**

The client sent me the main car image for the first redesign. It's a little bit small, so we'll have to do some manipulation to make it large enough to fill the cover space. The car also needs to be knocked out of its background so it can be more prominent. A vector path will work well to meet this goal because you can edit it at any time without losing quality.

You're going to use a combination of styles, filters, and effects on the background and inset images. Photoshop's Smart Object capabilities will be a significant advantage in this task because we can edit the effects and filters if the client isn't thrilled with the initial effort.

I've also already created a template in Illustrator with the magazine nameplate and text elements; we'll repurpose the same file every month with the different text for each issue. You can place that file directly into Photoshop as a linked file so that any last-minute changes in the file will automatically appear in the final composite cover.

**project objectives**

To complete this project, you will:

❑ Resize and resample an existing source image

❑ Edit the canvas size

❑ Create a vector-based layer mask

❑ Create a vector shape layer

❑ Create a clipping mask

❑ Add texture to a shape layer

❑ Apply custom layer effects

❑ Use the Filter Gallery

❑ Liquify a layer

❑ Use the Eyedropper tool

❑ Create a custom gradient

❑ Print a composite proof

# STAGE 1 / Enlarging Source Files

Any project that you build in Photoshop requires some amount of zooming in and out to various view percentages, as well as navigating around the document within its window. As we show you how to complete different stages of the workflow, we usually won't tell you when to change your view percentage because that's largely a matter of personal preference. Nonetheless, you should understand the different options for navigating around a Photoshop file so you can easily and efficiently get to what you want, when you want to get there.

To review information from the Interface chapter, keep in mind that you have a number of options for navigating around a document:

- Click with the Hand tool to drag the image around in the document window.

- Click with the Zoom tool to zoom in; Option/Alt-click to zoom out.

- Use the View Percentage field in the bottom-left corner of the document window.

- Use the options in the View menu (or the corresponding keyboard shortcuts).

- Use the Navigator panel.

*Note:*

*As you complete the exercises in this project, use any of these methods to zoom in or out on different areas of the file.*

## Resize and Resample the Existing Source Image

This project — like many others you will build throughout your career — starts with an existing image, which you will open and use as the basis for the rest of the project. Whenever you start with an existing file, it's best to evaluate what you already have before you make any changes.

1. **Expand the Cars_PS22_RF.zip archive in your WIP folder (Macintosh) or copy the archive contents into your WIP folder (Windows).**

   This results in a folder named **Cars**, which contains the files you need for this project. You should also use this folder to save the files you create in this project.

2. **In Photoshop, choose File>Open. Navigate to the file amg.jpg in your WIP>Cars folder and click Open.**

3. **Choose View>Fit on Screen so you can see the entire image, and make sure rulers are visible (View>Rulers).**

4. **Choose Image>Image Size.**

   The amg.jpg file is 25″ wide by 18.75″ high, with a resolution of 72 pixels/ inch. Commercial printing typically requires 300 pixels/inch, so this image would not be considered "print quality" at its current size.

   The first step is to resize the image using the principle of effective resolution to achieve the 300 pixels/ inch required for commercial printing.

5. **At the bottom of the dialog box, uncheck the Resample option and change the Resolution field to 300.**

Remember, when resampling is not active, the image retains the same number of pixels when you change the size or resolution fields. The image's physical size is now smaller since you compressed 300 pixels into an inch instead of the original 72 ppi.

Uncheck the Resample option.

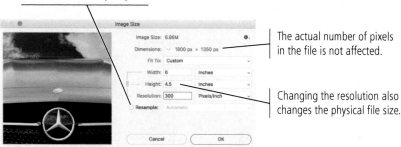

The actual number of pixels in the file is not affected.

Changing the resolution also changes the physical file size.

6. **Click OK to resize the source image.**

As you can see, the image view in the document window does not change because the image still has the same number of pixels. The rulers at the left and top edges of the document window show the new measurements that are associated with the resized image.

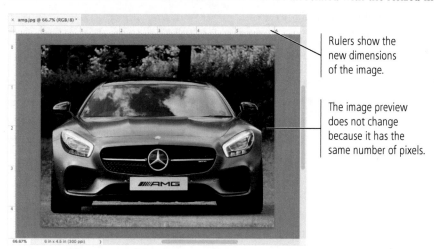

Rulers show the new dimensions of the image.

The image preview does not change because it has the same number of pixels.

**Note:**

*At the time of writing, there is a bug in the software that might prevent the rulers from showing the new image size. If you don't see the new file dimensions, change the view percentage of the file; the rulers will change.*

7. **Choose Image>Image Size again.**

Because you already defined the appropriate resolution for this image, you now need to make the image large enough to meet the overall job requirements.

Resampling adds or removes pixels to create the size you define without affecting the defined resolution.

8. **Click in the Preview window and drag until the logo on the car's grill is visible.**

Areas of greater detail are the most prone to distortion when you enlarge an image. The Image Size preview area allows you to review the results before finalizing the process.

9. **At the bottom of the dialog box, check the Resample option.**

When the Resample option is checked, you can change the actual number of pixels in the image without affecting its resolution.

10. **Open the Resample menu and choose Preserve Details (enlargement).**

Although you should try to capture images at the size you will need them, this is not always possible when working with client-supplied images. The Preserve Details option significantly improves the results of artificially enlarging an existing image.

11. **Make sure the Constrain option is active.**

12. **With the units menus set to Inches, change the Width field to 8.25.**

The overall project requires a finished image that is 8.25″ wide by 10.25″ high. If you enlarged the picture to match the required height, it would be too wide for the entire car to fit into the composition. Instead, you are enlarging the image to match the required width; you will later adjust the canvas to suit the project's height requirement.

As you can see, increasing the image's physical size with resampling adds more pixels to the image. This also significantly increases the file weight (its size in bytes).

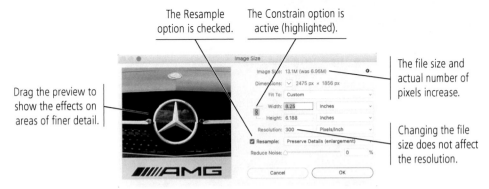

The Resample option is checked.

The Constrain option is active (highlighted).

The file size and actual number of pixels increase.

Drag the preview to show the effects on areas of finer detail.

Changing the file size does not affect the resolution.

13. **Drag in the Preview window to show an area with flat areas of color near a high-contrast edge.**

Artificially enlarging an image often results in small pixels of varying color, especially in areas of solid color and near high-contrast edges. When you choose the Preserve Details option, you can use the Reduce Noise slider to help reduce those artifacts.

14. **Change the Reduce Noise slider to 20%.**

The Preview window shows the results that will be achieved when you finalize the resampling.

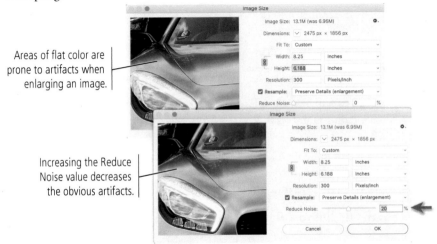

Areas of flat color are prone to artifacts when enlarging an image.

Increasing the Reduce Noise value decreases the obvious artifacts.

**15. Click OK to finalize the resampling.**

Resampling the image (enlarging) adds pixels to the file. The image no longer fits in the document window at the current view percentage.

The image now has more pixels, so less of the image is visible in the document window.

*Note:*

*You're adding a sizeable amount of information to this file, so the resampling process might take a few seconds. Depending on the power and speed of your computer, you might see a progress bar as the image size is remapped.*

**16. Choose View>Fit on Screen to show the entire image.**

**17. Choose File>Save As. Save the file as a native Photoshop file named magazine.psd in your WIP>Cars folder.**

**18. Continue to the next exercise.**

## Sharpen the Enlarged Image

When you enlarge an image in Photoshop, the application must generate new data. The algorithm underlying the Preserve Details option does a significantly better job of generating new pixels than was available in previous versions, but the pixels are still not original to the image. This can result in a loss of detail, especially near apparent edges or areas of high contrast. Whenever you enlarge an image, **sharpening** can help to restore detail and make the image appear more crisp.

*Note:*

*The Sharpen, Sharpen More, and Sharpen Edges filters apply sharpening with no user control.*

**1. With magazine.psd open, choose Filter>Sharpen>Unsharp Mask.**

**2. Make sure the Preview check box is active in the dialog box.**

Unsharp masking sharpens an image by increasing contrast along apparent edges in the image.

- **Amount** determines how much the contrast in edges will increase. Typically, 150–200% creates good results in high-resolution images.

- **Radius** determines how many pixels will be included in the edge comparison. Higher radius values result in more pronounced edge effects.

- **Threshold** defines the difference that is required for Photoshop to identify an edge. A threshold of 15 means that colors must be more than 15 levels different.

Drag here or click in the document window to change the visible area in the preview window.

**3. Change the Amount to 100%, the Radius to 2.0 pixels, and the Threshold to 3 levels.**

4. **Toggle the Preview option off and on to review the results in the document window.**

Sharpening is most obvious in areas of high contrast.

5. **Click OK to apply the Unsharp Mask filter.**

6. **Save the file and continue to the next exercise.**

 ## Edit the Canvas Size

As you learned in the project meeting, the final artwork for this project needs to be 8.25" wide by 10.25" high. You already accomplished the required width when you resampled the source file. In this exercise, you are going to enlarge the canvas to meet the project's height requirement.

*Watch the video* ***Changing the Canvas Size in Photoshop*** *in your online student resources.*

1. **With magazine.psd open, make the Layers panel visible.**

   Photos and scans almost always default to exist on the Background layer when you first open them.

2. **Choose Image>Canvas Size.**

   In Photoshop, **canvas** refers to the overall image area — like the surface of a canvas used by traditional artists. It is not directly connected to the content of most layers (except for the Background layer).

   You can use this dialog box to change the size of the canvas to specific measurements.

### 3. Choose the top-center anchor option.

The Anchor area shows the reference point around which the canvas will be enlarged or cropped. Using this option, all new pixels will be added at the bottom of the image.

### 4. Change the Height field to 10.25 [Inches], and choose White in the Canvas Extension Color menu.

This menu defines what color will appear in the new pixels on the Background layer.

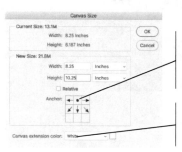

Anchoring the top edge means new pixels will be added to the bottom of the existing canvas.

Use this menu to define the color of new pixels on the Background layer.

*Note:*

*If you define smaller measurements, you are basically accomplishing the same thing as using the Crop tool.*

*Note:*

*If you reduce the canvas size, clicking OK in the Canvas Size dialog box results in a warning that some clipping will occur.*

*Content on the Background layer that is outside the new canvas size is permanently removed from the layer. Content on other layers is maintained.*

### 5. Click OK to apply the change, then choose View>Fit On Screen.

As you can see, new pixels were added to the bottom of the canvas. Because the existing image content exists on the Background layer, and the Background layer cannot contain transparent pixels, the new pixels are filled with white.

Because the photo existed on the locked Background layer, new pixels are filled with white.

### 6. Choose Edit>Undo Canvas Size.

Press Command/Control-Z to undo the previous action.

### 7. In the Layers panel, click the Lock icon to unlock the Background layer.

### 8. Double-click the Layer 0 name, type Car to rename the layer, then press Return/Enter.

9. **Choose Image>Canvas Size again. Select the top-center Anchor option, then change the Height field to 10.25 [Inches].**

This menu is not available because the file no longer has a locked Background layer.

**Note:**

*If you check the Relative option, you can change the canvas size by specific amounts. For example, to make the canvas one inch narrower, you would type −1 in the Width field. Photoshop automatically calculates the resulting canvas size based on the selected Anchor position.*

10. **Click OK to apply the change.**

Regular layers support transparency, so the new pixels are not filled with a solid color. The gray-and-white checked pattern identifies transparent areas of the visible layer.

Because regular layers can include transparency, no color appears in the area of the new pixels.

11. **Save the file. With Maximize Compatibility checked, click OK in the Photoshop Format Options dialog box.**

Because you converted the Background layer to a regular image layer, you see the dialog box that asks if you want to maximize compatibility the first time you save the file.

12. **Continue to the next stage of the project.**

# STAGE 2 / Working with Vector Tools

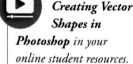

*Watch the video **Creating Vector Shapes in Photoshop** in your online student resources.*

Vector paths, also called Bézier curves, are defined mathematically based on the position of anchor points and the length and angle of direction handles that are connected to those anchor points. Unlike the pixels in a raster image, vector paths do not have a defined resolution until they are output. Because of this, vector paths can be edited at any time without any loss of quality.

> **Note:**
>
> *The Type tool is also technically a vector-based tool because digital type uses vectors to define the character shapes.*

Photoshop includes a number of tools for creating vector paths:

- The **Pen tool** places individual anchor points each time you click; line segments connect each point. If you click and drag, you create a point with direction handles, which precisely control the shape of the connecting segments.

- The **Freeform Pen tool** draws vector paths wherever you drag, just as you would draw with a pencil on paper.

- The **Rectangle** and **Ellipse tools** create shapes that you would expect based on the tool names. If you press Shift while you click and drag, you create a shape with equal height and width (a square or circle, respectively).

You can also single-click with these tools to open a dialog box, where you can define settings for the new shape.

In the Create Rectangle dialog box, you can define width and height values, as well as corner-radius values for each corner of the resulting shape.

In the Create Ellipse dialog box, you can define overall width and height values for the new shape (in other words, the size of the shape's bounding box).

If you check the From Center option, the new shape will be centered on the point where you clicked to open the dialog box. If this option is not checked, the top-left corner of shape's bounding box will be placed at the point where you click.

- The **Triangle tool** creates a three-sided polygon. Clinking once with the tool opens the Create Triangle dialog box, where you can define the specific settings of the triangle you want to draw.

The Width and Height fields determine the outside dimensions of the overall shape (the size of the shape's bounding box).

If you check the Equilateral option, all three sides of the shape will have the same length; the height and width fields automatically adjust as necessary to create the equal-sided triangle.

You can use the Corner Radius option to automatically add rounded corners to the resulting triangle.

If you check the From Center option, the new triangle shape will be centered on the point where you clicked to open the dialog box. If this option is not checked, the top-left corner of shape's bounding box will be placed at the point where you click.

You can also click and drag with the Triangle tool to create the new shape with the last-used equilateral and corner-radius settings.

- The **Polygon tool** creates a shape with any number of sides. Clicking once opens a dialog box where you can define the number of sides on the resulting shape.

  If you check the **Smooth Corners** option, each anchor point has direction handles that make the corners rounded instead of sharp.

  If you choose the **Star** option, the **Indent Sides By** value determines where the inner points of the star appear relative to the overall shape diameter.

  You can also check the **Smooth Indents** option to create smooth curves on the inside points of the shape, instead of corner points.

  Of you click and drag with the tool, the new shape is created with the last-used settings (number of sides, smooth corners, star, and indents)

| Polygon created with all options unchecked | Polygon created with the Star option checked | Polygon (star) created with the Smooth Corners option checked | Polygon (star) created with the Smooth Corners and Smooth Indents options checked |

- The **Line tool** creates open straight lines with two points — one at each end. When first created, the points have no direction handles and the connecting segment is a straight line.

- The **Custom Shape tool** creates vector-based shapes from built-in or external libraries.

When you use the vector drawing tools, you have the option to create a new shape, path, or pixels.

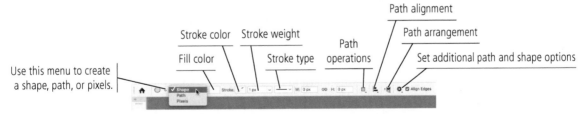

- If you choose Shape, the shape is placed on a vector-based shape layer.

- If you choose Path, the shape exists only as a work path in the Paths panel.

- If you choose Pixels, the resulting shape is created as pixels on the previously selected layer; no vector path is created. (The Pixels option is not available when you use the Pen tools.)

Use the Freeform Pen Tool

The Freeform Pen tool creates a vector path based on where you drag the cursor. The application creates anchor points and direction handles as necessary to create the shape that you draw.

1. **With magazine.psd open, show the image at 100% in the document window.**

   Ideally, you should work at 100% while you complete this exercise.

2. **Choose the Freeform Pen tool (nested under the Pen tool) in the Tools panel.**

3. **In the Options bar, choose the Path option in the left menu.**

   When you choose Path in the tool mode menu, the vector path that you draw is stored in the Paths panel.

4. **Open the Path Operations menu and choose the Combine Shapes option.**

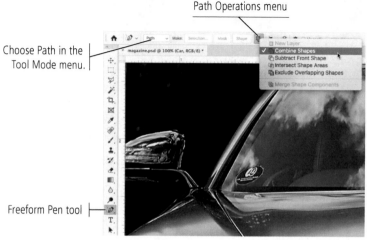

*Note:*

*The Pen Pressure option only applies if you have a pressure-sensitive graphics tablet. When this option is turned on, higher pressure decreases the Width tolerance.*

These options define how a new path will interact with any existing paths. (Illustrator and InDesign users might recognize these as options from the Pathfinder panel.)

- **New Layer**, available when Layer is selected in the Tool Mode menu, creates a new shape layer every time you draw a new path.

- **Combine Shapes** adds new paths to an already selected path or shape layer. Each path's shape is maintained as a separate vector path. If you want a new path to include only areas inside the path you draw, you should choose this option before you begin drawing a new path.

- **Subtract Front Shape** removes the area of secondary shapes from existing shapes.

- **Intersect Shape Areas** results in a shape that is only the area where a new shape overlaps an existing shape.

- **Exclude Overlapping Shapes** is similar to Subtract; overlapping areas are removed from the existing shape, but non-overlapping areas of the new shape are filled with the shape color.

- The **Merge Shape Components** option, available when a single path contains more than one shape, results in a single (possibly compound) shape. Any overlapping paths are combined into one shape/path.

5. **Check the Magnetic option in the Options bar, then click the Set Additional Path and Shape Options button.**

   When you draw with the Pen tool, the default path appears in the document window as a thin, medium blue line. You can use the Thickness and Color options to change the appearance of the path. (The settings here do not affect the actual stroke color and width of a path; they refer only to the appearance of paths in the document window.)

   - **Curve Fit** determines how closely the curves will match the path that you drag with the mouse cursor. When the Magnetic option is active, you can also define settings that control how the magnetic function behaves:
   - **Width** determines how far from an edge you have to drag (1–256 pixels) for Photoshop to still find the edge.
   - **Contrast** determines how much variation (1–100%) must exist between pixels for Photoshop to define an edge.
   - **Frequency** determines the rate at which Photoshop places anchor points. Higher values (up to 100) create anchor points faster than lower values (down to 0).

6. **Define the following settings in the pop-up menu, then press Return/ Enter to apply them:**

   | | |
   |---|---|
   | **Thickness:** | **2 px** |
   | **Color:** | **Light Red** |
   | **Curve Fit:** | **2 px** |
   | **Width:** | **15 px** |
   | **Contrast:** | **10%** |
   | **Frequency:** | **25** |

   Open this menu.    Check this option.

   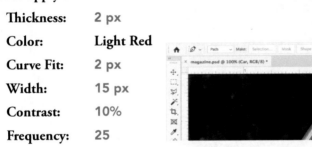

   *Note:*

   *The default path color is very similar to the colors in the image you're working with; you are changing it to a thicker red path so it will be easier to see as you work through this project.*

7. **Click at the corner where the left side mirror meets the car to place the first anchor point. Drag up and around the car shape.**

   You don't have to hold down the mouse button when you draw with the Freeform Pen tool in Magnetic mode.

   As you drag, the magnetic function creates anchor points to define a vector path around obvious edges where you drag.

   Magnetic Freeform Pen tool cursor

   The path snaps to the high-contrast edges near where you drag.

   Click here to place the first anchor point for the path.

   *Note:*

   *When you draw by holding down a button (mouse button or the button on a graphics tablet/pen) it is not uncommon for the line to "jump" where you don't want it to jump. If this happens, press Esc to remove your selection or path, and start drawing again.*

8. **Continue dragging around the car shape to create the initial outline.**

   Skip the tires for now, and don't worry if the path is not perfect as you outline the car shape. You will fine-tune the path in the next few exercises.

you can't see the entire car in the document window, press the Spacebar to temporarily access the Hand tool, then click and drag to move the image so you can see the edges that you need to follow.

The Spacebar temporarily switches to the Hand tool, so you can drag the image in the window, even while working on another task. When you release the Spacebar, you return to the previously selected tool, so you can continue drawing the path of the car's shape.

If you drag past the edge of the document window, Photoshop automatically scrolls the visible area of the image. Manually repositioning with the Hand tool gives you better control over exactly what you see.

**Note:**

*Some users report processor-related issues when temporarily switching to the Hand tool while drawing with the Freeform Pen tool in Magnetic mode.*

*If you experience performance problems, try zooming out and in with the keyboard commands instead of dragging with the Hand tool.*

Press the Spacebar to temporarily access the Hand tool.

10. **When you reach an obvious corner in the car's outline, click to place a specific anchor point.**

    Although Photoshop automatically creates anchor points based on the defined magnetic behavior, you can also click to place anchor points in specific locations.

Click to manually place an anchor point at obvious corners.

11. **Continue outlining the car shape. When you get back to your original starting point, click to create a closed path.**

    When the tool cursor is over the original starting point, a hollow circle in the icon indicates that clicking will close the path.

The hollow circle indicates that clicking will close the path.

## 12. Open the Layers and Paths panels.

As you can see, no layer has been added. The path you drew is stored in the Paths panel as the Work Path, which is a temporary path that exists only until you create another path.

Some parts of the car are not included inside the path.

No layer is added to the file.

The path you drew is stored as the Work Path.

## 13. With the Work Path selected in the Paths panel, open the panel Options menu and choose Save Path.

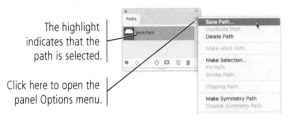

The highlight indicates that the path is selected.

Click here to open the panel Options menu.

---

# More about Working with the Paths Panel

In the Paths panel options menu, you can choose **Make Selection** to make a marching-ants selection based on the path shape. You can use the resulting dialog box to define the details of the selection.

If you choose **Fill Path** in the Options menu, you can use the resulting dialog box to determine how the fill will be created. You can choose a color or pattern, blending mode and opacity, and whether to feather the edge of the fill so it blends smoothly into underlying layers.

If you choose the **Stroke Path** option, you must also choose which tool will create the stroke. The applied stroke will have the last-used settings for the selected tool. In other words, you have to define the tool options (brush size, hardness, etc.) that you want before using this option.

The Fill Path and Stroke Path options add the resulting pixels to the currently active layer — an important distinction from the Shape Layer option, which creates a new layer when you begin drawing the vector path. It is also important to remember that although the path remains a vector path, color applied to the fill or stroke of the path is raster-based and it does not have the same scalability as a vector shape layer.

If you choose the **Clipping Path** option, the selected path will become a clipping path, which is essentially a vector mask that can define the visible area of an image. The white area in the path thumbnail defines the visible areas.

Buttons across the bottom of the panel provide quick access to many of the available options. They are, from left:

- Fill path with foreground color
- Stroke path with brush
- Load path as a selection
- Make work path from selection
- Add layer mask
- Create new path
- Delete path

---

**14.** **Type Car Outline in the resulting dialog box, then click OK.**

After you save the path, the new name appears instead of "Work Path"; this path will remain in the file even if you create a different temporary Work Path.

The saved path is permanent.

## Understanding Anchor Points and Handles

An **anchor point** marks the end of a line **segment**, and the point **handles** determine the shape of that segment. That's the basic definition of a vector, but there is a bit more to it than that. (The Photoshop Help files refer to handles as direction lines and distinguishes different types of points. Our aim here is to explain the overall concept of vector paths, so we use the generic industry-standard terms. For more information on Adobe's terminology, refer to the Photoshop Help files.)

Each segment in a path has two anchor points and can have two associated handles.

You can create corner points by simply clicking with the Pen tool, instead of clicking and dragging. Corner points do not have their own handles; the connected segments are controlled by the handles of the other associated points.

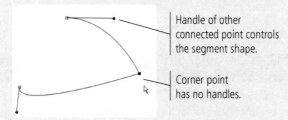

Handle of other connected point controls the segment shape.

Corner point has no handles.

In the image shown here, we first clicked to create Point A and dragged (without releasing the mouse button) to create Handle A1. We then clicked and dragged to create Point B and Handle B1. Handle B2 was automatically created as a reflection of B1. Point B is a **symmetrical point**.

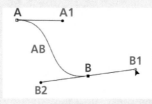

This image shows the result of dragging Handle B1 to the left instead of to the right when we created the initial curve. Notice the difference in the curve here, compared to the curve above. When you drag a handle, the connecting segment arcs away from the direction you drag.

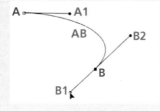

It's important to understand that every line segment is connected to two handles. In this example, Handle A1 and Handle B2 determine the shape of Segment AB. Dragging either handle affects the shape of the connected segment.

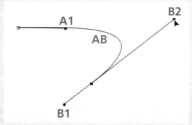

When you use the Pen tool, clicking and dragging a point creates a symmetrical (smooth) point; both handles start out at equal length, directly opposite one another. Changing the angle of one handle of a symmetrical point also changes the opposing handle of that point. In the example here, repositioning Handle B1 also moves Handle B2, which affects the shape of Segment AB. You can, however, change the length of one handle without affecting the length of the other handle.

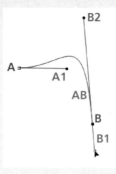

**15. Click the bottom area of the Paths panel to deselect the path.**

When the path is not selected, you can't see its anchor points and connecting segments in the document window.

When the path is not selected, you can't see it in the document window.

**16. Save the file and continue to the next exercise.**

# Add to an Existing Path

In the previous exercise, you intentionally skipped the wheels in the image because the Freeform Pen tool's magnetic properties perform better with higher-contrast edges than what is evident where the tires meet the pavement. In this exercise, you will use the Pen tool to add the wheels to the existing path.

*Watch the video* ***Using the Pen Tool in Photoshop*** *in your online student resources.*

**1. With magazine.psd open, make sure the view percentage is 100% and position the image so the right wheel is entirely visible.**

**2. Choose the Pen tool (nested under the Freeform Pen tool) in the Tools panel.**

When you choose a nested tool, it becomes the default option in that position of the Tools panel. To access the original default tool — the Pen tool, in this case — you have to click the tool and hold down the mouse button to access the nested tools menu.

**3. In the Paths panel, click the Car Outline path to make it visible in the document window.**

You want to add more shapes to the existing path, so the path needs to be selected and visible in the document window.

**4. In the Options bar, choose Path in the Tool Mode menu.**

**5. Click the Path Operations button and choose Combine Shapes (if it is not already selected).**

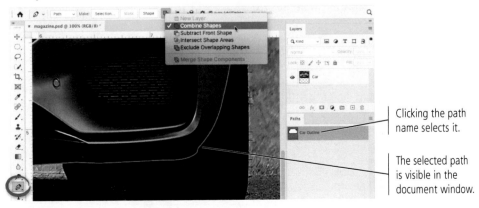

Clicking the path name selects it.

The selected path is visible in the document window.

6. **Click the Pen tool in the Tools panel to hide the anchor points of the existing path (if necessary).**

If the existing path's anchor points are visible, you can use the Pen tool to add anchor points to the existing path. You want to create a second shape in the same path, so you need to turn off the existing path's anchor points.

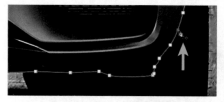

If the existing path's anchor points are visible, clicking would add a new point to the existing path.

If the existing path's anchor points are not visible, clicking creates a new shape that is part of the same path.

7. **Click with the Pen tool cursor where the rear tire meets the car undercarriage.**

Clicking once with the Pen tool creates a corner anchor point with no direction handles.

8. **Move the cursor down and right along the tire edge (as shown in Step 9).**

9. **Click to create an anchor point, hold down the mouse button, and drag down and right to create direction handles for the point.**

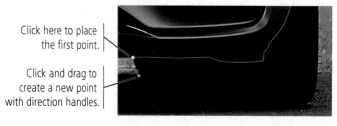

Click here to place the first point.

Click and drag to create a new point with direction handles.

*Note:*

*Don't worry if the curve isn't quite perfect — you will learn how to edit anchor points and handles in the next exercise.*

10. **When the shape of the connecting segment between the two points matches the shape of the tire, release the mouse button.**

When you click and drag with the Pen tool, you create a smooth point with symmetrical direction handles. As you drag, you can see the handles extend equal distances from both sides of the point you just created. The length and angle of the direction handles control the shape of segments that connect two anchor points.

As long as you hold down the mouse button, you can drag to change the length and angle of the point's handles, which also changes the shape of the connecting segment.

11. **Move the cursor to the right, following the bottom edge of the rear tire. Click and drag to create another anchor point with symmetrical direction handles. When the connecting segment matches the shape of the tire, release the mouse button.**

When you click-drag to create a smooth point, the point is automatically symmetrical. In other words, the handles on each side of the point are the same length.

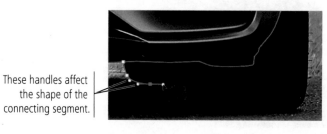

These handles affect the shape of the connecting segment.

**12.** Click without dragging where the rear tire meets the front tire.

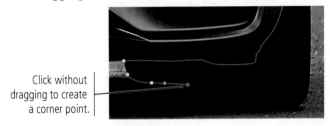

Click without dragging to create a corner point.

**13.** Continue adding symmetrical smooth points to the path, placing the final point where the front tire meets the body of the car.

Add a point where the tire meets the body.

**14.** Click and drag to place another smooth point inside the area of the bumper.

You are intentionally overlapping the new path with the existing one. Later, you will combine the multiple separate shapes into a single path.

**15.** Move the cursor over the original starting point. When you see a hollow circle in the cursor icon, click to close the path.

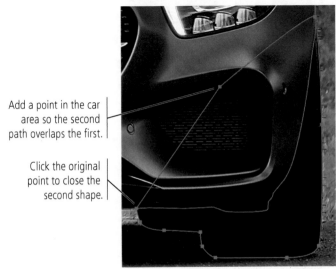

Add a point in the car area so the second path overlaps the first.

Click the original point to close the second shape.

16. **Repeat the process from this exercise to add a path around the left wheels.**

Remember, clicking without dragging creates a corner point, which does not have direction handles.

The Car Outline path is still selected.

17. **Change your view percentage so you can see the entire car in the document window.**

18. **With the Car Outline path selected in the Paths panel, make sure the Pen tool is still active.**

19. **Open the Path Operations menu in the Options bar and choose Merge Shape Components.**

The three original paths are combined into a single shape. Photoshop adds anchor points where necessary and removes overlapping segments from the original paths.

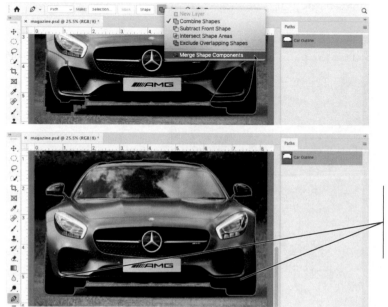

After merging shapes, the three separate paths are combined into a single path that is the outermost path of each component.

20. **Save the file and continue to the next exercise.**

# Edit Vector Paths

You probably noticed that the path you created in the previous exercises is not a perfect outline of the car. The Freeform Pen tool can be a very good starting point for creating odd-shaped paths, but you will almost always need to edit and fine-tune the results to accurately reflect the path you want. Fortunately, Photoshop offers a number of options for editing vector paths.

You can use the **Path Selection tool** ( ) to select an entire path or the **Direct Selection tool** ( ) to select a specific anchor point or segment.

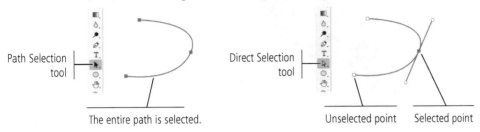

Path Selection tool — The entire path is selected.

Direct Selection tool — Unselected point    Selected point

The **Add Anchor Point tool** ( ) adds a new anchor point to an existing path. Photoshop automatically creates handles for the new point and adjusts handles for existing points to maintain the existing path shape.

You can use the **Delete Anchor Point tool** ( ) to remove an existing point from a path. Photoshop removes the selected point and adjusts the handles of remaining points to try to maintain the original path shape.

Clicking a smooth point with the **Convert Point tool** ( ) converts that point to a corner point by removing its handles (below left). Clicking and dragging from a corner point with this tool converts it to a smooth, symmetrical point (below right).

You can add a handle to only one side of a corner point by Option/Alt-clicking a point with the Convert Point tool and dragging (below left). You can also click a handle with the Convert Point tool and drag to move only one handle of the point, resulting in a corner point with asymmetrical handles (below right).

*Note:*

*When the Pen tool is active, placing the cursor over an existing selected path automatically shows the Add Anchor Point tool cursor.*

*Note:*

*When the Pen tool is active, placing the cursor over an existing point on a selected path automatically shows the Delete Anchor Point tool cursor.*

*Note:*

*When the Pen tool is active, you can press Option/Alt to temporarily access the Convert Point tool cursor.*

1. **With magazine.psd open, set your view percentage to at least 100%.**

2. **Drag around the image to review the Car Outline path.**

   Although your results might differ from our screen captures, the path almost certainly does not accurately outline the car. You must use what you learned on Page 106 and Page 111 to edit the path to exactly match the car's shape.

The Magnetic Freeform Pen tool path excluded some areas that must be inside the path.

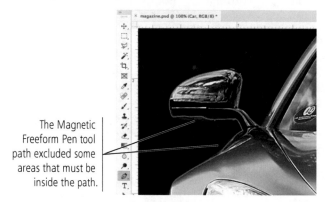

3. **Use the following information to fine-tune your Car Outline path.**

   In this instance, we can't give you specific instructions because everyone's path will be a bit different. Keep the following points in mind as you refine your shape:

   - Use the Direct Selection tool to select and edit specific segments or points on the path. You can move points to a new position by dragging (or using the Arrow keys) or moving their handles to change segment shapes.

   - Use the Add Anchor Point tool to add a point to the path.

   - Use the Delete Anchor Point tool to remove a point from the path.

   - Use the Convert Point tool to change a corner point to a smooth point and vice versa.

4. **Save the file and continue to the next exercise.**

# Create a Vector-Based Layer Mask

Now that your car outline shape is nearly complete, you are going to use the path to create a vector-based layer mask, which will remove the car from the surrounding background. The edges of a vector mask are defined by a vector path, which means they cannot have degrees of transparency. To edit the mask edge, you have to edit the vector path.

1. **With magazine.psd open, set your view percentage so you can see the entire car in the document window.**

2. **Select the Car Outline path in the Paths panel and select the Car layer in the Layers panel.**

3. **Choose Layer>Vector Mask>Current Path.**

As you can see, a new path is added to the Paths panel. The name, "Car Vector Mask" identifies this path as a vector mask for the layer named, "Car." This temporary path only appears in the panel when the masked layer is selected.

Nothing is added to the Channels panel because channels are raster-based; they do not store vector-based path information.

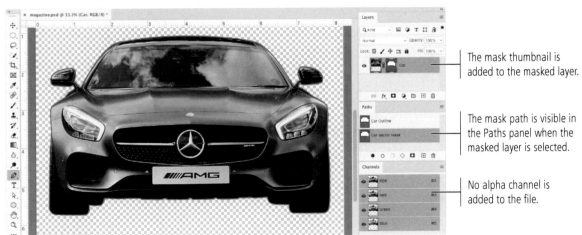

4. **Click the empty area at the bottom of the Layers panel to deselect the layer.**

   When the masked layer is not selected, the mask path does not appear in the Paths panel. This is an important distinction — if you want to edit the mask path, you have to make sure the correct path is selected first. Editing the original Car Outline path will have no effect on the mask path.

When the masked layer is not selected, the mask path does not appear in the Paths panel.

5. **Save the file and continue to the next exercise.**

## Drawing with the Curvature Pen Tool

The Curvature Pen tool, nested under the regular Pen tool, can be used to create and edit complex paths without manually manipulating anchor points.

Using the Curvature Pen tool, begin by clicking to place points in a new path. As you drag after creating the first two points, the software shows a rubber-band preview of the path that will be created by clicking again.

If you don't see the rubber-band behavior, open the Set Additional Pen and Path Options menu in the Options bar and make sure Rubber Band is checked.

As long as the Curvature Pen tool is active, you do not need to change tools to edit the path:

- Option/Alt-click to create a corner point.
- Click anywhere along an existing path to add a new anchor point.
- Double-click any point to toggle it between a smooth and corner point.
- Click a point to select it.
- Drag a selected point to move it.
- Press Delete to remove the selected point. The existing curve is maintained.
- Press the Esc key to stop drawing the current shape.

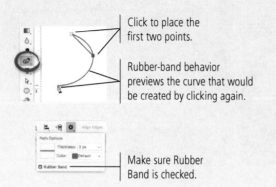

Click to place the first two points.

Rubber-band behavior previews the curve that would be created by clicking again.

Make sure Rubber Band is checked.

# Create a Vector Shape Layer

A shape layer is a special type of Photoshop layer that retains vector path information. The vector shape functions as a mask, revealing the defined fill color for the shape. Any vector paths can have defined stroke properties (color, width, and type/style), and can be edited using the same tools that you used to edit the paths in the previous exercises.

In this exercise, you will build a compound vector shape that will provide a background for the magazine's "In This Issue" text.

1. **With magazine.psd open, hide the Car layer.**

2. **In the Tools panel, choose the Rectangle tool.**

3. **In the Options bar, choose Shape in the Pick tool mode menu.**

*Note:*

*If a tool is missing from its default spot in the Tools panel, check in the Edit Toolbar menu* ... *at the bottom of the Tools panel. You can also reset the Essentials workspace to show all tools in their default locations.*

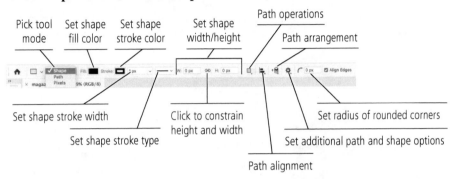

Pick tool mode | Set shape fill color | Set shape stroke color | Set shape width/height | Path operations | Path arrangement

Set shape stroke width | Click to constrain height and width | Set radius of rounded corners

Set shape stroke type | Set additional path and shape options

Path alignment

4. **Click the Fill color swatch to open the pop-up Swatches panel. Click the arrow to the left of the CMYK group, then click the CMYK Blue swatch to select it as the fill color.**

You can define separate fill and stroke colors of a vector shape layer, just as you might do for an object you create in Adobe Illustrator or InDesign. Clicking the Fill or Stroke color swatch opens a pop-up panel, where you can select a specific swatch to use as the attribute's color. Four buttons at the top of the panel change the attribute to (from left): None, Solid, a Gradient, or a Pattern. Predefined color swatches are organized into folders by category. You can also click the Color Picker button to define any color that is not already in the Swatches panel.

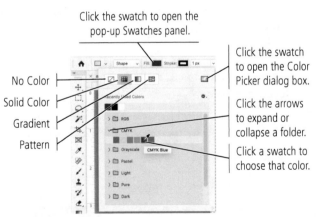

Click the swatch to open the pop-up Swatches panel.

No Color
Solid Color
Gradient
Pattern

Click the swatch to open the Color Picker dialog box.

Click the arrows to expand or collapse a folder.

Click a swatch to choose that color.

5. **Click the Stroke swatch and choose No Color in the pop-up Swatches panel.**

## 6. Change the Radius field to 50 px.

A rounded-corner rectangle is simply a rectangle with the corners cut at a specific distance from the end (the corner radius). The two sides are connected with one-fourth of a circle, which has a radius equal to the amount of the rounding.

> This imaginary circle has a 50-px radius.

## 7. Click in the top-right area of the canvas, then drag down and right to create the new shape.

When you release the mouse button, the shape you drew fills with the defined Fill color. Because you chose None as the Stroke color, the shape you drew has no applied stroke. The red color you see around the shape is the color you defined earlier as the path color when you drew the car path.

When you use the Shape option in the Tool Mode menu, the resulting vector shape exists by default on its own layer.

*Note:*

*The color you are using here is temporary, because you will later apply a built-in graphic style to this shape.*

> The shape appears on a new shape layer.

> This icon identifies a vector shape layer.

## 8. Click the empty space at the bottom of the Layers panel to deselect the Rectangle layer.

When you deselect the layer, you can see the actual shape without the heavy red vector path. You can now see that the shape you created has no defined stroke color.

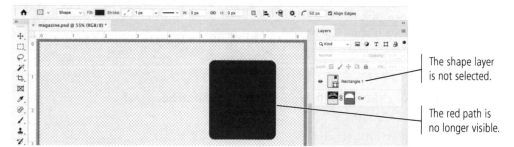

> The shape layer is not selected.

> The red path is no longer visible.

## 9. Click the Rectangle 1 layer to select it again.

When the shape layer is selected, you can again see the vector path that makes up the shape.

# Understanding On-Screen Controls for Vector Shapes

When you create a vector shape in Photoshop, a number of on-screen controls appear on that shape.

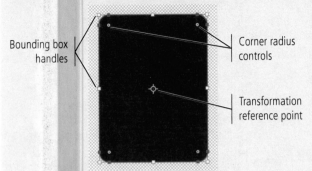

Bounding box handles

Corner radius controls

Transformation reference point

You can click and drag any of the corner radius controls to change the corner radius of all corners in the active shape. If you press Option/Alt before you click a corner radius control, you can drag to change the radius of only that corner.

Click and drag a corner radius handle to change the radius of all corners on the shape:

Option/Alt-click and drag a corner raduis handle to change the radius of only that corner:

You can click and drag any of the bounding box handles to change the size of the shape.

If you move the mouse cursor outside one of the corner handles, it changes to the Rotate cursor. You can click and drag to rotate the shape around the transformation reference point, which defaults to the shape's center.

You can also click and drag the transformation reference point to move it. Transformations such as rotation will then apply around the repositioned reference point.

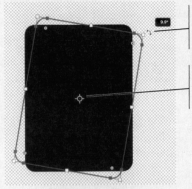

Click outside a corner handle and drag to rotate the shape.

The object rotates around the transformation reference point.

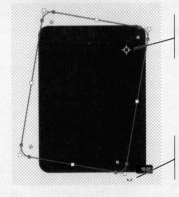

Click and drag the transformation reference point to move it.

Transformations apply around the repositioned reference point.

**10.** **Make sure the rulers are visible (View>Rulers). Control/right-click the top ruler and choose Pixels as the unit of measurement.**

Photoshop has a minor bug that might cause various panels to display measurements in pixels instead of the working default unit. To avoid confusion of different units in different UI areas,

we change the units to pixels in this step to be sure you see the same measurements in all areas of the interface.

**11.** **Review the information in the Properties panel.**

This panel automatically appears when you create a new shape with one of the vector shape tools. It shows the dimensions and position of the resulting shape, as well as other properties that were not available in the Options bar before you created the shape.

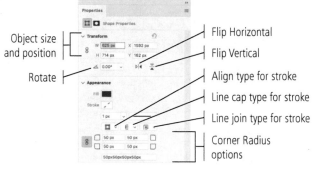

Because you are creating a vector shape, you can edit its properties at any time, without losing quality or pixel integrity (as would happen for pixel-based, raster data).

**12.** **In the Transform section of the Properties panel, make sure the Constrain option is turned off.**

When the Constrain button is active (highlighted), changing one field — width or height — applies a proportional change to the other object dimension.

Because you need to define specific sizes to each dimension without maintaining a specific proportion, you are turning this option off for the next few steps.

Constrain is active (highlighted)  Constrain is inactive (not highlighted)

**13.** **Highlight the current W field and type 500. Press Tab to highlight the H field, then type 1230. Press Return/Enter to apply the change.**

The W and H fields define the object's physical dimensions.

The Properties panel defaults to use pixels for shape layers, regardless of the default units for the active file. You can, however, type values in other units of measurement, as long as you include the appropriate unit in the value you type (for example, "2 in" or "4 cm").

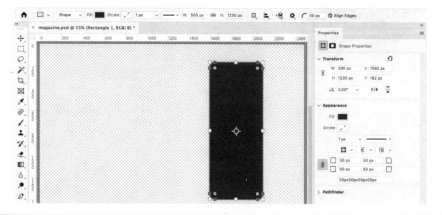

14. **Place the Mouse cursor over the X field until you see the scrubby slider cursor.**

15. **Click and drag right or left until the X field shows 1865 px (the shape is approximately 3/8″ from the right edge of the canvas).**

The X and Y fields in the Properties panel define the object's position based on its top-left corner. Unlike transforming objects in the Options panel, you cannot select a different reference point around which to anchor the transformation.

**Scrubby sliders**, available in most Photoshop panels, offer a dynamic way to change field values. You can click the field name and drag left to decrease the value, or drag right to increase the value.

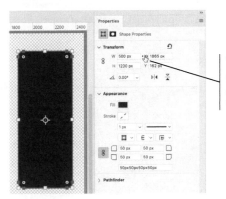

When you see this scrubby slider, click and drag to change the related field value.

16. **Using either the scrubby slider or the field, change the Y position to 0 px.**

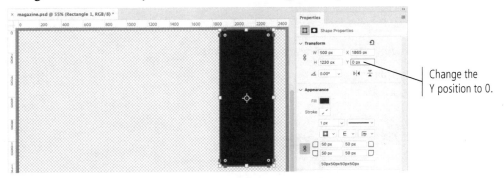

Change the Y position to 0.

17. **In the Layers panel, click the empty area at the bottom of the panel to deselect the Rectangle 1 layer.**

18. **Click the Rectangle 1 layer in the Layers panel to select it again.**

If you do not perform this step, a minor bug in the software (at the time of writing) will cause the rectangle shape to invert when you complete Step 19.

19. **In the Options bar, open the Path Operations menu and choose Subtract Front Shape.**

If no shape layer is currently selected, the Path Operations menu defaults to New Layer. As long as a shape layer is selected and one of the shape layer tools is active, the menu retains the last-used option. You can continue subtracting as many new shapes as you like until you switch to a different tool — the Direct Selection tool, for example, to modify a specific anchor point.

*Note:*

*The Path Operations menu retains the last-used selection, as long as the same tool remains active. If you switch to a different tool, the path operation reverts back to the New Layer option.*

**20. Click and drag to create another rectangle inside the area of the first.**

Using the Subtract Front Shape option, the second shape removes the overlapping area of underlying shapes, creating a compound path that results in a "window" effect. (A **compound path** is any single shape made up of more than one closed path.)

Options for the basic Shape tools remember the last-used settings, so the new shape automatically has the 50-px corner radius that you defined for the first shape.

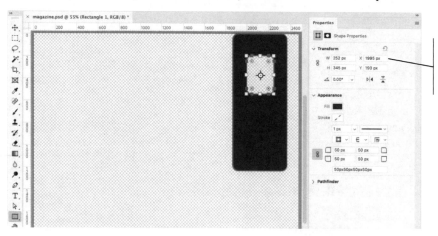

The Properties panel shows options for the selected vector path, not the overall shape.

**21. In the Properties panel, change the new shape's parameters to:**

|  |  |
|---|---|
| W: 300 px | X: 1965 px |
| H: 300 px | Y: 135 px |

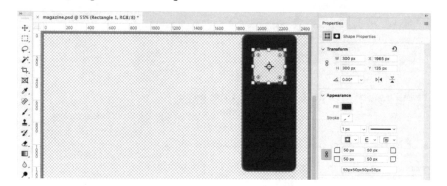

22. **In the lower half of the Properties panel, make sure the four corner radius fields are linked.**

When the link icon is highlighted (active), changing any one radius value affects the other three corners.

23. **Type 10 in the top-left field, then press Return/Enter to apply your changes.**

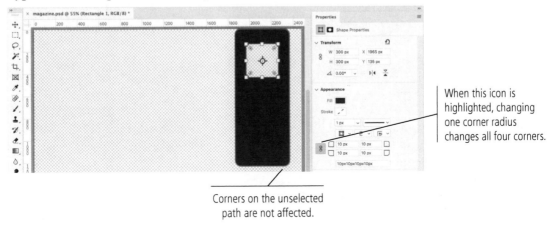

When this icon is highlighted, changing one corner radius changes all four corners.

Corners on the unselected path are not affected.

24. **Choose the Path Selection tool in the Tools panel, then click the outer path of the compound shape to select it.**

Each component path of the overall shape is still an independent vector path, which means you can select and edit its properties in the Properties panel at any time.

25. **In the Properties panel, unlink the four corner radius fields, then change the top-left and top-right corner radius fields to 0 px.**

Although rounded-corner shapes always start with four identical corners, you can use this panel to change each corner radius individually.

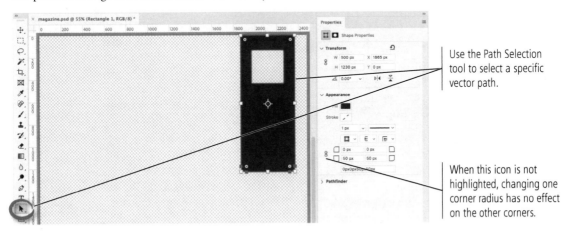

Use the Path Selection tool to select a specific vector path.

When this icon is not highlighted, changing one corner radius has no effect on the other corners.

26. **Save the file and continue to the next exercise.**

## Stroke Types

When a vector drawing tool is active, you can use the Stroke Type menu in the Options bar to choose a preset stroke style (solid, dashed, or dotted).

- The Align menu changes the stroke's alignment relative to the path. The icons in the menu suggest the result.

- The Caps menu determines how the stroke aligns to the ends of the path.

- The Corners menu defines the way the stroke appears at corners on the path.

If you click the More Options button, you can define a custom dash pattern.

### Align

- Align stroke to inside of path
- Align stroke to center of path
- Align stroke to outside of path

### Caps

- No end cap
- Rounded end cap
- Square end cap

### Corners

- Miter join
- Rounded join
- Beveled join

## Path Alignment

You can use the **Path Alignment** to align or distribute multiple shapes on the same layer. For these options to work properly, you must use the Path Selection tool to select the paths you want to align, and then choose an option from the menu. When Canvas is selected in the Align To menu, you can align one or more paths in relation to the overall canvas.

## Pen and Path Options

### Pen Tool

For the Pen tool, you can check the Rubber Band option in the Pen and Path Options menu to show a preview of the path curve as you move the cursor.

### Rectangle and Ellipse Tools

When **Unconstrained** is selected, you can simply click and drag to create a rectangle of any size.

If you choose the **Square** option (or Circle for the Ellipse tool), the shape you draw will be constrained to equal width and height (1:1 aspect ratio).

Rectangle tool

Ellipse tool

You can use the **Fixed Size** option to create a shape at a specific width and height. When you click in the canvas, you see a preview of the shape that will be created. You can drag around to determine where the shape will be placed when you release the mouse button.

You can also use the **Proportional** option to define the aspect ratio of the shape you will create. When you click and drag, the shape is constrained to the proportions you define.

If you choose the **From Center** option, the center of the shape you create will be placed where you first click.

### Polygon Tool

Path options for this tool are the same as those that are available when you click the tool to define the shape you want to create (see Page 101).

### Line Tool

When you draw with the Line tool, you can use the Geometry Options menu to add arrowheads to the start and/or end of the line. The Width and Length fields define those attributes of the arrowheads as a percentage of the line weight. The Concavity field defines the arrowheads' inset as a percentage of its length.

### Custom Shape Tool

The Custom Shape tool makes it easy to create custom vector shapes from one of several defined libraries. You can open the Shape panel in the Options bar to access the built-in libraries of shapes.

Path options for the Custom Shape tool are the same as those for the Rectangle and Ellipse tools.

# Understanding Vector Path Operations

## New Layer

When you first choose one of the vector drawing tools — Pen, Freeform Pen, or one of the Shape tools — the Path Operations menu defaults to **New Layer**. When this option is active, every new path will be created on a separate layer.

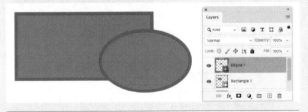

## Combining Shapes

**Combine Shapes** creates the new path on the existing (selected) shape layer.

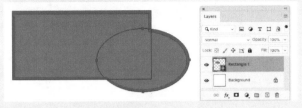

**Subtract Front Shape** creates the new path on the existing (selected) layer and removes overlapping areas of the new shape from the existing shape.

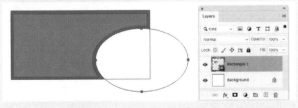

**Intersect Shape Areas** results in the shape of only overlapping areas in the existing and new shapes.

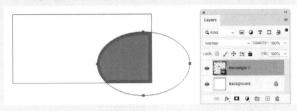

**Exclude Overlapping Areas** removes overlapping areas between the existing and new shapes.

## Merge Shape Components

It is important to note that with the four Combine options explained to the left, the result is the appearance of a single shape, but the original paths of each shape are maintained. You can still manipulate each component path independently.

To make the interaction of overlapping shapes permanent, you can select the paths you want to affect and choose **Merge Shape Components**. This results in a single shape that is the combination of any selected paths; unselected paths are not affected.

The actual result of this command depends on the interaction of the selected paths. In the example below, the top shape has been created with the Intersect Shape Areas operation. After applying the Merge Shape Components operation, anchor points were removed where the original paths did not intersect (as shown in the bottom image).

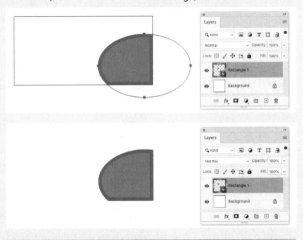

## Merging Shape Layers

If multiple shape layers are selected in the Layers panel, you can combine them by choosing Merge Shapes in the Layers panel Options menu.

This command combines the shapes on all selected layers into a single shape layer — basically the same as using the Combine Shapes path operation. The new combined layer adopts the name of the highest layer in the previous selection.

**Important note:** Don't confuse this Merge option with the Merge Shape Components option in the Path Operations menu. The Merge Shapes option in the Layers panel actually combines the various shapes into a single layer, but maintains all of the existing paths.

## Selecting and Modifying Paths

When you draw vector paths, you can use the Path Selection tool to select and move specific paths on a layer.

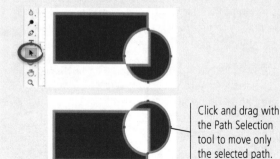

Click and drag with the Path Selection tool to move only the selected path.

Because the path operations affect underlying shapes, you should also understand the concept of **stacking order**. When you create multiple shapes on the same shape layer, they exist from bottom-to-top in the order in which you create them — the first shape is on the bottom, and then the next shape is above, and so on, until the last shape created is at the top of the stack. You can use the **Path Arrangement** menu to control the stacking order of selected paths on the same shape layer.

You can also select a specific shape to change the path operation that applies to it (in either the Options or Properties panel). In the example below, the rectangle was created first, and then the oval was created with the Combine Shapes path operation. We then used the Path Selection tool to select the oval, and chose the Intersect Front Shape operation. Unless you merge the paths into a single shape, you can always select an individual path and change the way it interacts with underlying shapes.

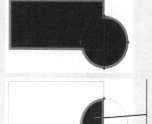

Changing the path operation of the selected path changes the way it interacts with the bottom path.

 ## Clone and Align Layers

If you need more than one version of the same layer, you can create a copy by choosing Duplicate Layer in the layer's contextual menu. This command results in a copy of the original layer in exactly the same position as the original.

You can also use the Move tool to **clone** a layer, which results in a duplicate copy of the original, in the position where you drag to make the clone. In this exercise, you will use cloning to create three rectangle shape layers across the bottom of the canvas. You will then distribute those shape layers evenly across the canvas. These shapes will be used to hold additional inset photos to enhance the visual interest of the overall composition.

1. **With magazine.psd open, click the empty area at the bottom of the layers panel to deselect the existing shape layer.**

   If you don't first deselect the shape layer, your stroke color changes in the next few steps would affect the existing shape.

2. **Choose the Rectangle tool. In the Options bar, define the following settings:**

| Fill Color: | White (in the Grayscale folder) |
| Stroke Color: | Dark Red (in the Dark folder) |
| Stroke Width: | 15 px |

Click here to define the Fill color.

Click here to define the Stroke color.

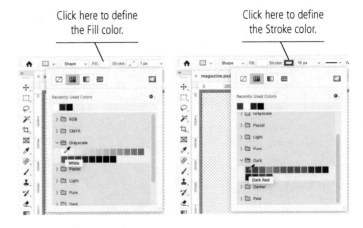

3. **Open the Path Operations menu and review the options.**

The Path Operations menu defaults to the New Layer option if an existing shape layer is not selected.

4. **Open the Set Additional Shape and Path Options menu. Define a 1 px thickness and use the Default color.**

Because you are creating a shape with an actual red stroke, the red path you defined earlier is not a good choice. In this case, the thinner Default (blue) option will be far less distracting.

5. **In the Options bar, reset the Radius field to 0 px.**

6. **Click and drag to create a rectangle in the lower half of the canvas. Using the Properties panel, define the new shape's parameters as:**

| W: 600 px | X: 200 px |
| H: 500 px | Y: 2430 px |

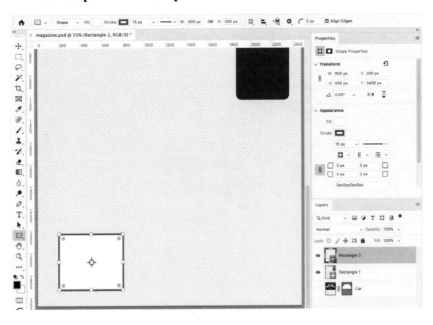

7. **Choose the Move tool in the Tools panel. Press Option/Alt, then click inside the smaller rectangle shape and drag right to clone it.**

Pressing Option/Alt while dragging a selection clones that selection. Because the shape layer is the active selection, the entire shape layer is cloned. The Smart Guides help you maintain the cloned layer's horizontal alignment to the original. If you decide to hide Smart Guides, pressing Shift constrains the movement to 45° angles.

The new cloned layer appears immediately above the original in the Layers panel, with the name, "Rectangle 2 Copy."

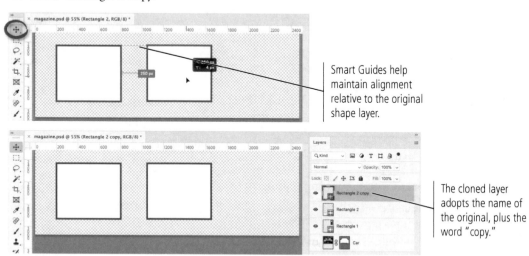

Smart Guides help maintain alignment relative to the original shape layer.

The cloned layer adopts the name of the original, plus the word "copy."

8. **Double-click the name of the Rectangle 2 layer to highlight it. Type Left Inset, then press Return/Enter to change the layer name.**

Even though you will have only three copies of this shape layer, it could become very confusing later if you don't use meaningful names to differentiate the layers.

9. **Double-click the name of the cloned layer to highlight it. Type Center Inset, then press Return/Enter to change the layer name.**

10. **Repeat Step 7 to create a third shape layer at the bottom of the canvas. Name this new layer Right Inset.**

11. **In the Properties panel, change the X position of the active shape to 1700 px.**

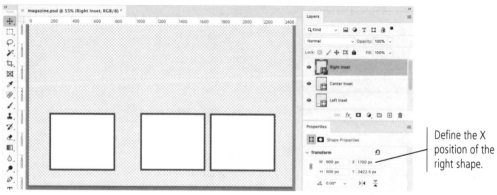

Define the X position of the right shape.

12. **In the Layers panel, Shift-click to select all three Inset shape layers.**

When multiple layers are selected in the Layers panel, a number of alignment options become available in the Options bar. These are very useful for aligning or distributing the content of multiple layers relative to one another.

13. **With the Move tool active, click the Align Top and Distribute Horizontally buttons in the Options bar.**

When the Move tool is active and multiple layers are selected, you can use the Options bar to align the contents of the selected layers relative to one another. The Distribute Horizontal Centers option places an equal amount of space between the center pixel of each selected layer; the positions of layers containing the outermost pixels in the selection are not affected.

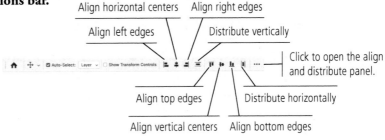

*Note:*

*You can click the Align and Distribute button to access options for distributing based on specific edges or centers.*

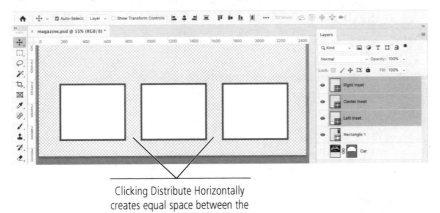

Clicking Distribute Horizontally creates equal space between the content of selected layers.

14. **Save the file and continue to the next exercise.**

# Auto-Select Layers

When your files have more than a few layers — a common occurrence — selecting exactly the layer you want can be difficult. As you already learned, the Move tool defaults to affect the layer that is selected in the Layers panel. Using the Auto-Select option, you can automatically select a specific layer by clicking pixels in the document window, rather than manually selecting a layer in the panel first.

1. **With magazine.psd open, choose File>Place Embedded.**

2. **Navigate to inset1.jpg (in your WIP>Cars folder) and click place. When the image appears on the canvas, press Return/Enter to finalize the placement.**

   New Smart Object layers appear immediately above the previously selected layer. In this case, it is at the top of the layer stack.

3. **In the Layers panel, drag inset1 to appear immediately above the Left Inset layer.**

4. **Repeat Steps 1–3 to place inset2.jpg as an embedded file, and position the inset2 layer immediately above the Center Inset layer.**

   Unfortunately, you can only select one file at a time in the Place dialog box.

5. **Repeat Steps 1–3 to place inset3.jpg as an embedded file, and position the inset3 layer immediately above the Right Inset layer.**

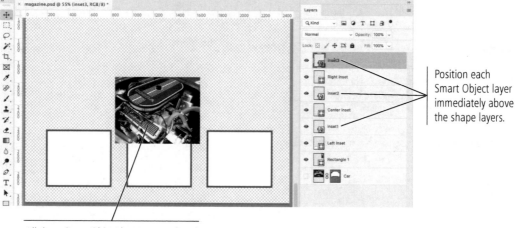

Position each Smart Object layer immediately above the shape layers.

All three Smart Object layers were placed in the center of the document window.

6. **Choose the Move tool in the Tools panel. In the Options bar, check the Auto-Select option.**

7. **Click in the area of the placed images and drag until the inset3 image entirely obscures the bottom-right rectangle shape.**

When Auto-Select is active, clicking in the canvas automatically selects the layer containing the pixel where you clicked. Because the inset3 image is on top of the other two, clicking in the area of the placed images automatically selects the inset3 layer.

Check the Auto-Select option.

Drag the inset3 layer into the area of the Right Inset shape layer.

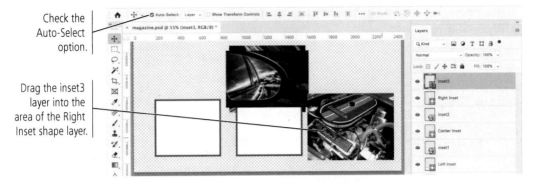

8. **Click again in the original area of the placed images, and drag to move the inset2 image until it entirely obscures the center rectangle.**

Again, clicking automatically selects the relevant layer. Using the Auto-Select option makes it easier to manage layer contents, even when you are not sure which layer contains the pixels you want to affect.

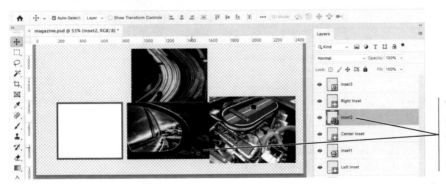

When Auto-Select is checked, clicking automatically selects the layer containing the pixel on which you clicked.

9. **Move the inset1 image until it entirely obscures the left rectangle.**

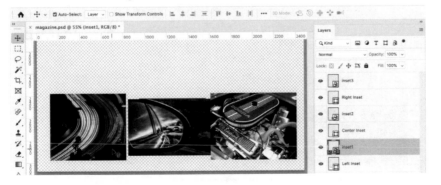

**Note:**

*Remember, if the Auto-Select option is checked in the Options bar, you can simply click pixels of the layer you want to move without first selecting the layer.*

10. **Save the file and continue to the next exercise.**

# Create Clipping Masks

As you can see, the placed images completely hide the underlying layer content. To make the inset images appear only within the area of the underlying shapes, you need to create clipping masks. This task is relatively easy to accomplish.

1. **With magazine.psd open, Control/right-click the inset1 layer to open the layer's contextual menu.**

   Remember, to access the contextual menu for a specific layer, you have to Control/right-click in the area to the right of the layer name.

2. **Choose Create Clipping Mask from the contextual menu.**

   A clipping mask is another way to show only certain areas of a layer; in this case, using the shape of one layer (Left Inset) to show parts of the layer above it (inset1).

   The Layers panel shows that the inset1 layer is clipped by the Left Inset layer.

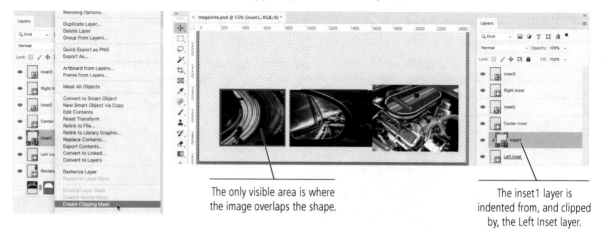

The only visible area is where the image overlaps the shape.

The inset1 layer is indented from, and clipped by, the Left Inset layer.

3. **With the Move tool active, click in the area of the left inset image and drag until you are satisfied with the visible area of the image.**

   Even though a layer is clipped, you can still move it without affecting the position of the clipping layer. Unlike a layer mask, the clipping and clipped layers are not automatically linked.

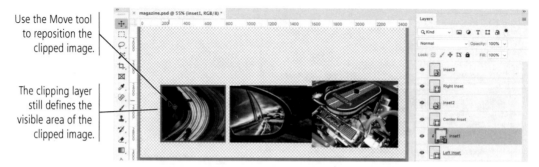

Use the Move tool to reposition the clipped image.

The clipping layer still defines the visible area of the clipped image.

As with layer masks, clipping masks do not permanently modify the pixels in the layer. You can choose Release Clipping Mask in the clipped layer's contextual menu to undo a clipping mask, without altering the affected layers.

4. **Repeat Steps 1–3 to clip the inset2 and inset3 images to their underlying layers.**

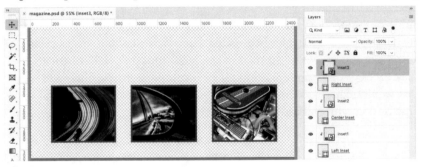

5. **In the Layers panel, show the Car layer, and then move it to the top of the layer stack.**

6. **Using the Move tool, position the car so it slightly overlaps the three shape layers at the bottom of the page.**

   Use the following image as a guide.

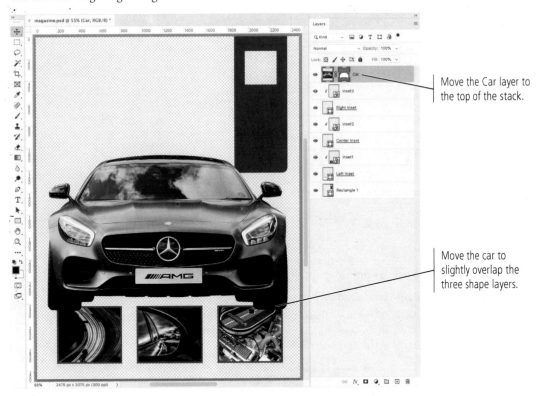

Move the Car layer to the top of the stack.

Move the car to slightly overlap the three shape layers.

7. **Save the file, and then continue to the next stage of the project.**

# STAGE 3 / Applying Styles and Filters

Photoshop includes a large number of options for creating artistic effects, including built-in patterns, styles, and filters. You can add texture to the flat fill color of a vector shape layer or apply effects, such as drop shadows or beveling, to add the appearance of depth. You can make images look like pencil sketches, paintings, or any of the dozens of other options. You can even compound these filters and styles to create unique effects that would require extreme skill using traditional art techniques, such as oil painting. In this stage of the project, you will use a number of these options to enhance your overall composition.

##  Add Texture to a Shape Layer

Aside from their usefulness as scalable vector paths, shape layers can be filled with solid colors (as the background shape is now), with other images (as the smaller inset shapes are now), or with styles or patterns (which you will add in this exercise).

1. **With magazine.psd open, choose Window>Styles to open the Styles panel.**

   This panel shows the predefined styles that can be applied to a shape layer. The icons give you an idea of each style's results.

2. **Click the button in the top-right corner of the Styles panel and choose Small List from the Options menu.**

   After the few default styles that appear at the top of the panel, the built-in styles include a number of sets or **style groups**. You can click the arrow to the left of any group name to expand it and see the individual styles in that group.

   By default, styles appear in the Large Thumbnail view. We prefer the list view because the style names provide a better idea of what the styles do.

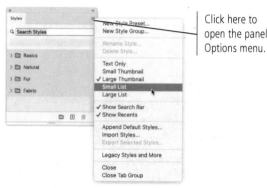

Click here to open the panel Options menu.

3. **Open the Styles panel Options menu again and choose Legacy Styles and More.**

   In the 2020 release, Photoshop made significant changes to the way assets such as styles are managed; part of this re-tooling included removing a large number of built-in styles from the default panel. Those styles are still useful, though, and can be accessed by choosing the Legacy Styles and More option.

Access recently used styles in this bar.

Click the arrows to expand a style set.

Click here and drag down to expand the panel.

*Note:*

*You can click the bottom edge of the panel and drag to resize the panel, showing more styles and sets at one time.*

4. **In the Styles panel, expand the Legacy Styles and More folder, then expand the All Legacy Default Styles and Web Styles subfolders.**

5. **Select the Rectangle 1 shape layer in the Layers panel, then click the Black Anodized Metal style in the Styles panel to apply the style to the shape layer.**

   The layers panel shows that a series of effects (those which make up the style) has been applied to the layer.

   Photoshop styles are non-destructive, which means you can change or delete them without affecting the original layer content. You can temporarily disable all effects by clicking the eye icon to the left of the word "Effects" or disable individual effects by clicking the icon for a specific item in the panel.

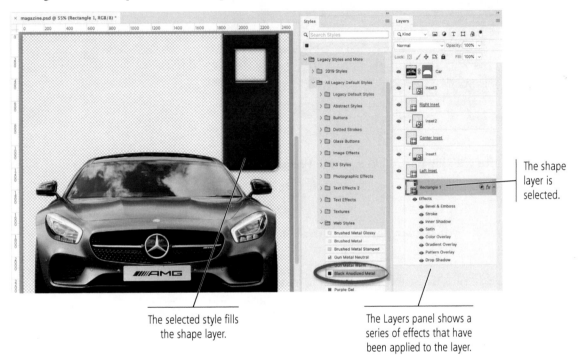

The selected style fills
the shape layer.

The shape
layer is
selected.

The Layers panel shows a
series of effects that have
been applied to the layer.

6. **In the Layers panel, click the arrow to the right of the fx icon of the Rectangle 1 layer.**

   This collapses the list of applied effects, which helps keep the Layers panel easier to manage.

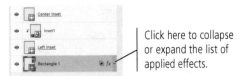

Click here to collapse
or expand the list of
applied effects.

7. **Save the file and continue to the next exercise.**

# Apply Custom Layer Styles

A style is simply a saved group of effects that can be applied with a single click. You can also create your own styles using the Layer Style dialog box, which you will do in this exercise.

1. **With magazine.psd open, choose the Left Inset layer.**

2. **Choose Layer>Layer Style>Drop Shadow.**

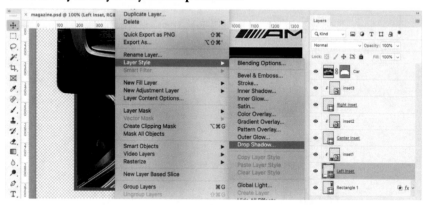

3. **In the resulting dialog box, make sure the Preview option is checked.**

   The Preview option allows you to see the results of your settings while the dialog box is still open.

4. **In the Layer Style dialog box, make sure the Use Global Light option is checked.**

   This option is checked by default, so you should not have to make any change.

   The Angle field defines the position of the effect in relation to the layer. When the Global Light option is checked, changing the style Angle applies the same change to any other layer for which an effect using the Use Global Light option is applied.

5. **Make the following changes to the default settings in the dialog box:**

| Opacity: | 50% | This setting controls the transparency of pixels created by the style. |
| Distance: | 10 px | This setting offsets the effect relative to the layer content. |
| Spread: | 5% | This setting is the percentage the effect expands beyond the layer content. |
| Size: | 10 px | This setting controls the amount of blurring applied to the effect. |

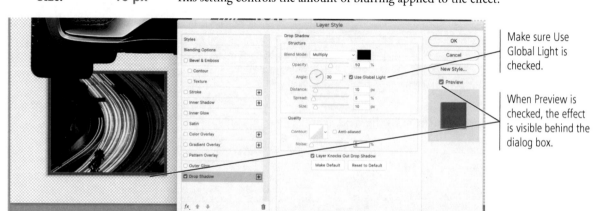

Make sure Use Global Light is checked.

When Preview is checked, the effect is visible behind the dialog box.

**6.** **Click the + button to the right of the Drop Shadow layer style.**

You can apply more than one instance of certain layer styles (those identified with a "+"). When you click the + button, a new instance of the style appears in the list.

*Note:*

*You can use the buttons at the bottom of the effects list to change the order of applied effects, as well as delete a specific (selected) effect.*

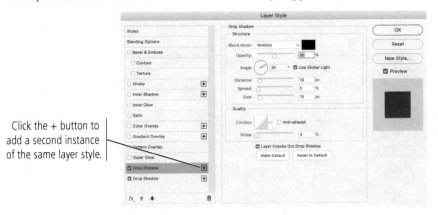

Click the + button to add a second instance of the same layer style.

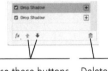

Use these buttons to reorder applied effects.    Delete Effect

**7.** **With the top Drop Shadow item selected in the list, click the color swatch to the right of the Blend Mode menu.**

**8.** **When the Color Picker appears, move the mouse cursor over the dark blue color on the car's windshield and click to sample that color. Click OK to close the Color Picker dialog box.**

Click the swatch to open the Color Picker for the style.

Click to sample a color that you want to use for the style.

**9.** **Uncheck the Use Global Light option, then change the Angle field to -150°.**

If you change the angle field while the Use Global Light option is checked, you would change the global angle and that change would apply to any other applied layer style that uses the global light angle. You want to change the angle for only this style instance, so you must uncheck Use Global Light *before* changing the angle field.

10. **Make the following changes to the settings in the dialog box:**

| | |
|---|---|
| Opacity: | 75% |
| Distance: | 20 px |
| Spread: | 10% |
| Size: | 20 px |

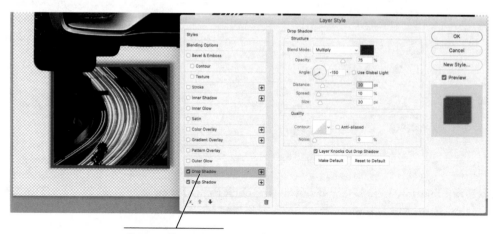

Changes affect only the
selected style instance.

11. **Click OK to apply the layer style.**

    In the Layers panel, the drop shadow
    styles appear as effects for the Left Inset
    layer. As with the built-in style you
    applied in the previous exercise, custom
    layer styles are non-destructive.

Layer styles are
non-destructive;
use the Eye icons to
turn effects on or off.

12. **Press Option/Alt, then click the word "Effects" in the Layers panel and
    drag it to the Center Inset layer.**

    Just as you cloned a layer in an earlier exercise, pressing Option/Alt allows you to
    clone effects from one layer to another. This offers an easy way to apply exactly the
    same effects to multiple layers in your file.

The cursor shows you are
cloning the applied effects.

The cloned effects now apply
to the Center Inset layer.

13. **Repeat Step 12 to add the Drop Shadow effects to the Right Inset layer.**

## Bevel and Emboss

This style has five variations:

- **Outer Bevel** creates a bevel on the outside edges of the layer contents.
- **Inner Bevel** creates a bevel on the inside edges.
- **Emboss** creates the effect of embossing the layer contents against the underlying layers.
- **Pillow Emboss** creates the effect of stamping the edges of the layer into the underlying layers.
- **Stroke Emboss** applies an embossed effect to a stroke applied to the layer. (The Stroke Emboss effect is not available if you haven't applied a stroke to the layer.)

Any of these styles can be applied as **Smooth** (blurs the edges of the effect), **Chisel Hard** (creates a distinct edge), or **Chisel Soft** (creates a distinct but slightly blurred edge).

You can change the **Direction** of the bevel effect. **Up** creates the appearance of the layer coming out of the image; **Down** creates the appearance of something stamped into the image.

The **Size** slider makes the effect smaller or larger, and the **Soften** slider blurs the edges of the effect.

In the Shading area, you can control the light source **Angle** and **Altitude** (think of how shadows differ as the sun moves). You can also apply a **Gloss Contour** (see the following explanation of Contours). Finally, you can change the Blending Mode, Opacity, and Color settings of highlights and shadows created in effects.

When a Bevel and Emboss style is applied, you can also apply Contour and Texture effects.

## Stroke

The **Stroke** style adds an outline of a specific number of pixels to the layer. The Stroke effect can be added at the outside or inside of the layer edge, or it can be centered over the edge (half the stroke will be inside and half outside the actual layer edge). You can adjust the Blending Mode and Opacity setting of the stroke, and you can also define a specific color, gradient, or pattern to apply to the stroke.

## Satin

The Satin options apply interior shading to create a satiny appearance. You can change the Blending Mode, Color, and Opacity settings of the effect, as well as the Angle, Distance, and Size settings.

## Drop Shadow and Inner Shadow

**Drop Shadow** adds a shadow behind the layer. **Inner Shadow** adds a shadow inside the edges of the layer's content. For both types, you can define the blending mode, color, opacity, angle, distance, and size of the shadow.

- **Distance** is the offset of the shadow, or how far away the shadow will be from the original layer.
- **Spread** (for Drop Shadows) is the percentage the shadow expands beyond the original layer.
- **Choke** (for Inner Shadows) is the percentage the shadow shrinks into the original layer.
- **Size** is the blur amount applied to the shadow.

You can also adjust the Contour, Anti-aliasing, and Noise settings in the shadow effect. (See the Contours section later in this discussion for further explanation.)

When checked, the Layer Knocks Out Drop Shadow option removes the drop shadow underneath the original layer area. This is particularly important if you convert a shadow style to a separate layer that you move to a different position, or if the layer is semi-transparent above its shadow.

**Global Light.** The Use Global Light check box is available for Drop Shadow, Inner Shadow, and Bevel and Emboss styles. When this option is checked, the style is linked to the "master" light source angle for the entire file. Changing the global light affects any linked style applied to any layer in the entire file. You can change the Global Light setting in any of the Layer Style fields, or by choosing Layer>Layer Style>Global Light.

## Outer Glow and Inner Glow

**Outer Glow** and **Inner Glow** styles add glow effects to the outside and inside (respectively) edges of the layer. For either, you can define the Blending Mode, Opacity, and Noise values, as well as whether to use a solid color or a gradient.

- For either kind of glow, you can define the **Technique** as Precise or Softer. **Precise** creates a glow at a specific distance. **Softer** creates a blurred glow and does not preserve detail as well as Precise.
- For Inner Glows, you can also define the **Source** of the glow (Center or Edge). **Center** applies a glow starting from the center of the layer. **Edge** applies the glow starting from the inside edges of the layer.
- The **Spread** and **Choke** sliders affect the percentages of the glow effects.
- The **Size** slider makes the effect smaller or larger.

### Contours

Contour options control the shape of the applied styles. Drop Shadow, Inner Shadow, Inner Glow, Outer Glow, Bevel and Emboss, and Satin styles all include Contour options. The default option for all but the Satin style is Linear, which applies a linear effect from solid to 100% transparent.

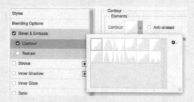

The easiest way to understand the Contour options is through examples. In the following series of images, the same Inner Bevel style was applied in all three examples. In the top image, you can clearly see the size and depth of the bevel. In the center and bottom images, the only difference is the applied contour. If you look carefully at the shape edge, you should be able to see how the applied contour shape maps to the beveled edge in the image.

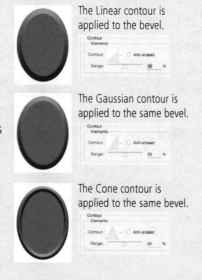

The Linear contour is applied to the bevel.

The Gaussian contour is applied to the same bevel.

The Cone contour is applied to the same bevel.

When you apply a contour, the **Range** slider controls which part of the effect is contoured. For Outer Glow or Inner Glow, you can add variation to the contour color and opacity using the **Jitter** slider.

### Textures

The Textures options allow you to create texture effects using the built-in patterns.

- The **Scale** slider varies the size of the applied pattern.
- The **Depth** slider varies the apparent depth of the applied pattern.
- The **Invert** option (as the name implies) inverts the applied pattern.
- If you check the **Link with Layer** option, the pattern's position is locked to the layer so you can move the two together. If this option is unchecked, different parts of the pattern are visible if you move the associated layer.
- When you create a texture, you can drag in the image window (behind the Layer Style dialog box) to move the texture. When the Link with Layer option is checked, clicking the **Snap to Origin** button positions the pattern origin at the upper-left corner of the layer. If Link with Layers is unchecked, clicking the Snap to Origin button positions the pattern at the image origin point.

### Color Overlay, Gradient Overlay, Pattern Overlay

A **color overlay** is simply a solid color with a specific Blending Mode and Opacity value applied. A color overlay can be used to change an entire layer to a solid color (with the Normal blending mode at 100% opacity), or to create unique effects using different Blending Mode and Opacity settings.

A **gradient overlay** is basically the same as a color overlay, except you use a gradient instead of a solid color. You can choose an existing gradient or define a new one, change the Blending Mode and Opacity value of the gradient, apply any of the available gradient styles (Linear, Radial, etc.), or change the Angle and Scale values of the gradient.

A **pattern overlay** is similar to the Texture options for a Bevel and Emboss style. You can choose a specific pattern, change the Blending Mode and Opacity value, or change the applied pattern scale. You can also link the pattern to the layer and snap the pattern to the layer or the file origin.

**14.** **Press Option/Alt, then click the second (bottom) instance of the Drop Shadow and drag it to the Car layer.**

If you remember, you edited the top instance to use blue as the shadow color. The bottom instance — the one you are cloning here — applies a black shadow at a 30° angle (the global angle).

You can clone an entire set of effects by Option/Alt-dragging the word "Effects," or clone only specific effects by Option/Alt-dragging an individual item in the list.

The cursor shows you are cloning only one drop shadow effect.

The single cloned effect now applies to the Car layer.

**15.** **In the Layers panel, double-click the Drop Shadow effect for the Car layer.**

Double-clicking an effect in the panel opens the dialog box, where you can make changes to the settings that define the effect for the active layer.

**16.** **Click in the document window (behind the dialog box) and drag down until the drop shadow is much more prominent behind the car layer.**

When you drag in the document window, the dialog box dynamically changes to reflect the new angle and distance for the effect.

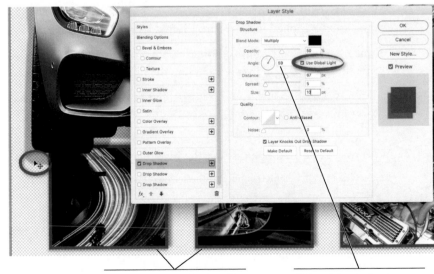

As you dynamically change the angle, you should also notice the effect on the three Inset layers. Because the Use Global Light option is checked for all four layers, changing the angle for one of these layers applies the same change to all four layers.

Changing the angle for one effect changes the angle for all that use the Global Light option.

Click and drag in the document window to dynamically change the effect settings.

You should also notice, however, that the altered Distance value does not apply to the other three layers in which the Drop Shadow effect is applied. Only the Angle of the effects is synchronized between the various layers.

17. **Change the size field to 50 px, then click OK to apply the changed settings.**

18. **In the Layers panel, click the arrow buttons to the right of each fx icon to collapse the effects for all layers.**

**Note:**

*If you double-click the word "Effects" in the Layers panel, the dialog box opens to the Blending Options: Default screen. Double-clicking a specific effect opens the dialog box directly to the settings for the effect on which you clicked.*

19. **Save the file and continue to the next exercise.**

 ## Use the Filter Gallery

You can apply filters to specific selections, individual layers, or even individual channels depending on what you need to accomplish. If you combine filters with Smart Objects, you can apply non-destructive filters, and then change the settings or turn off the filters to experiment with different results.

In addition to the options in the Filter Gallery, a wide range of other filters can be accessed in the various Filter submenus. We encourage you to explore the various settings. Any filter that includes an ellipsis (...) in the menu command opens a secondary dialog box, where you can control the filter's specific settings.

Keep the following points in mind when you use filters:

- Filters can be applied to the entire selected layer or to an active selection.

- Some filters work only on RGB images. If you are in a different color mode, some (or all) filter options — including the Filter Gallery — will be unavailable.

- All filters can be applied to 8-bit images but options are limited for 16- and 32-bit images.

**Note:**

*Photoshop ships with more than 100 filters divided into 13 categories; some of these are functional while others are purely decorative.*

1. **With magazine.psd open, select the inset3 layer in the Layers panel.**

   Like styles and effects, filters apply to the selected layer, not to the entire file.

2. **Choose Filter>Filter Gallery.**

   If the Filter menu includes the Filter Gallery at the top of the list, the top command applies the last-used filter gallery settings to the selected layer. To open the Filter Gallery dialog box, you have to choose the Filter Gallery command at the third spot in the menu.

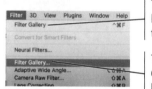

This command applies the last-used filter without opening the Filter Gallery dialog box.

This command opens the Filter Gallery dialog box with the last-used settings applied.

3. **If necessary, adjust the view percentage and position in the dialog box so you can see the inset3 image.**

4. **In the middle pane of the dialog box, expand the Artistic collection of filters and click the Plastic Wrap thumbnail.**

The left side of the dialog box shows a preview of the applied filter(s). You can use the options in the bottom-left corner to change the preview view percentage.

In the middle column, available filters are broken into six categories. Inside each folder, thumbnails show a small preview of each filter.

On the right, the top half shows settings specific to the selected filter (from the middle column). The bottom shows the filters that are applied to the selected layer.

You can apply more than one filter to a layer by clicking the New Effect Layer button in the bottom-right corner of the Filter Gallery dialog box.

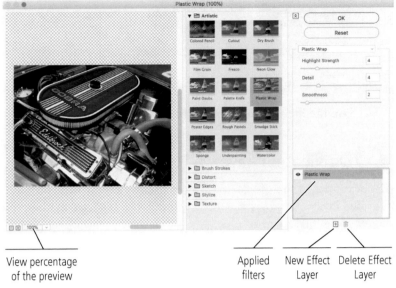

View percentage of the preview

Applied filters    New Effect Layer    Delete Effect Layer

5. **Adjust the filter options until you are satisfied with the result, then click OK to apply the filter.**

Because the inset3 layer is a Smart Object layer, the filter is applied non-destructively as a Smart Filter. If you apply a filter to a regular layer, it is destructive, and cannot be changed or turned off.

The filter is applied to the Smart Object layer as a Smart Filter.

6. **Press Option/Alt, then click the Filter Gallery listing in the Layers panel and drag it to the inset2 layer.**

As with layer styles, this method allows you to apply the same Smart Filter to multiple layers, without opening any dialog boxes.

The cursor shows you are cloning the Smart Filter.

7. **Repeat Step 6 to apply the Smart Filter to the inset1 layer.**

The Smart Filters have been cloned, but the lists do not automatically expand in the panel.

8. **Collapse the Smart Filters listing for the inset3 layer.**

9. **Save the file and continue to the next exercise.**

 ## Duplicate a Layer

The next piece of this project is a custom background, which you will create from a provided image. In this exercise, you will use the Duplicate method to move layer content from one file to another.

1. **With magazine.psd open, open tires.jpg from your WIP>Cars folder.**

2. **Control/right-click the Background layer in the tires.jpg file and choose Duplicate Layer in the contextual menu.**

3. **In the resulting dialog box, choose magazine.psd in the Destination Document menu, then click OK.**

The Duplicate command provides an easy method for copying an entire layer — either in the current file, any other open file, or a new file. If you choose the current file as the destination, you can define a new name for the duplicated layer.

Choose where you want the duplicate layer in this menu.

4. **Close the tires.jpg file and review the current magazine.psd file.**

   The Background layer from the tires file is copied into the magazine file. It is placed immediately above the previously selected layer.

   Although it is still named "Background" because of the file from which it was copied, it is neither locked nor placed at the bottom of the layer stack.

   If you continued directly from the previous exercise, the inset3 layer was selected so the Background layer appears immediately above that layer. Don't worry if it appears in a different location, because you will intentionally move it in the layer stacking order in the next step.

The duplicated layer is placed above the previously selected layer.

5. **Click the Background layer in the Layers panel and drag it to the bottom of the layer stack.**

6. **Double-click the layer name to highlight it. Type Tires as the new layer name, then press Return/Enter to finalize the new name.**

Rename the layer and move it to the bottom of the stack.

7. **Save the file and then continue to the next exercise.**

# Liquify a Layer

Rather than just using the stacked-tires image as the background, you are going to use the Liquify filter to push around layer pixels in a freeform style to create a unique background for the magazine cover.

1. **With magazine.psd open, hide all but the Tires layer.**

   You can Option/Alt-click the eye icon for a layer to hide all other layers.

2. **With the Tires layer selected in the Layers panel, choose Filter>Liquify.**

   The Liquify filter has its own interface and tools. Depending on which tool you select, different options become available in the right side of the dialog box.

3. **In the bottom-left corner of the dialog box, open the View Percentage menu and choose Fit In View.**

4. **On the left side of the dialog box, choose the Forward Warp tool.**

5. **On the right side of the dialog box, define a large brush with medium density and medium pressure.**

   For any of the distortion tools, you have to define a brush size, density (feathering around the edges), and pressure. Some tools also allow you to define the brush rate (how fast distortions are made).

   For this exercise, we used a 500-pixel brush with 50% density and 75% pressure.

6. **Make sure the Pin Edges option is checked.**

   When checked, this option prevents transparent pixels from appearing at the canvas edges.

7. **Click and drag in the preview to warp the tire pattern away from the neat stack in the original image.**

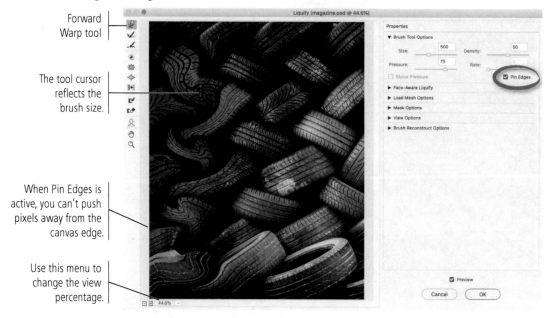

Forward Warp tool

The tool cursor reflects the brush size.

When Pin Edges is active, you can't push pixels away from the canvas edge.

Use this menu to change the view percentage.

# More About the Liquify Filter

Tools in the Liquify filter distort the brush area when you drag. The distortion is concentrated at the center of the brush area, and the effect intensifies as you hold down the mouse button or repeatedly drag over an area. (The **Hand** and **Zoom tools** function the same as they do in the main Photoshop interface.)

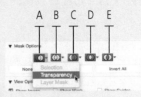

A. The **Forward Warp tool** pushes pixels as you drag.

B. The **Reconstruct tool** restores distorted pixels.

C. The **Smooth tool** smoothes jagged edges.

D. The **Twirl Clockwise tool** rotates pixels clockwise as you hold down the mouse button or drag. Press Option/Alt to twirl pixels counterclockwise.

E. The **Pucker tool** moves pixels toward the center of the brush, creating a zoomed-out effect if you simply hold down the mouse button without dragging.

F. The **Bloat tool** moves pixels away from the center of the brush, creating a zoomed-in effect.

G. The **Push Left tool** moves pixels left when you drag up, and right when you drag down. You can also drag clockwise around an object to increase its size, or drag counterclockwise to decrease its size.

H. The **Freeze Mask tool** protects areas where you paint.

I. The **Thaw Mask tool** removes the protection created by the Freeze Mask tool.

J. The **Face tool** reveals on-screen controls for changing the shape of various facial features. For example, you can click and drag to change the shape of the forehead, chin height, jawline, and face width when the overall face shape is selected.

## Face-Aware Liquify Options

If an image includes faces, the Liquify filter automatically recognizes them, and provides options for manipulating the individual eyes, nose, mouth, and overall face shape. You can use the controls on the right side of the dialog box, or use the Face tool to drag on-screen controls in the preview area.

If more than one face exists in the overall image, you can use the Select Face menu to determine which one you want to edit using the slider controls.

## Mask Options

Mask Options allow you to freeze areas in the Liquify preview to protect them from distortion. You can use the Mask options to freeze areas based on existing selections, transparent areas, or layer masks in the original image.

A. **Replace Selection**

B. **Add to Selection**

C. **Subtract from Selection**

D. **Intersect with Selection**

E. **Invert Selection**

You can click the **None** button to thaw all masked areas. Click the **Mask All** button to mask the entire image or the **Invert All** button to reverse the current mask.

## Brush Reconstruct Options

When the Liquify dialog box is open, pressing Command/Control-Z

undoes your last brush stroke. Clicking **Restore All** has the same effect as using the Undo keyboard shortcut.

You can also use the **Reconstruct** button to affect the last-applied stroke. Rather than undoing the entire stroke, you can use the resulting dialog box to lessen the effect by a specific percentage.

## View Options

**Show Image**, active by default, shows the active layer in the filter's preview area. If you check the **Show Mesh** option, the preview also shows a grid that defaults to small, gray lines. You can use the Mesh Size and Mesh Color menus to change the appearance of the grid.

When **Show Mask** is checked, any mask you paint with the Freeze Mask tool appears in the filter's preview area. You can use the Mask Color menu to change the color of that mask.

When **Show Backdrop** is checked, you can include other layers in the filter's preview area. The Use menu also lists individual layers in the file so you can show only a certain layer in the preview. You can use the Mode and Opacity menus to change how extra layers appear in the preview.

8. **Continue clicking and dragging to push pixels until you are satisfied with your results.**

   If necessary, you can press Command/Control-Z to undo your last brush stroke in the Liquify dialog box.

9. **Click OK to return to the image.**

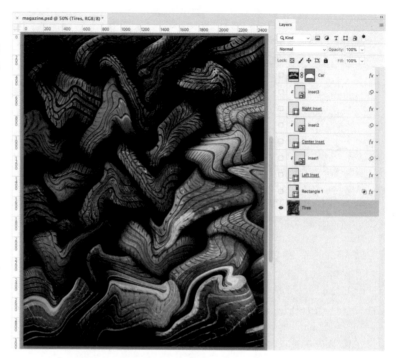

   Depending on the size of the layer you are liquifying, the process might take a while to complete; be patient.

   The Liquify filter is not a smart filter, and cannot be applied to a Smart Object layer; it permanently alters the pixels in the layer to which it is applied.

10. **Save the file and continue to the next exercise.**

## Use the Eyedropper Tool

In Photoshop, there is almost always more than one way to complete a task. In this exercise, you use the Eyedropper tool to change the Foreground and Background colors by sampling from the original car image. You will then use those colors to create a gradient background for the overall composition.

1. **With magazine.psd open, hide all but the Car layer.**

   You can hide multiple layers by clicking and dragging over the eye icons of each layer that you want to hide.

2. **Choose the Eyedropper tool in the Tools panel.**

3. **In the Options bar, choose 5 by 5 Average in the Sample Size menu and choose All Layers in the Sample menu. Make sure the Show Sampling Ring option is checked.**

   The default Eyedropper option — Point Sample — selects the color of the single pixel where you click. Using one of the average values avoids the possibility of sampling an errant artifact color because the tool finds the average color in a range of adjacent pixels.

   By default, the sample will be selected from All [visible] Layers. You can choose Current Layer in the Sample menu to choose a color from only the active layer.

4. **Move the cursor over the light silver color near the left edge of the car (as shown in the following image). Click to change the foreground color.**

When you click with the Eyedropper tool, the sampling ring appears and shows the previous foreground color on the bottom, and the current sample color on the top half.

If you hold down the mouse button, you can drag around the image to find the color you want. The sampling ring previews which color will be selected if you release the mouse button.

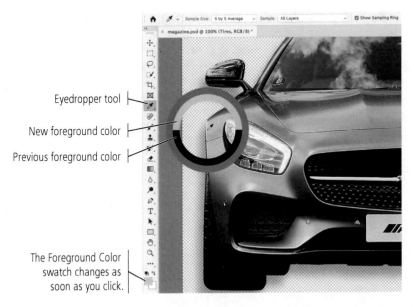

Eyedropper tool

New foreground color

Previous foreground color

The Foreground Color swatch changes as soon as you click.

5. **Move the cursor over the yellow/greenish tones in the bottom part of the headlight (as shown in the image below). Option/Alt-click to change the background color.**

Pressing Option/Alt while you click with the Eyedropper tool changes the Background color. In this case, the sampling ring shows the previous background color on the bottom and the current selection on the top.

New background color

Previous background color

The Background Color swatch changes as soon as you Option/Alt-click.

6. **Save the file and continue to the next exercise.**

# Create a Custom Gradient

A **gradient** (sometimes called a blend) is a fill that creates a smooth transition from one color to another. Photoshop can create several different kinds of gradients (linear, radial, etc.), and you can access a number of built-in gradients. You can also create your own custom gradients, which you will do in this exercise.

1. **With magazine.psd open, choose the Gradient tool in the Tools panel.**

2. **Choose Window>Gradients to open the Gradients panel.**

3. **Click the arrow to the left of the Basics folder to expand that set.**

4. **Click the button in the top-right corner of the Gradients panel, then choose Small List view from the panel Options menu.**

   Like the built-in styles, Photoshop includes a number of predefined gradients organized in groups. The Basic set includes foreground-to-background, foreground-to-transparent, and black-to-white. The names are useful for understanding the result of each.

*Note:*

*You can click the bottom edge of the panel and drag to resize the panel, showing more gradients and sets at one time.*

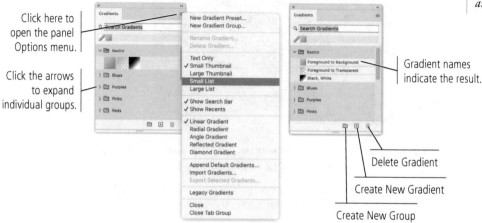

5. **Click the Create New Gradient button at the bottom of the Gradient panel.**

   This button opens the Gradient Editor dialog box, which you can use to edit existing gradients or create new ones.

6. **In the Presets section of the dialog box, expand the Basics set and then click the left gradient swatch to select the Foreground to Background gradient.**

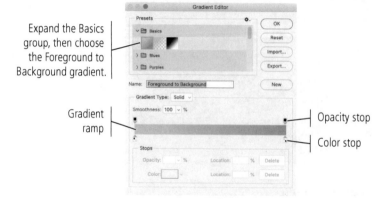

7. **Click the right color stop below the gradient ramp. Drag left until the Location field shows 60%.**

After you move the color stop, the name changes to Custom because you're defining a custom gradient.

Open this menu to set the stop color to the active Foreground or Background color.

Click the swatch to open the Color Picker for the selected stop.

Click a stop to select it.

Verify the stop position as you drag it across the ramp.

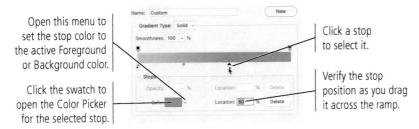

8. **Double-click the moved stop to open the Color Picker dialog box. Change the stop color to C: 25%, M: 40%, Y: 80%, K: 5%, then click OK.**

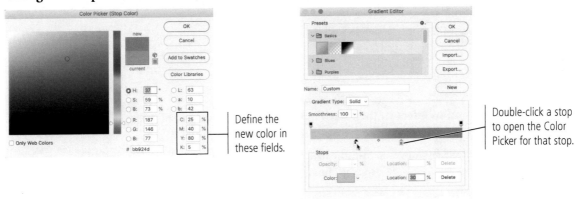

Define the new color in these fields.

Double-click a stop to open the Color Picker for that stop.

9. **Click the left stop to select it. Drag right until the Location field shows 30%.**

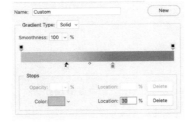

10. **Click the small diamond icon between the first and second stops. Drag right until the Location field shows 80%.**

This point indicates where the colors of the two surrounding stops are equally mixed. Dragging this point extends the gradient on one side of the point and compresses the gradient on the other.

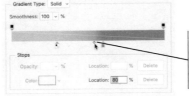

Drag this icon to change the midpoint between the two surrounding stops.

11. **Click below the right side of the ramp. Drag the new stop until the location field shows 80%.**

   Clicking below the ramp adds a new stop to the gradient, using the same color settings as the last-selected stop.

   Click below the ramp to add a new stop.

   The new stop adopts the color of the last-selected stop.

12. **Click below the left end of the gradient ramp to add a new stop. Set its location to 0%.**

13. **Double-click the new stop to open the Color Picker dialog box. Change the stop color to white (C: 0%, M: 0%, Y: 0%, K: 0%), then click OK.**

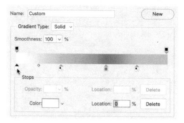

*Note:*

*Whenever the Color Picker dialog box is open, you can use the Eyedropper cursor to sample a color from the image in the document window.*

14. **Click the left stop to select it, then click below the right end of the gradient ramp to add another new stop. Set its location to 100%.**

   If you didn't click the leftmost stop first, the new stop from this step would have the same color settings as the last-selected stop (from Step 11).

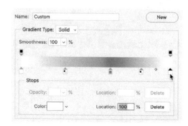

*Note:*

*Drag a stop off the gradient ramp to remove it from the gradient.*

15. **Type Car Background in the Name field and click the New button.**

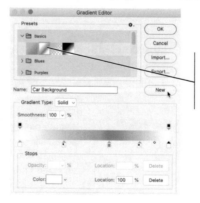

   Clicking the New button adds the new swatch to the list of gradient options.

16. **Click OK to close the dialog box.**

17. **Save the file and continue to the next exercise.**

Create a Gradient Fill Layer

Once you define the gradient you want, applying it is fairly easy: add a layer (if necessary), select the type of gradient you want to create, and then click and drag.

1. **With magazine.psd open, make sure the Tires layer is selected.**

2. **Click the Create a New Layer button at the bottom of the Layers panel. Name the new layer Shading.**

   When you add a new layer, it is automatically added directly above the selected layer.

Create a New Layer button

3. **Choose the Gradient tool in the Tools panel, then review the options in the Options bar.**

4. **In the Options bar, click the arrow button to open the Gradient Picker panel.**

   The Gradient Picker panel has the same options that are available in the standalone Gradients panel.

5. **Expand the Basics set, then click the Car Background gradient swatch to select it. Make sure the Linear Gradient option is active to the right of the Gradient Picker.**

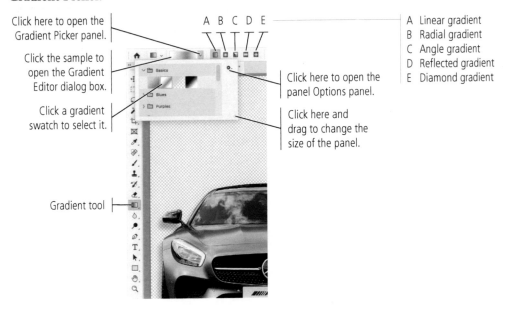

Click here to open the Gradient Picker panel.

Click the sample to open the Gradient Editor dialog box.

Click a gradient swatch to select it.

Gradient tool

A B C D E

Click here to open the panel Options panel.

Click here and drag to change the size of the panel.

A  Linear gradient
B  Radial gradient
C  Angle gradient
D  Reflected gradient
E  Diamond gradient

**6.** **Click in the top-left area of the canvas and drag to the bottom-right area of the canvas (as shown in the following image).**

When you release the mouse button, the layer fills with the gradient. Areas before and after the line drawn with the Gradient tool fill with the start and stop colors of the gradient (in this case, they're both white).

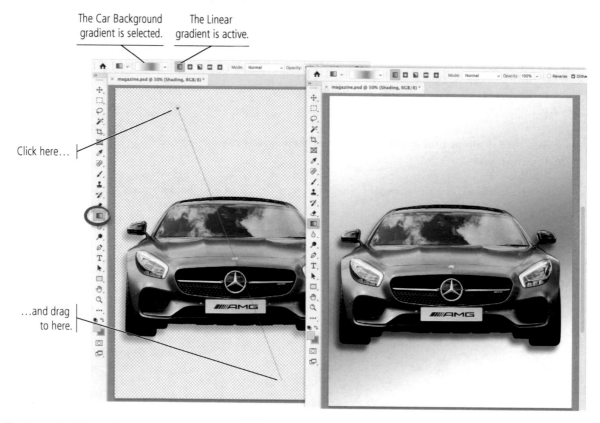

The Car Background gradient is selected.

The Linear gradient is active.

Click here...

...and drag to here.

**7.** **Save the file and continue to the next exercise.**

# Adjust Blending Mode and Layer Opacity

The final step to creating your custom background is to blend the gradient you just created into the liquified tires. Photoshop includes a number of options for making this type of adjustment.

1. **With magazine.psd open, show all layers in the file and then select the Shading layer as the active one.**

2. **Open the Blending Mode menu in the Layers panel and choose Overlay.**

   Photoshop provides access to 27 different layer blending modes; the default is Normal, or no blending applied. As you move your mouse cursor over each option in the menu, the document window shows a dynamic preview of that mode. Using the Overlay mode, colors in the gradient are blended onto the pixels in the underlying Tires layer.

   Blending Mode menu

3. **Select the Tires layer in the Layers panel, then change the Opacity field to 10%.**

   Reducing the layer opacity reduces the strength of the layer content so that it no longer overpowers other elements in the composition. You can now better see the effect created by the blended gradient.

   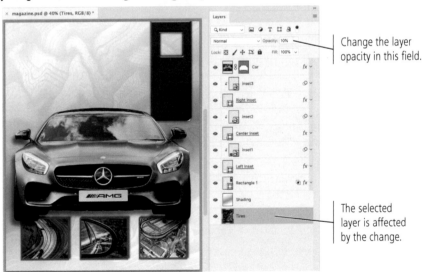

   Change the layer opacity in this field.

   The selected layer is affected by the change.

4. **Save the file and continue to the next exercise.**

# Distinguishing Photoshop Blending Modes

When working with blending modes, think of the top layer as the "blend" layer and the next lowest layer as the "base."

- **Normal** is the default mode (no blending applied).
- **Dissolve** results in a random scattering of pixels of both the blend and base colors.
- **Darken** returns the darker of the blend or base color. Base pixels that are lighter than the blend color are replaced. Base pixels that are darker than the blend color remain unchanged.
- **Multiply** multiplies (hence, the name) the base color by the blend color, resulting in a darker color. Multiplying any color with black produces black. Multiplying any color with white leaves the color unchanged (think of math — any number times 0 equals 0).
- **Color Burn** darkens the base color by increasing the contrast. Blend colors darker than 50% significantly darken the base color by increasing saturation and reducing brightness. Blending with white has no effect.
- **Linear Burn** darkens the base color similar to Color Burn. Using Linear Burn, the brightness is reduced about twice as much for blend colors in the mid-tone range.
- **Darker Color** compares the channel values of the blend and base colors, resulting in the lower value.
- **Lighten** returns whichever is the lighter color (base or blend). Base pixels that are darker than the blend color are replaced. Base pixels that are lighter than the blend color remain unchanged.
- **Screen** is basically the inverse of Multiply, always returning a lighter color. Screening with black has no effect; screening with white produces white.
- **Color Dodge** brightens the base color. Blend colors lighter than 50% significantly increase brightness. Blending with black has no effect.
- **Linear Dodge (Add)** is similar to Color Dodge, but creates smoother transitions from areas of high brightness to areas of low brightness.
- **Lighter Color** compares channel values of the blend and base colors, resulting in the higher value.
- **Overlay** multiplies or screens the blend color to preserve the original lightness or darkness of the base.
- **Soft Light** darkens or lightens base colors depending on the blend color. Blend colors lighter than 50% lighten the base color (as if dodged). Blend colors darker than 50% darken the base color (as if burned).
- **Hard Light** combines the Multiply and Screen modes. Blend colors darker than 50% are multiplied, and blend colors lighter than 50% are screened.
- **Vivid Light** combines the Color Dodge and Color Burn modes. Blend colors lighter than 50% lighten the base by decreasing contrast. Blend colors darker than 50% darken the base by increasing contrast.
- **Linear Light** combines the Linear Dodge and Linear Burn modes. If the blend color is lighter than 50%, the result is lightened by increasing the base brightness. If the blend color is darker than 50%, the result is darkened by decreasing the base brightness.
- **Pin Light** preserves the brightest and darkest areas of the blend color. Blend colors in the mid-tone range have little (if any) effect.
- **Hard Mix** pushes all pixels in the resulting blend to either all or nothing. The base and blend values of each pixel in each channel are added together (e.g., R 45 [blend] + R 230 [base] = R 275). Pixels with totals over 255 are shown at 255; pixels with a total lower than 255 are dropped to 0.
- **Difference** inverts base color values according to the brightness value in the blend layer. Lower brightness values in the blend layer have less of an effect on the result. Blending with black has no effect.
- **Exclusion** is very similar to Difference, except that mid-tone values in the base color are completely desaturated.
- **Subtract** removes the blend color from the base color.
- **Divide** looks at the color information in each channel and divides the blend color from the base color.
- **Hue** results in a color with the luminance and saturation of the base color, and the hue of the blend color.
- **Saturation** results in a color with the luminance and hue of the base color, and the saturation of the blend color.
- **Color** results in a color with the luminance of the base color, and the hue and saturation of the blend color.
- **Luminosity** results in a color with the hue and saturation of the base color, and the luminance of the blend color (basically, the opposite of the Color mode).

# Finish the Magazine Cover

The final piece required for this job is the nameplate and text treatment, which is created every month from a template in Adobe Illustrator. In this exercise, you will place and position the required file to complete the project.

1. **With magazine.psd open, choose File>Place Linked.**

   You are using the Place Linked option so that any changes in the cover treatment file (a common occurrence in professional design environments) will automatically reflect in your Photoshop file.

2. **Navigate to driver-mag.ai (in your WIP>Cars folder) and click Place.**

3. **Choose Bounding Box in the Crop To menu of the Open as Smart Object dialog box, then click OK.**

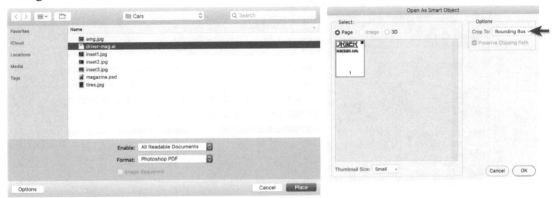

When you place files in Photoshop, either linked or embedded, they are commonly placed at slightly other than 100%. You should always verify — and correct, if necessary — the scaling of the placed content.

4. **In the Options bar, change the W and H values to 100%, then press Return/Enter to finalize the placement.**

5. **In the Layers panel, move the driver-mag layer to the top of the layer stack.**

6. **Using the Properties panel, change the position of the placed content to X: 115 px, Y: 115 px.**

   The value of 115 pixels is the equivalent of 0.375″.

   Alternatively, you could change the file rulers back to inches and then type the actual value in inches in the Properties panel fields. If you use this method, you should know that the Properties panel only displays two decimal values, so after typing the new position, the fields show only "0.38 in". This is a minor flaw in the software, but one that is worth noting.

7. **Save the file and then continue to the final exercise.**

## Sharing Photoshop Files

If you are connected to the Internet, you can use the Share an Image button to easily send a JPEG version of your file through a variety of communication media. If you choose Mail in the menu, for example, the image automatically appears in a new mail message in your email client software. If you choose one of the social media outlets, you can create your post directly through a window in the Photoshop interface; you do not need to interact with a browser or separate application to share an image from Photoshop. Keep in mind that you must have defined accounts in your system preferences for each of the various social media outlets. If an account is not defined, you will be prompted to add one before you can use these options in Photoshop.

# Print a Composite Proof

The last stage of most jobs — after the client has approved the work — is printing a proof. A printed proof is basically the output provider's roadmap of how the final job should look. As more processes move to all-digital workflows, a printed proof is not always required — especially if you're submitting files digitally. But some output providers still require a printed proof, and you might want to print samples of your work at various stages of development.

To output this file at 100%, you need a sheet at least tabloid size (11″ × 17″). If you don't have that option, you can use the Photoshop Print dialog box to fit the job onto letter-size paper. Keep in mind, however, that many of the effects that you created with filters will lose some of their impact when you reduce the file to fit onto a letter-size page.

1. **With magazine.psd open, choose File>Print.**

2. **In the Printer menu of the Print dialog box, choose the printer you're using.**

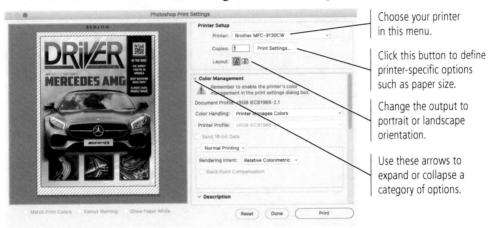

Choose your printer in this menu.

Click this button to define printer-specific options such as paper size.

Change the output to portrait or landscape orientation.

Use these arrows to expand or collapse a category of options.

3. **Choose the Portrait layout option (below the number of copies).**

   Ideally, you should always print proofs at 100%. If this is not possible, however, you can print a sample content proof by scaling the page to fit the available paper size.

4. **Review the options in the scrolling pane below the Printer Setup options.**

   Different types of output jobs require different settings. If you are simply printing a desktop proof, you can leave most of these options at their default values.

   As a general rule, proofs should be printed at 100% of the actual file size. If you are printing a file that is larger than the paper size your printer can handle, you can use the Scaled Print Size options to fit the job on the available paper size. Alternatively, you can use the Print Selected Area option to output different portions of the image onto separate sheets, and then manually assemble the multiple sheets into a single page.

   > *Note:*
   >
   > *If you submit a scaled proof with a print job, make sure you note the scale percentage prominently on the proof.*

5. **Click Print to output the file. If you see a warning about ColorSync matching, click OK to continue the print process.**

6. **When the output process is complete, close the file without saving.**

## Color Management Options

- **Color Handling** determines whether color management is applied by the printer or by Photoshop.
- **Printer Profile** defines the known color characteristics of the output device you are using.
- **Normal Printing** simply prints the file to your printer, using no defined output profile for color management.
  - **Rendering Intent** defines how colors are shifted to fit inside the printer's output capabilities.
  - **Black Point Compression** adjusts for differences in the black point (the darkest possible black area) between the file and the output device.
- **Hard Proofing** simulates the color output properties of another printer, based on the defined profile in the Proof Setup menu.
  - **Simulate Paper Color** applies the absolute colorimetric rendering intent to simulate the appearance of color on the actual paper and output device that will be used (for example, newsprint on a web press).
  - **Simulate Black Ink** simulates the brightness of dark colors as they would appear on the defined output device. If not checked, dark colors are printed as dark as possible on the actual printer you are using.

## Position and Size Options

- **Position** defines the location of the output on the paper. It is centered by default. You can use the Top and Left fields to position the output at a specific distance from the paper corner. You can also click in the preview area and drag to reposition the image on the paper.
- **Scale** defaults to 100%, creating a full-size print. The **Height** and **Width** fields define the size of the image being printed. If you change the Scale field, the Height and Width fields reflect the proportional size. You can also define a specific size in the Height and Width fields; in this case, the Scale field is adjusted accordingly.
- If you check **Scale to Fit Media**, the image is automatically scaled to fit inside the printable area on the selected paper size.
- **Print Resolution** defines the resolution that will be sent to the output device. Remember the principle of effective resolution: if you print a 300-ppi image at 200%, the printer has only 150 ppi with which to work.
- If you check **Print Selected Area**, handles appear in the preview area. You can drag those handles to define the image area that will be output.

## Printing Marks

- **Corner Crop Marks** adds crop marks to show the edges of the image where it should be cut.
- **Center Crop Marks** adds a crop mark at the center of each edge of the image.
- **Registration Marks** adds bulls-eye targets and star targets that are used to align color separations on a printing press. (Calibration bars and star target registration marks require a PostScript printer.)
- **Description** adds description text (from the File>File Info dialog box) outside the trim area in 9-pt Helvetica.
- **Labels** adds the file name above the image.

## Functions

- **Emulsion Down** reverses the image on the output. This option is primarily used for output to a filmsetter or imagesetter.
- **Negative** inverts the color values of the entire output. This option is typically used if you are outputting directly to film, which will then be used to image a photo-sensitive printing plate (a slowly disappearing workflow).
- The **Background** option allows you to add a background color that will print outside the image area.
- The **Border** option adds a black border around an image. You can define a specific width (in points) for the border.
- The **Bleed** option moves crop marks inside the image by a specific measurement.

## PostScript Options

- **Calibration Bars** adds swatches of black in 10% increments (starting at 0% and ending at 100%).
- The **Interpolation** option can help reduce the jagged appearance of low-resolution images by automatically resampling up when you print. This option is only available on PostScript Level 2 or 3 printers.
- The **Include Vector Data** option sends vector information in the output stream for a PostScript printer, so the vector data can be output at the highest possible resolution of the output device.

If your printer is not PostScript compatible, the PostScript options will not be available.

1. _____ sharpens an image by increasing contrast along the edges in an image.

2. _____ refers to the overall image area, like the surface used by traditional painters.

3. The _____ tool is used to draw freeform, vector-based shapes and paths.

4. A _____ is a special type of Photoshop layer that retains vector path information.

5. _____ control the shape of a curve between two anchor points.

6. The _____ option is used to link the angle of styles to the "master" angle for the entire file. Changing it affects any linked style applied to any layer in the entire file.

7. A _____ is a smooth transition from one color to another.

8. The _____ command is used to show only areas of one layer that fall within the area of the underlying layer.

9. In the Liquify filter, the _____ tool can be used to protect specific areas from being liquified.

10. The _____ allows you to experiment with different filters and filter settings, and to compound multiple filters to create unique artistic effects.

1. Briefly explain the difference between vectors and pixels.

2. Briefly describe two different tool modes when using a vector drawing tool.

3. Briefly explain the difference between the Path Selection tool and the Direct Selection tool.

Use what you have learned in this project to complete the following freeform exercise.
Carefully read the art director and client comments, then create your own design to meet the needs of the project.
Use the space below to sketch ideas. When finished, write a brief explanation of the reasoning behind your final design.

## art director comments

Against The Clock is considering a new design for the covers of its *Professional Portfolio* series of books. You have been hired to design a new cover comp for the Photoshop book.

❑ Create a new cover design using the following page specifications:

- Trim: 8″ wide × 10.15″ high
- Bleeds: 0.125″ all four sides
- Margins: 0.25″ top, bottom, and right 0.75″ left

❑ The client's logo, as well as text that must appear on the cover, is included in the **Covers_PS22_PB.zip** archive (in your student resources).

❑ Locate or create compelling artwork to illustrate the concept of the book title.

❑ Design the cover to meet commercial printing requirements.

## client comments

We really like the existing cover design, but after ten editions, we're starting to think a fresh look might be a good thing.

Obviously, the most important element of the cover is the title. Adobe differentiates each software release using the year instead of a version or edition number, so the release year needs to be incorporated somewhere in the cover design.

In the last few versions of the covers, we've used an urban theme — cityscapes, museum buildings, architectural macros, and so on — as a representation of places where graphic designers find jobs. We don't really have any set ideas for new imagery, but there should be some connection between graphic design and the concept you create.

Finally, keep in mind that the design should allow for repurposing for the other titles in the series.

## project justification

Vectors offer an advantage over pixel-based images because they can be freely scaled and edited, without losing quality. This project focused on many different options related to working with vectors in Photoshop — drawing paths, creating shape layers, and editing vector shape properties. You used vectors in this project to create a custom layer mask, as well as vector shapes that you filled with other images and a custom artistic pattern.

This project also introduced some of the creative tools that can turn photos and flat colors into painting-like artwork. You learned to use the Filter Gallery, the Liquify filter, custom gradients, and layer blending modes. You will use these options many times in your career as you complete different types of projects in Photoshop.

Create a compound vector shape layer

Edit corner properties of vector shapes

Apply a style to a vector shape layer

Use a vector mask to remove an image from its background

Use gradients to create a custom background

Liquify pixels to create unique effects

Adjust blending mode and opacity to blend one layer into another

Create clipping masks to isolate specific image areas

Apply filters to images to create artistic effects

# 3 Museum Image Correction

Your client is curator at the local Museum of Art and History. The institution wants to create a printed brochure of photos from a recently acquired collection of antiquities. Your job is to adjust the supplied images as necessary to achieve the best possible result when the final brochure is printed.

This project incorporates the following skills:

❏ Repairing damaged images
❏ Understanding the relationship between tonal range and contrast
❏ Correcting image lighting and exposure problems
❏ Understanding how gray balance affects overall image color
❏ Correcting minor and severe image color problems
❏ Preparing corrected images for printing
❏ Combining exposures into an HDR image

## Videos to Watch

Access these helpful videos in your online student resources:

▶▶ Museum Image Correction Project Introduction

▶▶ Using the Clone Stamp Tool

▶▶ Correcting Tonal Range and Contrast with Levels

## client comments

The Museum of Art and History recently received a large donation from a wealthy patron's estate. We are going to create a printed catalog that will showcase some of the collection's stars, as well as explain the history behind the various pieces.

We've selected seven photos that we want to include in the catalog. We want you to make sure they will look as good as possible when printed.

We have a photo of one of the family's patriarchs, who was responsible for building much of the family's collection. The picture is a bit grainy and has some damage, though, and we'd like you to clean it up as much as possible.

Finally, we also want to include a picture of the new museum on the back of the catalog. We are proud of the new space, and would like the photo to also be a work of art.

 **Watch the video** Museum Image Correction Project Introduction **in your online student resources.**

1 - JR Touch up / Fix Damage
2 - Silver - brighten, increase contrast
3 - Amethyst - improve contrast
4 - Bronze - correct underexposure
5 - Jade - remove yellow cast
6 - Gold - remove red cast, bump contrast
7 - Diamonds - fix overall contrast
8 - Faience - check for shift
9 - MOAH - combine exposures / HDR

## art director comments

Digital images come from a wide variety of sources — scanned photographs and digital cameras are the two most common — as is the case with the client's images for this project. Some images can be used as is, or with only minor corrections.

Unfortunately, not every project involves a professional photographer. Consumer-level digital cameras and smartphones are common sources of photography that is submitted for professional design work. This means many images require a bit of help — and some require a lot.

Even when a professional photographer is involved, not every image comes from a perfectly lit studio. Location shots — where a subject is photographed in a "real-world" setting — can't always be captured perfectly. Those images usually need work, as well. Fortunately, Photoshop provides a powerful toolset for solving most image problems, or at least improving the worst of them.

## project objectives

To complete this project, you will:

❏ Remove grain with blur and sharpen techniques

❏ Heal severe scratches

❏ Clone out major damage

❏ Correct minor problems with the Brightness/Contrast adjustment

❏ Correct tonal range with the Levels adjustment

❏ Correct lighting problems with the Exposure adjustment

❏ Correct overall color problems with the Color Balance adjustment

❏ Correct precise color values with the Curves adjustment

❏ Correct an RGB image to CMYK gamut limits

❏ Embed color profile information in a file

❏ Combine multiple exposures with the Merge to HDR Pro utility

# STAGE 1 / Retouching Damaged Images

**Image repair** is the process of fixing damaged images, while **retouching** is the technique of changing an image by adding something that wasn't there or removing something that was there. Damage can come from a wide range of sources: creases, scratches, water spots, and tape marks, to name just a few. Other image problems such as photographic grain are a natural part of photographs (especially older ones), and dust is common (if not inevitable) whenever photographs are scanned.

There are many different ways to approach image repairs. As you complete the exercises in this stage of the project, you will use several tools to clean up damage in a portrait from the 1940s.

##  Remove Grain with Blur and Sharpen Techniques

Photographic film is made up of microscopic grains of light-sensitive material. These grains capture the image information, which is eventually processed into a print or transparency. While not usually apparent in a standard photographic print, the grain in a photograph can become pronounced when scanned with a high-resolution scanner. Enlarging an image during scanning further enhances any grain that already exists.

When grain is evident in a digital image, it can destroy fine detail and create a mottled appearance in areas of solid color or subtle tone variation.

Blurring and Sharpening techniques are the best methods for removing photographic grain. The techniques you use in this exercise work for any image with grain. Older images — such as the one your client wants to use — almost always have obvious grain problems that can be fixed to some degree, but there are limits to how much can be corrected. The techniques you learn in this project produce very good results if you need to remove grain from modern scanned images.

*Note:*

*Slower-rated film typically has the smallest and least-evident grain, while faster film can produce significant graininess.*

1. **Expand the MOAH_PS22_RF.zip archive in your WIP folder (Macintosh) or copy the archive contents into your WIP folder (Windows).**

   This results in a folder named **MOAH**, which contains the files you need for this project. You should also use this folder to save the files you create in this project.

2. **Open the file rossi.jpg from your WIP>MOAH folder.**

The corner has been torn off.

Water damage is evident in the background.

Scratches cut into the man's jacket.

The image has been creased in storage.

**3. Choose View>100% to show the image at the actual size.**

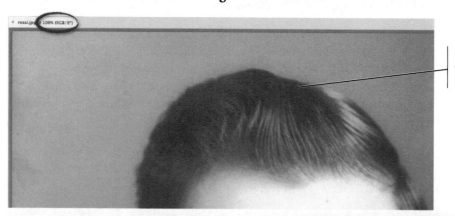

Grain is more obvious when you view the image at 100%.

## Understanding the Noise Filters

**Noise** is defined as random pixels that stand out from the surrounding pixels, either hurting the overall appearance of the image (as in the case of visible grains in an old photograph) or helping to prevent printing problems (as in the case of a gradient that extends across a large area). Photoshop includes several filters (Filters>Noise) that can add or remove noise.

The **Add Noise** filter applies random pixels to the image. Uniform distributes color values of noise between 0 and the defined amount. Gaussian distributes color values of noise along a bell-shaped curve. Monochromatic adds random pixels without affecting the colors in the image.

The **Despeckle** filter detects the edges in an image and blurs everything except those edges.

The **Reduce Noise** filter provides far greater control over different aspects of noise correction. In Basic mode, you can remove luminance noise and color noise in the composite image. **Luminance noise**, also called grayscale noise, makes an image appear grainy. **Color noise** usually appears as color artifacts in the image.

In Advanced mode, you can remove noise from individual color channels.

The **Dust & Scratches** filter reduces noise by comparing the contrast of pixels within the defined radius. Pixels outside the defined threshold are adjusted.

The **Median** filter reduces noise by blending the brightness of pixels within a selection. The filter compares the brightness of pixels within the defined radius, and replaces those that differ too much from the surrounding pixels with the median brightness value of the compared pixels.

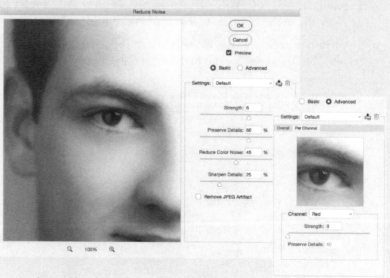

- **Strength** controls the amount of luminance noise reduction.

- **Preserve Details** controls how carefully the filter compares the difference in luminance between adjacent pixels. Lower values remove more noise, but result in less detail.

- **Reduce Color Noise** removes random color pixels from the image.

- **Sharpen Details** sharpens the image. Because the noise reduction process inherently blurs the image, this option applies the same kind of sharpening that is available in the Photoshop Sharpen filters.

- **Remove JPEG Artifact** removes artifacts and halos caused by saving an image with a low JPEG quality setting (in other words, using a high lossy compression scheme).

4. **Choose Filter>Blur>Gaussian Blur.**

5. **In the image behind the dialog box, click the area between the man's right eye and eyebrow.**

    When many filter dialog boxes are open, clicking the image (behind the dialog box) changes the visible preview area in the dialog box. You can also click inside the dialog box preview area and drag to change the visible preview area.

6. **Make sure Preview is checked in the dialog box and change the Radius field to 2.0 pixels.**

    The **Radius** field defines (in pixels) the amount of blurring that will be applied. Photoshop uses this value to average the brightness of a pixel with that of surrounding pixels. A small radius value can soften an image and remove most photographic grain.

*Note:*

*All Photoshop blur filters work in essentially the same way: they average the brightness values of contiguous pixels to soften the image.*

Click the image to change the visible preview area in the dialog box.

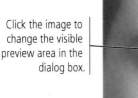 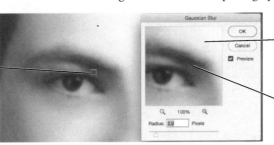

A small amount of Gaussian blur removes most of the photographic grain.

Areas of fine detail are also slightly blurred by the Gaussian Blur filter.

7. **Click OK to apply the Gaussian Blur to the image.**

    To remove the photographic grain, you had to blur the entire image. This means that areas of fine detail were also blurred. You can use a second technique — sharpening — to restore some of the lost edge detail.

## Understanding the Blur Filters

The Filter>Blur menu includes a number of choices for applying corrective or artistic blurs to an image or selection.

**Average** finds the average color of an image or selection, and then fills the image or selection with that color to create a smooth appearance.

**Blur** and **Blur More** smooth transitions by averaging the pixels next to the hard edges of defined lines and shaded areas. When you apply these filters, you have no additional control: Blur is roughly equivalent to a 0.3-pixel radius blur, and Blur More uses approximately a 0.7-pixel radius.

**Box Blur** averages the color value of neighboring pixels. You can adjust the size of the area used to calculate the average value. A larger radius value results in more blurring.

**Gaussian Blur** blurs the selection by a specific amount.

**Lens Blur** adds blur to an image to create the effect of a narrower depth of field, so some objects in the image remain in focus, while others areas are blurred.

**Motion Blur** includes an option for changing the blur angle, as well as a Distance value, or the number of pixels to blur.

**Radial Blur** either spins the pixel around the center point of the image, or zooms the pixel around the center point based on the Amount setting. The farther a pixel is from the center point, the more the pixel is blurred. You can drag in the Blur Center window to move the center point of the blur.

**Shape Blur** uses a specific shape, or **kernel**, to create the blur. Radius determines the size of the kernel — the larger the kernel, the greater the blur.

**Smart Blur** blurs tones closely related in value without affecting edge quality. Threshold determines how closely pixels must be related in tone before being blurred. You can also specify a Quality level and change the Mode setting. Using Edge Only mode, edges are outlined in white and the image is forced to black. Using Overlay Edges mode, the color image is blurred and edges are outlined in white.

**Surface Blur** blurs an image, while trying to preserve edges. The Radius option specifies the size of the blur in whole numbers. Threshold controls how much the tonal values of neighboring pixels must differ before being blurred.

8. **Choose Filter>Sharpen>Smart Sharpen.**

The Smart Sharpen filter allows you to sharpen an image based on a specific amount and radius. You can also limit the sharpening that occurs in shadow and highlight areas.

9. **If you don't see the entire dialog box, click the arrow to the left of Shadows/Highlights to show all the available options.**

10. **Make the man's right eye visible in the dialog box preview area.**

11. **Define the following settings in the dialog box:**

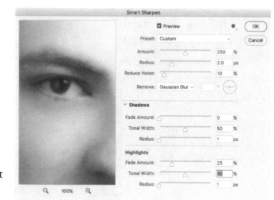

- **Set the Amount to 250%.**

  **Amount** defines how much sharpening to apply. A higher amount increases contrast between edge pixels, giving the appearance of greater sharpness. Be careful — if this is set too high, it can result in halos at apparent edges.

- **Set the Radius to 2.0 px.**

  **Radius** defines the number of pixels around edge pixels that will be affected by the sharpening. Higher radius values result in more obvious sharpening.

- **Set the Reduce Noise slider to 10%.**

  **Reduce Noise** helps to avoid sharpening any noise that still exists in the image.

- **Choose Gaussian Blur in the Remove menu.**

  The **Remove** menu defines the type of blur you want to remove. Because you applied a Gaussian blur to remove the heavy noise, you are now using the Smart Sharpen filter to remove that blur and restore image detail.

  Lens Blur detects edges and detail, and provides finer sharpening of detail and reduced halos. Motion Blur attempts to reduce the effects of blur caused by camera movement. You can also define a specific angle of the blur to remove.

- **In the Highlights section, set the Fade Amount to 25%.**

  In the Shadows and Highlights sections, you can adjust sharpening that will be applied in those areas of the image.

  - **Fade Amount** adjusts the amount of sharpening. By reducing the sharpening in the highlights of this image, you help to further remove the noise that remains in the lighter portions (the faces and background).

  - **Tonal Width** controls the range of tones that will be modified. Smaller values restrict the adjustments to darker regions for shadows, and lighter regions for highlights.

  - **Radius** defines the size of the area around each pixel used to determine whether a pixel is in the shadows or highlights.

12. **Click OK to sharpen the image.**

13. **Choose File>Save As. Save the file as a native Photoshop file named rossi.psd in your WIP>MOAH folder. Continue to the next exercise.**

Remember, you have to choose File>Save As to save the file with a different name or format.

*Note:*

*If a setting is not mentioned here, leave it at the default value.*

# Understanding the Shake Reduction Filter

As the name suggests, the Shake Reduction filter (Filter> Sharpen>Shake Reduction) was designed to reduce blur caused by a shaking camera — for example, images photographed with a slow shutter speed or without a flash.

This filter was not designed to remove blur caused by a moving subject. It also does not work well on images with specular highlights or noise. It works best to reduce shake in specific areas, not over an entire image.

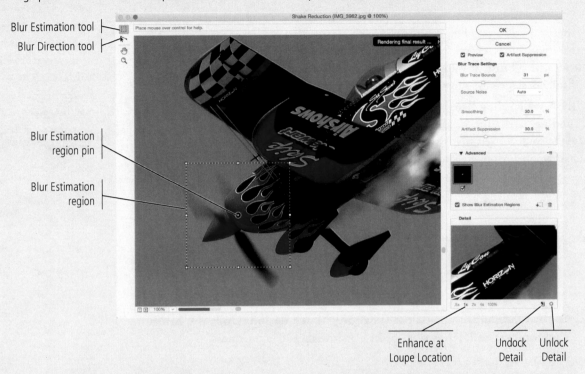

Blur Estimation tool
Blur Direction tool

Blur Estimation region pin

Blur Estimation region

Enhance at Loupe Location

Undock Detail

Unlock Detail

When you first open the filter, the image is automatically analyzed. The software determines a "region of interest," and calculates the shape and direction of the blur.

If necessary, you can adjust the automatically defined settings on the right side of the dialog box:

- **Blur Trace Bounds** is the extent of blur size introduced by the camera shake.
- **Source Noise** defines the noise level of the Source image: Auto, Low, Medium, or High.
- **Smoothing** reduces high-frequency sharpening noise.
- **Artifact Suppression** reduces larger artifacts that might be enhanced by sharpening.

You can use the Blur Estimation tool to add more than one blur estimation region to the image, or use the Blur Direction tool to specify the direction and length of a straight blur.

When Advanced options are expanded, the small icons show previews of the blur shape that was defined for each region.

You can select a specific region to make it active in the larger preview pane. Click the handles on the marquee to resize it, and click the pin in the center of a region to move it.

## Using the Detail Loupe

You can use the Detail loupe (pane) to analyze specific areas of the image. You can enlarge the detail preview using the options at the bottom of the pane: .5x, 1x, 2x, or 4x.

To change the preview area, click inside the pane while it is docked. You can also undock the Detail pane and drag it over the image to enhance a specific area.

If you click the Enhance at Loupe Location button, the filter creates a new blur estimation region based on what is visible in the Detail pane.

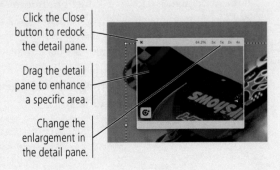

Click the Close button to redock the detail pane.

Drag the detail pane to enhance a specific area.

Change the enlargement in the detail pane.

# Heal Random Color Spots

The blur and sharpen routine from the previous exercise improved the client's image — the obvious grain is gone. Even though the edges are slightly less sharp than the original scan, they are sharp enough to produce good results when the image is printed. If you're working with images that aren't 70 years old, you will be able to produce far sharper edges using these same techniques.

There are still a number of problems in the image that require intervention. Photoshop includes several tools for changing the pixels in an image — from painting with a brush or nudging selections on a layer, to using repair tools specifically designed to adjust pixels based on the others in the image.

The **Spot Healing Brush tool** allows you to remove imperfections by blending surrounding pixels. The **Healing Brush tool** has a similar function, except you can define the source pixels that will be used to heal an area. The **Patch tool** allows you to repair an area with pixels from another area by dragging the selection area.

**Note:**

*Whenever you need to clean up blemishes on images and make other adjustments that require looking at very small areas, it can be very helpful to clean your monitor so you don't mistake on-screen dust or smudges for flaws in the images.*

1. **With rossi.psd open, set up the document window so you can see the man's forehead.**

2. **Select the Spot Healing Brush tool in the Tools panel.**

3. **In the Options bar, choose the Proximity Match option. Open the Brush Preset picker and define a 20-pixel brush with 100% hardness.**

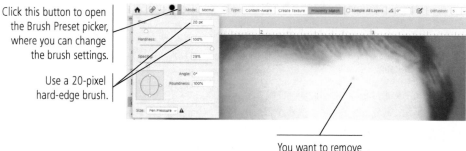

Click this button to open the Brush Preset picker, where you can change the brush settings.

Use a 20-pixel hard-edge brush.

You want to remove this blemish.

**Note:**

*You will work extensively with brushes and brush settings in Project 7: House Painting.*

The **Proximity Match** method uses the pixels around the edge of the selection to find an image area to use as a patch for the selected area. The **Create Texture** method uses all the pixels in the selection to create a texture for repairing the area. **Content Aware** mode attempts to match the detail in surrounding areas, while healing pixels (this method does not work well for areas with hard edges or sharp contrast). If you select **Sample All Layers**, the tool pulls pixel data from all visible layers.

4. **Place the cursor over the orange spot on the man's forehead. Click immediately over the spot to heal it.**

The Spot Healing Brush tool shows the size of the selected brush.

5. **Make the man's chin visible in the document window, then choose the Healing Brush tool (nested under the Spot Healing Brush tool).**

It might help to zoom in when you want to heal small areas such as this white spot on the man's chin. We are working at 200% in the following screen shots.

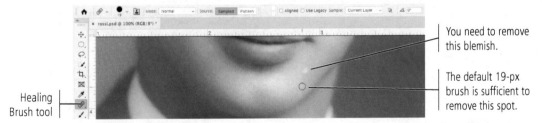

You need to remove this blemish.

The default 19-px brush is sufficient to remove this spot.

Healing Brush tool

For the Healing Brush tool, you can define brush settings just as you did for the Spot Healing Brush tool. As the tool cursor shows in the document window, the default 19-px brush size is sufficient to cover the white spot on the man's chin.

The Mode menu determines the blending mode used to heal an area. The default option (Normal) samples the source color and transparency to blend the new pixels smoothly into the area being healed. The Replace mode preserves texture in the healed area when you use a soft-edge brush. Multiple, Screen, Darken, Lighten, Color, and Luminosity modes have the same function as the blending modes for specific layers and brushes.

*Note:*

*You can use the bracket keys to enlarge (]) or reduce ([) the Healing Brush tool brush size.*

6. **Place the cursor directly below the spot you want to heal. Press Option/Alt and click to define the healing source.**

Pressing Option/Alt with the Healing Brush tool changes the cursor icon to a crosshair, which you can click to select the source of the brush (the pixels that will be used to heal the spot where you next click).

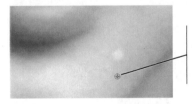

Pressing Option/Alt allows you to define the source pixels that will be used to heal the next spot you click.

7. **Place the cursor over the blemish on the man's chin and click.**

Unlike the Spot Healing Brush tool, the Healing Brush tool allows you to define the source of the healing. By choosing nearby pixels as the healing source, the blemish on the man's chin disappears, and that spot blends nicely into the surrounding pixels.

The Healing Brush tool blends colors from the source pixels (which you defined in Step 6) with colors in the area where you click. You can also change the source from Sampled (the pixels you defined by Option/Alt-clicking) to Pattern, which uses pixels from a defined pattern to heal the area — a good choice for creating artistic effects, rather than healing blemishes in a photo.

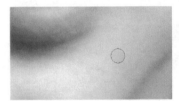 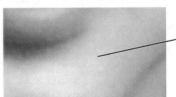

After clicking, the spot is healed using the source pixels.

8. **Save the file and continue to the next exercise.**

When you work with the Healing Brush and Clone Stamp tools, you have the option to align the healing source to the cursor. If the Align option is turned off, the source starting point will be relative to the image; each successive click uses the same source point. If the Align option is turned on, the source starting point will be relative to the cursor.

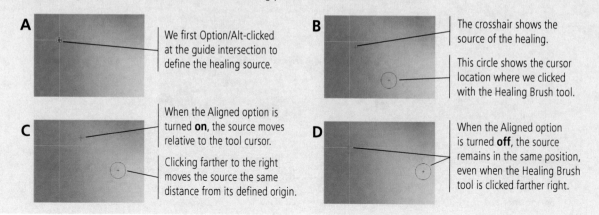

**A** We first Option/Alt-clicked at the guide intersection to define the healing source.

**B** The crosshair shows the source of the healing.

This circle shows the cursor location where we clicked with the Healing Brush tool.

**C** When the Aligned option is turned **on**, the source moves relative to the tool cursor.

Clicking farther to the right moves the source the same distance from its defined origin.

**D** When the Aligned option is turned **off**, the source remains in the same position, even when the Healing Brush tool is clicked farther right.

##  Clone out Major Damage

The client's image has definitely been improved by removing the grain and healing the small blemishes, but several major areas of damage still need to be fixed. In this exercise you will use the Fill dialog box to fix the damage in the image background, and then use the Clone Stamp tool to fix the scratch on the man's shoulder.

*Watch the video* **Using the Clone Stamp Tool in Photoshop** *in your online student resources.*

1. **With the file rossi.psd open, zoom into the top-right of the image (where the corner has been ripped off).**

2. **Using the Rectangular Marquee tool, draw a selection around the torn-off corner.**

3. **With the new marquee active, choose Edit>Fill.**

   In the Fill dialog box, the Contents menu determines what will fill the active selection when you click OK. You can choose any of the following options as the content with which to fill the selection: the active foreground or background color; any Color selected from the Color Picker dialog box when you choose the Color option; white, gray or black; a defined pattern; or a specific state in the History panel. If you use the Content-Aware option, you allow Photoshop to evaluate the image and surrounding pixels to determine what should fill the selection.

   In the case of this image, the backdrop is a slightly mottled gradient. The Content-Aware option is an excellent choice for fixing the torn-off corner.

4. **Choose Content-Aware in the Contents menu, then click OK.**

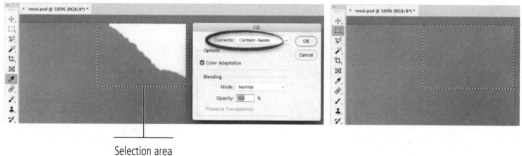

Selection area

**Note:**

*Press Command/
Control-D to turn off a
selection marquee.*

5. **Choose Select>Deselect to turn off the active selection marquee.**

6. **Repeat the process from Steps 2–5 to remove the crease on the right edge
   and the water damage on the left edge of the image.**

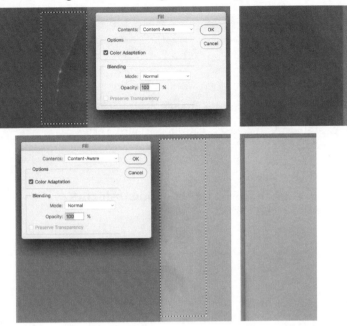

7. **Make the man's shoulder visible in the document window, then choose the
   Clone Stamp tool.**

   Content-Aware Fill works very well on areas of subtle shading, such as the backdrop
   in this image, or other areas where you do not need to maintain fine detail or edges in
   the selected area. If you try to use this option on a sharp edge, however, the Content-
   Aware Fill results are unpredictable. Other tools, such as the Clone Stamp tool, work
   better for retouching distinct edges.

   The Clone Stamp tool paints one part of an image over another, which is useful for
   duplicating objects or removing defects in an image. When you are using the Clone
   Stamp tool, the Options bar combines brush options (brush size, blending mode,
   opacity, and flow) with healing options (alignment and sample source, which you used
   in the previous exercise).

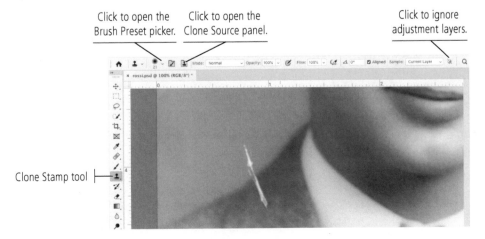

Click to open the Brush Preset picker.    Click to open the Clone Source panel.      Click to ignore adjustment layers.

Clone Stamp tool

8. **Open the Brush Preset picker in the Options bar. Define a 50-pixel brush with 50% hardness.**

   This brush size is large enough to cover the scratch on the man's shoulder.

   When using the Clone Stamp tool, hard-edge brushes can result in harsh lines where you clone pixels. The reduced hardness creates a soft-edged brush, which will help to prevent hard edges in areas where you clone pixels.

*Note:*

*You can use the bracket keys to enlarge (]) or reduce ([) the Clone Stamp brush size.*

9. **In the Options bar, make sure the Aligned option is turned on (checked).**

   As with the Healing Brush tool, you can define the source that will be cloned when you click with the Clone Stamp tool; the difference is that whole pixels are copied, not just their color values.

10. **Place the cursor over the edge you want to reproduce and Option/Alt-click to define the source.**

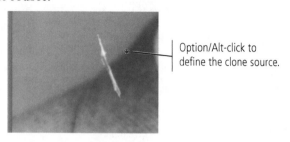

Option/Alt-click to define the clone source.

*Note:*

*When you are cloning, it's usually a good idea to clone in small strokes, or even single clicks. This can help you avoid cloning in patterns or "railroad tracks" that do more damage than good. When cloning large areas, it's also a good idea to frequently resample the clone source to avoid cloning the same pixels into a new, noticeable pattern.*

11. **Place the cursor over the scratched pixels on the man's shoulder.**

   As you move the Clone Stamp tool cursor, the source pixels move along with the tool cursor to give you a preview of what will happen when you click.

12. **Click without dragging when the cloned pixels appear to align properly with the area behind the scratch.**

   Clicking without dragging clones a 50-pixel area. Because the brush we chose has 50% hardness, the center (the edge of the man's shoulder) is clear, but the outside parts of the brush are feathered into the surrounding area.

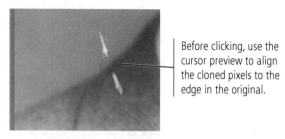

Before clicking, use the cursor preview to align the cloned pixels to the edge in the original.

*Note:*

*If you're not happy with the result of a clone, simply undo the action (Command/Control-Z, or using the History panel) and try again. Cloning — especially edges — often takes more than one try to achieve the desired result.*

13. **Choose the Lasso tool in the Tools panel. Draw a marquee around the scratches in the background, above the man's shoulder.**

   Be careful to avoid the man's shoulder in the selection area.

14. **Choose Edit>Fill. Choose Content-Aware in the Contents menu and click OK.**

    Photoshop evaluates the image and determines what should be created inside the selection area. The fill might take a few seconds to process, so be patient.

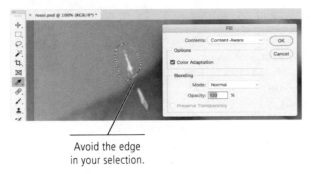

Avoid the edge
in your selection.

15. **Turn off the active selection (Select>Deselect).**

16. **Use the same method from Steps 13–15 to remove the scratches from the man's coat.**

17. **Choose File>Save As. Change the file name to rossi-fixed.psd and save it in your WIP>MOAH folder.**

18. **Close the file and continue to the next stage of the project.**

# The Clone Source Panel in Depth

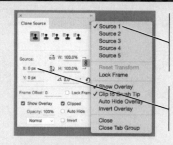

The Clone Source panel (Window>Clone Source) allows you to store up to five sources for the Clone Stamp or Healing Brush tool. These sources can be from any layer of any open image, which allows you to combine pixels from multiple layers or multiple files.

Store and access up to five sources from any layer of any open image.

The Show Overlay options show (at the defined opacity) the source pixels on top of the area where you are cloning. Say you want to clone a parachutist onto a plane photo. You would first define a clone source in the parachutist image and then make the plane image active.

Transform the offset, size, and angle of the clone source.

With the Show Overlay option checked, placing the Clone Stamp cursor over the plane image shows the parachutist on top of the plane image. When you click in the plane image with the Clone Stamp tool, that area of the parachutist image will be cloned into the plane image. The overlay allows you to preview the source areas that will be cloned into the plane image.

If the Auto Hide option is checked, the overlay is only visible when the mouse button is not clicked. The Invert option reverses the overlay into a negative representation of the source image. You can also change the blending mode of the overlay from the default Normal to Darken, Lighten, or Difference.

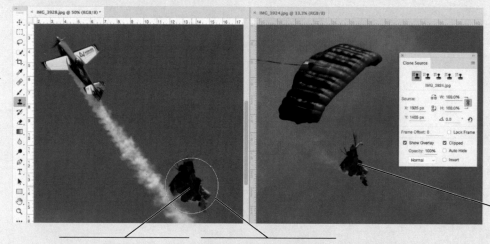

We defined a clone source here.

Using Show Overlay, the Clone Stamp cursor shows the pixels that will be cloned by clicking.

If the Clipped option is checked, the clone source appears only within the tool cursor area.

We turned off the Clipped option and reduced the opacity to 50% to show the entire source file over the image where the cloning is taking place.

# STAGE 2 / **Correcting Lighting Problems**

Before you start correcting problems with lighting and color, you should understand the different parts of an image, as well as the terms used to describe these areas.

- **Highlights** are defined as the lightest areas of the image that include detail. Direct sources of light such as a light bulb or reflected sunlight on water are called **specular highlights**; they should not be considered the highlights of an image.

- **Shadows** are the darkest areas of the image that still contain some detail. Areas of solid black are not considered shadow tones.

- The shades between the highlights and shadows are the **midtones** (or **gamma**) of the image.

Contrast and saturation play an integral role in reproducing high-quality images. **Contrast** refers to the tonal variation in adjacent image pixels, which distinguishes one object from another. An image with a strong detail in the highlight, midtone, and shadow ranges is considered a high-contrast image; an image with good detail in the midtone range but little highlight and shadow detail is called a low-contrast image.

**Saturation** refers to the intensity of a color or its variation away from gray. The saturation of individual colors in an image, and the correct saturation of different colors in relation to one another, affects the overall image contrast. If an image is under- or oversaturated, the contrast suffers.

##  Correct Problems with Brightness/Contrast

Several tools are available for correcting problems related to images that are either too dark or too light. The most basic adjustment option — Brightness/Contrast — can fix images that need overall adjustment to brightness, contrast, or both.

1. **Open the file silver.jpg from your WIP>MOAH folder.**

2. **Choose Image>Adjustments>Brightness/Contrast and make sure the Preview option is checked.**

3. **Drag the Brightness slider to 40.**

   Increasing the overall brightness creates an immediate improvement in this image, although some areas of detail are still muddy.

*Note:*

*Image adjustments can be applied directly to the image pixels, or as non-destructive adjustment layers using the Adjustments panel. In this project, you edit the actual image pixels. You use the adjustment layer method in Project 6: Advertising Samples.*

## 4. Drag the Contrast slider to 20.

Increasing the contrast brings out more detail in the overall object.

## 5. Click OK to apply the change.

## 6. Save the file in your WIP>MOAH folder as a native Photoshop file named silver-fixed.psd.

## 7. Close the file and continue to the next exercise.

## Correct Contrast and Tonal Range with Levels

The **tonal range** of an image is the amount of variation between the lightest highlight and the darkest shadow in a particular image. A grayscale image can contain 256 possible shades of gray. Each channel of a color image can also contain 256 possible shades of gray. To achieve the best contrast in an image, the tonal range of the image should include as many levels of gray as are available.

While the Brightness/Contrast option is a good choice for making basic adjustments, the Levels adjustment is the best approach for enhancing image detail throughout the entire tonal range. Using Levels, adjusting contrast is a three-step process:

- Determine the image's highlight areas (the lightest areas that contain detail).

- Determine the image's shadow areas (the darkest areas that contain detail).

- Adjust the gamma (the contrast in midtones of an image) to determine the proportion of darker tones to lighter tones.

*Watch the video* ***Correcting Tonal Range and Contrast with Levels*** *in your online student resources.*

1. **Open the file amethyst.jpg from the WIP>MOAH folder.**

2. **Display the Histogram panel (Window>Histogram), and then choose Expanded View from the panel Options menu.**

   The Histogram panel shows the distribution of pixels — or, more accurately, the tonal values of those pixels — from the darkest to the lightest portions of an image, for the entire image or for individual color channels. The Histogram panel can help identify problems that need to be corrected.

   When you first display the panel, it probably appears in Compact view, which shows only the graphs for the individual color channels and the composite image. In Expanded view, you can see more information about how pixels are distributed in the image (from shadows on the left to highlights on the right).

   - The **Mean** value is an average point of the brightness values. A Mean of 128 usually identifies a well-balanced image. Images with a Mean of 170 to 255 are light; images with a Mean lower than 90 are very dark.

   *If you see a warning icon, click it to reset the cache.*

   - The **Standard Deviation** (Std Dev) value represents how widely the brightness values vary.

   - The **Median** value shows the middle value in the range of color values.

   - The **Pixels** value displays the total number of pixels used for the graphic displayed on the histogram.

   - The **Level** statistic displays the intensity level of the pixels below the mouse cursor if you click in the Histogram (in the top section of the panel).

   - **Count** shows the number of pixels in the area below the cursor if you click in the Histogram (in the top section of the panel).

   - **Percentile** represents the percentage of pixels to the left of the cursor location if you click in the Histogram (in the top section of the panel).

   - The **Cache Level** is determined by the Performance preferences, and is related to the Cache Refresh and Warning icons. The larger your cache, the more you can do before the image and disk cache don't match. On the other hand, a larger cache requires more RAM for the application to run smoothly.

3. **In the Histogram panel, change the Channel menu to RGB.**

The histogram — the chart that shows the distribution of tones — can display a single graph for the entire composite image (all channels combined) or for individual channels. The white space at the left and right sides of the histogram indicate that some of the tones in the available range are not being used in this image.

Empty spaces on the ends of the histogram indicate that some tones are not being used.

4. **If you see a Warning icon (⚠) in the upper-right corner of the Histogram panel, click it to reset the cache.**

Every time you zoom in or out of an image, Photoshop stores the results of the display in a **cache** (a drive location that keeps track of what you're doing). The image you're looking at on the histogram often doesn't match the results on the drive. The Warning icon shows there's a problem; clicking it resets the image and rereads the cache.

**Note:**

*In the Histogram panel, you can use the Channels menu to view the histogram for individual channels.*

5. **Choose Image>Adjustments>Levels and make sure Preview is checked.**

The Levels dialog box shows a histogram like the one shown in the Histogram panel.

Two sets of sliders control input and output levels. Each set has a black slider for adjusting the shadows and a white slider to adjust highlights. The Input Levels slider also has a gray triangle in the center of the slider bar for adjusting gamma or midtones.

Sample in image to set White Point

Sample in image to set Gray Point

Sample in image to set Black Point

The Input sliders in the Levels dialog box correspond to the tonal range of the image. Any pixels that exist to the left of the Input Shadow slider are reproduced as solid black, and have no detail. Any pixels that exist to the right of the Input Highlight slider are reproduced as pure white.

6. **Move the Input Shadow slider to the right until it touches the left edge of the curve.**

**Note:**

*In the Levels dialog box, you can use the Channel menu to access and adjust the levels for a specific color channel.*

**7.** **Move the Input Highlight slider to the left until it touches the right edge of the curve.**

The adjustments in Steps 6 and 7 extend the colors in the image to take advantage of all 256 possible tones.

**Note:**

*You can change input and output levels by moving the sliders, entering actual values in the boxes below the slider sets, or by using the eyedroppers to select the brightest and darkest points in the image.*

**8.** **Move the Input Gamma slider to the left until the middle box below the slider shows approximately 1.10.**

The Input Gamma slider controls the proportion of darker to lighter tones in the midtones of an image. If you increase gamma, you increase the proportion of lighter grays in the image. This effectively increases contrast in lighter shades and lightens the entire image. If you decrease gamma, you extend the tonal range of darker shades. This allows those areas of the image to be reproduced with a larger range of shades, which increases the contrast in darker shades.

Dragging the Input Gamma slider extends the range between the midtone and the highlights, creating greater contrast and showing more detail throughout the image.

To decrease contrast in an image, you can adjust the Output sliders. This method effectively compresses the range of possible tones that can be reproduced, forcing all areas of the image into a smaller tonal range. Areas originally set to 0 are reproduced at the value of the Output Shadow slider. Areas originally set to 255 are output at the value of the Output Highlight slider.

9. **Click OK to close the Levels dialog box.**

10. **Save the file in your WIP>MOAH folder as a native Photoshop file named**
amethyst-fixed.psd.

11. **Close the file and then continue to the next exercise.**

## Identifying Shadows and Highlights

When you move the Shadow and Highlight sliders in the Levels dialog box, you change the **black point** and **white point** of the image — the points at which pixels become black or white. The goal is to find highlight and shadow points that maintain detail. Choosing a point that has no detail causes the area to turn totally white (highlight) or black (shadow), with no detail reproduced. In some images, it can be difficult to visually identify the black and white points. In these cases, you can use the Levels dialog box to help you find those areas.

If you press Option/Alt while dragging the Input Shadow or Input Highlight slider, the image turns entirely white or black (respectively). As you drag, the first pixels that become visible are the darkest shadow and the lightest highlight.

Once you identify the highlight and shadow points in the image, select the White Point eyedropper. Click the highlight, select the Black Point eyedropper, and then click the shadow to define those two areas of the image.

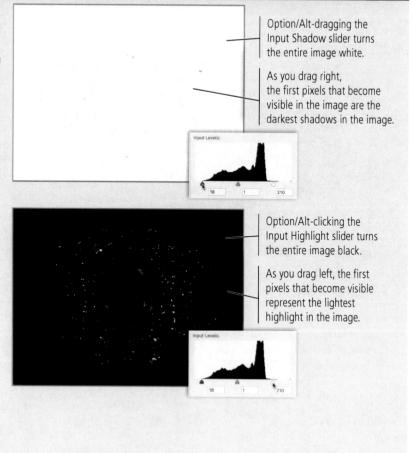

Option/Alt-dragging the Input Shadow slider turns the entire image white.

As you drag right, the first pixels that become visible in the image are the darkest shadows in the image.

Option/Alt-clicking the Input Highlight slider turns the entire image black.

As you drag left, the first pixels that become visible represent the lightest highlight in the image.

## Understanding the Gradient Map Adjustment

The **Gradient Map adjustment** (Image>Adjustments>Gradient Map) enables you to create interesting artistic effects by mapping the tones of an image to the shades in a defined gradient.

In the Gradient Map dialog box, you can apply any defined gradient by clicking the arrow to the right of the gradient sample. You can then choose from the pop-up menu or edit the selected gradient by clicking the sample gradient ramp. The **Dither** option adds random noise to the effect. If you check the **Reverse** option, image highlights map to the left end of the gradient, and image shadows map to the right, effectively reversing the gradient map.

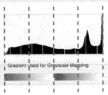

The composite histogram of an RGB image starts at the darkest point and ends at the lightest point with 256 total possible tonal values. If you think of the gradient as having 256 steps from one end to the other, then you can see how the shades of the gradient map to the tones of the original image.

# Correct Lighting Problems with the Exposure Adjustment

Many images are either over- or underexposed when photographed. If an image is underexposed, it appears dark and lacks detail in the shadows. If an image is overexposed, it appears too light and lacks detail in the highlights. You can use the Exposure adjustment to correct exposure, and thus, the overall detail and contrast in the image.

Keep in mind, however, that Photoshop cannot create information that doesn't exist. If you have an underexposed image with no detail in the shadow areas, Photoshop cannot generate that detail for you. Some problems are simply beyond fixing.

The Exposure dialog box is designed to make tonal adjustments to 32- and 64-bit HDR (high dynamic range) images, but it also works with 8- and 16-bit images. The Exposure adjustment works by performing calculations in a linear color space (gamma 1.0), rather than the image's current color space.

*Note:*

*HDR refers to high-dynamic range (32- or 64-bit) images.*

1. **Open bronze.jpg from your WIP>MOAH folder.**

2. **Choose Image>Adjustments>Exposure and make sure Preview is checked.**

**3. Choose the White Point eyedropper in the dialog box, and then click the lightest highlight on the left bead.**

The eyedroppers in the Exposure dialog box adjust the image's luminance (or the degree of lightness, from white to black). By adjusting the luminance only, you can change the lightness of the image without affecting the color.

- Clicking with the Black Point eyedropper shifts the point you click to black (0 luminance).

- Clicking with the White Point eyedropper shifts the point you click to white (100 luminance).

- Clicking with the Gray Point eyedropper shifts the point you click to gray (50 luminance).

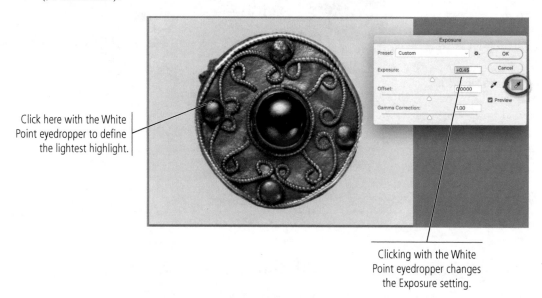

Click here with the White Point eyedropper to define the lightest highlight.

Clicking with the White Point eyedropper changes the Exposure setting.

**4. Drag the Gamma Correction slider left to extend the midtone range, which increases contrast and brings out detail in the image. (We used a setting of 1.15.)**

The Gamma slider adjusts the image midtones. Dragging the slider left lightens the image, improving contrast and detail in the midtones-to-highlight range. Dragging the slider right darkens the image, extending the range and increasing detail in the midtone-to-shadow range.

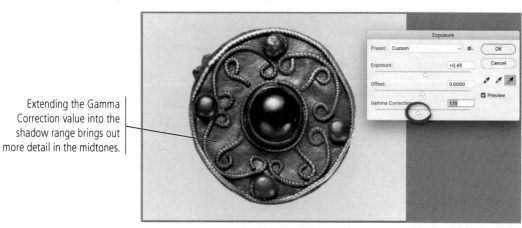

Extending the Gamma Correction value into the shadow range brings out more detail in the midtones.

5. **Click the Offset slider and drag very slightly left to add detail back into the midtones and shadows.**

The Offset slider lightens (when dragged to the right) or darkens (when dragged to the left) the shadows and midtones of the image. The white point (highlight) remains unaffected, but all other pixels are affected.

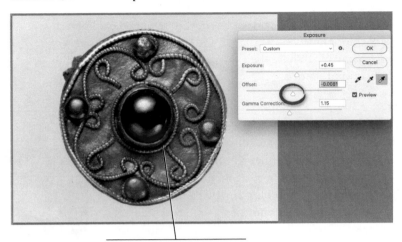

Decreasing the Offset value adds detail back into the shadows.

6. **Click OK to finalize the adjustment.**

7. **Save the file as a native Photoshop file named bronze-fixed.psd in your WIP>MOAH folder.**

 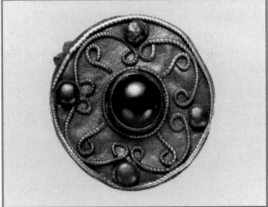

8. **Close the file and continue to the next stage of the project.**

# STAGE 3 / Correcting Color Problems

You can't accurately reproduce color without a basic understanding of color theory, so we present a very basic introduction in this project. Be aware that there are entire, weighty books written about color science. We're providing the condensed version of what you absolutely must know to work effectively with files in any color mode.

Before starting to color-correct an image, you should understand how different colors interact with one another. There are two primary color models — RGB and CMYK — used to output digital images. Other models, such as LAB and HSB, have their own purposes in color conversion and correction, but they are not typically output models.

## Additive vs. Subtractive Color

The most important thing to remember about color theory is that color is light, and light is color. Without light, you can't see — and without light, there is no color.

The **additive color** model (RGB) is based on the idea that all colors can be reproduced by combining pure red, green, and blue light in varying intensities. These three colors are considered the **additive primaries**. Combining any two additive primaries at full strength produces one of the **additive secondaries** — red and blue light combine to produce magenta; red and green combine to produce yellow; and blue and green combine to produce cyan. Although it is considered a color, black is the absence of light, and therefore, also the absence of color.

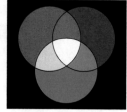

Additive color model

White is the sum of all colors, produced when all three additive primaries are combined at full strength. Additive color theory is practically applied in computer monitors, which are black when turned off; when the power is turned on, light in the monitor illuminates at different intensities to create the range of colors that you see.

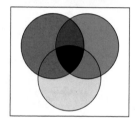

Subtractive color model

Printing pigmented inks on a substrate is a very different method of reproducing color. Reproducing color on paper requires **subtractive color theory**, which is essentially the inverse of additive color theory. Instead of adding red, green, and blue light to create the range of colors, subtractive color begins with a white surface that reflects red, green, and blue light at equal and full strength. To reflect (reproduce) a specific color, you add pigments that subtract or absorb only certain wavelengths from the white light. To reflect only red, for example, the surface must subtract (or absorb) the green and blue light.

Remember that the additive primaries (red, green, and blue) combine to create the additive secondaries (cyan, magenta, and yellow). Those additive secondaries are also called the **subtractive primaries**; because each subtracts one-third of the light spectrum and reflects the other two-thirds:

- Cyan absorbs red light, reflecting only blue and green light.

- Magenta absorbs green light, reflecting only red and blue light.

- Yellow absorbs blue light, reflecting only red and green light.

A combination of two subtractive primaries, then, absorbs two-thirds of the light spectrum and reflects only one-third. As an example, a combination of yellow and magenta absorbs both blue and green light, reflecting only red.

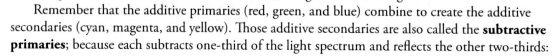

Color printing is a practical application of subtractive color theory. The pigments in the cyan, magenta, yellow, and black (CMYK) inks are combined to absorb different wavelengths of light. By combining different amounts of the subtractive primaries, it's possible to produce a large range (or gamut) of colors.

Although the RGB and CMYK models handle color in different ways, these two color models are definitely linked. RGB colors are directly inverse (opposite) to CMY colors, referring to the position of each color on a color wheel. The relationship between primary colors is the basis for all color correction.

Referencing a basic color wheel can help you understand how RGB colors relate to CMY colors. If you center an equilateral triangle over the color wheel, the points of the triangle touch either the RGB primaries or the CMY primaries. Adding together two points of the triangle results in the color between the two points. Red and blue combine to form magenta, yellow and cyan combine to form green, and so on.

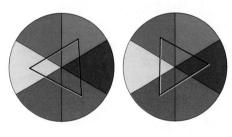

Opposite colors on the color wheel are called **color complements**. Using subtractive color theory, a color's complement absorbs or subtracts that color from visible white light. For example, cyan is opposite red on the color wheel; cyan absorbs red light and reflects green and blue. If you know green and blue light combine to create cyan, you can begin to understand how the two theories are related.

How does all this apply to color correction?

If you want to add a specific color to an image, you have three options: add the color; add equal parts of the color's constituent colors; or remove some of the color's complement color. For example, to add red, you can add red, add yellow and magenta, or remove cyan. Conversely, this means that to remove a color from an image, you can remove the color itself, remove equal parts of its constituents, or add its complement. To remove cyan, for example, you can remove cyan, remove blue and green, or add red.

Make sure you understand the relationships between complementary colors:

- To add red, add yellow and magenta, or remove cyan.
- To add blue, add cyan and magenta, or remove yellow.
- To add green, add cyan and yellow, or remove magenta.
- To remove cyan, remove blue and green, or add red.
- To remove yellow, remove green and red, or add blue.
- To remove magenta, remove blue and red, or add green.

### Understanding Gray Balance

Understanding the concept of neutral gray is also fundamental to effective color correction. Once you correct the contrast (tonal range) of an image, many of the remaining problems can be, at least partially, fixed by correcting the **gray balance**, or the component elements of neutral grays.

In the RGB color model, equal parts of red, green, and blue light combine to create a shade of gray that is equal to the percentage of each component — R=0 G=0 B=0 creates pure black; R=255 G=255 B=255 creates pure white. To correct an image in RGB mode, you should evaluate and correct the neutral grays so that they contain equal percentages of the three primary colors.

Using the CMYK color model, equal percentages of cyan, magenta, and yellow *theoretically* combine to produce an equal shade of gray. For example, C=0 M=0 Y=0 creates white; C=100 M=100 Y=100 creates black. In practice, however, the impurities of ink pigments (specifically cyan) do not live up to this theory. When you print equal parts cyan, magenta, and yellow, the result is a muddy brown because the cyan pigments are impure. To compensate for those impurities, neutral grays must be adjusted to contain equal parts of magenta and yellow, and a slightly higher percentage of cyan.

**Note:**

*Because white is a combination of all colors of light, white paper should (theoretically) reflect equal percentages of all light wavelengths. However, different papers absorb or reflect varying percentages of some wavelengths, thus defining the paper's apparent color. The paper's color affects the appearance of inks printed on it.*

**Note:**

*It might seem easiest to simply add or subtract the color in question. However, a better result might be achieved by adding one color and subtracting another. For example, if an image needs less blue, simply removing cyan can cause reds to appear pink or cyan to appear green. Adding magenta and yellow to better balance the existing cyan often creates a better result.*

**Note:**

*An important point to remember is that any color correction requires compromise. If you add or remove a color to correct a certain area, you also affect other areas of the image.*

# Understanding Color Terms

Many vague and technical-sounding terms are mentioned when discussing color. Is hue the same as color? The same as value? As tone? What's the difference between lightness and brightness? What is chroma? And where does saturation fit in?

This problem has resulted in several attempts to normalize color communication. A number of systems have been developed to define color according to specific criteria, including Hue, Saturation, and Brightness (HSB); Hue, Saturation, and Lightness (HSL); Hue, Saturation, and Value (HSV); and Lightness, Chroma, and Hue (LCH). Each of these models or systems plots color on a three-dimensional diagram, based on the elements of human color perception — hue, intensity, and brightness.

**Hue** is what most people think of as color — red, green, purple, and so on. Hue is defined according to a color's position on a color wheel, beginning from red (0°) and traveling counterclockwise.

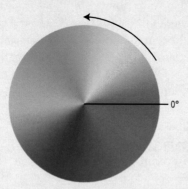

**Saturation** (also called "intensity") refers to the color's difference from neutral gray. Highly saturated colors are more vivid than those with low saturation. Saturation is plotted from the center of the color wheel. Color at the center is neutral gray and has a saturation value of 0; color at the edge of the wheel is the most intense value of that hue and has a saturation value of 100.

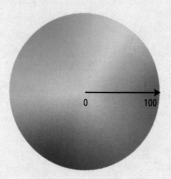

If you bisect the color wheel with a straight line, the line creates a saturation axis for two complementary colors. A color is dulled by the introduction of its complement. Red, for example, is neutralized by the addition of cyan (blue and green). Near the center of the axis, the result is neutral gray.

**Chroma** is similar to saturation, but chroma factors in a reference white. In any viewing situation, colors appear less vivid as the light source dims. The process of chromatic adaptation, however, allows the human eye to adjust to changes in light, and still differentiate colors according to the relative saturation.

**Brightness** is the amount of light reflected off an object. As an element of color reproduction, brightness is typically judged by comparing the color to the lightest nearby object (such as an unprinted area of white paper).

**Lightness** is the amount of white or black added to the pure color. Lightness (also called "luminance" or "value") is the relative brightness based purely on the black-white value of a color. A lightness value of 0 means there is no addition of white or black. Lightness of +100 is pure white; lightness of −100 is pure black.

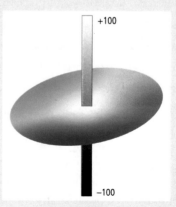

All hues are affected equally by changes in lightness.

Correct Color Cast with the Color Balance Adjustment

**Color cast** is the result of improper gray balance, when one channel is significantly stronger or weaker than the others. An image with improper gray balance has an overall predominance of one color, which is most visible in the highlight areas. The image that you will correct in this exercise has a strong yellow cast that needs to be removed.

1. **Open the file jade.jpg from your WIP>MOAH folder.**

2. **Display the Info panel (Window>Info).**

3. **If you don't see both RGB and CMYK color modes in the Info panel, choose Panel Options in the Info panel Options menu. In the resulting dialog box, choose Actual Color for the First Color Readout and CMYK Color for the Second Color Readout, then click OK.**

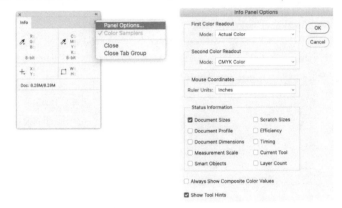

**Note:**

*This exercise relies purely on numbers to correct gray balance. To see an accurate preview of image color on screen, you should calibrate your monitor and create a monitor profile that you can load into Photoshop.*

4. **Choose the Color Sampler tool (nested under the Eyedropper tool).**

5. **In the Options bar, choose 3 by 3 Average in the Sample Size menu.**

   Instead of correcting based on individual pixel values, you can average a group of contiguous pixels as the sample value. Doing so prevents accidentally correcting an image based on a single anomalous pixel (a dust spot, for example).

**Note:**

*The Color Sampler tool can place up to ten sample points per image.*

**Note:**

*To delete an existing sample point, make the Color Sampler tool active, press Option/Alt, and click a point when the cursor icon changes to a pair of scissors.*

6. **Click the cursor in the top-right corner of the image, away from the brooch.**

   As you can see in the Info panel, the sample shows a significantly lower percentage of blue, which leads to a strong yellow color cast.

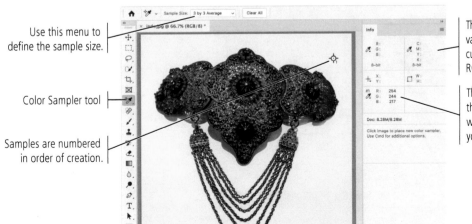

Use this menu to define the sample size.

Color Sampler tool

Samples are numbered in order of creation.

The Info panel shows color values for the current cursor location, in both RGB and CMYK modes.

The Info panel shows the values associated with the sample point you created.

7. **Choose Image>Adjustments>Color Balance.**

Color Balance is a basic correction tool that can effectively remove overall color cast. The Color Balance dialog box presents a separate slider for each pair of complementary colors. You can adjust the highlights, shadows, or midtones of an image by selecting the appropriate radio button. The Preserve Luminosity check box ensures that only the colors shift, leaving the tonal balance of the image unchanged.

8. **Click the Highlights radio button in the Tone Balance section at the bottom of the Color Balance dialog box.**

The background of this image, which should be a neutral shade, is much lighter than the subject of the photo. By adjusting only the highlights, you can remove the color cast in the background without significantly affecting the photo subject.

9. **Drag the Yellow/Blue slider right until the right field shows +40.**

Remember, adding a color's complement is one method for neutralizing that color. Increasing blue in the highlight areas neutralizes the yellow color cast. You might notice, however, that there is now a slight red cast — an issue confirmed by the sample numbers in the Info panel.

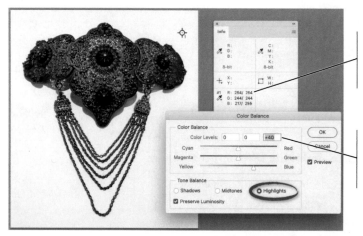

The values after the slash (/) show the result of the changes. These will become the actual sample values if you click OK.

These fields correspond to the three color sliders. The right field shows the Yellow/Blue adjustment.

10. **Drag the Magenta/Green slider right until the center field shows +10.**

Increasing the green value in the highlights brings the three sample values much closer together, resulting in a more neutral background.

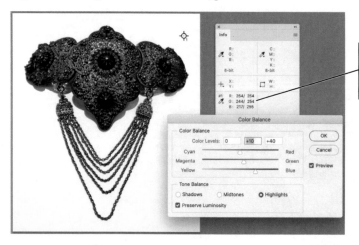

The three values after the slash are very close to equal, which means the yellow cast has been removed from the sample.

**11.** Click OK to apply the adjustment.

**12.** Save the file in your WIP>MOAH folder as a native Photoshop file named
jade-fixed.psd.

**13.** Close the file and continue to the next exercise.

 # Correct Gray Balance with Curves

The Curves adjustment is the most powerful color-correction tool in Photoshop.
If you understand the ideas behind curves, you can use this tool to remove color cast,
enhance overall contrast, and even modify color values in individual channels.

The diagram in the Curves dialog box is the heart of the Curves adjustment.
When you open the Curves dialog box, a straight diagonal line in the graph
represents the existing color in the image.

The horizontal axis represents the input color value, and the vertical axis
represents the output color value. The upper-right point is the maximum value for
that color mode (255 for RGB images and 100 for CMYK images). The bottom-left
corner of the curves grid is the zero point.

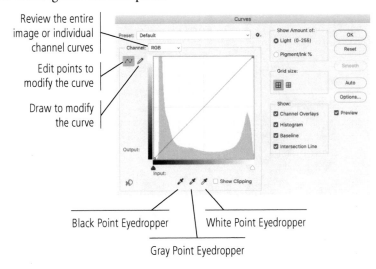

Review the entire image or individual channel curves

Edit points to modify the curve

Draw to modify the curve

Black Point Eyedropper

Gray Point Eyedropper

White Point Eyedropper

The color mode of the image determines the direction of the input and output scales. In both CMYK and RGB, 0 means "none of that color." However, remember the difference between the two color modes:

- The additive RGB color model starts at black and adds values of each channel to produce different colors, so 0, 0, 0 in RGB equals black.

- The subtractive CMYK model starts with white (paper) and adds percentages of each ink (channel) to produce different colors, so 0, 0, 0, 0 in CMYK equals white.

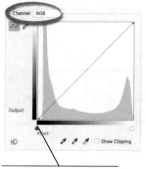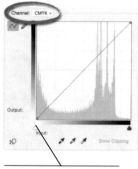

In RGB, the zero point represents the black point, or image shadows.

In CMYK images, the zero point represents the white point, or image highlights.

Every curve is automatically anchored by a black point and a white point. (For RGB, the black point is at the bottom left and the white point is at the top right.) You can add points along the curve by simply clicking the curve. You can also move any point on the curve by clicking and dragging.

When you move points on the curve of an image (whether for the whole image or for an individual channel), you are telling Photoshop to, "Map every pixel that was [this] input value to [that] output value." In other words, using the image at right as an example, a pixel that was 137 (the input value) will now be 115 (the output value). Because curves are just that — curves, and not individual points — adjusting one point on a curve changes the shape of the curve as necessary.

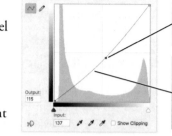

This point changes the input value of 137 to an output value of 115.

On either side of the adjusted point, the curve is adjusted to smoothly meet the other points on the curve (in this case, the black and white points).

## Adjusting Curves On-Screen

The On-Image Adjustment tool in the Curves dialog box allows you to make curve adjustments by interacting directly with the image (behind the dialog box).

When the On-Image Adjustment tool is active, clicking in the image places a point on the curve based on the pixel data where you clicked. You can then drag up or down within the image area to move that point of the curve (i.e., change the output value of the selected input value).

You can add 14 points on a curve, and delete points by pressing Command/Control-delete.

The open circle shows the curve point related to the cursor.

On-Image Adjustment tool cursor

The On-Image Adjustment tool is active.

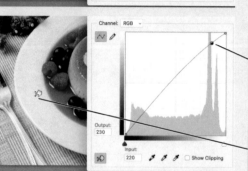

Clicking with the On-Image Adjustment tool adds a point at the appropriate spot on the curve.

Drag up or down in the image to adjust the curve at the added point.

1. **Open the file gold.jpg from the WIP>MOAH folder.**

2. **Using the Color Sampler tool, place a sample point in the empty area outside the brooch.**

   Recognizable "neutral" areas — such as the surrounding area in this image — are the best places to look for global color problems; fixing these will also fix many problem areas that you might not immediately recognize.

   This image has a strong red cast that needs to be neutralized. You can correct cast by removing the cast color or adjusting the other two primaries. The goal is equal (or nearly equal) parts of red, green, and blue in the neutral areas.

   In the Info panel, our sample values show that the red channel has a value of 185, the green channel has a value of 166, and the blue channel has a value of 168. To fix the cast in this image, you will use the middle of these values (the blue channel) as the target and adjust the other two curves.

The sample shows a
strong red cast in what
should be a neutral area.

3. **Choose Image>Adjustments>Curves and make sure the Preview option is checked in the Curves dialog box.**

4. **Choose Red in the Channel menu to display the curve for only the Red channel, and then click the line on the graph to place a point near the three-quarter grid intersection.**

   After you adjust a curve (including adding the point, as you did in this step) the Info panel shows two values for the placed color sample. Numbers before the slash are the original values. Numbers after the slash are the values that result from changes in the Curves dialog box.

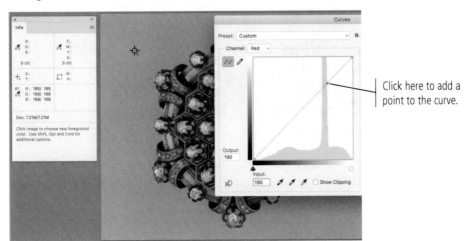

Click here to add a
point to the curve.

5. **With the new point selected on the curve, type the original Red value in the Input field (ours is 185).**

6. **Type the target value in the Output field (ours is the Blue value of 168).**

   In the Info panel, the number after the slash shows that the Red value for this sample will be equal to the Blue value when you click OK.

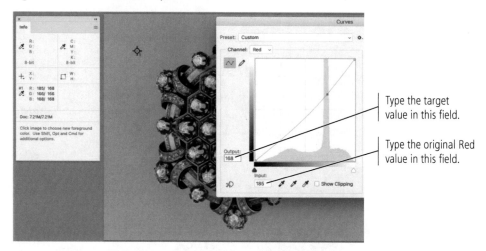

Type the target value in this field.

Type the original Red value in this field.

7. **In the Channel menu, choose the other channel that you need to adjust based on your sample values (ours is Green). Add a point to the curve, and then adjust the input value to match your target output value (the original Blue value, in our example).**

   Using our sample point, we adjusted the Input value of 166 to an Output value of 168.

   You can add the point anywhere along the curve. When you change the Input and Output values, the point automatically moves to that location along the curve.

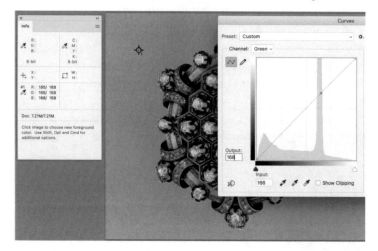

8. **Click OK to apply the changes and close the Curves dialog box.**

You can see how simply correcting gray balance has a significant impact on the image:

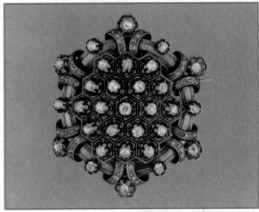

9. **Save the file in your WIP>MOAH folder as a native Photoshop file named** gold-fixed.psd.

10. **Close the file and continue to the next exercise.**

 ## Correct Contrast with Curves

Remember, contrast is essentially the difference between the values in an image. By adjusting the points on the curve, you increase the tonal range between those points — which means you also increase the contrast in that same range.

In the following image, Point A has an Input value of 167 and an Output value of 182. Point B has an Input value of 87 and an Output value of 62. Mathematically:

- Original tonal range (Input values): 167 to 87 = 80 available tones

- New tonal range (Output values): 182 to 62 = 120 available tones

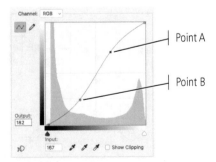

Making these two curve adjustments significantly increases the tonal range available for the image's midtones, which means the contrast in the midtones is also significantly increased. A steeper curve indicates increased tonal range and increased contrast. Notice, however, that the curves before Point B and after Point A are much shallower than the original curves, which means this change also significantly reduces the contrast in the shadow and highlight areas.

## Things to Remember about Curves

Curves are very powerful tools, and they can be intimidating. To simplify the process and make it less daunting, keep these points in mind:

- Aim for neutral grays.

- You can adjust the curve for an entire image, or you can adjust the individual curves for each channel of the image.

- The horizontal tone scale shows the Input value, and the vertical tone scale shows the Output value.

- Changes made to one area of a curve affect all other areas of the image.

- The steeper the curve, the greater the contrast.

- Increasing contrast in one area inherently decreases contrast in other areas.

## Understanding Curve Display Options

Options on the right side of the dialog box allow you to control what is visible in the graph.

The Show Amount Of radio buttons reverse the input and output tone scales. Light is the default setting for RGB images; Pigment/Ink % is the default setting for CMYK images.

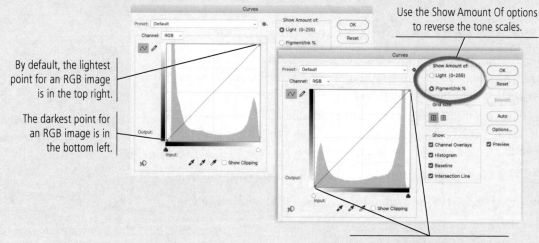

By default, the lightest point for an RGB image is in the top right.

The darkest point for an RGB image is in the bottom left.

Use the Show Amount Of options to reverse the tone scales.

For a CMYK image, the lightest point moves to the bottom left and the darkest point moves to the top right.

The Show options determine what is visible in the actual graph:

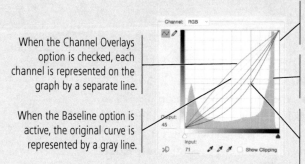

When the Channel Overlays option is checked, each channel is represented on the graph by a separate line.

When the Baseline option is active, the original curve is represented by a gray line.

Use the Grid Size options to show the grid in quartertone or 10% increments.

When the Histogram option is active, the image's tonal range is represented behind the graph.

When the Intersection Line option is active, crosshairs appear when you drag a point in the graph, which can help you more precisely adjust curve points.

1. Open the file **diamonds.jpg** from the **WIP>MOAH folder**.

2. Choose **Image>Adjustments>Curves** and make sure Preview is checked.

The empty areas on the left and right sides of the histogram indicate that this image is not using the entire available tonal range. Before addressing contrast, you should correct the tonal range problem.

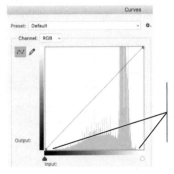

The empty area to the right of the histogram shows that the image does not use the entire available tonal range.

3. Activate the **Show Clipping** option. Click the black-point slider on the bottom-left end of the graph, and drag right until some pixels start to appear in the image (behind the dialog box).

We dragged the Input Black point just past the point where the histogram shows the darkest shadows in the image. (You performed this same action in the Levels dialog box when you adjusted the Input Shadow slider.) The Input and Output fields show that any pixels with an Input value of 26 will be output as 0. In other words, anything with an Input value lower than 26 will be clipped to solid black.

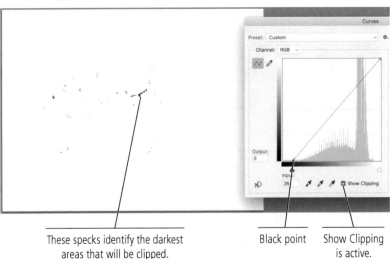

These specks identify the darkest areas that will be clipped.

Black point

Show Clipping is active.

4. Click the **white-point slider** on the bottom-right corner of the graph, and then drag left until some pixels start to appear in the image.

We dragged the Input White point just past the point where the histogram shows the lightest highlights in the image. (You performed this same action in the Levels dialog box when you adjusted the Input Highlight slider.) The Input and Output fields show that any pixels with an Input value of 235 will be output as 255. In other words, anything with an Input value higher than 235 will be clipped to solid white.

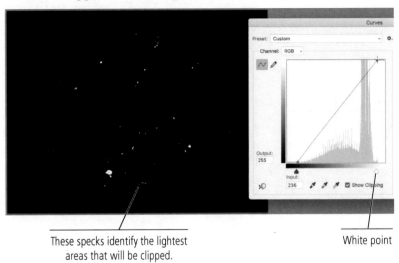

These specks identify the lightest areas that will be clipped.

White point

5. **Turn off the Show Clipping option so you can see the actual image behind the dialog box.**

   Even this small change improved the image, but the midtones need some additional contrast. To accomplish that change, you need to steepen the curve in the middle of the graph.

6. **Click the curve to create a point at the quartertone gridline and drag it slightly to the right.**

   We adjusted the curve point from an Input value of 95 to an Output value of 65.

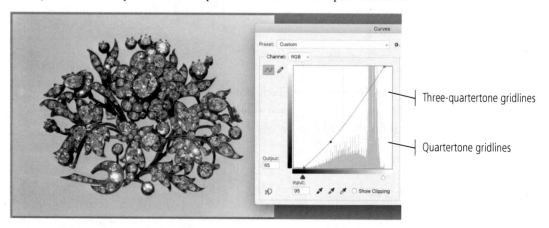

Three-quartertone gridlines

Quartertone gridlines

7. **Click the curve at the three-quartertone gridline and drag the point to the left.**

   We adjusted the Input value of 175 to an Output value of 190.

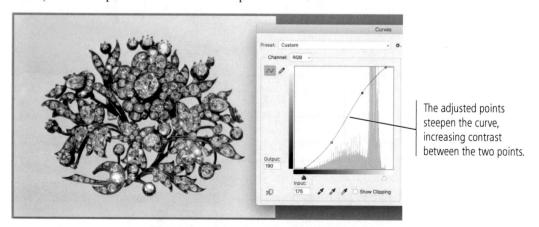

The adjusted points steepen the curve, increasing contrast between the two points.

8. **Click OK to apply the changes and close the dialog box.**

   Adjusting the contrast with curves improved the detail in the image and enhanced the overall image color.

 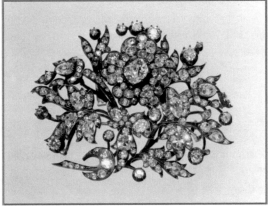

9. **Save the file in your WIP>MOAH folder as a native Photoshop file named diamonds-fixed.psd.**

10. **Close the file and continue to the next stage of the project.**

## Understanding Automatic Color Correction

Clicking Options in the right side of the Curves dialog box opens the Auto Color Correction Options dialog box. These settings apply if you click Auto in the Levels or Curves dialog box.

The Algorithms options determine how Photoshop will adjust an image's tonal range:

- **Enhance Monochromatic Contrast** clips all channels identically, preserving overall color while making highlights appear lighter and shadows darker. This is effectively the same as choosing Image>Adjustments>Auto Contrast.

- **Enhance Per Channel Contrast** maximizes the tonal range in each channel by moving the darkest shadow to 0 (or 100 for CMYK images), and the lightest highlight to 255 (or 0 for CMYK images). The overall color relationship is not maintained, which might result in color cast in the adjusted image. This is effectively the same as Image>Adjustments>Auto Tone.

- **Find Dark & Light Colors** uses the average lightest and darkest pixels to maximize contrast and minimize clipping. When selected, you can also activate **Snap Neutral Midtones**. This finds an average neutral color, and then adjusts midtone (gamma) values to make that color neutral. This is effectively the same as Image>Adjustments>Auto Color.

- **Enhance Brightness and Contrast** allows Photoshop to use content-aware monochromatic adjustments to produce smoother results across the entire tonal range.

The **Target Colors & Clipping** options are available when one of the first three algorithms is selected. You can define the target shadow, midtone, and highlight values by clicking the appropriate color swatch. The Clip fields determine how much of the darkest shadow and lightest highlight will be clipped. For example, a Shadow Clip setting of 1% means Photoshop will ignore the first 1% of the darkest pixels when adjusting the image.

## Understanding the Match Color Adjustment

The Match Color adjustment (Image>Adjustments>Match Color) allows you to match colors between multiple RGB images, layers, or selections. In the Match Color dialog box, the Target shows the image, layer, or selection you are modifying. The changes are based on values from the source image and layer selected in the Image Statistics area. You can change the luminance or color intensity of the target image, fade the adjustment, and neutralize color cast caused by the adjustment.

The Destination Image Target is the active image (and selected layer, if applicable) when you open the dialog box. If the target image has an active selection area, you can check the Ignore Selection... option to apply the change to the entire target image instead of the selected area only.

- The **Luminance** slider affects the brightness in the target image; higher values lighten the image.

- The **Color Intensity** slider adjusts the color saturation in the target image; higher values increase the color saturation.

- The **Fade** slider changes the amount of adjustment applied to the target image; higher values (i.e., more fade) reduce the amount of the adjustment.

- The **Neutralize** check box automatically removes color cast in the target image.

In the Image Statistics section of the dialog box, choose the source image and layer to which the target will be matched. You can use the two check boxes to apply changes based on the selected area only (if the target or source image has an active selection area).

# STAGE 4 / **Preparing Images for Print**

You might have noticed that all the images for this project are in the RGB color mode. Printing, however, relies on the CMYK mode to output color images.

Although a full discussion of color science and management can be extremely complex, and is beyond the needs of most graphic designers, applying color management in Photoshop is more intimidating than difficult. We believe this foundational information on color management will make you a more effective and practically grounded designer.

## *Understanding Gamut*

Different color models have different ranges, or **gamuts**, of possible colors. The RGB model has the largest gamut of the output models. The CMYK gamut is far more limited; many of the brightest and most saturated colors that can be reproduced using light cannot be reproduced using pigmented inks.

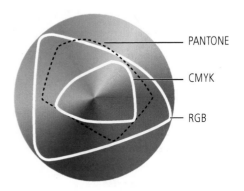

This difference in gamut is one of the biggest problems graphic designers face when working with color images. Digital image-capture devices (including scanners and digital cameras) work in the RGB space, which, with its larger gamut, can more closely mirror the range of colors in the original scene. Printing, however, requires images to first be converted or **separated** into the CMYK color space.

The usual goal in color reproduction is to achieve a color appearance equivalent to the original. Depending on the image, at least some colors in the RGB color model likely cannot be reproduced in the more limited gamut of the CMYK color model. These **out-of-gamut** colors pose a challenge to faithfully reproducing the original image. If the conversion from RGB to CMYK is not carefully controlled, **color shift** can result in drastic differences between the original and printed images.

## *Color Management in Brief*

**Color management** is intended to preserve color predictability and consistency as a file is moved from one color mode to another throughout the reproduction process. Color management can also eliminate ambiguity when a color is only specified by some numbers. For example, you might create a royal purple in the Photoshop Color Picker, but without color management, that same set of RGB numbers might look more lilac (or even gray) when converted to CMYK for printing. A well-tuned color-management system can translate the numbers that define a color in one space to numbers that can better represent that same color in another space.

It's important to have realistic expectations for color management, and realize that color management isn't a replacement for a thorough knowledge of the color-reproduction process. Even at its best, color management can't fix bad scans or photos — all it can do is introduce consistency and predictability to a process that, otherwise, rarely has either.

Color management relies on **color profiles**, which are data sets that define the reproduction characteristics of a specific device. A profile is essentially a recipe that contains the ingredients for reproducing a specific color in a given color space. The color recipes in profiles are known as **look-up tables** (LUTs), which are essentially cross-reference systems for finding matching color values in different color spaces.

*Note:*

*Color shift can also result when converting from one type of CMYK to another, or (though less likely) from one version of RGB to another. Whatever models are being used, color management gives you better control over the conversion process.*

*Note:*

*Color profiles are sometimes also called "ICC profiles," named after the International Color Consortium (ICC), which developed the standard for creating color profiles.*

**Source profiles** are the profiles of the devices (scanners, digital cameras, etc.) used to capture an image. **Destination profiles** are the profiles of output devices. LAB (or L*a*b*, or CIELAB) is a theoretical color space that represents the full visible spectrum. This device-independent color space can represent any possible color. By moving device-dependent RGB and CMYK colors into LAB as an intermediary space, you can convert color from any one space to any other space.

The **Color Management Module** (CMM) is the engine that drives color conversions via the LUT numbers. The engine doesn't do much other than look up numbers and cross-reference them to another set of numbers. The mechanics of color-managed conversions are quite simple. Regardless of the specific input and output spaces in use, the same basic process is followed for every pixel:

1. The CMM looks up the color values of a pixel in the input-space profile to find a matching set of LAB values.

2. The CMM looks up the LAB values in the output-space profile to find the matching set of values that will display the color of that pixel most accurately.

*Note:*

*Most professional-level devices come with profiles you can install when you install the hardware. A number of generic and industry-specific destination profiles are also built into Photoshop.*

## Color Management in Theory and Practice

RGB and CMYK are very different entities. The two color models have distinct capabilities, advantages, and limitations. There is no way to exactly reproduce RGB color using the CMYK gamut because many of the colors in the RGB gamut are simply too bright or too saturated. Rather than claiming to produce an exact (impossible) match from your monitor to a printed page, the true goal of color management is to produce the best possible representation of the color using the gamut of the chosen output device.

A theoretically ideal color-managed workflow resembles the following:

- Image-capture devices (scanners and digital cameras) are profiled to create a look-up table that defines the device's color-capturing characteristics.

- Images are acquired using a calibrated, profiled device. The profile of the capturing device is tagged to every image captured.

- The image is opened in Photoshop and viewed on a calibrated monitor. The monitor's profile is defined in Photoshop as your working space.

- Photoshop translates the image profile to your working space profile.

- You define a destination (CMYK) profile for the calibrated output device that will be used for your final job.

- The image is converted from RGB to CMYK, based on the defined working space and destination profiles.

Notice that three of the "ideal workflow" steps mention a form of the word, "calibrate." To **calibrate** something means to check and correct a device's characteristics. Calibration is an essential element in a color-managed workflow, and it is fundamentally important to achieving consistent and predictable output.

You cannot check or correct the color characteristics of a device without having something with which you can compare them. To calibrate a device, a known target — usually a sequence of distinct and varying color patches — is reproduced using the device. The color values of the reproduction are measured and compared to the values of the known target. Precise calibration requires adjusting the device until the reproduction matches the original.

As long as your devices are accurately calibrated to the same target values, the color acquired by your RGB scanner will exactly match the colors displayed on your RGB monitor and the colors printed by your desktop printer. Of course, most devices (especially consumer-level, desktop devices that are gaining a larger market share in the commercial graphics world) are not accurately calibrated, and very few are calibrated to the same set of known target values.

Keeping in mind these ideals and realities, the true goals of color management are to:

- Compensate for variations in the different devices

- Accurately translate one color space to another

- Compensate for limitations in the output process

- Better predict the result when an image is reproduced

## Understanding Color Modes

**Bitmap color** reproduces all pixels in the image as either black or white; there are no shades of gray.

**Grayscale color** reproduces all tones in the file as shades of gray. This type of image has only one channel (you were introduced to color channels in Project 1: New Music Artwork, and will learn more in subsequent projects).

**RGB** creates color by combining different intensities of red, green, and blue light (collectively referred to as the "additive primaries"). Computer monitors and television sets display color in RGB, which has a **gamut** (or range) of more than 16.7 million different colors. An RGB file has three color channels, one for each of the additive primaries.

**LAB color** is device independent; the colors it describes don't depend upon the characteristics of a particular printer, monitor, or scanner. In theory, LAB bridges the gap between the various color models and devices. It is used in the background when converting images from one color space to another.

**CMYK** ("process") **color** is based on the absorption and reflection of light. Four process inks — cyan, magenta, yellow, and black — are used in varying combinations and percentages to produce the range of printable colors in most commercial printing. A CMYK file has four color channels — one for each subtractive primary and one for black.

Theoretically, a mixture of equal parts of cyan, magenta, and yellow would produce black. Pigments, however, are not pure, so the result of mixing these colors is a muddy brown (called **hue error**). To obtain vibrant colors (and so elements, such as type, can be printed cleanly), black ink is added to the three primaries. Black is represented by the letter "K" for "key color."

The problem with using RGB for print jobs is that the RGB colors eventually need to be converted to CMYK separations for a commercial printing press. Photoshop includes sophisticated tools that allow you to control this conversion.

Your client's catalog will be printed, which means the image files ultimately have to be in the CMYK color mode. In this stage of the project, you will learn how to control and correct for the conversion process from RGB to CMYK — a very common process in professional graphic design. (In a professional environment, you would actually have to convert all of the images you have used in this project; we are only working with one for the sake of illustration.)

 ## Define Color Settings

Photoshop's color management system allows you to set up a fully managed color workflow — from input device through output device. You can use Adobe's predefined color settings or create custom settings that pertain to the equipment you use.

1. **With no file open in Photoshop, choose Edit>Color Settings.**

    The Color Settings dialog box defines default working spaces for RGB, CMYK, gray, and spot colors, as well as general color management policies.

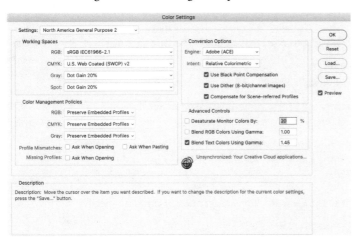

**2. Choose North America Prepress 2 in the Settings menu.**

Photoshop includes four saved groups of options that are common in North America, which can be accessed in the Settings menu. You can also make your own choices and save those settings as a new preset by clicking Save, or you can import settings files created by another user by clicking Load.

**3. In the Working Spaces area, choose the RGB profile for your monitor. If your specific monitor isn't available, choose Adobe RGB (1998).**

If you use a color-managed workflow, each color mode must be defined as a particular type of color space. Because there are different types of monitors, there are different types of RGB color spaces; the same is true of the other color spaces. The Working Space menus define exactly which version of each space is used to define color within that space.

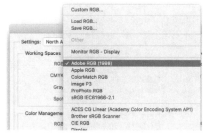

For color management to work properly, you must have accurate, device-specific profiles for every device in the workflow. However, you can use generic settings, such as Adobe RGB (1998), in a "better-than-nothing" color environment — which is almost a direct contradiction to the concept of color management. We're showing you *how* to use the tools in Photoshop, but it's up to you to implement true color management by profiling your devices and using those profiles for specific jobs.

*Note:*

*In Photoshop, a **working space** is the default profile used for each of the different color modes.*

*Note:*

*When you choose a profile that isn't part of the saved settings, the Settings menu automatically changes to "Custom."*

**4. In the CMYK menu, choose U.S. Sheetfed Coated v2.**

There are many CMYK profiles — each different printer and press has a gamut unique to that individual device.

This is a United States industry-standard profile for a common type of printing (sheetfed printing on coated paper). In a truly color-managed workflow, you would actually use a profile for the specific printing press/paper/ink combination being used for the job. Again, we're using the default profiles to show you how the process works.

Use the Load CMYK option to access profiles that are supplied by your output provider.

*Note:*

*We assume this catalog will be printed on a sheetfed press. However, always ask your output provider which profile to use for a specific job.*

*Note:*

*If you convert an image's color space using the Image>Mode menu, Photoshop converts the image to the default working space for the mode you choose.*

**5. Leave the Gray and Spot working space menus at their default settings.**

The Gray working space defines how grayscale images will translate when the images are printed. Gray working space options include:

- **Dot Gain** (of varying percentages). These options compensate for the spread of a halftone dot in a grayscale image.
- **Gray Gamma.** This option allows you to set the monitor's gamma to compensate for differences between the monitor's presentation of an image and the actual grayscale image on press.

The Spot working space is similar to the Gray working space, but you can only specify dot gain percentages (not gamma).

6. **In the Color Management Policies area, make sure RGB is turned off, Preserve Embedded Profiles is selected for CMYK and Gray, and all three check boxes are selected.**

These options tell Photoshop what to do when you open an existing image. When an option here is turned off, color is not managed for that mode. If you choose Preserve Embedded Profiles, images that have a defined profile retain that profile; images with no profile use the current working space. If you choose Convert to Working Space, all images, even those with an embedded profile, are converted to the current working profile; images with no profile are assigned the current working profile.

For profile mismatches, you can display a warning when opening or pasting an image with a different embedded profile. When an image doesn't have an embedded profile, you can display a warning by checking the Ask When Opening option.

7. **Review the options in the right side of the dialog box.**

**Engine** determines the system and color-matching method used to convert between color spaces – **Adobe (ACE)** or Adobe Color Engine; **Apple CMM** (Macintosh only); or **Microsoft ICM** (Windows only).

The **Intent** menu defines how the engine translates source colors outside the gamut of the destination profile.

- **Perceptual** presents a visually pleasing representation of the image, preserving visual relationships between colors. All colors, including those available in the destination gamut, shift to maintain a proportional relationship.

- **Saturation** compares the saturation of colors in the source profile and shifts them to the nearest-possible saturated color in the destination profile. The focus is on saturation instead of actual color value. This method can produce drastic color shift.

- **Relative Colorimetric** maintains any colors that are in both the source and destination profiles; source colors outside the destination gamut shift to fit. This method adjusts for the whiteness of the media.

- **Absolute Colorimetric** maintains colors in both the source and destination profiles. Colors outside the destination gamut are shifted to a color within the destination gamut, without considering the white point of the media.

When **Use Black Point Compensation** is selected, the full range of the source space is mapped into the destination space. This method is most useful when the black point of the source is darker than that of the destination.

When **Use Dither** is selected, colors in the destination space are mixed to simulate missing colors from the source space. This can result in larger file sizes for web images.

**Compensate for Scene-Referred Profiles** relates to the increasingly popular use of Photoshop to perform color correction (and profile matching) for video enhancement.

**Desaturate Monitor Colors** is useful for visualizing the full range of color, including colors outside the monitor's range. When this option is deselected, colors that were previously distinct might appear as a single color.

**Blend RGB Colors Using Gamma** inputs a gamma curve to avoid artifacts. A gamma of 1.00 is considered "colorimetrically correct."

**Blend Text Colors Using Gamma** applies the defined gamma to text layers.

*Note:*

*Web printing is done on larger presses and fed from huge rolls of paper, with the actual pages being cut off the roll only after the ink has been laid down. Although web presses are typically cheaper to operate for long print runs, they generally do not produce the same quality of color as their sheetfed counterparts.*

*Sheetfed presses place ink on sheets of paper that have already been cut to press-sheet size from a large roll of paper. Sheetfed presses are typically considered higher quality, with appropriately higher costs associated with the job.*

8. **Click Save in the Color Settings dialog box. In the resulting navigation dialog box, navigate to your WIP>MOAH folder as the location where you want to save the file.**

By default, custom color settings are saved in a Settings folder in a specific location where your system stores user preferences for different applications. Settings files saved in the application's default location are available in the Settings menu of the Color Settings dialog box.

If you are working on a shared computer or a network where you can't save to the system files, you have to save the custom Color Settings file in your WIP folder. In this case, you would have to click the Load button to locate the CSF file if you wanted to use the profile again later.

9. **Change the Save As/File Name field to museum.csf and click Save.**

Color management settings files use the ".csf" extension.

10. **In the Color Settings Comment dialog box, type** Use this option for Photoshop museum image adjustment project.

11. **Click OK to return to the Color Settings dialog box.**

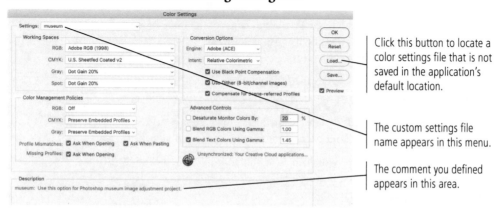

Click this button to locate a color settings file that is not saved in the application's default location.

The custom settings file name appears in this menu.

The comment you defined appears in this area.

12. **Click OK to close the Color Settings dialog box and apply your settings, and then continue to the next exercise.**

**Identify Out-of-Gamut Colors**

Fortunately, Photoshop contains the necessary tools for previewing out-of-gamut colors, which means you can correct colors *before* converting an image. If you have no out-of-gamut colors, then there is nothing to shift, and you can be fairly confident that your color images will be reproduced as you intended.

1. **Open the file faience.jpg from the WIP>MOAH folder.**

2. **When you see the profile mismatch warning, choose Use the Embedded Profile and click OK.**

   Remember, color management relies on profiles to accurately translate color from one model to another. This dialog box shows you the starting point — the embedded image profile. As a general rule, you should use the embedded profile whenever one is available.

*Note:*

*You can choose Edit>Assign Profile to define a specific profile for the active image.*

3. **Choose View>Proof Colors to toggle that option on.**

   This toggle provides a quick preview of what will happen when the image is converted to the CMYK working-space profile, without affecting the actual file data. In this case, you will see slight color shift in the brightest blue (out-of-gamut) areas, but it does not significantly affect the overall image quality.

*Note:*

*Command/Control-Y toggles the Proof Colors view on or off.*

*Shift-Command/ Control-Y toggles the Gamut Warning View.*

**Original color**

**Proof color**

4. **Choose View>Proof Colors again to toggle the option off.**

5. **Choose View>Gamut Warning.**

   When the Gamut Warning is visible, areas of color shift are highlighted with a gray overlay. In this case, the highlight shows that only the brightest blue and red areas will be affected.

   A gray highlight overlays areas where color shift will occur.

*Note:*

*You can change the color of the gamut warning overlay in the Transparency & Gamut pane of the Preferences dialog box.*

6. **Continue to the next exercise.**

Adjust Highlight and Shadow Points for Print

For images that will be commercially printed, some allowance must be made in the highlight and shadow areas for the mechanics of the printing process. Images are printed as a pattern of closely spaced dots called a **halftone**. Those dots create the illusion of continuous color. Different sizes of dots create different shades of color — larger dots create darker shades and smaller dots create lighter shades.

There is a limit to the smallest size dot that can be consistently reproduced. The mechanical aspect of the printing process causes anything specified as a 1% dot to drop out, resulting in highlights that lack detail and contrast. The **minimum printable dot** is the smallest printable dot, and should be specified for highlights in a CMYK image. There is some debate over the appropriate highlight setting because different presses and imaging equipment have varying capabilities. To be sure your highlights will work on most printing equipment, you should define the highlight as C=5 M=3 Y=3 K=0.

**Note:**

*The larger cyan percentage is to compensate for the typically weaker characteristics of cyan printing ink.*

**Maximum printable dot** is the opposite of minimum printable dot. Paper's absorption rate, speed of the press, and other mechanical factors limit the amount of ink that can be placed on the same area. If too much ink is printed, the result is a dark blob with no visible detail; heavy layers of ink also result in drying problems and a number of other issues.

**Total ink coverage** is the largest percentage of ink that can be safely printed on a single area, and therefore dictates the shadow dot you define in Photoshop. This number, similar to minimum printable dot, varies according to the ink/paper/press combination being used for a given job. The Specifications for Web Offset Publications (SWOP) indicates a 300% maximum value. Many sheetfed printers require 280% maximum, while the number for newspapers is usually around 240% because the lower-quality paper absorbs more ink.

1. **With faience.jpg open and the gamut warning visible, choose Image>Adjustments>Curves.**

2. **Double-click the White Point Eyedropper.**

3. **In the resulting Color Picker (Target Highlight Color) dialog box, change the CMYK values to C=5 M=3 Y=3 K=0, and then click OK.**

Double-click the White Point Eyedropper to open the Color Picker (Target Highlight Color) dialog box.

Change the Target Highlight Color in these fields.

4. **With the White Point Eyedropper selected, click a white area in the image background.**

You should typically choose the lightest highlight in the image where you want to maintain detail. Because the image subject in this case does not include any actual white pixels, you must use the image background.

We selected this area as the white point.

5. **Double-click the Black Point Eyedropper. Change the CMYK target shadow values to C=80 M=70 Y=70 K=70, and then click OK.**

Unless your images will be printed in a newspaper, 290% is an acceptable shadow for most applications. You can safely define shadows as C=80 M=70 Y=70 K=70. If you need to adjust a lower or higher number for specific projects, you can do so at any time.

Double-click the Black Point Eyedropper to open the Color Picker (Target Shadow Color) dialog box.

Change the Target Shadow Color in these fields.

6. **With the Black Point Eyedropper selected, click the darkest area of the image where you want to maintain shadow detail.**

By defining the target highlight and shadow points in the image, you can see that the gray gamut warning is nearly gone in all but the brightest blue areas. As you saw when you used the Proof Colors option, the shift will be minimal. No further correction is required for this image.

**Note:**

*You can turn the gamut warning off and on while the Curves dialog box is open.*

We selected this area as the black point.

7. **Click OK to apply your changes.**

8. **Click No in the warning message.**

If you change the target Black Point, Gray Point, or White Point Eyedropper values, Photoshop asks if you want to save the new target values as the default settings when you click OK to close the Curves dialog box.

9. **Choose View>Gamut Warning to toggle that option off.**

10. **Continue to the next exercise.**

Because the RGB gamut is so much larger than the CMYK gamut, you can expect colors to be far less brilliant (especially in the outer ranges of saturation) when corrected to the CMYK gamut. It's better to know this will happen and control it, rather than simply allowing the color management engine to shift colors where it deems best.

# Converting Image Color Modes

Although many modern workflows convert RGB images to CMYK during the output process (called "on-the-fly" or "in-RIP" conversion), there are times when you need to manually convert RGB images to CMYK. This is a fairly simple process, especially if you have corrected your images to meet the requirements of the printing process.

1. **With the corrected faience image open from the previous exercise, choose Image>Mode>CMYK Color.**

   This option converts the image to the CMYK color mode using the current working space. Since you intentionally defined the working profile and corrected the image to that profile, you can safely use this menu option to convert the RGB image to CMYK.

2. **Click OK in the resulting warning dialog box.**

3. **Choose File>Save As. If necessary, navigate to WIP>MOAH as the target location.**

4. **Change the Format/Save As Type menu to Photoshop, and then add -CMYK to the end of the existing file name.**

5. **Macintosh users: In the bottom half of the Save As dialog box, make sure the Embed Color Profile: U.S. Sheetfed Coated v2 option is checked.**

   **Windows users: In the bottom half of the Save As dialog box, make sure the ICC Profile: U.S. Sheetfed Coated v2 option is checked.**

   By embedding the profile into the Photoshop file, other applications and devices with color management capabilities will be able to correctly process the image color data in the file, based on the embedded profile.

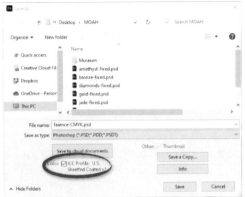

6. **Click Save, then close the file.**

> **Note:**
>
> *You can also convert an image to a different color model by choosing Edit>Convert to Profile, and then choosing any available profile in the Destination Space Profile menu.*

> **Note**
>
> *If you haven't completed the process in the previous series of exercises, you shouldn't convert the image color mode. Color mode is not something that should be switched on a whim; rather, it is the final stage of a specific process.*

7. **With no file open in Photoshop, choose Edit>Color Settings.**

8. **In the Color Settings dialog box, choose North America General Purpose 2 in the Settings menu, then click OK.**

   This option effectively resets the default color settings for the application. This step will prevent unnecessary warning messages when you open files in later projects.

Reset this menu to North America General Purpose 2.

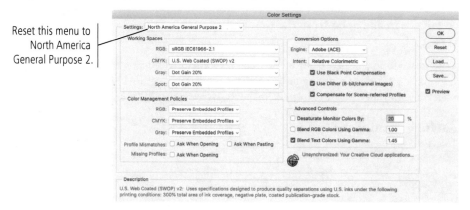

9. **Continue to the final stage of the project.**

# STAGE 5 / Working with HDR Images

The human eye is extremely sensitive to subtle changes in light. In general, we can perceive detail in both light and dark areas — and areas in-between — with a single glance. Camera sensors, on the other hand, are not as perceptive. If you look at most photographs, they typically have sharp detail in one of the ranges — highlights, midtones, or shadows — depending on the exposure and other settings used to capture the image. If a photograph favors highlights, details in shadow areas are lost (and vice versa).

To solve this problem, the concept of HDR (**high dynamic range**) images combines multiple photographs of different exposures into a single image to enhance the detail throughout the entire image. HDR images combine highlight, shadow, and midtone detail from various exposures to create an image more like what the human eye is capable of observing, rather than the more limited range that characterizes a digital camera's sensors.

The phrase "dynamic range" refers to the difference between the darkest shadow and the lightest highlight in an image.

- A regular 8-bit RGB photo has a dynamic range of 0–255 for each color channel ($2^8$ or 256 possible values). In other words, each pixel can have one of 256 possible values to describe the lightness of that color in that specific location.

- A 16-bit RGB photo allows 16 bits of information to describe the information in each pixel, allowing a dynamic range of $2^{16}$ or 65,536 possible values in each color channel.

- A 32-bit, or HDR, image allows $2^{32}$ possible values — more than 4 billion, which is significantly larger than the visible spectrum of 16.7 million colors (thus, 32-bit dynamic range is sometimes referred to as "infinite").

# Use Merge to HDR Pro

The last piece required to complete this project is an image of the new museum's exterior. The photographer suggested using high dynamic range (HDR) photo techniques to capture the most possible detail in the scene, and has provided you with five photos taken at the same time, using different exposure settings.

1. **With no file open, choose File>Automate>Merge to HDR Pro.**

2. **In the resulting Merge to HDR Pro dialog box, choose Folder in the Use menu and then click the Browse button.**

   This option makes it easy to identify the folder that contains all component images for the HDR merge.

*Note:*

*You can merge up to seven images with the Merge to HDR Pro utility.*

3. **Navigate to WIP>MOAH>Museum, then click Open/OK.**

4. **Make sure the Attempt to Automatically Align Source Images box at the bottom of the dialog box is checked, then click OK.**

   Because you are merging multiple images into one, there is a chance that one or more images might be slightly misaligned. Even using a tripod, a stiff breeze can affect the camera just enough to make the different exposures slightly different. When Attempt to Automatically Align Source Images is checked, Photoshop compares details in each image and adjusts them as necessary to create the resulting merged image.

*Note:*

*The merge process might take a minute or two to complete, so be patient.*

5. **If you don't see a histogram on the right side of the dialog box, open the Mode menu and choose 32 Bit.**

   The resulting dialog box shows each selected image as a thumbnail at the bottom. By default, all selected images are included in the merge. You can exclude specific exposures by unchecking the box for that image.

   If you work with HDR, you need to realize that most computer monitors are not capable of displaying 32-bit image depth. When you merge to a 32-bit image, you can use the White Point Preview slider to change the dynamic range that is visible on your screen, but this has no effect on the actual data in the file — it affects only the current display of the image data.

6. **Check the Remove Ghosts option on the right side of the dialog box.**

   When an HDR image contains movement, merging the individual exposures can blur the areas where that movement occurs. When you check Remove Ghosts, the software uses one of the exposures (highlighted in green) to define detail in the area of motion, such as the moving car in this image. You can change the key exposure by simply clicking a different image in the lower pane.

Check Remove Ghosts to eliminate blurring in areas that differ from one exposure to another.

When Remove Ghosts is checked, details in areas of movement are defined by the selected exposure.

7. **Open the Mode menu and choose 8 Bit.**

   32-bit images can store a tremendous amount of information, which creates images with far more detail than you see in a conventional 8-bit photograph. However, one significant disadvantage of such images is that they cannot be separated for commercial printing. If you're going to use an HDR image in a print application — such as the cover of this catalog — you need to apply the process of **tone mapping** to define how the high dynamic range will be compressed into the lower dynamic range required by the output process.

8. **Leave the secondary menu set to Local Adaptation.**

   You can use the other options to apply less specific tone mapping to the image. Equalize Histogram and Highlight Compression have no further options. The Exposure and Gamma option allows you to define specific values for only those two settings.

   When the Local Adaptation method is selected, you can change the values for a number of specific options to map the tones in the HDR image to a lower dynamic range.

## 9. Open the Preset menu and choose Surrealistic.

The application has a number of standard settings, including several variations of monochromatic, photorealistic, and surrealistic. Each preset changes the values of the Local Adaptation sliders to create the desired effect.

You can create your own presets by clicking the button to the right of the Preset menu and choosing Save Preset in the resulting menu.

## 10. Experiment with the different sliders until you are satisfied with the result.

Tone mapping is a largely subjective process, and different end uses can influence the settings that you apply to a specific image. You should understand the following information as you experiment with the various settings:

- **Radius** defines the size of the glowing effect in areas of localized brightness.

- **Strength** determines the required tolerance between tonal values before pixels are no longer considered part of the same brightness region.

- **Gamma** values lower than 1.0 increase details in the midtones, while higher values emphasize details in the highlights and shadows.

- **Exposure** affects the overall lightness or darkness of the image.

- **Detail** increases or decreases the overall sharpness of the image.

- **Shadow** and **Highlight** affect the amount of detail in those areas of the image. Higher values increase detail and lower values reduce detail.

- **Vibrance** affects the intensity of subtle colors, while minimizing clipping of highly saturated colors.

- **Saturation** affects the intensity of all colors from –100 (monochrome) to +100 (double saturation).

**11. Click OK to finalize the process.**

Because you chose 8 Bit in the Mode menu of the Merge to HDR Pro dialog box, the resulting image is an 8-bit RGB image (as you can see in the document tab).

× Untitled_HDR-2 @ 75% (RGB/8) *

*Note:*

*The original exposures for this image were captured by Charlie Essers.*

**12. Save the file in your WIP>MOAH folder as a native Photoshop file named museum-merged.psd, then close it.**

# Converting Images to Grayscale

An RGB image has three channels and a CMYK image has four. Each channel is a grayscale representation of the tones of that color throughout. A **grayscale image** has only one channel, and the grayscale tones in that channel are the tones in the entire image. Choosing Image>Mode>Grayscale simply flattens the component color channels, throwing away the color information to create the gray channel.

The **Desaturate** adjustment (Image>Adjustments> Desaturate) has a similar effect, but maintains the same number of channels as the original image. This adjustment averages the individual channel values for each pixel and applies the average value in each channel. (Remember, equal values of red, green, and blue combine to create a neutral gray value.)

If you need to convert a color image to grayscale, you might want to carefully consider which data to use for generating the gray channel. The **Black & White** adjustment (Image> Adjustments>Black & White) enables you to control the conversion process. In the Black and White dialog box, you can either choose one of the built-in presets, or drag the individual color sliders to determine how dark that color component will be in the resulting image.

If you move the mouse cursor over the image, it changes to an eyedropper. You can click an area in the image to highlight the predominant color in that area. Click within the image and drag to dynamically change the slider associated with that area of the image.

Remember, equal parts red, green, and blue combine to create a neutral gray. Applying the Black & White filter maintains the existing color channels, with exactly the same data in all three channels. Because the adjusted image is still technically in a color mode (not Grayscale), you can also use the Tint options in the Black & White dialog box to apply a hue or saturation tint to the grayscale image. After using the Black & White dialog box to control the conversion of colors to grayscale, you can safely discard the color data by choosing Image>Mode>Grayscale.

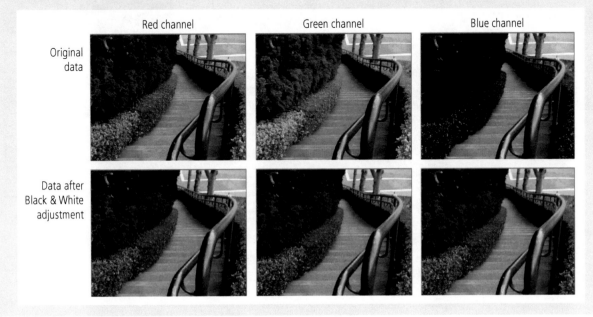

You can use the **Channel Mixer** adjustment to change the values of individual channels in an image, affecting overall color balance and contrast.

The **Output Channel** menu determines which channel you are changing. The Source Channels sliders determine how much of the original channels will be used to create the new output channel values.

The Constant slider adjusts the overall grayscale value of the output channel. Negative values add more black to the channel (reducing the target color in the overall image), and positive

 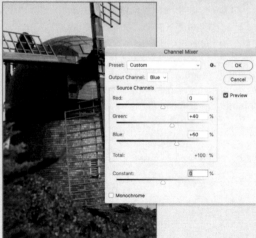

Replacing 40% of the Blue channel with data from the Green channel reduces some of the yellow color cast.

values add more white to the channel (increasing the target color in the overall image).

You can also use the Channel Mixer to control the conversion to grayscale. If you check the Monochrome option at the bottom of the dialog box, the output channel automatically changes to gray.

When the **Monochrome** option is checked, you can change the percentage of each component channel that will be used to generate the grayscale values. If the combined channel values are higher than 100%, Photoshop displays a warning icon next to the total.

The "Output Channel: Gray" option is deceptive, since there is no Gray channel in either an RGB or CMYK image. As with the Black and White adjustment, the Channel Mixer results in a color image with the same

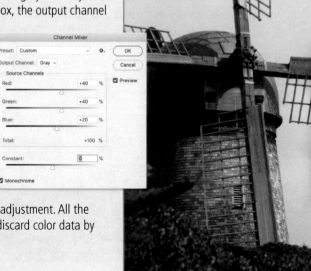

number of color channels that it had before you applied the adjustment. All the color channels have equal data, however, so you can safely discard color data by choosing Image>Mode>Grayscale.

1. The _____ filter blurs an image by a selected pixel radius.

2. _____ is defined as random pixels that stand out from the surrounding pixels.

3. The _____ blends colors from user-defined source pixels with colors in the area in which you click.

4. The _____ paints one part of an image over another part, which is useful for duplicating specific objects or removing defects in an image.

5. _____ are direct sources of light, such as a light bulb or reflected sunlight on water; they should not be considered the highlights of an image.

6. _____ refers to the tonal variation within an image.

7. A _____ is a visual depiction of the distribution of colors in an image.

8. _____ is defined according to a color's position on a color wheel, beginning from red (0°) and traveling counterclockwise.

9. _____ (also called "intensity") refers to the color's difference from neutral gray.

10. _____ (also called "luminance" or "value") is the amount of white or black added to the pure color.

1. Explain the concept of neutral gray.

2. List three important points to remember when working with curves.

3. Briefly explain the concepts of minimum printable dot and maximum ink coverage.

# PORTFOLIO BUILDER PROJECT

Use what you have learned in this project to complete the following freeform exercise.
Carefully read the art director and client comments, then create your own design to meet the needs of the project.
Use the space below to sketch ideas. When finished, write a brief explanation of the reasoning behind your final design.

## art director comments

The director of the local tourism board recently saw your work for the museum, and has hired you to work on a new project about local architecture.

To complete this project, you should:

❑ Find at least 10 photos of different architectural styles throughout the Los Angeles metropolitan area.

❑ Use photo retouching techniques to clean up any graffiti and trash that is visible in the images.

❑ Use correction techniques to adjust the tonal range and gray balance of the images.

❑ Correct and convert all images based on the U.S. Sheetfed Coated v2 CMYK destination profile.

## client comments

Over the next year, we're planning on publishing a series of promotional booklets to show tourists that L.A. is more than just Hollywood.

Each issue will focus on an "area of interest" such as architecture, which is the first topic. The city has a diverse architectural mix, from eighteenth-century Spanish missions and 1920s bungalows, to the Disney Concert Hall designed by Frank Gehry in the 1990s.

We'd like at least 10 pictures of different landmarks or architectural styles, corrected and optimized for printing on a sheetfed press. If possible, we'd also like some historical images to include in a "building a metropolis" section on the first couple of pages.

Of course, Los Angeles is a large city, and cities have their problems — not the least of which are graffiti and garbage. We are trying to attract tourists. Make sure none of the images show any graffiti or blatant litter. If these problems are visible in the images you select, give them a good digital cleaning.

## project justification

As with many other skills, it takes time and practice to master image correction techniques. Understanding the relationship between brightness and contrast, and how these two values affect the quality of reproduction in digital images, is the first, and possibly, most critical factor in creating a high-quality image. An image that has too much contrast (a "sharp" image) or not enough contrast (a "flat" image) translates to an unsatisfactory print.

A basic understanding of color theory (specifically, complementary color) is the foundation of accurate color correction. Effective color correction relies on the numbers, rather than what you think you see on your monitor. As you gain experience in correcting images, you will be better able to predict the corrections required to achieve the best possible output.

Remove photographic grain with blur and sharpen techniques

Use the Healing Brush and Spot Healing Brush tools to correct scratches

Use the Clone Stamp tool to remove major damage

Use Merge to HDR Pro to find detail in multiple exposures

Correct minor problems with the Brightness/Contrast adjustment

Correct overall color cast using the Color Balance adjustment

Correct contrast and tonal range with the Levels adjustment

Correct lighting problems with the Exposure adjustment

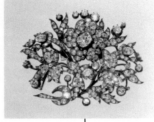

Correct gray balance with the Curves adjustment

Correct contrast with the Curves adjustment

Correct and convert an image using the defined destination CMYK profile

# 4 City Promotion Cards

Your client is the Redevelopment Authority for the city of Lancaster, in the California high desert north of Los Angeles. You have been hired to create a series of promotional post-cards featuring the improvements that have been made over the last two years, with the goal of driving tourism to the area.

This project incorporates the following skills:

❏ Managing missing and mismatched profiles

❏ Working with content-aware tools

❏ Adding effects in the Blur Gallery

❏ Creating and managing different types of text layers

❏ Using paragraph styles to format text

❏ Creating layer comps

## Videos to Watch

Access these helpful videos in your online student resources:

▶▶ City Promotion Cards Project Introduction

▶▶ Applying Content-Aware Scaling

▶▶ Using the Content-Aware Move Tool

▶▶ Type Basics in Photoshop

**client comments**

We want to feature two of our proudest achievements in a postcard campaign that we're hoping will help drive tourism to the area.

More than $50 million of public and private funding has been spent revitalizing the downtown area. The BLVD, an outdoor shopping and dining destination, is lined with a unique mix of dining, shopping, arts, and entertainment venues.

The Poppy Festival is attended by more than 20,000 visitors every year. It's an award-winning festival that celebrates California's state flower, which is fitting, since we're also the home of the Antelope Valley Poppy Preserve.

The images you create will be used in a range of digital advertising, but we also plan to print them in a larger promotional package that we send to conference coordinators around the country.

**Watch the video** City Promotion Cards Project Introduction **in your online student resources.**

**art director comments**

The client wants to create these files for both digital and print applications, so you should define the file size to meet the print specs:

Trim: 5″ high × 7″ wide

Bleed requirement: 0.125″ on all four sides

Each postcard will feature two main images, but the photos we have will require some manipulation to work in the overall composition. For the BLVD card, the clients also wants to include a secondary inset image, but they aren't sure which one they want to use. You can put all three options in place, and we'll give them the three samples to choose from.

Although compositing type and images is typically done in a page layout application, there isn't a lot of text to include on these postcards. You can use the Photoshop type tools to do what you need, without requiring a separate file.

When you're finished, save each version as a JPEG that we can email for approval.

**project objectives**

To complete this project, you will:

- ❏ Create a new color-managed file
- ❏ Apply content-aware scaling
- ❏ Use the Content-Aware Move tool
- ❏ Apply a tilt-shift blur effect
- ❏ Apply an iris blur effect
- ❏ Place and format point text
- ❏ Create and control area type
- ❏ Work with paragraph styles
- ❏ Create a solid-color fill layer
- ❏ Create layer comps

# STAGE 1 / **Creating New Files**

The basic process of creating a new file is relatively easy. However, you have a number of options that affect what you will see when you begin working. The first stage of this project explores a number of these issues, including color management settings and controlling the background layer.

 ## Create a New Color-Managed File

The Color Settings dialog box defines the default working spaces for RGB, CMYK, Gray, and Spot Color spaces. Once you've made your choices in the Color Settings dialog box, those working spaces are automatically applied when you create a new file.

1. **Expand the Cards_PS22_RF.zip archive in your WIP folder (Macintosh) or copy the archive contents into your WIP folder (Windows).**

   This results in a folder named **Cards**, which contains the files you need for this project. You should also use this folder to save the files you create in this project.

2. **In Photoshop, choose Edit>Color Settings.**

3. **In the resulting dialog box, choose the appropriate profile for your monitor in the Working Spaces: RGB menu.**

4. **Set all three Color Management Policies menus to Preserve Embedded Profiles, and check all three boxes for Profile Mismatches and Missing Profiles.**

   You can display a warning when opening or pasting an image with an embedded profile that does not match the working profile. You can also display a warning when opening an image that doesn't have an embedded profile.

   Choose your monitor profile here.

   Check all three of these options.

5. **Click OK to apply your changes.**

6. **Choose File>New.**

   You have several options for creating a new file:
   - Choose File>New
   - Use the associated keyboard shortcut, Command/Control-N
   - Click the New File button in the Start workspace

   If the Home workspace is visible, click the New File button to open the New Document dialog box.

7. **Click the Print option at the top of the resulting New Document dialog box.**

8. **Click the bottom edge of the New Document dialog box and drag down until you can see all of the options in the Preset Details section.**

The New Document dialog box presents a number of preset sizes, broken into categories based on the intended output.

When you choose the Print category, you see common page sizes such as Letter. Each preset includes a unit of measurement (for example, 8.5 × 11 in for the Letter preset or 210 × 297 mm for the A4 preset). The defined unit of measurement for each preset is set in the Preset Details section of the dialog box.

The Photo, Print, and Art & Illustration presets all default to 300 Pixels/Inch resolution. The Web, Mobile, and Film & Video presets default to 72 Pixels/Inch.

The **color mode** defines the structure of the colors in your file. All presets in all categories default to 8-bit RGB color mode. Although the file will eventually be printed, you are going to work in the RGB space to preserve the widest-possible gamut during the development stage.

Click a category name to show related presets.

Click to select an existing preset size.

Drag the bottom edge of the dialog box to show all the available options.

9. **In the Preset Details section, type** festival **in the Name field.**

10. **Highlight the existing Width field value, and then type 7.25.**

Because this file will eventually be printed, you are defining the width to include the required bleed (1/8″) area on each side.

11. **Press Tab two times to highlight the Height field.**

Like most applications, you can press Tab to move through the options and fields in a dialog box. Pressing Shift-Tab moves to the previous field in the dialog box.

12. **Change the highlighted Height field to 5.25.**

Again, this size includes the required 1/8″ bleed for the top and bottom edges.

13. **Choose Transparent in the Background Contents menu.**

If you choose White or Background Color in this menu, the new file will include a default locked Background layer. If you choose Transparent, the new file will have a default, unlocked Layer 1.

14. **Expand the Advanced options (if necessary) and choose Working RGB: [Profile Name] in the Color Profile menu.**

This option defines the working RGB space that you selected in the Color Settings dialog box. Options in the Pixel Aspect Ratio menu are primarily used for editing video. Since this is a print project, you don't want to alter the pixel ratio.

**15. Click Create to create the new file.**

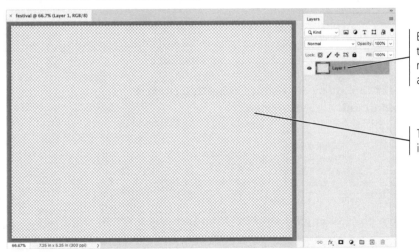

Because you chose Transparent in the Background Color menu, the new file has one regular layer and no locked Background layer.

The checked pattern identifies transparent areas.

**16. Choose File>Save As. If necessary, navigate to your WIP>Cards folder as the location for saving this file.**

Because you named the file when you created it (in the New Document dialog box), the Save As/File Name field is automatically set to the file name you already assigned. The extension is automatically added on both Macintosh and Windows computers.

**17. Make sure Photoshop is selected in the Format/Save As Type menu and click Save.**

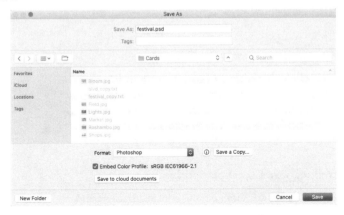

**18. Read the resulting warning message, then click OK.**

This warning appears as soon as a file has at least one regular layer. This file has no locked background layer, so the only layer is a regular layer by default.

**19. Continue to the next exercise.**

# Control the Background Layer

When you create a new file, the background of the canvas depends on your selection in the New dialog box. You should understand how that choice affects not only the color of the canvas, but also the existence (or inexistence) of a background layer.

1. **With festival.psd open, make sure rulers are visible (View>Rulers), and make sure inches are the default unit of measurement.**

Control/right-click the ruler and make sure Inches is selected.

2. **Using any method you prefer, place ruler guides 0.125″ from each edge.**

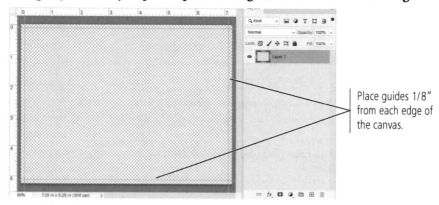

Place guides 1/8″ from each edge of the canvas.

3. **Save the file.**

4. **At the bottom of the Tools panel, click the Default Foreground and Background Colors button.**

5. **At the bottom of the Tools panel, click the Switch Foreground and Background Colors button.**

6. **With the default Layer 1 selected, choose Layer>Flatten Image.**

   When you flatten an image, all layers in the file are flattened into a locked Background layer. Because this file currently has only one layer, the new Background layer is simply a solid white fill. It is important to note that the defined Background color is not applied as the color of the resulting Background layer.

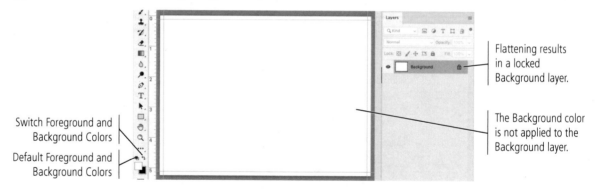

Switch Foreground and Background Colors

Default Foreground and Background Colors

Flattening results in a locked Background layer.

The Background color is not applied to the Background layer.

7. **With the Background layer selected, choose Edit>Fill.**

   You can fill a selection with a number of options:

   - Choose the defined foreground or background color.

   - Choose Color to define a specific color in the Color Picker dialog box.

   - Choose Content Aware to fill an area with pixels from surrounding image areas.

   - Choose Pattern, and then choose a specific pattern in the pop-up menu.

   - Choose History to fill the object with a specific history state (if possible).

   - Choose Black, 50% Gray, or White.

   You can also define a specific blending mode and opacity for the filled pixels. Using layers for different elements, however, is typically a better option than changing the fill transparency settings because you can adjust the layer blending mode and opacity as often as necessary.

*Note:*

*Press Shift-Delete/Backspace to open the Fill dialog box.*

8. **In the Fill dialog box, choose Background Color in the Contents menu and then click OK.**

   Because you did not draw a specific selection area, the entire selected layer (the Background layer) is filled.

9. **Choose File>Save As. In the Save As dialog box, change the file name to blvd.psd and click Save.**

   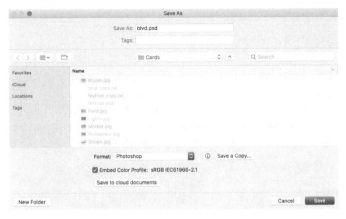

10. **Continue to the next exercise.**

# Control Missing and Mismatched Profiles

In the Color Settings dialog box, you told Photoshop how to handle images with profiles that don't match your working profiles, as well as images that don't have embedded profiles. These issues become important any time you work with files from more than a single source — and especially with client-supplied images, which often come from a wide variety of sources.

1. **With blvd.psd open, open Lights.jpg from your WIP>Cards folder.**

   This image does not have an embedded profile, so (as you defined in the Color Settings dialog box) Photoshop asks how you want to handle the file.

*Note:*

*It's quite common to find images that don't have embedded color profiles, especially when you work with older (legacy) files. In this case, color management will be imperfect, at best, since you don't know how the image was captured.*

2. **Choose Leave As Is and click OK.**

3. **With Lights.jpg open, chose Select>All. Choose Edit>Copy, then close the file.**

4. **With blvd.psd active, choose Edit>Paste.**

   Because the file's locked Background layer was selected, the pasted contents are added as a new layer immediately above the existing (selected) layer. Remember, you can't paste content onto a locked layer.

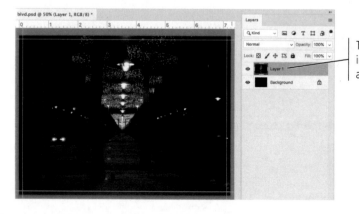

The pasted image is added as a new layer.

*Note:*

*Refer back to Project 1: New Music Artwork for a more detailed explanation of the Background layer.*

5. **In the Layers panel, rename Layer 1 as Lights.**

6. **Choose File>Save. Click OK in the Maximize Compatibility warning.**

   As we already explained, this warning appears the first time you save a file that has at least one regular layer.

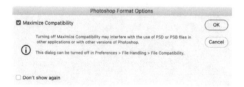

7. **Open the file festival.psd from your WIP>Cards folder.**

8. **Open the file Bloom.jpg, and read the resulting warning.**

   This file has an embedded profile, but it does not match your defined working RGB profile. Again, you told the application to show a warning when opening a file with a mismatched profile.

9. **Choose the option to use the embedded profile, then click OK.**

10. **Copy the contents of the file, then close it.**

11. **With festival.psd open, choose Edit>Paste.**

    In the Color Settings dialog box, you told the application to warn you if profiles do not match when you paste layer content. Photoshop cannot manage more than one profile for a single color space within the same file.

    The Convert option converts the pasted image colors to the color profile of the file into which you're pasting, preserving the color appearance. The Don't Convert option preserves the color data, but not the actual profile, in the pasted information.

12. **In the Paste Profile Mismatch dialog box, choose the Convert option, and then click OK.**

    Because this file has no Background layer, the pasted image is pasted into the active Layer 1.

    The pasted content is added to the selected Layer 1.

13. **In the Layers panel, rename Layer 1 as Bloom.**

14. **Save the file and continue to the next stage of the project.**

# STAGE 2 / Manipulating Pixels

Before digital image-editing software, a photo was a photo. If you wanted a different angle or arrangement, you simply took another photo. Digital photo editing makes it much easier to manipulate the actual content of an image — from scaling specific objects to a different size or moving them to a new location, to changing the image's entire focal point. In this stage of the project, you will learn a number of techniques for changing the content in the client's supplied images to better meet the needs of the project.

## Apply Content-Aware Scaling

When you scale a selection, you are stretching or squashing the pixels in that selection. This can produce the result you want, but it can also badly distort the image. Content-aware scaling intends to correct this problem by analyzing the image and preserving areas of detail when you scale the image.

*Watch the video* **Applying Content-Aware Scaling in Photoshop** *in your online student resources.*

1. **Make blvd.psd the active file.**

   The focus of this image is directly down the center. Because you are going to add type and other images to complete the entire postcard composition, you first need to move the image's focal point to create room for the textual elements.

2. **Choose the Move tool in the Tools panel.**

3. **With the Lights layer selected in the Layers panel, click in the document window to activate it. Press Shift, then click and drag to the left until the path in the image is approximately one-third of the way across the canvas.**

   As you can see, moving a layer's contents reveals the underlying layer. The right edge of the path image creates a harsh line.

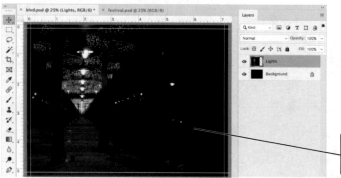

Just moving the layer reveals the content of underlying layers.

**Note:**

*The black background does not appear clearly in our screen captures, however, you should be able to see the edge on your monitor.*

4. **Choose Edit>Undo Move.**

   Rather than simply moving the image to the position you want, you are going to scale it to fill the entire space, while moving the lighted path into the left half of the image.

5. **With the Lights layer still selected, choose Edit>Transform>Scale.**

   When you enter into transformation mode by calling any of the Transform submenu options, the selection (or entire layer, if you don't have a specific area selected) is surrounded by a bounding box and handles, which you can use to control the transformation. The Options bar also includes fields for numerically transforming the selection.

6. **In the Options bar, turn off the Maintain Aspect Ration option between the W and H field.**

7. **Click the left-center handle on the image layer and drag left until the path in the image is approximately one-third of the way across the canvas.**

   When Maintain Aspect Ration is inactive, you can scale a selection in one direction (in this case, width) without affecting the other dimension (in this case, height).

   It can be helpful to reduce the view percentage so you can see more area around the defined canvas.

   Transformations alter the pixels in the layer. As you can see, the lights are distorted by scaling the layer in only one direction.

   Maintain Aspect Ratio is not active.   Scaling in only one direction distorts the image content.

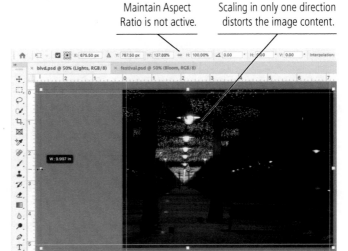

8. **In the Options bar, click the Cancel Transform button (or press ESC).**

   As long as the transformation handles remain visible, you can cancel any changes you made. By cancelling the transformation, the layer is restored to its original state.

**Note:**

*If Maintain Aspect Ration is active, you can press the Shift key and drag a transformation handle to transform a selection away from its original aspect ratio.*

9. **With the Lights layer selected, choose Edit>Content-Aware Scale.**

   Again, you see the transformation handles. The process is virtually the same as regular scaling, but it identifies and tries to protect areas of detail when you scale the image.

10. **In the Options bar, turn off the Maintain Aspect Ration option between the W and H field.**

11. **Click the left-center handle on the layer and drag left until the path in the image is approximately one-third of the way across the canvas.**

    As you can see, some distortion still occurs. However, the lights hanging over the path — the most obvious point of detail — are not noticeably distorted. Other areas of detail — the trees and bench, for example — are somewhat distorted, but not nearly as badly as they were from the regular scale transformation.

    Maintain Aspect Ratio is not active.   Content-aware scaling attempts to preserve areas of detail.

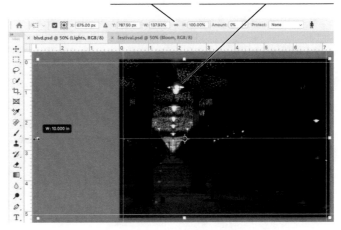

12. **Press Return/Enter to finalize the transformation.**

13. **Save the file and continue to the next exercise.**

## More About Content-Aware Scaling

Content-aware scaling identifies areas of detail when it determines what to protect. In some cases, though, the image focus might have little or no detail within the shape areas, like the white bird in the following images. To solve this problem, you can identify a specific mask area to protect when you use content-aware scaling.

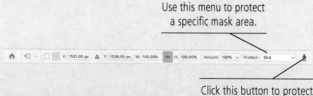

Use this menu to protect a specific mask area.

Click this button to protect skin tones from scaling.

Original image

Image scaled using
Transform>Scale mode

Image scaled using
Content-Aware Scale mode

Image scaled using
Content-Aware Scale mode, but with
the bird area protected by a mask.

## Use the Content-Aware Move Tool

Photoshop makes it easy to move content around on the canvas. If an entire layer is selected, you can easily use the Move tool to move all the content on that layer to a different location. If you create a specific selection area using one of the marquee or lasso tools, you can also move only the selected area to another location on the active layer. It's important to realize, however, that this process actually removes the area under the original selection area, which might not be what you want. The Content-Aware Move tool allows you to move a selection and fill the original selection area with detail instead of leaving an empty hole.

*Watch the video* ***Using the Content-Aware Move Tool in Photoshop*** *in your online student resources.*

1. **Make festival.psd the active file.**

   The main focus of the poppy image is nicely centered in the canvas. To make room for the other pieces of the composition, you need the flower to be on the right side of the image.

2. **Choose the Lasso tool in the Tools panel.**

3. **Draw a marquee that roughly selects the flower in the center of the image.**

Lasso tool

Draw a loose selection around the entire flower.

**Note:**

*Make sure your selection area is well away from the flower petals to avoid unwanted remnants after you move the selection.*

4. **Choose the Move tool in the Tools panel.**

5. **Click inside the selection area, then drag it to the right side of the canvas.**

When you use the Move tool with a specific selection marquee, you are moving all of the pixels within that selection area. The area of the original selection is removed from that layer, so you can see underlying layers (or transparent gray-and-white checkerboard, if there is no underlying layer).

Move tool

Moving the selection reveals the underlying layers (or transparent area if there is no underlying layer).

You should notice that the moved pixels remain on the same layer. As long as the selection marquee remains active, you can continue to move the selected pixels around the same layer without affecting the other pixels on that layer. If you deselect, however, the underlying pixels will be permanently replaced by the pixels you moved.

To get around this problem, it's fairly common practice to move selected pixels to another layer before dragging with the Move tool:

1. Make a selection.
2. Choose Edit>Cut to remove the selected pixels from the original layer or choose Edit>Copy to keep the selected pixels on the original layer.
3. Choose Edit>Paste to add the cut/copied pixels onto a new layer.

6. **Choose Edit>Undo Move to restore all the pixels to their original positions.**

7. **With the same marquee still selected, choose the Content-Aware Move tool (nested under the Spot Healing Brush tool).**

You can draw a new marquee with the Content-Aware Move tool, but in this case it isn't necessary because you already defined the selection area with the Lasso tool.

**Note:**

*If you leave the selection marquee in place before choosing Edit>Paste, the cut/copied pixels are pasted in exactly the same position they were in when you cut/copied them.*

8. **In the Options bar, make sure Move is selected in the Mode menu and the Transform On Drop option is selected.**

When the Content-Aware Move tool is active, the Mode menu in the Options bar determines whether you will move or extend the selection area.

The Structure and Color fields determine how closely the software analyzes the image to create the final result. Structure is defined on a 1–7 scale and Color is defined on a 0–10 scale.

When the Transform On Drop option is active, releasing the mouse button results in a bounding box around the moved selection. You can use the bounding-box handles to adjust the moved selection's size. The movement is not finalized until you press Return/Enter or click the Commit Transform button in the Options bar. If Transform On Drop is *not* checked, the movement is finalized as soon as you release the mouse button.

9. **Click inside the selection area and drag the selected flower to the right side of the canvas.**

Content-Aware Move tool

Transform On Drop is checked by default.

When you release the mouse button, bounding-box handles are available to transform the moved selection.

Moving the selection does not reveal the underlying layers.

10. **Press Return/Enter to finalize the move.**

When the process is complete, the original selection area is filled with pixels that seamlessly blend into the surrounding area. The edges of the moved area are also blended into their new surrounding area.

**Note:**

*The process might take a while to complete because Photoshop has to analyze and determine which pixels to create. Be patient.*

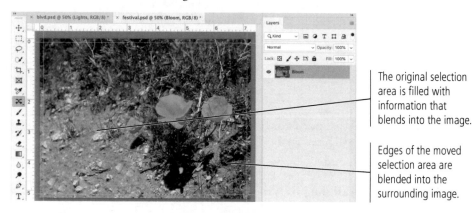

The original selection area is filled with information that blends into the image.

Edges of the moved selection area are blended into the surrounding image.

11. **Turn off the active selection (Select>Deselect).**

12. **Save the file and continue to the next exercise.**

## More About the Content-Aware Move Tool

You can also use the Content-Aware Move tool in Extend mode to enlarge objects in a linear direction, as you can see in the images to the right.

Tighter selection marquees generally produce better results than a loose area that includes a lot of background pixels.

Original image

Image after extending the building with the Content-Aware Move tool.

##  Apply a Tilt-Shift Blur Effect

Many of the Blur filters can be used for functional purposes, such as removing noise with the Gaussian Blur filter. Others have more artistic purposes, and include far more specific controls than a simple dialog box interface. Photoshop includes five sophisticated blur filters, which are controlled in a specialized workspace that contains only the tools you need to apply the filters.

1. **Make the blvd.psd file active, and make sure the Lights layer is selected in the Layers panel.**

2. **Choose Filter>Blur Gallery>Tilt-Shift.**

   The Tilt-Shift filter applies a linear blur out from a center line. You can use on-screen controls in the Blur Gallery to change the angle and position of the blur, as well as a number of other options.

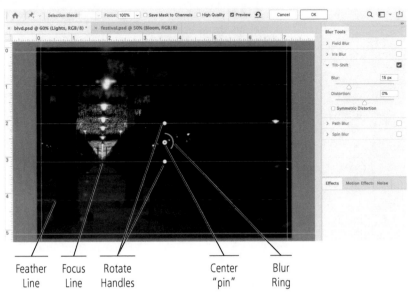

Feather Line    Focus Line    Rotate Handles    Center "pin"    Blur Ring

3. **Move the cursor over either Rotate Handle. Press Shift, then click and drag until the cursor feedback shows the angle of 90°.**

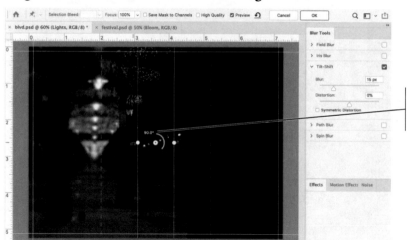

**Note:**

*Pressing Shift constrains the rotation to 22.5° increments.*

Heads-up display shows the blur rotation angle.

4. **Click the center "pin" of the blur control and drag left until the row of lights is between the two focus lines.**

   Anything between the two focus lines will be preserved without a blur.

5. **Click the left Focus Line (the solid line) away from the Rotate Handle, and drag left until the line is close to the right side of the left palm tree.**

6. **Click the left Feather Line (the dotted line) and drag until the line is just past the left side of the same palm tree.**

   The Feather Lines define the distance from unblurred (at the Focus Line) and completely blurred pixels.

**Note:**

*In the Effects panel, you can control **bokeh** effects — the aesthetic qualities of blurred points of light — for a field, iris, or tilt-shift blur.*

***Light Bokeh** brightens blurred areas of an image.*

***Bokeh Color** changes the color of lightened areas in the image from neutral (0%) to colorful (100%).*

***Light Range** determines which brightness values are affected by the Light Bokeh.*

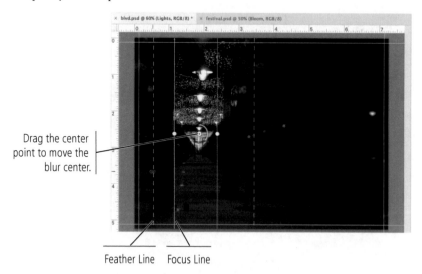

Drag the center point to move the blur center.

Feather Line    Focus Line

7. **Repeat Steps 5–6 to position the right Focus and Feather lines relative to the right palm tree.**

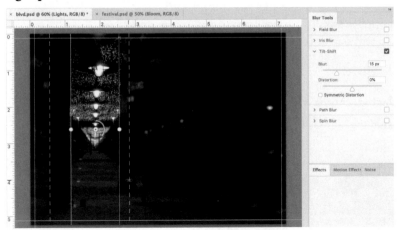

**Note:**

*The Distortion option in the Blur Tools panel defines the shape of the blur that is applied. You can also check the Symmetric Distortion option to apply the distortion amount to both sides of the blur.*

8. **Click the Blur Ring and drag the white area until the cursor feedback shows Blur: 20.**

Changing intensity of the blur using the on-screen control applies the same change in the Blur field in the Blur Tools panel.

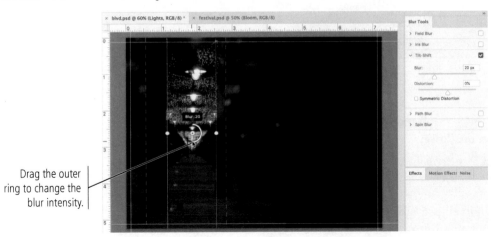

Drag the outer ring to change the blur intensity.

9. **Click OK in the Options bar to apply the blur.**

When you finalize the blur, the process can take a while to render. Be patient.

Because the Lights layer is a regular layer, the Blur Gallery filter is applied destructively. If you apply these filters to a Smart Object layer, they are remembered as Smart Filters and can be edited.

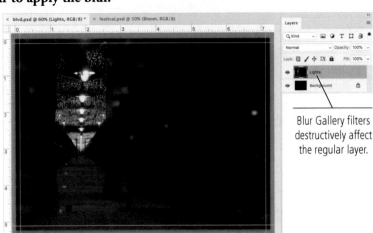

Blur Gallery filters destructively affect the regular layer.

10. **Save the file and continue to the next exercise.**

Apply an Iris Blur Effect

The Iris Blur filter mimics the effect of changing the aperture, focal length, and focus distance with a camera. The blur applies around a central point; you can use on-screen controls to define the shape and size of the blur.

1. **Make the festival.psd file active.**

2. **With the Bloom layer selected, choose Filter>Blur Gallery>Iris Blur.**

   The Iris blur is also controlled in the Blur Gallery interface.

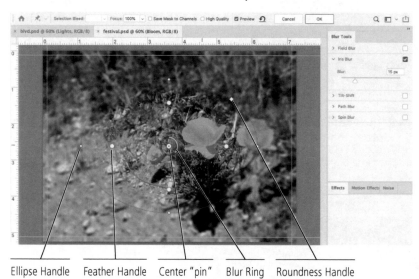

Ellipse Handle    Feather Handle    Center "pin"    Blur Ring    Roundness Handle

3. **Click the center "pin" and drag to position the blur so it is approximately centered on the flower.**

   You can click away from the existing blur controls to add a new pin, which means you can define more than one focal point on the same layer.

4. **Click the right ellipse handle and drag left to make the ellipse narrower. Release the mouse button when the ellipse is approximately the same height and width.**

   If you click the ellipse *away* from the handle, you can enlarge or shrink the existing ellipse without affecting its proportional shape.

Drag the pin to move the focal point of the blur.

Drag the Ellipse Handle to rotate or change the shape of the blur ellipse.

Drag the Ellipse to resize the blur without changing its shape.

*Note:*

*You can apply a blur to only certain parts of a layer by drawing a selection marquee before opening the Blur Gallery. In this case, you can use the Selection Bleed option (in the Options bar) to determine how much the selected area blends with the unselected areas.*

*Note:*

*Click the Roundness Handle and drag to make the blur shape more or less rectangular.*

5. **Click the top Feather Handle and drag down until it is placed at the top edge of the center flower.**

The distance between the Feather Handle and the outer ellipse defines the length of the blur. When you click and drag one handle, all four move symmetrically.

Drag any Feather Handle to change the distance from unblurred to entirely blurred pixels.

When you drag one Feather Handle, all four move the same distance.

6. **Press Option/Alt, then click the bottom Feather Handle and drag up to increase the blur distance on only the bottom of the flower. Release the mouse button when the Feather handle is almost touching the Blur Ring.**

Pressing Option/Alt allows you to move one Feather Handle independently of the others.

Option/Alt-drag a Feather Handle to move it independently of the other handles.

*Note:*

*You can use the Save Mask to Channels option (in the Blur Gallery Options bar) to create an alpha channel mask from the defined blur. Solid areas in the mask show areas that are unblurred; white areas of the mask show areas that are entirely blurred.*

7. **Click the Blur Ring and drag around to increase the intensity to 20 px.**

*Note:*

*The Focus option in the Options bar defines the clarity of the area in the focus zone. For a Tilt-Shift blur, this is the area between the two Focus Lines. For an Iris blur, this is the area inside the Feather Handles.*

8. **Click OK in the Options bar to apply the blur.**

9. **Save the file and continue to the next stage of the project.**

# More About the Blur Gallery

FOUNDATIONS

## Field Blur

The Field Blur filter applies an overall blur that affects the entire layer. Changing the blur intensity changes the amount of blur that is applied to that layer.

You can also place multiple focus points to change the blur in different areas of the layer. In the image to the right, we applied a 25-px blur to the pin at the top of the image and a 0-px blur to the pin in the center portion of the image. The 0-px pin prevents the blur from affecting the entire image, so the front of the bridge appears in focus.

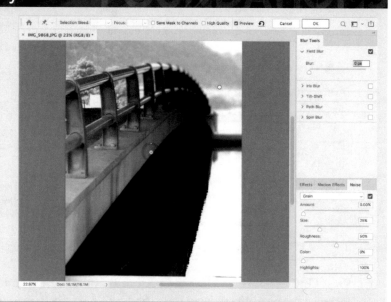

## Spin Blur

The Spin Blur filter creates a rotational blur around a defined point. The blur angle controls the amount of blur that is applied.

You can click and drag the rotation point to move the blur's center point. If you Option/Alt-click and drag the rotation point, you can move it away from the center of the blur ring to create an off-center spin blur.

The feather handles define the outer edge of the area affected by the blur.

Clicking and dragging the blur ring away from the ellipse handles resizes the blur ring proportionally. You can also click and drag one of the ellipse handles to resize the blur ring in only one direction.

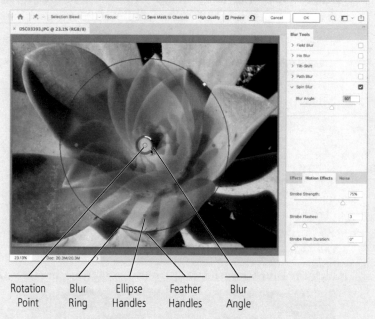

Rotation Point    Blur Ring    Ellipse Handles    Feather Handles    Blur Angle

You can also use the Motion Effects panel to change the strength of the blur:

- **Strobe Flashes** defines the number of exposures that will be visible.
- **Strobe Strength** defines how much blurring is visible between strobe flash exposures. A setting of 0% (the default) means no strobe effect is visible. A setting of 100% results in very little blur between exposures.
- **Strobe Flash Duration** defines the length of the strobe flash exposure in degrees, which controls the distance of the blur around the blur circumference.

Applying a spin blur with an increased Stroke Strength effect creates the appearance of the blade in motion. Because Strobe Flashes effect is set to 3, you can see three ghosted versions of the plant's center leaves in the image above.

# More About the Blur Gallery (continued)

## Path Blur

The Path Blur filter creates a motion blur based on a path that you define.

Clicking and dragging in the gallery window creates the initial blur path. You can click anywhere along the blue path to create a path midpoint and bend the path in a specific direction.

In the Blur Tools panel, you can use the top menu to define a basic blur or rear sync flash blur (this simulates the effect of a flash fired at the end of an exposure).

The Speed slider defines the overall blur amount for all defined blur paths.

The Taper slider adjusts the edge fading of blurs. Higher values allow the blur to fade gradually.

The Centered Blur option creates stable blurs by centering the blur shape for any pixel on the defined path.

Each end point on the blur path can have a different speed, or the degree of blur that is applied at that point. If **Edit Blur Shapes** is checked in the Blur Tools panel, you can drag a red arrow to change the speed (length) of the blur and bend the red arrow to change the direction of the blur that is applied along the blur path.

In the Motion Effects panel, Strobe Flashes defines the number of exposures of the virtual strobe flash light. Strobe Strength defines how much blurring is visible between strobe flash exposures.

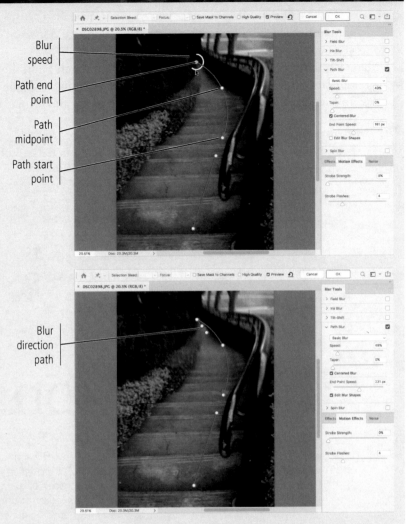

Blur speed

Path end point

Path midpoint

Path start point

Blur direction path

In the above images, we created two separate blur paths. The first defines a curved blur that follows the shape of the lower stairs; the starting point has a rather high blur speed and the end point has a blur speed of 0 px. Because the 0-px blur speed does not eliminate all blurring at the end point, we added a second straight blur path with 0-px blur speeds at both ends to eliminate all blurring in that area (the top of the staircase) of the image.

# STAGE 3 / **Working with Type**

Type is a vector-based element. As long as you maintain type as vectors, the letter shapes can be resized and transformed without losing quality. As you know, Photoshop can combine raster and vector objects into a single composition.

Many Photoshop jobs require some kind of type. Although Photoshop is not a typesetting tool by definition, its type capabilities are robust enough for creating and manipulating type in a variety of ways. To complete these postcards, you are going to create and format several type elements.

## *The Anatomy of Type*

Before we jump into the exercises in this section, you should understand the terms that you will often hear when people talk about type:

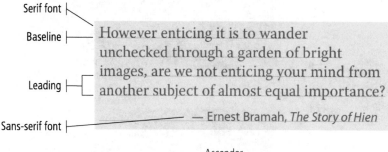

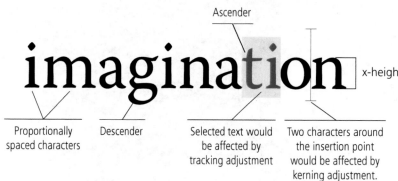

Type is typically divided into two basic categories: serif and sans serif. **Serif type** has small flourishes on the ends of the letterforms; **sans-serif** has no such decorations (*sans* is French for "without"). The actual shape of letters is determined by the specific **font** you use. Each **character** in a font is referred to as a **glyph**.

Fonts can be monospaced or proportionally spaced. In a monospace font, each character takes up the same amount of space on a line. In other words, a lowercase "i" and "w" will occupy the same horizontal width. In a proportionally spaced font, different characters occupy different amounts of horizontal space as necessary.

When you set type in a digital application, the letters rest on a nonprinting line called the **baseline**. If a type element has more than one line in a single paragraph, the distance from one baseline to the next is called **leading** (pronounced, "ledding"). Most applications set the default leading as 120% of the type size, but you can change the leading to any value you prefer.

The **x-height** of type is the height of the lowercase letter "x." Elements that extend below the baseline are called **descenders** (as in, "g," "j," and "p"). Elements that extend above the x-height are called **ascenders** (as in, "b," "d," and "k").

The size of type is usually measured in **points** (there are approximately 72 points in an inch). When you define a specific type size, you determine the distance from the bottom of the descenders to the top of the ascenders, plus a small extra space above the ascenders called the **body clearance**.

Place and Format Point Type

You can create two basic kinds of type in Photoshop: point type and area type. **Point type** is created by simply clicking in the image window with one of the Type tools. A point type element can exist on one or multiple lines. Point type can continue into apparent infinity without starting a new line. If you want to start a new line, you have to manually tell Photoshop where to create the break.

1. **With festival.psd active, choose the Horizontal Type tool.**

   You can access the basic type options in the Options bar. Additional options are available in the Character and Paragraph panels.

2. **In the Tools panel, click the Default Foreground and Background Colors button.**

   Type automatically adopts the active foreground color — in this case, black.

3. **In the Options bar, change the Font Size to 28 pt.**

   If you define type settings before you create a type layer, those settings automatically apply to the layer you create.

*Watch the video* **Type Basics in Photoshop** *in your online student resources.*

*Note:*

*As of November 2021, Photoshop's 3D features no longer function properly, and they are in the process of being deprecated (removed) from the program. Do not use the Create 3D from text button.*

A  Toggle Text Orientation
B  Font Family
C  Font Style
D  Font Size
E  Anti-Aliasing Method
F  Left Align Text
G  Center Align Text
H  Right Align Text
I  Text Color
J  Create Warped Text
K  Toggle the Character and Pararaph Panels

Horizontal Type tool

4. **Click anywhere in the canvas to create a type layer.**

   When you create a new type layer, it is automatically filled with placeholder text, which is highlighted. You can immediately see the formatting that is currently applied to the new type layer.

*Note:*

*You can turn off the automatic placeholder text in the Type pane of the Preferences dialog box.*

Cancel any current edits     Commit any current edits

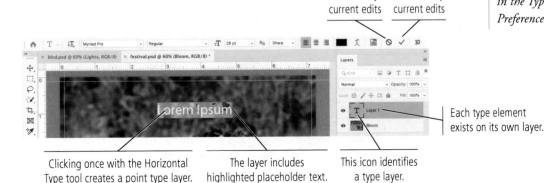

Each type element exists on its own layer.

Clicking once with the Horizontal Type tool creates a point type layer.

The layer includes highlighted placeholder text.

This icon identifies a type layer.

5. **With the placeholder text selected, type Antelope Valley.**

   When text is selected on a type layer, typing replaces the previously highlighted text with whatever you type.

6. **In the Options bar, click the Commit button to finalize your changes to the active Type layer.**

   You can also choose a different tool, or select a different layer to finalize your changes.

*Note:*

*You must install the ATC fonts from the Student Files website to complete the rest of this project.*

After committing the edits, the type layer adopts its name based on the text in the layer.

7. **With the new type layer selected, click the Font menu to highlight it and type atc g.**

   Typing in the Font menu returns a list of all fonts that contain the defined search string. The resulting font names do not need to exactly match the search string. In this case, any fonts that include the characters "atc" and "g" are returned.

*Note:*

*If you're working with the insertion point flashing in a type layer or you have characters on a type layer selected, you can't use the keyboard shortcuts to access different tools.*

8. **Move the mouse cursor over the first font in the resulting list.**

   Photoshop includes a live font preview that automatically shows the selected text in the font where your mouse cursor is currently hovering.

Type in this field to search for specific fonts.　Click this button to show all fonts that are available on your computer.

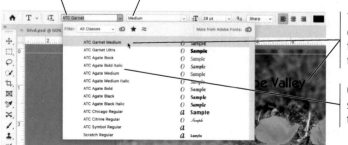

The active type layer changes to show the font that is active under the mouse cursor.

Only fonts matching the search criteria appear in the resulting menu.

9. **Click ATC Garnet Medium in the menu to change the font of the active type layer.**

10. **Click with the Horizontal Type tool again (away from the existing type) to create a second type layer, then type Poppy Festival.**

    Clicking places the insertion point in a new point type element, creating a new type layer.

The Type tools remember the last formatting options you defined.

Clicking again creates a separate type layer.

**11. With the insertion point flashing in the second type layer, choose Select>All.**

When the insertion point is flashing, this command highlights (selects) all of the text in the active type layer.

You can also click and drag to select specific characters, double-click to select an entire word, triple-click to select an entire line, or quadruple-click to select an entire paragraph.

**12. In the Options bar, change the Font Style to Ultra and change the Font Size to 72 pt.**

If you type in the field, you have to Press Return/Enter (or click the Commit button) to finalize the new formatting. If you choose a defined size from the attached menu, you do not need to press Return/Enter.

Character attributes such as font size affect all selected characters.

Point type exists on a single line unless you manually insert a line break.

**13. Press the Left Arrow key to deselect the characters and move the insertion point to the beginning of the type. With the insertion point still flashing in the type, press and hold Command/Control to access the type layer bounding box.**

Pressing Command/Control temporarily switches to the Move tool, so you can move a type layer without switching away from the Horizontal Type tool.

Press Command/Control while the insertion point is flashing to access the layer's transformation bounding box.

**14. Click inside the bounding-box area and drag to move the type until it is centered horizontally on the canvas, approximately 0.25″ from the top ruler guide.**

The pink smart guides identify when the dragged content is centered on the canvas. On Windows, the smart guides do not appear while you are pressing the Control key. You can release that key after you start dragging so that the smart guides identify when the type is centered horizontally.

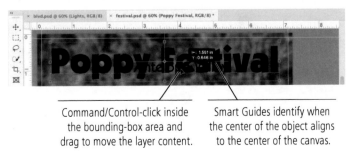

Command/Control-click inside the bounding-box area and drag to move the layer content.

Smart Guides identify when the center of the object aligns to the center of the canvas.

**15. Use the Layers panel to hide the Antelope Valley layer.**

This will allow you to better see the effects of your changes in the next few steps.

You can click the arrow to the right of the Font Family menu to open the Font panel, which provides a number of options for finding fonts you want to use in your design. (The same options are available wherever you see a Font Family menu — the Character panel, the Options bar, and the Properties panel.)

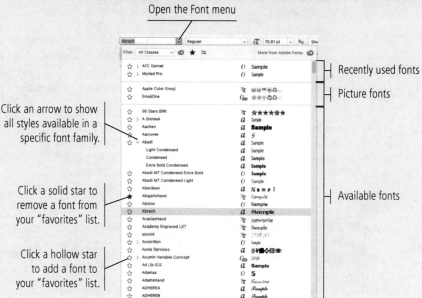

Open the Font menu

Recently used fonts

Picture fonts

Available fonts

Click an arrow to show all styles available in a specific font family.

Click a solid star to remove a font from your "favorites" list.

Click a hollow star to add a font to your "favorites" list.

The top section of the menu lists up to ten of the most recently used fonts. These appear in the order in which they were used, with the most recent at the top of the menu. You can change the number of displayed fonts in the Type pane of the Preferences dialog box.

The second section lists SVG fonts.
The third section lists all other fonts that are available to Photoshop.

The font family names in each section appear in alphabetical order. An arrow to the left of a font name indicates that a specific font family includes more than one style. You can click the arrow to show all possible styles in the panel.

If you apply a font that includes more than one style, the style you choose appears in the Font Style menu. You can open the Font Style menu to change the style, without changing the font family.

Above the list of fonts in the Font panel, you can use the Filter menu to show only certain classes of fonts. You can also use the three filter buttons to show only certain fonts in the panel. Simply click an active button to turn off that filter.

&#9673; Show Adobe Fonts

&#9733; Show Favorite Fonts

&#8776; Show Similar Fonts

The right column in the Font menu shows a sample of the font, as well as an icon to identify the type of font:

*a* **PostScript (Type 1) fonts** have two file components (outline and printer) that are required for output.

**T̲r** **TrueType fonts** have a single file, but (until recently) were primarily used on the Windows platform.

*O* **OpenType fonts** are contained in a single file that can include more than 60,000 glyphs (characters) in a single font. OpenType fonts are cross-platform; they can be used on both Macintosh and Windows systems.

**G̲ₛᵥ₉** **OpenType SVG fonts** allow font glyphs to be created as SVG (scalable vector graphics) artwork, which means glyphs can include multiple colors and gradients. These fonts, which are relatively new, are most commonly used for emojis.

**G̲ᵥₐᵣ** **OpenType Variable fonts**, introduced in 2016, were developed jointly by Adobe, Apple, Google, and Microsoft to allow a single font file to store a continuous range of variants. If you apply a variable font, you can adjust the width and weight of the applied font, without the need for different font files for variations, such as Bold, Black, Condensed, or Extended.

&#9673; **Adobe fonts** (previously called Typekit fonts) are those that have been activated from Adobe servers through your Creative Cloud account. (Adobe fonts are explained in greater detail in Project 5: Calendar Cover.)

16. **Click to place the insertion point between the "F" and "e" in the word Festival.**

17. **In the Options bar, click the button to toggle open the Character and Paragraph panels.**

    You can also choose Window>Character or Type>Panels>Character to open the Character panel. Changes made in the Character panel apply only to selected text.

18. **In the Character panel, change the Kerning field to –30.**

    Kerning and tracking control the spacing between individual characters. **Kerning** adjusts the spacing between two specific characters (called a **kerning pair**). **Tracking** (also called range kerning) is applied over a range of selected type.

    Kerning values are based, by default, on the type **metrics** (the values stored in the font data). Professional-quality fonts include predefined kerning and tracking tables in the font data. The **Optical** option in the Kerning menu is useful for fonts that don't have built-in kerning values. Photoshop applies kerning based on how it perceives letter shapes.

    You should always check the letter spacing when you set headline type, use All Caps or Small Caps type styles, or apply any other artificial manipulation.

    **Note:**

    *Kerning and tracking are largely matters of personal taste. In this project, you want the letters to be tightly spaced, but not touching.*

    Click here to toggle the Character and Paragraph panels.

    Kerning applies to the space between two characters, where the insertion point is placed.

19. **Continue adjusting the kerning between the letter pairs until you are satisfied with the results.**

    **Note:**

    *Press Option/Alt-Left Arrow to apply –20 kerning units or Option/Alt-Right Arrow to apply +20 kerning units at the insertion point.*

20. **With the insertion point flashing in the Type layer, press Command/Control to access the type layer's bounding box and handles.**

21. **While still holding the Command/Control key, click the bottom-right bounding-box handle, press Shift, and drag down. Resize the type until its right edge is approximately 0.25″ from the right ruler guide.**

    Because the Type tool is active, the Options bar does not include an option to Maintain Aspect Ratio during this kind of transformation. To scale the type layer proportionally, you have to press the Shift key while dragging one of the handles.

    Drag the handles to resize or transform the type layer disproportionally.

Changes to character formatting affect only selected characters. If you make changes before typing, the changes apply to all characters you type from the insertion point.

All of the character formatting options that are available in the Options bar are also available in the Character panel. However, the Character panel includes a number of other options that control the appearance of type in your document.

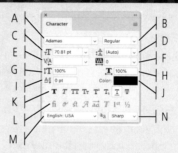

A **Font Family** is the general font that is applied, such as Minion or Warnock Pro.

B **Font Style** is the specific variation of the applied font, such as Italic, Bold, or Light.

C **Font Size** is the size of the type in points.

D **Leading** is the distance from one baseline to the next. Adobe applications treat leading as a character attribute, even though leading controls the space between lines of an individual paragraph. (Space between paragraphs is controlled using the Space Before and Space After options in the Paragraph panel.) To change leading for an entire paragraph, you must first select the entire paragraph.

If you increase the leading for only certain characters in a line, keep in mind that the adjusted leading applies to the entire line where adjusted characters exist. For example:

> In this sentence, we changed the leading
>
> for only the <u>underlined</u> word; all text in the same line moves to accommodate the adjusted leading of the characters.

E **Kerning** increases or decreases the space between pairs of letters. Kerning is used in cases in which particular letters in specific fonts need to be manually spread apart or brought together to eliminate a crowded or spread-out appearance. Manual kerning is usually necessary in headlines or other large type elements. Many commercial fonts have built-in kerning pairs, so you won't need to apply much hands-on intervention with kerning. Adobe applications default to the kerning values stored in the **font metrics**.

F **Tracking**, also known as "range kerning," refers to the overall tightness or looseness across a range of characters. Tracking and kerning are applied in thousandths of an **em** — the width of the applied type size in points.

G, H **Vertical Scale** and **Horizontal Scale** artificially stretch or contract the selected characters. This scaling is a quick way of achieving condensed or expanded type if those variations of a font don't exist. (Type that has been artificially condensed or expanded too much looks bad because the scaling destroys the type's metrics.)

I **Baseline Shift** raises characters above or below the baseline where other characters rest, such as you might use for an exponent ($x^4$) or chemical symbol ($H_2O$).

J **Character Color** moves the selected type above or below the baseline by a specific number of points. Positive numbers move the characters up; negative values move the characters down.

K Type Styles — **All Caps**, **Small Caps**, **Superscript**, **Subscript**, **Underline**, and **Strikethrough** — change the appearance of selected characters.

L **OpenType Attributes** give you access to alternate glyphs, such as ligatures, stylistic alternates, and fractions. These options are only available if the active font is an OpenType font, which can store more than 65,000 glyphs or characters in a single font. Not all stylistic alternates are available for all OpenType fonts.

M **Language Dictionary** defines the language that is used to check spelling in the story.

N **Anti-Aliasing** can be used to help smooth the apparent edges of type when it is rendered (rasterized) — even if that doesn't happen until the final output. Anti-aliasing produces smooth-edge type by partially filling the edge pixels, which allows the edges of the type to better blend into the background when the type is rendered. (Be aware that anti-aliasing small type might distort the letter shapes.) Photoshop supports the following five options for anti-aliasing type, the effects of which are best viewed at higher zoom percentages:

- None applies no anti-aliasing.
- Sharp creates the sharpest type.
- Crisp makes type appear slightly sharp.
- Strong makes type appear heavier.
- Smooth makes type edges appear very smooth.

**22. When you finish resizing the type, release the Command/Control key.**

Because the Type tool is still active, the insertion point still flashes in the active type layer. The Font Size field in the Character panel and Options bar shows the new size that resulted from scaling the type.

The Font Size field shows the change that was created by scaling the type layer.

**23. Save the file and continue to the next exercise.**

 ## Use the Move Tool with Type Layers

Type layers in Photoshop are similar to most other layers. You can drag and transform type layers using most of the same tools that you use to transform other kinds of layers. You can scale or skew type layers; change their opacity, fill, and blending modes; apply layer styles; and even add warp effects, while still maintaining the editable type.

1. **With festival.psd active, make the Antelope Valley type layer visible. Click the Antelope Valley layer in the Layers panel to select it.**

2. **Choose the Move tool.**

Using the Move tool, you can move and manipulate type layers like any other layer, but you can't edit the actual type.

3. **With the Auto-Select option turned off in the Options bar, click and drag to move the type so the first letter in the layer appears just above the "o" in the word "Poppy."**

If you don't turn off the Auto-Select option, you must click exactly on the rather thin letters in the type. When this option is not checked, you can click anywhere in the canvas to drag the selected layer.

As you can see, the 28-pt text is too large to fit in the space. The type runs directly behind the "F" in the word "Festival" because the "Poppy Festival" type layer is higher in the layer stacking order.

*Note:*

*The only options you can't apply to live text are the Distort and Perspective transformations, custom warps (although you can use the built-in warp shapes), and filters. To use these features, you must rasterize the type layer.*

*Note:*

*Feel free to toggle rulers on and off as necessary while working on this (and all) projects.*

4. **In the Character panel, click the Color swatch to open the Color Picker for the text color.**

   The insertion point does not need to be flashing to change the formatting of the active type layer. Keep in mind, however, that any change you make while the insertion point is *not* flashing applies to all type in the layer. If you want to change the formatting of only some type on a layer, you first have to use the Type tool to select the characters you want to affect.

5. **Move the Eyedropper cursor over a bright orange color in the poppy image and click to sample that color. Click OK to change the type color.**

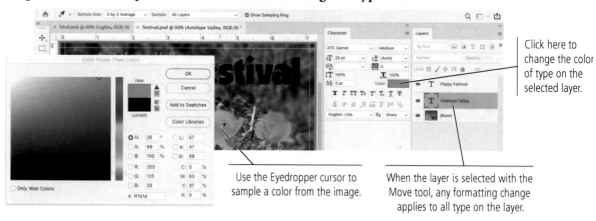

Click here to change the color of type on the selected layer.

Use the Eyedropper cursor to sample a color from the image.

When the layer is selected with the Move tool, any formatting change applies to all type on the layer.

6. **In the Character panel, reduce the font size to 22 pt.**

   This layer uses left paragraph alignment, and the origin point of the layer remains in place when you change the formatting.

This type layer is still selected.

7. **Select the Poppy Festival type layer, then use the Character panel to change the type color to white.**

8. **Save the file and continue to the next exercise.**

## The Paragraph Panel in Depth

You can change a number of paragraph attributes, including alignment and justification, indents, and space above and below paragraphs. The Justification options are only available when you work with area type (which you will do shortly), and some options are not relevant for point type that only occupies a single line.

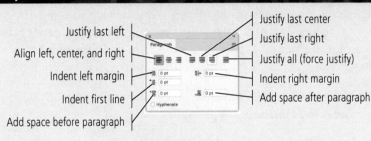

Justify last left
Align left, center, and right
Indent left margin
Indent first line
Add space before paragraph

Justify last center
Justify last right
Justify all (force justify)
Indent right margin
Add space after paragraph

### Hyphenation Options

When the Hyphenate option is selected, text in area type hyphenates automatically, based on the Hyphenation options in the Paragraph panel Options menu. You can control the minimum length of a word before it can be hyphenated, as well as the minimum number of characters that must appear before or after a hyphen.

The **Hyphen Limit** field defines how many hyphens can appear at the ends of consecutive lines. Formal rules of typography recommend limiting consecutive hyphens to three, but preferably, no more than two.

The **Hyphenation Zone** determines the distance from the right edge of a type area where automatic hyphens can exist. If this field is set to 1/2″, for example, the automatic hyphen would have to fall within half an inch of the type area edge for a word to be automatically hyphenated.

The final option, **Hyphenate Capitalized Words**, can be turned off to prevent automatic hyphenation in proper nouns such as corporate or product names — many companies seriously frown on their trademarks being split across lines.

### Justification Options

When you work with area type, you can justify paragraphs inside the type area. Justified type stretches horizontally to fill the width of the area. The last line of the paragraph can be aligned left, centered, or right, or it can be stretched based on your choice in the Paragraph panel. When text is justified, it's stretched based on the defined Justification options, which can be changed by choosing Justification in the Paragraph panel Options menu.

The Minimum and Maximum values define the acceptable spacing for justified paragraphs. The Desired value defines the *preferred* spacing for paragraphs:

- The **Word Spacing** fields control the space between words (anywhere you press the space bar). A 100% value uses the word spacing that is designed into the font data.

- The **Letter Spacing** fields control the space between letters, including kerning and tracking values. A 0% value means the letter spacing remains the same when you justify a paragraph.

- The **Glyph Scaling** fields control the width of individual characters. A 100% value means they are not stretched.

The **Auto Leading** field applies to both area type and point type that occupy more than one line. By default, automatic leading is set to 120% of the type size. You can change this automatic value, but it is usually better to change the leading for individual type instances instead.

# Create Vertically Oriented Type

Although most type (in English, at least) is oriented left-to-right, row-to-row, there are times when you want to orient type vertically — each character below the next. You can use the Vertical Type tool to accomplish this goal, whether for a foreign-language design or simply for artistic purposes.

1. **Make blvd.psd the active file, then choose the Vertical Type tool (nested under the Horizontal Type tool).**

2. **In the Character panel, choose ATC Garnet Ultra as the font, define the size as 72 pt, and choose white as the type color.**

3. **Open the Leading menu and choose Auto.**

   **Leading** is the distance from one baseline to the next. Adobe applications treat leading as a character attribute, even though leading controls the space between lines of an individual paragraph.

4. **Click to create a new type layer, then type BLVD.**

   When you use the Vertical Type tool, each letter appears below the previous one.

   As you can see, the left edges of the letters (especially B and L) do not align. Vertical type orientation does not recognize the edges of lettershapes for the sake of alignment.

   In the Options bar, the paragraph alignment options for vertical type affect the position of type relative to the point at which you click. You can align the type below, centered on, or above the origin point. You cannot, however, align the left or right edges of the letters.

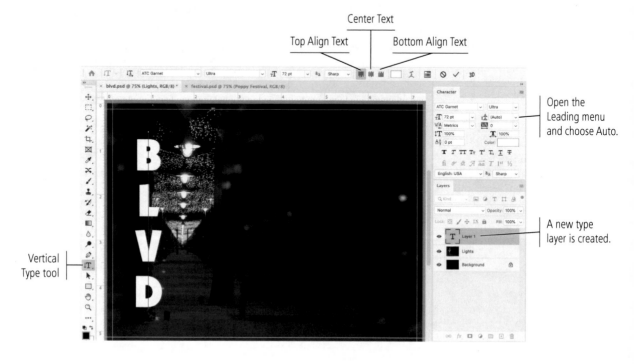

Center Text
Top Align Text
Bottom Align Text
Open the Leading menu and choose Auto.
A new type layer is created.
Vertical Type tool

**5. Click the Toggle Text Orientation button in the Options bar.**

This button switches the type between vertically and horizontally oriented type.

**6. Click to place the insertion point after the "B" and press Return/Enter to start a new paragraph.**

**7. Repeat this process to move each character onto a separate line.**

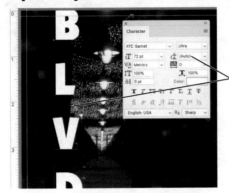

For horizontally oriented type, the default (auto) leading creates a large space from one baseline to the next.

**8. Place the insertion point before the "B." In the Options bar or Character panel, change the type size to 12 pt. Type THE and then press Return/Enter.**

Changes to character formatting apply only to the insertion point and the new type that you add from that point.

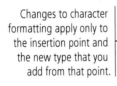

**9. Select the four letters in "BLVD." In the Character panel, change the Leading field to 55 pt.**

Although leading appears to apply to paragraphs, it is a character property. To change the leading for an entire paragraph, you have to select all characters in that paragraph.

Reduced leading reduces the space from one baseline to the next.

Changes to character formatting apply only to the highlighted type.

10. **Choose the Move tool. With the type layer selected, move it so the type begins in the top-left corner of the canvas, approximately 1/4" from the ruler guides.**

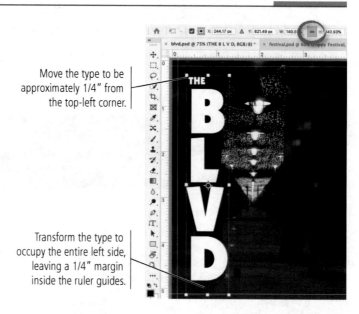

Move the type to be approximately 1/4" from the top-left corner.

11. **Choose Edit>Free Transform.**

12. **With Maintain Aspect Ratio active in the Options bar, click and drag the bottom-right handle until the letters occupy the entire left side of the canvas.**

    Leave approximately 1/4" from the bottom ruler guide, as shown in the image to the right.

Transform the type to occupy the entire left side, leaving a 1/4" margin inside the ruler guides.

13. **Press Return/Enter to finalize the transformation.**

14. **Double-click any of the characters on the type layer to highlight all of it.**

    You do not need to manually switch to the Type tool to access the characters in a type layer. Simply double-click the characters to highlight all characters on the layer; the Horizontal Type tool is automatically activated for you.

15. **Click to place the insertion point anywhere in the word "THE" (the first paragraph).**

16. **In the Paragraph panel, change the Indent Left Margin field to 4 pt.**

    You can choose Window>Paragraph to open the Paragraph panel, or click the Toggle the Character and Paragraph Panels button in the Options bar.

    The Indent values affect the position of the type relative to the layer's orientation point. This better aligns the "T" in "THE" with the left edge of the "B" in "BLVD."

    When you work with point type, paragraph attributes apply to all type on a single line. If you have more than one paragraph — as you do in this type layer — you can apply different paragraph format options to each paragraph.

17. **Change the Add Space After Paragraph field to −3 pt.**

    Leading affects the space from one baseline to the next, even within a single paragraph. The Space Before Paragraph and Space After Paragraph options relate to an entire paragraph. By reducing this value, you are closing up the space between the first paragraph ("THE") and the second paragraph ("B").

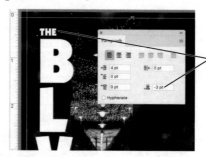

Paragraph formatting options apply to the entire paragraph in which the insertion point is flashing.

18. **Save the file and continue to the next exercise.**

# Create and Control Area Type

In many cases, your clients will provide specific text to include in a design; that text might be part of an email message or saved in a word-processing file. If the client-supplied text is only a couple of words, it's easier to retype the text into your Photoshop file. However, when the supplied text is longer, there's no point in making extra work by retyping.

The final type element you need for each postcard is a two- or three-paragraph blurb of promotional copy. You are going to create these as area-type layers so that you can better control the line breaks and alignment, and more easily fit them into a specific amount of space.

1. **On your desktop, double-click the file festival_copy.txt (in your WIP>Cards folder) to open the text file in a text-editing application.**

    You can't place or import external text files directly into a Photoshop file. If you want to use text from an external file, you simply open the file in a text editor, copy it, and paste it into a Photoshop type layer.

*Note:*

*We used Macintosh TextEdit as our word processor.*

2. **Select all text in the file, copy it, then close the file.**

3. **With festival.psd active in Photoshop, choose the Horizontal Type tool in the Tools panel.**

4. **Click the empty area at the bottom of the Layers panel to deselect all layers.**

5. **In the Characters panel, define the following type formatting options:**

    | | |
    |---|---|
    | Font Family: | ATC Onyx |
    | Font Style: | Italic |
    | Font Size: | 11 pt. |
    | Leading: | 14 pt. |
    | Type Color: | White |

6. **In the Paragraph panel, make sure all fields are set to 0:**

    If you did not deselect any of the existing type layers in Step 4, these changes would affect whatever layer was selected. Instead, these settings will apply to the next type layer you create.

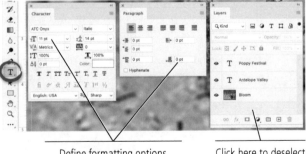

Define formatting options before creating a new type layer.

Click here to deselect existing layers.

7. **Click below the "P" in "Poppy," and drag down and right to create a type area (as shown in the following image).**

When you release the mouse button, a new type layer is created for the type area.

Because you defined the type formatting before you created the type area, placeholder text in the new area is automatically formatted with the settings you defined.

When the insertion point is placed (or text is selected) in a type area, the area shows eight bounding-box handles that you can drag to change the area's shape.

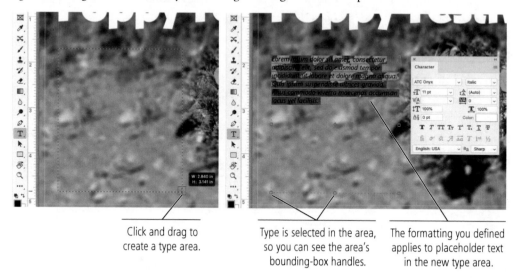

Click and drag to create a type area.

Type is selected in the area, so you can see the area's bounding-box handles.

The formatting you defined applies to placeholder text in the new type area.

8. **With the placeholder text selected, choose Edit>Paste.**

9. **With the Horizontal Type tool still active, click the right-center bounding-box handle of the type area and drag so the right edge of the area is between the "y" in "Poppy" and the "F" in "Festival."**

When you resize the type area by dragging the bounding-box handles, you do not affect the type; you change the type *container*, which allows more (or less, depending on how you drag) of the type to show.

Type also wraps within the type area. You don't have to manually define where new lines begin — simply press Return/Enter to start a new paragraph.

10. **Click the bottom-center handle and drag down to the bottom ruler guide.**

Dragging a type area handle with the Horizontal Type tool changes the size of the area without resizing the type.

*Note:*

*Make sure to use the Horizontal Type tool when you want to change the dimensions of a type area. If you press Command/Control-T or choose Edit>Free Transform, stretching or otherwise resizing the type area bounding box resizes the type it contains.*

11. **Click and drag to select at least part of the first two paragraphs in the area. In the Paragraph panel, change the Add Space After Paragraph field to 8 pt.**

Paragraph formatting attributes apply to any paragraph that is even partially selected. If no characters are highlighted, any paragraph formatting changes apply to the paragraph in which the insertion point is currently placed.

12. **Drag the top-center handle of the type area until the last paragraph is approximately 1/4″ from the bottom guide.**

Drag this handle down to make the area shorter.

13. **Select the entire last paragraph in the area. In the Character panel, change the font to ATC Onyx Normal, and change the size to 13 pt. In the Paragraph panel, click the Center Text button.**

Remember that character attributes, such as font and size, apply only to selected characters. To change these for the entire paragraph, you must first select the entire paragraph.

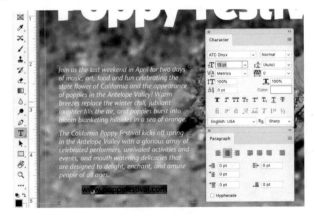

14. **Save the file and continue to the next exercise.**

# Create Paragraph Styles

When you work with longer blocks of text, many of the same formatting options are applied to different text elements (such as headings) throughout the story, or to different elements in similar pieces of a campaign. To simplify the workflow, you can use styles to store and apply multiple formatting options with a single click.

Another powerful benefit of styles is that when you change the options applied in a style, any text formatted with that style reflects the newly defined options. In other words, you can change multiple instances of noncontiguous text in a single process, instead of selecting each block and making the same changes repeatedly.

1. **With festival.psd active, select the entire first paragraph in the type area.**

2. **Open the Paragraph Styles panel (Window>Paragraph Styles).**

   The Paragraph Styles panel shows that the selected type is formatted with the Basic Paragraph style.

The Basic Paragraph option is included in every file.

3. **Click the Create New Paragraph Style button at the bottom of the panel.**

   When you create a new style, it defaults to include all formatting options that are applied to the currently selected type.

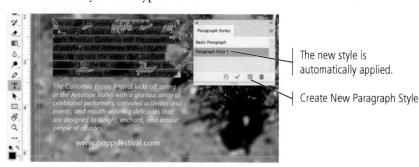

The new style is automatically applied.

Create New Paragraph Style

If you have used type styles in InDesign or Illustrator, you need to be aware of a difference in the way you create styles based on existing formatting. In those applications, a new style adopts the formatting of the current insertion point, which means you do not have to select specific type to create a style.

In Photoshop, however, you do have to select at least part of a paragraph to create a style based on that paragraph's formatting. Also, you cannot select multiple paragraphs with the same formatting to create a style based on those options.

*Note:*

*Photoshop also supports character styles, which can be used to store any character-formatting options that can be applied to selected characters.*

*Note:*

*You can delete a style by dragging it to the panel's Delete button. If the style had been applied, you would see a warning message, asking you to confirm the deletion. (You do not have the opportunity to replace the applied style with another, as you do in Adobe InDesign.)*

**4. Double-click the new style in the panel to review its settings.**

Double-clicking a style opens the Paragraph Style Options dialog box for that style, so you can edit its stored settings. Different options are available in the right side of the dialog box, depending on what is selected in the list of categories.

*Note:*

*You can also choose Style Options in the panel Options menu to open this dialog box.*

Checking the Preview option allows you to immediately see the effect of your changes in the layout before you finalize them.

**5. Change the style name to Body Copy and click OK.**

**6. Select the entire second paragraph, then click the Body Copy style in the Paragraph Styles panel to apply it to the active paragraph.**

The plus sign next to the style name indicates that formatting other than what is defined by the style is applied. You have to click the Clear Override button to apply only the style's formatting to the selected type.

**7. With the same type selected, click the Clear Override button at the bottom of the Paragraph Styles panel.**

If you do not clear the overrides, later changes to the applied style might not correctly reflect in type formatted with the style. Whenever you work with styles, check the applied styles to see if a plus sign appears where you know it shouldn't.

*Note:*

*You could also choose Clear Override in the Paragraph panel Options menu.*

*Note:*

*If the applied style shows a plus sign in the name, you can click the Redefine button to change the selected style's formatting to match that of the current text selection.*

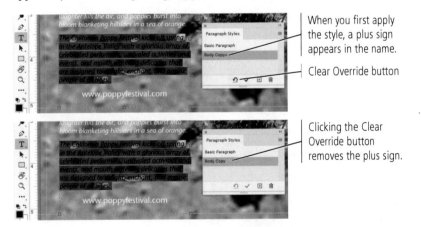

When you first apply the style, a plus sign appears in the name.

Clear Override button

Clicking the Clear Override button removes the plus sign.

**8. Repeat this process to create a new paragraph style named Web Address based on the formatting of the last paragraph in the type area.**

**9. Save the file and continue to the next exercise.**

# Load Paragraph Styles from Another File

Once you create styles, you can apply them to any text on any layer. You can also import styles from other Photoshop files so they can be used for different projects.

1. **On your desktop, open the file blvd_copy.txt (from your WIP>Cards folder) in a text editor application.**

2. **Select all the text in the file, copy it, then close the file.**

3. **In Photoshop, open the blvd.psd file if necessary.**

4. **In the Layers panel, click the empty area below the existing layers to deselect all layers in the file.**

   Deselecting the existing layers prevents you from accidentally changing the type formatting that is applied to the existing type layer.

5. **In the Paragraph Styles panel Options menu, choose Load Paragraph Styles. Navigate to festival.psd (in your WIP>Cards folder) and click Open/Load.**

*Note:*

*Don't worry if your formatting doesn't match what you see here. You're going to change it in the next few steps.*

Click below the layers to deselect all layers in the file.

6. **Click the Body Copy style in the panel to select it.**

7. **Using the Horizontal Type tool, click and drag to create a type area in the top-right corner of the canvas.**

*Note:*

*Loading styles from one Photoshop file to another is an all-or-nothing choice; you can't select certain styles to import.*

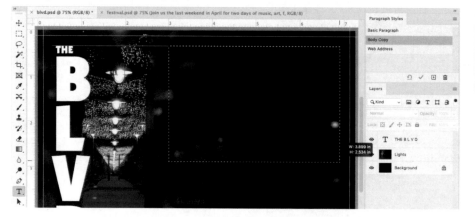

If you click a type style before creating a new type layer, as you did in Step 6, the new type layer automatically adopts the formatting defined in the selected style.

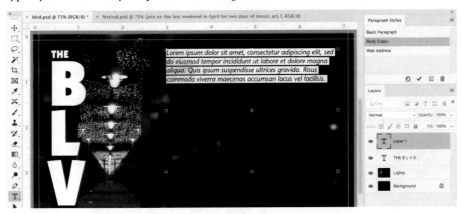

8. **With the placeholder copy in the new area highlighted, paste the text that you copied in Step 2.**

9. **If necessary, adjust the handles of the area so all the type in the story appears in the type area.**

10. **Select the entire last paragraph in the type area. Click Web Address in the Paragraph Styles panel, then click the Clear Override button.**

11. **Adjust the type area handles until you are satisfied with the text appearance.**

12. **Save the file and continue to the final stage of the project.**

In some cases, maintaining a type layer with live text is either unnecessary (e.g., you know the book title isn't going to change), or it prevents you from applying certain changes (e.g., you can't apply filters to a type layer). When you find an effect or change that won't work with live text, you must convert the type layer.

You can simply rasterize a type layer by choosing Type>Rasterize Type Layer, which converts the editable, vector-based type to a regular, pixel-based layer. Once rasterized, you can't edit the text, but you can apply filters and use the layer as a clipping mask.

Rasterizing type results in a regular, pixel-based layer.

You should understand that type is fundamentally based on vectors. Rather than simply rasterizing type, you can convert a type layer to a vector-based shape layer by choosing Type>Convert to Shape. Converting a type layer to a shape means the type is no longer editable, but you can still manipulate the letterforms as you would any other vector shape layer. By converting type to a shape layer, you can use the Distort or Perspective transformation to create custom warps for the layer. You still can't apply filters, however, since filters only work on rasterized layers.

The resulting shape layer adopts the original text color as the fill color.

If you need to apply filters, custom warps, or transformations to type, but you want to maintain the type layer as live (editable) text, you can convert the type layer to a Smart Object in the layer's contextual menu. You can apply filters or transformations in the main document, but still edit the text in the Smart Object file.

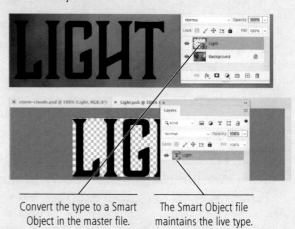

Convert the type to a Smart Object in the master file.  The Smart Object file maintains the live type.

Finally, you can use the vector information of type to create a work path (Type>Create Work Path), which you can then save as a regular path in the Paths panel. In this case, the type layer is maintained as an editable type layer, but you can use the path for any purpose you choose.

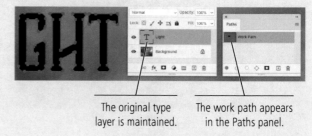

The original type layer is maintained.  The work path appears in the Paths panel.

### Creating Type Selections

You can use one of the Type Mask tools (horizontal or vertical) to create a selection in the shape of letters. When you click with one of these tools, you automatically enter a kind of Quick Mask mode; letters you type are removed from the mask to show what will be selected. (If you press Command/Control while the red mask is visible, you can drag the type selection around in the image window.)

When you have finished typing, switching to the Move tool shows the marching ants that make up the type-shaped selection. No layer, path, or channel is automatically created when you use the Type Mask tools.

# STAGE 4 / Creating Layer Comps

The basic structure of the two cards for this project is essentially complete. Each card, however, still needs a bit more work to be considered finished. To complete the Poppy Festival card, you are going to add a solid-color fill layer to improve the visibility of text. For the BLVD card, you will add several different inset images for the client to choose from.

## Create a Solid-Color Fill Layer

A solid-color fill layer is exactly what it sounds like — a layer of colored pixels, which obscure all underlying layers. Like a vector shape layer, the fill layer's thumbnail shows a swatch of the current fill color; you can double-click that swatch to change the color. A fill layer also has an attached (pixel-based) layer mask, which you can use to define where the fill color will be visible.

1. **With festival.psd open, select the Bloom layer in the Layers panel.**

2. **Click the Create New Fill or Adjustment Layer button at the bottom of the Layers panel and choose Solid Color in the resulting menu.**

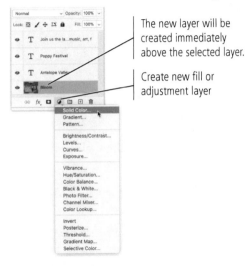

The new layer will be created immediately above the selected layer.

Create new fill or adjustment layer

3. **Click OK in the Color Picker dialog box to accept the default color value.**

The fill color defaults to the active foreground color. Don't worry if yours is different than what you see in our images; you will change the color in the next few steps.

The solid color of the fill obscures the underlying image layer.

The Color Picker automatically opens when you add a solid-color fill layer.

4. **In the Layers panel, click the eye icon to hide the Color Fill layer.**

   To sample a color from the underlying image, you first have to hide the fill layer.

5. **Double-click the Color Fill 1 layer's thumbnail to reopen the Color Picker dialog box.**

   You can change the Color Fill layer color even though it isn't currently visible.

6. **With the Color Picker dialog box open, click in the image (behind the dialog box) with the eyedropper cursor to sample a medium-dark green area of the image as the layer's fill color.**

Because the Color Fill layer is hidden, you can sample a color from the underlying layer.

Double-click the color icon to change the layer's fill color.

7. **Click OK to close the Color Picker dialog box, then make the Color Fill layer visible again.**

8. **In the Layers panel, click to select the mask thumbnail for the Color Fill layer.**

   Color fill and adjustment layers automatically include a mask, which you can use to define where the fill is visible. This is similar to the vector shape layers, where the vector path(s) define where the color is visible. The fill layer's mask, however, is pixel-based, which means it can include shades of gray.

   Remember, black areas of a mask are transparent and white areas are opaque. In this case, white areas of the mask result in full strength of the fill layer's color. Shades of gray indicate varying degrees of the fill color.

*Note:*

*You could have accomplished the same basic goal by creating a new layer, filling it with a solid color, and then manually adding a pixel mask. When you add a solid-color fill layer, the mask is automatically added for you. You can also double-click the color swatch in the layer icon to change the color that fills the layer.*

9. **Choose the Gradient tool in the Tools panel. Reset the foreground and background colors (so that white is the Foreground and black is the Background Color), then choose the Foreground to Background gradient in the Options bar.**

Choose the Linear Gradient option.

Click here to choose the gradient you want to use.

Use this menu to view the gradients as a list instead of swatches.

The mask is selected.

Default foreground and background colors for a mask are white and black, respectively.

10. **Make sure the Linear Gradient option is selected. Click near the right edge of the type area (with the body copy), then drag right to the right edge of the canvas.**

We dragged the gradient from here...        ...to here.

**11. Choose Multiply in the Blending Mode menu at the top of the Layers panel.**

Multiplying the dark color with the underlying image allows the white type to stand out more clearly against the background. The result, however, is too dark — it almost entirely obscures the underlying image.

The Multiply blending mode mixes the color of the fill layer with colors in the underlying layer.

**12. Change the layer's opacity to 75%.**

Reducing the fill layer's opacity allows more of the underlying image to show through. You can type the new value in the field, use the attached menu, or use the scrubby slider for the field's label.

The **Opacity** percentage changes the opacity of the entire layer, including applied effects and styles. The **Fill** percentage changes the opacity of the actual layer pixels, but none of the applied effects or styles. In this case, the layer doesn't yet have any applied styles or effects, so both controls would have the same effect.

Reducing the fill layer's opacity reduces the darkness created by the multiplied colors.

*Note:*

*If the Opacity field is unavailable, check the Lock options. When you use the Lock All option, you can't change the layer opacity.*

*Note:*

*When a layer is selected and the insertion point is not flashing in a Type layer, you can press the number keys to change the active layer's opacity in 10% increments:*

| | |
|---|---|
| *1 = 10%* | *6 = 60%* |
| *2 = 20%* | *7 = 70%* |
| *3 = 30%* | *8 = 80%* |
| *4 = 40%* | *9 = 90%* |
| *5 = 50%* | *0 = 100%* |

13. **Select the Bloom layer in the Layers panel, then click the Lock All button at the top of the Layers panel.**

The Bloom layer is technically the postcard background, even though it is not a formal Background layer. By locking all properties, you prevent the layer from being moved, painted on, or otherwise edited.

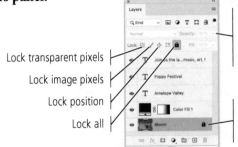

Lock transparent pixels

Lock image pixels

Lock position

Lock all

When the entire layer is locked, the opacity, fill, and blending mode options are not available.

The solid lock icon indicates that all properties of the layer are locked.

14. **Select the three type layers, then click the Lock Position button.**

By locking the layers' positions, you prevent them from accidentally being moved as you continue working. Since only the position is locked, however, you can still apply effects that do not affect the position of the layer content.

You cannot, by definition, lock the image pixels or transparent pixels of a type layer. If you activate the Lock All button for a Type layer, you will not be able to apply styles to those layers in the next steps.

The hollow lock icon indicates that some, but not all, properties of the layer are locked.

*Note:*

*For all but type layers, you can lock three different attributes individually, or you can lock the entire layer at once.*

15. **Save the file and then continue to the next exercise.**

## Transform Multiple Layers at One Time

You are going to create three different variations of the BLVD card using different inset images. The placement of each inset, however, will be exactly the same on the different variations. Accomplishing this task is made easier because you can select and transform multiple layers at one time, ensuring that the same transformations are applied to each layer.

1. **Make the blvd.psd file active, then click the top layer in the Layers panel to make it active.**

New layers, including those created by placing embedded images, are added immediately above the previously selected layer.

2. **Choose File>Place Embedded. Select the file Market.jpg (in your WIP>Cards folder) and click Place. When the image appears in the file, press Return/Enter to finalize the placement.**

Remember, the Place Embedded command places the image contents as a Smart Object layer.

3. **Repeat Step 2 to place the file Roshambo.jpg into the file.**

4. **Repeat Step 2 again to place the file Shops.jpg into the file.**

When you place images into a file as Smart Object layers, they are automatically placed in the center of the document window. All three of the placed images are now exactly on top of each other.

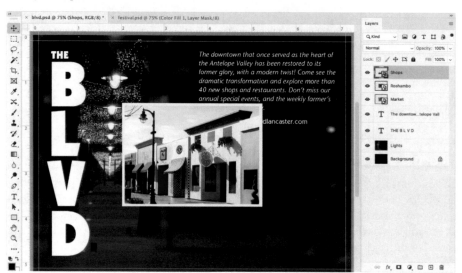

5. **In the Layers panel, click to select the Shops layer.**

6. **Press the Shift key and click the Market layer in the panel.**

Pressing the Shift key selects all consecutive layers in the panel, including any layers between the two you click.

You can also press the Command/Control key and click layers to select multiple non-consecutive layers.

7. **Choose the Move tool. With all three layers selected in the Layers panel, click inside the inset image area, then drag to move the placed layer to the empty area in the bottom-right corner of the canvas.**

Use the following image as a guide.

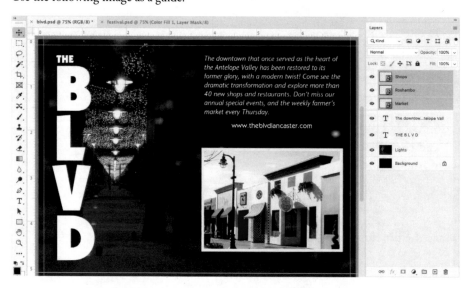

8. **With all three layers still selected in the panel, choose Edit>Free Transform.**

9. **In the Options bar, change the Rotate field to 3°.**

   Because all three layers are selected, this step rotates all three layers.

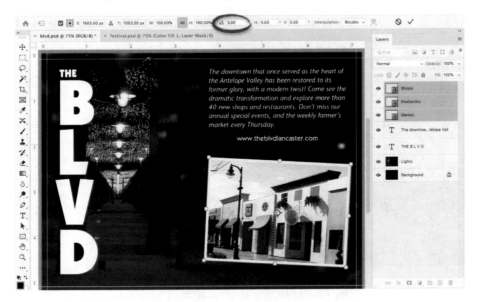

10. **Press Return/Enter to finalize the transformation.**

11. **In the Layers panel, click to select only the Shops layer.**

    To complete the cards, you are going to add a drop shadow to each inset layer. Unfortunately, however, you cannot apply a layer style such as a drop shadow to more than one layer at a time. To accomplish the task, you must apply the style to each individual layer.

12. **With the Shops layer selected, choose Layer>Layer Style>Drop Shadow.**

13. **In the resulting dialog box, define the following settings:**

    | | |
    |---|---|
    | **Opacity:** | 50% |
    | **Angle:** | 45° |
    | **Distance:** | 50 px |
    | **Spread:** | 5% |
    | **Size:** | 50% |

**14. Click OK to apply the layer style.**

As we explained, you can apply a layer style to only one layer at a time. The drop shadow now appears on the Shops layer. You still need to apply it to the other two inset layers. Fortunately, you can easily copy a layer style from one layer to another, which makes the process much easier.

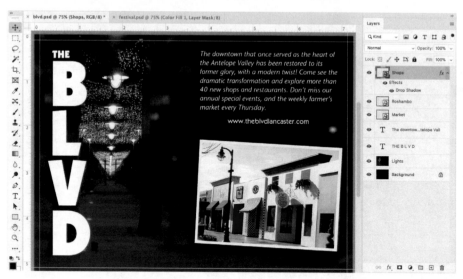

**15. Press the Option/Alt key, then click the Effects listing in the Layers panel and drag to the Roshambo layer.**

When you release the mouse button, the Effect listing is copied to the Roshambo layer.

Option/Alt-click and drag the Effects listing from the Shops layer to the Roshambo layer.

**16. Repeat Step 15 to copy the drop shadow to the Market layer.**

**17. In the Layers panel, click the arrow buttons to collapse the applied Effects listings for each of the inset layers.**

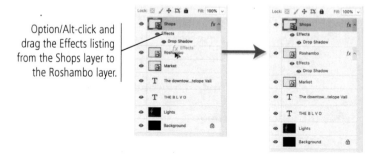

Click the arrow buttons to collapse the Effects listings for each layer.

**18. Save the file and continue to the next exercise.**

Create Layer Comps

A layer comp can store the position and visibility of individual layers, as well as any effects applied. This feature is useful when you want to experiment with the position of specific layers, but you want to keep a record of earlier positions of the layers. In this case, you want to present two versions of a file — one with a layer visible and one with a layer hidden.

**Note:**

*Layer comps do not store pixel information; modifying the actual pixel data on a layer will not be undone by reverting to an earlier layer comp. To undo that kind of change, you must use the History panel and snapshots (assuming you haven't closed the file since you created the snapshots).*

1. **With blvd.psd open, click the Eye icons in the Layers panel to hide the Shops and Roshambo layers.**

2. **Open the Layer Comps panel (Window>Layer Comps).**

   When no layer comps exist in the file, or you make changes that do not match what is saved as an existing layer comp, the panel shows the Last Document State as active. Buttons at the bottom of the panel enable a number of options:

   A   Apply Next Selected Layer Comp

   B   Update Visibilities of Selected Layer Comps and Layers

   C   Update Positions of Selected Layer Comps and Layers

   D   Update Appearances of Selected Layer Comps and Layers

   E   Update Layer Comp Selection for Smart Objects of Selected Layer Comps and Layers

   F   Update Layer Comp

   G   Create New Layer Comp

   H   Delete Layer Comp

3. **Click the Create New Layer Comp button at the bottom of the Layer Comps panel.**

4. **In the New Layer Comp dialog box, name the comp BLVD-market.**

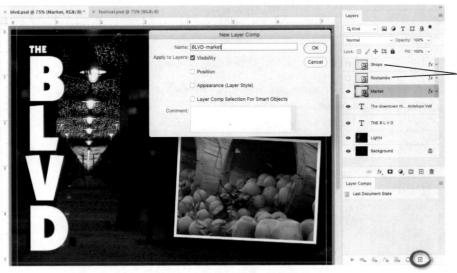

The Shops and Roshambo layers are hidden.

5. **Make sure the Visibility option is checked, and then click OK.**

When you choose the Visibility option, only the currently visible layers will be included in the comp.

When you close the dialog box, the new comp has been added to the panel. It is active because you haven't made any changes to layers since saving the layer comp.

This icon shows the currently active comp.

Only the visibility property is stored in the layer comp.

Icons to the right of the layer comp identify which attributes — visibility, position, and appearance — are stored in the layer comp. If an icon is grayed out, it is not part of that comp. You can click these icons to toggle each attribute on or off for a selected comp.

6. **In the Layers panel, hide the Market layer and show the Roshambo layer.**

When you make changes in the file after creating a layer comp, the Active icon on the left side of the panel automatically switches to Last Document State.

7. **Repeat Steps 4–5 to create a new layer comp named BLVD-roshambo.**

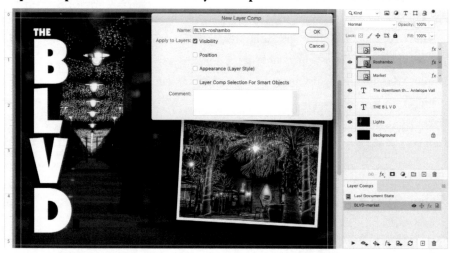

8. **In the Layers panel, hide the Roshambo layer and show the Shops layer.**

9. **Repeat Steps 4–5 to create a new layer comp named BLVD-shops.**

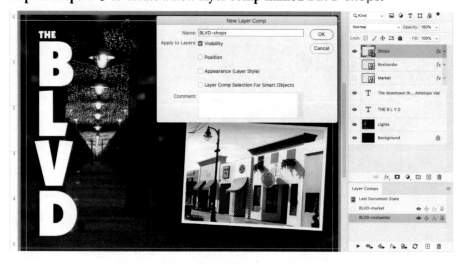

10. **Choose File>Export>Layer Comps to Files.**

This script creates separate files for each layer comp. The target location defaults to the same location as the working file, and the file name defaults to the current file name.

**Note:**

*You can select a specific layer comp in the panel and click the buttons at the bottom to change the layer properties that are stored in that comp. The first three buttons affect only one attribute (visibility, position, or appearance); the Update Layer Comp button updates all three attributes at once.*

11. **In the Layer Comps to Files dialog box, make sure the WIP>Cards folder is selected in the Destination field.**

12. **Delete the text in the File Name Prefix field, and uncheck the File Name Prefix checkbox.**

Because you included the text "BLVD" in the layer comp names, you do not need to include a file name prefix in the resulting files.

13. **Choose JPEG in the File Type menu, and leave the remaining options at their default values.**

14. **Click Run.**

The process could take a while to complete; don't panic and don't get impatient. When the file is done, you will see the message shown here.

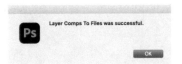

15. **Click OK to close the message, and then save and close the Photoshop file.**

16. **If necessary, close the festival.psd file.**

17. **With no file open in Photoshop, choose Edit>Color Settings.**

18. **In the Color Settings dialog box, choose North America General Purpose 2 in the Settings menu, then click OK.**

This option effectively resets the default color settings for the application. This step will prevent unnecessary warning messages when you open files in later projects.

Reset this menu to North America General Purpose 2.

1. _____ identifies and tries to protect areas of detail when you scale the image.

2. _____ allows you to move a selection, filling the original selection area with detail, instead of leaving an empty hole.

3. A _____ effect applies a consistent blur over the entire selected layer.

4. _____ is created by simply clicking (without dragging) with one of the Type tools.

5. _____ is the distance from one baseline to the next in a paragraph of type.

6. The _____ tools can be used to create selections in the shape of individual characters or entire words.

7. _____ describes the space between individual type characters (where the insertion point is placed).

8. _____ cannot be applied to type layers; you must first rasterize a type layer to apply them.

9. A color fill layer automatically includes a _____, which you can use to define where the fill is visible.

10. A(n) _____ stores the visibility of specific layers at a given point.

1. Briefly describe the result of moving a selection with the Move tool.

2. Briefly explain the difference between point type and area type.

3. Briefly explain the advantages of creating paragraph styles.

Use what you have learned in this project to complete the following freeform exercise.
Carefully read the art director and client comments, then create your own design to meet the needs of the project.
Use the space below to sketch ideas. When finished, write a brief explanation of the reasoning behind your final design.

**art director comments**

As a freelance designer, you have been hired by the band Midnight Sun to create a logo and cover artwork for their forthcoming CD release.

To complete this project, you should:

❏ Design an interesting logotype for the band.

❏ Determine the appropriate size for the cover that is inserted into a CD jewel case.

❏ Locate or create artwork or images to illustrate the CD title.

❏ Create the CD cover art for commercial printing requirements.

**client comments**

We're originally from Alaska. We all had full-time jobs when we first started, so we practiced late at night (no surprise!) until we decided we would get more exposure in Seattle. Since we spent so much time awake in the middle of the night, we named the band Midnight Sun.

We haven't had much luck yet finding a label, so we're going to self-publish an EP to help promote the band and, hopefully, raise some money. We're calling the disc "The Lower 48," because all of the songs are about our journey to where we are now.

We want the cover art to represent the type of music we play — primarily rock, but with other genres thrown in. Blues, international beats, and even orchestrated undertones all make an appearance.

We have a very unique sound, and we're an eclectic group of people. We're hoping you can create cover art that says who we are, without using a boring group photo.

**project justification**

Completing this project required a number of new skills for manipulating layer content — scaling and moving selections, applying blur effects, and working with layer styles. By now you should understand the difference between working with an entire layer and working with only a selected area, and be able to choose the appropriate tools to affect only what you want to change.

You also did a considerable amount of work with type, which can be either created from scratch or pasted from a text editor. Although the type controls in Photoshop are not quite as robust as those in formal page layout applications — which are specifically designed to create and control large blocks of type — they are certainly useful for a range of different applications.

You learned how to create both point and area type, as well as the different formatting options that are available for selected characters or entire paragraphs. You also worked with a number of tools that create unique artistic effects from a Photoshop type layer — sampling colors from an image to format type, applying styles to type layers, and changing layer opacity and blending modes.

Finally, you learned how to create layer comps to create multiple layout variations in a single file. This function makes it easier to manage different options in a single Photoshop file, so you have fewer files to organize and maintain.

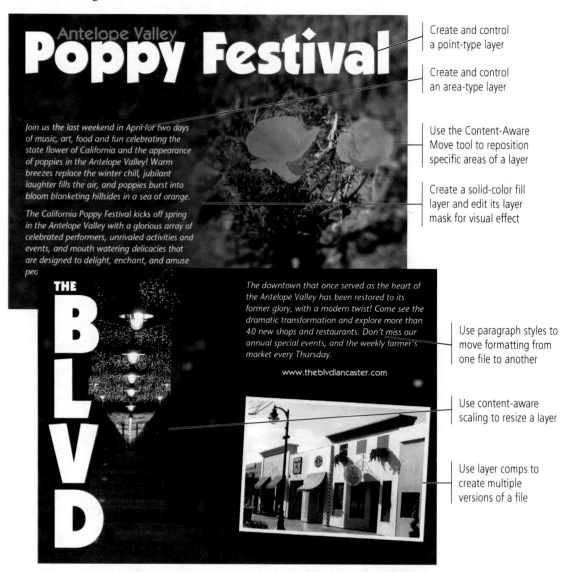

Create and control a point-type layer

Create and control an area-type layer

Use the Content-Aware Move tool to reposition specific areas of a layer

Create a solid-color fill layer and edit its layer mask for visual effect

Use paragraph styles to move formatting from one file to another

Use content-aware scaling to resize a layer

Use layer comps to create multiple versions of a file

# 5 Calendar Cover

Your client is a performing arts center that is preparing to publish its schedule for the upcoming Fall/Winter season. The annual mailing drives a significant portion of season ticket subscriptions, so it is one of the most important pieces of their overall marketing campaign. Although your agency has been hired to produce the entire booklet, your job is to complete only the cover.

This project incorporates the following skills:

❏ Managing missing fonts
❏ Creating a complex mask
❏ Creating custom vector shapes
❏ Working with spot channels

## Videos to Watch

Access these helpful videos in your online student resources:

▶▶ Calendar Cover Project Introduction

▶▶ Managing Missing Fonts

▶▶ Creating and Editing Pixel Masks

▶▶ Creating Custom Vector Shapes

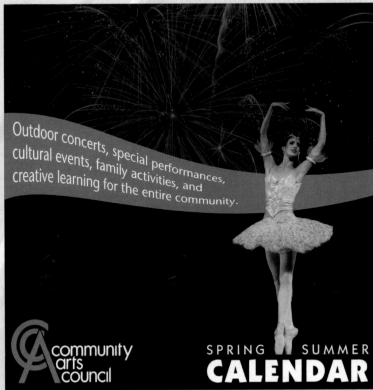

Outdoor concerts, special performances, cultural events, family activities, and creative learning for the entire community.

community arts council

SPRING SUMMER
**CALENDAR**

Our calendar mailings are the number-one driver of annual subscriptions. We send out the Spring/Summer schedule in early December, so it is in subscribers' hands before the holiday season.

We anticipate one of this year's biggest performances to be The Golden Fleece, which is a new symphony and ballet telling the story of Jason and the Argonauts. The Royal Ballet Company has committed to two weekends at the end of April for the performance, and we hope to sell out all six shows. We sent you an image from the ballet company's media files; we want that image to be featured prominently on the calendar cover.

Our calendars are printed on a six-color press. The sixth press unit runs a flood varnish, and we have the budget to use a spot color on the other press unit if you think it will enhance the design.

**Watch the video** Calendar Cover Project Introduction in your online student resources.

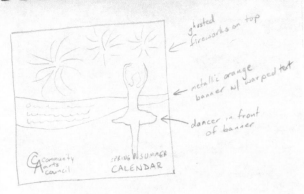

I already started work on the cover, but I need to move over to the interior layout, so I want you to finish it. I used two different fonts in the file, but if you don't have them, you can substitute similar fonts.

There are several tasks that remain to be completed on the cover image.

Create a banner shape that extends the entire width of the piece, behind the dancer, but in front of the background images, to hide the bottom edge of the fireworks layer.

Create a complex selection to remove the main dancer from her background.

For the fifth color, we will use Pantone 8943 from the metallic ink set — metallic orange, which will work nicely as the orange in the client's logo. Be aware that using spot colors in Photoshop requires a few tricks and work-arounds that are different from what you do when you work with regular image channels.

To complete this project, you will:

- ❏ Manage missing fonts
- ❏ Create a custom shape layer
- ❏ Create warped text
- ❏ Manually edit an Alpha channel
- ❏ Use Select and Mask to refine a complex selection
- ❏ Define a new spot channel
- ❏ Copy layer information to a spot channel
- ❏ Save the file with and without spot-color information

# STAGE 1 / **Managing Missing Fonts**

When you work with type in a Photoshop file, it is important to understand that fonts are external files of data that describe the font for on-screen display and for the output device. The fonts you use in a layout need to be available on any computer that will be used to open the file. Photoshop stores a reference to used fonts, but it does not store the actual font data.

##  Evaluate Project Requirements

Because this project includes a partially completed file, your first task is to evaluate the existing file and determine what needs to be accomplished.

*Watch the video* **Managing Missing Fonts** *in Photoshop in your online student resources.*

1. **Expand the Calendar_PS22_RF.zip archive in your WIP folder (Macintosh), or copy the archive contents into your WIP folder (Windows).**

   This results in a folder named **Calendar**, which contains the file you need for this project. You should also use this folder to save the files you create in this project.

2. **In Photoshop, open the file ballet-cover.psd from the WIP>Calendar folder.**

3. **Review the Layers panel.**

   This file includes several type layers. Two of those show a warning icon, which indicates that the layer requires a font that is not available on your computer.

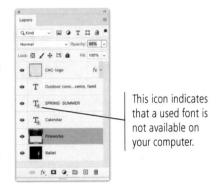

This icon indicates that a used font is not available on your computer.

4. **Choose Type>Manage Missing Fonts.**

   This dialog box lists the missing fonts that are required by the active Photoshop file.

**Note:**

*If a file uses an Adobe Font that is not currently active in your Creative Cloud account, Photoshop automatically activates the required font for you so that those fonts do not show missing warnings.*

5. **Open the menu to the right of the ATCMapleMedium font and choose ATC Onyx Normal.**

   The replacement menus list the default font for the application (Myriad Pro), as well as any other fonts that are used in the current file.

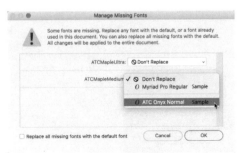

6. **Click OK to apply the replacement.**

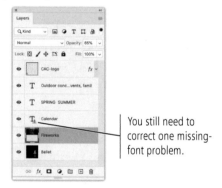

You still need to correct one missing-font problem.

7. **Choose the Horizontal Type tool in the Tools panel.**

8. **Click anywhere in the word "CALENDAR" at the bottom of the canvas to place the insertion point.**

   You do not need to first select a specific type layer to place the insertion point in an existing type layer.

9. **Read the resulting message, then click Replace.**

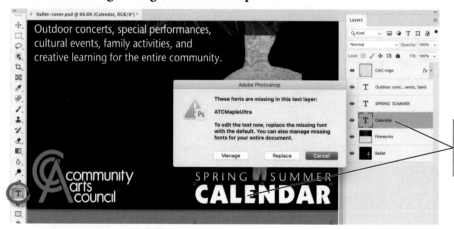

Clicking with the Horizontal Type tool places the insertion point in the type layer.

   Clicking Manage opens the Manage Missing Fonts dialog box that you just used. Because the font you want to use for this layer is not yet used in the file, you can't use that method to correct the second missing font warning; you need to replace that font manually.

   After dismissing the warning message, the missing font on the selected layer is replaced by the application's default font (typically, Myriad Pro Regular).

10. **Select all the type on the active layer and change the font to ATC Garnet Ultra.**

11. **Click the Commit button in the Options bar to finalize the change and remove the insertion point from the active type layer.**

   After committing the change, the layer is still selected in the Layers panel, but the insertion point is no longer flashing in the related type.

12. **Save the file, then continue to the next stage of the project.**

## Working with Adobe Fonts

Adobe Fonts (formerly called Typekit) is an online library of high-quality fonts that are available to anyone with a Creative Cloud subscription.

You can use the Adobe Fonts website to browse through available fonts, and even filter those fonts based on specific attributes and/or uses (for example, show only serif fonts that are available for desktop use). When you find fonts you want to use, you can activate them in your Creative Cloud subscription; those fonts will then be available on any machine where you log into your Creative Cloud account.

When Adobe fonts are available on your desktop, you can filter the application's font menus to show only those fonts in the menu.

### Verify Your Adobe ID

To use Adobe fonts, you must first verify that you are signed in using the username and password that is associated with your individual user subscription. (Adobe Fonts functionality is not available if you are working on a computer that has an Adobe software Device license instead of an individual user subscription, or if you do not have administrative access for the computer you are using.)

If you open the Help menu, you will see an option to either Sign In or Sign Out. The Sign Out menu option also shows the email address (username) that is currently signed in.

If you see your own username, you are already signed in, and can use the Adobe Fonts functionality. If you see a different username, you should choose the Sign Out option. All Adobe open applications, including Photoshop, will quit. Then, when you relaunch Photoshop, you will be asked to sign in with your own username and password.

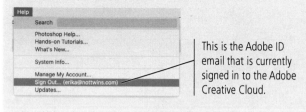

This is the Adobe ID email that is currently signed in to the Adobe Creative Cloud.

### Activating Adobe Fonts

Clicking the More From Adobe Fonts button in Photoshop launches your default browser and shows the Browse Fonts page of the Adobe Fonts website.

Because you launch the site from your Creative Cloud application, you are automatically logged in to your account.

If you are looking for a specific font, you can use the Search field at the top of the browser window.

On the left side of the browser window, you can use the buttons to filter the available fonts based on a number of criteria. (Filter buttons are toggles; when they are filled, they are active. Active filters remain active until you turn them off.)

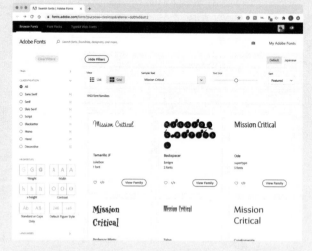

If you click a preview in the list to show that font's details page, you can review the individual fonts in that family. You can use the Activate Font switches in this screen for any single font within a family.

# STAGE 2 / Creating Custom Vector Shapes

The first stated goal of this project is to create a banner shape that hides the bottom edge of the fireworks layer content, and helps the call-to-action text stand out from the background image. In this stage of the project, you will create that custom banner shape, and then adjust the existing text layer to make the two elements work together.

Photoshop includes a number of built-in custom shape libraries, which make it very easy to add complex vector graphics into any Photoshop file. The Shapes panel (Window>Shapes) shows all the built-in shapes, grouped into logical sets. Clicking the arrow to the left of a set name expands the set and shows the available shapes.

To add a custom shape to your file, simply click the shape in the panel and drag onto the canvas. The new shape is added as a vector shape layer at whatever default size is defined in the saved library item. Because it's a vector shape layer, however, it can be transformed and edited like any other vector element in a Photoshop file.

*Watch the video* **Creating Custom Vector Shapes in Photoshop** *in your online student resources.*

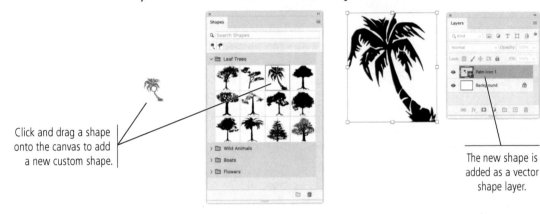

Click and drag a shape onto the canvas to add a new custom shape.

The new shape is added as a vector shape layer.

If you choose the Custom Shape tool in the Tools panel, you can access the same saved custom shapes in the Options bar. Once you choose a shape in the pop-up panel, you can click and drag to add the new vector shape at any size you need.

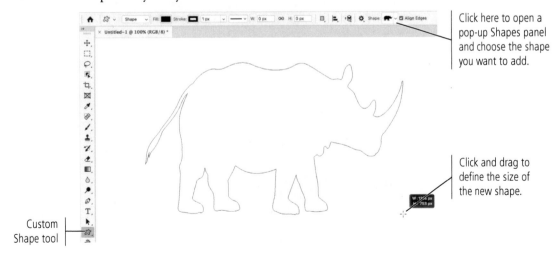

Click here to open a pop-up Shapes panel and choose the shape you want to add.

Click and drag to define the size of the new shape.

Custom Shape tool

# Create and Warp a Shape Layer

For this project, you need a banner shape, which is not available in any of the built-in shape libraries. Instead, you will create a rectangle shape layer and use other methods to warp it into the shape you need. (Remember, you can define fill and stroke colors for vector shape layers, as well as edit the anchor points that make up the vector shape to best suit the job at hand.)

1. **With ballet-cover.psd open, make the Fireworks layer active in the Layers panel.**

   New layers are created immediately above the previously selected layer. By first selecting the Fireworks layer, the shape layer you are about to create will automatically appear directly above the Fireworks layer.

2. **Choose the Rectangle tool in the Tools panel.**

3. **In the Options bar, make sure the Shape option is selected.**

   Like the Pen tool, the shape tools can be used to create a vector-based shape layer, a path, or pixels of a solid color. In this case, you want to create a new shape layer.

4. **Click the Stroke swatch in the Options bar and choose the No Color option.**

5. **Click the Fill swatch in the Options bar. Click the button to open the Color Picker, then use the Eyedropper cursor to sample the color in the logo (in the bottom-left corner). Click OK to close the Color Picker.**

   Ultimately, the shape you are creating will be moved to a spot channel to reproduce the banner in a specific color of ink, so it really doesn't matter what color you use in this step. We're working with the logo color because both the logo and the banner will eventually be created with the same spot color.

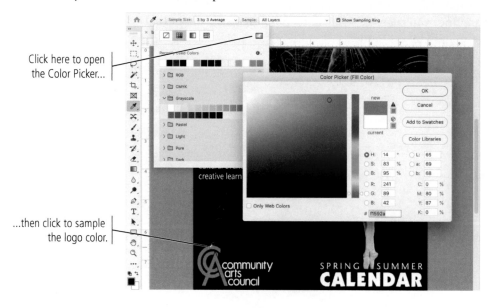

Click here to open the Color Picker...

...then click to sample the logo color.

6. **Make sure the Radius field is set to 0 px.**

   The Rectangle tool remembers the last-used settings, so it is possible your corner radius is set to a different value from a previous project. This step ensures that your new rectangle shape has square corners.

7. **Click at the left edge of the document window, above the "Outdoor..." text layer and drag to the right canvas edge below the banner text. (Use the following image as a guide.)**

   The Shape tools create a vector path based on the shape you select. The new shape layer is added to the Layers panel.

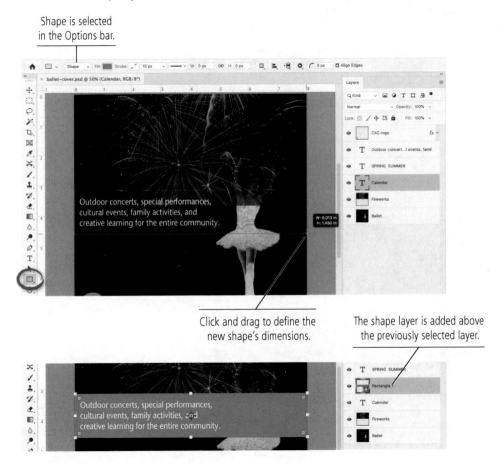

Shape is selected in the Options bar.

Click and drag to define the new shape's dimensions.

The shape layer is added above the previously selected layer.

8. **With the new Rectangle 1 layer selected, choose Edit>Transform Path>Warp.**

   You have a number of options for warping layer content, from calling one of the built-in warp styles to defining completely custom warp "quilts".

9. **In the Options bar, open the Warp menu and choose the Rise option.**

    Photoshop includes 15 built-in warp styles. The icon next to each style name suggests the result of applying that style.

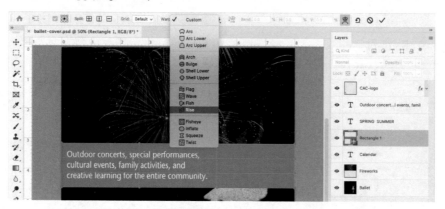

10. **Change the Bend value to –40% and change the Horizontal Distortion (H) value to –25%.**

Use these fields to change
the dynamics of the warp.

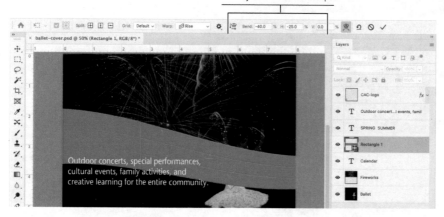

11. **Click the Commit Transform button (or press Return/Enter) to apply the change.**

12. **Read the resulting warning, then click Yes.**

    When you use the basic shape tools, Photoshop recognizes the shapes you draw by their geometric names (rectangle, ellipse, etc.). If you modify the vectors that make up a basic shape, it is no longer that shape and so Photoshop warns you.

    Don't worry, the shape is still a vector path. It is simply no longer a true rectangle (even though Photoshop does not change the layer name.)

*Note:*

*If you use the Return/ Enter key, you have to press the key two times: once to apply the change in the Horizontal Distortion field, and then again to finalize the overall type transformation.*

13. **If necessary, the Move tool to drag the Rectangle 1 layer so it covers the entire bottom edge of the Fireworks layer content.**

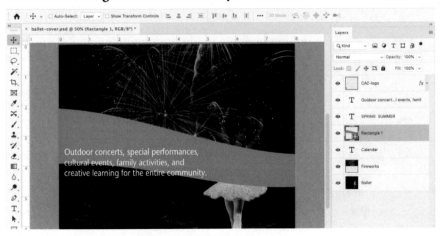

14. **Save the file and continue to the next exercise.**

 Create Warped Text

In this exercise, you are going to warp the call-to-action text so it follows the contour of the banner shape you created in the previous exercise. This is easily accomplished with the built-in Warp Text options that change the shape of text without rasterizing it.

1. **With ballet-cover.psd open, choose the Horizontal Type tool in the Tools panel.**

2. **In the Layers panel, click to select the "Outdoor concerts..." type layer.**

3. **In the Options bar, click the Create Warped Text button.**

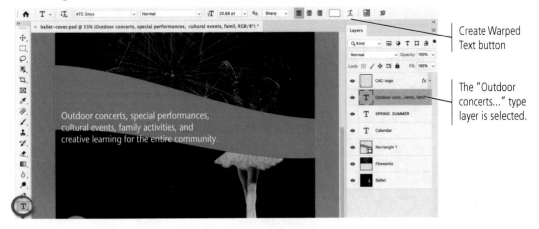

Create Warped Text button

The "Outdoor concerts..." type layer is selected.

4. **In the Warp Text dialog box, choose Rise from the Style menu.**

As long as text remains editable, your warping options are limited to the list of predefined shapes.

5. **Define a –40 Bend and –25 Horizontal Distortion value.**

**Note:**

*If you work with raster-ized text (or any other pixel-based selection), you can create custom warps.*

6. **Click OK to close the Warp Text dialog box.**

Although you used the same warp values for the text as you did for the banner shape, the two warps do not exactly match because the text and the banner are different widths. The built-in warp styles apply only across the width of the selected content, not the entire canvas. You can solve this problem by editing the vectors that make up the banner shape.

7. **In the Layers panel, click the Rectangle 1 layer to select it.**

8. **Using the Direct Selection tool, adjust the shape's anchor points and handles to better match the shape and contour of the warped text.**

Make sure the shape entirely obscures the bottom edge of the Fireworks layer content.

9. **Save the file and continue to the next stage of the project.**

# STAGE 3 / Creating a Complex Mask

You should already understand a number of different ways to make selections, from basic shape selections with a marquee to color-based selections. Some images, however, defy these tools — specifically, images with various colors, thin lines, and complex edges can be difficult to isolate. The background photo for this project is a perfect example of this type of image.

 ## Select the Focus Area

In this exercise, you are going to use the Select Focus Area option to create a mask that allows the dancer in the foreground to appear in front of other elements. You will then edit the mask to fine-tune the selection.

1. **With ballet-cover.psd open, hide all but the Ballet layer. Make the Ballet layer active in the Layers panel.**

2. **Choose Select>Focus Area.**

   This function automatically evaluates the image and determines areas that are in focus. You can adjust the In-Focus Range parameter to broaden or narrow the selection. A range of 0 selects the entire image, while high range (near the right side of the slider scale) selects only the parts of the image that are in clearest focus. If the selection area has noise, you can use the Image Noise Level slider to control how that noise affects the selection.

3. **With the Preview option checked in the resulting dialog box, open the View Mode menu and choose On Layers.**

   The preview options allow you to change the way your image appears in the document window while you refine your selection with the dialog box tools. On Layers shows the transparent checkerboard pattern behind the selected areas.

   When there is a clear focal point in an image, the Focus Area tool produces excellent results with very little intervention. As in the case of the image you are using in this project, however, you should understand that many photos will defy 100% automatic selections. You can still use the Focus Area selection as a starting point, and then make whatever adjustments are necessary using other tools.

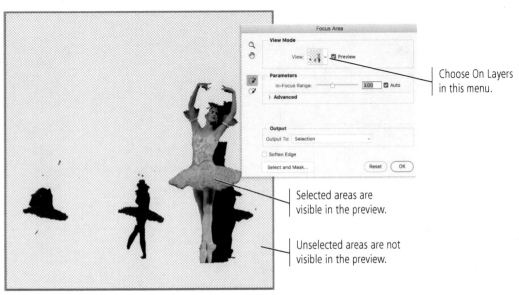

Choose On Layers in this menu.

Selected areas are visible in the preview.

Unselected areas are not visible in the preview.

4. **Select the Focus Area Subtract Tool in the left side of the dialog box.**

    This tool allows you to paint on the image to remove areas from the current selection.

5. **Click and drag down the dark selected area to the right of the dancer's legs.**

Focus Area
Subtract tool

Drag over an area
to remove it from
the selection.

When you release the mouse button, the software identifies contiguous areas of similar focus and color to remove from the selection.

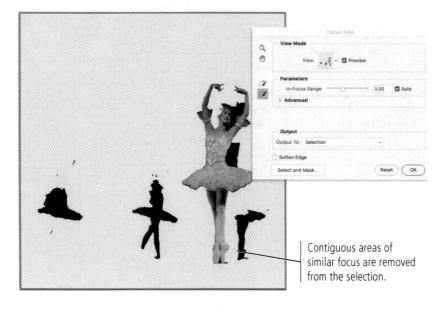

Contiguous areas of
similar focus are removed
from the selection.

6. **Continue painting with the Focus Area Subtract Tool to remove as much of the dark background that touches the front dancer as possible.**

7. **At the bottom of the Focus Area dialog box, choose the New Layer with Layer Mask option in the Output To menu.**

Your ultimate goal is to place the logotype layer group between the foreground and background elements in this image. The foreground elements need to exist on a separate layer to accomplish this goal, so you are using the dialog box to automatically create a new layer that shows only the selected foreground elements.

8. **Click OK to finalize your selection.**

Because you chose the New Layer with Layer Mask option in the Output To menu, the unselected areas are now masked on the new Ballet copy layer.

A new masked layer is the result of the Focus Area selection.

9. **Save the file and continue to the next exercise.**

# Erase and Paint the Alpha Channel

Although automatic results are usually a good start, you should almost never rely entirely on the software to accomplish your goals. Most automatic features will require at least some manual adjustment or intervention.

 *Watch the video* ***Creating and Editing Pixel Masks*** *in your online student resources.*

We intentionally chose the Backstage image you are using in this project to highlight this point. The foreground elements are not entirely in clear focus (especially around the dancer's tiara), so the Focus Area dialog box was not able to create a perfect selection.

Now that you have created the initial mask, you can use other tools to fine-tune the mask and determine exactly what will be visible on the layer. In this exercise, you will use painting tools to add to and subtract from the existing layer mask.

1. **With ballet-cover.psd open, make sure the Ballet copy layer is selected in the Layers panel and then open the Channels panel.**

    This file uses the RGB color mode, so you have three channels — one for each of the three primary colors. When a masked layer is selected, the Channels panel also includes an alpha channel that contains the selected layer's mask.

2. **In the Channels panel, click the empty space to the left of the Ballet copy Mask to make it visible in the document window.**

Some areas need to be added to the mask.

Click here to show the mask in the document window.

3. **If your mask channel is not semi-transparent, double-click the Ballet copy Mask channel to open the Layer Mask Display Options dialog box. Set the Opacity field to 50%, then click OK.**

    Mask opacity remembers the last-used settings.

4. **If necessary, click the empty space on the left side of the Channels panel to make the Ballet copy Mask channel visible again.**

There is a minor bug in the software that might cause the mask channel to be hidden when you change the mask opacity.

5. **In the Layers panel, click the Ballet copy layer mask icon to select the mask.**

You must select the actual mask in the panel before you can paint to edit the mask.

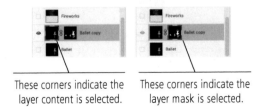

These corners indicate the     These corners indicate the
layer content is selected.     layer mask is selected.

6. **In the Tools panel, click the button to restore the default foreground and background colors to black and white (respectively).**

You have to paint with black to add to a mask (hide areas), or paint with white to subtract from a mask (reveal areas).

7. **Select the Brush tool in the Tools panel. In the Options bar, choose a 100-px brush with 100% hardness, 100% opacity, and 100% flow.**

Open the Brush Preset Picker to
define the brush size and hardness.

Make sure the actual
mask is selected.

Reset the default
Foreground and
Background colors.

8. **Click and drag over any isolated background areas that are not masked.**

Paint with black to add to the mask area.

9. **Zoom in to the dancer's feet. Continue painting with the Brush tool to add to the mask area (remove the background pixels around the feet).**

When using any tool that has a brush size, you can press the Left Bracket key ( [ ) to dynamically decrease the brush size or press the Right Bracket key ( ] ) to increase the brush size.

Don't worry about the dark artifact pixels that surround most of the selection at this point; you will use another technique to refine the selection edge.

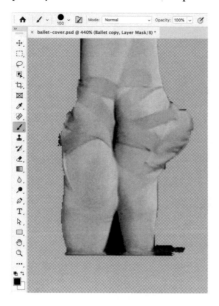 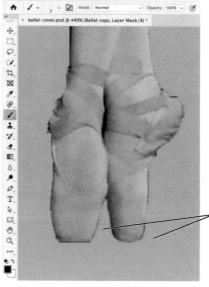

Paint to mask the background pixels from around the dancer's feet.

10. **Zoom in to the dancer's head.**

This is an excellent example of a case in which algorithms are no substitute for human subjectivity. The dancer's dark hair blends into the dark background in the original image. The automatic selection algorithms used in the Focus Area utility are not able to determine the difference between the two areas. You have to use your best judgment to define the area where the dancer's hair ends.

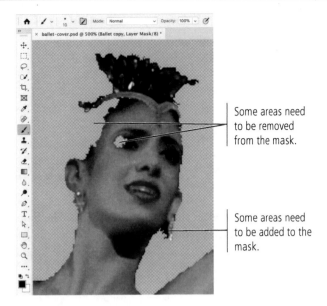

Some areas need to be removed from the mask.

Some areas need to be added to the mask.

11. **Paint with black to add any necessary areas to the mask.**

12. **Click the Switch Foreground and Background Colors button at the bottom of the Tools panel.**

Remember, paint with white to remove areas from the mask.

13. **Paint to the layer mask with white to remove any areas of the dancer's face and head.**

Change the brush size as necessary to accomplish your goal.

Paint with white to remove pixels from the mask area.

14. **In the Channels panel, click the eye icon to hide the Ballet copy Mask channel.**

    The mask channel can be confusing when you use various view methods in the Select and Mask workspace, which you will do in the next few steps.

Click to hide the mask in the document window.

15. **With the mask selected in the layers panel, click the Select and Mask button in the Properties panel.**

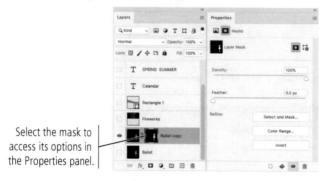

Select the mask to access its options in the Properties panel.

16. **Choose the On Layers option in the View Mode menu.**

    The Select and Mask workspace provides more sophisticated tools for refining a complicated mask like the one you are creating in this project.

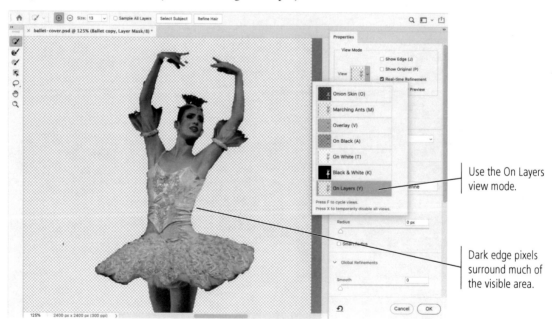

Use the On Layers view mode.

Dark edge pixels surround much of the visible area.

17. **On the right side of the workspace, change the Edge Detection Radius value to 1 px.**

    Increasing the Radius value results in a slightly softer edge, removing most of the dark artifact pixels that resulted from the Focus Area selection.

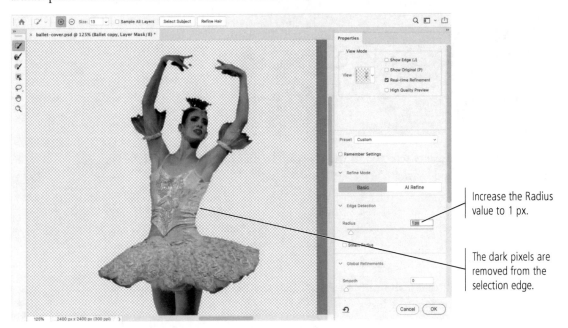

Increase the Radius value to 1 px.

The dark pixels are removed from the selection edge.

18. **Choose the Onion Skin view mode and set the transparency to 25%. Review the rest of your selection.**

    Different viewing modes have different uses. With the Onion Skin mode, the masked areas appear partially transparent; this allows you to see what you still need to add or remove from the mask.

19. **Choose the Brush tool in the top-left corner of the workspace, and choose the option to add to the selected area.**

    In our example, part of the dancer's hand is masked. You can use the Brush tool directly in the Select and Mask workspace to paint — either adding to or removing from the mask.

Add to selected area

Remove from selected area

Onion Skin mode shows the masked areas as semi-transparent.

Brush tool

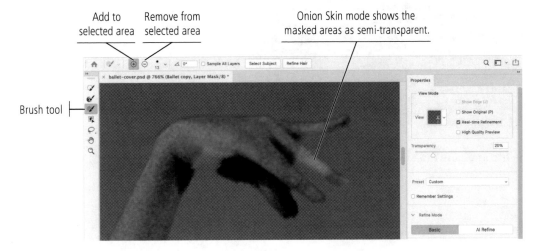

**20.** **Paint over any areas that need to be added to the selection.**

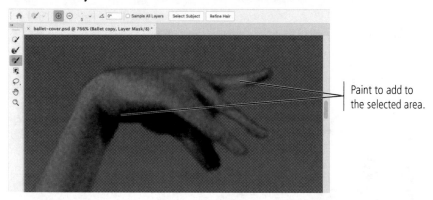

Paint to add to the selected area.

**21.** **Make sure Layer Mask is selected in the Output To menu, then click OK to finalize the revised mask.**

**22.** **In the Layers panel, make all layers visible. Click the Ballet copy layer and drag it above the Rectangle 1 layer.**

The dancer in the foreground, which you isolated from the background using a variety of techniques, now appears in front of the custom shape banner and the fireworks.

**23.** **Save the file and continue to the final stage of the project.**

# STAGE 4 / Working with Spot Channels

Spot colors are frequently used to produce a special look, to match an exact color, or to highlight a certain aspect of a job (for example, with varnish or some other special coating). Spot-color inks are opaque, so they produce the desired result with a single printing unit, instead of by combining varying percentages of the four process inks. If you want to create a certain look, or if a color must be the same on every printed job, a spot color is usually the best choice. You should be aware, however, that adding spot color to a process job adds to the cost, and budgets are usually a consideration when designing a print project.

Every designer should own a set of spot-color guides, such as those produced by Pantone. (Pantone is the most common spot-color system in the United States, but ask your printer which one they use before building spot colors in any design.) These printed spot-color guides usually show coated and uncoated samples. Some also show the process-color combination that produces the closest possible match to the spot ink. If you want to approximate a special ink color, you can use those ink percentages to designate the process color in a layout or illustration program.

**Note:**

*Spot colors are typically selected from printed swatch books that show the exact color of the ink. Don't rely on the on-screen previews when you select a spot color.*

##  Define a New Spot Channel

To work with spot colors in Photoshop, you have to create a new channel to include the information for that ink. Anything printed in the spot color needs to be placed or copied onto the spot channel.

1. **With ballet-cover.psd open, click at the bottom of the Layers panel to deselect all layers in the file.**

2. **Choose Edit>Color Settings. Choose U.S. Sheetfed Coated v2 in the CMYK Working Space menu, then click OK.**

   Before you create the required spot color channel, you will convert the file to the CMYK color mode for printing. When you make the conversion, the file is converted to whatever is defined as the working CMYK space.

3. **Choose Image>Mode>CMYK Color. Read the resulting message, then click Don't Merge.**

   As the warning suggests, changing the color mode of a file can affect the appearance of individual layers. You are given the option to flatten the file before converting the colors.

   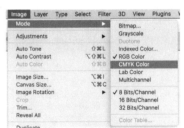

4. **Read the resulting warning, then click OK.**

Because you already defined the destination profile you want to use, you can safely click OK to dismiss the warning.

5. **Display the Channels panel. Open the Channels panel Options menu and choose Panel Options.**

6. **In the resulting dialog box, select the large thumbnail, and then click OK.**

The larger thumbnail makes it easier to see the channel contents in the panel.

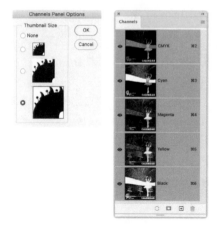

7. **Open the Channels panel Options menu again and choose New Spot Channel.**

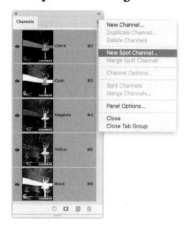

8. **In the New Spot Channel dialog box, click the Color swatch to open the Color Picker (Spot Color) dialog box.**

Click this swatch to open the Color Picker (Spot Color) dialog box.

Click this button to access the built-in spot-color libraries.

9. **Click the Color Libraries button to access the built-in spot-color libraries.**

10. **In the Book menu, choose PANTONE+ Metallic Coated. Type 8943 to scroll quickly to the color that the client selected for this job.**

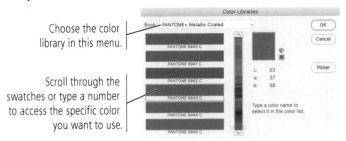

Choose the color library in this menu.

Scroll through the swatches or type a number to access the specific color you want to use.

*Note:*

*This is the color your art director defined in the original project meeting.*

11. **Click OK to return to the New Spot Channel dialog box.**

12. **Set the Solidity to 100%.**

Solidity for a spot channel is similar to layer opacity. If the ink channel is not entirely opaque (with a 100% Solidity value), CMYK elements under the spot areas will be visible through the spot ink. In this case, you want the spot-ink areas to completely obscure underlying CMYK elements, so you have to use a 100% Solidity value.

*Note:*

*Double-clicking a spot-color channel thumbnail on the Channels panel opens the same dialog box you see when you first create a new spot channel.*

13. **Click OK to add the new spot channel to the file.**

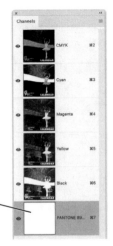

The newly added Pantone spot-color channel doesn't contain anything yet.

14. **Save the file and continue to the next exercise.**

# Copy Layer Information to a Spot Channel

There is no easy way to map specific layer content to a specific spot channel. To ensure that specific objects print in a spot color, you have to manually cut the content from its layer and paste it directly onto the appropriate spot-color channel. It is also important to understand that there are certain limitations to working with spot colors in Photoshop. You can't apply effects to a spot channel, such as the drop shadow behind the client's logo in the bottom-left corner. You also can't store vector information on a spot channel, which means vector shape and type layers must be rasterized if you place that content on a spot channel.

1. **With ballet-cover.psd open, drag the CAC-logo layer in the Layers panel to the Create a New Layer button to duplicate the layer.**

   You are duplicating the layer so that the original will be available later, in case you need to make changes.

Drag a layer to the Create New Layer button to duplicate it.

2. **Hide the original CAC-logo layer, then expand the effects listing for the CAC-logo copy layer.**

3. **Control/right-click the Drop Shadow effect for the CAC-logo copy layer and choose Create Layer from the contextual menu.**

   As we stated at the beginning of this exercise, you can't apply effects to spot-channel content. To maintain the drop shadow after the banner has been moved to the spot channel, you have to create an independent layer from the drop shadow effect.

Duplicate the CAC-logo layer, then hide the original.

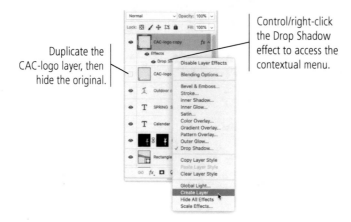

Control/right-click the Drop Shadow effect to access the contextual menu.

4. **If you see a warning about effects not being reproduced by layers, click OK.**

   Drop shadows can be reproduced with layers, so you can dismiss the warning.

5. **Using the Lasso tool, draw a marquee that surrounds only the orange elements of the client's logo.**

6. **Make sure the CMYK (composite) channel is selected in the Channels panel and the CAC-logo copy layer is selected in the Layers panel.**

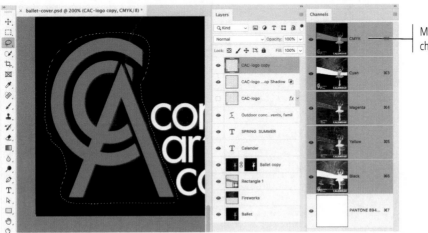

Make sure the CMYK channel is selected.

7. **Choose Edit>Cut.**

The pixels inside the previous marquee are removed from the CAC-logo copy layer and the CMYK channel.

8. **Select the PANTONE 8943 C channel in the Channels panel, then choose Edit>Paste Special>Paste in Place.**

   This command places the pasted content in the exact position it was in when you cut it, but on the selected Pantone 8943 C channel.

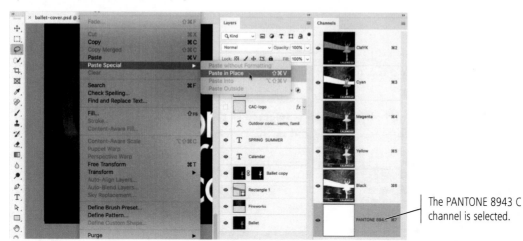

The PANTONE 8943 C channel is selected.

You should notice that the pasted content is not at full strength, because the original orange color maps to a medium gray on the spot channel.

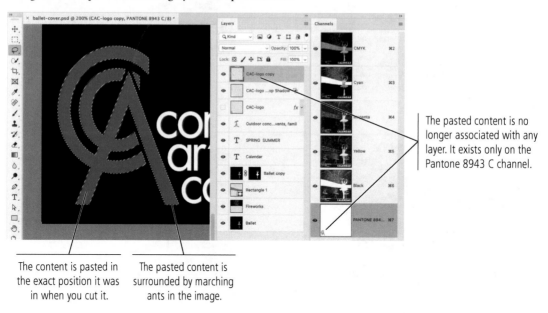

The pasted content is no longer associated with any layer. It exists only on the Pantone 8943 C channel.

The content is pasted in the exact position it was in when you cut it.

The pasted content is surrounded by marching ants in the image.

9. **Deselect the active selection area.**

   Press Command/Control-D to deselect.

10. **In the Layers panel, drag the Rectangle 1 layer to the Create a New Layer button to duplicate it. Hide the original Rectangle 1 layer.**

11. **Control/right-click the Rectangle 1 copy layer and choose Rasterize Layer from the contextual menu.**

    To move part of this object to the spot-color channel, you first have to rasterize the vector object.

Duplicate the Rectangle 1 layer, then hide the original.

Control/right-click the layer to access the contextual menu.

12. **With the rasterized layer selected, choose Select>Color Range.**

13. **Click the Eyedropper cursor anywhere in the orange banner shape.**

    The Color Range dialog box makes selections based on all visible layers. Because the Outdoor content... type layer is visible, the area selected excludes the type and the space where the dancer's torso appears in front of the banner.

    If you selected the entire shape area (including the area behind the type and the dancer), the content pasted onto the spot-color channel would be printed over the CMYK separations, obscuring both the type and the dancer's torso.

    The logo is also not selected; it is no longer the same orange color as the banner since you removed it from the original layer and pasted it onto the spot-color channel.

**14.** **Click OK to finalize the selection.**

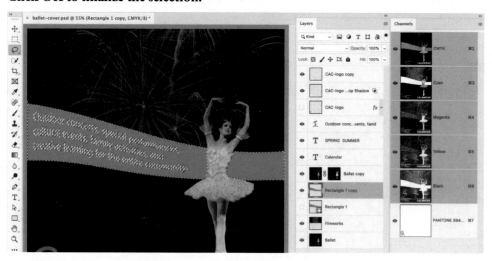

**15.** **With the CMYK channels selected in the Channels panel, choose Edit>Cut to remove the selected pixels from the active layer.**

**16.** **Choose the PANTONE 8943 C channel in the Channels panel, then choose Edit>Paste Special>Paste in Place.**

**17. Deselect the active selection area.**

Press Command/Control-D to deselect.

The selected area from Step 13 — the rasterized banner, excluding the area behind the dancer — is pasted in place onto the spot-color channel.

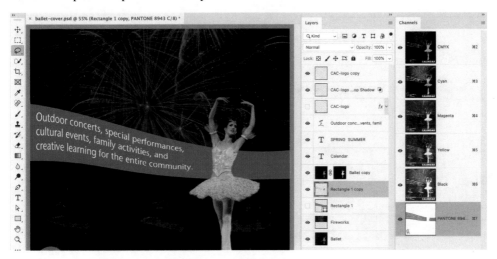

**18. Press Command/Control, and click the thumbnail for the PANTONE 8943 C channel.**

This method results in a selection that includes all pixels on the channel.

**19. With all the pixels on the spot-color channel selected, choose Edit>Fill. Choose Black in the Contents menu, make sure the Mode is set to Normal, set the Opacity to 100%, and then click OK.**

Remember, each channel is a grayscale representation of one color separation. When you pasted the banner pixels onto the channel, the original orange was converted to a shade of gray as part of that channel data. For the banner to be at full strength of the spot color, it must be filled with solid black on the channel.

*Note:*

*The same method works in the Layers panel: Command/Control-click a layer thumbnail to select all pixels on that layer.*

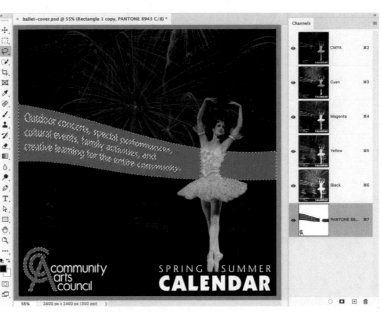

**20.** **Repeat Step 19 two more times.**

There appears to be a bug in the software that does not accurately fill the selection with 100% Black. We found it necessary to repeat the fill process two additional times to change the spot-channel pixels to Black instead of a shade of gray.

**21.** **Deselect the active selection area.**

**22.** **In the Channels panel, hide the CMYK channels and review the contents of the Pantone 8943 C channel.**

*Note:*

*Spot color information can also be saved in the PDF, EPS, or DCS file formats.*

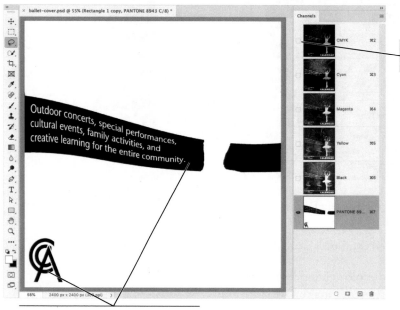

Click here to hide the CMYK channels.

The logo and banner should reproduce as full strength of the spot ink, so they appear as solid black on the spot-color channel.

**23.** **Show the CMYK channels again, save the file, and then continue to the final exercise.**

## Understanding Duotones

Spot colors are sometimes used to print monotone, duotone, tritone, and quadtone images. **Monotones** are grayscale images printed with one ink (typically, not black). **Duotones**, **tritones**, and **quadtones** are grayscale images printed with two, three, and four inks (respectively).

Of the four types of images, duotones are the most common. In many cases, duotones are printed with black ink for the shadows, and midtones and one other color for the highlights. This technique produces an image with a slight tint that adds visual interest to images in a two-color print job. In Photoshop, duotones are treated as single-channel, 8-bit grayscale images. You can convert any 8-bit grayscale image by choosing Image>Mode>Duotone.

Choose Monotone, Duotone, Tritone, or Quadtone in this menu.

Click these icons to change the curve associated with each ink.

Click a swatch to change the colors of the duotone.

In a duotone image, you can't access the individual ink channels in the Channels panel. You can, however, manipulate the channels through the curves in the Duotone Options dialog box.

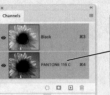

You can't use the Channels panel to access the individual inks in a duotone image.

Each ink has a curve that specifies how the color is distributed across shadows and highlights. This curve maps each grayscale value in the original image to a specific ink percentage. The default curve (a straight, diagonal line) indicates that the grayscale values in the original image map to an equal percentage of ink. For example, a 50% midtone pixel becomes a 50% tint of the ink.

If you need direct access to the individual channels in a duotone, you can convert it to Multichannel mode (Image>Mode> Multichannel).

After converting to Multichannel mode, the individual ink separations are available in the Channels panel.

Save the File without Spot-Color Information

When you use spot colors, you have to use a file format that can store the spot-channel information. The native Photoshop format (PSD) obviously stores the spot channels, and that format will be used for most print-based applications. A smaller file, such as JPEG, is usually preferred for digital distribution. However, JPEG does not support spot-color channels. If a file has spot channels, you need to merge the spot color data into the primary channels before saving a JPEG file; if you omit this step, information on the spot channels will simply be removed.

1. **With ballet-cover.psd open, select the PANTONE 8943 C channel in the Channels panel.**

2. **Open the Channels panel Options menu and choose Merge Spot Channel.**

   This command moves the spot-channel data into the primary color channels. The software creates a nearest-possible color match for any spot color that is outside the primary color gamut.

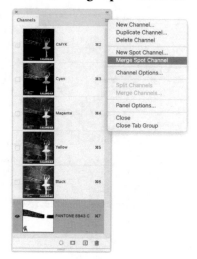

3. **Read the resulting message, then click OK.**

   Merging the spot channel requires the entire file to be flattened, which means you lose all individual layer data and future editability. You should take this step only after a file is absolutely finished, and always save it with a different name, so you can preserve editability in the original, unmerged file.

4. **With the merged file open, choose File>Save a copy.**

5. **Choose JPEG in the Format/Save As Type menu, then click Save.**

6. **In the JPEG Options dialog box, set the Quality field to 10, and then click OK.**

7. **Close any open file.**

## Working with Adobe CC Libraries

If you have an individual-user subscription to the Adobe Creative Cloud, you have access to CC Library functionality, which allows you to easily share assets across various Adobe applications. This technology makes it very easy to maintain consistency across a design campaign — for example, using the same color swatches for all pieces, whether created in Illustrator, InDesign, or Photoshop.

When you first open the Libraries panel you see a list of all libraries that exist in your Adobe account. You can:

- Click an existing library name to open it in the panel.
- Click the Create New Library button to add a new one to your account.
- Click Browse Shared Libraries to view libraries that other users have shared with you.
- Click Find Public Libraries to find assets that have been created by other users and shared publicly.

You can access these same options by clicking the + button in the bottom-right corner of the panel.

This menu also includes an option to create a New Library from Document. If you use this option, the new library automatically adopts the name of the file from which the library is created. Any character styles, defined color swatches, applied layer styles, and smart object layers are added to the new library by default.

Once you create a library, it is stored in your Creative Cloud account so you can access the same assets in other Adobe applications.

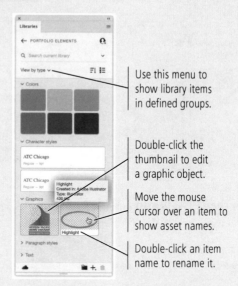

Use this menu to show library items in defined groups.

Double-click the thumbnail to edit a graphic object.

Move the mouse cursor over an item to show asset names.

Double-click an item name to rename it.

When a library is open in the panel, several buttons at the bottom of the panel can be used to manage the elements in the active library.

- Library Sync Status shows whether the active library is currently synced to your Adobe account.
- Create New Group adds a folder to the library, which you can use to manually group elements based on whatever criteria you determine.
- Add Elements opens a menu that you can use to add various types of library items. The options here depend on the selected layer in active file; if a type layer is selected, for example, this menu would also include options to add character and/or paragraph styles based on the type formatting applied to that layer.

- Delete removes the selected element(s) from the active library.

## Working with Library Items

Clicking a color swatch in the library changes the active foreground color in Photoshop.

Clicking a layer style in the library applies the stored layer styles to the active layer in the Layers panel.

Clicking a character style applies the defined formatting options to all text on the active type layer. (You cannot apply a library character style to only certain characters on a type layer.)

To place a graphic from a library, simply drag it from the Libraries panel onto the Photoshop canvas. This creates a linked Smart Object layer — in this case, it is linked to the Library item instead of to an external file on your desktop. Linked Smart Object layers in Photoshop are identified by a special icon in the Layers panel.

This icon identifies a Smart Object layer that is linked to a library item.

By default, objects placed from a library are linked to the library file. Any changes you make to the library item will reflect in all placed instances.

Say you change the color of text in a logo. Any instance of that logo that has been placed from the library, in any Adobe application, will automatically reflect the new type color as long as the library link is active.

If you press Option/Alt when you drag an object from the panel, you create a non-linked, regular layer with the content from the object you dragged onto the canvas. In this case, there is no dynamic link to the library.

## Sharing and Collaboration

Libraries also offer a powerful opportunity to communicate assets with other users.

You can click the Invite People button at the top of the Libraries panel to share a library with specific other users. Clicking this button navigates to your online Adobe account in the Creative Cloud desktop application, and automatically asks for the email addresses of those you want to share with.

You can click the arrow to the left of the "Can Edit" text to determine whether invited users can edit the library or simply view it.

1. True or False: Used fonts are embedded into the Photoshop file, so that they will be available for any user who opens that file. _____

2. The _____ option adjusts the degree of clarity that is selected by the Focus Area dialog box.

3. True or False: An Alpha channel visible in the document window is always 100% opaque. _____

4. Paint with _____ on a mask to remove from the mask area.

5. Paint with _____ on a mask to add to the mask area.

6. The Custom Shape tool can be used to create _____ from built-in or external libraries.

7. _____ are special inks used to print specific colors — often those that are outside the CMYK gamut.

8. A _____ is an image with only two channels — typically, black and one other spot color.

9. Spot-color information is stored in a _____; it is not associated with any Photoshop layer.

10. Images with spot-color channels should be saved in the _____ format.

1. Briefly describe the relationship between a layer mask and an Alpha channel.

2. Briefly explain the process of painting directly on a channel.

3. Briefly explain why spot colors are used in commercial graphic design.

# PORTFOLIO BUILDER PROJECT

Use what you have learned in this project to complete the following freeform exercise.
Carefully read the art director and client comments, then create your own design to meet the needs of the project.
Use the space below to sketch ideas. When finished, write a brief explanation of the reasoning behind your final design.

art director comments

The publisher you work for is creating a new title, SportsXtreme magazine, which will feature extreme sports such as BMX, skydiving, and whitewater rafting. As the in-house designer, you will be in charge of creating cover concepts for each edition of the magazine.

To complete this project, you should:

❏ Design an 8.25″ × 10.75″ cover concept that can be repurposed for each edition of the magazine.

❏ Create a nameplate that includes the magazine title, as well as the issue number, volume number, and date of the issue.

❏ Find or create artwork and images to illustrate each of the first two planned issues.

❏ Include placeholder text for three article titles on the cover.

client comments

Extreme sports are a big business, so we're going to publish this magazine to capitalize on a very large market. The target demographics in this area are very favorable for marketing companies, and we've already presold enough advertising space to make each issue at least 96 pages.

Each issue will focus on a variety of sports, but will have a main cover story that features a specific event. The first two issues will highlight skateboarding and wind surfing (respectively).

I want you to create a cover concept for the new magazine that will appeal to people who are interested in extreme sports — something bright, exciting, and dynamic that will speak to their adrenaline-junkie nature.

project justification

This project highlighted a number of aesthetic and technical issues associated with building a unified composition from a set of disparate elements. Many on-the-job projects include complex selections, such as the one you created in this project. Although the tools available in Photoshop make the process far easier than painting every pixel by hand, you should be prepared to do some manual clean-up to perfect the fine details of a selection mask. Patience and attention to detail separate great work from average work.

Create a custom
vector shape layer

Warp a
type layer

Use a complex selection to
isolate an image element from
its photographic background

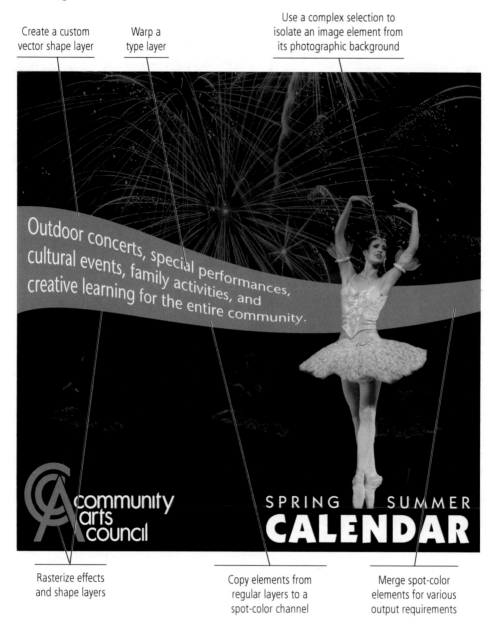

Rasterize effects
and shape layers

Copy elements from
regular layers to a
spot-color channel

Merge spot-color
elements for various
output requirements

# 6 Advertising Samples

You are the in-house designer for a printing company, so your client is the new accounts manager, who is pitching your company's new large-format printing services to a potential customer. She asked you to morph an existing sample ad onto a number of different photos to help promote the company's new "Advertise Anywhere!" services.

This project incorporates the following skills:

❏ Patching a photo to remove unwanted elements

❏ Replacing colors in a photo to change the appearance of an object

❏ Using adjustment layers to change hue/saturation for specific objects

❏ Adjusting an image's shadows and highlights to correct bad lighting

❏ Transforming a layer using one- and two-point perspective

❏ Warping a layer around irregular, non-flat surfaces

## Videos to Watch

Access these helpful videos in your online student resources:

▶▶ Advertising Samples Project Introduction

▶▶ Using the Patch Tool

▶▶ Using the Replace Color Adjustment

▶▶ Working with Adjustment Layers

**client comments**

Our "Advertise Anywhere!" campaign is designed to help our clients promote their products by placing large ads in unusual places — on a bench, on paint strips in parking lots, wrapped around a city bus, and in other nontraditional locations.

The promoter for a music festival, which draws more than 50,000 people every year, is very interested, but wants to see some samples. He asked me to do a presentation in two weeks for his marketing committee. If they like what they see, this contract could evolve into a much bigger one.

We already created a sample ad for the concert, and I asked my assistant to gather some photos to use in the presentation. We have pictures of two local buildings, as well as two less common examples — a large water tank by the freeway and a hot air balloon.

▶ **Watch the video** Advertising Samples Project Introduction **in your online student resources.**

**art director comments**

Since the "Advertise Anywhere!" program is new for our company, the owner is excited about presenting to the first potential client. All the pictures they want to use need some help to make them as attractive as possible.

In the water tank photo, there's a bunch of litter I want you to remove.

The bright yellow in the balloon is going to detract attention from the sample ad. Remove the yellow from the balloon body and mute the other colors a bit so the sample ad stands out.

One of the building photos isn't bad, but it has been painted since we took the photo. To personalize the presentation, convert the brown front façade to dark red and clean up any marks.

The office building photo is fairly dark, so I want you to adjust the photo's overall lighting. That photo also has some lens distortion, so you need to correct that before you wrap the ad around the building.

**project objectives**

To complete this project, you will:

❏ Use the Patch tool to replace one area of an image with pixels from another area

❏ Use the Replace Color adjustment to change selected colors in an image

❏ Use adjustment layers to apply color changes to specific areas of an image

❏ Use the Shadow/Highlight adjustment to correct a shadow-filled image

❏ Use Free Transform mode to match a layer to the perspective in the background image

❏ Use the Vanishing Point filter to wrap a layer in perspective around a sharp corner

❏ Create a custom warp transformation to morph a sample ad onto a round shape

# STAGE 1 / Cleaning and Adjusting Images

Photoshop includes a number of tools for creating irregular composite images — such as warping a flat ad around the shape of a water tank along the desert highway, or placing an ad on a hot-air balloon floating in the distance. Before you composite the images for this project, however, you need to do some clean-up work on the background photos. The best approach is to fix the images first, and then morph the ad onto the corrected files.

##  Remove Unwanted Image Elements

The Healing Brush and Spot Healing Brush tools are excellent choices for cleaning up marks and blemishes, and the Clone Stamp tool can effectively copy pixels from one location to another. The Patch tool can be used to replace one area with another and blend the area edges for smoother results.

*Watch the video **Using the Patch Tool in Photoshop** in your online student resources.*

1. **Expand the** Outdoors_PS22_RF.zip **archive in your WIP folder (Macintosh), or copy the archive contents into your WIP folder (Windows).**

   This results in a folder named **Outdoors**, which contains the files you need for this project. You should also use this folder to save the files you create in this project.

2. **In Photoshop, open** tanks.jpg **from the WIP>Outdoors folder.**

This image will make a better client sample without the annoying litter along the edge of the road.

3. **Zoom in to the large white object in the bottom center of the image.**

4. **Choose the Patch tool in the Tools panel (nested under the Spot Healing Brush tool).**

   If you don't see the Patch tool, look in the Edit Toolbar ( ... ) menu at the bottom of the Tools panel, or call the default Essentials workspace to reset all tools to their default positions in the Tools panel.

   The Patch tool allows you to repair a selected area with a texture, pixels from another specified area, or a pattern. It matches texture, lighting, and shading of the sampled pixels to the source (selected) pixels. This option gives you more control than the Content-Aware Fill dialog box because you choose the area to be filled *and* the pixels that will be used to fill that area.

5. **Using the Patch tool, draw a selection marquee that entirely surrounds the piece of trash.**

Unwanted area

Selection marquee

Because of the texture and detail in the surrounding area, the other repair tools are not the best choices for removing this object from the roadside. The Patch tool, on the other hand, allows you to sample pixels from other areas of the image and blend them smoothly over the selected area.

6. **In the Options bar, open the Patch Mode menu and choose Content-Aware.**

When the Patch mode menu is set to Normal (the default), you have two additional options: Source and Destination. These buttons define what the selection marquee represents.

- If Source is active, the original marquee represents the area that will be patched.

- If Destination is active, the original selection marquee represents the pixels that will be copied to another area.

If the Patch Mode menu is set to Content-Aware, Photoshop evaluates the image pixels and fills the original selection marquee with content from the area you drag to (similar to the Source option in Normal mode). In Content-Aware mode, you can determine how closely the software analyzes the Structure (on a scale of 1–7) and Color (on a scale of 1–10) of the image to create the final result. Higher structure and color values mean the patched pixels will more closely resemble the detail in the patching pixels; they take longer to process, but can produce more accurate results.

7. **Using the default tool settings, place the Patch tool cursor inside the selection marquee, and then click and drag to the left. When you are satisfied with the preview, release the mouse button.**

The pixels inside the second marquee (where you drag to) are used to fill the original location. This tool shows a dynamic preview; as you drag the marquee, the original selection changes to show the result that will be created when you release the mouse button.

When you release the mouse button, the Patch tool blends the selection edge smoothly into the surrounding area, preventing unwanted harsh edges around the patch.

*Note:*

*If you aren't satisfied with the result, undo the patch selection and try again.*

8. **Press Command/Control-D to turn off the selection marquee so you can better review your results.**

# Using Content-Aware Fill

The Edit>Content-Aware Fill command opens a dedicated workspace with tools and options for filling a selection with content sampled from another part of the image.

Within the Content-Aware Fill workspace, the document window shows the default sampling area, or the area that will be used to fill the selection, as a green overlay mask over the image. You can change the opacity and color of the mask, as well as whether the mask shows the sampling area (default) or the excluded area, in the Content-Aware Fill panel on the right side of the workspace.

You can paint with the Sampling Brush Tool to change the sampling area. When this tool is active, you can use the Options bar to determine whether you are adding to, or subtracting from, the sampling area. You can also use the Size option to change the sampling brush size, or press the Left Bracket or Right Bracket keys to reduce, or enlarge, the brush.

You can use the Lasso and (nested) Polygonal Lasso tools to modify the selection area that will be filled. Options for these tools in the Content-Aware Fill workspace are the same as those for the Lasso tools in the main Photoshop workspace. You can also use the Expand and Contract options to enlarge or shrink the selection by a defined number of pixels.

The Hand and Zoom tools have the same functions here as in the main Photoshop interface.

The Preview panel in the center of the screen shows a live preview of the fill results based on the active sampling area.

You can specify Fill settings in the Content-Aware Fill panel on the right side of workspace.

**Color Adaptation** allows contrast and brightness to adapt for a better match when filling content with gradual color or texture changes.

**Rotation Adaptation** allows content rotation for a better match when filling content with rotated or curved patterns.

**Scale** allows content resizing for a better match when filling content with repeating patterns of different sizes, or under perspective.

**Mirror** allows content to be flipped horizontally for a better match when filling content with horizontal symmetry.

The **Output To** menu defines what results from clicking OK:

- Current Layer applies the fill directly to the active layer.
- New Layer adds only the fill area to a new layer, immediately above the previously selected layer.
- Duplicate Layer creates a new layer, with both the content of the previously selected layer and the new filled area.

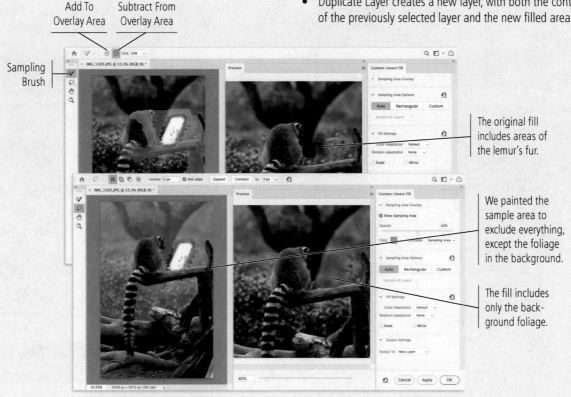

Add To Overlay Area

Subtract From Overlay Area

Sampling Brush

The original fill includes areas of the lemur's fur.

We painted the sample area to exclude everything, except the foliage in the background.

The fill includes only the background foliage.

In addition to the tools you have used throughout this book, a number of tools in the Tools panel can be used to make basic corrections.

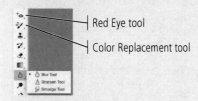

Red Eye tool

Color Replacement tool

The **Red Eye tool** (nested under the Spot Healing Brush tool) removes the red-eye effect caused by flash photography.

In the Options bar, the **Pupil Size** menu controls the size of the area affected by the tool. The **Darken Amount** option sets the darkness of the correction.

The **Blur tool** softens hard edges and reduces detail.

The **Sharpen tool** increases contrast at edges to increase apparent sharpness.

The **Smudge tool** allows you to push pixels around in an image, as if you were dragging your finger across wet (digital) paint.

All three of these tools use a selected brush preset to affect the image. You can choose a specific blending mode, as well as the strength of the effect as you paint a brush stroke. Multiple brush strokes increase the tool's effect.

If the **Sample All Layers** option is checked, you can affect the selected layer using data from all layers in the file. For the Smudge tool, the Finger Painting option adds the foreground color to the beginning of the brush stroke.

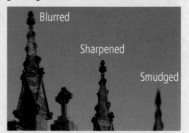

The **Color Replacement tool** (nested under the Brush tool) attempts to simplify replacement of specific colors in your image. You can define the brush you want to use, and then paint over a targeted color to replace it with the foreground color.

You can replace the color, or you can choose Hue, Saturation, or Luminosity in the Mode menu. The sampling options determine how color will be replaced:

- **Continuous** samples colors as you drag.
- **Once** replaces color only in areas of the color that you first click.
- **Background Swatch** replaces only areas of the current background color.

The Limits menu determines how the tool's effect can be constrained:

- **Discontiguous** replaces the sampled color under the brush tip.
- **Contiguous** replaces color contiguous with the color under the brush tip.
- **Find Edges** replaces connected areas of the sampled color, attempting to preserve the sharpness of shape edges.

**Tolerance** defines how much variance from the sample will be affected. The **Anti-alias** option smoothes edges of the affected areas.

The Color Replacement tool works best for images with high-contrast edges.

# Painting Image Exposure and Saturation

The **Dodge** and **Burn tools** are used to lighten or darken, respectively, areas of an image. These tools are based on traditional photographic techniques for exposing specific areas of a print. Photographers hold back light to lighten an area on the print (**dodging**) or increase the exposure to darken areas on a print (**burning**).

You define a brush in the Options bar, as well as the image range you want to affect (highlights, midtones, or shadows) and the degree of exposure.

The **Sponge tool** changes the color saturation of an area. As with the Dodge and Burn tools, you can define a specific brush to use. You can also define the mode of the Sponge tool — Saturate or Desaturate — and the flow rate for the effect.

The original image shows the view through a guard house window at Alcatraz Island in San Francisco Bay.

The post on the left was painted with the Dodge tool to lighten the shadows and reveal details in the concrete.

Original Image

The foliage at the bottom opening was painted with the Burn tool to darken the shadows, effectively removing all detail in that area.

The opening in the wall was painted with the Sponge tool in Saturate mode to enhance the blue of the water.

9. **Using the same technique, remove the rest of the litter from the foreground of this image.**

**Note:**

*When using the Patch tool, use the smallest selection area possible to achieve the best results.*

10. **Save the file as a native Photoshop file named** studio.jpg — tanks-clean.psd **in your WIP>Outdoors folder.**

11. **Close the file, then continue to the next exercise.**

## Replace Colors in Parts of an Image

The Replace Color adjustment allows you to select and replace a specific range of colors in an image. This adjustment option is a simple method for making overall changes to hue, saturation, or lightness in selected areas, without having to experiment with layer blending modes.

*Watch the video* **Using the Replace Color Adjustment in Photoshop** *in your online student resources.*

1. **Open the file** studio.jpg **from the WIP>Outdoors folder.**

On the actual building, this façade has been repainted a deep red.

The fresh paint removed these white streaks.

2. **Choose Image>Adjustments>Replace Color.**

3. **Using the Eyedropper tool from the Replace Color dialog box, click in the image (behind the dialog box) to select the brown stucco façade of the building.**

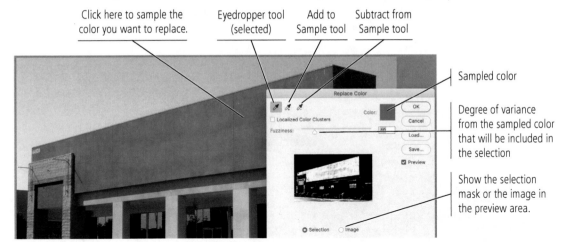

Click here to sample the color you want to replace.

Eyedropper tool (selected)

Add to Sample tool

Subtract from Sample tool

Sampled color

Degree of variance from the sampled color that will be included in the selection

Show the selection mask or the image in the preview area.

4. **Drag the Fuzziness slider right to increase the selection tolerance.**

As you increase the fuzziness, you can see other areas of the image being added to the selection. Various areas in this image share many of the same earth tones, which means you can't select the façade color without affecting some other areas of the image — at least, not without a couple of extra steps.

Increasing fuzziness adds more areas to the selection.

5. **Click Cancel to close the Replace Color dialog box.**

6. **In the Layers panel, Control/right-click the Background layer and choose Duplicate Layer from the contextual menu. Click OK in the Duplicate Layer dialog box to accept the default layer name.**

*Note:*

*When you Control/ right-click a layer and select Duplicate Layer, you can use the Destination options to place the duplicate layer in the stack for the current (open) image, any open image, or a new image.*

7. **With the Background Copy layer selected in the Layers panel, choose Image>Adjustments>Replace Color.**

8. **Click in the image to sample the same brown as the selection color, and then move the Fuzziness slider all the way to the right.**

    The preview shows that a large portion of the image is selected, including areas that you don't want to change. That's okay, since you'll use a layer mask to eliminate those areas from the duplicate layer.

9. **In the lower half of the dialog box, experiment with the Hue, Saturation, and Lightness sliders until you find a dark red color.**

Note:

You can also click the Result color swatch and define a replacement color in the Color Picker dialog box.

Much of the building has some shade of brown, so full Fuzziness selects most of the building face.

Use these options to change the color of the selected pixels.

10. **Click OK to apply the change to the selected layer.**

11. **Using any method you prefer, draw a selection marquee around the edges of the façade (as shown in the following image).**

    Since this selection has straight edges, the Polygonal Lasso tool will do a fine job of creating the selection. You could also draw a work path with the Pen tool, and then make a selection based on the work path.

Note:

It's important to understand that image adjustments apply to the selected area or layer only. These adjustments do not apply to all layers in an image.

**12.** **With the selection active (you can see the marching ants), click the Add Layer Mask button at the bottom of the Layers panel.**

When you add a layer mask with an active selection, the areas outside the selection are automatically masked.

Add Layer Mask button

## Understanding the Selective Color Adjustment

The **Selective Color** adjustment (Image>Adjustments>Selective Color) allows you to change ink values in specific colors or neutrals without affecting other colors.

For example, if water looks too yellow, as it does in the image on the left below, you should remove yellow to produce a more inviting blue color. If you reduce the overall amount of yellow, however, you might affect other areas, such as the pier and island. The Selective Color option allows you to adjust the yellow component of only blues or cyans, so you can fix the water without affecting other areas.

The Relative method changes the existing amount of cyan, magenta, yellow, or black by its percentage of the total. For example, if you start with a pixel that is 70% yellow and remove 10%, then 7% is removed from the yellow (10% of 70% = 7%). The Absolute method adjusts the color in absolute values. If you start with a pixel that is 70% yellow and remove 10%, the yellow pixel is set to 60%.

Water in the original image has a strong yellow cast.

Adjusting ink percentages of only the cyans made the water more inviting without affecting the pilings in the foreground.

The Preset menu at the top of the Selective Color dialog box is useful if you need to make the same adjustment to multiple images — for example, if you know photos from a particular digital camera always have a yellow cast in the blue areas. (The same Preset options are available in all adjustment dialog boxes.)

13. **Zoom in to the edges of the façade and make sure the mask covers exactly what you want it to cover. Use the Brush and/or Eraser tool to clean up the mask edges if necessary.**

Remember, when you paint on a mask, black adds to the mask and white removes areas from the mask. You should also make sure to select the mask in the Layers panel (instead of the layer thumbnail) before painting on it, or you will mistakenly paint on the actual image layer.

14. **In the Layers panel, Control/right-click the Background Copy layer name and choose Merge Down from the contextual menu.**

**Merge Down** combines the selected layer with the next layer down in the Layers panel. **Merge Visible** combines all visible layers into a single layer. **Flatten Image** combines all layers into the Background layer, giving you the option to discard hidden layers.

Because the next layer down is the Background layer, merging the selected layer down combines the Background Copy layer into the Background layer.

15. **Use any technique you prefer to remove the white streaks from the building's façade.**

The Replace Color function only affected areas of color within the selected range (Step 9). These spots are drastically different than the selected brown shades, so they still need to be corrected.

We used a combination of the Spot Healing tool to clean up the spots on the face, and the Clone Stamp and Patch tools to clean up the edges.

16. **Save the file as a native Photoshop file named studio-clean.psd in your WIP>Outdoors folder.**

17. **Close the file, then continue to the next exercise.**

## Adjust Hue and Saturation with an Adjustment Layer

Correcting the previous image highlighted one of the potential drawbacks of using image adjustments: you might change areas you don't want to change, requiring a work-around (in this case, a duplicate layer with a mask) to achieve the effect you want.

The process you used in the previous exercise is so common that Photoshop includes built-in options for creating adjustment layers, which effectively achieve the same result that you accomplished manually in the previous exercise. An adjustment layer is an empty layer containing an adjustment (such as a Levels or Curves adjustment) that modifies the layers below it.

**Adjustment layers** are non-destructive; rather than permanently affecting the pixels in your image, adjustment layers store the adjustment settings, so you can change the settings or toggle the adjustment on or off at any point.

You can add an adjustment layer using the buttons in the Adjustments panel, or the menu at the bottom of the Layers panel. Once an adjustment layer is added, you can use the Properties panel to change the settings of the adjustment.

*Watch the video **Working with Adjustment Layers** in your online student resources.*

**Note:**

*You can use adjustment layers for most of the adjustments available in the Image>Adjustments menu. (For some reason, a few adjustments — including the Replace Color adjustment you used in the previous exercise — have been left out of this panel.)*

Create New Fill or Adjustment Layer

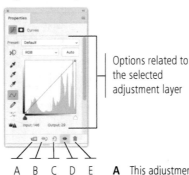

Options related to the selected adjustment layer

A  B  C  D  E

**A**  This adjustment affects all layers below (click to clip to layer)
**B**  Press to view previous state
**C**  Reset to adjustment defaults
**D**  Toggle [adjustment] layer visibility
**E**  Delete this adjustment layer

Icons in the Adjustments panel match the icons that identify an adjustment layer:

| | | | |
|---|---|---|---|
| ☀ Brightness/Contrast | 📷 Photo Filter | ▽ Vibrance | ▨ Posterize |
| ▥ Levels | ◐ Channel Mixer | ▦ Hue/Saturation | ▨ Threshold |
| ▦ Curves | ▦ Color Lookup | ⚴ Color Balance | ▧ Selective Color |
| ▨ Exposure | ▨ Invert | ◨ Black & White | ▭ Gradient Map |

1. **Open the file balloon.jpg from the WIP>Outdoors folder.**

   The art director wants this yellow balloon to be white, so it doesn't distract from the sample ad. The Hue/Saturation adjustment, which allows you to change the Hue, Saturation, and Lightness values of specific primary colors, is perfectly suited for changing this yellow balloon to white.

2. **Open the Adjustments panel and click the Hue/Saturation button.**

   The Hue/Saturation adjustment can be extremely useful for shifting the Hue, Saturation, or Lightness value of an entire image or for selected primary colors.

   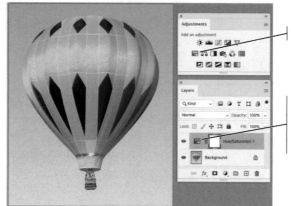

   Hue/Saturation button

   The adjustment layer icon matches the Hue/Saturation button in the Adjustments panel.

   Adding an adjustment layer creates a new layer on top of the currently selected one. This allows you to easily show or hide the adjustment, apply multiple adjustments to the same layer, or even delete an adjustment from the file without permanently changing the pixels on the original layer. The adjustment from an adjustment layer is not permanent unless you merge the adjustment layer with one or more underlying layers.

   Keep in mind that adjustment layers affect all underlying layers. If you want an adjustment layer to affect only the next layer down, Control/right-click the adjustment layer and choose Create Clipping Mask from the contextual menu.

3. **In the Properties panel, choose Yellows in the Edit menu (which defaults to Master) and drag the Lightness slider all the way to the right.**

   When an adjustment layer is selected in the Layers panel, the Properties panel contains options specific to the selected adjustment layer.

   **Lightness** is the position of a color along the black/white scale. Lightness of 0 adds no white or black to the hue. Lightness of –100 is solid black (obscuring all other color). Lightness of +100 is pure white (removing all color).

   Since the balloon was pure yellow, increasing the yellow lightness to +100 converts the yellow parts of the balloon to pure white.

   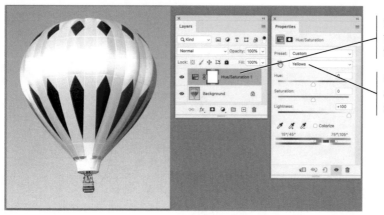

   Select the adjustment layer to show related settings in the Properties panel.

   Choose from this menu to adjust the entire image, or specific primary colors.

4. **In the Layers panel, click the Adjustment Layer Mask thumbnail to select it.**

   Adjustment layers automatically include a layer mask, which allows you to isolate portions of an image for correction. Adjustment layers are also helpful for experimenting with corrections without permanently affecting the underlying layer.

5. **Choose the Brush tool in the Tools panel. Open the Brush Preset picker in the Options bar and define a 70-pixel brush with 100% hardness.**

6. **Click the Default Foreground and Background Colors button in the Tools panel, then click the Switch Foreground and Background Colors button.**

   This sets the foreground color to black, which you must use on an adjustment layer mask to protect certain areas from the adjustment.

7. **With the adjustment layer mask selected in the Layers panel, paint over the area of the basket to protect that area from the increased Lightness setting for yellows.**

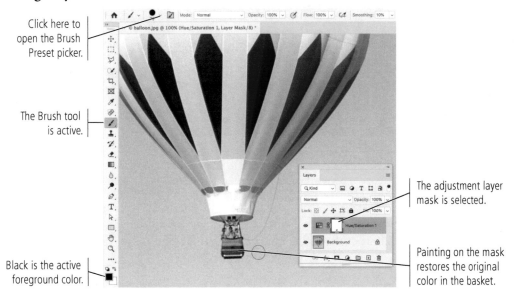

Click here to open the Brush Preset picker.

The Brush tool is active.

Black is the active foreground color.

The adjustment layer mask is selected.

Painting on the mask restores the original color in the basket.

8. **Save the file as a native Photoshop file named balloon-clean.psd in your WIP>Outdoors folder. Click OK in the Photoshop Format Options dialog box when asked to maximize compatibility.**

   You were not asked to maximize compatibility with the previous files, because all of those still have only one layer.

9. **Close the file and continue to the next exercise.**

*Note:*

*You can change the opacity, order, or blending mode of an adjustment layer, just as you can with a regular layer.*

# Adjust Image Shadows and Highlights

The Shadows/Highlights adjustment is well suited for correcting highlight and shadow areas of an image. Photoshop calculates the changes based on the values of surrounding pixels. Using the basic settings, you can adjust the values of shadows and highlights independently.

When the Show More Options box is checked in the Shadows/Highlights dialog box, you can fine-tune the adjustments for both shadows and highlights, as well as modify the options for color correction and midtone contrast.

- **Tone** defines the part of the tonal range that will be modified by the adjustment. Set to 100%, the adjustment will be applied to half of the tonal range. Smaller values restrict the adjustment to smaller regions of the related area (shadows or highlights).

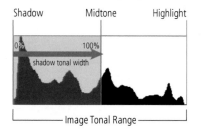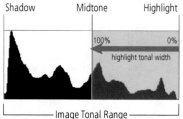

- **Radius** controls the size of the area around each pixel that is used to determine whether a pixel is in the shadows or highlights.

- **Color** fine-tunes the colors in areas that are changed by your choices in the Shadows and Highlights sections of the dialog box. Higher values tend to produce more saturated colors.

- **Midtone** adjusts the contrast in the midtones, similar to the Input Gamma slider in the Levels dialog box.

- **Black Clip** and **White Clip** determine how much of the extreme shadows and highlights are clipped, just as with the Clip options in the Auto Color Correction Options dialog box.

1. Open the file **office.jpg** from the WIP>Outdoors folder.

This overall image is extremely dark; much of the building is in shadows.

2. Choose **Image>Adjustments>Shadows/Highlights.**

3. **Reduce the Shadow Amount value to 15% to lighten the shadows in the image.**

   An Amount value of 0% means no change will be applied to that area. Larger values result in lighter shadows or darker highlights.

Drag this slider right to lighten the shadows.

Drag this slider right to darken the highlights.

4. **Click OK to apply the change.**

5. **Save the file as a native Photoshop file named office-clean.psd in your WIP>Outdoors folder.**

6. **Close the file, then continue to the next stage of the project.**

# STAGE 2 / **Working in Perspective**

Many compositing jobs will be straightforward copy-and-paste jobs — putting multiple images together, and then possibly adjusting size, clipping edges, or blending edges into other elements — such as the work you completed in the earlier projects of this book.

Other jobs are more complex, especially those that require you to make one object appear to be a seamless part of another image. When your goal is to merge one element with another existing image, you need to pay close attention to details, such as size, angle, and depth, so the composited element appears to blend naturally with the background image.

 ## Transform the Perspective of a Layer

Basic transformations, such as scale, rotation, skew, and perspective, can all be accomplished in Free Transform mode. For skewing a flat ad onto a flat surface, Free Transform mode is the simplest choice.

1. **Open the file studio-clean.psd from your WIP>Outdoors folder.**

2. **Choose File>Place Embedded. Select the file banner.tif from the WIP>Outdoors folder and click Place.**

   The Place Embedded command adds the selected file as a Smart Object layer.

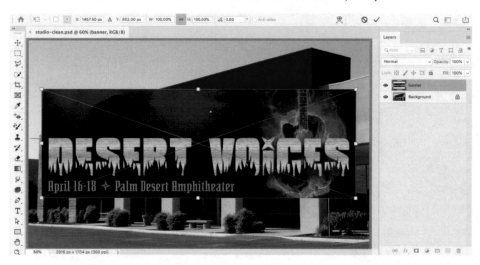

3. **Using the Options bar, scale the layer to 73% proportionally, and then drag the banner so that its top-right corner is near the top-right corner of the studio façade.**

Use the W and H fields to resize the banner graphic to 73% of its original size.

Position the top-right corner near the top-right corner of the façade.

4. **Command/Control-click the center-left transformation handle and drag down to skew the layer. Align the bottom-left corner of the banner to the bottom-left corner of the building façade (as shown here).**

Simply dragging a center handle stretches or shrinks the selection. Pressing the Command/Control key allows you to skew a selection, instead of changing its horizontal or vertical size.

Press Shift while Command/Control-dragging to skew the object exactly vertical or exactly horizontal.

Press Command/Control and drag the center handle to skew the selection.

5. **Command/Control-click the top-left transformation handle and drag down to distort the perspective of the layer.**

Simply dragging a corner handle stretches or shrinks the selection. Pressing the Command/Control key allows you to distort the image's shape, which affects perspective when you drag straight corners in this manner.

Press Shift while Command/Control-dragging to constrain the movement of the transformation handle to 45° angles.

Press Command/Control and drag the corner handle to alter the perspective of the selection.

6. **If necessary, adjust the bottom corner handles so that the banner fits entirely within the front of the façade.**

7. **When you're satisfied with the position, size, and perspective of the banner, press Return/Enter to finalize the transformation.**

8. **Apply a slight drop shadow to the banner layer (Layer>Layer Style>Drop Shadow). We used the following settings:**

| Blend Mode: | Multiply Black | Distance: | 10 |
|---|---|---|---|
| Opacity: | 75% | Spread: | 0 |
| Angle: | 125° | Size: | 5 |

*Note:*

*We used the 125° angle for the drop shadow to approximate the angle of shadows that already exist in the image.*

9. **Save the file as studio-ad.psd in your WIP>Outdoors folder. Click OK when asked to maximize compatibility.**

10. **Close the file, and then continue to the next exercise.**

## Understanding Free Transform Options

You can transform any layer or selection using the options in the Edit>Transform menu, or by choosing Edit>Free Transform. (Most of the options in the Edit>Transform submenu — Scale, Rotate, Skew, and Distort — can also be applied using the Free Transform option, making these choices redundant.)

When you choose Edit>Free Transform, the selection is surrounded by handles that allow you to control the transformation.

When you enter Free Transform mode, the Maintain Aspect Ratio in the Options bar option is checked by default. The following images summarize the transformation behavior when the Maintain Aspect Ratio option is active:

| Drag a handle to proportionally stretch or shrink the selection. | Command/Control-drag a corner handle to distort the selection in both directions. | Command/Control-drag a center handle to skew the selection in both directions. | Click slightly outside a corner handle to rotate the selection. |
| --- | --- | --- | --- |

| Shift-drag a handle to disproportionally stretch or shrink the selection. | Command/Control-Shift-drag a corner handle to distort the selection in one direction. | Command/Control-Shift-drag a center handle to skew the selection in one direction. |
| --- | --- | --- |

*Pressing Option/Alt while making any of these transformations applies the change equally on both sides of the selection center.

If you turn off the Maintain Aspect Ratio option, the default behavior reverses: You can simply click and drag a handle to transform a layer disproportionally. To transform the layer while maintaining the original aspect ratio, you must press Shift while dragging the handles.

**Important note:** If you are transforming a vector shape layer, the software does not automatically maintain the selection's aspect ratio when you drag a handle. In this case, you have to press Shift and drag to maintain the selection's original aspect ratio.

---

If you choose Edit>Transform>Perspective, dragging a side handle has the same effect as pressing Command/Control-Shift when in Free Transform mode. Dragging a corner handle has the same effect as pressing Command-Option/Control-Alt when working in Free Transform mode.

The advantage to Perspective transformation mode is that you don't have to use the modifier keys. The disadvantage is that you can't change anything other than the horizontal or vertical skew, and the reflective horizontal or vertical distortion of the selection.

| Drag a center handle to skew the selection. | Drag a corner handle to distort that side of the selection around the center point. |
| --- | --- |

# Apply a Perspective Warp

In the next exercise, you are going to place the banner ad in perspective around the office building. Before you do that, however, you are going to use the powerful Perspective Warp utility in this exercise to straighten the lines in the photo, and reduce some of the distortion caused by the photographer's angle relative to the building.

1. **Open the file office-clean.psd from the WIP>Outdoors folder.**

2. **With the Background layer selected in the Layers panel, choose Edit>Perspective Warp.**

3. **If you see a pop-up message, read it, and then click the Close button.**

   When you enter Perspective Warp mode for the first time, Photoshop shows helpful tips for using the filter. If someone else has already closed these messages, you can reshow them by clicking the Reset All Warning Dialogs in the General pane of the Preferences dialog box.

Perspective Warp initially opens in Layout mode, where you define perspective planes.

Remove All Quads

Cancel Perspective Warp

Commit Perspective Warp

Click here to close the pop-up message.

4. **Click anywhere in the document window to create a perspective plane grid.**

   Photoshop's Help materials sometimes refer to perspective planes as quads. We use the term "planes" to maintain consistency throughout our discussion of perspective.

Click to create a new perspective grid plane.

Drag the plane's corners or edges to define the exact perspective grid.

5. **Click and drag the four corners of the perspective plane to match the apparent corners on the right side of the building.**

6. **At the bottom of the image, make sure all visible pieces of the building are included inside the plane grid. (Use the following image as a guide.)**

   Anything outside the grid boundaries will not be transformed when you later warp the perspective grid. To avoid unusual results, you must include the entire bottom edge of the building — including the pillars — inside the perspective warp grid.

Drag the corners to apparent corners in the image.

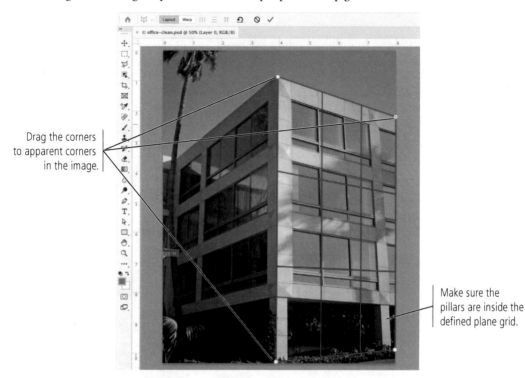

Make sure the pillars are inside the defined plane grid.

7. **Click again to create a second perspective plane.**

8. **If you see a pop-up message, read it, and then click the Close button to dismiss the message.**

Click again to create a second plane grid.

9. **Click the bottom-right corner of the second grid. Drag that point down and right until you see a heavy line along the left edge of the first plane grid.**

Photoshop identifies and connects the edges of adjacent planes if you drag one edge near enough to another. The highlight indicates that releasing the mouse button will automatically connect the two planes along that line; you don't need to drag the top-right corner because it automatically snaps into place.

10. **Click and drag the left corners of the second plane to match the apparent corners in the image. Again, use the following image as a guide.**

We dragged the bottom-left corner to the image's bottom-left corner, so that the entire image foreground will be included in the warp. If you exclude any part of the shrubbery or palm tree, your end result could produce some unnaturally twisted vegetation.

**11.** In the Options bar, click the Warp button. If you see a pop-up message, read it and then click the Close button to dismiss it.

**12.** Click the top-left corner on the left plane grid. Drag left until the vertical lines of the building appear to be truly vertical.

Use the canvas edge as a guide for an exact 90° vertical line.

You are now working in Warp mode.

Drag the top-left grid corner until this line appears to be exactly vertical.

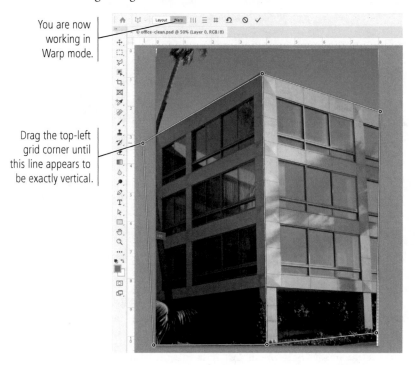

**Note:**

*Three buttons in the Options bar can be used to (from left) automatically straighten near vertical lines, automatically level near horizontal lines, or auto warp to horizontal and vertical.*

**13.** Repeat Step 12 for the top-right corner on the right plane grid.

You can drag any perspective grid corner to warp the image inside the plane grid.

Drag the top-right grid corner until this line appears to be exactly vertical.

**Note:**

*You can Shift-click an edge of the perspective plane to straighten that edge. The affected edge remains locked at a 90° angle unless you Shift-click the same edge again to unlock it. (Straight edges appear yellow in the document window.) Keep in mind that this action straightens the edge line in the perspective grid, and disregards apparent lines in the actual image content.*

14. **Click the Commit button in the Options bar (or press Return/Enter) to finalize the warp.**

   The Remove Warp button restores the image and any perspective planes to their original state; Perspective Warp mode remains active so you can readjust the warp. The Cancel Perspective Warp button cancels the entire process and exits Perspective Warp mode.

15. **Choose the Crop tool in the Tools panel. In the Options bar, make sure the Delete Cropped Pixels option is checked.**

16. **Drag the crop area handles until the visible area does not include any transparent pixels.**

   Pay particular attention to the top corners when you crop the image; you don't want any "empty" areas where there should be blue sky.

Adjust the crop handles until there are no transparent pixels inside the crop area.

The Crop Preview shows how the image was warped in previous steps.

17. **Click the Commit button in the Options bar (or press Return/Enter) to finalize the crop.**

18. **Save the file. Click OK when asked to maximize file compatibility.**

19. **Continue to the next exercise.**

# Use the Vanishing Point Filter (Macintosh)

The studio image used **one-point perspective** — an artistic principle, in which all horizontal lines in an image ultimately meet at a single vanishing point (possibly outside the edges of the image). To effectively merge one image into another, the new image must be adjusted to use the same vanishing point as the original. The Free Transform option is usually enough to combine images in one-point perspective.

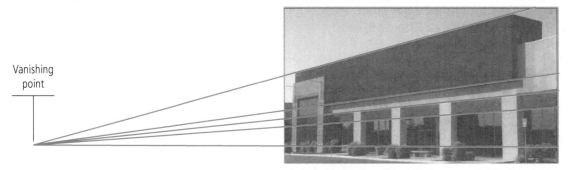

Vanishing
point

Many images have more than one side (or plane), where lines go off in two different directions. This type of image has **two-point perspective**, because there are two different vanishing points. Combining images in two-point perspective (such as wrapping a selection around a corner) is a bit more difficult to manage using the Free Transform option. Fortunately, the Vanishing Point filter makes the process relatively easy, once you understand how it works.

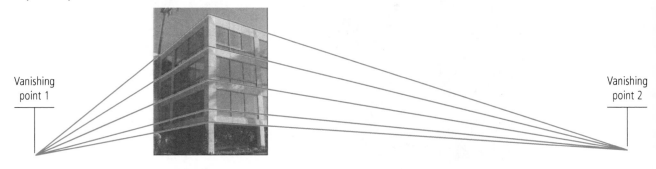

Vanishing
point 1

Vanishing
point 2

1. **Macintosh users: Open the file banner.tif from the WIP>Outdoors folder. Windows users: Skip to the next exercise.**

   At the time of this writing, the Vanishing Point filter on Windows has significant bugs; it does not work properly or predictably when creating a two-point perspective grid. While we expect this to be fixed in future releases, we include an alternate "work-around" exercise that allows Windows users to achieve the same basic effect of wrapping the sample ad around the corner of the office building.

2. **Activate the Move tool, then select the entire banner file (Command/Control-A) and copy it to the Clipboard.**

   The object that you want to put into perspective — in this case, the banner artwork — needs to be copied before you open the Vanishing Point filter.

## Understanding Vanishing Point Controls

The **Vanishing Point** dialog box might seem intimidating at first, but it's fairly easy to use once you understand the tools. Most of these tools perform the same functions as those in the main Photoshop interface; the Marquee tool, however, is the most notable difference.

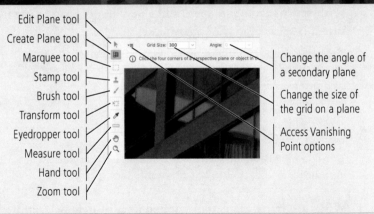

Edit Plane tool
Create Plane tool
Marquee tool
Stamp tool
Brush tool
Transform tool
Eyedropper tool
Measure tool
Hand tool
Zoom tool

Change the angle of a secondary plane

Change the size of the grid on a plane

Access Vanishing Point options

---

In addition to pasting a selection from the Clipboard, you can use the Marquee tool to make selections within the perspective planes in the Vanishing Point dialog box. Once you've drawn a selection, a number of options become available above the preview.

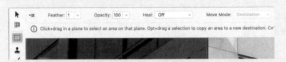

- The **Feather** option defines how many pixels at the selection edges are blurred to help smooth the transition from the copied pixels to the original pixels.

- The **Opacity** option allows you to adjust the opacity of moved pixels (useful if you aren't building the filter onto a new layer).

- The **Heal** menu defines the blending mode for moved pixels (also useful if you aren't building the filter onto a new layer).

- The **Move Mode** menu is similar to the Patch tool Source and Destination options.

  – If **Destination** is selected, clicking inside a selection marquee and dragging moves the marquee to a new position, maintaining the same perspective defined in the plane. (You can press Command/Control and drag from inside a Destination mode marquee to fill the selection with pixels from another area.)

  – If **Source** is selected, clicking inside a selection marquee and dragging fills the marquee with pixels from the destination.

Once you have moved pixels into a selection, you can use the **Transform** tool to rotate or scale the selection, as well as flip it horizontally or vertically using the check boxes that appear over the preview image.

First, we defined the perspective plane, identified here by the red outline. Then using the Marquee tool, we defined the original selection to be large enough to fit the entire window.

With the marquee in Destination Move mode, we dragged the marquee to the place we wanted to create a new window. The size of the marquee is altered to match the defined perspective plane.

We then switched to Source Move mode and dragged back over the original selection to create a second window.

3. **Close the banner file.**

4. **With office-clean.psd open, add a new empty layer to the file and make sure it is selected in the Layers panel.**

   The results of the Vanishing Point filter will become part of the selected layer. If you don't add a new layer before using the filter, the sample ad will be automatically flattened into the background.

   Click here to create a new layer.

5. **Choose Filter>Vanishing Point.**

   The Vanishing Point filter has its own interface, where you can define the perspective in an image and place other selections onto those planes.

6. **With the Create Plane tool selected (it is by default), set the Grid Size to 100 pixels.**

7. **Click at the top corner where the two sides of the building meet to anchor the plane.**

8. **Release the mouse button and move the cursor to the right. Click again at the right edge of the building (at the canvas edge).**

   Don't hold down the mouse button (click-and-drag) to create a perspective plane.

9. **Use the lines in the image to draw the rest of the perspective plane (as shown in the following image).**

   The Create Plane tool defines the first perspective plane of the image. When you define the perspective plane, make sure you follow the path of lines in the image so the vanishing point of your plane matches the vanishing point in the image.

   When you define the third corner of the plane, lines automatically connect the first and third points with the mouse cursor. Simply click to anchor the fourth corner point.

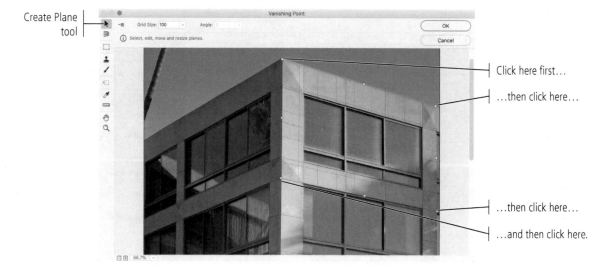

Create Plane tool

Click here first…

…then click here…

…then click here…

…and then click here.

10. **With the Edit Plane tool selected, drag the top-, bottom-, and right-center handles in toward the center of the concrete surrounding the first section of windows, so the plane edges are about halfway between the surrounding windows. (Leave the left edge at the building corner.)**

*Note:*

*If the grid of a perspective plane is yellow or red, the software does not recognize that plane as valid. Drag the corner handles until the grid turns blue, identifying a valid plane.*

Edit
Plane
tool

Drag the top, right, and bottom handles in, toward the center of the concrete blocks surrounding the first bank of windows.

11. **Press Command/Control, click the left-center handle, and then drag left to create a secondary plane that is perpendicular to the first.**

If you click the handle before pressing the Command/Control key, this step won't work. Make sure you press the modifier key before you click and drag the handle.

Press Command/
Control, and then
drag this handle to
add a secondary plane.

12. **Click the arrow to access the Angle slider, then adjust the slider until the second plane matches the angle of the left building face.**

We found approximately 300 to be the best-matched angle for the second plane.

Adjust the plane
angle until the left
grid appears to match
the image perspective.

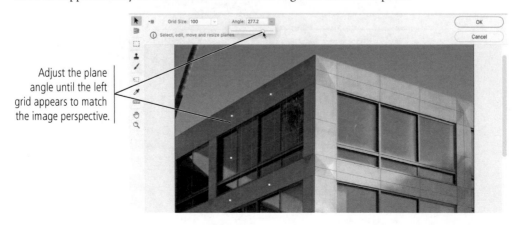

13. **Drag the left-center handle on the second plane until the left edge is halfway between the two columns of windows (use the following image as a guide).**

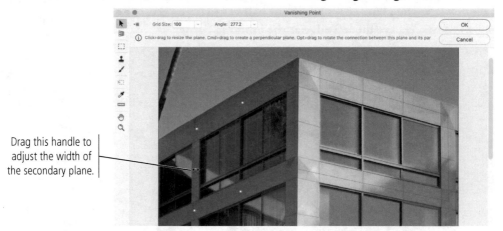

Drag this handle to adjust the width of the secondary plane.

14. **Press Command/Control-V to paste the copied pixels from the Clipboard (the banner file that you copied in Step 2).**

The pasted pixels appear in the top-left corner of the preview, surrounded by a selection marquee.

15. **Click inside the selection marquee and drag onto any part of the perspective plane. Drag the selection until the top-right corner of the ad matches the top-right corner of the plane.**

The selection is dropped into the perspective plane, cleanly wrapped around both sides of the building.

16. **Open the Settings and Commands for the Vanishing Point menu. Turn off the Clip Operations to Surface Edges option (it should be unchecked).**

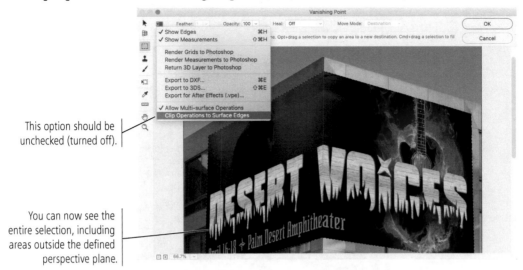

This option should be unchecked (turned off).

You can now see the entire selection, including areas outside the defined perspective plane.

17. **Select the Transform tool in the left side of the Vanishing Point filter dialog box.**

18. **Zoom out until you can see the handle on the bottom-left corner of the banner graphic.**

Transform tool

You need to be able to access this handle.

19. **Drag the bottom-right handle of the selection until all of the banner fits within the defined plane edge.**

    Even though you are scaling out of proportion to fit the banner within the allowed space, the perspective planes still produce a very good result,

Drag this handle until it matches the corner of the perspective plane grid.

20. **Reactivate the Clip Operations to Surface Edges option.**

21. **Click OK to apply the Vanishing Point filter.**

22. **Apply a drop shadow to Layer 1 using the following settings:**

    | Blend mode: | Multiply Black | Distance: | 5 |
    |---|---|---|---|
    | Opacity: | 75% | Spread: | 0 |
    | Angle: | 40° | Size: | 10 |

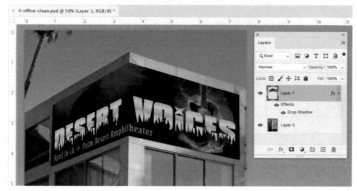

**Note:**

*The 40° angle helps match the drop shadow angle to the apparent light source in the office image.*

23. **Save the file as a native Photoshop file named office-ad.psd in your WIP>Outdoors folder. Click OK if asked to maximize compatibility.**

24. **Close the file, and then continue to the next exercise.**

Place the Ad in Two-Point Perspective (Windows)

As we explained at the beginning of the previous exercise, there are significant functional problems with the Vanishing Point filter on Windows. To work around these issues, we include this alternative exercise so that Windows users can achieve the same basic effect of wrapping the sample ad around the office-building corner.

1. **Windows users: Open the file banner.tif from the WIP>Outdoors folder. Macintosh users: Skip to the next exercise.**

2. **Activate the Move tool, then select the entire banner file (Command/Control-A) and copy it to the Clipboard.**

    The object that you want to put into perspective — in this case, the banner artwork — needs to be copied before you open the Vanishing Point filter.

3. **Close the banner file.**

4. **With office-clean.psd open (from your WIP folder), choose Edit>Paste to paste the banner artwork as a new layer in the file. Rename the new layer Banner Left in the Layers panel.**

5. **With the Banner Left layer selected, choose Edit>Free Transform. Scale the layer to 80% proportionally. Drag the layer until the banner content is centered horizontally on the canvas, and the top and bottom edges cover the top row of windows on the office (use the following image as a guide).**

Maintain Aspect
Ratio is active.

Center the layer content horizontally on the canvas.

Center the layer content vertically over the top row of windows.

6. **Press Return/Enter to finalize the transformation.**

7. In the Layers panel, Right-click the Banner Left layer and choose Duplicate Layer in the contextual menu.

8. In the resulting dialog box, change the duplicate layer name to Banner Right, and then click OK.

9. Using the Rectangle Marquee tool, draw a selection area over the right half of the banner. Make sure the selection edge is exactly aligned with the building corner.

It might help to zoom in so that you can precisely place the selection edge on the building corner.

10. Select the Banner Left layer in the Layers panel, then press the Backspace key on your keyboard.

You are essentially cutting the banner into two pieces, which you can then transform individually to achieve the ultimate effect of two-point perspective.

Align the left edge of the marquee to the corner of the building.

Everything inside the marquee is deleted from the Banner Left layer.

11. With the same selection marquee active, choose Select>Inverse.

This command reverses the active selection, effectively selecting everything that was not previously selected.

**12.** In the Layers panel, click to make the Banner Right layer active and then press the Backspace key on your keyboard.

You now have the two necessary layers, each containing approximately half the sample banner image.

The Select>Inverse command reverses the active selection.

Everything inside the marquee is deleted from the Banner Right layer.

**13.** Choose Select>Deselect to turnoff the active selection area.

**14.** Make the Banner Left layer active, then press Control-T to enter into Free Transform mode.

**15.** In the Options bar, turn off the Maintain Aspect Ratio option. Drag the left handle of the banner until it appears within the bricks between the two banks of windows (use the following image as a guide).

Maintain Aspect Ratio is not active.

Drag the center-left handle to the middle of this row of bricks.

16. **Press the Control and Shift keys. While holding down the two modifier keys, click the bottom-left transformation handle and drag down until the bottom edge of the banner is centered in the bricks below the top row of windows.**

Pressing the Control and Shift keys while dragging a transformation handle allows you to distort content in one direction — you are using this technique to distort the active layer content so that it appears to exist in perspective on the building's left plane.

Control-Shift-drag the bottom-left handle to the middle of this row of bricks.

17. **Repeat Step 16 to adjust the top edge of the banner, as shown in the following image.**

Control-Shift-drag the top-left handle to the middle of this row of bricks.

18. **Press Enter to finalize the transformation.**

19. **Select the Banner Right layer in the Layers panel and then enter into Free Transform mode.**

20. Repeat the process from Steps 15–18 to adjust the perspective of the right half of the banner.

21. In the Layers panel, Shift-click the Banner Left layer to select both banner layers.

22. Right-click either of the two selected layers and choose Merge Layers in the contextual menu.

If you do not merge the two layers back together, the drop shadow you apply in the next step will apply separately to each layer.

23. Apply a drop shadow to the Banner Right layer using the following settings:

| | | | |
|---|---|---|---|
| Blend mode: | Multiply Black | Distance: | 5 |
| Opacity: | 75% | Spread: | 0 |
| Angle: | 40° | Size: | 10 |

24. Save the file as a native Photoshop file named office-ad.psd in your WIP>Outdoors folder. Click OK if asked to maximize compatibility.

25. Close the file, and then continue to the next exercise.

# Warp the Sample Ad

Linear perspective, such as the two examples you just created, is fairly easy to adjust, especially using the Vanishing Point filter. However, the world is not entirely linear; objects with curves also have depth and perspective. Compositing onto rounded objects is slightly more complicated than linear perspective, but you can accomplish the task with patience and attention to detail.

1. **Open the file tanks-clean.psd from your WIP>Outdoors folder.**

2. **Place the banner.tif file as an embedded Smart Object layer into the tanks file.**

3. **Scale the placed ad to 35% and position it in the center of the front water tank (above the top of the fence).**

4. **With the banner layer selected, choose Edit>Transform>Warp.**

   When you warp anything other than text, you have more options and better control.

Cancel Transform    Commit Transform

When warping anything other than text, handles appear for controlling the warp.

5. **In the Options bar, choose Arc Upper from the Warp menu.**

   The same predefined options are available for warping an object as those for warping text. In this case, the background image — the water tank — is only slightly curved. A minor Arc Upper warp should be enough to add perspective to the ad layer.

The default Bend value (50%) is obviously too much for compositing these two images.

6. **Experiment with Bend values until you're satisfied with the result. (We used a 5% bend.)**

   The Bend value changes only the edges affected by the warp you apply. In the case of Arc Upper, only the top edge changes when you modify the Bend value.

7. **In the Options bar, click the Commit button to finalize the transformation (or press Return/Enter).**

8. **Apply a drop shadow to the layer using the following settings:**

   | | | | |
   |---|---|---|---|
   | Blend mode: | Multiply Black | Distance: | 2 |
   | Opacity: | 75% | Spread: | 0 |
   | Angle: | 90° | Size: | 5 |

**Note:**

*The 90° angle helps match the drop shadow angle to the apparent light source in the tanks image.*

9. **Save the file as a native Photoshop file named tanks-ad.psd in your WIP>Outdoors folder. Click OK when asked to maximize compatibility.**

10. **Close the file, then continue to the next exercise.**

Apply a Custom Warp

In some cases, the predefined warp styles are adequate. In other cases — such as warping the ad around the balloon in this exercise — the existing styles do not work. In these cases, Photoshop provides a powerful toolset for defining custom warp shapes.

1. **Open the file balloon-clean.psd from your WIP>Outdoors folder.**

2. **Place the banner.tif file into the balloon file as an embedded Smart Object.**

3. **Scale the banner layer to 40% proportionally and position it as shown in the following image:**

4. **Choose Edit>Transform>Warp. Apply the Arch warp to the ad layer with a 12% bend.**

5. **If necessary, drag the layer (still in Warp Transform mode) so the banner appears within the white area (as shown here).**

   As you can see, this warp shape is flat; it does not reflect the roundness of the balloon.

6. **Choose Custom in the Warp menu on the Options bar.**

   Anchor points (and their attached handles) are now visible at the corners of the warped shape. You can move these points and handles to adjust the exact shape of the warp to better align it to the balloon's shape.

These handles control the warp curves between points on the grid.

7. **Drag the corner points on the left side of the warp grid to be directly inside the second seam line on the balloon.**

Position the left corner points directly inside this seam line.

8. **Drag the handles on the left side of the grid to bloat the left edge of the ad layer.**

Handles on a warp grid are just like handles on a vector path (created with the Pen tool). Curves follow the direction in which you drag the connected handles.

Drag these two handles left so the left edge of the ad follows the line of the seam.

## More About Custom Warps

The Grid menu in the Options bar adds evenly spaced horizontal and vertical gridlines inside the warp shape. If you choose the Custom option in the menu, you can define different numbers for horizontal and vertical gridlines. An anchor point is added at each place where gridlines meet; you can drag those points and adjust the related handles to change the warp characteristics of content inside the warp area.

You can also use the Split buttons to add warp gridlines anywhere in the warp.

- Split the Warp Crosswise adds a horizontal and vertical gridline at the same time.
- Split the Warp Vertically adds only a vertical gridline.
- Split the Warp Horizontally adds only a horizontal gridline.

Split the Warp Vertically

Split the Warp Crosswise          Split the Warp Horizontally

Click and drag a grid point to warp the interior of the selection.

9. **Repeat Steps 7–8 for the right side of the ad.**

10. **Adjust the top and bottom handles to fit the edges vertically within the area between the color patches.**

Use this seam to align the ad's right edge.

Use this seam to align the ad's top edge.

Use this seam to align the ad's bottom edge.

11. **Press Return/Enter to finalize the transformation, and then apply a drop shadow using the following settings:**

| Blend mode: | Multiply Black | Distance: | 3 |
|---|---|---|---|
| Opacity: | 75% | Spread: | 0 |
| Angle: | 120° | Size: | 5 |

*Note:*

*The 120° angle helps match the drop shadow angle to the apparent light source in the balloon image.*

12. **Save the file as a native Photoshop file named balloon-ad.psd in your WIP>Outdoors folder.**

13. **Close the file.**

The **Clouds** filter (Filters>Render>Clouds) fills the currently selected layer with a random, cloud-like pattern that varies between the foreground and background colors. The **Difference Clouds** filter (Filters>Render>Difference Clouds) does the same thing, but returns a cloud pattern that looks as though it was affected by the Difference blending mode. Because these filters replace the content of the current layer, they are best applied on a separate layer that you can mask and blend to create the look you want.

The Clouds filter is applied to a separate layer behind the masked foreground layer. The clouds are a mixture of the defined foreground and background colors.

The Difference Clouds filter is applied to the same layer. The resulting colors are the effect of the Difference blending mode applied to the foreground and background colors.

The **Fibers** filter (Filters>Render>Fibers) fills the currently selected layer with a pattern that looks like woven fibers of the foreground and background colors. The Variance option controls how the colors vary (a low value produces long streaks of color, and a high value results in very short fibers).

The Strength option controls how each fiber looks. Low strength produces a loose weave, and high strength produces a tighter weave. The Randomize button changes the pattern randomly; you can keep clicking the button to generate new patterns until you find one that you like.

The **Lens Flare** filter (Filters>Render>Lens Flare) simulates the refraction caused by shining a bright light into a camera lens. You can drag the crosshair in the small preview image to change the position of the flare center, change the brightness of the flare, and define the type of lens to simulate.

1. When using the Patch tool, choose the _____ option to select an area that will be copied to another area (where you drag the marquee).

2. The _____ adjustment changes the ink values in specific primary colors or neutrals, without affecting other colors.

3. The _____ adjustment allows you to change the Hue, Saturation, and Lightness values of specific primary colors.

4. A/an _____ non-destructively applies changes such as Levels or Curves to the selected layer.

5. The _____ tool attempts to simplify replacement of specific colors in your image; you can paint over a targeted color to replace it with the foreground color.

6. The _____ tool mimics a process used in traditional photo development, and is used to lighten an area of a photograph.

7. When working in perspective, the _____ is the invisible point at which horizontal lines meet.

8. In _____ perspective, all lines in an image move toward a single spot on the horizon.

9. The _____ provides an easy interface for transforming layer content onto a perspective plane.

10. The _____ transformation can be used to distort a flat, rectangular object into a custom shape, such as around the side of a balloon.

1. Briefly explain the advantages to using adjustment layers, rather than applying adjustments to regular layers from the Image>Adjustments menu.

2. Briefly explain how a mask relates to an adjustment layer.

3. Briefly explain the concept of a vanishing point..

Use what you have learned in this project to complete the following freeform exercise.
Carefully read the art director and client comments, then create your own design to meet the needs of the project.
Use the space below to sketch ideas. When finished, write a brief explanation of the reasoning behind your final design.

**art director comments**

Your company's sales manager has another potential client for the Advertise Anywhere! program, and would like to build a personalized presentation similar to the one you did for the music festival.

To complete this project, you should:

❑ Build a sample ad for the Go Green clean energy initiative.

❑ Find interesting background images on which you can composite the sample ad.

❑ Clean up or adjust the background images as necessary to create the best possible samples.

❑ Composite the sample ad onto the different backgrounds. Adjust perspective as necessary to make the samples appear as natural as possible.

**client comments**

The director of the Go Green clean energy initiative saw the Desert Voices festival ads that we placed around the city, and called the show's marketing director to find out where they were created. I just got off the phone with her, and we have a meeting scheduled next week to present some ideas for advertising the Go Green campaign.

I need you to create a sample ad at the same size as the Desert Voices sample. It should include imagery that supports the idea of clean energy — hydroelectricity, windmills, etc. The only text for the ad should be the words "Go Green!" and the website address (www.ggenergy.org).

For the backgrounds, find a variety of images. Methods of public transportation, buildings, and large outdoor signs are all good options, but we also want to highlight the "anywhere" part of Advertise Anywhere! services. Get creative with these samples — think up unusual locations where ads might be seen by large numbers of people.

**project justification**

_____
_____
_____
_____
_____
_____
_____
_____
_____
_____
_____
_____
_____
_____
_____

Compositing images like those in this project is part skill (applying necessary corrections), part judgment (determining the perspective in the background images), and part experimentation (exploring the transformation and filter options to find the best possible solution to the specific problem). Being able to manipulate images with the correction and transformation tools you used to create these samples will be invaluable during your graphic design career.

Correct camera distortion with a perspective warp

Use the Patch tool to clean up digital garbage

Composite the ad layer with a built-in warp transformation

Correct lighting with the Shadow/Highlight adjustment

Composite the ad layer with the Vanishing Point filter

Composite the ad layer with a custom warp transformation

Use a Hue/Saturation adjustment layer to change the balloon color

Use the Replace Color adjustment to apply a fresh coat of digital paint

Composite the ad layer in Free Transform mode

# 7 House Painting

Your client, a real estate developer, is planning a new presales campaign for the company's latest master plan community. He has line-art sketches of the completed houses, but he wants color "paintings" to show prospective buyers what the finished houses might look like. You were hired to create a full-color digital rendering based on one of the artist's black-and-white sketches.

This project incorporates the following skills:

❑ Converting an image from bitmap to RGB color mode

❑ Loading a custom swatch panel to access approved colors

❑ Using fill and stroke techniques to create the basic artwork

❑ Using hard and soft brushes to create detail in the painting

❑ Using blending modes to achieve special effects, such as shadows

❑ Creating and applying custom patterns

❑ Setting brush options to randomize strokes and paint "nature"

## Videos to Watch

Access these helpful videos in your online student resources:

▶▶ House Painting Project Introduction

▶▶ Understanding Basic Brush Settings

▶▶ Using the Eraser Tools

▶▶ Understanding Brush Presets

<br />

In three months we break ground on a new master planned community. We are installing an on-site sales office soon so we can start preselling, and we want to be able to show potential buyers what finished houses will look like.

Our architect gave us pen-and-ink renderings, but we want something more realistic — like a painting — in color. If you can create a painting, we can print copies to frame in the office. When we get closer to building the houses, we might also launch a direct mail campaign and do some other print advertising.

We worked with an environmental designer to create the community plan, and have finalized everything from down to the stucco and trim colors that will be used on the finished houses. I showed your art director paint chips; we want you to use those to create the digital painting.

**Watch the video** House Painting Project Introduction **in your online student resources.**

Most people in our field will tell you that high-quality art is part creativity and part technique. Your role in this project is to provide technique, since the actual artwork was drawn by the architect.

The client isn't sure what he's going to do with the final artwork. He knows it's going to be printed and framed for the sales office, and possibly used in print brochures and on his website.

For all these possible uses, you need to produce a versatile file that can support many file formats. The RGB color space is larger than CMYK, so create the painting in RGB and start with high enough resolution for print.

The large-format output company has switched to an all-PDF workflow for output. They don't accept any native application files, so you'll have to save the final painting as a high-resolution PDF file. The service rep also said their output devices convert color on the fly, and they get better results from RGB than images already converted to CMYK.

project objectives

To complete this project, you will:

- ❏ Convert a bitmap image to RGB
- ❏ Import custom swatches
- ❏ Create fill shapes
- ❏ Fill areas with the Paint Bucket tool
- ❏ Use hard- and soft-edge brushes
- ❏ Clone repeating drawing elements
- ❏ Create texture with a faux-finish brush
- ❏ Use opacity and blending modes to create deep shadows
- ❏ Define and save a custom pattern
- ❏ Change brush settings to paint random elements
- ❏ Create and save a brush preset
- ❏ Export a PDF file for print

# STAGE 1 / **Filling Solid Areas**

Some of the skills you will learn in this project, including painting with brushes, are normally used by creative designers to develop original digital artwork — starting with nothing other than an idea. By starting with an existing line-art drawing, however, you can use the same tools and techniques to build a full-color artistic rendering, even if you don't have the natural painting ability of da Vinci.

The easiest way to start a project like this one is to create the basic shapes that make up the object you are painting. You can make a basic selection and simply fill it with a color, use the Paint Bucket tool to fill areas of similar color, or use brushes and painting techniques to color specific areas. When you combine these techniques with layers, you can also use transparency and blending modes to create images that appear as though they were painted on a traditional canvas with brushes.

##  Import Custom Swatches

The Swatches panel stores colors that you use frequently; you can access a color by simply clicking a swatch in the panel. Rather than randomly picking colors for the various elements of the house, you will use a set of custom swatches based on the color scheme defined in the community master plan.

1.  **Expand the Houses_PS22_RF.zip archive in your WIP folder (Macintosh) or copy the archive contents into your WIP folder (Windows).**

    This results in a folder named **Houses**, which contains the files you need for this project. You should also use this folder to save the files you create in this project.

2.  **In Photoshop, click the Photoshop icon in the top-left corner of the Home screen.**

    Clicking this icon enters into the Photoshop workspace, so you can access the various panels, even when no file is open.

    Click this icon in the Home screen to enter the Photoshop workspace.

3.  **Display the Swatches panel (Window>Swatches).**

    Photoshop includes a number of default swatches, showing by default in the large thumbnail view.

4.  **In the Swatches panel Options menu, choose Import Swatches.**

    You can use this menu to create a new swatch preset or group, change the panel view, or open built-in swatch libraries.

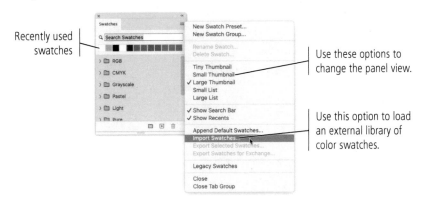

Recently used swatches

Use these options to change the panel view.

Use this option to load an external library of color swatches.

5. **Windows users: Choose Swatch Exchange (\*.ASE) in the Files of Type menu.**

6. **Navigate to the file Home Color.ase in the WIP>Houses folder, then click Open/Load.**

   The ASE extension identifies an Adobe Swatch Exchange file, which is a special format for sharing swatch libraries between Adobe applications.

   You can save custom swatch sets to be used in other Adobe applications by choosing Save Swatches for Exchange in the Swatches panel Options menu. To save a swatch library for only Photoshop, you can use the Save Swatches command to save the swatch library with the ".aco" extension.

On Windows, you have to choose Swatch Exchange in the Files of Type menu.

7. **Using the Swatches panel Options menu, change the panel to Small List view.**

8. **Scroll to the bottom of the panel to find the Home Color swatch group. Click the arrow to expand that group.**

9. **Click the bottom/right corner of the panel and drag down until you can see all the swatches in the imported group.**

   These swatches were created specifically for this project, using basic names that will make it easier to complete the house painting.

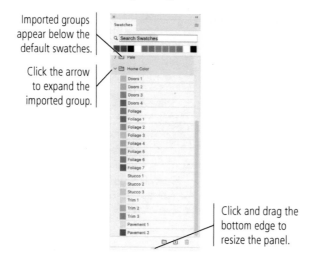

Imported groups appear below the default swatches.

Click the arrow to expand the imported group.

Click and drag the bottom edge to resize the panel.

10. **Continue to the next exercise.**

# Create Fill Shapes

In this exercise, you use standard selection tools to paint the house's front walls — large and relatively simple areas that you can fill with "stucco" colored paint.

1. **Open the file house.tif from the WIP>Houses folder.**

2. **In the Layers panel, unlock the Background layer.**

   As soon as you unlock the Background layer, it becomes a regular layer named Layer 0.

   Click here to unlock the layer.

3. **Double-click the unlocked Layer 0 layer name to highlight it, then type Sketch to rename it. Press Return/Enter to finalize the new name.**

4. **In the Layers panel, click the Lock All icon to lock the renamed Sketch layer.**

   You're going to use this layer as a template for your painting. Locking the layer prevents you from accidentally moving or altering the original artwork.

   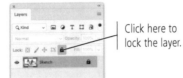

   Click here to lock the layer.

5. **Create a new layer named Walls, and make it the active layer.**

6. **Use the Rectangular Marquee tool to draw a selection around the front of the garage face, including the pillars to the sides of the garage door.**

   Don't worry if your selection covers parts of the bushes and doesn't include the pieces that stick out from the basic rectangular shape. You will refine the selection in the following steps, and you will paint the bushes on higher layers later in this project.

   We outlined the selection with a red overlay to make it more visible in these images. Yours will be visible as "marching ants" in the document window.

   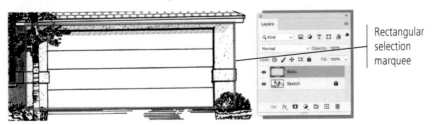

   Rectangular selection marquee

*Note:*

*As hard as we tried to get this image exactly square on the scanner bed, no scans are perfect. There's a chance that the straight lines, paths, and guides you create in Photoshop will not exactly match the horizontal, vertical, or angled lines in your scans. A very slight difference is nothing to worry about. The finished product will look fine because the original scan will ultimately be deleted.*

7. **Using the Add to Selection and Subtract from Selection options, draw additional selection marquees to select the entire face of the house.**

Zooming in might make it easier to refine the selection, especially in the smaller areas where the house shape extends slightly.

8. **Click the Stucco 2 swatch in the Swatches panel to define that swatch as the foreground color.**

Clicking a color in the Swatches panel changes the active foreground color.

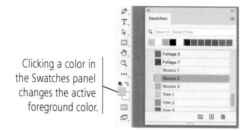

**Note:**

*Dragging a swatch from the panel fills the active selection area. The result is a solid-color fill layer with a mask based on the selection marquee.*

9. **Choose Edit>Fill. Choose Foreground Color in the Contents menu of the Fill dialog box.**

10. **Click OK to fill the wall selection.**

11. **With the Walls layer selected in the Layers panel, change the Opacity setting to 80%.**

The finished artwork will be at full opacity. While you're working, however, it helps to see through various layers.

Semi-transparent fills make it possible to see and continue painting the elements of the original artwork. When you're finished with the project, you can return this layer to 100% opacity. If you had changed the fill opacity to 80% in the Fill dialog box, you would be unable to change it back to 100%.

12. **Turn off the current selection (Select>Deselect).**

13. **Save the file as a native Photoshop file named** house-working.psd **in your WIP>Houses folder. When asked, click OK in the Photoshop Format Options dialog box to maximize file compatibility.**

14. **Continue to the next exercise.**

 ## Fill Areas with the Paint Bucket Tool

The Paint Bucket tool has the same basic functionality as the Fill dialog box — you click the tool cursor to fill an area with the current foreground color. In the Options bar, you can choose the color, blending mode, and opacity of the fill.

1. **With** house-working.psd **open, hide the Walls layer and add a new layer named** Front Trim **at the top of the layer stack.**

2. **Choose the Paint Bucket tool (nested under the Gradient tool) in the Tools panel. In the Options bar, type** 30 **in the Tolerance field, and activate the Contiguous and All Layers options.**

Unlike the Fill dialog box, the Paint Bucket tool creates fills based on the defined sample tolerance (like the settings used to create a selection based on a color range).

In addition to the fill color, blending mode, and opacity, the Options bar includes settings for tool tolerance and anti-aliasing, as well as whether to fill only contiguous pixels within the defined tolerance. The All Layers option allows you to sample pixels from all visible layers, instead of only the selected layer.

3. **Change the foreground color to the Trim 1 swatch.**

4. **Click the Paint Bucket tool on a white area of the trim board on the left side of the house.**

The Paint Bucket tool fills areas with the selected foreground color. Because the Contiguous option is checked in the Options bar, only the area inside the "board" edges is filled.

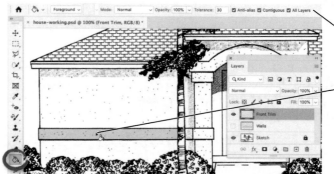

Use these settings to determine the sensitivity of the Paint Bucket tool.

Use the arrow tip to determine which area will be filled.

The tool's cursor can be confusing. Watch the top of the pointer in the cursor — not the drop of paint falling from the bucket — to identify the area that will be filled.

5. **Click inside each of the trim areas on the front of the house. (Use the following image as a guide for the areas you should fill.)**

Make sure you click on both sides of the trees, and don't forget the windowsill. In some segments, you might need to click several times to fill the primary shapes.

6. **Zoom into the trim on the right side of the window.**

Because of the way the illustrator created shadows, you need to use a slightly different method to fill in the shadowed pieces of trim.

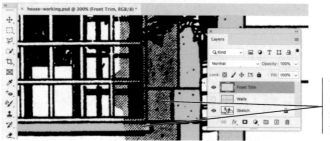

The penned shadows make it impossible to simply click to fill these two areas.

7. **Draw a rectangle marquee around the shadowed trim. Select the Paint Bucket tool, turn off the All Layers option in the Options bar, then click inside the selection marquee.**

Select this shadowed area, turn off the All Layers option, and then click to fill the selection.

**8.** Repeat Step 7 to fill the
shadowed section of the
windowsill.

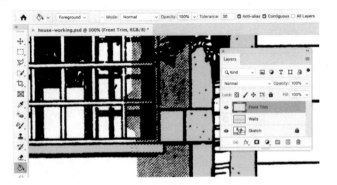

**9.** **Turn off the active selection, then hide the Sketch layer.**

Because of the points used to create texture in the sketch, the Paint Bucket tool did
not fill all the shapes. That's okay, though, because you will later use the empty spots
to create texture of your own. Also, don't worry about the areas where trees and bushes
cover the house; you're going to paint trees that will cover those areas.

**10.** **Show the Sketch layer again.**

**11.** **Create a new layer named Fascia at the top of the layer stack. Select the
new layer as the active one.**

**12.** **Using the Paint Bucket tool with the All Layers option active, fill the
upper parts of the fascia boards with the Trim 2 swatch.**

**13.** **Fill the lower parts of the fascia boards with the Trim 3 swatch.**

14. **Create a new layer named Garage Door at the top of the layer stack and select it. Use the Paint Bucket tool with the All Layers option active to fill the four panels on the garage door with the Doors 3 swatch.**

Because of the sketched shading, you might need to increase the tool's tolerance to fill most of the top garage door panel. Alternatively, you can use the selection marquee technique to fill the appropriate area.

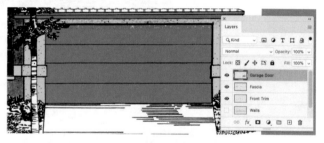

15. **Create a new layer named Pavement at the top of the layer stack and select it. Use the Polygonal Lasso tool to draw a marquee around the driveway area, then use the Paint Bucket tool to fill the selected area with the Pavement 1 swatch.**

In the sketch, the driveway area doesn't have a solid edge, so simply clicking with the Paint Bucket tool would fill most of the layer with gray. If you have defined a selection area, clicking inside the selection marquee only fills the selected area.

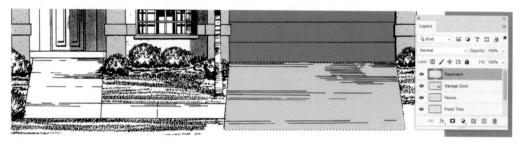

16. **Turn off the active selection area, then use the Paint Bucket tool to fill in the remaining areas of sidewalk.**

You don't need to draw a selection marquee for the sidewalk because the lines in the sketch form solid edges that limit the results from clicking with the Paint Bucket tool.

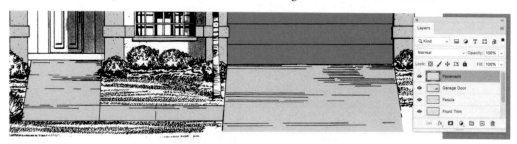

17. **Deselect any active marquee, save the file, and then continue to the next stage of the project.**

# STAGE 2 / **Painting with Brushes**

 *Watch the video* ***Understanding Basic Brush Settings in Photoshop*** *in your online student resources.*

Filling a selection area is one of the more basic techniques for painting in Photoshop. To create complex custom artwork, you can use Photoshop brushes in the digital workspace, just as you would traditional brushes on canvas. The built-in brushes come in hundreds of shapes and sizes; combining these with options, such as opacity, flow, and blending mode, provides an almost infinite array of choices for painting pixels in a Photoshop layout.

As you might have guessed, there is far more to using brushes than what you have already learned throughout this book's earlier projects. Painting the house in this project requires several different types of brushes, as well as controlling the brush options to complete various areas of the painting.

When you choose the Brush tool, you must first select a specific brush. You can choose one of the built-in brush presets from the Options bar, or you can define your own brush by changing the Size and Hardness settings in the Brush Preset Picker. You can also use the Options bar to change a number of settings that affect how a specific brush works.

**Note:**

*In addition to the hundreds of built-in Photoshop brushes, you can access hundreds of additional brushes by choosing Get More Brushes in the Brush Preset Picker Options menu.*

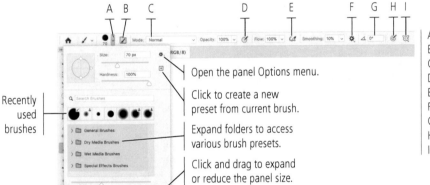

A   Click to open the Brush Preset picker
B   Click to open the Brush panel
C   Brush blending mode
D   Tablet pressure controls opacity
E   Enable Airbrush mode
F   Set additional smoothing options
G   Set the brush angle
H   Tablet pressure controls size
I   Set symmetry options

You learned about blending modes and opacity in an earlier project. The other brush options require a little bit of explanation.

- **Size** is the size of the brush tip, measured in pixels.

- **Hardness** is the percentage of the brush that's completely opaque. For example, a Hardness setting of 50% for a brush with a 10-pixel diameter means 5 pixels in the brush center are hard, and the remaining diameter has a feathered edge.

**Note:**

*Pressure sensitivity becomes an issue when you use a drawing tablet. The harder you press, the more "paint" is applied. Many of the painting tools in Photoshop — including the Brush tool — include options that allow pressure sensitivity while you paint.*

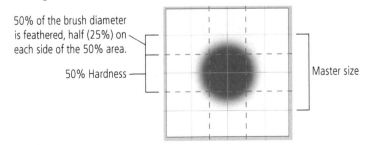

- **Flow** sets the rate at which color is applied as you paint repeatedly over the same area. As you do this (while holding down the mouse button), the amount of color "builds up."

In the following example, we set the brush color to C=100 M=50, with a Flow setting of 50%. Each successive click moved the color values 50% closer to the brush color.

Contrary to what many people think, the Flow setting does not apply hard percentages of the brush color. The first click resulted in 25% magenta, or 50% of the brush color value. The second click produced 38% magenta, which is the result of adding 50% of the difference between the first click (25% magenta) and the brush color (50% magenta) — or one half of the difference between 25 and 50 (25 / 2 = 12.5).

For the third click, 50% of the difference between 38 (the previous value) and 50 (the brush value) is added: $50 - 38 = 12 / 2 = 6 + 38 = 44$

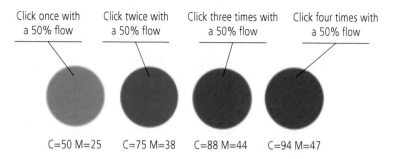

| Click once with a 50% flow | Click twice with a 50% flow | Click three times with a 50% flow | Click four times with a 50% flow |
| --- | --- | --- | --- |
| C=50 M=25 | C=75 M=38 | C=88 M=44 | C=94 M=47 |

- **Airbrush mode** simulates painting with an airbrush. If you hold down the mouse button, or move the cursor back and forth over the same area, more color builds up in the same location. Brush hardness, opacity, and flow options control how fast and how much "paint" is applied.

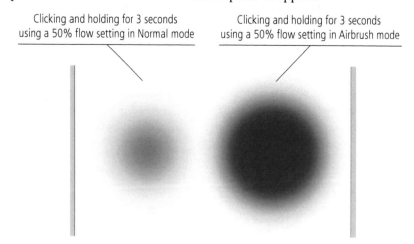

Clicking and holding for 3 seconds using a 50% flow setting in Normal mode

Clicking and holding for 3 seconds using a 50% flow setting in Airbrush mode

*Note:*

*Press the Left Bracket key ( [ ) or Right Bracket key ( ] ) to decrease or increase (respectively) the current brush diameter to the next, predetermined size.*

*Press Shift-[ to decrease brush hardness, or Shift-] to increase it in 25% increments.*

*Note:*

*Color values are always whole numbers, which is why the magenta value is rounded to 38 instead of the mathematical 50% value of 37.5.*

*Note:*

*Press a number key to define the brush opacity setting in increments of 10% (e.g., pressing 6 sets the opacity to 60%).*

*Note:*

*Press Shift and a number key to define the brush flow setting in increments of 10% (e.g., pressing Shift-6 sets the flow to 60%).*

- **Smoothing** helps to prevent jags on a brush stroke that result from slight jumps of a mouse cursor or stylus. Higher smoothing values (up to 100%) result in smoother brush strokes. You can click the Set Additional Smoothing Options button to control the way Photoshop applies smoothing.

In the Cursors pane of the Preferences dialog box, you can turn on a brush "leash," which shows the actual path that you drag while painting. You can use the swatch to change the brush leash color from the default pink.

When **Pulled String Mode** is active in the Smoothing Options menu, clicking reveals a pink "safe zone." Increasing the Smoothing value increases the size of the safe zone. Cursor movement within the safe zone does not add to the stroke. If it is enabled, the leash (string) curves to show the movement. If you drag past the safe-zone area, the leash is straightened and cursor movement adds to the stroke.

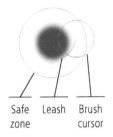
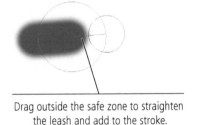

Safe  Leash  Brush
zone         cursor

Drag outside the safe zone to straighten the leash and add to the stroke.

**Note:**

*Smoothing is available when using the Brush, Pencil, Mixer Brush, or Eraser tool.*

If you turn off Pulled String Mode, you can use the Catch Up options to control how strokes are created when you drag faster than the software is able to paint.

If **Stroke Catch Up** is active, the stroke you're painting will extend to the position of the cursor if you pause while dragging. If this option is not active, the stroke painting ends when you pause; it does not necessarily extend to match the current cursor position.

Stroke Catch Up is NOT active.

Stroke Catch Up is active.

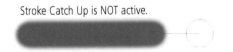

**Catch-Up On Stroke End** is similar to Stroke Catch Up, but relates to how a stroke is finished when you actually *release* the mouse cursor. In the following examples, the top image shows the point at which we released the brush cursor. The bottom image shows the resulting stroke after releasing the mouse button.

Catch Up on Stroke End is active.

Catch Up on Stroke End is NOT active.

If **Adjust For Zoom** is active, zooming in decreases smoothing, and zooming out increases it.

## Painting with Symmetry

When the Brush, Mixer Brush, Eraser, or Pencil tool is selected, you can activate Symmetry Mode in the Options bar to paint symmetrically around defined paths.

Click this button to choose a symmetry path.

When you click the Set Symmetry Options button in the Options bar, you can choose the symmetry path you want to use. You can also Control/right-click any path in the Paths panel and choose Make Symmetry Path from the contextual menu to make that path a symmetry path.

Symmetry paths are stored in the Paths panel so you can call them again later. Keep in mind, however, that your painting is not dynamically attached to the path. If you edit the path after painting, the painting does not transform along with the path.

New symmetry paths default to Transform mode. You can drag the handles to resize or reshape the path, using the same free transform options as a regular selection. Click anywhere inside the bounding box, and drag to move the path. After you are satisfied with your path shape and position, pressing Return/Enter finalizes the path so you can begin to paint.

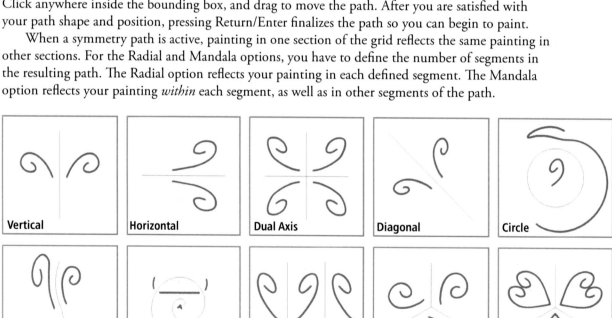

When a symmetry path is active, painting in one section of the grid reflects the same painting in other sections. For the Radial and Mandala options, you have to define the number of segments in the resulting path. The Radial option reflects your painting in each defined segment. The Mandala option reflects your painting *within* each segment, as well as in other segments of the path.

**Vertical**

**Horizontal**

**Dual Axis**

**Diagonal**

**Circle**

**Wavy**

**Spiral**

**Parallel Lines**

**Mandala**

**Radial**

# Use Hard Brushes

The brush Hardness setting allows you to paint either sharp lines or lines with soft, feathered edges. Most painting projects — including this one — require a combination of hard- and soft-edge brushes.

1. **With house-working.psd open, create two new layers at the top of the layer stack — one named Front Door and one named FD Panels. Make sure the FD Panels layer is higher in the layer stack.**

   The Front Door layer will hold the overall door area. The FD Panels layer will hold the painted lines that form the shapes of the raised panels within the front door.

2. **Open the Cursors pane of the Preferences dialog box (in the Photoshop menu on Macintosh, or the Edit menu on Windows).**

3. **In the Painting Cursors area, choose the Full Size Brush Tip option and activate the Show Crosshair in Brush Tip option. Click OK to apply the change.**

   The Full Size Brush Tip option changes the cursor to include the entire brush area, including the feathered part of soft-edge brushes.

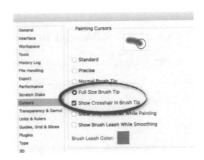

*Note:*

*When using the Brush tool, you can activate Caps Lock on your keyboard to temporarily switch to the Precise cursor mode. If you are already in Precise cursor mode, activating the Caps Lock key switches to the Normal Brush Tip cursor.*

4. **Make the Front Door layer active, then draw a rectangular selection around the front door. Make sure all door edges, but not the door frame, are included in the selection (see the image after Step 6).**

5. **Change the foreground color to the Doors 3 swatch, then choose the Paint Bucket tool in the Tools panel. Uncheck the All Layers option in the Options bar.**

   If the All Layers option is selected, clicking with the Paint Bucket tool would sample from the Sketch layer, and some of the selected area wouldn't be entirely filled.

6. **With the Front Door layer active, click the Paint Bucket tool inside the selection marquee.**

   Since the active layer (Front Door) has no current content, the Tolerance setting is irrelevant. The entire selection area fills with the Doors 3 color.

The All Layers option is turned off.

The Front Door layer has no other content, so clicking paints all pixels inside the selection area.

7. **Deselect the active selection marquee. Change the Front Door layer Opacity value to 50% so you can see the underlying sketch.**

8. **Make the FD Panels layer active, and then choose the Brush tool in the Tools panel.**

9. **Change the foreground color to the Doors 4 swatch.**

10. **In the Options bar, click the arrow button to open the Brush Preset Picker. Set the brush size to 10 px and the Hardness to 100%.**

Click to open the Brush Preset picker.    Click to open the Brush Settings panel.

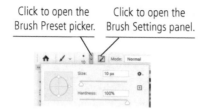

11. **Press Return/Enter to close the Brush Preset Picker.**

12. **Place the cursor over the inset line on the top-left panel of the front door.**

   The default brush cursor shows the size of the selected brush tip. In this case, the 10-pixel brush is clearly wider than the line you want to paint.

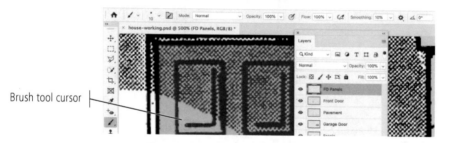

Brush tool cursor

**Note:**

*Zooming in helps when you're working on the smaller details of a painting (such as the door inset panels).*

13. **Press [ six times to reduce the brush size to 4 pixels.**

   You can press [ and ] to decrease or increase the brush size to the next defined preset. Under ten pixels, the bracket key shortcuts change the brush size by 1 pixel at a time.

14. **Click at the top-right corner of the panel inset, press Shift, and then click at the lower-right corner of the panel inset.**

15. **Press Shift and click at the lower-left corner of the panel inset.**

   Pressing Shift and then clicking again connects the first and second points with a straight line of the brush color. You can also press Shift while dragging to paint a perfectly horizontal or vertical line.

Click here…

…then Shift-click here…

…then Shift-click here.

16. **Save the file and continue to the next exercise.**

# Use Soft Brushes

Painting with a hard brush results in colored pixels edged by white pixels. In the real world, however, there are very few perfectly hard edges with no variation in shades. Soft-edge brushes are far more useful for creating artwork that includes the subtle color variations found in a real object.

1. **With house-working.psd open, draw a rectangular selection marquee around the front door panel where you painted the inset.**

   Always remember that when you have an active selection, you can only affect the area inside the selection.

2. **Make sure the FD Panels layer is selected and Doors 4 is the current foreground color.**

3. **Choose the Brush tool. Using the Options bar, open the Brush Preset Picker and change the brush Size to 15 px and the Hardness to 0%. Press Return/Enter to finalize your selections and close the Brush Preset Picker.**

4. **Place the cursor so the crosshairs are exactly on top of the selection marquee.**

5. **Click at the top-right corner of the selection marquee, press Shift, and drag down to paint the panel's right edge.**

   Even though half the cursor is outside the selection marquee, areas outside the marquee are not painted. The reduced hardness gives a softer edge to the brush stroke.

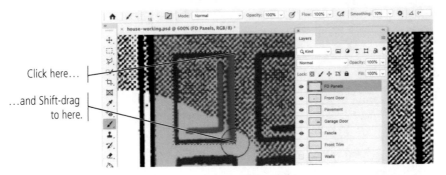

Click here...

...and Shift-drag to here.

These screen captures show the art at a relatively high view percentage, which naturally causes even hard edges to appear soft. However, you should be able to see the difference between the hard- and soft-edge lines.

6. Using the same technique, paint a stroke at the top edge of the panel.

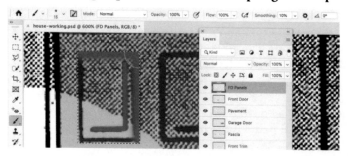

7. Change the foreground color to Doors 2, and reduce the brush size to 10 px. Paint the left and bottom edges of the panel.

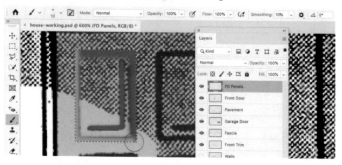

8. Turn off the active selection.

9. Use the same processes outlined in this and the previous exercise to create the lower-left inset panel of the door.

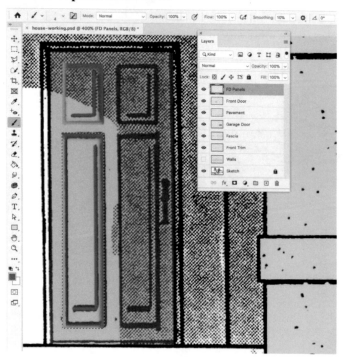

10. Deselect the active marquee, save the file, and then continue to the next exercise.

Paint Strokes Around Selections

In addition to the techniques you have already applied, a number of other options can be used to paint color into a digital file. In this exercise, you will use the Stroke dialog box to outline the front door.

1. **With house-working.psd open, make sure the FD Panels layer is selected.**

2. **With the Move tool active, make sure the Auto-Select option is turned off in the Options bar.**

3. **Press Option/Alt-Shift, and then click-drag right. Position the cloned layer to match the raised panels on the right side of the door.**

   This method of copying a selection (or layer, if there is no specific selection marquee) is called **cloning**. When you clone an entire layer, the result is a copy of the existing layer. If you clone a selection marquee, the cloned content becomes part of the active layer.

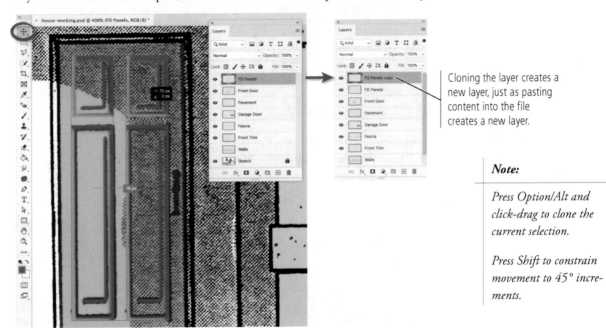

Cloning the layer creates a new layer, just as pasting content into the file creates a new layer.

*Note:*

*Press Option/Alt and click-drag to clone the current selection.*

*Press Shift to constrain movement to 45° increments.*

4. **Use a small, hard brush with a black foreground color to create the door handle on the Front Door layer.**

5. **Change the Front Door layer opacity back to 100%.**

6. **Select the FD Panels copy, FD Panels, and Front Door layers. With all three layers selected, click the Create a New Group button at the bottom of the panel.**

   You could also merge the selected layers into a single layer using the Merge Layers command. However, that option permanently flattens the merged layers, so you can no longer edit individual component layers. In many real-world projects, professionals often prefer to maintain individual components as long as possible, in case changes need to be made at a later time.

7. **Rename the new layer group** Front Door.

8. **In the Layers panel, expand the Front Door layer group. Click the Front Door layer (not the layer group) to make it the active layer.**

9. **Press Command/Control, then click the layer thumbnail for the Front Door layer (not the layer group).**

This shortcut makes a new selection that encompasses all pixels on the layer you click.

You could also use the Magic Wand tool to select the unpainted area of the layer, then choose Select>Inverse to invert the active selection.

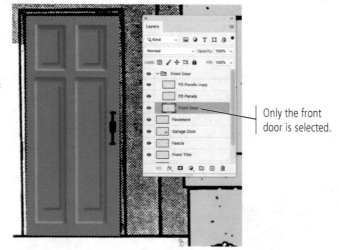

Only the front door is selected.

10. **Change the foreground color to the Doors 4 swatch.**

11. **Choose Edit>Stroke. In the Stroke dialog box, set the Width value to 3 px and the Location to Center. Leave the Blending Mode menu set to Normal, then click OK to apply the stroke.**

The Stroke dialog box is similar to the Fill dialog box, except you use it to define the stroke for the current selection.

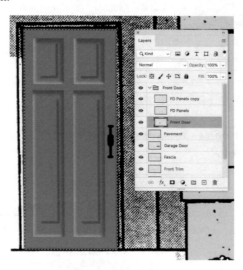

***Note:***

*The Location value of the stroke determines the placement of the stroke width in relation to the selection marquee.*

Inside

Center

Outside

12. **Using the Rectangular Marquee tool, draw a new selection area around the outer door. Use the Stroke dialog box to apply a 5-px stroke to the new selection.**

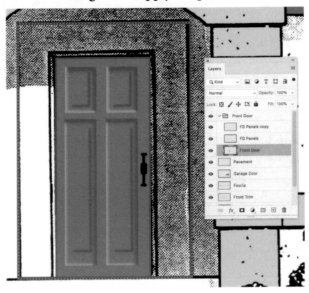

13. **Deselect the current selection.**

14. **Choose the Brush tool, and define a 5-px brush with 100% hardness.**

15. **Place the cursor over the bottom-left corner of the stroke created in Step 11. Click, then Shift-drag left to create the line that marks the top of the stoop.**

    Use the brush cursor preview to align the brush with the existing stroke.

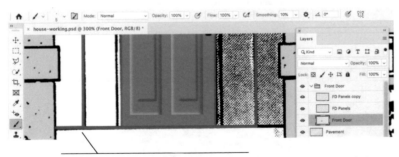

Use the brush cursor to align the new stroke
with the bottom of the existing stroke.

16. **Repeat Step 15 to create the line on the right side of the door.**

17. **In the Layers panel, collapse the Front Door layer group.**

18. **Save the file and continue to the next exercise.**

Apply Strokes to Closed Paths

The window on the front of the house includes a bit more detail than most other elements in this painting. To create this detail, you will use a combination of methods to add strokes to both closed and open paths.

1. With **house-working.psd** open, create a new layer named **Window** at the top of the layer stack. Hide all layers but the Window and Sketch layers, and make the Window layer active.

2. **Choose the Pen tool. In the Options bar, choose Path in the left menu. Open the Set Additional... menu and make sure the Rubber Band option is not checked.**

   When the Rubber Band option is checked, you will see a preview of the line you are drawing when you move the mouse cursor. Because you are only creating basic shapes in this exercise, the feature is not useful, and can actually become confusing (especially drawing over a black-and-white image layer, such as the sketch you are using here).

Use this option to create a path with the Pen tool.

Make sure the Rubber Band option is not active.

3. **Draw the top curved portion of the window.**

   The Pen tool makes it easier to draw a path that matches the window curve. You can then use this path to create a selection that you can use to apply a stroke. (We highlighted the path in red here to show you which path you need to create; yours will not have a colored stroke.)

Draw this path.

The path is stored in the Paths panel as the Work Path.

4. **With the work path selected in the Paths panel (Window>Paths), click the Load Path as Selection button at the bottom of the panel.**

Load Path as Selection

5. **Set the Foreground color to Black, then choose Edit>Stroke. Apply a 6-px black stroke centered on the selection marquee and click OK.**

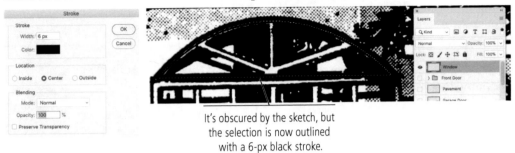

It's obscured by the sketch, but
the selection is now outlined
with a 6-px black stroke.

6. **Set the Foreground color to White, then immediately choose Edit>Stroke again. Apply a 3-px white stroke centered on the selection marquee, then click OK.**

7. **Turn off the active selection marquee.**

8. **Use the same 6-px-black/3-px-white sequence of strokes to create the outer frame of the square window.**

   In this case, you can simply use the Rectangular Marquee tool to draw the selection.

9. **Turn off any active selection, then hide the Sketch layer and review your work.**

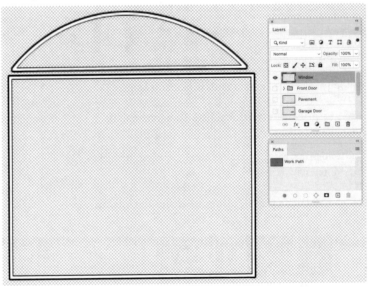

10. **Save the file and continue to the next exercise.**

## Apply Strokes to Open Paths

The rest of the window lines are basically straight, which are easy to create. However, these lines do not create closed shapes from which you can make a selection, so you will use a slightly different technique to create the inner lines of the window.

1. **With house-working.psd open, show the Sketch layer, and then create a new layer immediately above the Window layer.**

   You will use this layer as a temporary workspace, so it isn't necessary to name it.

2. **Choose the Pencil tool (nested under the Brush tool in the Tools panel), and then reset the default foreground and background colors.**

3. **In the Options bar, open the Brush Preset Picker and change the size to 5 px. Press Return/Enter to close the picker.**

   The Pencil tool is similar to the Brush tool, except it only creates a hard edge. In the Options bar, you can select a brush preset from any of the available hard-edge brushes. You can also define the blending mode, opacity, and smoothing to use for the stroke.

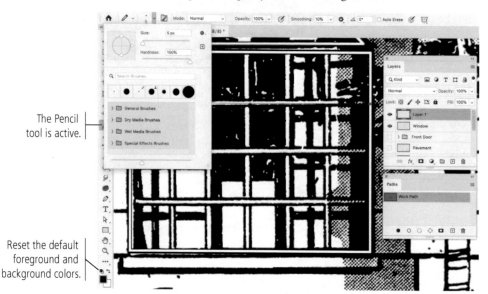

The Pencil tool is active.

Reset the default foreground and background colors.

*Note:*

*If **Auto Erase** is checked in the Options bar, the Pencil tool paints based on the defined foreground and background colors, relative to the color of pixels under the tool cursor. If you draw over an area that contains the foreground color, that area is erased to the background color. If you draw over an area that does not include the foreground color, the Pencil tool simply applies the foreground color.*

Although you are not going to use the Pencil tool to actually draw, you need to set the tool's attributes, so that you can apply those settings to a path in the next few steps.

4. **Use the Pen tool in Path mode to draw a horizontal line that represents the top horizontal division of the window.**

   Because this is an open path (i.e., it doesn't create an actual shape), creating the black-and-white effect requires a slightly different method.

5. **With the work path selected in the Paths panel, choose Stroke Path from the panel Options menu.**

Using the Pen tool, draw this line as the path.

6. **In the resulting Stroke Path dialog box, choose Pencil, and then click OK.**

Using this method, you can define a specific tool to use for the stroke. The current characteristics of the selected tool will be applied, which is why you set the Pencil tool options in Steps 2 and 3.

7. **Choose the Pencil tool again, change the brush size to 3 px, and then swap the foreground and background colors.**

The brush size is now 3 px.

The Pencil tool is selected again.

The same work path is still active.

Click here to swap the foreground and background colors.

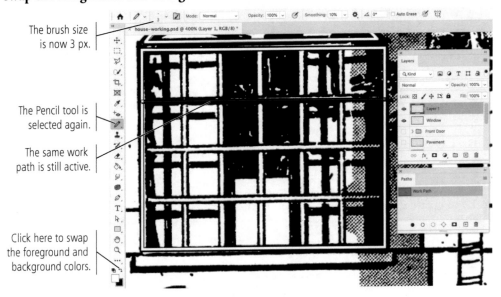

8. **With the work path still selected in the Paths panel, choose Stroke Path from the panel Options menu.**

9. **Choose Pencil in the resulting dialog box and click OK.**

10. **Click the empty area of the Paths panel to turn off the work path.**

11. **Hide the Sketch layer and review your work.**

12. **Select the Move tool. With the Layer 1 layer active in the Layers panel, press Option/Alt-Shift, and then click and drag down to clone the horizontal line.**

If you had not deselected in Step 10, this step would create the cloned line on the existing Layer 1, instead of creating a new layer.

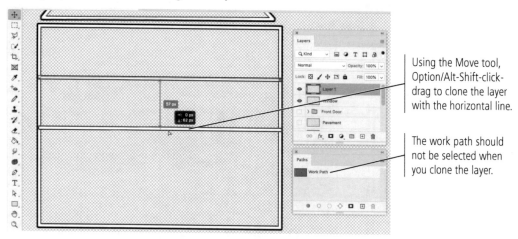

Using the Move tool, Option/Alt-Shift-click-drag to clone the layer with the horizontal line.

The work path should not be selected when you clone the layer.

13. **Repeat Step 12 to create the remaining horizontal line.**

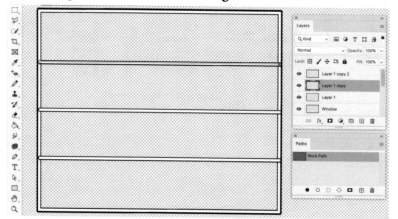

*Note:*

*You should show and hide the Sketch layer as necessary to create these lines and put them in the correct position.*

14. **Use any method you prefer to create the remaining lines of the window, including the lines in the arched window area.**

Whenever possible, clone elements to save yourself work. For example, you could clone one of the layers with a horizontal line, and then transform (rotate and scale) that clone to create a vertical line — which you can then clone to create all the necessary vertical lines.

You can use the same process to create the angled lines in the arched window, rotating the layers as necessary to approximate the correct angles.

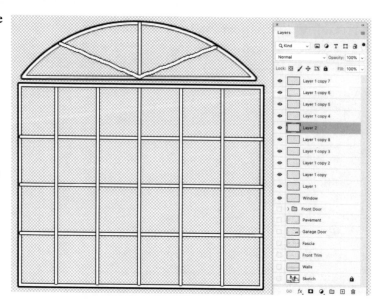

**15. Move the Window layer to the top of the layer stack.**

This hides the ends of the open lines behind the closed paths. If any line ends are visible, select the appropriate layer with the Move tool, and then use the Arrow keys to nudge it into place.

**16. Select all temporary layers and the Window layer. Open the Layers panel Options menu and choose Merge Layers.**

The topmost layer attributes — including the name — are applied to the merged layer. The entire element is now contained on the single Window layer.

As with the Front Door layer, you might prefer to store the component layers in a layer group, so you could more easily make changes to the component layers at a later point. In this case, it really isn't necessary, so you are merging all the component layers into a single Window layer.

**Note:**

*The document tab displays the name of the active layer. This tab can be very helpful when you're working on complex files with multiple layers.*

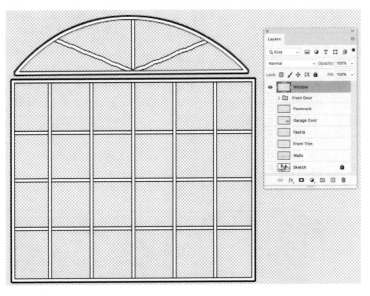

**17. Save the file and continue to the next exercise.**

## Paint Behind Existing Color

The Behind blending mode is only available when you are creating pixels (painting, adding a fill or stroke to a selection, and so on). This blending mode adds new pixels behind the existing pixels. Any existing pixels that are fully opaque will entirely hide the new pixels. This technique is extremely useful for filling spaces and lining edges of existing areas. In this exercise, you will use the Behind method to create the lines that surround the garage door panels.

**1. With house-working.psd open, hide all but the Sketch and Garage Door layers, and then select the Garage Door layer as the active layer.**

**2. Change the foreground color to the Doors 4 swatch.**

3. **Choose the Brush tool (nested under the Pencil tool if you continued directly from the previous exercise) and define a 25-px brush size with 100% hardness. In the Options bar, open the Blending Mode menu and choose Behind.**

4. **Click and drag across the top dividing line in the garage door.**

Use a 25-px hard round brush.

Choose the Behind blending mode.

Click and drag across this line.

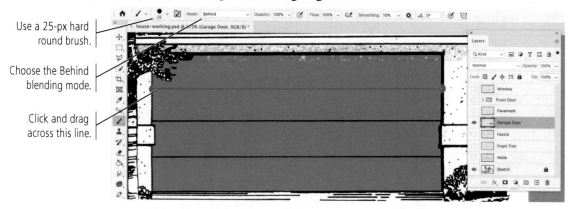

5. **Repeat Step 4 to fill in the other dividing lines in the door, the space above the door, and the space on the right and left sides of the door.**

6. **Show the Front Trim layer, and drag it to the top of the layer stack.**

The Behind blending mode only applies to the active layer; other layers are obscured by painted areas. To create the appropriate effect, you have to change the layer stacking order so the trim appears in front of the entire Garage Door layer.

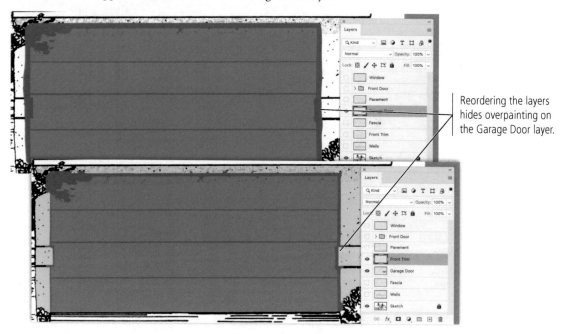

Reordering the layers hides overpainting on the Garage Door layer.

7. **Save the file and continue to the next exercise.**

# Modify Selections to Fill Behind Color

Much of the remaining work is more of the same — you need to fill in the empty areas and apply a stroke around the house trim, fascia, and pavement. You could accomplish this with brushes, carefully painting individual strokes, as necessary, to all the different pieces. However, another method based on selections can accomplish the same general result in a fraction of the time.

1. **With house-working.psd open, make sure the Front Trim layer is selected.**

2. **Create a selection that contains only the filled area of the Front Trim layer.**

   To accomplish this, simply Command/Control-click the Front Trim layer thumbnail in the Layers panel.

The selection excludes
all of the inner areas.

3. **Choose Select>Modify>Expand. In the resulting dialog box, type 4 in the field and click OK.**

   This enlarges the original selection area by 4 pixels. When you fill the enlarged selection, the result will be an apparent edge around the objects on the Front Trim layer.

Expanding the selection includes
most of the inner areas of the trim.

4. **Choose Select>Modify>Feather. In the resulting dialog box, type 3 in the field and click OK.**

Feathering the selection creates a softer edge, which will result in more natural shadows.

5. **Set the foreground color to Doors 4, if it is not already.**

6. **With the selection active, choose Edit>Fill. In the Fill dialog box, choose Foreground Color in the Contents menu and choose Behind in the Blending Mode menu, then click OK.**

The Behind blending mode in this dialog box has the same effect as painting with the Brush tool using the Behind blending mode.

7. **Deselect the active selection, then hide the Sketch layer to review the results.**

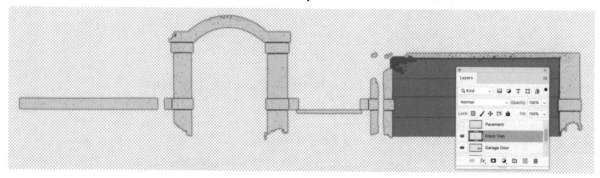

8. **Show the Fascia layer, and then drag it to the top of the layer stack.**

9. **Repeat Steps 2–7 for the Fascia layer, using the same Doors 4 color.**

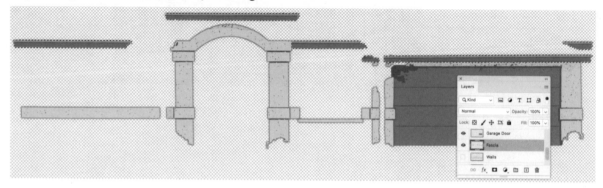

10. **Show the Pavement layer, and then drag it below the Garage Door layer.**

11. **Repeat the same general process (without the feathering) for the Pavement layer, using the Pavement 2 swatch as the fill color.**

We did not feather this selection before filling it because pavement typically does not have a softened edge.

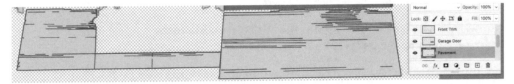

12. **Deselect any active marquee.**

13. **Choose the Brush tool and define a hard, round brush. Using the Behind blending mode, fill in the pavement areas that were not filled in by Step 11.**

Click-Shift-click to create straight lines that connect the two points where you click. This method allows you to cleanly paint the pavement edges. You can then more easily fill in the empty areas.

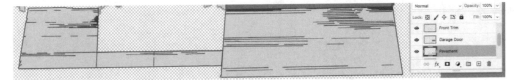

14. **Save the file and continue to the next exercise.**

## Painting with the Mixer Brush

The **Mixer Brush tool** simulates realistic painting techniques, such as mixing colors on a canvas, combining colors on a brush, and varying paint wetness across a stroke.

In the Options bar, the **Current Brush Load** shows which color is currently loaded in the brush. You can click the swatch to open the color picker, or Option/Alt-click the screen to sample a load color from the existing image.

If you click the arrow button to the right of the Current Brush Load swatch, you can choose **Clean Brush** to empty all color from the brush, or choose **Load Brush** to fill the brush with the defined load color. **Load Solid Colors Only** prevents the brush from loading multiple "paint" colors.

If **Load Brush After Each Stroke** is toggled on, the brush load is restored to full capacity after each stroke.

If the **Clean Brush After Each Stroke** option is toggled on, the brush is restored to only the load color after each stroke. When this option is toggled off, the brush "picks up" and holds color from the canvas.

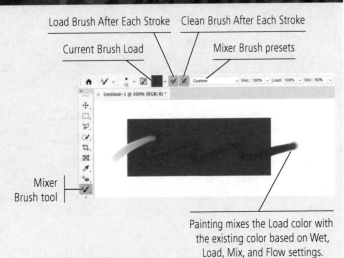

Painting mixes the Load color with the existing color based on Wet, Load, Mix, and Flow settings.

The **Wet** setting defines how much paint the brush picks up from the canvas; higher settings produce longer streaks.

The **Load** setting defines the amount of paint loaded in the reservoir. At low values, strokes dry out more quickly.

The **Mix** setting defines the ratio of canvas paint to reservoir paint. At 100%, all paint is picked up from the canvas; at 0%, all paint comes from the reservoir.

# Create Texture with a Faux Finish Brush

Textures can be sampled from other images, copied and pasted into place, and created from scratch using combinations of brush styles and options. In this exercise, you use a textured brush to turn what are now simple brown walls into realistic-looking stone.

1. **With house-working.psd open, hide all but the Walls layer. Make the Walls layer active, then change its layer opacity to 100%.**

2. **Command/Control-click the Walls layer thumbnail to select all pixels on that layer.**

3. **Choose the Brush tool. In the Options bar, set the brush blending mode to Normal.**

4. **Open the Brush Preset Picker from the Options bar.**

5. **Open the panel Options menu and choose Legacy Brushes.**

The four default brush sets, which appear at the bottom of the Brush Preset Picker by default, are a very limited set of random brushes.

You still have access to hundreds of predefined brushes that were available in previous versions of the software, in addition to more than a thousand that are now available to download from the Adobe website by choosing Get More Brushes.

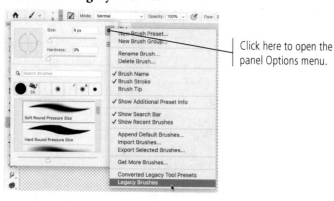

Click here to open the panel Options menu.

6. **In the warning message, click OK to restore the legacy brushes to the panel.**

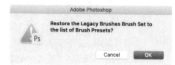

7. **In the Brush Preset Picker, expand the length of the panel so you can see more options, and then expand the Legacy Brushes folder.**

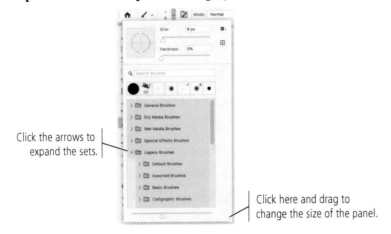

Click the arrows to expand the sets.

Click here and drag to change the size of the panel.

8. **Expand the Faux Finish Brushes in the panel, and then scroll through the list until you find the Stencil Sponge - Wet brush.**

The list of brushes includes a preview of the brush stroke that will be created. You can use the slider at the bottom of the panel to change the size of the brush previews.

9. **Select the Stencil Sponge – Wet preset. Make the brush size large enough to cover the highest part of the fill in the Walls layer.**

A 700-px brush is large enough to cover the entire area in one brush stroke.

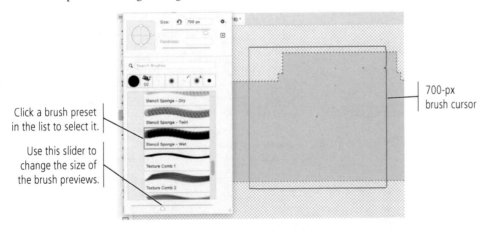

Click a brush preset in the list to select it.

Use this slider to change the size of the brush previews.

700-px brush cursor

10. **Change the foreground color to the Stucco 3 swatch, and then click and drag from left to right to paint the texture into the selection area.**

11. **Deselect the active selection, save the file, and continue to the next exercise.**

# Use Opacity and Blending Modes to Create Shadows

In many cases, it works well to paint on a separate layer and adjust the layer's blend options (blending mode and opacity). In other cases, adjusting the specific brush settings makes it easier to create subtle elements, such as the shadows on the front of the house.

1. With **house-working.psd** open, make all layers visible.

2. Reduce the Walls layer opacity to 50%, so that you can see the sketch through the walls.

3. Create a new layer named House Shadows immediately below the Front Trim layer.

4. Choose the Brush tool and set the foreground color to Doors 3.

5. Using the Brush Preset Picker in the Options bar, choose the Soft Round brush in the General Brushes set, and set the size to 100 px.

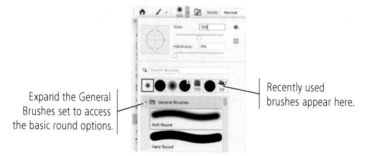

Expand the General Brushes set to access the basic round options.

Recently used brushes appear here.

6. In the Options bar, define the following options:

| | |
|---|---|
| **Blending Mode:** | **Multiply** |
| **Opacity:** | **25%** |
| **Enable Airbrush-Style Build-Up Effects:** | **Active** |

7. Use the shadows in the Sketch layer as a guide to paint the shadow strokes on the House Shadows layer.

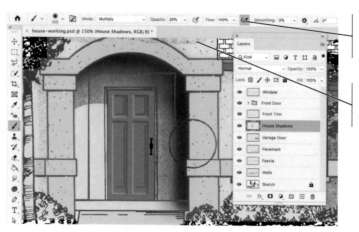

Because you are using Airbrush mode, each successive brush stroke applies more color. Use multiple strokes to build darker shadows near the house edges that cast the shadows.

Using reduced brush opacity and the Multiply blending mode, you can build darker shadows without completely obscuring the color and texture of the wall — just as actual shadows appear in real life.

Enable Airbrush-Style Build-up Effects

The shadows on the sketch define where you need to paint.

8. **Hide the Sketch layer and review your results.**

It can be helpful to frequently toggle the visibility of the Sketch layer as you paint in the shadows, so you can see where your shadows still need work.

9. **Continue painting the shadows until you are satisfied with your result.**

10. **Create a new layer named Window Inside below the Window layer. Fill the window area with black, and set the layer opacity to 35%.**

11. **Create another new layer named Window Shadows below the Window layer but above the Window Inside layer.**

12. **Use a soft round brush with black as the foreground color to paint the shadows that fall inside the house. Change the brush size, flow, and opacity as necessary to create the shadows.**

We used a 20-px brush with 50% hardness, Normal blending mode, 100% opacity, and 25% flow for the horizontal lines, and a slightly smaller brush size for the vertical lines.

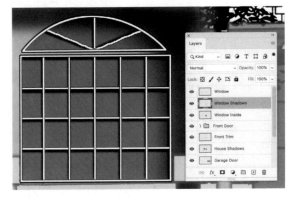

13. **Show all layers, and set the Walls layer to 100% opacity.**

14. **Save the file and continue to the next stage of the project.**

The **History Brush tool** allows you to restore specific areas of an image back to a previous state. In the Options bar, you can choose the brush preset and brush settings that you want to use. When you paint with the History Brush tool, areas where you paint return to the target state or snapshot in the History panel. (The same effect can be achieved using any of the regular Eraser tools with the Erase to History option active.)

In the image shown here, we opened a file and made a number of adjustments to the image color and contrast. We then applied a filter to make the building look like a line-art drawing. In the final step, we selected the adjusted, unfiltered state, and then used the History Brush tool to restore only the upper section of the building back to the photographic pixels.

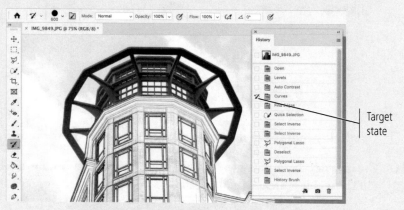

Target state

The **Art History Brush tool** paints with stylized strokes, using the targeted history state (or snapshot) as the source data for the painting. (We can't say the tool "restores" the data, because results from the artistic style of the brush could hardly be called "restorative.")

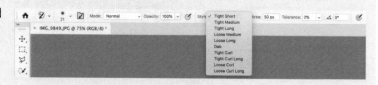

In the Options bar, you can define the brush preset, blending mode, and opacity, as well as a specific style that will be used for the brush marks. The Area option defines the area that will be covered with the brush marks. Larger area values result in a greater area covered, as well as more brush marks created by the stroke. Tolerance limits the area in which brush strokes can be applied. Higher tolerance values limit painting to areas that significantly differ from colors in the targeted state of the snapshot.

In the series of images shown here, we targeted the original image snapshot in the History panel, and then restored the top floors by using the Art History Brush with different style settings.

Painted with the Tight Short style

Painted with the Loose Medium style

Painted with the Dab style

Painted with the Tight Curl style

# STAGE 3 / **Working with Patterns**

The only element of the house left to paint is the roof. Manually drawing every shingle would take hours, and it would be difficult (if not impossible) to create the uniformity that is part of real roofing shingles. A better solution is to use a pattern fill. Unfortunately, the built-in Photoshop pattern sets do not include a roof tile pattern, so in this exercise, you will create your own.

 **Define a Pattern from Existing Artwork**

The trick to creating a good repeating tile is placing or creating elements in such a way that apparent edges align properly when the pattern is tiled. Once you have defined the tile, creating and applying the pattern is fairly easy.

1. **Open the file tiles.psd from the WIP>Houses folder.**

    This file was created as a 1-inch square. Each edge of the square has half of the blurred lines that make up the tile edges.

2. **Open the Patterns panel (Window>Patterns) and review the available options.**

    Like the Swatches, Gradients, and Styles panels, Photoshop includes a number of built-in patterns that are grouped into logical sets. You can click the arrow to the left of each group name to see the patterns that are included in a particular group.

    Default patterns include a number of existing groups.

    Create New Group

    Create New Pattern

    Delete Pattern

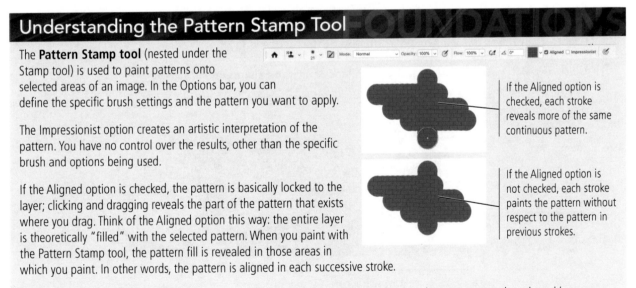

## Understanding the Pattern Stamp Tool

The **Pattern Stamp tool** (nested under the Stamp tool) is used to paint patterns onto selected areas of an image. In the Options bar, you can define the specific brush settings and the pattern you want to apply.

The Impressionist option creates an artistic interpretation of the pattern. You have no control over the results, other than the specific brush and options being used.

If the Aligned option is checked, the pattern is basically locked to the layer; clicking and dragging reveals the part of the pattern that exists where you drag. Think of the Aligned option this way: the entire layer is theoretically "filled" with the selected pattern. When you paint with the Pattern Stamp tool, the pattern fill is revealed in those areas in which you paint. In other words, the pattern is aligned in each successive stroke.

If the Aligned option is checked, each stroke reveals more of the same continuous pattern.

If the Aligned option is not checked, each stroke paints the pattern without respect to the pattern in previous strokes.

When the Aligned option is not checked, each stroke of the Pattern Stamp tool paints the pattern onto the selected layer. The pattern is not aligned from one stroke to the next.

### 3. Click the Create New Pattern button at the bottom of the Patterns panel.

This button creates a new pattern from the active selection. Because you did not select a specific area of the file, the entire selected layer will become the new pattern.

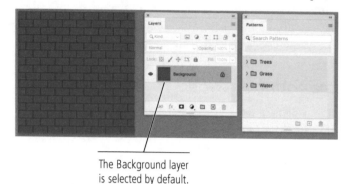

The Background layer is selected by default.

### 4. In the Resulting Pattern Name dialog box, type Shingles, and then click OK.

Your new custom pattern is created, and is listed at the bottom of the Patterns panel.

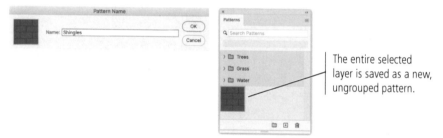

The entire selected layer is saved as a new, ungrouped pattern.

### 5. Close the tiles image without saving it.

### 6. Make the house-working.psd file active in the document window.

### 7. Create a new layer named Roof 1 at the top of the layer stack.

### 8. Using the Polygonal Lasso tool, draw a selection around the main roof area.

You might have to make some assumptions in the top corners, where the sketched trees obscure the roof corners.

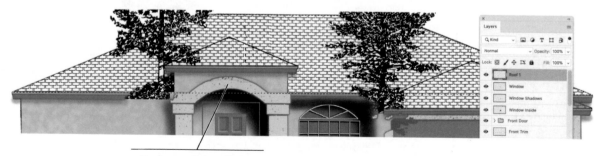

Don't worry if the selection covers some of the house; you will fix potential problems later.

9. **Choose Edit>Fill, and choose Pattern in the Contents menu. Open the Custom Pattern menu and choose the Shingles pattern.**

   This pattern you created was added to the existing options in the Patterns panel.

10. **Make sure the Blending Mode menu is set to Normal and the Opacity is set to 100%, then click OK to fill the selection area with the pattern.**

    As you can see, the lines on the pattern tile align seamlessly in the pattern fill.

    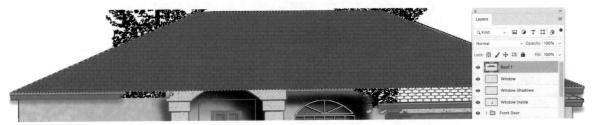

11. **Deselect the active selection, then hide the Roof 1 layer.**

12. **Use the same process to create the two remaining sections of the roof, each on its own layer (named Roof 2 and Roof 3).**

    Use the Polygonal Lasso tool to make a selection, and then use the Fill dialog box to add the pattern fill.

13. **Show the Roof 1 layer.**

    With all three roof sections showing, you can now see two problems. First, the main roof is obscuring the porch covering and fascia. Second, all three pieces of the roof were created with the same pattern, so all three pieces merge seamlessly together.

14. **Drag the Fascia and Front Trim layers to the top of the layer stack.**

    It's common to lock, hide, and move layers as necessary when working on a complex assignment like this one. At times, the position of specific layers becomes critical, as does making sure you're working on the correct layer. When you work on a complex file, plan your work, and then carefully follow those plans.

15. **Set the Roof 1 layer opacity to 50% so you can see the underlying layers.**

16. **Using the Rectangular Marquee tool, draw a selection marquee around the area of the house that is obscured by the Roof 1 layer content.**

Select only the roof area that obscures the house.

17. **With the Roof 1 layer selected, press Delete/Backspace to remove all pixels inside the selection area.**

Pressing Delete/Backspace removes selected pixels from the selected layer.

18. **Restore the Roof 1 layer to 100% opacity.**

19. **Use any method you prefer to add a dark, soft edge around each roof section. Sample the dark color in the tile pattern to use as the edge color.**

    You can use the Paint Behind method with a soft-edge brush, or use the modified-selection fill technique you used for the front trim.

20. **Save the file and continue to the next exercise.**

# Erasing Pixels

 *Watch the video **Using the Eraser Tools in Photoshop** in your online student resources.*

The **Eraser tool** removes pixels where you click. If you erase from the Background layer or in a regular layer with transparency locked, the background color shows through where you erased.

If the **Erase to History** option is checked, dragging with the Eraser tool (in any mode) reveals the selected state in the History panel.

- The default Block mode simply erases the area under the square cursor; you can't control the size, shape, opacity, or flow of the tool. When using the Eraser tool, the opacity setting determines the strength of the tool; 100% opacity entirely erases pixels.

- If you choose Brush mode, you can define the specific brush preset, opacity, and flow, as well as use the Eraser brush in Airbrush mode.

- If you choose Pencil mode, you can define the specific brush and opacity. Pencil mode does not offer flow control or Airbrush mode.

The **Magic Eraser tool** (nested under the Eraser tool) works on the same principle as the Magic Wand tool. Clicking with the tool erases all pixels within the defined tolerance.

Clicking with the Magic Eraser tool removes all pixels within the defined tolerance.

The **Background Eraser tool** (nested under the Eraser tool) erases pixels, while attempting to maintain the edges of an object in the foreground. The Background Eraser samples color at the brush center, and deletes that color where it appears inside the brush. In the Options bar, you can define the brush size and settings. You can also specify different sampling and tolerance options to control the range of pixels that are affected.

The sampling options determine how color will be replaced:

- **Continuous** samples colors as you drag.
- **Once** erases color only in areas containing the color that you first click.
- **Background Swatch** erases only areas containing the current background color.

The Limits menu constrains the tool's effect:

- **Discontiguous** erases the sampled color where it occurs under the brush.
- **Contiguous** erases colors that are adjacent to the color immediately under the brush tip.
- **Find Edges** erases connected areas of the sampled color, attempting to preserve edge sharpness.

**Tolerance** defines how much variance from the sample will be affected. If the **Protect Foreground Color** option is checked, pixels of the defined foreground color in the Tools panel will be protected from erasure.

Clicking and dragging with the Background Eraser tool removes pixels within the defined tolerance.

## Save a Custom Pattern

You never know when a particular pattern or other asset might be useful. By default, when you quit Photoshop you lose any custom assets unless you intentionally save them. Since you have taken the time to create the pattern for a tiled roof, it's a good idea to save it so you can use it again later.

1. **With house-working.psd open, click the Create New Group button at the bottom of the Patterns panel.**

2. **In the resulting dialog box, type Portfolio Patterns as the new group name.**

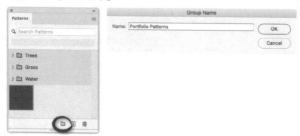

3. **Click OK to create the new pattern group.**

   Your new group appears below the existing patterns in the panel.

4. **Click the Shingles pattern tile and drag it onto the Portfolio Patterns group.**

5. **Click to select the Portfolio Patterns folder in the panel, then open the Patterns panel Options menu and choose Export Selected Patterns.**

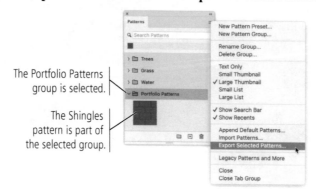

The Portfolio Patterns group is selected.

The Shingles pattern is part of the selected group.

**Note:**

*There is a bug in the Windows software that might cause the Export Selected Patterns option to be unavailable. If the Export option is unavailable, close the panel, then reopen it, and try again.*

6. **In the resulting dialog box, navigate to your WIP>Houses folder as the target location.**

The Save/Save As dialog box defaults to the application's Presets>Patterns folder. The extension (.pat) is automatically added for you.

If you are using a shared computer, you might not be able to save files in the application's default location. Saving the file directly to your WIP folder makes it readily available whenever you need it.

7. **Change the Save As field to Portfolio Patterns.pat, and then click Save.**

**Note:**

*After a pattern group has been saved, you can access those patterns again by choosing Import Patterns in the Patterns panel Options menu.*

8. **Continue to the next stage of the project.**

# STAGE 4 / Painting Nature

Some elements of this painting are far less structured than the house. The trees, bushes, grass, and other natural elements can't be created by filling and painting with basic brushes — or at least, you can't make them look natural with the tools you have learned so far. These elements should be painted more randomly so they look as natural as possible.

##  Use a Filter to Create Trees

When it comes to painting the landscaping, it helps to have an eye for art in general, more so than for any other component of this project. That's not to say, however, that you need to be Michelangelo to finish this project. The easiest place to start is with a built-in filter for creating the trees in the painting.

1. **With house-working.psd open, create a new layer named Tree 1 at the top of the layer stack. Hide all other layers, except the Sketch layer.**

You're going to use a series of different layers to create the various landscaping elements. Doing so will allow you to control the different pieces, including rearranging or merging them together, as necessary, to create the best possible result. These layers should be on top of the layer stack because most of the trees and bushes are in the sketch foreground (i.e., in front of the house).

2. **Using the Rectangular Marquee tool, draw a selection that roughly encompasses the tree on the left side of the sketch.**

Drawing a selection marquee before calling the Tree filter limits the area in which the filter artwork can exist. (We outlined the selection area in red to make it more visible in our image.)

3. **With the Tree 1 layer selected, choose Filter>Render>Tree.**

This filter does exactly what its name suggests — creates realistic trees, using built-in artwork and randomizing settings.

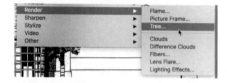

4. **Open the Basic Tree Type menu and review the options.**

You can choose from a variety of specific species. You can create a pine forest or a palm garden, or simply choose a tree with the look you want to achieve.

5. **Choose Populus Nigra in the Basic Tree Type menu.**

We chose this option because it has the tall and narrow characteristics of the one in the sketch. The preview window on the left side of the dialog box shows what the resulting artwork will look like when you click OK.

6. **Experiment with the settings in the lower half of the dialog box until you are satisfied with the results.**

- **Light Direction.** Changing this value moves the apparent light source left (0) to right (180).

- **Leaves Amount.** Increasing this value adds more leaves, while decreasing it reduces the number of leaves. A value of 0, for example, would create a winter tree with no leaves at all.

- **Leaves Size.** Smaller size values result in smaller leaves, almost creating the look of a tree beginning to bud in early Spring.

- **Branches Height.** Increasing this value moves the first protruding branches farther up the tree trunk.

- **Branches Thickness.** Increasing this value results in a thicker trunk and branches throughout the artwork.

- **Default Leaves.** Each tree uses a specific leaf shape as the default — for example, maple trees use a maple leaf shape. If you uncheck the Default Leaves option, you can change the shape that will be used for the leaves in your resulting tree.

- **Randomize Shapes.** If checked, this option randomly creates the tree artwork, regardless of your other settings.

- **Arrangement.** When Randomize Shapes is not checked, you can increase this value to adjust the shape of branches and leaves in the resulting artwork.

7. **Click OK to create the new tree artwork.**

The resulting artwork is scaled to fit inside the marquee that you drew before you called the filter. If you don't first make a selection area, the artwork would fill the most available space based on the dimensions of the tree you define in the filter dialog box.

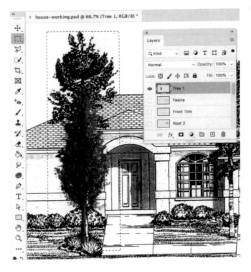

8. Turn off the active selection, and then choose Edit>Free Transform. Use the bounding-box handles to adjust the size of the tree artwork to better match the sketched tree. Press Return/Enter when you are satisfied with the result.

9. Create another new layer named Tree 2. Repeat this same general process to create the second tree in the sketch.

10. Save the file, and then continue to the next exercise.

Change Brush Settings to Paint Random Elements

The randomness of shapes, colors, and textures occurring in nature simply cannot be painted using basic lines, regardless of the brush size, flow, opacity, and other options. For this reason, we can't provide specific step-by-step instructions to create every required brush stroke in this exercise. To create the shrubs and grass, we can only provide advice on how to select the best tool settings for the job. Every person will end up with different results.

1. **With house-working.psd open, create a new layer named Shrubs immediately below the Tree 1 layer. Make the Shrubs layer active.**

2. **Select the Brush tool. In the Options bar, choose Normal in the Mode menu, and set the Opacity and Flow to 100%.**

3. **In the Brush Preset Picker choose the Stencil Sponge-Twirl brush in the Faux Finishes set (inside the Legacy Brushes set).**

   This brush is the starting point; you will change the settings based on this selected preset.

Click to open the Brush Preset Picker.    Click to open the Brush Settings panel.

*Note:*

*Refer to Page 396 if you need to again restore the Legacy Brushes set.*

4. **In the Options bar, click the button to open the Brush Settings panel.**

5. **Choose Brush Tip Shape in the list of options. Set the Size to 40 px, change the Angle to 30°, and set the Roundness to 70%.**

   Leaves are rarely straight up-and-down, so your brush strokes shouldn't be either.

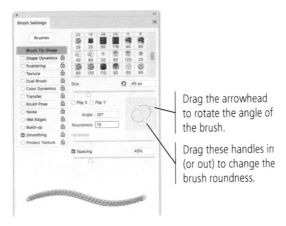

Drag the arrowhead to rotate the angle of the brush.

Drag these handles in (or out) to change the brush roundness.

6. **Select Shape Dynamics in the list on the left. Change all the Jitter sliders to 50%, and then set all the Control menus to Off.**

   Real shrubbery has leaves in many different shapes and sizes. By jittering all these settings, you allow Photoshop to randomize the brush marks that will create the leaves.

Notice the new preview, which dynamically shows the results of your settings.

7. **In the Scattering options, allow Photoshop to scatter the marks along both axes, using a 150% setting.**

   By scattering along both axes, you get a more random result than if brush marks only move perpendicularly from the brush stroke. Watch the preview to evaluate the results of different scatter values.

8. **Set the Count value to 2 to limit the number of brush marks in the same area.**

   You can use multiple brush strokes to build up more marks in the same space.

9. **In the Color Dynamics options, check the Apply Per Tip option, and apply a 100% Foreground/Background Jitter setting.**

   You could manually vary the colors by frequently switching the foreground color, but this option speeds up the process by varying the colors in a single brush stroke, without choosing new paint colors.

10. **In the Transfer options, apply 15% opacity jitter.**

    A slight variation in the stroke opacity will further increase the randomness of the brush marks. Because some marks will be semi-transparent, overlapping areas will produce an even broader range of color, without manually changing the brush color.

11. **In the Tools panel, set the foreground color to the Foliage 2 swatch and the background color to the Foliage 1 swatch.**

12. **With the Shrubs layer active, click with the brush and drag to paint the shrubs in the sketch. Use multiple brush strokes to add a greater variety of color throughout the shrubs.**

   The settings you applied allow you to easily create a random set of brush marks, differing in size, angle, roundness, position, color, and opacity.

   As you paint, don't forget about the History panel. You can step back up to 20 brush strokes, or you can create new History snapshots at regular intervals, so you can return to earlier stages of your work.

13. **Show all layers in the file and review your work. Paint shrubs over any areas where the house is not perfectly painted.**

14. **Save the file and continue to the next exercise.**

# Understanding the Brush Settings Panel

## Brush Tip Shape

**Size** controls the diameter (in pixels) of the brush.

**Flip X** and **Flip Y** change the direction of a brush tip on the X (horizontal) or Y (vertical) axis.

**Angle** defines the angle for an elliptical brush.

**Roundness** controls the ratio between the short and long axes of the brush; 100% creates a round brush, 0% creates a linear brush, and middle values create elliptical brushes.

**Hardness** controls the size of the brush's hard center. This is the same as the Hardness setting in the Options bar.

**Spacing** controls the distance between brush marks in a stroke. The spacing is a percentage of the brush diameter.

## Shape Dynamics

**Size Jitter** varies the size of brush marks in a stroke, based on the maximum percentage defined here. You can also use the Control menu to vary the size of brush marks:

- Off provides no control over the variation.
- Fade varies the size of brush marks between the initial diameter and the minimum diameter in a specified number of steps (from 1 to 9,999).
- Pen Pressure, Pen Tilt, Stylus Wheel, and Rotation vary the size of brush marks when using a drawing tablet/pen.

**Minimum Diameter** defines the minimum brush (as a percentage of brush diameter) when Size Jitter is used.

**Tilt Scale** specifies the scale factor for brush height when Pen Tilt is active in the Control menu.

**Angle Jitter** varies the angle of brush marks in a stroke (as a percentage of 360°). The Control menu specifies how you control the angle variance of brush marks:

- Off, Fade, Pen Pressure, Pen Tilt, and Stylus Wheel have the same meanings as those for Size Jitter (above).
- Initial Direction bases the angle of brush marks on the initial direction of the brush stroke.
- Direction bases the angle of brush marks on the overall direction of the brush stroke.

**Roundness Jitter** varies the roundness of brush marks in a stroke as a percentage of the ratio between the brush height and width.

**Minimum Roundness** specifies the minimum roundness for brush marks when Roundness Jitter is enabled.

**Flip X Jitter** and **Flip Y Jitter** allow the flip behavior (when enabled) to be randomized.

## Scattering

**Scatter** controls how brush marks are distributed in a stroke. If Both Axes is active, brush marks are distributed radially. If Both Axes is not active, brush marks are distributed perpendicular to the stroke path.

**Count** defines the number of brush marks applied at each spacing interval.

**Count Jitter** varies the number of brush marks for each spacing interval, based on the defined maximum percentage.

## Texture

Textured brushes use patterns to make strokes look as though they were painted on paper or canvas. After you choose a pattern, you can set many of the same options that are available when applying a texture effect to a layer.

**Invert** reverses the high (light) and low (dark) points in the texture. When Invert is selected, the lightest areas are the low points and the darkest areas are the high points.

**Scale** defines the size of the pattern texture as a percentage of the original pattern size.

**Texture Each Tip** applies the selected texture to each brush mark, rather than to the brush stroke as a whole.

**Mode** defines the blending mode that combines the brush and the pattern.

**Depth** defines how deeply color affects the texture. At 0%, all points receive the same amount of color, which obscures the texture. At 100%, low points are not painted.

**Minimum Depth** specifies the minimum depth to which color can penetrate.

**Depth Jitter** varies the depth (when Texture Each Tip is selected), based on the maximum percentage defined here.

## Dual Brush

A dual brush combines two brush tips. The second brush texture is applied within the stroke of the primary brush. Only areas where both brush strokes intersect are painted.

**Mode** defines the blending mode that will combine marks from the two brushes.

**Size** defines the diameter of the dual tip (in pixels).

**Spacing** defines the distance between the dual-tip brush marks in a stroke as a percentage of the brush diameter.

**Scatter** determines how dual-tip brush marks are distributed in a stroke. (See Scattering above.)

**Count** defines the number of dual-tip brush marks at each spacing interval.

# Understanding the Brush Settings Panel (continued)

## Color Dynamics

Color dynamics determine how the color of paint changes over the course of a stroke.

**Apply Per Tip** allows color dynamics to change across a single brush stroke. If this option is not checked, the color is varied only between multiple strokes with the same brush.

**Foreground/Background Jitter** varies between the foreground and background colors.

**Hue Jitter** varies the hue in a stroke. Lower percentages create less hue variation across the stroke.

**Saturation Jitter** varies the saturation in a stroke. Lower percentages create less saturation variation across the stroke.

**Brightness Jitter** varies the brightness in a stroke. Lower percentages create less brightness variation across the stroke.

**Purity** increases or decreases the saturation of the color, between –100% (fully desaturated) and 100% (fully saturated).

## Transfer

**Opacity Jitter** varies the opacity of color in a stroke, up to the opacity value defined in the Options bar.

**Flow Jitter** varies the flow of color in a brush stroke.

**Wetness Jitter** varies the wetness setting of a Wet Mixer brush.

**Mix Jitter** varies the mixing quality of a Wet Mixer brush.

## Brush Pose

These options — Tilt X, Tilt Y, Rotation, and Pressure — allow you to define settings that mimic the behavior of a drawing tablet/stylus if you are using a mouse. If you are using a digital drawing tablet, you can check the Override options to prevent stylus properties from affecting the brush stroke.

## Other Brush Options

**Noise** adds randomness to brush tips that contain shades of gray (e.g., soft tips).

**Wet Edges** causes paint to build up along the edges of the brush stroke, creating a watercolor effect.

**Build-up** applies gradual tones to an image, simulating traditional airbrush techniques (this is the same as the Airbrush button in the Options bar).

**Smoothing**, which creates smoother curves in brush strokes, is most useful if you are using a drawing tablet.

**Protect Texture** applies the same pattern and scale to all textured brushes to simulate a consistent canvas texture throughout the entire image.

## Create a Brush Preset

As with custom patterns, you must save custom brush presets if you want to be able to use them again later after quitting and relaunching Photoshop. You have a lot of shrubs to paint in this image, so it's a good idea to save the brush you defined in the previous exercise.

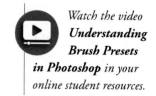

*Watch the video **Understanding Brush Presets in Photoshop** in your online student resources.*

1. **With house-working.psd open, open the Brush Settings panel Options menu and choose New Brush Preset.**

2. **In the Brush Name dialog box, name the new preset Shrubbery. Check the Include Tool Settings and Include Color options, and then click OK.**

**Note:**

*If you changed your Brush Settings panel or quit Photoshop since the previous exercise, you might have to go back and re-create the Shrubbery brush for this exercise to work properly.*

3. **Click the Create New Group button at the bottom of the Brushes panel.**

4. **In the resulting dialog box, type Portfolio Brushes as the new group name.**

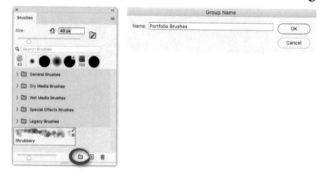

5. **Click OK to create the new brush group.**

   Your new group appears below the existing brushes in the panel.

6. **Click the Shrubbery brush and drag it onto the Portfolio Brushes group.**

7. **With the Portfolio Brushes group selected, open the Brushes panel Options menu and choose Export Selected Brushes.**

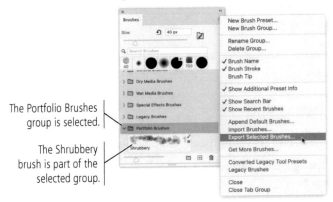

The Portfolio Brushes group is selected.

The Shrubbery brush is part of the selected group.

*Note:*

*There is a bug in the Windows software that might cause the Export Selected Brushes option to be unavailable. If the Export option is unavailable, close the panel, then reopen it, and try again.*

8. **In the resulting dialog box, navigate to your WIP>Houses folder as the target location.**

The Save/Save As dialog box defaults to the application's Presets>Patterns folder. The extension (.abr) is automatically added for you. If you are using a shared computer, you might not be able to save files in the application's default location. Saving the file directly to your WIP folder makes it readily available whenever you need it.

*Note:*

*After a brush group has been saved, you can access those brushes again by choosing Import Brushes in the Brushes panel Options menu.*

9. **Change the Save As field to Portfolio Brushes.abr, and then click Save.**

10. **Continue to the next exercise.**

## Understanding the Tool Presets Panel

Just as saving a custom brush preset allows you to access that brush again later, tool presets allow you to save and reuse settings for any Photoshop tool. **Tool presets** can be accessed in the Options bar or in the Tool Presets panel (Window>Tool Presets). The structure of the panel Options menu offers the same options as other asset panels — you can control what is visible in the panel, load and save custom sets, and access built-in sets of tool presets.

To save your own tool presets, simply choose New Tool Preset from the panel Options menu or click the Create New Tool Preset button at the bottom of the panel. The new tool preset will include whatever tool and options are currently selected.

Click here to access tool presets.

View presets for all tools or for only the currently selected tool.

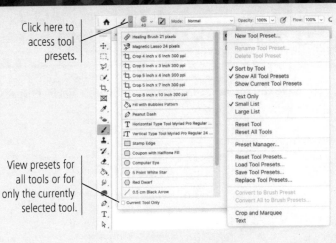

Finish the Painting

Using the skills and techniques you just learned, paint the rest of the landscaping in the image. Keep the following steps in mind as you paint these elements.

1. **Create, rearrange, and merge layers as necessary to produce the best result.**

   You should experiment with the different brush settings as you paint these elements. Use layers liberally as you create the various elements so you can easily turn off or delete objects, and try again.

2. **Grass — especially new sod — has far less randomness than leaves.**

   - **Choose foreground and background colors that are only slightly different (try Foliage 6 and Foliage 7).**

   - **Start with a brush preset that looks like a blade of grass (try one of the veining brushes in the Faux Finish Brushes set).**

   - **Use a small brush size with a small amount of size and angle jitter, and allow the marks to flip horizontally (Flip X Jitter option).**

   - **Experiment with different settings for foreground/background and opacity jitter.**

3. **When you're finished, add a new layer immediately above the Sketch layer, and fill it with solid white.**

4. **Save the file as house-final.psd in your WIP>Houses folder and continue to the final exercise.**

Export a PDF File for Print

The Portable Document Format (PDF) was created by Adobe to facilitate cross-platform transportation of documents, independent of the fonts used, linked files, or even the originating application. The format offers a number of advantages:

- Data in a PDF file can be high or low resolution, and it can be compressed to reduce file size.

- PDF files are device-independent, which means you don't need the originating application or the same platform to open and print the file.

- PDF files are also page-independent, which means a PDF document can contain rotated pages, and even pages of different sizes.

1. **With house-final.psd open, choose File>Save As. Navigate to your WIP>Houses folder as the target destination.**

2. **Choose Photoshop PDF in the Format/Save As Type menu, and then click Save.**

Choose Photoshop PDF as the file format.

3. **Click OK in the resulting warning message.**

   Before the PDF is saved, you have to define the settings that will be used to generate the PDF file. Some options (such as color profile information) can be changed in the Save Adobe PDF dialog box; those choices will override the selections in the Save As dialog box.

4. **Choose High Quality Print in the Adobe PDF Preset menu.**

   The Adobe PDF Preset menu includes six PDF presets (in brackets) that meet common output requirements. Other options might also be available if another user created custom presets in Photoshop or another Adobe application.

   Because there are so many ways to create a PDF, the potential benefits of the format are often undermined. The PDF/X specification was created to help solve some of the problems associated with bad PDF files entering the prepress workflow. Ask your output provider whether you should apply a PDF/X standard to your files.

   The Compatibility menu determines which version of the PDF format you create. This is particularly important if your file uses transparency. PDF 1.3 does not support transparency, so the file will require flattening. If you save the file to be compatible with PDF 1.4 or later, the transparency information will be maintained in the PDF file. It will have to be flattened later in the output process (after it leaves your desk).

## 5. In the General pane, uncheck all but Optimize for Fast Web Preview.

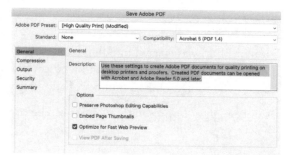

As soon as you change an option away from the defined preset, the menu changes to [High Quality Print] (Modified).

## 6. Review the Compression options.

The Compression options determine what data will be included in the PDF file. If you're creating a file for commercial print, resolution is more important than file size. If your goal is a PDF for use on the web, file size and image quality are equally important.

**Note:**

*Since you chose the High Quality Print preset, these options default to settings that will produce the best results for most commercial printing applications.*

**Note:**

*The Output options relate to color management and PDF/X settings. Ask your output provider if you need to change anything for those options.*

You can define a specific compression scheme for color, grayscale, and monochrome images. Different options are available, depending on the image type:

- ZIP compression is lossless, which means all file data is maintained in the compressed file.

- JPEG compression options are lossy, which means data is discarded to create a smaller file. When you use one of the JPEG options, you can also define an Image Quality option (from Low to Maximum).

## 7. Click Save PDF. When the process is finished, close the Photoshop file.

## 8. Read the resulting error message, then click Don't Save.

When you save a file as a PDF, the resulting PDF is the one that is open in the document window. The PDF format does not store all editable Photoshop information, so you are warned to save a native Photoshop file if you want to maintain full editability. Because you saved the finished Photoshop file at the end of the previous exercise, you can safely close the file.

1. The _____ command can be used to share color swatches between Photoshop and other Adobe applications.

2. The _____ tool is used to fill areas with a solid color or pattern by clicking the area you want to fill.

3. _____ is the percentage of a brush's diameter that is completely opaque.

4. The _____ option can be used to help prevent jags on a brush stroke that result from slight jumps of a mouse cursor or stylus.

5. The _____ brush mode option is useful for filling gaps left by other painting methods.

6. The _____ removes pixels from an image, while attempting to maintain edges of an object in the foreground.

7. The _____ can be used to restore specific areas of an image to a previous state.

8. The _____ tool is similar to the Brush tool, but can only create hard edges.

9. The _____ tool is used to paint with patterns, by either painting a stroke of the pattern or revealing more of the solid pattern with each brush stroke.

10. _____ store specific settings for a specific tool; they can be accessed in the menu on the left end of the Options bar.

1. Briefly explain the difference between the Size, Hardness, and Flow settings when using the Brush tool.

2. Briefly explain how layers made it easier to complete this complex project.

3. Briefly explain three advantages of the PDF file format.

Use what you have learned in this project to complete the following freeform exercise.
Carefully read the art director and client comments, then create your own design to meet the needs of the project.
Use the space below to sketch ideas. When finished, write a brief explanation of the reasoning behind your final design.

**art director comments**

As part of the annual International Classic Surfing Competition, the Honolulu Marketing Group (a major event sponsor) is holding a surfboard decoration contest.

To complete this project, you should:

❏ Use the file **surfboard.psd** in the **Boards_PS22_PB.zip** archive (in your student resources) as the basis for your work.

❏ Create a custom digital painting to decorate the surfboard shape.

❏ If necessary, rotate the surfboard canvas to paint your design vertically.

**client comments**

This year is the 30th anniversary of the Classic, and we're planning a contest for people to submit personal, custom surfboard designs.

In addition to people who will paint actual surfboards and send photos, we're allowing people to create virtual entries using the surfboard vector shape in the provided file.

There isn't really a theme, but we will divide the entries into several groups: fantasy, graffiti-style, abstract, and realistic. The winner of each category will receive a $250 gift certificate from the ATC Board Company, and be entered in the best-of-show judging round.

The best-of-show winner will receive an all-expenses-paid trip for two to Honolulu to attend the International Classic, as well as a custom surfboard, handpainted with the winning design.

**project justification**

Drawing and painting from scratch requires some degree of creativity and natural artistic talent; however, learning the technical aspects of drawing and painting will help you as you complete many different types of projects — and might even help you develop and refine natural artistic skills.

Creating original artwork in Photoshop — including artwork that starts as a black-and-white pen sketch — can be a time-consuming, and sometimes, repetitive process. If you learn how to use the painting and drawing tools, you will have an advantage when you need to create something unique. Mastering these skills also gives you a competitive edge because few people take the time to learn the intricacies of creating original digital artwork.

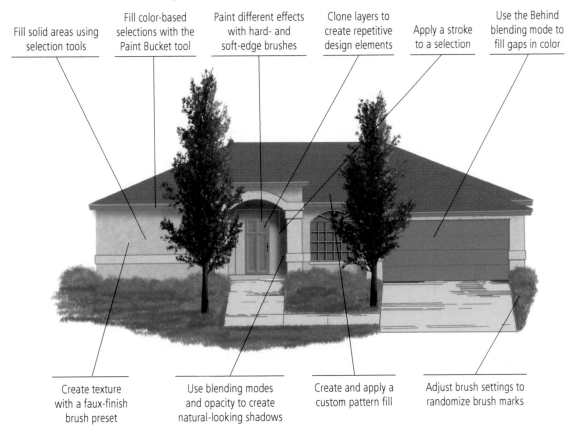

Fill solid areas using selection tools

Fill color-based selections with the Paint Bucket tool

Paint different effects with hard- and soft-edge brushes

Clone layers to create repetitive design elements

Apply a stroke to a selection

Use the Behind blending mode to fill gaps in color

Create texture with a faux-finish brush preset

Use blending modes and opacity to create natural-looking shadows

Create and apply a custom pattern fill

Adjust brush settings to randomize brush marks

# 8

# Web Page Design

Your client is a costume designer who is launching a new online presence to grow her business. Your job is to take the first draft, and apply a number of finishing touches to add visual appeal to the overall site. You must then generate the required pieces that will be used by a web developer to create the functioning HTML.

This project incorporates the following skills:

❑ Using actions and batches to automate repetitive processes and improve productivity

❑ Adding depth and visual interest with puppet warping

❑ Generating image assets from Photoshop layers and layer groups, as required by the HTML developer

❑ Communicating design intent using cascading style sheets

## Videos to Watch

Access these helpful videos in your online student resources:

▶▶ Web Page Design
Project Introduction

▶▶ Creating Frames

▶▶ Applying a Puppet Warp

My business model has largely been word-of-mouth until now, but I've finally decided to take the next step and formalize a plan with all the requisite professional elements.

I'm naming my new company, "Silk Road Costume Design." I have very little for you to work with, other than photos of the work I've done in the past. Those are really the best way to communicate what I do, so I want them to be included in a digital slideshow somewhere on the new website.

I don't want a lot of text, especially not on the site's Welcome page — probably just a heading and one or two short paragraphs. I haven't written the text yet, so can you just use some nonsense text to come up with a design?

▶ **Watch the video** Web Page Design Project Introduction **in your online student resources.**

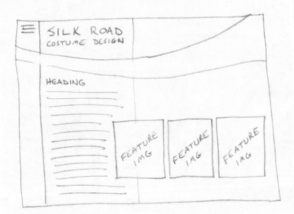

First, the web designer tells me that the images for the slideshow should be optimized to no more than 1,000 pixels high. Since there are so many of them (and likely to be more, over time), you should develop an action to resize the images automatically, without having to manually open each one.

The client liked the initial Welcome page comp, but I think there is some room for improvement.

Although we only spec'd space for one image, the client selected three that she wants to feature on the Welcome page. You'll need to break up the defined space to fit the three feature images.

Finally, the silk pattern is too straight. Try warping it to create more of a "flowing cloth" feel, and to help break up the overall blockiness of the page.

To complete this project, you will:

❏ Save an action set

❏ Create a new action

❏ Batch-process files

❏ Use frames to define image position and size

❏ Use Puppet Warp to transform a layer

❏ Generate image assets from layers

❏ Copy CSS for text layers

❏ Create alternate layers with artboards

# STAGE 1 / Automating Repetitive Tasks

**Actions** are some of the most powerful (yet underused) productivity tools in Photoshop. In the simplest terms, actions are miniature programs that run a sequence of commands on a particular image or selected area. An action can initiate most of the commands available in Photoshop — alone or in sequence — to automate repetitive, and potentially time-consuming tasks.

Running an action is a fairly simple process: highlight the appropriate action in the Actions panel, and then click the Play button at the bottom of the panel. Some actions work on an entire image, while others require some initial selection. If you use the actions that shipped with the Photoshop application, the action name tells you (in parentheses) what type of element the action was designed to affect. In most cases, however, you can run an action on other elements without a problem.

## The Actions Panel in Depth

The default **Actions panel** (Window> Actions) shows the Default Actions set, which contains several pre-built actions. A folder icon indicates an **action set**, which is used to create logical groupings of actions. You can expand an action set to show the actions contained within that set, and you can expand a specific action to show the steps that are saved in that action. Any step in an action marked with an arrow can be further expanded to see the details of that step.

The left column of the Actions panel shows a check mark next to each action set, individual action, and step within an expanded action. All elements of prerecorded actions are active by default, which means that playing an action initiates each step within that action. You can deactivate specific steps of an action by clicking the related check mark. If the check mark next to an action is black, all elements of that action are active. If the check mark is red, one or more steps of that action are inactive.

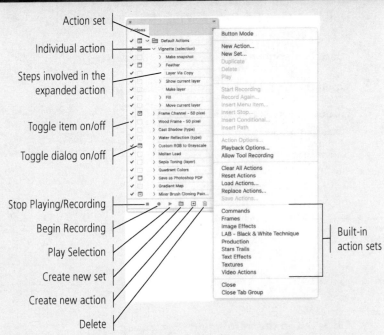

### Modal Controls

The second column in the Actions panel controls the degree of user interaction required when running an action. If an icon appears in this column, the Photoshop dialog box relevant to that step opens when the action runs. These are called **modal controls**; the action pauses until you take some required action. You can deactivate modal controls by clicking the dialog box icon for an entire action set, a specific action, or a single step within an action.

If the modal controls are turned off, Photoshop applies the values that were used when the action was recorded. This increases the automatic functionality of the action, but also offers less control over the action's behavior.

Some actions require a certain degree of user interaction, in which case modal controls can't be entirely deactivated. In this case, the dialog box icon appears grayed out in the panel, even when the remaining modal controls are turned off. If an action shows a black dialog box icon, all modal controls within that action are active. If an action shows a red dialog box icon, one or more modal controls within that action have been turned off.

### Button Mode

Choosing Button Mode at the top of the panel Options menu makes running an action one step easier. Each action is represented as a colored button, which you can simply click to run the action.

## Save an Action Set

Whenever you need to perform the same task more than twice, it's a good idea to automate as much of the process as possible. This project requires you to create thumbnails from a number of images, which requires multiple steps. Rather than performing each step for each image, you can streamline the process using an action, which you have to record only once.

**Note:**

*It's important to remember when creating actions that, "just because you can, doesn't mean you should." There are many powerful tools in Photoshop that require human judgment and intervention if they are to be effective. Color correction, for example, is different for every image, and should never be left entirely to a computer to implement.*

1. **Expand the Silk_PS22_RF.zip archive in your WIP folder (Macintosh) or copy the archive contents into your WIP folder (Windows).**

   This results in a folder named **Silk**, which contains all of the files you need for this project. You should also use this folder to save the files you create in this project.

2. **In Photoshop with no file open, click the Photoshop icon in the top-left corner of the Home screen.**

   Clicking this icon enters into the Photoshop workspace so you can access the various panels, even when no file is open.

Click this icon to enter the Photoshop workspace.

3. **Open the Actions panel (Window>Actions).**

4. **Choose Clear All Actions from the Actions panel Options menu.**

   Rather than editing an existing action set, you are going to create your own action set to store the action you define. If you did not clear the existing actions, the set you define would include all of the default actions, as well as the one you create.

**Note:**

*You can add actions to the Actions panel by choosing a defined set, or by choosing **Load Actions** in the panel Options menu.*

***Reset Actions** restores the default set to the Actions panel. You have the option to replace the existing actions, or append the default set to the current sets.*

***Replace Actions** replaces the current action sets with the set you load in the resulting dialog box.*

5. **Click OK in the warning message dialog box.**

   **Clear All Actions** removes everything from the Actions panel. You can also remove a specific action or set from the panel by highlighting the item in the panel, and then clicking the Delete button, or by choosing Delete from the Actions

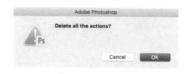

   panel Options menu. These commands remove the actions or sets from the panel, but they do not permanently delete saved actions or sets. If you delete an action from one of the built-in sets, you can reload the set to restore all items that originally existed in the set.

6. **Click the Create New Set button at the bottom of the Actions panel.**

7. **In the New Set dialog box, name the new set Portfolio Actions, and then click OK.**

You can name the set whatever you prefer, but it should indicate what the set contains, whether it's a set of actions for a specific type of project, for a specific client, or any other logical group.

Create New Set

8. **Continue to the next exercise.**

 Create a New Action

Recording an action is a fairly simple process: open a file, click the Record button in the Actions panel, and then perform the steps you want to save in the action. Click the Stop button to stop recording. If you stop recording, you can later select the last step in the existing action, and start recording again by clicking the Record button.

1. **In Photoshop, open culture1.jpg from your WIP>Silk>costumes folder.**

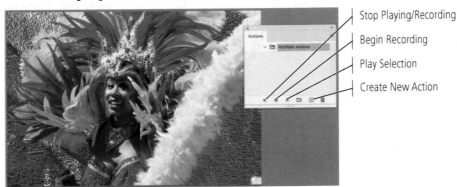

Stop Playing/Recording

Begin Recording

Play Selection

Create New Action

*Note:*

*You can change the name, keyboard shortcut, and/or button color of any action by selecting it in the Actions panel, and then choosing Action Options from the panel Options menu.*

2. **Open the Actions panel if necessary, and click the Create New Action button at the bottom of the panel.**

3. **In the New Action dialog box, type Optimize For Slides in the Name field.**

By default, new actions are added to the currently selected set. You can add the action to any open set by choosing from the Set menu. The Function Key menu allows you to assign a keyboard shortcut to the action, so, for example, an "F" key (with or without modifiers) can initiate that action. The Color menu defines the color of the button when the Actions panel is viewed in Button mode.

*Note:*

*As with any user-defined element, you should use descriptive names for your actions.*

4. **Click Record to close the dialog box.**

In the Actions panel, the Record button automatically becomes red, indicating that you are now recording. Anything you do from this point forward is recorded as a step in the action until you intentionally stop the recording by clicking the Stop button at the bottom of the Actions panel.

The red button indicates that the action is currently being recorded.

5. **With culture1.jpg open, choose Image>Image Size.**

6. **Make sure the Resample option is checked.**

   You want the slides to be proportionally sized, and you want them to remain at 72 ppi.

7. **With the Constrain Aspect Ratio option active, choose Pixels in the Height Units menu, and then change the Pixel Dimensions height to 1000 pixels.**

   Because the Resample option is active, reducing the number of pixels results in a proportionally smaller document size.

Make sure the Resample option is checked. | Change this value to 1000 pixels. | The image's physical dimensions are reduced proprtionally.

8. **Click OK to close the Image Size dialog box and apply the change.**

9. **In the Actions panel, click the Stop Playing/Recording button.**

10. **Expand the Image Size item in the Optimize for Slides action.**

The things you did in Steps 5–8 are included in the action.

11. **Click Portfolio Actions in the Actions panel to select the set, and then choose Save Actions in the panel Options menu.**

   If you make changes to a set — whether you delete an existing action from the set or add your own custom actions — without saving the altered set, you will have to repeat your work the next time you launch Photoshop.

**12. In the resulting dialog box, navigate to your WIP>Silk folder as the target location.**

The dialog box defaults to the application's Presets>Actions folder. If you are using a shared computer, you might not be able to save files in the application's default location. Saving the file directly to your WIP folder makes it readily available whenever you need it.

**13. Leave the Save As field at the default value, then click Save.**

The default file name is the same as the set name that you defined when you created the set. The extension (.atn) is automatically added for you.

**14. Close the culture1.jpg file without saving.**

You don't need to save the changes, as this file will be processed when you run the action on the entire images folder.

**15. Continue to the next exercise.**

 Batch-Process Files

The ability to batch-process files further enhances and automates productivity. If you have a large group of files that all require the same adjustments, you can build an action, set up a batch, and go to lunch (or, depending on your computer processor and number of files, go home for the night).

For example, when we write the Portfolio books, we take screen shots in RGB mode at 100%. Before the books are laid out for print production, the screen captures are converted to the U.S. Web Coated (SWOP) v2 CMYK profile, and resized (not resampled) to 40%. As you have probably noticed, there are a lot of screen captures in these books. Rather than sitting for several days and modifying each file (or even sitting for one full day and running an action on each file), we set up a batch that converts all screen captures for an entire book in about 25 minutes.

**1. In Photoshop, choose File>Automate>Batch.**

At the top of the Batch dialog box, the Set and Action menus default to the active selection in the Actions panel. In this case, there is only one available choice, so the Optimize for Slides action is already selected. You can choose to run a batch for any action in any open set.

## Action Stops

When you record actions, you can insert an intentional pause by choosing **Insert Stop** from the Actions panel Options menu. When you insert a stop, the Record Stop dialog box allows you to type a message — for example, specific instructions or reminders to the user — that displays when the action runs.

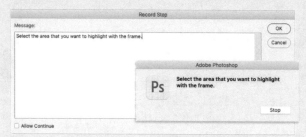

When a user runs the action and the action reaches a stop, the message you entered into the Record Stop dialog box appears. The user must click Stop, perform the required step, and then click the Play button in the Actions panel to complete the rest of the action. If you check the Allow Continue option when you define the Stop, the resulting message includes a Continue button; if the user clicks Continue, the action resumes.

## Menu Items

You can cause an action to open a specific dialog box or execute a menu command by choosing **Insert Menu Item** from the Actions panel Options menu. When the Insert Menu Item dialog box appears, you can make a selection from the application menus, and then click OK. When a user runs the action, the specified dialog box opens or the menu command executes.

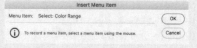

When you insert a menu item that opens a dialog box (such as, Select>Color Range), you are adding a modal command that can't be turned off. When a user runs the action, even with modal commands turned off, the dialog box opens and requires user interaction. Although an action can automate many steps in a repetitive process, there are still some things that can't be entirely automatic.

## Conditional Actions

You can also define steps in an action that occur if a specific condition is met by choosing **Insert Conditional** from the Actions panel Options menu. In the Conditional Actions dialog box:

- If Current defines the condition that will be evaluated. You can choose from the available list conditions.

- Then Play Action menu defines what will occur if the condition is true. You can choose any action that exists in the same set as the action you are recording.

- Else Play Action defines what happens if the condition is *not* true. You can choose any action that exists in the same set as the action you are recording.

2. **Choose Folder in the Source menu.**

The Source menu allows you to choose which files are batched:

- **Folder** processes a complete group of images arranged within a single folder on your computer.

- **Import** acquires and processes a group of images from a scanner or digital camera.

- **Open Files** processes all files currently open in the application.

- **File Browser** processes files selected in the File Browser.

When Folder is selected, you can also choose to override "Open" commands that are recorded in the selected action, include subfolders within the selected folder, and suppress color profile warnings for the files being processed.

3. **Click the Choose button and navigate to the WIP>Silk>costumes folder. Click Choose/Select Folder to return to the Batch dialog box.**

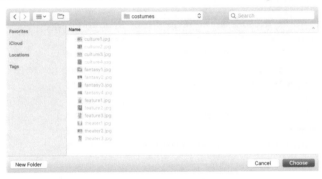

4. **Make sure the Suppress Color Profile Warnings option is checked to prevent the batch from stopping if color management policies are violated.**

This is a matter of some debate, but when processing images for the web, color management is not considered as critical as it is for print.

5. **Choose Folder in the Destination menu.**

The Destination menu in the Batch dialog box presents three options:

- **None** simply means that the action will run. If the action saves and closes the files, those commands will be completed. If the action does not save and close the files, you might end up with a large number of open files and, eventually, crash your computer.

- **Save and Close** saves the modified file in the same location with the same name, overwriting the original file.

- **Folder** allows you to specify a target folder for the files after they have been processed. This option is particularly useful because it saves the processed files as copies of the originals in the defined folder; the original files remain intact.

6. **Click the Choose button (in the Destination area), navigate to the WIP>Silk>slides folder, and click Choose/Select Folder.**

7. **In the File Naming area, open the menu for the first field and choose document name (lowercase) from the menu.**

The File Naming fields, available when Folder is selected in the Destination menu, allow you to redefine file names for the modified files. You can choose a variable from the pop-up menu, type specific text in a field, or use a combination of both. The example in the File Naming area shows the result of your choices in these menus.

8. **In the second field (below "document name"), type -slide.**

This identifies the images as the versions for the slideshow, differentiating them from the full-size images with the same names.

9. **Choose extension (lowercase) from the menu for the third field.**

10. **Click OK to run the batch.**

When the process is complete, you will have 14 images in your WIP>Silk>slides folder.

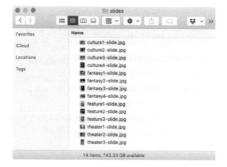

11. **Continue to the next stage of the project.**

*Note:*

*You can create a **droplet**, which allows you to run an action using a basic drag-and-drop technique (as long as Photoshop is running). The Create Droplet dialog box (File>Automate>Create Droplet) presents most of the same options as the Batch dialog box, with a few exceptions. Clicking Choose at the top of the dialog box allows you to define the name of the droplet and the location in which to save it. The dialog box does not include Source options because the source is defined when you drag files onto the droplet.*

Optimize Slides

*Note:*

*The Errors section of the Batch dialog box determines what happens if an error occurs during a batch. **Stop for Errors** (the default setting) interrupts the batch and displays a warning dialog box. **Log Errors to File** batch-processes every file and saves a record of all problems.*

# STAGE 2 / Editing Layers for Visual Effect

At the meeting, your art director defined three tasks that need to be completed in the client's Welcome page design. Photoshop offers a number of tools for manipulating layers, from simple transformations to liquifying pixels. If you completed the other projects in this book, you have already used many of these techniques to fulfill specific project goals. In this stage of the project, you use three more options for managing and transforming layer content to achieve effects that can't easily be created with other methods.

##  Use Frames to Place Images

The Frame tool offers another option for defining the visible area of a placed image. If you have used a page-layout application such as Adobe InDesign, you should be familiar with the concept of frames.

In this exercise, you will create frames to present three images that the client wants to feature on her site's Welcome page. Rather than simply placing the feature images into the layout, you will use frames to define the image areas, so that you can more easily change the images inside the frames without affecting the actual frames that define the location for those images.

*Watch the video **Creating Frames in Photoshop** in your online student resources.*

1. **Open the file silk-road.psd from your WIP>Silk folder.**

2. **Make sure rulers are visible (View>Rulers).**

3. **Control/right-click the horizontal ruler at the top of the document window and make sure Pixels is checked as the unit of measurement.**

4. **In the Layers panel, click to select the Menu Icon layer. With that layer selected, Command/Control-click to select the other four pixel-based (non-type) layers:**

   **SILK ROAD       Silk       Text Background       Background Image**

5. **With all five layers selected, click the Lock All button at the top of the Layers panel.**

   When you draw a new frame, it automatically applies to the topmost pixel-based layer in the file. Because you don't want the new frame to affect the existing layers, you are locking those layers to prevent them from becoming attached to the frame.

   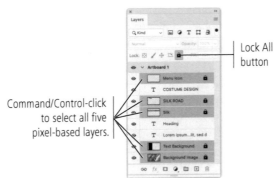

   Lock All button

   Command/Control-click to select all five pixel-based layers.

6. **Choose the Frame tool in the Tools panel. In the Options bar, make sure the Rectangle option is selected.**

   When the Frame tool is active, you can use the Options bar to determine whether you are creating a rectangle or ellipse frame.

*Note:*

*If you don't see the Frame tool in the main Tools panel, check in the Edit Toolbar menu ··· at the bottom of the Tools panel.*

7. **Click at the top-left corner where the ruler guides meet, and drag down and right to the bottom-right intersection of the ruler guides.**

   If you don't see the page guides, choose View>Show>Guides.

   Clicking and dragging creates the selected frame shape. A new layer for the frame shape is added to the Layers panel.

Create a new rectangular frame.  Create a new elliptical frame.

Frame tool

Create the frame in the area defined by the ruler guides.

Empty frames show crossed diagonal lines.

The new Frame layer is created above the highest last-selected layer.

8. **In the Properties panel, open the Inset Image menu and choose Place from Local Disk - Embedded.**

   You can use this menu to place an image directly from the Adobe Stock library, from an open CC Library file, or from your local drive as an Embedded or Linked Smart object. You can also drag images into a frame from the Libraries panel or from a Finder window.

   You can also create a frame from an existing layer. For vector-based layers, Control/right-click the layer name and choose Convert to Frame. For regular layers, choose Frame from Layers in the contextual menu; in this case, you can define the new frame name, as well as change the frame dimensions away from the existing frame content.

*Note:*

*If you place a file that includes layer comps, you can use the Properties panel to determine which comp should be used in the frame.*

9. **In the resulting dialog box, navigate to the file feature1.jpg in the WIP>Silk>costumes folder and click Place.**

After you define the image to inset into a frame, the frame layer shows two thumbnails — the actual frame on the left and the inset image on the right. Brackets surround the thumbnail of the active element. Be sure to check which is active before you make changes.

By default, the placed image is automatically scaled to fill the frame. Image areas outside the frame dimensions are hidden, but they are not permanently removed.

You can use the Properties panel to change the X and Y position of the image relative to the top-left corner of the canvas. Keep in mind, these values do not refer to the image's position within the containing frame.

The image in the frame is active.

The image is scaled to fill the frame.

Image areas outside the frame are not visible.

The light boundary shows the actual image dimensions.

10. **In the Layers panel, click the Frame thumbnail to select the actual frame, then review the Properties panel. Note the frame height.**

When the frame is selected and the Frame tool or Move tool is active, bounding-box handles surround the frame. You can drag those handles to change the frame size. You can also use the Properties panel to define the frame height, width, and position relative to the overall canvas.

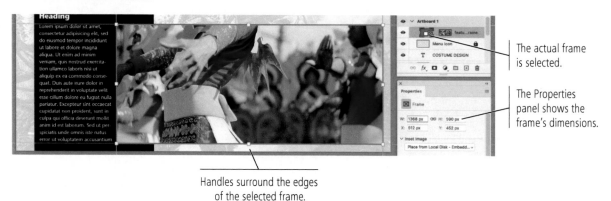

The actual frame is selected.

The Properties panel shows the frame's dimensions.

Handles surround the edges of the selected frame.

11. **In the Layers panel, click the placed image thumbnail to select the image inside the frame.**

12. **With the placed image selected in the Layers panel, press Command/Control-T to enter Free Transform mode.**

When the frame content is active, you can simply click and drag to change the visible portion of the placed image. You can also enter Free Transform mode to scale or otherwise transform the placed content.

13. **In the Options bar, make sure the Maintain Aspect Ratio option is active. Highlight the existing H field value and type 590 px, then press Return/Enter to finalize the change.**

The final result will probably be slightly different than 590 px after you press Return/Enter. This appears to be a minor bug in the software, but it should not affect the end result of your work in this project.

*Note:*

*You can use the Edit Contents button to open the Smart Object file, or use the Convert To Linked button to save the embedded file on your computer and link that content to that file as a linked Smart Object.*

Maintain Aspect Ratio should be active.

Change the image height to match the frame height.

The image in the frame is selected.

14. **In the Layers panel, click to select the containing frame.**

15. **Click the left-center handle and drag right until the frame edge meets the edge of the placed content.**

16. **Click the right-center handle and drag left until the frame edge meets the edge of the placed content.**

Drag the handles to match the size of the placed image.

The actual frame is again selected.

17. **In the Layers panel, click the name of the frame layer to select the entire layer (frame and content).**

18. **Click inside the frame boundaries and drag left until the frame snaps to the left ruler guide.**

    Because you selected the entire layer before dragging, both the frame and its contents move.

Click inside the frame boundary and drag to move the frame and its content.

The entire layer (frame and content) is selected.

19. **Using the Frame tool, click to the right of the existing frame and drag to create a second empty frame. Drag the frame's bounding-box handles to match the height of the space defined by the ruler guides.**

    You can't click inside an existing frame's boundaries to create a new frame.

20. Using the Properties panel, place the file **feature2.jpg** into the frame as an embedded image.

21. Repeat the process from Steps 10–16 to resize the placed content to fit the frame height, then adjust the frame to fit the resized content.

22. In the Layers panel, click the name of the frame layer to select the entire layer (frame and content). Click inside the frame area and drag left until the second frame meets the right edge of the first frame.

23. Repeat the frame-creation process to add a third frame with the image **feature3.jpg**. Scale this placed image to 590 px high, but do not adjust the width of the frame.

24. Position this frame so its right edge snaps to the right edge of the space defined by the ruler guides.

Align the third frame to the right ruler guide.

25. **In the Layers panel, Shift-click to select all three Frame layers.**

26. **Choose the Move tool. In the Options bar, click the Align Top Edges button and then click the Distribute Horizontally button.**

    Align and distribute buttons are available in the Options bar when the Move tool is active, and more than one layer is selected. The Align Top Edges button ensures that all three frames are exactly aligned (making up for any slight movement that occurred when you moved the frame layers). The Distribute Horizontally button places an equal amount of space between the content of selected layers.

    Align Top Edges      Distribute Horizontally

    All three frame layers are selected.

27. **Save the file, then continue to the next exercise.**

## Use Puppet Warp to Transform a Layer

Puppet Warp provides a way to transform and distort specific areas of a layer, without affecting other areas of the same layer. It is called "puppet" warp because it's based on the concept of pinning certain areas in place, and then bending other areas around those pin locations — mimicking the way a puppet's joints pivot. In this exercise, you use puppet warping to bend and distort the top Silk image layer.

*Watch the video* ***Applying a Puppet Warp in Photoshop*** *in your online student resources.*

1. **With silk-road.psd open, choose View>Show>Guides to hide page guides.**

   The guides are not necessary for this stage of the project; hiding them helps to minimize unnecessary elements on the screen.

2. **Unlock the Silk layer in the Layers panel.**

3. **Control/right-click the Silk layer in the Layers panel. Choose Convert to Smart Object from the contextual menu.**

   By first converting this layer to a Smart Object, you can apply the puppet warp non-destructively.

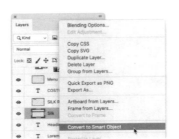

4. **With the Silk Smart Object layer selected in the Layers panel, choose Edit>Puppet Warp.**

   When you enter Puppet Warp mode, a mesh overlays the active layer content. This mesh represents the joints in the shape that can bend when you warp the layer content.

   This mesh shows the area that can be warped.

   The Silk layer is now a Smart Object layer.

5. **In the Options bar, make sure Show Mesh is checked. Choose Distort in the Mode menu and choose Fewer Points in the Density menu.**

   Choose the Distort mode.

   Choose Fewer Points.

6. **Click the mesh near the center of the Silk layer content to place an anchoring pin.**

   Clicking the mesh places a pin, which anchors the layer at that location.

7. **Click the top-right corner of the mesh and, without releasing the mouse button, drag up above the top edge of the image.**

   Clicking and dragging places a new pin, and rotates the image around the location of the existing pin. Because you have placed one other pin on the layer, the entire shape rotates around the first pin location.

   Clicking and dragging places a new pin, and rotates the layer around the existing pin.

   This is the pin you placed in Step 6.

8. **Click near the top-left corner of the Silk image and drag up to bend the layer content around the center pin.**

**Note:**

*Pressing Command/ Control-Z while working in Puppet Warp mode undoes the last action you performed inside the puppet warp mesh. You can only undo one action; after you finalize the warp, the Undo command undoes the entire warp — everything you did since you entered Puppet Warp mode.*

9. **Add another pin to the bottom-right corner of the layer. Drag the new point until the pin is just past the canvas edge (as shown here).**

10. **Click the center pin and drag left to change the distorted shape.**

Moving a pin changes the distortion shape because of the distance between various pins on the shape.

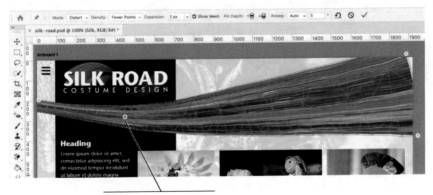

Moving a pin changes the overall shape distortion.

11. **Continue manipulating the filmstrip warp until you are satisfied with the result. Keep the following points in mind:**

- **Click to add new pins at any point in the process.**
- **Option/Alt-click an existing, selected pin to remove it from the mesh.**
- **Press Option/Alt to change the selected pin from an Auto rotation angle to a Fixed rotation angle.**
- **With a specific pin selected, press Option/Alt, click the rotation proxy, and drag to change the angle of that pin.**
- **Uncheck the Show Mesh option to get a better preview of your warp.**

Our solution is shown here.

*Note:*

*The Expansion option in the Options bar determines how far the mesh extends beyond the edge of the layer content.*

*Note:*

*If you warp a layer so that the mesh overlaps, you can use the Pin Depth buttons in the Options bar to show pins on underlying layers.*

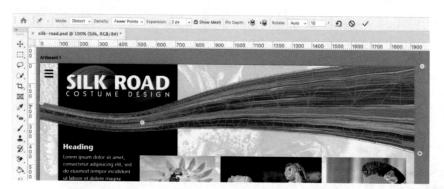

12. **Press Return/Enter to finalize the warp.**

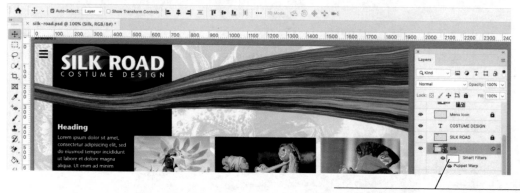

Because you converted the layer to a Smart Object, you can double-click the Puppet Warp effect to change the warp settings.

13. **Click the arrow button in the Layers panel to collapse the Smart Filters for the Silk layer.**

Click here to collapse the Smart Filters.

14. **Save the file, then continue to the next stage of the project.**

# STAGE 3 / Generating Web-Ready Assets

It is common practice to create the look and feel of a website in Photoshop, and then hand off the pieces for a programmer to assemble in a web design application, such as Adobe Dreamweaver. In this stage of the project, you complete a number of tasks to create the necessary pieces for the final website, including the different styles that will be used to properly format various elements in the resulting HTML page.

This site is a very simple example, using only a few elements to illustrate the process of properly mapping Photoshop objects to create the pieces that are necessary in an HTML page. We kept the site design basic to minimize the amount of repetition required to complete the project. The skills and concepts you complete in this project would apply equally to more complex sites.

##  Examine a Photoshop Artboard

Responsive design is a term used to describe how page layouts change based on the size of display being used to show a specific web page. This technique typically requires different settings for various elements (type size, alignment, etc.), and even different content that will — or will not — appear in different-size displays (for example, removing images from extra-small or phone display sizes).

Photoshop artboards are a special type of layer group that make it easier to manage content for multiple display sizes within a single Photoshop file. In this exercise, you are going to examine the artboard concept in the silk-road.psd file, which was designed specifically for large display sizes. In a later exercise, you will duplicate and modify the existing layout elements to create the required files for a different size display.

1. **With silk-road.psd open, unlock all layers in the Layers panel.**

2. **Choose the Artboard tool (nested under the Move tool).**

   If you don't see the Artboard tool, call and reset the Essentials workspace in the Workspace switcher. Some of the built-in workspaces, such as the 3D workspace, do not include the Artboard tool.

   When you create a new document using any of the Mobile or Web presets, the file automatically includes an Artboard that matches the defined canvas size.

   This layout was created using the Web Large preset in the New Document dialog box. When the Artboard tool is active, you can see the artboard size and orientation. If you change the size away from one of the built-in presets, or define a custom size when you create the file, the size menu shows "Custom," indicating that the artboard is no longer one of the predefined web or mobile sizes.

### 3. Review the Layers panel.

In the Layers panel, a special Artboard folder contains all the layers with content that appears, at least partially, within the artboard bounds.

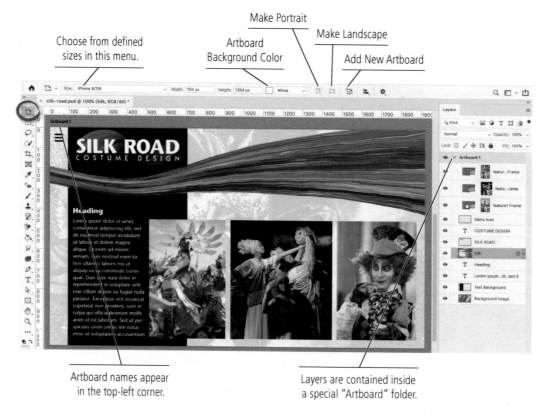

Choose from defined sizes in this menu.

Artboard Background Color

Make Portrait

Make Landscape

Add New Artboard

Artboard names appear in the top-left corner.

Layers are contained inside a special "Artboard" folder.

### 4. In the Layer panel, double-click the Artboard 1 name to highlight it. Type Web Large, then press Return/Enter to finalize the new artboard name.

Like other assets, meaningful artboard names are more useful than the default "Artboard 1."

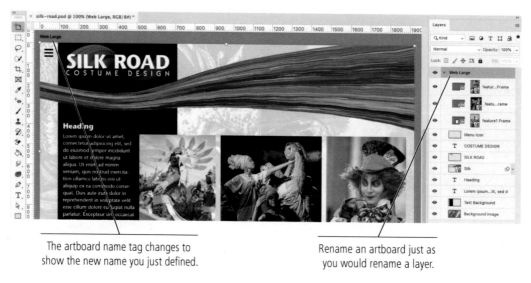

The artboard name tag changes to show the new name you just defined.

Rename an artboard just as you would rename a layer.

### 5. Save the file, then continue to the next exercise.

Generate Image Assets from Layers

Adobe Generator is a Photoshop plug-in that makes it easy to create the required web-ready assets from layers in any Photoshop file. Any transformations applied to layer content are processed and become a permanent part of the generated asset.

Three image formats are primarily used for digital delivery:

- **JPEG** (Joint Photographic Experts Group), which supports 24-bit color, is used primarily for continuous-tone images, with subtle changes in color, such as photographs or other images that are created in Adobe Photoshop. The JPEG format incorporates **lossy compression**, which means that pixels are thrown away in order to reduce file size. When areas of flat color are highly compressed, speckles of other colors (called artifacts) often appear, which negatively impacts the quality of the design.

- **GIF** (Graphics Interchange Format), which supports only 8-bit color and basic, on-or-off transparency, is best used for graphics with areas of solid color, such as logos or other basic illustrations. The GIF format uses **lossless compression** to reduce file size, while ensuring that no information is lost during the compression.

- **PNG** (Portable Network Graphics), which supports 8- and 24-bit color, as well as a special 32-bit format allowing support for various degrees of transparency, can be used for both illustrations and continuous-tone images. The PNG format uses lossless compression to create smaller file size without losing image data.

In this exercise, you will create the required assets for images that were manipulated or created directly in Adobe Photoshop. You do not need to export the three feature images. Those files already exist in the client's supplied files. Even though you scaled them into the Photoshop frames, the web developer who implements the site in HTML can use code to adjust the images to fit into the necessary spaces.

1. **With silk-road.psd open, open the Plugins pane of the Preferences dialog box.**

2. **Make sure the Enable Generator option is checked (active), then click OK.**

**3. Choose File>Generate>Image Assets to activate that option.**

If this menu item is already checked, simply move your mouse cursor away and click to close the menu.

**4. In the Layers panel, select both the COSTUME DESIGN and SILK ROAD layers. Click the Create a New Group button at the bottom of the Layers panel.**

You want the two layers to function together as a single logo in the web page, so you are grouping them together.

Create a New Group button

Selected layers are automatically placed in the new group.

**5. Double-click the new layer group name to select it. Type logotype.png as the new name, and then press Return/Enter.**

Renaming a layer group is the same process as renaming a layer.

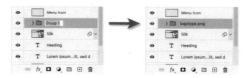

**6. On your desktop, open the WIP>Silk folder.**

Adobe Generator creates new web assets as soon as you define a layer name that includes an appropriate extension (.jpg, .gif, or .png). A new folder — silk-road-assets — has been added. The logotype.png file, which was generated as soon as you defined the layer group name, exists inside that folder.

**7. In Photoshop, double-click the Silk layer name to highlight it. Type silk-lg.png as the new layer name, and then press Return/Enter.**

You are using the "-lg" designation to differentiate this file from the one you will create for a smaller display in a later exercise.

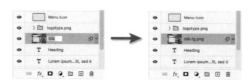

---

*Note:*

***Bit depth*** *refers to how many bits define the color value of a particular pixel. A* ***bit*** *is a unit of information that is either on or off (represented as 1 and 0, respectively). One bit has two states, or colors; eight bits have 256 possible colors (2×2×2×2×2×2×2=256); and 24 bits have 16,777,216 ($2^{24}$) possible colors.*

*In an RGB photograph, three color channels define how much of each primary color (red, green, and blue) makes up each pixel. Each channel requires 8 bits, resulting in a total of 24 bits for each pixel ("true color").*

*Note:*

*If you are using Adobe Dreamweaver to build a site's HTML files, you can use the Extract functionality inside of Dreamweaver to create the assets you need directly from native Photoshop layers. The Generator functionality is useful if the required assets will be needed in some other web design environment.*

8. **Repeat Step 7 for the following layers:**

| Layer | Rename as: |
|---|---|
| Menu Icon: | menu-icon.gif |
| Text Background: | text-bkg.jpg |
| Background Image: | body-bkg.jpg |

9. **On your desktop, review the contents of the silk-road-assets folder.**

*Note:*

*To disable image asset generation for the active file, deselect File>Generate>Image Assets.*

*To disable image asset generation for all Photoshop files, uncheck the Enable Generator option in the Plug-Ins pane of the Preferences dialog box.*

10. **In Photoshop, save silk-road.psd and then continue to the next exercise.**

## More about Adobe Generator

### Creating Multiple Files

You can also use Generator to create multiple files from a single layer by separating asset names with a comma in the Layers panel. For example, the layer name:

> menu-bar.jpg, menu-bar.png

creates two separate files in the metro-site-assets folder.

### Changing Asset Size Settings

You can also use layer names to define a specific size for the generated assets. Simply add the desired output size — relative or specific — as a prefix to the asset name. Remember to add a space character between the prefix and the asset name. For example:

> 200% menu-bar.jpg
>
> 10in x 2in logotype.png
>
> 50 x 25 menu-icon.gif

If you specify the size in pixels, you can omit the unit; other units must be included in the layer name prefix.

### Creating Asset Subfolders

If you want to create subfolders inside the main assets folder, simply include the subfolder name and a forward slash in the modified layer name. For example:

> thumbnails/bridge_small.jpg

### Changing Asset Quality Settings

You can use complex layer/layer group names to define different compression, quality, and size options in the generated assets. By default:

- JPG assets are generated at 90% quality.
- PNG assets are generated as 32-bit images.
- GIF assets are generated with basic alpha transparency.

While renaming layers or layer groups in preparation for asset generation, you can customize quality and size.

For JPEG files, you can define a different quality setting by appending a number to the end of the layer name, such as filename.jpg(1-10) or filename.jpg(1-100%). For example:

> menu-bar.jpg50%

creates a JPEG file with medium image quality.

For PNG files, you can change the output quality by appending the number 8, 24, or 32 to the layer name. For example:

> filmstrip.png24

creates a 24-bit PNG file, instead of the default 32-bit file.

# Copy CSS for Text Layers

You do not need to be a web programmer to design a site in Photoshop. However, to best take advantage of some of the tools that are available for moving your work into a functional HTML page, you should understand at least the basics of HTML:

- An HTML page contains code that defines the **elements** making up that page.

- Individual page elements are defined with **tags**. For example, a <div> tag identifies a division or area of the page, and a <p> tag identifies a paragraph. Available tags are defined by HTML; you can't simply make them up.

- Specific elements can be identified with user-defined classes, which helps to differentiate them from other same-type elements. For example:

    **<div class="feature-image">**

- Cascading Style Sheets (CSS) are used to define the properties of HTML elements. CSS files define **selectors**, which contain **property:value pairs** to control the appearance of specific elements in an HTML page. For example:

    **header {**
        **width: 780px;**
    **}**

- Two types of CSS selectors are relevant to site design in Photoshop:

    - **Tag selectors** define the appearance of HTML tags. These selectors simply use the tag name as the selector name; for example, the **div** selector defines the appearance of all **<div>** tags.

    - **Class selectors** define the appearance of any tag that is identified with the defined class. These selector names always begin with a period. For example, the **.text-area** selector would apply to any element that has the **class="text-area"** attribute.

In this exercise, you will use Photoshop to create CSS classes, which the web designer can apply to various page elements, so that your design choices are maintained in the final HTML page.

1. **With silk-road.psd open in Photoshop, change the Heading type layer name to h1-lg.**

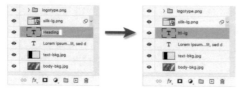

2. **Control/right-click the h1-lg type layer and choose Copy CSS from the contextual menu.**

3. **Using any text-editing application, open the file type-styles.css from the WIP>Silk folder.**

We use TextEdit on a Macintosh in our screen captures, but you can use any text editor to complete the following steps.

4. **Place the insertion point on the first empty line at the end of the file, then press Command/Control-V to paste the CSS that was copied in Step 2.**

All CSS copied from Photoshop is created as a class. The selector name, beginning with a period, is taken from the relevant Photoshop layer.

These lines are included in the original file.

These lines create a new class selector based on the settings applied to the h1-lg type layer in the Photoshop file.

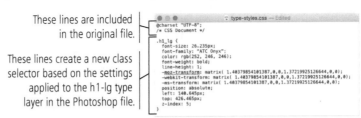

5. **Repeat Steps 1–4 to rename the remaining type layer ("Lorem...") as body-copy-lg in the Photoshop file. Add the required CSS for that layer to the type-styles.css file.**

6. **Save type-styles.css, then close it.**

7. **In Photoshop, collapse the Web Large artboard in the Layers panel.**

8. **Save the file, then continue to the next exercise.**

## Creating Image Slices

Although the **Slice tool** was intended to cut apart pieces of a web page comp for reassembly in a web design application, it can be used for any situation in which you need to cut a single image into multiple bits.

In addition to creating image assets from layers and layer groups, you can also create image slices. All visible layers in the slice area are included in the resulting images.

Photoshop offers a number of options for creating slices:

- Manually draw a slice area with the Slice tool.
- When the Slice tool is active, click Slices from Guides in the Options bar to automatically slice the file based on existing ruler guides.
- When the Slice Select tool is active and a specific slice is selected in the file, click Divide in the Options bar to divide the slice horizontally or vertically into a specific number of equal-size slices.
- Create a new slice based on specific layer content by selecting one or more layers in the Layers panel, and then choosing Layer>New Layer Based Slice.

Once slices are created, you can double-click to select a specific slice with the Slice Selection tool to edit its settings. In the resulting dialog box:

- Name is the file name of the image that is created from the slice.
- URL is the file that opens if a user clicks the slice.
- Target is the location where the URL opens when a user clicks the slice.
- Message Text appears in the browser's status bar.
- Alt Tag appears if image display is disabled.

URL, Target, and Message are better handled in a web design application such as Adobe Dreamweaver.

Dimensions fields are automatically filled with the size of the selected slice. You can also change the slice background type and color if the slice contains areas of transparency.

## Copy and Edit Artboard Sizes

As we explained earlier, a Photoshop artboard is basically a way of organizing and managing layers so you can create more than one layout in the same Photoshop file. In this exercise, you are going to create a second artboard to manage the elements you need for an iPhone display.

1. **With silk-road.psd open, make sure the Web Large artboard is selected in the Layers panel and then activate the Artboard tool in the Tools panel.**

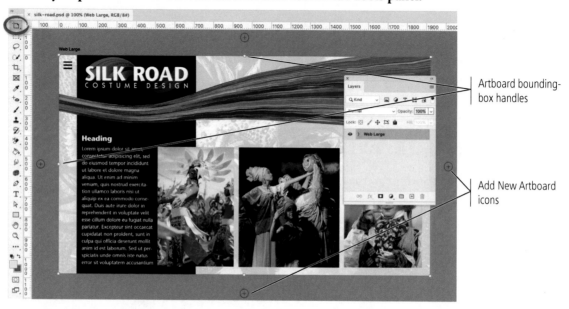

Artboard bounding-box handles

Add New Artboard icons

2. **Option/Alt-click the Add New Artboard icon to the right of the existing artboard.**

When the Artboard tool is active, the Add New Artboard icons appear on all four sides of the active artboard. Clicking one of these icons adds a new, blank artboard adjacent to the existing one (the new artboard appears on the same side as the icon you click).

If you Option/Alt-click one of the icons, the new artboard is a duplicate of the existing one, including all the layers that existed on the previous artboard.

3. **In the Layers panel, expand the Web Large copy artboard.**

Layers on the original artboard are duplicated in the new artboard.

4. **In the Layers panel, change the name of the Web Large copy artboard to iPhone V.**

Renaming artboards uses the same process as renaming layers and layer groups — double-click the existing name in the Layers panel, and then type the new name.

5. **With the iPhone V artboard active, choose iPhone 8/7/6 in the Options bar Size menu. Click the Make Portrait button to change the artboard orientation.**

When you change the size of an artboard, any layers that no longer have content within the bounds of the artboard are automatically moved outside the artboard group in the Layers panel.

Make Portrait    Make Landscape

The new artboard size is reflected in the document window.

Layers that don't touch the artboard are moved out of the group in the Layers panel.

Artboard size changes can affect which layers are part of the artboard group.

6. **Save the file and continue to the next exercise.**

Adjust Content for the Alternate Display Size

As you might have already guessed, the different sizes and orientations of various displays mean you will often have to define different content positions, sizes, and settings for different displays. In this exercise, you will make several necessary adjustments to the elements in the vertical iPhone layout.

1. **With silk-road.psd open, click to select the feature2 Frame layer in the Layers panel. Press the Shift key and click the feature3 Frame layer in the panel to select both layers.**

2. **With both layers selected, click the panel's Delete button. Click Yes to confirm the deletion.**

   On a small display size, such as an iPhone, it is common to use fewer images on a page than on a larger physical display. In this case, you will include only a single feature image on the vertical iPhone layout, instead of the row of three that is more appropriate in the large, horizontal display size.

3. **In the Layers panel, rename the silk-lg.png file in the iPhone V artboard as silk-iphone.png.**

   When you use Generator to export image assets, only the visible portion of the layer is included in the exported image (the resulting image is cropped at the artboard edges).

   In this case, the right half of the puppet-warped layer will not be part of the exported file. If you transformed the layer to fit entirely in horizontal space, it would be much smaller and might lose some of the effect. The left half of the layer that is currently visible in the iPhone V artboard still creates the desired "flowing silk" appearance, so it is sufficient to meet the visual needs of the project.

   The exported asset includes only what you see in the artboard bounds.

4. **Using the Horizontal Type tool, click to place the insertion point in the body-copy-lg type layer. Adjust the bottom-right type area handle until the cursor feedback shows W: 570 px, H: 250 px.**

Place the insertion point in the type area to access its bounding-box handles.

Drag the bottom-right handle until the area's dimensions are W: 570 px, H: 250 px.

*Note:*

*You might need to zoom in to adjust the frame to the correct size.*

5. **Activate the Move tool in the Tools panel. Turn off the Auto Select option in the Options bar.**

6. **In the Layers panel, click to select the feature1 Frame layer.**

Make sure you click the layer name to select the entire layer, instead of only the frame or only the contents.

7. **Using the Move tool, move the selected layer below the adjusted type area (as shown in the following image).**

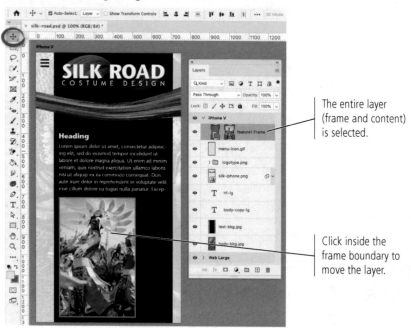

The entire layer (frame and content) is selected.

Click inside the frame boundary to move the layer.

8. **Press Command/Control-T to enter Free Transform mode. With the Maintain Aspect Ratio option active in the Options bar, click the bottom-right handle and drag down until only a small amount of the black background shows to the right of the frame.**

Because the entire layer is selected, you are transforming both the frame and the frame's contents.

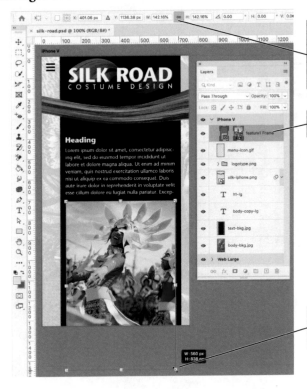

When Maintain Aspect Ratio is active, you don't need to press the Shift key to transform the layer proportionally.

The entire layer is still selected.

Free Transform mode scales the frame and its content.

9. **In the Layers panel, click to select only the frame on the layer you just transformed. Click the bottom-center bounding-box handle of the frame and drag up until a small area of the black background is visible below the frame.**

*Note:*

*You do not need to generate the image for this frame because it will be placed and scaled in the web page code.*

Remember, when the actual frame is selected in the Layers panel, the frame's bounding-box handles automatically appear in the document window if the Frame or Move tool is active.

Select only the frame to change its dimensions.

Drag the handle to change the frame's height.

10. **Click the body-copy-lg layer name to select the layer.**

11. **Using the Character or Properties panel, define a 32 pt font size with 44 pt leading.**

    Remember: When the layer is selected and the insertion point is not placed, changing type settings affects all text on the selected layer.

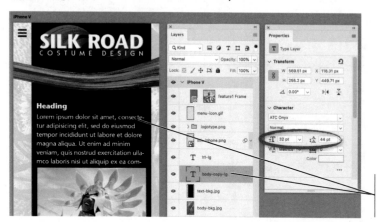

Formatting changes affect all type on the active type layer.

12. **In the Layers panel, change the body-copy-lg layer name to body-copy-iphone.**

13. **Control/right-click the body-copy-iphone layer and choose Copy CSS in the contextual menu.**

14. **If necessary, open type-styles.css (from your WIP>Silk folder) in a text-editing application.**

15. **Place the insertion point at the end of the existing copy and press Command/Control-V to paste the CSS from Step 13.**

```
type-styles.css — Edited
@charset "UTF-8";
/* CSS Document */

.h1_lg {
    font-size: 26.235px;
    font-family: "ATC Onyx";
    color: rgb(252, 246, 246);
    font-weight: bold;
    line-height: 1;
    -moz-transform: matrix( 1.40379854101387,0,0,1.37219925126644,0,0);
    -webkit-transform: matrix( 1.40379854101387,0,0,1.37219925126644,0,0);
    -ms-transform: matrix( 1.40379854101387,0,0,1.37219925126644,0,0);
    position: absolute;
    left: 140.645px;
    top: 426.465px;
    z-index: 5;
}

.body_copy_lg {
    font-size: 18.219px;
    font-family: "ATC Onyx";
    color: rgb(252, 246, 246);
    line-height: 1.4;
    -moz-transform: matrix( 1.40379854101387,0,0,1.37219925126644,0,0);
    -webkit-transform: matrix( 1.40379854101387,0,0,1.37219925126644,0,0);
    -ms-transform: matrix( 1.40379854101387,0,0,1.37219925126644,0,0);
    position: absolute;
    left: 171.969px;
    top: 555.969px;
    width: 263.911px;
    height: 426.979px;
    z-index: 4;
}

.body_copy_iphone {
    font-size: 23.32px;
    font-family: "ATC Onyx";
    color: rgb(252, 246, 246);
    line-height: 1.375;
    -moz-transform: matrix( 1.40379854101387,0,0,1.37219925126644,0,0);
    -webkit-transform: matrix( 1.40379854101387,0,0,1.37219925126644,0,0);
    -ms-transform: matrix( 1.40379854101387,0,0,1.37219925126644,0,0);
    position: absolute;
    left: 2218.149px;
    top: 517.079px;
    width: 394.579px;
    height: 184.201px;
    z-index: 25;
}
```

16. Repeat Steps 10–15 to change the font size on the **h1-lg** layer to **48 pt** with **48 pt** leading. Change the layer name to **h1-iphone**, then copy and paste the layer's CSS into the **type-styles.css** file.

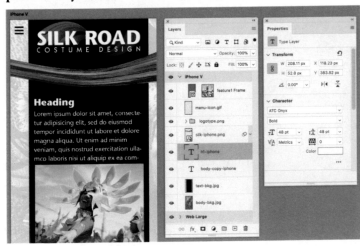

17. Save and close **text-styles.css**.

18. Save and close **silk-road.psd**.

1. The _____ command can be used to run an action on all files in a specific folder without user intervention.

2. Align options are available in the _____ when multiple layers are selected in the Layers panel.

3. True or False: A Puppet Warp is always destructive; you cannot edit the original, pre-warp pixels. _____

4. The _____ tool can be used to create more than one canvas in a single Photoshop file.

5. The _____ image format allows lossy compression and does not support transparency; it is best used for photos.

6. The _____ format supports only 8-bit color; it is best used for artwork or graphics with large areas of solid color.

7. The _____ format supports both continuous-tone color and degrees of transparency.

8. _____ are used to define the properties of HTML elements.

9. CSS files define _____, which contain property:value pairs to control the appearance of elements in an HTML page.

10. All CSS copied from Photoshop is created as a _____. The selector name, beginning with a period, is taken from the relevant Photoshop layer.

1. Briefly explain how actions can be used to improve workflow.

2. Briefly explain three file formats that are used for images on the web.

3. Briefly explain the concept of CSS in relation to web design.

# PORTFOLIO BUILDER PROJECT

Use what you have learned in this project to complete the following freeform exercise.
Carefully read the art director and client comments, then create your own design to meet the needs of the project.
Use the space below to sketch ideas. When finished, write a brief explanation of the reasoning behind your final design.

**art director comments**

Every professional designer needs a portfolio of their work. If you have completed the projects in this book, you should now have a number of different examples to show off your skills using Photoshop.

The projects in this book were specifically designed to include a broad range of *types* of projects; your portfolio should use the same principle.

Using the following suggestions, gather your best work, and create printed and digital versions of your portfolio.

**client comments**

❑ Include as many different types of work as possible — book covers, image retouching, art projects, etc.

❑ Print clean copies of each finished piece that you want to include.

❑ For correction or compositing jobs, include the "before" image as part of the sample.

❑ For each example in your portfolio, write a brief (one or two paragraphs) synopsis of the project. Explain the purpose of the piece, as well as your role in the creative and production process.

❑ Design a web page interface with thumbnails of your work.

❑ Create a portable version of your digital portfolio so you can present your work even when an Internet connection is not available — you never know when you might meet a potential employer.

**project justification**

_____
_____
_____
_____
_____
_____
_____
_____
_____
_____
_____
_____
_____
_____
_____

The graphic design workflow typically revolves around extremely short turnaround times, which means that any possible automation will only be a benefit. Photoshop actions can be useful whenever you need to apply the same sets of options to more than one or two images. Every click you save will allow you to do other work, meet tight deadlines, and satisfy your clients. In the case of running a batch on multiple images, you are completely freed to work on other projects, be in other places, or even (technically) "work" while you're gone for the evening.

Although many developers use dedicated web design software, like Adobe Dreamweaver, to build sophisticated websites, the images for those sites have to come from somewhere. It is very common for a designer to build the "look and feel" of a site in Photoshop, and then generate the pieces so the developer can more easily reassemble them in the web design application. As you saw by completing this project, Photoshop can even be used to create cascading style sheets (CSS) to communicate the type and object formatting that you define in Photoshop.

Create a 3D extrusion from a type layer

Use puppet warping to distort a layer

Define an action to resize images

Run a batch to resize and rename multiple images

Use artboards to create multiple versions in one file

Create CSS from type layers

Generate web assets based on layers and layer groups

# INDEX

## Symbols

# INDEX

# INDEX

# INDEX

# Use our portfolio to build yours.

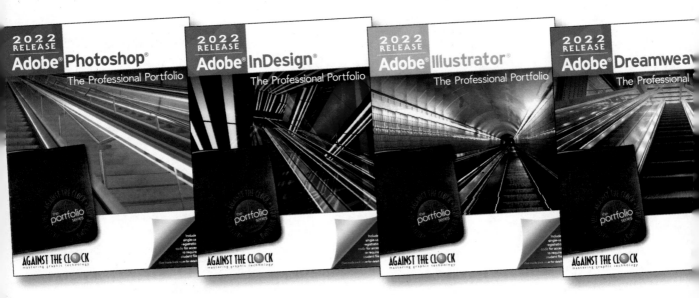

The Against The Clock Professional Portfolio Series walks you step-by-step through the tools and techniques of graphic design professionals.

Order online at www.againsttheclock.com
Use code **ATCEDU2022** for a 10% discount

Go to **www.againsttheclock.com** to enter our monthly drawing for a free book of your choice

*. . . a time to* SPEAK

From Ecclesiastes 3:1–7

# A Time to Speak

A Healing Journal for Post-Abortive Women

by Yvonne Florczak-Seeman

Love From Above, Inc.
P.O. Box 199
Clarendon Hills, IL 60514

General Editors: Rebekah Bailey, Sally Marcey, Betsy Schmitt

Scripture quotations marked GW are taken from GOD'S WORD. Copyright © 1995 by God's Word to the Nations Bible Society. All rights reserved. Quotations used by permission.

Scripture quotations marked NIV are taken from The Holy Bible, New International Version. Copyright © 1973, 1978, 1984, International Bible Society. Used by permission of Zondervan Bible Publishers.

Scripture quotations marked NLT are taken from the *Holy Bible,* New Living Translation, copyright © 1996. Used by permission of Tyndale House Publishers, Inc, Wheaton, Illinois 60189. All rights reserved.

Produced with the assistance of The Livingstone Corporation (www. LivingstoneCorporation.com). Project staff includes Betsy Schmitt, Kirk Luttrell, Ashley Taylor, Joel Bartlett and Mary Horner Collins.

ISBN 0-9768098-4-2

Printed in the United States of America

05 06 07 08 — 7 6 5 4 3 2 1

*Presented to* _____

*By* _____

*Date* _____

# { DEDICATION }

With all my love to my amazing grandmother, Ana Celia Morales. I will forever remember the endless prayers and tears that you sent up to heaven on my behalf. My prayer today is that through my walk of faith I will be given the opportunity to someday touch as many lives as you have. Your unyielding love and devotion to God and our family will always be remembered. I love you very much.

With all my love to my dear mother, Miriam Esther Cook. I know that our relationship has had its struggles. Many times through my healing process I would get stuck and take things out on you. You have always taught me that journaling is the freeing of our souls and that once written down, our thoughts and emotions can be turned over to the Almighty God. You are a very special person in my life.

And with all my love I dedicate this journal to my five children in heaven, Jennifer Lynne, Emily Joy, Rachel Maria, David Alexander and Jacob Jeremiah. Words can't even begin to tell you how much I love and miss you. Had it not been for your prayers in heaven mommy would never have been able to finish this project. You are all a part of my life, and clearly the evil that resulted in your deaths, God has graciously turned around for the good of life. Thank you for loving me when I was so hard to love.

Yvonne Florczak-Seeman
President, Love From Above, Inc.

# { Contents }

## { FOREWORD }

Almost forty years ago I first encountered the wounds that abortion leaves on the souls of women. A friend of mine had placed her first baby up for adoption. My friend later endured sexual abuse by a family member, which led to her second pregnancy. Her mother arranged for a safe but illegal abortion. Little did her mother know that she had bought her daughter a one-way ticket to hell.

Later in life she struggled with suicide attempts, an abusive marriage, chemical dependency, and became abusive to her other children. She always said, "I can live with the adoption. I can't live with the abortion." My search for answers to her pain led me to obtain a degree in psychology to become certified as a prenatal loss facilitator and a grief counselor, and to obtain certificates in trauma counseling and spiritual direction.

My friend's pain was a life-changing event for me, which eventually led me in 1984 to develop *Project Rachel*, the post-abortion healing ministry of the Catholic Church. The first organized ministry with a broad reaching scope, Project Rachel is a network of caregivers, including priests, mental health professionals, and others, who provide one-on-one care to those struggling after having an abortion. Over the past twenty years, I have trained thousands of caregivers here and abroad. Currently, Project Rachel is offered in almost all the Catholic dioceses throughout the United States. It is also growing in Canada, the Bahamas, Guam, New Zealand, and Australia. I have received invitations from Mexico, Venezuela, and the Ukraine as well.

The vision of Project Rachel is about proclaiming the love and mercy of God. The Holy Father John Paul II, in the *Gospel of Life*, invites women to healing. He first wrote about the aftermath of abortion in 1960 in his book *Love and Responsibility*. Project Rachel is the pastoral component of the Catholic Church's teaching that abortion is not good for women, men, or children.

As I write this foreword, we have just marked thirty-two years of legalized abortion in the United States. We do not know how many abortions have really occurred because abortion did not begin with the Supreme Court decision; we just began counting at that point. Many abortions happened during World War I, the Depression, and World War II. The oldest woman I have personally spoken with is ninety-four years old, grieving an abortion that happened more than seventy years ago. At one point the Allen Guttmacher Institute, Planned Parenthood's research arm, stated that "43 percent of women in America will have at least one abortion by age 45." This is a staggering number.

Pro-abortion organizations acknowledge that up to 10 percent of women who have had abortions may have serious psychiatric aftermath. If the abortion toll in our country is more than forty million and as high or higher than 46.5 million, the numbers of women just within that 10 percent range are frightening: more than 4 million women in our country may have serious psychiatric aftermath. In addition, the number of women who are struggling with abortion-related issues, but not severe enough to be classified as "serious psychiatric," is mind-boggling. By way of comparison, two million women are now living with diagnosed breast cancer and 929,985 Americans are currently diagnosed with AIDS. Countless research is being done in these areas. Abortion is one of the most frequently performed elective surgeries. Why is there no research being done on the consequences? Why is there no public outcry and research on something this big? Women who are suffering are being swept under the rug because this is a political hot potato. Women deserve better.

My experience is that there are multitudes of women who do not fit into the above 10 percent category. They are single and married, with other children and without. They are everywhere. Some have tucked the event away for years. Some have been trying to find ways to suppress the pain with medication. Others have wrestled with depression and anxiety disorders,

failed relationships, infertility, and pregnancy difficulties, and maybe have never made the connection.

We have done women a huge disservice by pretending that abortion erases the experience of pregnancy. In fact, there is much research on the fact that women carry cells of every child they ever conceive the rest of their lives. (The phenomena are called "human microchimerism.") Yet if you asked your doctor, he or she would likely say that they have never heard about this. This is why the reality of an abortion stays with that woman the rest of her life. It is impossible to forget because she carries these cells. I believe that this is why she often knows intuitively the sex of her lost child/children.

I do not use the language of Post-Abortion Syndrome that many people use. A "syndrome" implies pathology, the worst-case scenario if you will. But for many women the aftermath of abortion is not about physical pathology, but about grief and guilt. These feelings need spiritual and psychological healing. Both aspects need to be addressed in the healing process. Grief and guilt are normal reactions of a woman who has lost a child/children in a traumatic and unnatural fashion. That is the bottom line. How she is trying to cope may be where pathological issues come in. She may come to this pain immediately afterward or she may not come for many years, but something known as a "trigger incident" suddenly makes her aware of her need for healing.

This journal seeks to break the silence. This journal seeks to empower women to begin healing. This journal seeks to let women who are struggling know that they are not alone. There are women who have walked the path to healing. There are people across the country that can help.

People always ask me if I get depressed hearing all the painful stories that I hear. I never do because I KNOW that God will heal anyone who asks. God is alive and well. No one has ever called me and said it didn't happen, if they opened their heart to the Lord. In fact, women often give me a hug and whisper "thank you" in my ear. I recently met a woman whom I had counseled. With a huge smile she said, "You and I have known each other a long time!" And the joy in her eyes told me the merciful hand of God had touched her and made her whole. If you give God permission to heal you, it will happen, and you will be astonished at the "God happenings" in your life.

Vicki Thorn
Founder, Project Rachel and
National Office of Post-Abortion Reconciliation & Healing

## { PREFACE }

Many women suffer silently with the pain of abortion, unable or unwilling to speak out because of the shame and guilt associated with their choice. Years may go by as they continue to mourn the loss, but they haven't been able to reveal their pain to anyone. You and I know many of these women—at work, in our neighborhoods, in the church pew sitting next to us on Sunday mornings. Maybe this woman is even you.

Has the secret agony of abortion robbed you of time and peace? Have you felt that your life has been put on hold? The secret to peace with God is to discover, accept, and appreciate His perfect timing and His perfect forgiveness. Right now is the time to heal broken hearts and allow God to restore the treasures of our souls.

My name is Yvonne Florczak-Seeman, and I, too, have been robbed of time. I was sixteen years old when I made the agonizing decision to end the life of my unborn child. I still vividly remember the visit to the abortion clinic. I recall people telling me that my situation was "temporary" and that in just a few hours it would all be over. They couldn't have been more wrong. During the three hours I was at the clinic, I was never advised of what the long-term consequences would be. The true result of that abortion was the complete destruction of my life for the next seventeen years.

I wish I could say that I learned my proverbial lesson after that experience. However, the reality is that I not only survived that traumatic incident but also went on to have four additional abortions. You may wonder how someone could survive such a situation not just once, but five times? After the first abortion, my mind concluded that it was a necessary and reasonable response to my circumstances. The four abortions that followed were merely simple medical procedures. This self-serving scientific designation was created to hide the fact that my first abortion had not only removed "some harmless tissue" but had also succeeded in removing my very soul and personal identity.

Looking back, I believe that God allowed me to survive those terribly painful experiences so that I may tell others about the consequences of abortion. God has made it very clear that my life and my experiences are not things to be shrouded in silence and secrecy. I now exist as a powerful testimony to His mercy and grace. I realize that these revelations are beyond shocking. I share them not to make you uncomfortable or to tap into your sympathy, but rather to encourage you to begin your journey of healing and speak out. I urge you to join me—and all the amazing women who have found the strength to share their stories in this journal—as we walk toward healing and stand against this lie called "choice."

We must educate others on the lifelong consequences of our choices and clearly expose the lie that "choice protects women." Those of us who have experienced "choice" know the truth. Before we could embrace the truth, we had to deal with the years of guilt, shame, anger, regret, depression, endless crying episodes, remorse, and temper explosions. For some of us, drug and alcohol abuse was part of the package; all of us have experienced dysfunctional relationships. It is indeed "a time to speak," as Ecclesiastes 3 says.

My prayer as you begin this journey is that you realize *you are not alone.* There are many of us who feel what you feel, and there is hope for healing. Unfortunately the truth about abortion and its consequences isn't being discussed. We get more information about a tooth extraction than we do about abortion. I feel the calling and responsibility to educate and help those on the pro-choice side understand what is at stake when a woman makes the decision to abort her child. Thirty-two years ago we didn't know how legalized abortion would impact our society and future generations. Today we see the results all around us, yet refuse to acknowledge

and validate the inevitable truth. Abortion hurts women; it doesn't protect them. I believe this journal will shed some light on the deception about choosing abortion. Please join us as we stand together with one voice, finding strength in one another.

May God bless you on your journey, and may you find the forgiveness and freedom that comes through His great love and grace.

Yvonne Florczak-Seeman
Founder and President, Love From Above, Inc.

## { ACKNOWLEDGMENTS }

I would like to thank my wonderful, loving husband, Richard, who has supported me through this entire process. Your confidence and reassurance has been my sustaining courage to move forward into what God has called me to do. I love you very much. I would also like to thank my dear faithful prayer partner, mentor, and friend, Lauri Whamond, who has been there through my bouts of unbelief.

I would also like to thank Rebekah, Tommie, Elizabeth, Cathy, Lisa, Betsy, Jackie, Mary Kathryn, Carrie, and Maria—all the amazing women who shared their stories in this journal. I would not have been able to do this without your courage. I know that this was very painful, and I know that you agreed to this project because you wanted the evils in your life to be turned into good. God will bless you for it!

And last but not least I want to thank my three beautiful, amazing children. You are my gifts from God. Kevin Conrad, the day you were born mommy knew that a miracle had happened. Michael Thomas, they day you were born mommy started believing in angels again. Sarah Elizabeth, the day you were born I knew God's promises were fulfilled and that it was time for me to speak. Thank you so much for sharing mommy with so many people so that others can know the truth. I love all of you so very much!

## { INTRODUCTION }

This journal was written for *you*. Perhaps no one else knows what secrets you are carrying, what is happening right now in your life, or what wakes you up at night with tears on your face and no one to tell. This journal was created to be a safe place where you can begin to tell your own story, without feeling the need to edit your words or to worry about others' reactions. This is your place to dare to speak, perhaps for the first time, what is in your heart.

To help you begin, twelve women have courageously chosen to break the silence about what they have gone through. In these pages, they will share openly with you about the lies they believed and about their experiences before and after their abortions. Through their stories, they hope you will see that no matter what you have endured or what you have done, there is healing and hope.

You are invited to use this journal in a way that feels comfortable for you. After each story, you will find some journaling questions to help you start telling your own story. Feel free to begin with any question you wish and to use only those questions that seem relevant to you. Because the women who have chosen to tell their stories have found deep healing in God's love, care, and forgiveness for them, following each story is a section inviting you to go deeper in your own faith. When you are ready, feel free to use that section. Finally, there is a section in the back of the journal for further healing.

*Have compassion on me, L*ORD*, for I am weak.*

*Heal me, L*ORD*, for my body is in agony.*

(Psalm 6:2, NLT)

# Be Still My
# Little Girl

Oh, how I longed to hear the deepest thought of your heart.
Oh, how I wanted to tell you that I don't want us to be apart.
From the beginning of time My Precious Daughter
You have been what's on My mind.
I wondered how long it would be until
You would for Me find the time.
I am here to wash away the pain.
I will give you My peace and remove the shame
I will give you the strength and power to withstand
The deception and lies of the evil one's plan.
Come now, My Precious Little Girl, come sit on My lap.
Be still. Lay down. Maybe even take a nap.
The time is here and the time is now,
To set your life in motion; let Me show you how.
Oh, how I longed to be with you,
Oh, how I longed to give you
Instruction, and show you what to do.
Oh, will you stop and take your Daddy's hand.
I promise I will give you the strength to stand.
Our lives together will be forever as one.
For this was the purpose and plan for My Son.


Love, Your Daddy in heaven

# "It's a simple procedure; life will resume on Monday"

## { YVONNE'S STORY— DETERIORATION VS. RENEWAL }

It was the biggest day of my life—the Homecoming dance was finally here, and the cutest guy in the entire school had just asked me out. I was a sophomore in high school, and he was a junior. My girlfriends were happy for me, but jealous of my popularity because I was dating the cutest guy in the school! I felt that I was now in a "different league." I remember how special I felt in the beginning and how special he made me feel when I would see him in the hallway or in the lunchroom. On dates at the football games, all eyes were focused on us. Our relationship moved quickly, and before I knew it, we had been together for almost three months. He began telling me that he loved me, and that if I loved him, I would prove it.

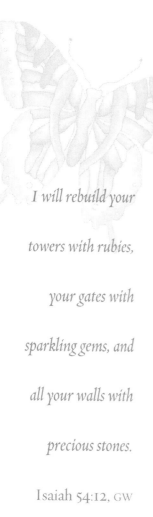

*I will rebuild your*

*towers with rubies,*

*your gates with*

*sparkling gems, and*

*all your walls with*

*precious stones.*

Isaiah 54:12, GW

At that time I really didn't understand what he was talking about because sex wasn't something we had talked about openly in my home. He told me that guys have certain needs. If I really loved him, I would be willing to meet those needs. He completely freaked me out with some of the things he wanted me to do. So I chose abstinence, which freaked him out and he broke up with me. I could not understand why, if he loved me, he would break up with me. I was devastated. But, three weeks later he asked me out again. This time I was determined not to lose him again. I was fully prepared to do whatever it took to keep him, even if that meant having sex with him. So having just turned sixteen, I made the choice to give him what he wanted.

I thought it was going to be okay because he loved me and he told me that it wouldn't hurt. I was very scared and nervous, but he used a condom so I felt safe. After we had sex, I just wanted to go home, take a shower, go to sleep, and never wake up again. I knew that what I had experienced was not something that I was truly prepared for, so I purposed in my heart that I wasn't going to do it again.

Unfortunately I became pregnant the very first time that I had sex. I woke up one morning feeling very sick. I was going out with my girlfriend that morning. I called her and told her that I had been nauseous, and she asked me if I was pregnant. I got angry and told her a lie—that I was a virgin. After I finished the phone call, I started thinking about whether or not she was right; could I be pregnant?

I thought getting pregnant after just one time of having sex and having used protection was impossible. I called my boyfriend, and after denying that he was the one who got me pregnant, he told me to take a pregnancy test. He hung up on me when I told him that I didn't know what to do next. I was forced to tell my mother about the pregnancy.

After discussing the situation, my mother decided that the best thing for me was to choose abortion. She scheduled the appointment with Planned Parenthood and took me to the clinic. I just wanted to die inside. Here I was, young and full of life, with so many wonderful things happening in school—being on the cheerleading squad, making the honor roll, and getting into the drama program. How could this have happened? I only had sex one time and I didn't even like it. Now I had to deal with something that was much bigger than I was. I so much needed my mother to tell me that it was going to be okay, that she would help me through this. But she was angry (we had a family history of three generations of teen crisis pregnancies) and centered on her own disappointments.

As I sat there in the waiting room, the minutes seemed like hours and the hours seemed like days. Then finally someone came out and called my name. I followed her into a room with six or seven other girls. She explained the "simple procedure" and said it wasn't going to be painful—like having some menstrual cramps—and "life would resume on Monday." Then we went into a locker room to change into the hospital gowns. After I changed, I walked into the next room and sat on the bench. There were about twenty girls already there waiting. One of the workers gave me a urine sample cup and a number, and told me where to put the cup when I was done. I did what she asked me to do.

I waited on that hard cold bench for about an hour; then they called my number. I remember feeling so afraid and wondering what they were going to do to me in there. *Why did it have to be this way? Why did I let this happen?* The questions seemed pointless but I couldn't stop them from running through my mind. The worker told me to lay back on the table and put my feet into the stirrups. I didn't know what stirrups were, so I didn't put my feet up. She curtly said, "Put your feet up." When I told her I didn't know where to put them, she became very irritated with me, as if I should have known better. I waited for another half-hour or so, and then a man came into the room. He never addressed me; he just started the procedure and turned on the vacuum. It was then I realized that something wasn't right.

However, I just stared at the ceiling as the tears rolled down my face. The pain was unbelievable and the burning felt endless. He finished and left the room, never saying a word. I continued to stare at the ceiling. The worker led me to the recovery room, where

I lay on a cot with a very thin, worn-out sheet. I fell asleep, until the pain woke me up. They gave me some pain medication and told me I was free to go. I stood up, but I fell because I was so weak. They told me to rest at home for a few hours. My mother was reading a book in the waiting room. I said, "It's finished. We can go now."

We left the clinic and never spoke about that day again. I fell into a deep depression. All the things that I once loved—cheerleading, drama, friends—I had no desire to pursue. Three months later I became pregnant again with the same boyfriend. My mother took me to the clinic again. It was on the third pregnancy that I ran away from home. I really thought that things would be different this time. I was living with my boyfriend, so it would be okay that I was pregnant. He was not happy, however, and told me to take care of it. So I called my mother and she took me to the same clinic, where I relived the same nightmare! By now I had pretty much lost all desire to live. My boyfriend and I continued to live together because I hated my mother and blamed her. I hoped that my miserable life would at least cause her life to be unhappy, too.

My depression got worse and I used drugs as much as I could to help numb the pain. The more drugs I used, the closer I got to death. After my second abortion I really tried to use better birth control protection. However, because of my depression, which led to my drug abuse, protection didn't work. I continued to get pregnant. By the time I was twenty, I had had five abortions.

It was on my fifth abortion when the slogan of "choice" became suspicious to me. When I became pregnant, I was in complete denial. Eight weeks turned into nine weeks, then ten weeks. Finally a few weeks later I went to the clinic. But this time, when I lay back and put my feet in the stirrups, I felt like I was going to throw up. I told the worker that I didn't feel good, and she told me to lie down because we didn't have much time left. A man came in and started the procedure. The pain was like never before and I told him to stop. He got very angry and said, "This is week thirteen. We need more money." He left the room. I was completely out of my mind at this point. I asked the worker what was happening, and she told me that I needed more money. She asked me for my boyfriend's name. She called him to see if he could get more money. We needed another $150. I talked to him, and he got more money and came right back.

Back in the room, I put my feet in the stirrups again. The same man came in and began a different procedure. He used some bigger instruments, and it seemed like a stronger vacuum with a bigger hose. As soon as he turned on the vacuum I cried out, "Please stop! I have changed my mind." He told me it was too late now and said, "Just lay back and don't move because you might hurt yourself." When he was done, he told me to go and get some pizza. I left the clinic and never returned again. I stopped eating pizza for about two years.

Three days after the abortion I began to hemorrhage. I ended up in the hospital emergency room. I told them I had had an abortion three days prior and that the bleeding wouldn't stop. Then I told them that I had had other abortions, but hemorrhaging had never happened before. The nurse asked me, "How many abortions have you had?" and I told her that was my fifth. Then they ran some tests and she informed me that the baby hadn't been completely removed.

I turned toward the nurse who had just given me this news and said, "What baby are you talking about? This was and is a blob of tissue!" She immediately realized what she had said and started to change her terminology. However, by that time it was too late! At that moment I realized for the first time what I was feeling. All the missing pieces in my life that my choice had brought now were finally starting to make sense. My depression, my desire to die, my missing something but not knowing what it was. At that moment the lie of choice was exposed; I realized that they were babies! By this time my life had hit rock bottom, and the few solid pieces that were left seemed to be crumbling into dust.

In this state of mind I turned to suicide as my solution. I figured no one would miss me. I really hadn't contributed anything to society other than five dead babies who would never, if given the opportunity, forgive me for the horrible mother that I was. I left the hospital that morning and walked all the way home thinking, *How had I managed to mess up my life so*

AT THAT MOMENT

I REALIZED FOR THE

FIRST TIME WHAT I

WAS FEELING. ALL THE

MISSING PIECES IN MY

LIFE THAT MY CHOICE

HAD BROUGHT NOW

WERE FINALLY STARTING

TO MAKE SENSE.

*I made you grow like*

*a plant of the field.*

*You grew up and*

*developed and became*

*the most beautiful of*

*jewels . . . you who*

*were naked and bare.*

Ezekiel 16:7, NIV

*badly?* I called my girlfriend and made plans to go out drinking that night. Then I would come home and take an overdose.

That night, I sat at the bar alone, thinking about dying and wondering if there was a God or a Higher Being. I questioned my childhood faith that was once a part of my life. I sat there asking this Higher Being, "Are You there? Why didn't You protect me?" Then a man who was about eighty years old came into the bar and sat next to me. He asked, "What is a beautiful young lady like you doing in a place like this all by herself?" I turned around and thought, *What a great pickup line.* I told him to please leave me alone. But he looked at me and said, "There is a reason why you are here tonight and why I came in here tonight." I turned around and said, "I suppose you are going to tell me this reason!" And he said, "Yes. God wants you to know that He has a plan for your life."

I just stared at this man as he continued to answer so many of my questions before I could even ask them. He visited with me for about fifteen minutes; I felt as if my whole life had just flashed before my eyes. As he turned to leave, I went to grab my purse, and then he was gone. I ran outside to thank him for his kind words, but there wasn't a soul in sight. I knew at that moment that I had been visited by an angel and that my life had a purpose.

Back in my bedroom, I fell on my knees and promised God if He could forgive me and put my life back on track, I would do whatever He asked of me. That night what was intended for evil in my life, God turned around for good. My journey and healing process has been painful and long. From the time of the first abortion to the beginning of my healing process it had been nineteen years. Since then, it's been five years of freedom! However, before the freedom came I had experienced many years of confusion, guilt, shame, anger, one trip into a cult for five years, and one failed marriage because I had not addressed the abortions yet. I was on my soon-to-be failed second marriage when I realized that I was trying to do it on my own and was not letting God be God in my life! I realized that I didn't have to do anything other than give it to God and He would put all the pieces back into place. It was hard at first but I finally learned how to embrace God's complete forgiveness, and through that forgiveness I have become FREE.

# Reflection

Yvonne began her story by describing her relationship with her boyfriend and why she felt pressured to have sex. Can you relate to being afraid of losing a relationship with a boyfriend or with someone that you are or were dating? Has this fear caused you to act in ways that do not fit with your personal beliefs?

Yvonne describes the experience of her first abortion in detail. How was her experience similar to your experience? How was it different?

How did Yvonne feel that her mother had let her down when she went for her abortion? What people in your life let you down during your abortion experience?

How did your family members or friends respond to you when you went for your abortion? Describe their reactions and your feelings below.

_____

_____

_____

_____

_____

_____

_____

_____

When the nurse in the hospital called the fetus "a baby," Yvonne suddenly realized why the other parts of her life were not making sense. She understood that her depression, her feelings of wanting to die, and her "missing something" were all related to her abortions. When did you come to that realization? How did you respond?

_____

_____

_____

_____

_____

_____

_____

_____

## { Yvonne's Story Continues }

Today I have been happily married to Richard for nine years. We have three beautiful children—Kevin (from my first marriage) who is eleven years old, Michael who is seven years old, and Sarah Elizabeth who is two years old. Can God work miracles? Absolutely! Doctors had told me that I couldn't have children after the fifth abortion because of all the scar tissue left in my womb from the scraping of the abortions. However, God is an Almighty God and for Him nothing is impossible!

He has given me a ministry called Love From Above. Through this ministry we have seen women set free from the guilt and condemnation that abortion leaves. We have been part of saving babies from abortion. We have helped single moms get to the next step in their lives, and we have helped women in crisis pregnancies find shelter in their time of need. Words can't begin to explain what God has in store for those who are willing to become vulnerable before His throne.

Having had five abortions and feeling that I had nothing to contribute to society, God has placed me today before Senators, House of Representatives, Cardinals, Archbishops, and Bishops. I have been on TV, radio, and interviewed by newspapers. Tens of thousands of students in middle schools and high schools have heard my story. God has done this because my story, along with your story, needs to be told. It's time to speak!

## { GOING DEEPER }

*God delights in taking the areas of our greatest weakness and changing us so that these areas become our greatest strengths. Yvonne went from wanting to die and feeling as if she had nothing to contribute to society to being able to offer hope through telling her story to thousands of students. Whatever you feel are your areas of weakness, they can be changed into strengths if you will, in Yvonne's words, "be vulnerable before the throne of God" and surrender your weakness to Him. Allow Him to take over and begin to transform these areas into strengths.*

{ GOD'S LOVE LETTER }

*My Little Girl,*

*Oh how I have longed to let you know how precious you are to Me. When I crafted all the earth, it was with the same beautiful miraculous detail that I formed you. Heaven is surrounded with many precious stones. You were the inspiration in which I was able to create diamonds, rubies, emeralds, and sapphires. I see a beauty in you that surpasses My greatest creation. You are My treasure and I love you!*

*Your Daddy in heaven*

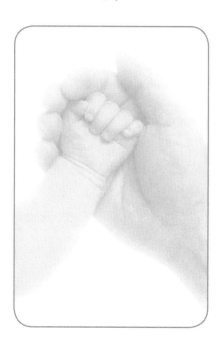

# Your Time to Speak

**Precious child, what is on your heart right now? Tell Me.**

# "It's not a baby; It's just a blob of tissue"

## { CATHY'S STORY—
## BROKENNESS VS. WHOLENESS }

I was the good child. The one with the 3.9 GPA in college and a full scholarship. The one with dreams of going to medical school and becoming a doctor. In minutes, all those dreams were shattered. I was pregnant. I didn't need a pregnancy test. I just knew. And I was afraid, really afraid.

I went to a close relative to talk about having an abortion. I had no idea that she had had an abortion a year earlier. She went with me to Planned Parenthood, where I received absolutely no real counseling. I believed that my life would be over if I had the baby, and the "counselor" played on that fear. The adoption option was never discussed. There was only one solution to this problem: *abortion.*

*But he was wounded*

*and crushed for our*

*sins. He was beaten*

*that we might have*

*peace. He was whipped,*

*and we were healed!*

Isaiah 53:5, NLT

I was too far along to have the abortion at the Planned Parenthood clinic. As I walked out of the office my friend pulled me down onto a sofa in the waiting room. She began to desperately rattle off the horrors of her experience. She told me she still had nightmares about the abortion and that she wished she had never had it. I didn't listen to her.

Looking back, I see how God was intervening in that situation. It was the Holy Spirit who prompted my friend to warn me of the consequences of using this as a method to solve my "problem." I have since graciously thanked my friend for having the courage to confront me. Her words of wisdom and experience will always stay in my heart. I have learned that it takes real love to confront sin, and real love is what she showed me that day as she pleaded with me not to take the same road she had taken.

My mother discovered that I was pregnant. She saw my growing stomach one day as I came out of the shower. I broke down into tears and told her that I wanted to have an abortion. My mom, a strong Christian, was unprepared to deal with my decision. She went to pro-life organizations for help and left a few pro-life pamphlets around the house. But she did not confront me. I now know that she was just as devastated as I was and had no idea how to handle the situation.

Having an abortion was the greatest tragedy of my life. Sometimes people describe tragic events as though they were all a blur. I remember this event as if it happened yesterday. I remember the faces, the sounds, the smells, and the pain.

I was five months pregnant and was told that the "procedure" would take two days. The first day, I wore a pink New York tee shirt. I still remember it because I ripped it to shreds in a rage of anger after the abortion. I wore the shirt because it was big, and I didn't want anyone to know that I was pregnant. I rode the bus and train for what seemed like hours before I got to the building. I met with a smiling lady who explained the abortion. Small cigarette-sized seaweed sticks would be inserted into my cervix. Over the next twenty-four hours they would expand,

and the abortion would then be performed the next day. I laid down on the table and the abortionist performed an ultrasound. When he walked out of the room, I could see my baby alive and well on the screen. That was the first and last time that I would see her alive.

On the ride home, I began to feel ill. An older woman on the train started fussing at some boys, telling them to get up and let the pregnant lady sit down. I felt like fainting. The smiling lady hadn't told me about this. Later that night, for hours, I could feel my baby thrashing around fighting for her life. I wanted so badly to rescue her, but they had told me that I couldn't change my mind. I began to vomit uncontrollably. My baby was dying, and it was my fault. I loved my baby, and in that instant, I realized that I had ended her life!

By the next day my baby was motionless, dead. I knew it, I felt it, and it was killing me. I wanted to die. That morning the anesthesiologist took my hand and told me to count backward. I am sure that he could see the fear and pain in my eyes. I started to count . . . ten . . . nine . . . eight . . . seven . . . I woke up sometime later, in a room full of women who had just aborted their children. It felt like a holding cell. We could all smell the denial in the air. I was still dazed from the anesthetic, but could hear people talking around me. Some women said that they were relieved. A few of them told stories about their previous abortions. One said that she really didn't believe in abortion, but she just made a mistake and needed to fix it. I think I accepted what I had done the night before, so I sat there in silence.

The nurse began to pass out birth control pills like they were candy. One girl asked how the nurse knew that the pills were the right prescription. The nurse calmly answered, "Well, you don't really know, but if you get pregnant again after this, you can have another abortion, and we'll up the dosage."

I deeply regretted the abortion, and I took it out on myself in the most destructive way. My grades dropped. I lost all self-esteem and self-confidence, and I started dating a very abusive person. I didn't feel worthy of anyone's love, and I went

HAVING AN ABORTION

WAS THE GREATEST

TRAGEDY OF MY LIFE.

SOMETIMES PEOPLE

DESCRIBE TRAGIC

EVENTS AS THOUGH

THEY WERE ALL A BLUR.

I REMEMBER THIS EVENT

AS IF IT HAPPENED

YESTERDAY.

*In just a short time,*

*he will restore us so we*

*can live in his presence.*

*Oh, that we might*

*know the LORD! Let us*

*press on to know him!*

Hosea 6:2–3a, NLT

through life wishing that I were dead. I wished that something bad would happen to me to take away the pain.

To make a long story short, I became just another statistic. I became pregnant again, this time by a very abusive person. The day that I realized that I was pregnant, I was neither happy nor sad; I was terrified. I wanted God to help me be the mother I was afraid to be. I also knew that it meant becoming a single mom.

I spoke with a woman at a crisis pregnancy center who hinted that I should get married. I started laughing inside and thought, *Not on your life.* I didn't want my child raised by an abusive atheist. I knew from the beginning of our relationship that he was *not* the one. The bottom line was that I chose a relationship with him because I was not ready to repent of my sin. I thought that somehow being with someone who rejected God would take away the guilt for what I had done. I could hear the words of 1 John 1:8–9, over and over in my head: "If we claim to be without sin, we deceive ourselves and the truth is not in us. If we confess our sins, he is faithful and just and will forgive us our sins and purify us from all unrighteousness" (NIV).

By this time the whole self-deception thing had worn off. It was time to grow up and take care of my baby, to be a good mom, and to ask for forgiveness from a loving God. I began to pray daily for God's will in my life. Shortly before leaving my son's father, I met a wonderful woman named Zelda, who had been through a crisis pregnancy. She shared her story with me, and she told me that abortion for her was never an option. I admired her strength and her love for God. She stayed in contact with me throughout my pregnancy, and we are still friends to this day. When I left my boyfriend, he stole everything that I owned. But it was okay. I knew I needed to trust God.

I went home to my family, and many of my family members and friends told me that I should have an abortion. I did not listen for a minute. I had been there, done that. This baby was mine, and I was going to take care of him. We would face life together—with the help of God and my mom, of course.

When I felt my baby move inside me for the first time, I panicked. One lady had told me that her abortion had left her infertile. What was going to happen to my baby? I worried that God was going to take my baby away for what I had done. All at once the guilt fell, and I could not escape it. The reality of the abortion set in. I had destroyed a life. I never believed that God was a "vindictive God," but I couldn't accept His forgiveness for this horrible crime that I had committed against my body, my family, my child, and my God. How could He ever forgive me?

Through Healing Hearts, I began post-abortion counseling. I accepted the reality of my sin, but I could not grieve. I had lost a child. I only saw her alive once on the ultrasound. I felt her move, but I never saw her eyes. I never saw her smile. There was no funeral, no body, and no grave. She didn't even have a name. I named her Danielle, after Daniel in the Bible, because Daniel had succeeded where I had failed. In the face of adversity, he stood his ground and trusted in God even though everyone around him worshiped false gods. The god that I had worshiped was my own pride and selfish ambition. I wanted her to have a name that showed that we, through the help of God, could stand firm and trust Him.

After a while, I placed pictures of myself and my family along with pictures of my unborn child's sonogram in a small box, and then I buried it. With it, I also buried the guilt, the pain, and the anguish. What I live with now is the memory of my experience, which God has used time and time again to encourage others to protect the lives of unborn children. With love and compassion, I want everyone to know that abortion should never be an option.

THE DAY THAT I

REALIZED THAT I WAS

PREGNANT, I WAS

NEITHER HAPPY NOR

SAD; I WAS TERRIFIED.

I WANTED GOD

TO HELP ME BE THE

MOTHER I WAS

AFRAID TO BE.

*Reflection*

How did you feel when you first found out that you were pregnant? How did you feel your life would be affected because of the pregnancy?

_____

_____

_____

_____

_____

Cathy told her best friend about her pregnancy. Who did you tell, and how did that person(s) respond?

_____

_____

_____

_____

In her story, Cathy shares some of the experiences that made her abortion difficult. What was the most difficult part of your abortion experience? How did you respond to that experience?

_____

_____

_____

_____

Cathy grieved the death of her first child by creating a way to remember her baby. First, she named her baby. Then she buried a box that contained pictures of herself, her family, and the sonogram. Have you planned some ways of grieving your abortion? What do you need to do to mourn?

Many of the women who have shared their stories in this journal have named their unborn child. They have also involved family and friends in the process. Involving others in our loss helps us to grieve differently and to move ahead. Who would you like to involve in your grieving and healing?

Hosea 6:2-3a (NLT) says, "In just a short time, he will restore us so we can live in his presence. Oh, that we might know the LORD! Let us press on to know him!" What parts of your life still need this restoration today?

## { Cathy's Story Continues }

But the story doesn't end there. On December 23, 1992, my post-abortion counselor called me to say that she wanted to drop off a gift for the baby. By that time, I was nine months pregnant and ready to deliver, so I was happy that she would be so kind (not to mention that I had not even put together the crib yet). She arrived with a truckload of baby clothes, baby bottles, formula, diapers, lotion, baby wipes, sippy cups— everything that a baby could need. I received so much that I had to give some away, and I did not have to buy my son clothes for two years. My labor coach who was a crisis pregnancy counselor came over to see all of the gifts. I was given more than anyone could believe.

Shortly afterward, I went into labor and gave birth to my son, Alexander, the following day, Christmas Eve. When I looked into his eyes for the first time, I thought of all that I had endured, and I was overcome with the way that God had shown mercy and kindness to me. Since then, God has continued to bless my life over and over again. My son is now eleven years old. He's a good-looking, intelligent kid—just like his mom. He rides his bike and is an avid snowboarder, rafter, and fisherman. As for me, I graduated from college and now have a successful career as a military officer. I am now planning to go back to school and become a dentist.

But I will never forget Danielle. A few years ago when I was stationed in Kuwait, I bought a tiny gold bangle bracelet made to fit the arm of the tiniest babies. I keep the bangle as a reminder of Danielle, my baby, and as a reminder of the importance and significance of every single life.

## { GOING DEEPER }

*It may not seem like it's possible to you now, but there is healing, hope, and even a life of blessing after having had an abortion. Cathy experienced all three in the birth of her son, the kindness of others, and the forgiveness and blessing of God. Like many women who have experienced an abortion, Cathy did not feel worthy of anyone's love and became self-destructive. After having an abortion, it will take real courage for you to accept God's forgiveness and to believe that your life can have meaning and purpose. As God's child, you are worthy of His love and care.*

**What are some of your dreams for your future? What are the desires of your heart? Take some time to write these down. Then, we encourage you to do two things with your list. First, pray about them frequently. Second, share them with one other person whom you trust.**

## { GOD'S LOVE LETTER }

*My Little Girl,*

*I know that you have been wounded and crushed. I was there when others were beating you down. The ugly words you have been told still echo in your memories. Let Me restore your past so that you can live in the present. My timing is your timing if you embrace it. Let Me help you help others as a result of your pain. I give you My word that I will protect you from harm.*

*Your Daddy in heaven*

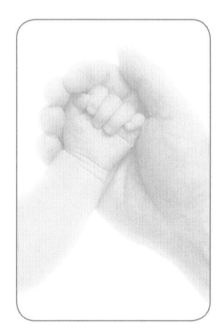

## Your Time to Speak

My little girl, what is on your heart right now? Share your pain with me.

_____

_____

_____

_____

_____

_____

_____

_____

_____

_____

_____

_____

_____

_____

_____

_____

_____

_____

_____

_____

# "It's okay; abortion is legal"

{ JACKIE'S STORY—
HIDING VS. HEALING }

I am fifty-two years old. I came from a godless blue-collar alcoholic/divorced home, complete with the assortment of abuses that come with that kind of environment. I learned very early that the best way to deal with my situation was to party my way through life. Every day I lived for the sole purpose of getting high! And the higher I got, the deeper the pit I dug for myself physically and emotionally. At my lowest point, when I was on the brink of suicide, a friend invited me to a "church" of sorts. The group met in a church building, stained glass windows and all. (I later realized this was a new age cult with just enough Jesus mixed in to sound legit.) They taught astrology classes, which appealed to me, being into the "hippie thing" as I was. I dragged my boyfriend there, and they loved and accepted us. They helped us get off drugs and taught us

*Delight yourself in*

*the* LORD, *and he*

*will give you the*

*desires of your heart.*

Psalm 37:4, NIV

some Bible. We got married and somehow managed to accept Jesus Christ as Lord along the way.

Because I had done so many illegal things, I was full of shame. Both my husband and I were looking for some way to rid ourselves of our bad reputation for "breaking the law" due to our drug habits. And just as every other cult, this one offered ways to earn your way to God. One way was complete mastery of your body through meditation and self-denial—and that included using the rhythm method of birth control. That, in my case, led to immediate pregnancy.

Embarrassed and ashamed—after all I was the one who convinced my husband we could do this—I knew we would be harshly criticized for not being able to control ourselves. Also we were very poor, just having left the drug culture lifestyle. We had nothing, except two kids (one from his previous marriage and the other from my previous relationship). We had added a third child to our family when we decided to help out a friend (who was still doing drugs) by taking care of her daughter. We were both working hard trying to come up with money for a house. The thoughts raced through my head, *How could we afford another child right now? This was not a good time; we are not ready.*

My biggest fear, though, was what my friends would think of us. I wouldn't be able to work. We would never own a home. These fears gave me the permission I was looking for to end the pregnancy. And besides, all my life I had been part of illegal practices; this time I was justified. It was my choice, and that choice was legal! I took responsibility for my situation for the first time in my life. But in my heart of hearts, I was longing for my husband to intervene at the last minute and say, "You don't have to do this; we will make it work." But he never did. After the procedure, we went home and buried it in our hearts, never speaking of it again.

I tried to stuff the whole experience deep down inside. Soon I began having unexplained crying spells, a secret death wish (I just wanted to plow my car into a viaduct for no apparent reason), and I had constant fear that something terrible would happen to my other children and did not allow them to leave our yard. I dealt with the experience by keeping very, very busy. I worked and worked and worked. Then I worked some more. I even tried to bury myself in church work. But in the end I still never felt good enough.

After years of silent suffering and endless attempts to try to "make it right" or cover it up, the Lord led me to a seminar called "Healing the Hurts." There I found other people who were just like me—hurting, filled with shame, and desperately wanting to feel forgiveness. During this seminar God really opened my festering wounds and gave me some relief, but most of all He gave me hope. Soon after that I went to a Bible study support group, which helped me deal with the issues in my life that had led me to make the abortion decision. It also helped me overcome my inability to experience God's forgiveness.

On one occasion the group leader encouraged us to do a life assessment exercise. We looked at our life as a "house": the main level represented our current circumstances, the upstairs our future, and the basement our past. Then in a guided prayer time, we prayerfully asked Jesus to go on a "tour" with us. As I walked with Jesus in my mind through my "basement," I felt Him saying that I was hiding something in the corner. I said, "Oh, You don't want to see that—it's terrible!" And He said, "Let Me go there." I said, "No. I can't bear it, because I can't forgive myself for it." Then He called my name and said, "Look at Me." When I did, I saw His face, as it was when they crucified Him, severely beaten and disfigured, full of blood. It was shocking and horrible. He said to me "Wasn't this enough?" I cried and cried and said, "It was enough. I would never want You to be hurt any further." Then I knew I was forgiven, and it was enough.

Since that time, God has slowly healed my broken heart and taken away my shame. I am free to share my story rather than hiding and burying a painful, shameful abortion experience that almost destroyed me. I was able to give my baby the human dignity he deserved, and I released him to Jesus in heaven, where one day I will see him again. I have been blessed to help others either not make the same mistake I did or find their way on the road to recovery.

BUT IN MY HEART OF HEARTS, I WAS LONGING FOR MY HUSBAND TO INTERVENE AT THE LAST MINUTE AND SAY, "YOU DON'T HAVE TO DO THIS; WE WILL MAKE IT WORK."

*Reflection*

When Jackie discovered that she was pregnant, she was filled with fears. What were some of her fears?

_____

_____

_____

_____

_____

After her abortion, Jackie tried to forget the entire experience. In what ways did you try to forget your experience?

_____

_____

_____

_____

_____

_____

What are some of the ways that you have also tried to cope with the pain of having had an abortion?

_____

_____

_____

_____

_____

_____

As part of her healing, Jackie did a life assessment exercise. She viewed her life as a house, with the main level representing her current circumstances; the upstairs, her future; and the basement, her past. If you looked at your life using that image, what would be in the main level (current circumstances) of your house?

What would be in the basement (your past)?

What do you hope the upstairs (your future) will be?

Jackie prayed and asked Jesus to go with her on a tour of her "house" and noted His responses to the contents there. If you feel comfortable doing so, take your answers from the questions above and, in prayer, ask Jesus to go with you on a tour of your house. What do you sense are His responses?

## { JACKIE'S STORY CONTINUES }

After my husband and I left the cult, God in His graciousness led us to the truth—His truth. We have accepted responsibility for not being there for the child that God gave us, and we have accepted the horrifying reality that we will never have another child together. Ironically, it was the one *legal* action that we took—the right to end the life of our only child together—that has hurt us the most. Our journey to complete healing and recovery through God's awesome love and forgiveness allowed us to accept the truth about the lie we believed—that abortion was okay because it was legal. Being accepted legally by the government doesn't mean that it is morally right before God.

Today my husband and I are both pastors of a church and have been given a full life of helping people and ministry. I have counseled hundreds of women struggling with issues of abuse and abortion. It is our sincerest desire and prayer for others to know, as Jesus claimed, that the "truth that will set them free"—free from making the same mistakes that we have; free from the shame and reproach that the evil one wants to paralyze us with; and ultimately, free from the consequences of being separated from God now and forever.

For years I believed that I wasn't good enough for anything. Today my calling as a wife, mother, pastor's wife, pastor, and counselor clearly shows how the evils in our lives can be turned around for good! Will you give God your life and allow Him to turn your ugliness into beauty?

## { GOING DEEPER }

*The irony of Jackie's story is that she believed she was taking responsibility for her pregnancy by ending it in a legal way. We are encouraged to take responsibility for our actions and to obey the law. Yet, even though Jackie did not break any laws, she suffered greatly and needed God's forgiveness and healing. It seems as though obeying our country's laws would always be the right thing to do. But we can't let others make our moral choices for us by their deciding what is legal and what isn't. Ultimately we are responsible for our own choices. Jackie realized that although something was legal, it wasn't necessarily right. It was only by submitting to God and His wisdom that she saw what was right in His eyes.*

## { GOD'S LOVE LETTER }

*My Little Girl,*

*I delight in you. You are precious and honored in My sight. There hasn't been a day that goes by that I don't smile when I think of you. On the days when you are feeling sad, I stop and wonder how I can make it better. Sometimes I try to get your attention, but you're so busy. Please let Me be a part of your day, week, month, year, and life. I long to talk to you.*

*Your Daddy in heaven*

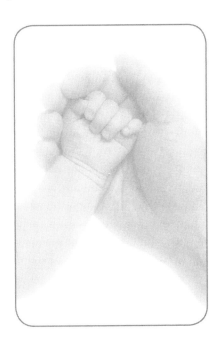

# Your Time to Speak

**Tell Me what is on your heart right now, precious one. I am listening.**

# "My life will be ruined if I have this baby"

## { Lisa's Story— Insignificant vs. Priceless }

I first noticed him in high school. He looked like he had walked out of the dream that I had had since childhood—tall, dark, handsome, and rich! I was certain that he was "Mr. Right," my very own Prince Charming. I thought he would provide my happily ever after. I couldn't wait for him to notice me and ask me out. And he did.

I grew up in a loving, white, middle class family as the third of five children. Being neither the first nor the last, but sandwiched between my four other siblings, I felt insignificant, even ordinary. I was a voice yearning to be heard but all too often drowned out by those who were older, louder, smaller, or cuter. I was the proverbial "lost child in the crowd," and from a very early age I began to long for some form of identity.

*He will shield you*

*with his wings. He*

*will shelter you with his*

*feathers. His faithful*

*promises are your*

*armor and protection.*

Psalm 91:4, NLT

For me, the hunger for significance drove me to try to be perfect. I was the "good girl" wanting desperately to please others in order to be noticed. And in my mind, good girls were defined by what they did not do. They did not do drugs, and they did not have sex before marriage. I made myself a promise to abide by those two rules.

But after a while in my relationship with "Mr. Right," I realized that what I thought was love between my boyfriend and me was nothing more than something selfish and immature—each of us vying with the other to get our own needs met. Yet I still believed in the dream, and despite what I was seeing, I found myself willing to do anything to perpetuate the dream. Before long I gave in to my boyfriend's pressure to have sex. Like so many other girls who have no self-esteem, I believed the lie that this was the only thing I had to offer him—and that if I didn't give it, the relationship would end.

I don't remember the first time we had sex. What I do remember, as we continued, was that it wasn't good. It felt dirty and degrading and was all about meeting his physical needs. My emotional needs were left by the wayside. I began to feel used, taken advantage of, and unloved.

What I had once believed would be fulfilling left me empty. A little voice inside me said, "If he really loved you, he wouldn't be doing this to you." But I shut out that voice, because the consequences of hearing it were too painful to consider. Over time a part of my heart shut, too. I began to feel numb and to close myself off from family and friends. The shame and humiliation that I was feeling caused me to be secretive and elusive.

And then the unthinkable happened. I found out that I was pregnant. At eighteen, I wasn't thinking of the consequences of unprotected sex. I was sure it wouldn't happen to me. But it did.

There was never any discussion about marriage or about keeping the baby. Instead, $100 and an appointment at Planned Parenthood seemed like the obvious answer. *No one was told. A simple procedure and then life could go on. High School. College. The rest of our lives.* A simple procedure. And it was gone. All gone.

But a piece of me was gone, too. And not just a piece of my tissue. What started out as a problem—an inconvenience, a bump in the road—was in reality, a baby. A life. A future. A voice waiting to be heard.

I believed that having the baby would ruin everything: my figure, my reputation, my relationship with my parents, my plans for college, my career, and my marriage. I also secretly feared that my boyfriend would abandon me, an unwed mother, unfit, damaged goods.

Ironically, after the abortion, the relationship ended anyway. My "happily ever after" disappeared. In its place was devastation and anger.

Life went on. I cloaked my despair, rage, and emptiness with busyness and shallow happiness. In time I met another man whom I hoped would take the place of my "knight in shining armor." We married, but it was only a matter of time before my sadness and unfinished business began to break through in this relationship. On the outside I remained my old fun self, but inside I felt broken, fearful, insecure, and unworthy. I desperately longed for a "do-over" in my life.

I got that chance. Circumstances in my life and in our marriage forced me to come face-to-face with my past—even my childhood—and to seek counseling. It was there that I was finally given permission to speak. And to be heard. In that journey came healing, reconciliation, and peace.

I wish I could say of my life, "And then we lived happily ever after." My *happily ever after* doesn't look as I thought it would. My husband doesn't come home on a white horse, and I don't wear a tiara. *Happily ever after* involves work and commitment and honest communication and vulnerability and trust. I can now say, though, that I am content. And I am grateful for the opportunity to share openly about my life and to encourage others to speak the truth and to be heard.

ON THE OUTSIDE I REMAINED MY OLD FUN SELF, BUT INSIDE I FELT BROKEN, FEARFUL, INSECURE, AND UNWORTHY. I DESPERATELY LONGED FOR A "DO-OVER" IN MY LIFE.

*Reflection*

How did you feel when you read Lisa's story? What, if any, of her experiences do you identify with?

_____

_____

_____

_____

_____

Growing up, Lisa felt insignificant, ordinary, and unnoticed. What were the times in your life that you also felt insignificant, ordinary, or unnoticed? What did you do?

_____

_____

_____

_____

_____

When Lisa found out that she was pregnant, she said she felt it was something she never thought would happen to her. What were the thoughts going through your mind when you found out that you were pregnant?

_____

_____

_____

_____

_____

Lisa describes her life after having the abortion as "a piece of her was gone." How would you describe your emotional life after having the abortion?

_____

_____

_____

_____

_____

_____

If you had an opportunity to say something about your experience to someone who was contemplating having an abortion, what would you say? Why?

_____

_____

_____

_____

_____

When in your life have you felt "a yearning to be heard"?

_____

_____

_____

_____

_____

_____

## { LISA'S STORY CONTINUES }

The lie that I believed about my abortion was that if I had the baby, my life would be ruined. The truth is, I actually did a pretty good job of messing up my life, in spite of the abortion, until God brought people into my life to show me another way. My pastor often encourages us to preach the gospel to ourselves: We are more sinful than we dare imagine and more loved than we can ever grasp. At different times in my life, I have grappled with both of those truths. "I'm not really *that* bad." Or conversely, "How could God love *me*?"

But the reality is that our Father longs to have a relationship with us, and He will go to great lengths to woo us to Him. It is in that place and there only where we find complete healing, acceptance, and peace. I found healing in that place, and I rediscovered my voice there when I learned that He was willing to listen and to love me, even when I felt unlovable. My hope for you is that you will find your voice and give yourself permission to speak. There you will find healing and peace.

## { GOING DEEPER }

*We heal in relationship. Most of us have never experienced what it means to be fully known and completely loved, with no strings attached and no need to earn love or approval. A relationship with our Father in heaven provides a steady stream of love and acceptance, flowing into our lives when we have not received love from others or are unable to give it to ourselves. Listen to God's words to you, His precious child, His little girl, and accept His words of love.*

## { GOD'S LOVE LETTER }

*My Little Girl,*

*You have always been precious to Me—unique and valuable. I have always been with you, even when you couldn't see Me, feel My presence, or open your heart to My love. You are made in My image and with a longing for Me in your soul. Even now, no matter what you have done, I want you to come back to Me. You are Mine. I am always ready, day or night, to hear your thoughts and desires and needs. I love you.*

*Your Daddy in heaven*

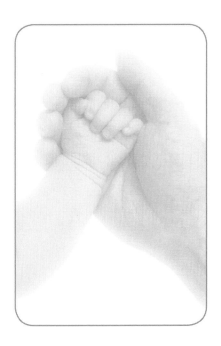

# Your Time to Speak

My daughter, take a few moments to tell Me what's on your heart right now. I want to hear from you.

# "It's *my* choice, *my* responsibility, *my* decision"

## { BETSY'S STORY— KEEPING SECRETS VS. CONFESSING }

I met him the fall of my sophomore year at college. We were together every possible moment. We studied together, went out on the weekends, and partied together. After three months of dating, I knew that he was the one—the man that I wanted to stay with for the rest of my life. And he felt the same way about me. So it only seemed natural that we would sleep together. It seemed like the right action to take. After all, I was making my own decisions now, not my parents or anyone else. And it was my choice to have sex with my boyfriend.

Of course, it never occurred to me that this choice could result in some fairly serious consequences. I thought that problems like getting pregnant happened to other people. Not me. But

*He heals the*

*brokenhearted and*

*binds up their wounds.*

Psalm 147:3, NIV

about six weeks later, after feeling crummy for a while and missing a period, I knew that something was up. I went to the Women's Center at the college where I took a pregnancy test. Even then it seemed so unreal. It was a complete shock when I received the results: *positive*.

I remember sitting in the small, stuffy third floor office and numbly trying to listen as the volunteer counselor explained my options. In great detail she outlined the procedure for ending the pregnancy—the nearest clinic, the cost, how to get an appointment, how much time it would take (about a half day), and what would be involved in the procedure (she never called it an abortion, but a procedure). Or, she said, I could have the baby. Period. No recommendations for agencies that might help with that decision or where I might go for further counseling if I decided to keep the baby. I would definitely be on my own if that was the course that I wanted to follow.

At that point in my life, however, I thought that there really was no other option. I was not ready to have a baby, and I certainly didn't want to get married. I had goals. I had my future career in mind. I knew what I wanted to do, and a baby was definitely not a part of that plan. It was my choice, my responsibility, and I was going to make my decision.

When I finally disclosed this news to my boyfriend, there really was no discussion except when to schedule the abortion. That was it. My mind was made up, and to be honest, I don't know if my boyfriend had any doubts about the decision. I know I didn't. At least I didn't allow myself to have any. I fully bought into the mantra of the women's rights movement during the 1970s: "My body, my choice."

With those words reinforcing my actions, we proceeded. I clearly remember certain aspects of that day. I remember sobbing because we had brought the wrong kind of money order. So we had to rush to a bank and hurry back to the abortion clinic, or I would have to reschedule and come back another day. I remember meeting a woman in the locker room area where we undressed and got into hospital gowns.

She was getting ready to leave. She had on an immaculate suit with lots of expensive jewelry, so I thought she was either a businesswoman or had a lot of money. She casually informed me that this was her third (maybe fourth?) abortion, and I had nothing to worry about. It was a breeze, she said.

I remember being led to a sterile room and feeling completely helpless and vulnerable as I lay on the table. I remember how impersonal it all felt. I never knew the doctor's name and he never even asked mine. In fact, he never said anything to me. I remember grasping tightly to the nurse's hand as she whispered words of encouragement to me as the baby was sucked out of my womb—the only person who even attempted to connect with me as a human. I remember feeling so empty as I was escorted to the recovery room where I joined about a dozen other women who were munching on crackers and drinking juice. Do you know what we talked about? We talked about what we felt like when we were pregnant—how tired we felt and how sick we were in the morning. Anything but what we had just gone through. Then I was handed a pack of antibiotics, told to take it easy the rest of the day, and to schedule a checkup in about a week. I was sent on my way.

My boyfriend and I left, and we never talked about the abortion again. The next night I went to a dance. My life resumed as before. I had messed up, but I had taken responsibility for my mistake. End of story. It was my life, my decision, and I was completely in charge.

Aside from telling my best friend, I never mentioned the experience to another person. I buried that experience deep, deep within me. Even when I became a Christian years later, it was something that I only confessed to God. God had forgiven me, so there was nothing more that I needed to do. I realized what I had done was morally wrong and repugnant to God, but again, it had been my choice and I was going to deal with it. I didn't really want God to deal with it in my life. I was going to do so on my own terms.

Then I met a woman associated with the ministry Love From Above. She shared with me what the ministry was all about and

I REALIZED WHAT I HAD DONE WAS MORALLY WRONG AND REPUGNANT TO GOD, BUT AGAIN, IT HAD BEEN MY CHOICE AND I WAS GOING TO DEAL WITH IT. I DIDN'T REALLY WANT GOD TO DEAL WITH IT IN MY LIFE. I WAS GOING TO DO SO ON MY OWN TERMS.

*The Lord is close*

*to the brokenhearted*

*and saves those who*

*are crushed in spirit.*

Psalm 34:18, NIV

her desire to publish a journal that would help post-abortive women find healing and hope. Within minutes of meeting her, with tears streaming down my face, I disclosed the secret that I had never uttered to another person for the past twenty-seven years. I was post-abortive. And I was in need of healing.

This had *not* been just *my* decision, *my* responsibility, and *my* choice, with no impact on anyone else. I began to discover that I needed forgiveness from my partner, from my baby whose life I had so callously ended, and from myself. I needed God to take this experience and redeem it for His purposes.

## Reflection

Betsy tells of keeping the reality of her abortion buried for many years before God brought her to a place of being able to share with a trusted person what had happened to her. We hope that this journal will be a place for you to begin to share what has happened to you—even if you, too, have kept what you have done a secret.

Why do you think Betsy kept her abortion a secret? In what ways have you kept your abortion a secret?

_____

_____

_____

_____

Betsy heard and followed the cultural message of "my body, my choice." What messages did you hear from society regarding abortion?

_____

_____

_____

_____

Having an abortion can seem like a way of taking responsibility for becoming pregnant. In what ways did you feel that you were taking responsibility for your actions?

_____

_____

_____

_____

On the day of her abortion, Betsy remembers sobbing because she brought the wrong money order and might not have been able to have the abortion that day. Why do you think she felt such a sense of urgency to have the abortion?

On that day that you went to the abortion clinic, what were some of the thoughts going through your mind?

Betsy describes asking God for forgiveness and receiving it. In her life, she couldn't keep her abortion a secret between herself and God and still receive deep healing; she needed to tell someone. Why is it so important to tell someone else the secret about your abortion? Have you told someone else? Why or why not? (These are very difficult questions. Perhaps you will want to re-read this part of her story, or come back to these questions more than once and see what new insights emerge.)

## { BETSY'S STORY CONTINUES }

It was truly God's direction that brought me in contact with Love From Above. I've found a community of sisters in Christ who have shared the same painful experience and who have received healing. Through their incredible stories, I realized the pain and guilt that I had pushed down to the deep recesses of my mind and soul. For the first time, I felt the freedom and release that comes with telling my story. I now recognize that the destructive behavior I engaged in throughout the years following my abortion was directly tied to that experience. I believe that God wants to take this experience and redeem it for His purposes. I thank God that He has brought people into my life who have encouraged me in my Christian walk and loved me enough to help me end my destructive patterns. God has graciously helped me see that He is the God of my past, my present, and my future. He can redeem this experience and use it for His glory. God's promise to do this is clearly given in His offer of forgiveness that was secured for all of us through His Son, Jesus. "He gave his life to free us from every kind of sin, to cleanse us, and to make us his very own people, totally committed to doing what is right" (Titus 2:14, NLT).

As I write this, I know I still have a long way to go in the healing process. I still struggle with totally relinquishing this experience to God, even as I know with all certainty that I must. I pray for the courage to do so, and I thank God that He is so very patient with me. I write my story with the hope that you will see yourself in my situation and will realize that it's okay to struggle. It's okay to be "in process." But my hope and prayer for you, as it is for myself, is that you will let go and let God bring healing and forgiveness.

## { GOING DEEPER }

*Betsy talked about God being the "God of the past, the present, and the future." This is one of the amazing realities of the healing that comes from God. Not only does He forgive our sins and heal us of past pain, but He also extends healing backward and forward from the event. As we experience His healing going backward, we will be able to forgive those in our past that we need to forgive. Those in need of forgiveness in Betsy's story were the people who presented her with limited options, including the volunteer at the women's center who didn't help her explore the possibility of keeping her baby, and the doctor who didn't take the trouble to even ask her name.*

*When we experience God's love and healing power extending forward, we can begin to forgive the person that might be the hardest to forgive— ourselves. As Betsy discovered, this is a process. Daily we need to take hold of God's grace and love and begin to treat ourselves as His precious daughters, fully forgiven and worthy and valuable in His eyes!*

*For those who are going through the process of healing themselves, there is a section in the back of this journal that provides five steps you can take to find healing from your abortion experience. Take time to explore those steps now, or at the end of your journaling experience.*

{ GOD'S LOVE LETTER }

*My Little Girl,*

*It makes Me sad to see your head hanging so low. Because when I made you it was your beautiful face I remember most. In the softness of your eyes I placed tomorrow's visions. In your smile I placed tomorrow's hope. In the softness of your skin I placed the beauty of My gentle touch. To know that you think I can't, or won't, forgive you hurts Me so much. All I have ever wanted was for you to understand that I forgive you and that I want to be your loving Daddy.*

*Your Daddy in heaven*

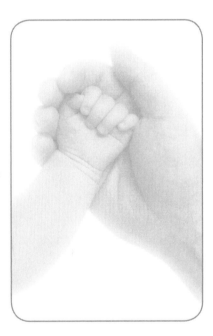

# Your Time to Speak

**Child, tell Me what's on your heart right now. I am listening.**

# "It's okay to have an abortion; there is something wrong with the baby"

## { MARIA'S STORY— REJECTION VS. ACCEPTANCE }

I grew up in a terribly dysfunctional household. I longed for acknowledgement that I was special and unique, but it never came. Distorted relationships were role-modeled for my siblings and me. The insecurity, anxiety, and depression we suffered followed me into adulthood.

I do not blame my parents for the mess my life became. I have forgiven them for what they know was wrong. Looking back, I finally understand that a desperate need for love and acceptance from others controlled my entire life. My dependency on others for affirmation resulted in a grief so intense that I thought I would die from it. I want to explain the influence that the past had on the decisions I made. The substitutes we choose to fill

*You will be a crown of*

*splendor in the LORD's*

*hand, a royal diadem in*

*the hand of your God.*

Isaiah 62:3, NIV

the deepest needs and longings of our hearts *will* eventually bring us down, over and over again.

I married young, had one child, and divorced after fifteen years of marriage. My ex and most of his family struggled with alcoholism. They were, and still are, good people who accepted me. Through them, I felt that I had worth. After the divorce, I felt rejection from the only "normal" family that I'd known. I was terrified of raising a child alone and of having no support system.

Soon after the split, I was involved with a successful, intelligent man who was attentive and made me feel like I mattered. But I still felt unworthy to be with someone of his caliber. He ended the relationship after two years. I was rejected again, experienced my first panic attack, and went on antidepressants.

I was aware of my need for male approval, but I was not promiscuous. I wondered if there was anyone out there for me who had a loving family background, who had no addictions, and who would provide the love and affirmation that I desired. Having a couple of good parents to adopt me would be nice, too. I was not unattractive. I was hard-working, fun, and would stand on my head for anyone who would love me. What was wrong with everyone?

It was eerie how quickly my wish came true. I met a too-good-to-be-true man who was attractive, athletic, well-educated, and had a great family. He proposed marriage quickly, and I was ecstatic. I finally felt loved by a man, welcomed by his parents and the rest of the close-knit, religious family. I was so eager to please, to prove that I was worthy enough to belong that I ignored warning signs and "gut" feelings. Then I found out I was pregnant . . . about the same time that he told me he didn't love me and didn't want to marry me. He urged me to terminate the pregnancy. I was horrified. He did not want the baby or me.

Rejected again.

Here I was, in my forties, pregnant by a man who didn't want our baby or me. I made it clear that I would not terminate the pregnancy unless there was a medical reason. He felt trapped, and I stopped making wedding plans. My life savings had been put into the down payment for the house that we had bought together, so we moved into our new home. I felt sick often, and concealed the pregnancy at work and at family gatherings so that no one would know. I worried about facing this. If he left me, would his family help with the baby? Probably not. I felt helpless.

Because of my age, I talked with a genetic counselor, who gave me statistics on the probability of having a child with cystic fibrosis or Down's syndrome. I sobbed as I told the counselor that the father wanted to terminate the pregnancy for no good reason. She said that "any reason to terminate was a good one to those who make that choice." I wanted to slap her.

I had to be sixteen weeks into the pregnancy for an amniocentesis to be performed. I was told that before twenty weeks, a D&C could be done. But after twenty weeks, labor could be induced and I could deliver a baby that might not survive. That was unthinkable to me. I worried that the longer I waited, the more time the blob of tissue had to become a baby. I went for a procedure called CVS (chronic villous sampling) that detects abnormalities at only eleven to twelve weeks gestation. The doctor was unable to complete the procedure because my tipped uterus made it impossible to get a sample of the placenta for DNA testing. At seventeen weeks I went for the amniocentesis and received beautiful ultrasound pictures of the baby. I stared at the fully formed arms, legs, ears, and nose. The baby was in just the right position in one picture, and we jokingly agreed that it was most likely a boy.

My doctor phoned with results one week later: Down's syndrome. I broke down and told her that I was relieved because the father didn't want the child anyway. As she gave me the necessary names and numbers, she assured me that she would make the same decision if she were in my position. I wasn't thinking clearly, but this was an "abnormality" and I had

I SOBBED AS I TOLD THE COUNSELOR THAT THE FATHER WANTED TO TERMINATE THE PREGNANCY FOR NO GOOD REASON. SHE SAID THAT "ANY REASON TO TERMINATE WAS A GOOD ONE TO THOSE WHO MAKE THAT CHOICE." I WANTED TO SLAP HER.

a good, medical reason to terminate. This made it acceptable to do what the father wanted to do all along. The procedure was scheduled for one week later. When I felt movement in my womb that week, I had the strange thought that the baby sensed what I was about to do. I asked God and the child to forgive me. I obsessed about the ultrasound pictures and what a fetus at this stage could feel.

I decided I had two choices: one, risk going completely nuts thinking these kinds of thoughts; or two, get tough, harden up, tell myself the movement was a five- to seven-inch defective blob of tissue and not a real baby. The mind must go into survival mode—shutting down the distorted thinking that occurs when faced with emotions too huge to handle. It worked and I got through the week.

At the hospital, the doctor said that there was no proof that the fetus feels anything because neural development isn't complete at this stage. She asked if we wanted to keep the body for a burial service afterward. I almost jumped out of my skin. *What?!* I couldn't comprehend what she said. *What body?* My brain snapped. I went into Survival Option #2: Go numb.

As a nurse explained the procedure to me again, I wondered if she thought I was a bad person. A mild sedative was injected into my IV and I felt dizzy. I was wheeled into the brightly lit surgery room and climbed onto the table. I was aware of everything but wasn't afraid. I fought back tears by joining two nurses in small talk. I felt the doctor put the instrument into me. There was no pain at all, only pressure. I chatted nervously expecting pain to come but it never did. It seemed like only five minutes had passed when the doctor said, "It's done," and removed the instrument. The tears flowed. I couldn't believe I got off this easy. No physical pain.

After an hour in the recovery area, I dressed and was assisted to the front of the hospital where my boyfriend was waiting with the car. We drove home in silence. Why wasn't he asking me how I felt? Why didn't he care? Could it be possible he was suffering remorse? At home I expected the pain that I deserved to come, but it didn't. I felt guilty for feeling fine. My boyfriend avoided me. Why did I keep wanting comfort from him? I felt continuous rejection and coldness. Did I expect too much and was that why he was always disappointing me? Was I nuts or was he?

The grief became so intense that I could not bear it. I knew I was at risk for post-partum depression, but this was different from the depression that I felt in the past. It was what hell must be like. The ultrasound pictures of my perfectly formed baby haunted me. Time went by in slow motion, prolonging the grief. Was this God's punishment for my terrible sin? I was not able to go numb so I was forced to face the guilt of what I had done.

I woke up every morning and the sting of it would hit me like salt poured into a wound. I deserved to suffer so I punished myself. I made myself look at the ultrasound pictures. Nothing could be worse than that. I knew I was teetering on the edge of sanity. A few days later I called the doctor that had performed the procedure and told her about the unbearable grief. I hoped she would console me. She gave me the number of a grief counselor that specialized in infant death. The counselor told me she would have made the same decision that I had and so would a friend of hers who had a Down's syndrome child. This made me feel slightly better.

Throughout the next few months, my boyfriend and I tried to have some happy days. But I felt guilty for laughing. Sometimes we went to church on Sunday; I think it made him feel like a good person to go. Hey, if God didn't strike him down first, then I was safe, too. I looked for signs of remorse from him. I could not bear all the guilt, and thought he should bear some, too. He just wanted to get on with life. I was going through hell, and he didn't care.

Something felt so terribly wrong it shook me to the core. I felt a powerful desperation, a strong need pulling me. I thought it was a desperate need to coax love from my partner; the harder I tried to get affection, the uglier he became. I just wanted love from him, acceptance, approval, a crumb . . . anything at all.

I KNEW I WAS AT RISK FOR POST-PARTUM DEPRESSION, BUT THIS WAS DIFFERENT FROM THE DEPRESSION THAT I FELT IN THE PAST. IT WAS WHAT HELL MUST BE LIKE.

Who do you call for that? I needed to ask someone something, someone who could help me. Finally it dawned on me: *Ask for forgiveness!*

I ran to the pastor of the church and spilled my story. What would it cost me, what it would take, how many millions of times did I have to say the Act of Contrition? I would do anything to earn forgiveness (if it were possible) for such a terrible sin.

Then I heard the truth. *The forgiveness was already there if I would accept it.* "That is why Jesus died on the cross," the pastor said. Those words were the beginning of hope for me. Hope that this living hell of guilt could end. Could I live without needing any human being to determine my worth and value? All this time I thought I was a "good person" who only wanted good things like love. But the Lord was the One who could fill the desperate need I felt. He alone could help me deal with the painful consequences of my actions. He knew that I was stubborn and wouldn't have been open to Him until I experienced the agony produced by the guilt of my sin.

*And when the Chief*

*Shepherd appears, you*

*will receive the crown*

*of glory that will*

*never fade away.*

1 Peter 5:4, NIV

## Reflection

Without the love and acceptance from our parents or caregivers, we grow up with a deep emptiness and need inside that we desperately try to fill. What was the way that Maria tried to fill the need for herself? What are some other ways that you have tried to fill the need for love and acceptance in your life?

_____

_____

_____

_____

_____

After her divorce, Maria was vulnerable and wanted the man she met to "be right" and ignored the warning signs and her "gut feelings" about him. Can you think of a situation when you wanted something so desperately to work that you also ignored the warning signs or your "gut feelings"? Describe the situation below.

_____

_____

_____

_____

Maria's "too-good-to-be-true" man responded by rejecting both Maria and the baby when he found out that she was pregnant. How did the man in your life respond? How did you feel as a result of that?

_____

_____

_____

_____

Maria refused to have an abortion unless her baby had a medical problem. She then found out that her baby had Down's syndrome. So in her mind, the abortion was justified. What justifications did you make for your abortion? What was the impact of those justifications for you?

After her abortion, Maria felt horrible grief and guilt. She turned to her boyfriend and the pastor of her church for help. Who did you turn to in dealing with your abortion? What was the response?

## { Maria's Story Continues }

It's been a year and a half. I still mourn over my unborn baby.
I have given him a name. I try to remember that he is in God's
hands. My dear friend keeps the ultrasound pictures safe with
her because I cannot bear having them near. It still hurts;
writing this hurts. Every year I will have to go through the
date of the termination and the due date five months later. My
abortion will affect my future forever.

Knowing that I'm forgiven for this horrible sin brings me to my
knees. I am so humbled, changed, and grateful. My life makes
more sense to me now. I understand why I spent my life trying
to fill a legitimate need that was never filled by anyone. I've
learned that *there is no substitute for my greatest need*—no man, no set
of perfect parents, no job, no object, nothing. Only God can fill
my emptiness.

## { GOING DEEPER }

*What is our greatest need? Is it love? Acceptance? To be known? To be
seen as valuable? To have a reason to live? When her early relationships
didn't meet those needs, Maria tried to meet those needs in relationships
first with her husband-to-be and his family. Eventually, she discovered
that only God could meet her deepest need. When she opened herself up
to a relationship with Him, she found the love and forgiveness that she
needed and hope for the future.*

*But, even if we came from a warm, caring family and those needs for love,
acceptance, and purpose were largely met, we will still live with feelings
of emptiness and longing. We are created in such a way that no human
relationship, no matter how wonderful, can fully meet those needs. Only by
opening up, as Maria did, to a relationship with our Creator will we find
that those needs are fully and deeply met. In relationship with God we find
the love to fill us and the hope for the future that we need to truly live!*

## { GOD'S LOVE LETTER }

*My Little Girl,*

*You are My princess! Every time I look at you, I see the beauty of who you are. When I close My eyes, I see you dancing with your baby doll giggling with the laughter of your innocence. On your head you are wearing a beautiful crown, like those reserved for a King's daughter. I am reminded of the crown My Son wore and how He wore **that** crown for you. I have built a special mansion for you! It looks like a castle. I long for us to be together forever in this place.*

*Your Daddy in heaven*

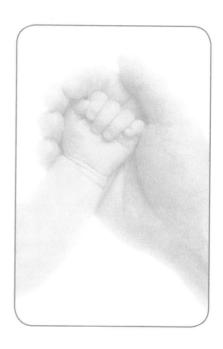

# Your Time to Speak

**My precious daughter, what is on your heart? Tell Me now.**

# "I am alone; no one cares about me"

## { Laura's Story—Despair vs. Hope }

Growing up, I believed that I was all alone and that no one really cared what happened to me. We were a divided family. My brother and I were not close. I did not feel safe at home. It was a nightmare most of the time from the time that I was nine years old. My energy was spent keeping the family secrets and pretending that everything was okay, even though there was constant fighting. Denial became my way of life. Remembering my past is like wearing a crown of thorns. With each memory there is a sharp pain and a wound that becomes exposed. My heart is covered with battle scars from that time.

The idea of commitment was an illusion. My parents were not committed to each other—just other things. Our family dynamics destroyed relationships. No one would stay around.

*And may you have the*

*power to understand, as*

*all God's people should,*

*how wide, how long,*

*how high, and how*

*deep his love really is.*

Ephesians 3:18, NLT

The message was, "I love you and now that you believe it, I will leave." I so wanted to be loved for just being me, flaws and all. I had a broken heart and felt so forsaken. I always had to perform to be perfect. To be loved was beyond my imagination.

Then some friends introduced me to a guy. On our first date he took me out to dinner to a really nice Italian restaurant. He opened up a new world to me that I did not know existed; he took me to nice restaurants, he taught me how to order off the menu. We spent time with his family at their cottage in Wisconsin. His friends became my friends. His mom made dinner every night, and his family was accepting of me. I felt that I wasn't alone anymore.

Soon I fell so in love that I gave him all of me—heart, mind, body, and soul. He had all that I valued. I loved him, and I so needed to belong and be loved by him. I truly believed that one day we would get married. We began having sex. Being Catholic, I knew that sex before marriage was a sin, but I felt that I would find the kind of love I needed in sex. My boyfriend said he loved me, and I know in some way that he did love me. Yet there were signs that the love I needed and desired most was not there. I ignored those signs because the desire to be loved and to believe in the dreams of marriage and having a family were so strong. Lacking the courage to stand firm and hold on to what I really wanted—a committed love in a marriage that would last for a lifetime—I settled for a love that was temporary.

Well that "love" brought me to a pregnancy clinic. Back at work, the person from the clinic phoned me with the results: "You are pregnant." I hung up the phone and ran to the bathroom to vomit. Everything I had been told when I was young came flooding back. Every thought pierced my mind: *My parents are going to kill me. No guy will ever want me again. Look at me—I go to the clubs all the time, dancing, drinking, smoking, and taking diet pills. There is no way this baby would be healthy if it were born.* I was alone, crushed, lost, and afraid.

My boyfriend and I discussed our pregnancy. He told me he was not ready to be a father and that he would pay for the abortion. So I went to the doctor and was told it would be a simple procedure, that the "fetus was tissue," and that I would be fine. The doctor said it was like a Pap smear. So I made the appointment. I felt alone with nowhere to go. I didn't even consider single parenting or adoption as options. As my one friend told me, "How can you support a baby when you can't even support yourself?" I was so confused and so isolated.

At the clinic, after my number was called, a lady led me into a room and asked me if I wanted to go through with this. I couldn't say it, but I wanted to run out of the door. She brought me to the next room to dress for my abortion. Dressed in a blue surgery gown, my baby and I were like lambs being led to the slaughter. As I lay there, the nurse held my hand as the doctor did the procedure. I remembered tears were falling down as I heard numbers being called out. I didn't realize it at the time, but they were counting to make sure they had all the baby's parts and had not left anything inside me. I felt so alone, empty, and condemned.

I thought my problems would be over after my abortion, but the torment was just beginning. The guilt, shame, fear, denial, depression, and anger were like grenades exploding into every part of my life. I gave permission for my baby to die. I did not protect my child, just as I was not protected as a child. I felt so dirty inside. I became numb. I had compromised everything I had ever believed that was good for this lie. I needed to deny that I had carried a live baby in my womb. So I believed that the baby was just a mass of tissue.

After the abortion was over, the relationship I had with my boyfriend was destroyed. The young man, who I thought had eyes that shined like diamonds, now had eyes filled with darkness. I became anorexic. My hair went to three different shades. I started to drink a lot and used cocaine as my drug of choice. I dressed provocatively. I had no self-respect or pride; but I did have rage, and I blamed everyone. I was crying out for help, but no one was listening. The word *abortion* would make me sick to my stomach. I was so scared, so paralyzed by the lies. Who would ever love me? I did not deserve to ever be loved.

> I REMEMBERED TEARS WERE FALLING DOWN AS I HEARD NUMBERS BEING CALLED OUT. I DIDN'T REALIZE IT AT THE TIME, BUT THEY WERE COUNTING TO MAKE SURE THEY HAD ALL THE BABY'S PARTS AND HAD NOT LEFT ANYTHING INSIDE ME.

*The LORD keeps*

*watch over you as you*

*come and go, both*

*now and forever.*

Psalm 121:8, NLT

My life had spun completely out of control. I was lashing out and I was hurting everyone who cared about me. I had hurt my boyfriend's mother badly because I had wanted to hurt my baby's father. Yet, she was the first person who taught me that the greatest measure of love is not what you give, but what you give up; and that is sacrifice. She forgave me and showed the love of Jesus Christ in the flesh. I started to heal, but I was still hurt.

I could not hold a job, and for some reason, no one ever really wanted to marry me. The dream of family was fading away. Some time passed and I met a new guy. I thought I was in love and that he loved me. Love meant being physical and before long I had bought a home pregnancy test. Just as I had suspected, I was pregnant. When I told him I was pregnant, my boyfriend was angry and wanted me to have an abortion. He said that if I loved him, I would have an abortion. But love does not ask you to end the life of another human being.

Then one day when I was taking a shower, the tears just started to flow. I was scrubbing my skin so hard that I wanted my skin to bleed. I wanted to take my fist and reach down into my throat and try to scrub clean the inside of my body. I could not get clean enough. I curled up into a fetal position as the hot water ran down my body and I wailed before God. How could God forgive me when I could not forgive myself? I thought that all the bad things that happened in my life were because God knew that I had allowed my baby to be terminated. My body was to bring forth life, not death. But my womb had become a tomb, and it only takes the beat of my heart to remember my choice and re-visit in my thoughts the gravesite of my first child.

I knew I had a choice: "Today, Laura, you can choose whom you will serve, life or death." I chose life. I went to church the next day and started my new life. This time I was going to protect my child, and I turned to God for help and forgiveness. I asked Him to forgive me, and He did just that. He breathed His life and hope into me! No longer hopeless, I became hopeful.

Over the next five months I was pressured by family and friends to abort my child. My boyfriend also pressured me to have an abortion. I told him no way. He emotionally and verbally abused me. He tried to bribe me with vacations if I would have an abortion. Finally he asked me to marry him. I told him no. I was not marrying someone like him. I asked God to shield me with His angels so that no one would see me pregnant and I would not have to deal with the guilt, shame, and gossip. I was alone and pregnant again, but I was with God.

I did not know if I was going to keep my baby or place my baby up for adoption. I continued to deal with the emotions of my earlier abortion. I had never grieved the death of my first baby. It was hard trying to make decisions with very little support or encouragement. I prayed and decided that the best decision for me was to keep my child.

I gave birth to a little girl and named her Hope. She has autism. It is hard being a single parent. I cannot go out when I want to or do what I want. I have a responsibility to my daughter. I am attending college. To do my homework, I have to get up at 4 AM or stay up late. I have a job doing home day care while taking care of my ill mother. I would *not* trade one day of my life or one tear I have shed for having my daughter, Hope, in my life. I love her more than I thought I could love any human being.

THIS TIME I WAS GOING TO PROTECT MY CHILD, AND I TURNED TO GOD FOR HELP AND FORGIVENESS. I ASKED HIM TO FORGIVE ME, AND HE DID JUST THAT. HE BREATHED HIS LIFE AND HOPE INTO ME! NO LONGER HOPELESS, I BECAME HOPEFUL.

## Reflection

Laura talks about her past as "wearing a crown of thorns," and telling her story is like being stabbed by past hurts. What were some of the ways that you have been hurt and mistreated in your past?

_____

_____

_____

_____

_____

_____

_____

_____

Laura's family did not show her what love meant. With her boyfriend, she confused love with need. In what ways did you confuse love with need in your relationship? How would you describe real love?

_____

_____

_____

_____

_____

_____

_____

_____

_____

In her story, Laura describes the ways that she felt all alone. In your situation, what are some of the ways that you have felt alone?

Laura became pregnant a second time and made a different choice. In carrying her second child, she also grieved the abortion she had had with her first child. If you have had a baby since your abortion, what was that pregnancy like for you?

## { LAURA'S STORY CONTINUES }

I have undergone intense abortion recovery that started five years ago when I met Grace Kern. She is a counselor who has listened to me cry and scream with no judgment or condemnation. She has prayed for me and has been my strength through my recovery. Through Grace, God started to open doors to let me speak to many people about what my abortion life has been like. I had the opportunity to speak in front of 40,000 youth and share my story. When I spoke in front of all those people, the message was called "A Love Beyond Imagination." I have met my Prince Charming and He is Jesus. His love for me is beyond my imagination.

The greatest measure of love is what Jesus did for me on the cross. God has placed some of His family in my life today to love me and care about me with the love of Jesus with skin on. They can tell me when I am getting too intense and help me slow down. I can receive it with love. I have been given wonderful friends who have stepped in for Hope, and I have a successful career, family, and church. I have Jesus.

## { GOING DEEPER }

*Laura named her daughter Hope. Hope is vital to our lives, for without hope we are in despair. In fact, when assessing depression, persistent feelings of hopelessness are a strong indicator of the possibility of suicide. We need hope to live!*

*Laura didn't have hope from the family that gave her birth nor did she find hope through the other students at her school. She wanted to find hope in the arms of her boyfriend and through his family, but that didn't happen either. Instead, she finally found her true hope in accepting the love of Jesus and in letting Him heal her. As she says, He gave her "hope in all ways." If you, like Laura, are also feeling alone and hopeless, our prayer for you is that you would also find hope—and find it in the arms of your Father in heaven. He is our hope!*

## { GOD'S LOVE LETTER }

*My Little Girl,*

*I have loved you from the beginning of time. Even before your mother and father knew of you, I loved you. I long for you to understand how wide, how long, and how deep My love for you is. I know that many in your life have failed you. I have seen and felt your pain all along. You have never been alone. I was always there. Will you let Me be a part of your life? I promise I won't let you down. I love you.*

*Your Daddy in heaven*

## *Your Time to Speak*

**Precious daughter, tell Me what you are feeling right now in response to My love for you.**

Myth 8

# "I don't deserve forgiveness; I knew it was wrong"

{ Tommie's Story—
Guilt vs. Forgiveness }

Twenty-seven years ago I ended my child's life by having an abortion. I had many reasons for doing it. I was married and had two teenagers and a four-year-old. I had taken a medication that could have harmed an unborn child while I was unknowingly pregnant. During the same time, my marriage was in chaos. My husband insisted that I get an abortion. He didn't want another child, let alone a "damaged" child. He badgered me, and I was weak enough to give in.

Even though I was raised Catholic and had gone to Catholic schools from grade school through college, the topic of abortion was never mentioned. I tended to believe the feminist agenda that abortion was the answer to crisis pregnancy, and now it was

*My guilt overwhelms*

*me—it is a burden*

*too heavy to bear.*

Psalm 38:4, NLT

safe and legal. I did not know at the time that although it was legal, it was never safe. I went along with the feminist and media lies, but deep in my heart I knew that abortion was wrong.

I did not want the abortion and did a lot of stalling, hoping that my husband would change his mind. I say *his* mind because at that time I did not have a mind of my own. Through many years of verbal abuse and diabolical mind-games on his part, I can say that I had lost the ability to think for myself. My husband demanded that I get the abortion or he would leave. I was too frightened to think that I could make it on my own without him.

I went to the abortion clinic alone. I can remember every detail twenty-seven years later. As I entered the "abortion mill," I was so alone and frightened. There were young couples, mothers with their daughters, and groups of women with their girlfriends. I was the only one without anyone with me. I was completely alone.

They took me into a room for counseling. The "counseling" consisted of a woman asking me why I wanted the abortion. I asked her if it was a baby. She laughed and said it was just a blob of tissue. I then asked if it would feel any pain. She asked, "How can a blob of tissue feel pain?" That was the end of the counseling session.

They led me into the room where the vacuum abortion procedure was to take place. The doctor came in and did an exam. Then he told them to take me out because I was too far along for this procedure. (At that time the Illinois law would only allow this procedure during the first eight weeks of pregnancy.) As I was leaving, I walked through a room where women were resting after their abortions. Most of them were weeping and seemed distraught. This really hit me hard.

I went to my personal doctor to verify the length of my pregnancy. He said I was under the eight-week mark, but he would not do an abortion. In fact, he advised me not to proceed with the abortion. I couldn't wait to tell my husband, but my husband was unrelenting and personally took me to Planned

Parenthood. By the time we went to Planned Parenthood, I was past the eight-week mark and so was sent to a hospital in Lansing, Michigan.

As they prepared me for the abortion, which had to be done in an operating room with a general anesthetic, the reality of what I was doing was devastating. I was about twelve weeks along. They had me line up in a hall outside the operating room, along with others waiting for the same procedure. By the time it was my turn, the anesthetic was wearing off. I told the nurses, and they gave me more. As they began the scraping, I could feel the scalpel inside of me.

The next thing I remember was becoming aware of the nurses slapping me and calling my name as they tried to revive me. I wasn't responding and they were panicking. I could hear their frightened voices and their remarks, but I couldn't move to respond. I remember thinking that this was my punishment from God for taking my child's life. I thought God would never forgive me nor would I ever be able to forgive myself.

My husband and I never spoke about it again, and I never told another person. My marriage did not last, and my baby's life was given up for nothing. I know now that I could have made it by myself, but it was too late to save my baby's life.

My road to forgiveness took quite a while. For a long time I wouldn't look at anything that would remind me of the abortion. I would take my son to the museum but would avoid the display of the development of an unborn baby within its mother's womb. I forced myself to watch the TV program called "The Silent Scream." It was a documentary, and it showed the ultrasound of the baby in the mother's womb. The lies and deception of the abortionist, the feminist, and the media became apparent to me. When I heard the pro-abortion representative on TV stating that abortion was good for women and that women were smart enough to make intelligent choices on their own, I became angry. I felt the word *choice* was a lie from the pit of hell. I was not pro-life then, but I knew that women could not make informed or intelligent "choices"

I REMEMBER THINKING THAT THIS WAS MY PUNISHMENT FROM GOD FOR TAKING MY CHILD'S LIFE. I THOUGHT GOD WOULD NEVER FORGIVE ME NOR WOULD I EVER BE ABLE TO FORGIVE MYSELF.

*Let us draw near to*

*God with a sincere*

*heart in full assurance*

*of faith, having our*

*hearts sprinkled to*

*cleanse us from a*

*guilty conscience.*

Hebrews 10:22a, NIV

because they were not being given the truth. The realization that the truth was not being taught began my journey toward forgiveness, recovery, and becoming pro-life.

I remember going back to the Catholic church, looking up to the image of the risen Christ on the altar, and saying, "If You are real and all that I am hearing about You is real, please show me and lead me to You." After that, people came into my life, planting "seeds" of faith, and leading me to the Lord. I met people in the strangest ways, some of whom led me to a faith-filled Christian prayer group. They began telling me about God's forgiveness and how it was attainable even for the most grievous of sins. This opened the door for me. I had never before confessed my sin of abortion.

I attended a church retreat, and the priest asked us to come and confess the one sin we had never confessed. I believed that he was talking directly to me. I had to confess the sin that I believed to be my most unpardonable sin: my abortion. I could only get the word out . . . *abortion*. After that, he told us to go to our rooms and ask the Lord to let us feel the love that He has for us. As I prayed in my room, I felt an overwhelming feeling of warmth and love, something that I had never experienced before. It was greater and more wonderful than anything imaginable. I knew that I had received God's forgiveness.

*Reflection*

Tommie felt pressured into having the abortion by her husband. What types of pressures did you feel to have an abortion? How did you respond?

_____

_____

_____

_____

_____

If you were married when you had your abortion, what was your husband's response?

_____

_____

_____

_____

_____

What were the pros and cons of having an abortion that you considered when making your decision?

_____

_____

_____

_____

_____

What were your thoughts about the "morality" of abortion before you had yours? How did those thoughts influence your decision?

Tommie said that she wasn't given the truth when she made her decision to have an abortion. What was the truth that she wished she had known? What do you wish you had known before you made your decision?

When, if ever, did you share about your pregnancy or abortion with the people from your church? How did they respond?

If you have been on a similar journey in search of forgiveness, what response have you received from your church? When you pray, what do you feel is God's response?

## { TOMMIE'S STORY CONTINUES }

It was still hard to forgive myself and to believe that my child would forgive me. But God did something amazing. At another church conference I attended, two priests presented a program on forgiveness. They told us to close our eyes and ask Jesus to bring us to someone that we needed to forgive, or from whom we needed forgiveness. I asked Jesus to bring me to my child whose life I chose to end.

I pictured Jesus standing with me on a hill filled with flowers, and as He waved His hand, a little girl came running over the hill. She was a beautiful three- or four-year-old girl with her arms outstretched running toward me. We embraced, and as I was begging her forgiveness, she kept patting me on my shoulder. I tilted my head and felt her little hands as she comforted me and made me feel forgiven. Whenever I think of her, I can still feel those little hands.

Forgiving myself was very difficult. It took time to realize that if God can forgive me and my daughter can forgive me, who am I not to forgive myself? I am not better or holier than they are. I now spend time with other women who have also endured the pain, shame, and guilt of abortion, helping them realize that we have a loving and forgiving God who sees our pain and will help us through it. We who have done the unimaginable can turn it into good, as we help others along the road to forgiveness.

## { GOING DEEPER }

*As part of her journey toward receiving forgiveness, Tommie participated in a program that used guided imagery in prayer. This can be a very powerful tool to receive forgiveness in a tangible way. One opportunity for you might be to find a prayer group that does this particular kind of prayer.*

*If you want to try praying with guided images, begin by picturing Jesus as you might imagine Him from a Bible story. He might be seated on a hillside teaching, or He might be walking with His disciples along the Sea of Galilee, or He might be alone in a quiet place praying. Then imagine yourself in the picture with Him. How does Jesus respond? What would you like to tell Him? What do you imagine He might say to you?*

## { GOD'S LOVE LETTER }

*My Little Girl,*

*I want to heal your broken heart. I want to mend the pieces together with My compassion.* **Through** *your pain and weakness I will make you strong. I know your guilt overwhelms you, and the burden is too heavy to bear. Let Me carry you through this. I long for you to understand that this was never a part of My plan for you. I am sorry that others have hurt you. Please let Me be your Daddy.*

*Your Daddy in heaven*

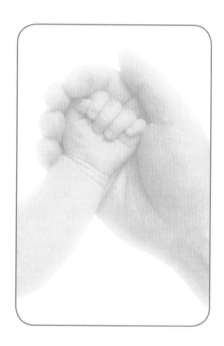

## Your Time to Speak

Pour out your heart, your thoughts, and your feelings to Me. I long to hear from you.

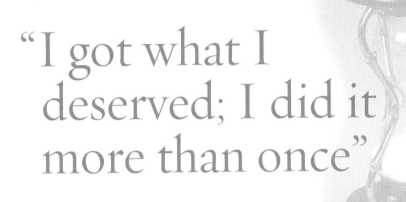

# "I got what I deserved; I did it more than once"

## { MARY KATHRYN'S STORY— BROKEN DREAMS VS. FULFILLMENT }

It is very difficult for me to look back over my life and tell my story. Today I am a forty-two-year-old professional who has worked full-time since I graduated from college in 1984. When I think of the life that I have lived, I wonder how and why I did what I did.

I grew up in a Christian home and went to church several times a week during my childhood. We were very strict Baptists. Then I went away to college and "cut loose" from the restrictions I had while growing up. I began to party and drink. Then I became sexually active and got involved with someone. It seems that once I opened "Pandora's box" of fun and pleasure, I wanted to keep it open.

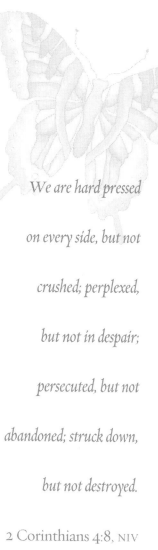

*We are hard pressed*

*on every side, but not*

*crushed; perplexed,*

*but not in despair;*

*persecuted, but not*

*abandoned; struck down,*

*but not destroyed.*

2 Corinthians 4:8, NIV

After I graduated from college, I began to work for a women's clothing store and quickly moved into management. When I received another promotion, I visited my old boyfriend from college to celebrate. It wasn't until several weeks later during a routine Pap smear that I discovered I was pregnant. I couldn't believe it! I even asked the doctor if I could have an abortion right away in his office after he gave me the news. I was certain that my family would hate me and would never forgive me (that's where the lies started!). I made an appointment to have an abortion the next week. When I arrived at the clinic, someone was standing outside of the building and asked me if I knew what I was doing. I didn't even acknowledge her. I didn't want to think about what I was doing, let alone discuss it with a stranger. I just wanted it to be over.

Inside the office, they gave me a consent form to sign and some Valium to take. Then the machine started. I cried as I lay there on the table. A nurse asked me if I was in pain, and I thought, *What a stupid question—the pain is in my head; I can't believe what I just did.* As I left the office with my girlfriend, she said, "Thank God, it's over." I agreed. But soon the torment of guilt began. I thought people looked at me differently. I saw myself as hideous, unforgiven, trash, useless, and unusable. I felt that I shouldn't even bother trying to have a relationship with God; He couldn't want me after what I had done.

I began dating a man who told me that I was beautiful, wonderful, and liked the fact that I went to church (a church big enough to sneak in and out of without anyone noticing me). He asked me if I had ever been pregnant, and I said I had. He then told me that two of his girlfriends had been pregnant and had had abortions. He accepted me and loved me, but still I was miserable.

We began sleeping together after three dates, and after only a couple of months, I suspected that he was cheating on me. When I questioned him, he told me some ridiculous story and reassured me that he loved me. I let myself believe him. A short while later I realized that I was pregnant. I made the arrangements to have another abortion. I soon found out that my boyfriend had been lying about other women, and I finally broke up with him. Throughout that time, I felt that I deserved what I got. Who would want me?

We had not been apart for long when my former boyfriend came to see me, and again I fell for the lies. Shortly thereafter I became pregnant yet again. I was living with my sister and brother-in-law at the time and decided to have by this time my fourth abortion. At this point in time I told my boyfriend that this abortion was my last. The next time I got pregnant we decided to get married. I was so ashamed to have to get married in Las Vegas without my family or friends. This was not the wedding I had dreamed about all of my life. It was, however, the wedding I thought I deserved. Shortly after we were married, my daughter was born. She was eight weeks premature. When I brought this beautiful little five-pound baby home, I realized what my abortions had actually done—ended the lives of those children. My guilt became unbearable, and it manifested itself in ways I never thought possible. I was assaulted daily by my own thoughts like

> *You can never have anyone good; you don't deserve it. You're a fraud. God will never forgive you. You're damaged goods. You're a loser. What would your family say if they knew the truth? You are an embarrassment. You can never let anyone know. Not even God can make this right. God doesn't want to make it right with you. God doesn't love you; He can't.*

I had no place to run or hide. I just knew that this was my lot in life and I was getting what I deserved.

To combat those negative thoughts in my head, I felt it necessary to look as good as I could on the outside. I wanted my house, my car, my hair, and makeup to be flawless. I reasoned that if I looked good on the outside, it would work its way in. I wanted everyone who knew me to think that I had it together. I needed to look and be a certain way and maintain my secret—the secret that ate at my soul. I found that because of my insecurities, I would look at others and find a reason to minimize their existence by putting them down. You see, gone was the concept that God created each of us and loved us

I DIDN'T WANT TO

THINK ABOUT WHAT

I WAS DOING, LET

ALONE DISCUSS IT WITH

A STRANGER. I JUST

WANTED IT TO BE OVER.

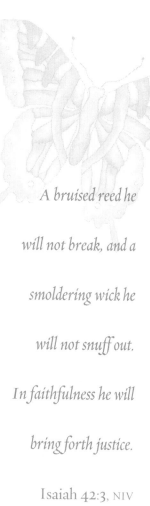

*A bruised reed he*

*will not break, and a*

*smoldering wick he*

*will not snuff out.*

*In faithfulness he will*

*bring forth justice.*

Isaiah 42:3, NIV

enough to die for us! I had a knack of making myself look better by judging others.

My son was born fifteen months after my daughter. I still was trying desperately to hold it together. I did not want anyone to know what was going wrong in my life and my marriage. My husband and I had a horrible relationship. For a while I listened to what he had to say about me—I was fat, ugly, stupid, lazy, a bad housekeeper, a bad cook, and a bad mom. I kept trying to do better, and the harder I tried, the worse that it got. I hated him and myself. Finally God gave me the courage to leave. I hadn't been able to leave my husband for myself, after all I got what I deserved. But I could leave for my children's sake.

## Reflection

When Mary Kathryn had her first abortion, she said she walked right by someone who wanted to talk to her about what she was doing. How willing were you to discuss your decision to have an abortion with others?

_____

_____

_____

_____

Here is a list of the lies that Mary Kathryn believed about herself. Circle the ones that you also believe. Then, take some time and write a true statement that counteracts each of the lies that you have circled.

You can never have anyone good or be in a good relationship; you don't deserve it.

You're a fraud.

God will never forgive you.

You're damaged goods.

You're a loser.

What would your family say if they knew the truth? You are an embarrassment.

You can never let anyone know.

Not even God can make this right.

God doesn't want to make it right with you.

God doesn't love you; He can't.

_____

_____

_____

Are there other lies that you believe about yourself? Write them down. Then take some time to write the truth beside each lie.

_____

_____

_____

_____

_____

We don't quickly believe the truth. Simply writing it down once won't automatically correct a lie, especially if we have believed it for a long time. One suggestion is to take some time to write the truths on small cards and carry them with you. At least twice daily read the cards aloud and remember the truth about yourself. This is an especially powerful exercise if you write down the truths from God's Word that correct the lies you have believed about yourself.

Here are some verses that offer the truth of God's promises of love, acceptance, and complete forgiveness for you. Look them up and write out God's promise to you.

Psalm 86:5

Psalm 103:11–14

Jeremiah 33:8

John 3:16–17

Colossians 1:13–14

Romans 5:8

Ephesians 2:4–8

1 John 1:9

Mary Kathryn's husband reinforced the lies she believed about herself. Is there someone in your life who is reinforcing the lies that you believe? What do you need to do about that relationship?

_____

_____

_____

_____

## { MARY KATHRYN'S STORY CONTINUES }

Two years later God began working in my life, using a friend's words to pierce my heart. My friend told me that when God looked at me, *He saw my purity*. That truth of God's love and acceptance broke through all the brick-and-mortar walls and exposed my heart—a heart that had been buried beneath years of lies and abuse, a heart that was impenetrable, and was now exposed. I am thankful to my friend who has opened up a vision of God's love for me and the truth of His Word.

I still look at these facts of my life and shudder. Yet I know that what Satan intended for harm, God will use for good. For this, I am truly thankful!

## { GOING DEEPER }

*This is a journal about healing and hope. One of the ways to experience healing is to give thanks. In fact, the Bible tells us that we grow in faith as we offer God thanks and praise for everything that occurs in our lives. Paul writes in Colossians, "Let your roots grow down into him and draw up nourishment from him, so you will grow in faith, strong and vigorous in the truth you were taught. Let your lives overflow with thanksgiving for all he has done" (Colossians 2:7, NLT). We are commanded to live lives full of thankfulness, "And you will always give thanks for everything to God the Father in the name of our Lord Jesus Christ" (Ephesians 5:20, NLT). As we focus on all that God has done for us through His Son, Jesus, we can begin to move past the pain and into healing.*

First, what are you thankful for right now in your *life?* Are there circumstances, friendships, family members, or unexplained positive "coincidences" that have brought you joy?

_____

_____

_____

_____

Second, what are you thankful for *about yourself?* This is not bragging. We all are made in God's image and we reflect Him. What do you see about yourself that you value? What do you like about yourself? "Nothing" is not an acceptable answer! Try to write down at least ten things that you appreciate about yourself.

_____

_____

_____

_____

Finally, what are you thankful for about *God's presence in your life?* Mary Kathryn was thankful that God saw her heart, her purity. She was also thankful for His love and the truth of His Word. God is also our Strength, our Refuge, our Healer and our Protector. He can be a source of wisdom and courage and hope. Take some time now to thank Him for who He is. Tell Him the ways you need Him to work in your life.

_____

_____

_____

_____

{ GOD'S LOVE LETTER }

*My Little Girl,*

*Please allow Me the opportunity to heal this ugliness. Let Me breathe life into this act of death. Your life has been shattered into millions of pieces. I know that you don't even know how to begin putting the pieces back together again. Let Me take your broken vessel back to the potter's wheel. I long for you to be whole again. I promise that when I am finished with you, My Son's resurrection from death will be your strength.*

*Your Daddy in heaven*

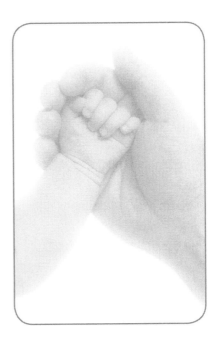

# *Your Time to Speak*

My precious child, tell Me what you are feeling right now in response to My lavish love for you.

# "This won't hurt; the pain will subside"

## { ELIZABETH'S STORY—PAIN VS. JOY }

They said it wouldn't hurt.

I was about eight weeks pregnant. I sat with a small group of women in an abortion facility in Cleveland, Ohio. We were looking at a plastic life-sized model of a uterus positioned before us. Someone asked the question that we were all thinking.

"Will it hurt?"

Quickly they assured us that there would be no pain, except for the "discomfort" of the injection in the cervix and a little pressure "like having your period." We were then encouraged to sign a very legal looking paper without reading it, as "there was

*And I am sure that*

*God, who began the*

*good work within*

*you, will continue his*

*work until it is finally*

*finished on that day*

*when Christ Jesus*

*comes back again.*

Philippians 1:6, NLT

not sufficient time and there was really nothing that could go wrong."

After the group session, I met with a counselor alone. The matronly woman who sat behind the desk was professional and domineering. I was very intimidated by her presence even though she spoke softly and smiled warmly. She asked about my religious background and if I knew the stand that my church took on abortion. I told her that I thought they would say it was wrong, hoping she would suggest that I call someone to ask. Instead, she again assured me that the procedure was not painful and that they were ready for me.

I wanted my husband to be with me. I had agreed before we were married to have an abortion if I became pregnant. But in the past few weeks I experienced mixed feelings about this decision, secretly wondering how I could keep the baby and not lose my husband's love. But my husband wasn't in the waiting room. The counselor hurried me along to the room across the hall, telling me that they were ready for me now. I reluctantly followed.

I was on my back, draped with a sheet, my feet up in the stirrups, when a man walked in. The woman at my side addressed him as "Doctor." He never looked at me. He sat down at my feet. I could see only the top of his head, dyed black hair, parted on the left side. The woman at my side put her hand on my left shoulder and spoke in a calming voice. The man spoke so softly I could hardly hear him. He pushed my knees wider apart and told me to slide down closer to the edge of the table. The woman at my side warned me the needle prick was about to happen. It did, and it was far more painful than a prick. I began to feel pressure, which kept intensifying. The hand on my shoulder became heavier and the woman's voice grew tenser as she told me to relax and be still. My insides screamed for me to get up and run away. Her hand kept me pinned to the table. The pain was like getting kicked by a horse (something that I had experienced), and I began to feel tears stream down my temple. Yet I remained quiet.

The loud vacuum was turned on and the pulling and the pressure intensified. I wanted to scream, but didn't. The pain was almost unbearable. The hand on my shoulder seemed to weigh a thousand pounds. I couldn't get away from the pain. The vacuum was turned off. The room was deafeningly quiet. The head at my knees said, "I'm finished." I was told to lie still. The man left the room. I was escorted down the hall and given an injection. I felt nauseous. I wanted to get out of that place.

I walked toward the exit, where my husband was waiting for me. I felt an overwhelming sense of hatred for him. I vowed that I would make him suffer as badly as I had just suffered.

We stopped at his sister's house on our way home and spent some time playing with her baby. I felt a deep pain that hurt so badly that I could hardly catch my breath. I looked at my sister-in-law and thought, *If you only knew what I just did, you would not allow me to even touch your baby.* At that moment, I began to close my heart to loving a child.

They lied to me that day.

I was told that the procedure would not hurt, but it did. The pain was excruciating. What I didn't know was that the pain would *continue* in a different way for the rest of my life. It has been twenty-eight years since my abortion, and it still hurts. I have never had the opportunity to have another child. They didn't tell me about the pain of remaining childless, or how it would feel when I first saw my friend's baby, born within a week of when my aborted child should have been born.

They said it would not hurt; yet it hurt my marriage. I caused my husband deep pain by acting out the feelings of anger and revenge that I felt toward him for not protecting me, for not protecting and welcoming the one unique gift that only I could give him—our baby. I lost any trust in my husband and refused to share with him on a deep emotional and spiritual level.

They said it would not hurt, but I wasn't told how painful it would be when my friends rejected me when they learned about

I WAS TOLD THAT

THE PROCEDURE

WOULD NOT HURT,

BUT IT DID. THE PAIN

WAS EXCRUCIATING.

WHAT I DIDN'T KNOW

WAS THAT THE PAIN

WOULD *CONTINUE* IN

A DIFFERENT WAY FOR

THE REST OF MY LIFE.

*Yes, dear friends, we are*

*already God's children,*

*and we can't even*

*imagine what we will be*

*like when Christ returns.*

*But we do know that*

*when he comes we will be*

*like him, for we will see*

*him as he really is.*

1 John 3:2, NLT

my abortion. They didn't tell me it would hurt when I realized that I had an awful secret that must be kept, and the only way that I could keep my secret was to withdraw from people. For several years after the abortion, I used vulgar and course vocabulary to keep people at a distance.

But most important, they didn't tell me that it would hurt every time I thought about God. When I was a child, I had believed in God and embraced the perfect sacrifice that He gave us in Jesus Christ. Now I could no longer embrace Him because of my guilt and shame.

Four years after the abortion God began working in my heart. I felt convicted about my lifestyle and choices and began seeking reconciliation with God. I began attending church services. But I still believed that if anyone knew the real me, they would reject me. I was on a roller coaster of emotions and mood swings. I became very controlling and demanding. I wanted to know God; yet I believed that He could never forgive me for what I had done. Abortion was not talked about in the churches I attended. So I firmly believed that God could not forgive abortion. Yet I yearned desperately for His forgiveness.

During this time I became more verbally abusive to my husband, tearing him down and going for days without speaking to him. For many years, we put on the "perfect couple" front for family and friends. But when we were alone, I was hardly civil to him. I used every opportunity to point out his inadequacies and failures. We became two people living in the same house, sharing the same bed, but not much else.

One day my husband asked me, "What will it take for you to walk away from this marriage?"

I was horrified. I thought, *You kill my baby and now you want me to walk away?* I ran to my room and closed the door, fell on my face, and cried out to God, *I hate this man, yet I can't lose him, how can I lose my child and him?*

The Spirit of God spoke to my heart that I was to tell my

husband that I loved him too much for him to not be in my life. I argued that it was a lie; yet I knew that was what I had to do. I am not sure my husband believed me, but he agreed that we would stay together and begin seeking help. Today, due to God's mercy and grace lavishly poured out on me, I can honestly tell you that I love my husband with a love deeper than anything I thought possible.

Fifteen years after the abortion I was introduced to a woman who walked the abortion-healing path with me. I was able to identify the hurt and the people who caused those hurts, and I was able to forgive them. Giving humanity to my child, whom I thought was a boy, gave me the freedom to grieve his ever so short life. Giving him a name, Brandon Anthony, allowed me to find closure and peace. I was finally able to share a few of my deep thoughts and feelings with my husband and allow him to grieve in his own way, which brought us closer together.

Finally, being able to accept God's forgiveness gave me the freedom to speak out about my own experience. I hope this will help others not to make the choice I made, and if they have, to walk the path of healing.

TODAY, DUE TO GOD'S MERCY AND GRACE LAVISHLY POURED OUT ON ME, I CAN HONESTLY TELL YOU THAT I LOVE MY HUSBAND WITH A LOVE DEEPER THAN ANYTHING I THOUGHT POSSIBLE.

*Reflection*

Elizabeth's abortion *did* hurt. Not only does she describe the physical pain of the abortion, but also the way she was treated at the abortion clinic. She was hurried through the counseling and not given time to think about the possible complications or the implications to her marriage and her faith. She was rushed through the procedure and was treated impersonally by the doctor. Can you relate to any of the pain that Elizabeth went through during her abortion?

Healing begins with telling the truth about our experiences. What lies were you told about the pain that occurs during an abortion? How were you treated?

Elizabeth candidly tells how she took out her anger and pain and betrayal on her husband, both by attacking him and refusing to open up to him. She felt he should have "protected her and their baby." Is there someone with whom you are angry as a result of your experience? How did that person let you down?

Elizabeth was afraid to let anyone know her. She felt that "if anyone knew the real me, they would reject me." When have you felt like that? What secrets are you keeping that you would be ashamed for close friends to know?

_____

_____

_____

_____

Elizabeth didn't believe that God could or would forgive her. She hadn't heard the message of forgiveness spoken in her church. What messages have you received in your church or place of worship about abortion?

_____

_____

_____

_____

Do you truthfully believe forgiveness is possible for someone after they have had an abortion? Why, or why not?

_____

_____

_____

_____

Elizabeth's healing began by asking and receiving God's forgiveness. Then, with a friend's help, she began to learn how to forgive herself and those who had hurt her. Forgiveness is a journey and requires us to be patient with our growth and ourselves. How will you begin your journey of forgiveness?

_____

_____

_____

_____

## { Elizabeth's Story Continues }

We don't know how the pain of abortion will continue to show up—the next week, the next year, or twenty years later. But even now, twenty-eight years after my abortion, it still hurts to know that I was so weak and fearful, and that I chose my own needs over the life of my child.

Seventeen years after the abortion, I felt the hurt of never having a child who would marry. I would not be the mother of a bridegroom, proudly taking my honored place at his wedding. The realization of this loss threw me into a deep depression. I cried into my husband's arms, asking him to just allow me to mourn. He was able to do so, assuring me of his love and devotion.

Because of the healing program, I knew what to do next. I allowed myself to fully embrace the loss, mourn it, and then ask, "Now what? How can God get the glory for this, too?" One day I will mourn never being a grandmother. I will allow myself to grieve and when I am finished, I will stand up and confidently ask, "How can this also be used to God's glory and my benefit?"

## { GOING DEEPER }

*Elizabeth's deep healing after her abortion has taken years. She mourned the loss of her baby, but she also needed to forgive those along the way who had lied to her, hurt her, and let her down. Amazingly God restored her marriage and renewed her faith.*

*Our hope is that you will find a way to start this process in your life, to find a place where you sense God's forgiveness for you and the hope of healing. This journal provides a beginning for your journey.*

## { GOD'S LOVE LETTER }

*My Little Girl,*

*I want to heal your broken heart. I want to mend the pieces together with My compassion and love. Through your pain and weakness, I will make you strong. I know your guilt overwhelms you, and the burden is too heavy to bear. Let Me carry you through this. I long for you to understand that this was never part of My plan for you. I am sorry that others have hurt you. Please let Me be your Daddy.*

*Your Daddy in heaven*

## *Your Time to Speak*

**My child, I want to know what is on your heart right now. Tell Me.**

# "It is my only option; he doesn't want the baby"

## { CARRIE'S STORY— MAN'S LOVE VS. GOD'S LOVE }

I was born in 1966, the middle child in a family of three girls. We were not raised in an environment of faith, although we attended a Presbyterian church when we were small children. We never discussed God as a family, and I don't recall Him being a part of our lives except for Sundays. My father had great difficulty expressing his love for me. As a result, I felt myself to be unworthy of love. As the head of our family, my father, like all human fathers, had the tremendous responsibility of representing and reflecting God's love to his children. His inability to do this had a traumatic effect on my relationship with God and my awareness of God's awesome and infinite love for me as His child. By the time I was eleven years old, my mother and father had drifted apart. My father eventually left us

*I can do everything*

*with the help of Christ*

*who gives me the*

*strength I need.*

Philippians 4:13, NLT

for another woman. I can still remember where my father and I were standing in our house, what he was wearing, and how sad I was as I squeezed him tightly to say good-bye.

I quickly began searching for an escape from my pain. I was in the seventh grade when I had my first experience with marijuana, alcohol, and cigarettes. Unfortunately it didn't end there. I began using those drugs as well as others to dull the pain and escape into a world where everything "felt good." Inevitably, my next choice would be to seek the love and attention of a boyfriend. I dated a boy much older than I was and lost my virginity at the age of thirteen. I can still remember my mother telling me that she would be happy to get me on "the pill" because "you're not bringing a baby in this house!" I had multiple partners from the time I was thirteen until I came to know Christ at the age of twenty-eight. Giving myself willingly to men and allowing them to use me to fulfill their lustful desires felt like love to me, but it was complete emptiness. This behavior led me into an even deeper depression. My mind was flooded with thoughts of a more permanent escape—suicide.

I had made a true attempt to end my life one evening by mixing large quantities of drugs with alcohol. I'm sure that my guardian angel was watching over me because I was brought out of this experience eight hours later. One other time when I felt desperate enough to make an attempt to end my life, I was the only one at home. Both of my sisters were away at college, and I called one of them to say good-bye. My sister knew that something was wrong and had a friend come over to stay with me until my mother and stepfather got home. I believe that because of my sister's ability to think and act quickly, I am still here today.

At the age of nineteen, I married for the first time with fantasies of having a "normal" family of my own. However, I was drawn to men who were abusive in one way or another— and my first husband was no exception. Abuse had become a way of life for me, so I sought to keep it that way. Needless to say, I was not prepared for this marriage and it ended eighteen months later.

After my divorce, I began abusing alcohol heavily. I was at a bar seven days a week and began using cocaine periodically (something I thought I would never do). I would experience frequent blackouts from my alcohol consumption, and I even got picked up for driving while intoxicated. This should have been a wake-up call for me, but it wasn't. The Lord knew that I had to bottom out, with nowhere else to turn, before I would respond to His call.

I met my next boyfriend at the bar. He was also a heavy drinker. He claimed to be an agnostic, and since I was living the life of a pagan, his lack of faith didn't bother me at all. Shortly after we had become intimately involved, I found out that I was pregnant. Deep in my heart I truly wanted this baby, even though I had no idea how to provide for her. I knew that abortion was wrong, so I searched in the *Yellow Pages* for help. I found a Catholic Charities organization and had great hope that they would be able to give me some direction. After my visit with one of their counselors, however, I left with a deep feeling of hopelessness. The counselor hadn't even bothered to talk to me about the facts of abortion or spend any time educating me toward another option, such as adoption. My boyfriend wanted me to have an abortion. This played a big role in my decision to go back to the *Yellow Pages* and find an abortion provider.

On the day that I was scheduled for the abortion, my boyfriend showed up at my door with a dozen red roses. We drove to the abortion clinic in silence. In the waiting area, I was instructed to sign a release form that clearly stated the danger I was about to undergo. This troubled me, but I had already fixed my mind on the fact that this was my only option. I have no recollection of anything else that took place while we were there. I was kept awake during the procedure, but can't recall anything about it. I do, however, remember leaving the abortion clinic and feeling lower than I had ever felt in my life. My sadness and depression had been instantly magnified. My alcohol consumption increased to an even higher level than before. But even more tormenting than this was that everywhere I went I was vividly aware of every baby and small child within my sight. They were so precious and innocent, all of them. I longed to undo what I

MY BOYFRIEND WANTED ME TO HAVE AN ABORTION. THIS PLAYED A BIG ROLE IN MY DECISION TO GO BACK TO THE *YELLOW PAGES* AND FIND AN ABORTION PROVIDER.

*"For I know the plans*

*I have for you," declares*

*the LORD, "plans to*

*prosper you and not to*

*harm you, plans to give*

*you hope and a future."*

Jeremiah 29:11, NIV

had done to my baby. I so desperately wanted to feel her in my arms and look upon her sweet little face. But I couldn't. This haunted me daily.

In His great mercy, God gave me a second chance. Two months later, I learned of my second pregnancy by the same boyfriend. He insisted on a second abortion. I did not want to go through that traumatic experience ever again. Three of my friends were desperately encouraging me to give birth to this baby. Debbie, who had two children of her own, said to me, "Look at my children. How could you do this to your child?" Gerri said, "Abortion is not a form of birth control. You can't continue to do this. When will you stop?" And Paula, my dearest friend, who normally held fast to a very pro-choice way of thinking, said, "There's something very special about this child." As Paula spoke these words to me, she placed her hand on my abdomen over the place where my baby was safely developing. Tears were streaming down her face. Her words were almost prophetic. Had she found herself in my situation at that time in her life, I believe that she would have chosen an abortion. Yet here she was trying to convince me to allow my baby to live. The loving concern of these three women and the truth in their words continued to flood my thoughts as I made my way once again to the abortion clinic.

Near the entrance, a group of nuns stood praying the rosary for my baby and me and anyone else who passed through the door. They asked me if I was going inside to have an abortion and I lied to them. I didn't want a discussion, yet their loving glances stuck with me as I entered the waiting area. My boyfriend and I waited three hours until finally the woman at the front desk informed us that the "doctor" (abortionist) had been called away on an emergency. We were then told to return the following day at the same time and we would be taken care of without any delay. I remember my first thought was, "Thank God!" I felt as though I had been given more time to be convinced that keeping this child was indeed the right thing to do.

Despite these feelings, I returned with my boyfriend the next day. A group of us went to a locker room to change into our gowns.

The room was cold and dim. While we were waiting to be called into our individual rooms, a young girl spoke up and said, "I'm really afraid." Another girl responded, "Oh it's nothing. This is my fifth one." I thought, *What? Your fifth abortion! How could you?* Then my conscience accused me as I thought, *This is your second, and you're no different than her!*

Shortly after that, we were taken to our rooms. I remember sitting on the table. The nurse asked me to put my feet in the stirrups so that she could prep me. I froze. I felt my whole body go numb. I literally could not move. Once again, she firmly repeated her instructions. I began to weep. She saw my tears and impatiently said, "I'll go get the doctor." I began to have visions of them tying me down since I wasn't cooperating. The abortionist entered the room alone. By this time I was sobbing uncontrollably. He was not at all what I had expected. He was full of compassion while he spoke to me. "Is someone making you do this?" he asked.

"Yes, kind of."

He then said, "I'm not going to force anyone to do this if they don't want to." He asked me for my boyfriend's name and left the room.

Returning a few moments later, he gently instructed me to go get my clothes on and go home. I couldn't believe what I was hearing. I felt an overwhelming sense of relief. All the worries and confusion about how I would provide for my baby left me completely. I had great peace. Eight months later, I gave birth to James, my firstborn son.

Looking back on this incident, I now realize that the Lord spoke to me through the words of the abortionist. It is very unusual for an abortionist to counsel anyone against going through with the procedure. I was so confused at the time that I easily could have been persuaded to go along with the abortion. I'm very grateful to the Lord for giving every person who interceded for me the courage to proclaim His truth with fearless confidence. The words of my friends, the prayers of

LOOKING BACK ON THIS INCIDENT, I NOW REALIZE THAT THE LORD SPOKE TO ME THROUGH THE WORDS OF THE ABORTIONIST.

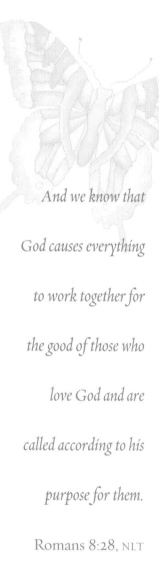

*And we know that*

*God causes everything*

*to work together for*

*the good of those who*

*love God and are*

*called according to his*

*purpose for them.*

Romans 8:28, NLT

the nuns, and even the abortionist himself were all miraculous events that saved my baby.

James' father and I married when James was six months old. I didn't want to marry him; I saw nothing wrong with living together and raising our son in that environment. After all, I knew many people who lived that way. I had not yet embraced our Lord or discovered the wisdom of His commandments. Our marriage and life with our new baby was a constant struggle. In about two years, we decided to end the pain and obtained a divorce. So here I was, a single mom, divorced twice before the age of twenty-five, with no idea how to financially support James and myself.

A girlfriend informed me about a "men's club" where I could work just two or three days a week as a "dancer" and make enough money to take care of all our needs. So, I soon started my new job that allowed me to spend time with James and pay the bills. I worked there for a year and a half before my conscience began accusing me again, telling me that what I was doing was very wrong. Each time I would go to work, the feeling would get stronger. One day I felt physically sick. My stomach hurt so badly that I was doubled over in pain. I knew what it was. I had to get out of that place. It overflowed with sin, and I was a willing contributor.

Thankfully, our Lord in His mercy and wisdom had placed a very special person in my life six months prior to this experience. Rick was a kind, gentle, and patient man. I had never experienced anyone like him before. Although he knew of my occupation, and eventually became aware of my entire past, he stood by my side. Looking back now and knowing how close his relationship was with our Lord, I cannot believe he didn't walk away. I was such a mess, and he knew it. He said that on many occasions he had wanted to distance himself from me, but the Lord kept showing him reasons to stay. Rick was a Roman Catholic, which meant nothing to me at the time. Yet he gave me such a beautiful example of unconditional love that without even realizing what was taking place, he was directing me toward Christ. Once I had made the decision to walk away from my sinful lifestyle, I began to desire what Rick had. He had something that I didn't, and I wanted it more than anything else.

I had no idea where our relationship was heading, but Rick believed that we were supposed to be married. Without telling me, Rick began praying daily for my conversion. He was praying that if I desired to convert, he would see it as the sign he needed to verify that I was the one with whom he was to spend the rest of his life. Not once did he ever make me aware of his thoughts or feelings about my conversion. He knew that he didn't have the power to change my heart, but he knew Who did.

During this time Jesus opened my mind to the knowledge of the truth and filled my heart with the fire of His love. In 1995, my son James and I were both received into the Church at the Easter Vigil Mass. This was such a special day for all of us! James and I had the privilege of receiving our sacraments during the same celebration. James, now four years old, was baptized, and I received the sacraments of Confession, Confirmation, and Holy Communion. Rick was my sponsor and also James' godfather.

RICK WAS A KIND, GENTLE, AND PATIENT MAN. I HAD NEVER EXPERIENCED ANYONE LIKE HIM BEFORE.

*Reflection*

Carrie felt that her father was not showing her unconditional love. When have you felt that you had not received unconditional love from the people in your life?

_____

_____

_____

_____

Carrie's relationship with her father was not what she needed or wanted. How would you describe your relationship with your father?

_____

_____

_____

_____

Carrie describes her sadness and depression, and how she felt such a strong longing for a second chance. Describe the times when you have experienced and felt those emotions.

_____

_____

_____

_____

Carrie talks about her "multiple partners" and how she stopped caring about herself. When have you felt like you didn't—or couldn't—respect yourself?

_____

_____

_____

_____

Carrie says that hanging out at a local bar added to her abuse of alcohol and other drugs. When have you struggled with any type of substance abuse? Why do you think you struggled with those abuses?

When Carrie met Rick, she mentioned that he was the first person to ever show her unconditional love. At first it was hard for her to understand why he would want to stick around because she was such a mess. Who in your life has been there for you—willing to stick around no matter what the circumstances? Why do you think that person(s) is still around?

For Carrie, Rick was an example of Christ in her life. Carrie realized that she needed Christ to help her deal with her day-to-day challenges. Think about your own situation. How do you respond to allowing Christ to stick around in your life? Who has been "Christ" for you?

## { CARRIE'S STORY CONTINUES }

Upon receiving Jesus in Holy Communion, I was flooded with peace and a sense of Christ's healing presence. I don't like to show my emotions in front of anyone, but on that day I could not control the tears as they streamed down my face. I had a very shallow idea as to what was taking place at this time, but I knew for certain that somehow my Lord and my God had united Himself to me in a way that I had never known before. I prayed to God, the Holy Spirit, to enlighten my mind as to what was taking place in this awesome mystery. I still pray that same prayer today. As He continues to draw me closer to a deeper understanding of His true presence and the abundance of grace He desires to offer me, I continue to long for Him even more. I believe that my faith and my longing to be closer to Christ are purely gifts from God. When I think back on my life just ten short years ago and the darkness that consumed my thoughts, I cannot believe what the Lord has done for me! He is overflowing with love and mercy.

Although I have made a sincere commitment to respond to God's grace and follow His call, I have learned that difficult times are not a thing of the past. The difference is that I now have the knowledge and hope that God is with me through these times. He loves me enough to stretch me spiritually so that I may grow closer in likeness to Him. When circumstances in my life seem overwhelming, I know I can rely on the Lord for the grace and the strength to walk with Him in obedience and love.

## { GOING DEEPER }

*God desires to bring us into a relationship with Him and to show us His love, the true love of a Father for His child. Carrie describes her experience of being in relationship with God as longing for more of His presence in her life, much as a daughter would long to spend time with a father who loves her.*

*However, God's plan for us goes beyond our receiving and living in His love. We were created to "grow up" in Him. His passion for us is that we would grow to be more like Him. Sometimes this happens in the gentlest ways as we sit in His presence and read His Word. But sometimes it happens through the problems and the struggles in our lives.*

*Once we know Christ, we can mistakenly think that we will not experience any more difficult times. Or when we do experience trouble and suffering, we can feel that God no longer loves us or cares about us. Carrie understood that the difficult times in her life were meant to "stretch her" spiritually and cause her to "grow up" in Christ. He is there for us when life is difficult and even overwhelming, and He urges us on in obedience to stretch our spiritual muscles and grow ever stronger in Him!*

### { GOD'S LOVE LETTER }

*My Little Girl,*

*Words can't even begin to describe how it hurts Me to know that your heart is so broken. I know that your pain is very deep, and the thought of something good coming out of this pain is impossible to understand. Please believe Me when I tell you that if you allow Me the privilege of having your heart, I will turn this "evil" into good. Let Me restore and mend your heart. I have the power to make the wrongs right. I love you, My precious daughter.*

*Your Daddy in heaven*

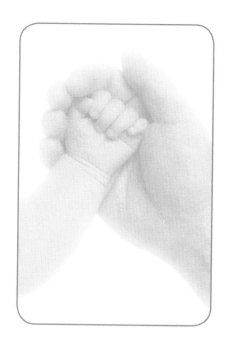

## Your Time to Speak

My precious child, I long to hear from you. Tell Me what is on your heart now.

# "It's okay in cases of rape or incest"

## { REBEKAH'S STORY—FEAR VS. TRUST }

I was eleven years old, and I was pregnant and scared. I believed that I had only one real option—to keep my secret. I had no idea how to deal with such a grown-up concept of being pregnant. More than anything, I was afraid that my father would find out. I really believed that he might kill me if he knew that I was pregnant. The only way to keep my baby and myself safe, I thought, was to keep him from finding out.

My father was also the father of my baby. He had molested me for most of my young life. I did not understand very much about pregnancy and knew even less about abortion. I did know that being pregnant meant that I would have a baby. Even though I knew I wasn't old enough to raise a baby, I very much wanted to have and keep the child. But I had no idea how to do that. If my

*Commit everything you do to the LORD. Trust him, and he will help you. . . Be still in the presence of the LORD, and wait patiently for him to act.*

Psalm 37:5, 7, NLT

father found out, I knew he would never let me have the baby. I didn't know that he could keep me from having the baby without killing *me*. I had no idea that he could kill only my baby.

I considered many options during the six and a half months that I was pregnant. I thought about running away. I thought that I might be able to find a safe place, but what if that place turned out to be worse than home? Because of that fear, I was afraid to run away. I thought about suicide. If I killed myself, I wouldn't have to worry about what would happen if other people found out what I had done. But then I realized that if I died, my baby would die, too. I couldn't do it. I thought about talking to other family members about the problem, but I feared that they would tell my dad. I considered talking with teachers or social workers, but I believed that they would take the baby away from me because I was so young. If there were other options available to me at the time, I did not know about them.

Looking back, I suspect that my father believed that he was exercising his only option as well. He must have known that he was the father of the baby that I carried. He also must have known, far better than I, how much trouble he would be in if anyone found out that he had gotten me pregnant. He knew he had to get rid of the baby to protect himself. I don't know if it was this fear of being found out or the reality that I was too far along, but he chose a "back alley" abortion for me instead of a clinical one.

Throughout my pregnancy, the only person I had talked to was an older foster sister. She took me to Planned Parenthood for a pregnancy test so that we could know for sure if I was pregnant. When we found out for sure that I was, she urged me to tell my parents. I did not do this and was very surprised when my dad picked me up from school one day for a doctor's appointment. My mother almost always took me to appointments, and she hadn't even mentioned this one to me. I wondered what was really going on, but was too afraid to ask.

My dad took me to a house, and we went down to the basement to meet the man he called the "doctor." Neither of the men told me what they planned to do. They told me to undress and what followed was the most excruciatingly painful procedure that I have ever experienced. I was not given any sort of anesthesia, and I thought I would die because it hurt so much. When they finished and I got dressed, the "doctor" told me that I wasn't pregnant. In spite of the continuing pain, I was relieved that they hadn't figured out my secret. I had been worried that a doctor would be able to tell I was pregnant and that he would tell my father. I had no idea that they had known all along and that what the doctor said was true. I really wasn't pregnant—anymore.

My father never talked to me about the situation. The only discussion that we had on the topic was when we pulled into the driveway after the procedure. He repeated the doctor's words to me, and I knew that he meant that this was the end of the subject. We would not discuss it any more, and I should not discuss it with anyone else. Aside from asking my foster sister about the bleeding and the pain that I felt after the abortion, I followed those implied instructions completely for a very long time. I never talked about any part of my experience until I was in college. I may not have talked about it even then, but I was having some health problems as a result of that experience for which I needed treatment.

The necessity of facing the issue medically brought the old issues to the surface, and I had to deal with them. I felt guilt and shame and fear, and just generally hated myself. I thought I needed to punish myself for letting them end the life of my baby. I struggled for a very long time before I realized that I wasn't responsible for my baby's death, and that even if I had been, Gods' grace covered even so heinous a sin. I had been terrified by the thought of anyone knowing what I had done, but I learned that people were more compassionate toward me than I was toward myself. I had tried to hide from God those hideous parts of my past that I thought would be displeasing to Him. I discovered that freedom and forgiveness come only from sharing all those evil things with Him, thereby allowing Him to fill me with cleansing and healing instead.

I HAD TRIED TO HIDE FROM GOD THOSE HIDEOUS PARTS OF MY PAST. . . . I DISCOVERED THAT FREEDOM AND FORGIVENESS COME ONLY FROM SHARING ALL THOSE EVIL THINGS WITH HIM, THEREBY ALLOWING HIM TO FILL ME WITH CLEANSING AND HEALING INSTEAD.

*He alone is my rock*

*and my salvation, my*

*fortress where I will*

*never be shaken.*

Psalm 62:2, NLT

It is probably true that my dad chose the only option that would keep him out of trouble. My choice to keep my secret was not the only choice that I had. There were other options, but my fear prevented me from choosing them. I was so afraid of how people would respond that I tried to figure everything out on my own. I still prefer to figure things out for myself and fear the responses of others to the problems that I encounter. As I have considered the events in my life that year, I have seen that there may have been quite a bit of help available to me if I had only been willing to trust someone enough to ask for help. I have been able to see how I might have been helped in other situations in my life also—if only I had asked. Scripture says, "Ask and you will receive" (Matthew 7:7). I'm afraid that I have missed out on some blessings because I have not done so.

*Reflection*

As you read Rebekah's story, what feelings do you have for the eleven-year-old girl that she once was? What would you have said to her? In what ways did you feel like this eleven-year-old?

_____

_____

_____

_____

_____

As you read again what you have written to the question above, are there any words of encouragement and comfort that you might have wanted to give to her that you can also give yourself?

_____

_____

_____

_____

_____

What were Rebekah's reasons for not asking for help? In what ways do you identify with her reasons?

_____

_____

_____

_____

Even though Rebekah was a child when she became pregnant, she looked back at her situation with courage, asking herself if she had had any other choice. In what ways did you feel that you didn't have any other choices?

Rebekah finally dealt with her abortion as an adult when she was in college. How long did it take you before you were able to deal with your abortion?

Rebekah struggled for a long time before she was able to trust God's grace to "cover so heinous a sin." She tried to hide from God the "hideous parts of her past" until she finally trusted Him enough to share those "evil things" with Him. What are you still hiding from God? Tell Him now.

## { Rebekah's Story Continues }

My prayer for each of you who read my story is that you will
know that *there are always options.* Like me, you may have had
other options than an abortion, but were unable or unwilling
to take them. More important, you have new choices right
now. Options that will give you a hope and a future that your
heavenly Father desires to give you (Jeremiah 29:11). Options
that will allow you to come out from hiding and to experience
the freedom that the truth will bring (John 8:32). I pray that
you will exercise the option your Father has given you to share
your burdens with Him (1 Peter 5:7), and to approach Him
with confidence to receive the help He offers (Hebrews 4:16).

## { GOING DEEPER }

*Rebekah's earthly father sexually abused her. One of the consequences
of that abuse was her pregnancy. She longed to know what to do, but
her fear and lack of trust of those around her prevented her from asking
for help. Then her father abused her further by subjecting her to a
"back alley" abortion, leaving her with the physical, emotional, and
spiritual consequences. One of the amazing realities of Rebekah's story
is that she refused to define herself as a victim, although she certainly
was. Instead, she pushed ahead with a great deal of courage and fought
for her own healing.*

*She confronted her guilt, fear, shame, and self-hatred and began to risk
other people's responses to her situation. She found more compassion
in their responses than she had been able to give herself. Finally, she
began to risk God's response. It was there, in a relationship with a
loving heavenly Father, that she found freedom and forgiveness. She
experienced the release that comes with telling the truth and letting
God know all of the "evil things" she had done and that had been done to
her. He wrapped her tightly in His love and care. Her earthly father's
abuse both caused her to become pregnant and tore away her baby, but
her heavenly Father's embrace filled her with "cleansing and healing"
and continues to fill her with His love.*

{ GOD'S LOVE LETTER }

*My Little Girl,*

*I know that trust and commitment have been very difficult for you. It breaks My heart to know that others have violated you so much that your trust no longer exists. As a little girl, you would trust so easily, without hesitation. I know that I am asking a lot. However, I promise you that if you allow Me the precious gift of your trust, I will place a fortress around you of safety and protection. And I will teach you how to trust others from that place. Please give Me your heart and let Me be your Protector.*

*Your Daddy in heaven*

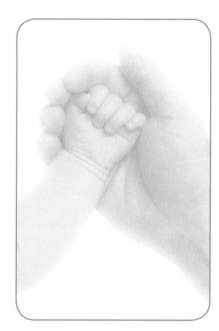

## Your Time to Speak

My precious little girl, what is on your heart right now? Talk to your daddy in heaven.

_____

_____

_____

_____

_____

_____

_____

_____

_____

_____

_____

_____

_____

_____

_____

_____

_____

_____

_____

_____

_____

_____

# Project Rachel:
# Five Steps of Healing

The process of healing involves forgiveness and reconciliation. We are called to work through the process of forgiving those who abandoned us or somehow wounded us during our abortion experience. In coming to forgive others, we are set free. If we can forgive those who hurt us so deeply, then our baby and God can forgive us, and indeed, forgiving ourselves might be possible.

Reconciliation is about rebuilding a damaged relationship, and we reconcile with our child, with God, and with ourselves. We need to grieve for our lost child/children, recognizing their sex, naming them, and grieving for them as our sons or daughters. Writing a letter to this child allows us to finally put on paper everything we have longed to say over the years. (I believe that these children are in the arms of God, praying for the healing of their family.) Because we need to remember, finding a way to memorialize this loss also helps us to heal. As part of the healing journey, we are called back to our relationship with God. It is hard to believe that God could forgive what we've done, but

*But we have this*

*treasure in jars of*

*clay to show that*

*this all-surpassing*

*power is from God*

*and not from us.*

2 Corinthians 4:7, NIV

God waits for us to come and give Him permission to heal us. God will never impose upon our free will.

For the Catholic woman this healing process includes the Sacrament of Reconciliation. Across the country there are specially trained priests who understand the aftermath of abortion and who can help you with your Confession. Tremendous grace is gained from this Sacrament. When God forgives us, it is as if He has blown out the flaming candle of our sin. We may continue to hold onto the candle, though, and try to re-ignite it with our guilt. It is for this reason that perhaps the most challenging part of the healing process is self-forgiveness. Eventually, we come to see ourselves as God sees us. And with God's help and grace, we are finally set free.

On the following pages are five steps of healing that we have developed through Project Rachel. With each step, there is an opportunity for you to respond as you work through the healing process. You may spend days, possibly weeks on one step. Take your time. Allow God to guide you as together you find the healing and the release that only He can give.

## { STEP ONE: RECONCILING WITH YOUR CHILD }

The first step you can take toward healing is reconciling with your child. One way to do this is to ask your baby to forgive you. The idea of asking your child for forgiveness may seem startling or painful at first; yet one aspect of healing the wounds caused by an abortion is facing the fact that *a child's life was lost.*

Our culture seems to deal with the sadness and guilt left after an abortion by simply urging people to forget about it. Society refuses to acknowledge our children by telling us:

"Get over it."

"It was just some tissue."

"You had the right."

This is unhelpful for those who are deeply hurt by an abortion. These women have no way of resolving their feelings of grief because the child is unacknowledged. When other people refuse to validate our loss, we buy the lie that "we don't have to mourn because the fetus is not a human being." If that is true, then why do we feel that something is missing in our lives? Why do we feel sad, depressed, guilty, or like a failure? We feel these things because the truth is that we lost a child through the act of "choice."

Naming the child is a way of honoring the memory of the one who was lost. Many women know instinctively whether their child was a boy or a girl. Once you have picked a name for your child, ask God to give you the strength to write a letter to your child. Tell your child the name you have chosen and why you chose it. Tell your child that you love him or her and that you think about your child often. Share why you felt you had to make the choice and how you have regretted it. Ask your child for forgiveness, and assure him or her that you will one day meet in heaven.

There is space here for you to write at least part of the letter. Please remember that the act of choice doesn't need to end in death. It can be turned around to an act of life.

*His divine power has given us everything we need for life and godliness through our knowledge of him who called us by his own glory and goodness.*

2 Peter 1:3, NIV

*To My Precious Child,*

_____

_____

_____

_____

_____

_____

_____

_____

_____

_____

_____

_____

_____

_____

_____

*Love,*

*Your Mom,* _____

## { GOD'S LOVE LETTER }

*My Little Girl,*

*You truly are My treasure! Your worth to Me was so great that it required the death of My Son. The price that was paid for you was one that only a mother's broken heart could understand. I know how much you love your child, and I want you to know that your child loves you, too. We talk about you often, and in every conversation, we pray that one day soon you will realize your true worth! You are priceless in our eyes!*

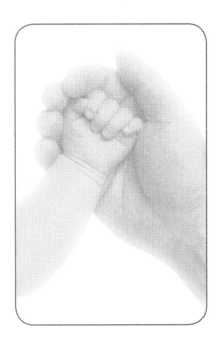

*Your Daddy in heaven*

*For if you forgive*

*men when they sin*

*against you, your*

*heavenly Father*

*will also forgive you.*

Matthew 6:14, NIV

## { STEP 2: GIVING FORGIVENESS TO OTHERS }

You probably will find this next step very difficult. It is hard to forgive someone who hasn't asked for forgiveness, who hasn't validated your pain. This step is a very important part of the process, but don't confuse it with making excuses or justifying someone's abusive treatment of you. Don't allow people to continue to hurt you. Forgiving all the individuals associated with the abortion, whether actively or passively involved, will allow you to start the process of letting go of the hurt that has been paralyzing you for so long.

One way to do this is make a list of all the people who have hurt you in any way, even reaching back into your childhood if necessary. If there is someone in your life now, or in the past, that you just can't bring yourself to forgive, then you can ask God to forgive that person for you until you are strong enough to do so yourself. In the Lord's Prayer we ask our heavenly Father to "forgive us our trespasses as we forgive those who trespass against us." Praying the Lord's Prayer every day is one way to find God's help in being merciful to those who have hurt us.

Use this space below to write a list of names of all the people who have hurt you.

---

---

---

---

---

---

## { GOD'S LOVE LETTER }

*My Little Girl,*

*My love for you brought me to forgiveness. Forgiveness is the essence of my being. My Child was brutally beaten and put to death for the sake of forgiveness. His death was more than I could bear! In fact, the pain caused me to turn away from him for a moment. I truly understand the pain of losing a child to a brutal death. I promise I will never turn away from you. Please let me love and forgive you!*

*Your Daddy in heaven*

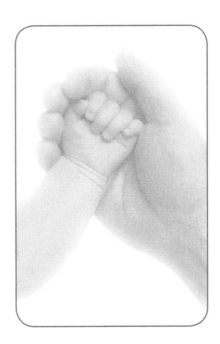

## { STEP 3: ASKING GOD'S FORGIVENESS }

In the Bible, Jesus says that He came into the world to seek those who are lost. His mercy and love are beautifully expressed in the reconciliation—being made right with God—that He offers. Through Christ's sacrifice, our sin is covered and we can all experience the tremendous mercy that God has for each of us. Some women are afraid to confess an abortion to God because they secretly believe that they have committed the "unforgivable sin" and fear that God won't forgive them.

Be assured that God's love is more powerful than any sin you can commit and that His grace is given in a special way through Jesus' sacrifice on the cross. It may be particularly helpful on this occasion to make a general confession, taking some time to reflect on your entire life. Reflect on any patterns that have led you into sin and away from God, even from the time you were a child.

Accepting God's mercy can take great courage, trust, and humility. A simple prayer thanking God for His loving-kindness can help to break down any lingering doubts about whether we are forgiven. Gratitude for the graces we have received can have a very healing and peaceful influence on us.

In the space provided, write your own prayer for forgiveness to God.

*It is for freedom that*

*Christ has set us free.*

*Stand firm, then, and*

*do not let yourselves*

*be burdened again*

*by a yoke of slavery.*

Galatians 5:1 NIV

Dear Daddy,

Love,

## { GOD'S LOVE LETTER }

*My Little Girl,*

*I have longed to share with you My secrets—the miracle of whom "I AM"—and share My plan for you. Will you bring Me your burdens and let Me help you through this? I see your disappointments, your sadness, your brokenness, and your hurt.*

*There isn't anything that I can't or won't fix. Give Me your silent secret and let Me work a miracle in you. I give you My word that you won't have any regrets.*

*Your Daddy in heaven*

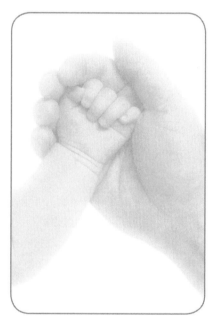

## { STEP 4: FORGIVING YOURSELF }

Some women have an especially hard time forgiving themselves for an abortion. They are plagued with feelings of guilt, depression, or fear. Some have spent years beating themselves up emotionally for an abortion. None of these responses is God's will for our lives. A guilty conscience can remind us that we have sinned and that we need God's help in building reconciliation. But after we have taken the steps to set things right, guilt can become a destructive force that tears down our ability to live a good and loving life.

At this point, you have asked the child for forgiveness, you have tried to forgive everyone in your life, and you have asked God to forgive you. Now you need to let go of the guilt.

God wants each of us to be a strong, compassionate Christian so that we can live a full life and help others who are in need of God's love. Letting guilt and self-hatred dominate you makes that kind of life very difficult. When Jesus asks us to love others as we love ourselves, He is telling us that we need to love ourselves.

Earlier you made a list of all the people you needed to forgive. Go back to that list and add *your own name*. Ask God to help you forgive yourself. When you feel guilty about the abortion, remember to keep going back to God and asking for His help. Give those feelings to God. He came to the earth to set us free from anything and everything that enslaves us. Praying, reading the Bible, and listening to Christian music are ways to change the direction of your thoughts toward God when you're stuck in the darkness of the past.

Tell God right now how you feel about yourself.

*Those who look*

*to him are radiant;*

*their faces are never*

*covered with shame.*

Psalm 34:5, NIV

Dear Daddy,

Love,

## { GOD'S LOVE LETTER }

*My Little Girl,*

*My plan for you was never to live in shame and guilt. I know that the power of regret stings very much. I also know that you had no idea what "choice" was going to do to your life. Whether you made the choice or it was made for you doesn't matter. Whether you made the choice once or more than once doesn't matter. What matters is that I have forgiven you! Please make the choice today to receive and accept my forgiveness. I promise you won't regret it!*

*Your Daddy in heaven*

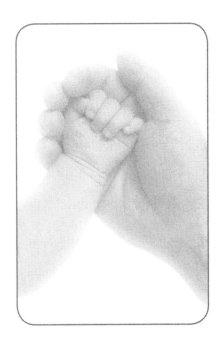

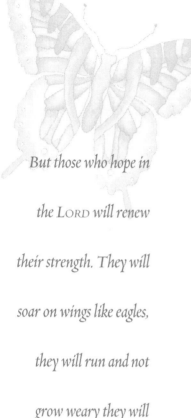

*But those who hope in*

*the LORD will renew*

*their strength. They will*

*soar on wings like eagles,*

*they will run and not*

*grow weary they will*

*walk and not be faint.*

Isaiah 40:31, NIV

## { STEP 5: HAVING A MEMORIAL SERVICE FOR YOUR CHILD }

The last step toward healing is to plan a memorial service for the lost child. This will also help the healing of your whole family. This can be similar to a funeral memorial service, where you can entrust the child to God's care until you meet again in heaven. Many women who have done this feel that this service was the most healing and freeing of the steps, helping to bring a sense of closure. This new anniversary "date" can take the place of more painful anniversaries that may have caused you grief in the past.

You may feel that you want to try some volunteer service or make other positive contributions to your community. These impulses are good, but you should be careful that you are not trying to "make up" for what was lost by taking on difficult challenges. Jesus Himself did all the work necessary for our salvation by living among us and taking our sins to the cross. Some women feel that simply accepting His forgiveness is "too easy," and they believe they must do some difficult work to earn forgiveness. But there is no work we can do that can change the past— trusting in the power of sacrifice of Jesus is all He asks of us. When you are ready, it may be good to express your thanks for God's mercy by working at a crisis pregnancy or a soup kitchen. Compassion given to others in need is one of the best ways of praising and thanking our God for all of His good gifts to us.

Take time to share your closing thoughts with your child and with God.

Dear

Love,

## { God's Love Letter }

*My Little Girl,*

*Bring me your broken wings. Allow me to repair them. I know you have been tossed to and fro by the heavy storms in your life. Every time you try to fly, something happens that prevents you from being able to let go and be free. I AM here now! You can let go. Your child is safe with me. I will make sure you don't come crashing down. You will learn to fly **now**, I promise.*

*Your Daddy in heaven*

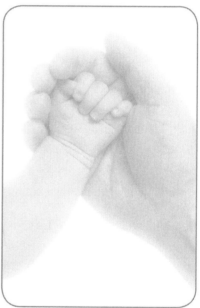

## { JOURNALING PAGES }

# Other Resources

ALL THE RESOURCES GIVEN ARE HELD WITH THE HIGHEST LEVEL OF CONFIDENTIALITY

To find out about Post-Abortion Healing call:

> Project Rachel
> Vicki Thorn, Executive Director/Founder
> National Office of Post-Abortion Reconciliation & Healing
> 1 (800) 5WE-CARE
> www.noparh.org

To find out about Crisis Pregnancies Shelters and Healing call:

> Word of Hope/Healing Hearts
> Grace Kern, Executive Director/Founder
> 1 (888) 217-8679
> www.wordofhope.org

To find out about Breast Cancer and its link to abortions call:

> Coalition on Abortion/Breast Cancer
> Karen Malec, President
> An International Women's Organization
> 1 (877) 803-0102
> www.response@abortionbreastcancer.com

To find out how to get involved with the Legal Team by signing an affidavit for the education of other woman call:

> Protector's of Women's Rights
> Tommie Romano, Chairman of the Board
> National Foundation for Life Legal Chief Counsel—Harold Cassidy
> 1 (732) 542-5700
> www.NFFLLP.org

To find out how to get involved with Time to Speak or join one of our "Slumber Parties" call:

> Time to Speak/Love From Above
> Yvonne Florczak-Seeman – President / Founder
> 1 (866) Time 2 Speak
> www.timetospeak.org or www.lovefromaboveinc.com

# The Perfect Sacrifice

As a woman I was designed to be the

perfect gift of God's plan. From the very beginning

I was created to give life. I represented the completion of

who God was and is. Yet something went terribly wrong.

I don't really know how, or even why, it happened. Before I could

even make sense of it, it was too late. By the time I realized what I

had done, you were gone. No one ever mourned for you, my precious child.

I was never asked how great my loss was. It seemed as if life just continued for

everyone. However, my life didn't continue; my life stopped! I remember feeling like I

had entered a bad dream. A dream with no end in sight because it had become a living

nightmare, day in and day out. I tried to forget about you by bearing the pain in

silence. The thought of anyone finding out what I had done to you was more than I

could bear. It was the beginning of my reality of HELL. I still remember everything

about the pain of death; the cold floors in the clinic and the stark white walls, the

beaming white lights hanging over my head as I lay on the hard metal table wondering

why the lights had to be so bright and feeling exposed by them, the thin sheets on the

cot in the recovery room, the lie that my life would go back to normal, the simple

medical procedure of removing some "harmless tissue." They lied to me! And devalued

"The Perfect Gift of Life" that you represented. "I AM SO SORRY" that I didn't protect

you from that horrible death sentence. I know that I can never truly give back to you

what I took from you—things like experiencing what it would be like to run in the

rain; having you pick your clothes for school; learning how to play sports and

making the varsity team; learning how to play an instrument with your heart, body, and

soul; getting the lead in the school play. Words will never express the pain of not

knowing who you would have become. Much time has passed, and many years have gone

by. When I look in the mirror, I don't see as many regrets any more. Now, I see new

beginnings, along with some wrinkles and gray hair. Time has healed the wounds

and has given me great courage. I talk about you often, and I find strength in

"Breaking the Silence" day in and day out. I have shared my regret with tens of

thousands who have experienced the same pain. I have come to realize the

"Greatest Revelation." Your death was not in vain for today the

pain your death once caused is giving others the strength to

accept forgiveness and the freedom to embrace

life and live again. Thank you for being . . .

"The Perfect Sacrifice."

Love, Your Mom
*Yvonne Florczak-Seeman*

# The Time to Speak Movement

*"Speak up for those who cannot speak for themselves;*
*ensure justice for those who are perishing."*
Proverbs 31:8, NLT

*Time to Speak* is an awareness and educational movement to promote help, hope, and healing for the post-abortive woman and all others who have been hurt by abortion.

## { PURPOSE }

*Time to Speak* is designed to encourage women who are ready to speak out about their abortion experience, with the hope that they can turn an evil into good. These women understand that awareness and education are the keys to exposing "choice" for what it truly is— a lie, that wasn't a "true choice," nor was it in the woman's best interest. Many women who have had abortions later feel that they didn't have any other options. They often feel alone, and in some instances, pressured into making the decision. The truth is that in this nation we are given more information about a tooth extraction than we are about this "simple procedure" of abortion, which for some becomes a final decision as some women are never able to conceive again.

Imagine for a moment that your thirteen-year-old daughter becomes pregnant and goes to an abortion clinic and receives a "simple procedure." No one is required by law to inform you of your child's decision. That same daughter grows up with all the depression and hopelessness that comes from her "legal" choice. She gets married and wants to start a family. However, because of her legal "choice," she is never able to have children again. We need to give our next generation a chance to live.

Hundreds of thousands of women have been hurt by abortion, yet many think that they are alone. Our mission is to provide hope by communicating that forgiveness and healing are possible. There is no set way that one is healed because we all have different journeys; the healing process can be different for everyone. It affects us emotionally, physically, psychologically, and spiritually. Our goal is to plant a seed of faith and hope among women and help them take the first steps towards recognizing their pain and eventually seeking further help. Too many women continue to suffer in silence. Many believe that the problems they are experiencing are unique to them. They are longing for help, but they don't know where to turn.

Some women can't begin the healing process because they are either in denial or they don't recognize the connection between their pain and the problems in their lives. Our freedom to choose a legal abortion comes with a lifetime of consequences. However, the process of healing can begin with the help of Almighty God. Our Daddy in heaven can restore what we have lost.

Through Time to Speak we offer overnight retreats that we refer to as "Slumber Parties." Why slumber parties? Early in the development of this movement God revealed to me that not only did women lose their child/children but they also lost the "little girl" that would laugh, giggle, play and enjoy life. Well what happens in slumber parties? Little girls get together and laugh, giggle, play and enjoy life! God also revealed to me that they share their secrets because they feel safe. In this safe place, we enjoy eating lots of pizza, fellowshipping, praying, sharing and making jewelry. At our parties we also do different activities that help us work through Project Rachel's five steps of healing.

Please contact us to become part of our ARMY of WOMEN who know the truth about abortion and help us educate the other side by telling them the truth.

Contact us by calling 1-866-TIME2SPEAK, or through our website, www.lovefromaboveinc. com.

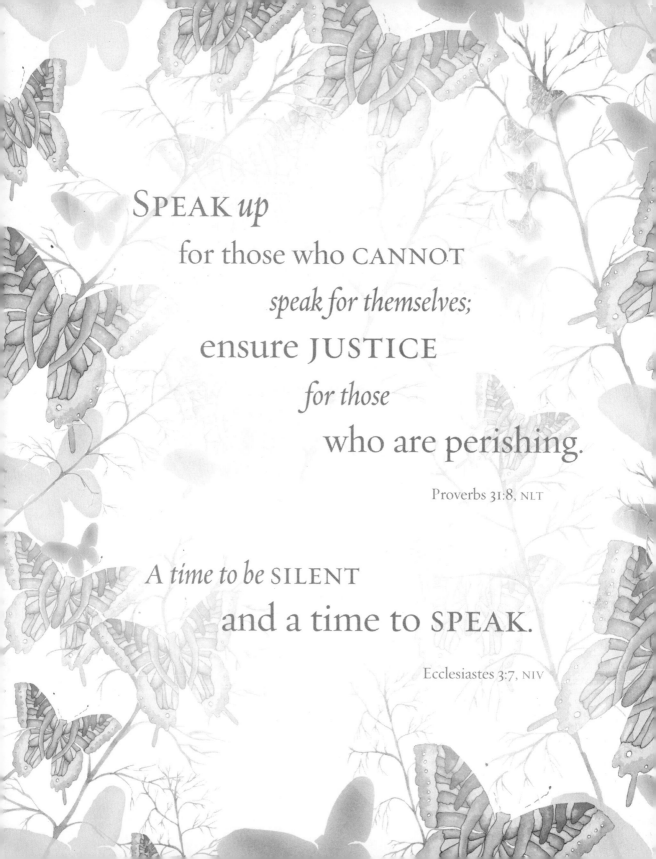

Speak *up*
for those who CANNOT
*speak for themselves;*
ensure JUSTICE
*for those*
who are perishing.

Proverbs 31:8, NLT

*A time to be* SILENT
and a time to SPEAK.

Ecclesiastes 3:7, NIV